THE LEGAL ENVIRONMENT OF BUSINESS:
BRIEFED CASE EDITION

Also available from McGraw-Hill

Schaum's Outline Series In Accounting, Business & Economics

Each outline includes basic theory, definitions and hundreds of solved problems and supplementary problems with answers.

Current List Includes:

Accounting I, 3d edition
Accounting II, 2d edition
Advanced Accounting
Advanced Business Law
Advertising
Bookkeeping & Accounting
Introduction to Business
Business Law
Business Mathematics
Introduction to Business Organization & Management
Business Statistics, 2d edition
College Business Law
Contemporary Mathematics of Finance
Cost Accounting I, 2d edition
Cost Accounting II
Development Economics
Financial Accounting
Intermediate Accounting I
International Economics, 2d edition
Macroeconomic Theory
Managerial Accounting
Managerial Finance
Marketing
Mathematics for Economists
Mathematics of Finance
Microeconomic Theory, 2d edition
Money and Banking
Operations Management
Personal Finance & Consumer Economics
Principles of Economics
Quantitative Methods in Management
Statistics and Econometrics
Tax Accounting

Available At Your College Bookstore

THE LEGAL ENVIRONMENT OF BUSINESS:

BRIEFED CASE EDITION

SECOND EDITION

Robert N. Corley
Distinguished Professor of Legal Studies Emeritus
University of Georgia

O. Lee Reed
Professor of Legal Studies
University of Georgia

McGRAW-HILL BOOK COMPANY

New York St. Louis San Francisco Auckland Bogotá
Caracas Colorado Springs Hamburg Lisbon London Madrid
Mexico Milan Montreal New Delhi Oklahoma City Panama Paris
San Juan São Paulo Singapore Sydney Tokyo Toronto

This book was set in Times Roman by the College Composition Unit
in cooperation with the William Byrd Press.
The editor was Michael Asher; the production supervisor was Salvador Gonzales;
the designer was Merrill Haber.
Project supervision was done by The Total Book.
R. R. Donnelley & Sons Company was printer and binder.

THE LEGAL ENVIRONMENT OF BUSINESS:
Briefed Case Edition

Copyright © 1989 by McGraw-Hill, Inc. All rights reserved.
Formerly published under the title of *Fundamentals of the Legal Environment of Business.*
Copyright © 1986 by McGraw-Hill Inc. All rights reserved.
Printed in the United States of America. Except as permitted under the United States Copyright Act of 1976, no part of this publication may be reproduced or distributed in any form or by any means, or stored in a data base or retrieval system, without the prior written permission of the publisher.

1 2 3 4 5 6 7 8 9 0   DOC DOC   8 9 3 2 1 0 9 8

ISBN 0-07-013277-1

Library of Congress Cataloging-in-Publication Data

Corley, Robert Neil.
  The legal environment of business:briefed
case edition/Robert N. Corley, O. Lee Reed. —2nd ed.
    p. cm.
  Rev. ed. of: Fundamentals of the legal environment
of business. 1986.
  Includes index.
  ISBN 0-07-013227-1
  1. Industrial laws and legislation—United States.
  2. Trade regulation—United States.
  3. Commercial law—United States. I. Reed, O. Lee (Omer Lee)
II. Corley, Robert Neil. Fundamentals of the legal environment of business. III. Title.
KF1600.C59 1989
346.73'07—dc19
[347.3067]   88-13274

ABOUT THE AUTHORS

Robert N. Corley is a Distinguished Professor of Legal Studies Emeritus of the University of Georgia. He received his J.D. and B.S. degrees from the University of Illinois, where he taught for eighteen years. He was admitted to the Illinois Bar in 1956. Professor Corley is past president of the American Business Law Association and a past member of the editorial board of the *American Business Law Journal*. In 1985 he was awarded the Senior Faculty Award of Excellence by the American Business Law Association.Winner of numerous teaching awards at both the undergraduate and graduate levels, he has also taught in several national executive development programs. Since 1964 he has been senior author of *The Legal Environment of Business*. His contributions have shaped the content of the entire legal environment of business field.

O. Lee Reed holds a J.D. degree from the University of Chicago and a B.A. degree from Birmingham-Southern College. Presently, he is Professor of Legal Studies at the University of Georgia. The author of many scholarly articles, he is former editor-in-chief of the *American Business Law Journal*. He also has served as president of the Southeastern Regional Business Law Association. Professor Reed has received teacher-of-the-year awards from both undergraduate and graduate student organizations. He has been co-author of *The Legal Environment of Business* since 1977.

CONTENTS

PREFACE	xxv
TO THE STUDENT	xxix

PART 1 INTRODUCTION

1 Introduction to Law — 3

OVERVIEW — 3
1. The Law and Business — 3
2. Definitions of Law — 4
3. Schools of Legal Thought — 6
4. The Rule of Law — 7
5. Lawyers — 8
6. General Classifications of Legal Subjects — 10
7. The Criminal Law — 11
8. The Law of Contracts — 15
9. The Law of Torts — 16
10. The Law of Property — 17
11. Sources of Law — 19
12. Other Influences on Behavior — 21
13. Law and Ethics — 22

REVIEW QUESTIONS — 25

2 The Powers and Functions of Courts — 27

OVERVIEW — 27
1. Introduction — 27
2. Judges and Justices — 28
3. The Jury — 29
4. Judicial Review — 31
5. Attitudes toward Judicial Review — 32
6. The Interpretation of Legislation — 36
7. Uniform Statutes — 38

CASE LAW — 39
8. Inherent Problems — 39
9. The Weight to Be Given Precedent — 41
10. Selecting the Applicable Case Law — 43
11. The Judicial Process — 45

REVIEW QUESTIONS — 48

3 Court Systems — 50

OVERVIEW — 50
1. Introduction — 50
2. The State Court System — 51
3. Small-Claims Courts — 53
4. The Federal Court System — 54
5. Diversity-of-Citizenship Cases — 56
6. Federal Reviewing Courts — 58
7. Transfer from the States to the Federal System — 59
8. The Law in the Federal Courts — 60
9. Law and Equity — 62
10. Equitable Procedures — 63
11. Contemporary Problems — 65
12. Delay: Some Solutions — 66

REVIEW QUESTIONS — 67

4 Litgation and other Methods for Resolving Disputes — 69

OVERVIEW — 69
1. Introduction — 69
2. Parties to Litigation — 70
3. Standing to Sue — 71
4. Class Action Suits — 73
5. Jurisdiction of Courts — 75
6. Venue — 78
7. Pleadings — 79
8. Motions — 79
9. Discovery Procedures — 81
10. Conduct of a Trial — 82
11. The Burden of Proof — 85
12. Rules of Evidence — 86
13. Appellate Procedure — 88
14. Enforcement of Judgments and Decrees — 90
15. Res Judicata — 91
16. Mediation and Arbitration — 91
17. Arbitration Proceedings — 93

REVIEW QUESTIONS — 95

PART 2 CONSTITUTIONAL AND ADMINISTRATIVE LAW

5 The Constitution and Business — 101

OVERVIEW — 101
1. Organization — 101
2. Separation of Powers — 102
3. The Supremacy Clause — 104
4. External Affairs — 105

5	The Contract Clause	107
6	The Taxing Power	108
7	The Import-Export Clause	109
8	States' Relation Article	111
THE COMMERCE CLAUSE		113
9	Introduction	113
10	Foreign Commerce	114
11	Interstate Commerce	114
12	The Commerce Clause and the State Police Power	117
13	The Commerce Clause and Taxation	121
REVIEW QUESTIONS		124

6 The Bill of Rights and Business — 127

OVERVIEW		127
1	Introduction	127
THE FIRST AMENDMENT		128
2	Freedom of Religion	128
3	Freedom of the Press	131
4	Freedom of Speech	133
5	Commercial Speech	135
6	Other First Amendment Freedoms	136
OTHER AMENDMENTS		138
7	The Fourth Amendment	138
8	The Fifth Amendment	140
9	The Sixth Amendment	143
10	The Seventh Amendment	144
THE FOURTEENTH AMENDMENT		144
11	Introduction	144
12	Due Process of Law	146
13	Equal Protection	148
REVIEW QUESTIONS		151

7 Administrative Law — 154

OVERVIEW		154
1	Introduction	155
2	Reasons for the Use of Administrative Agencies	155
3	Functions	158
4	Organization	161
5	Influencing Agency Decisions	163
JUDICIAL REVIEW of AGENCY DECISIONS		164
6	Introduction	164
7	Judicial Review of Agency Rule Making	165
8	Review of Adjudications: Procedural Aspects	167
9	Exhaustion of Remedies	168
10	Review of Agency's Determination of Facts	170

11	Agency Personnel and Damage Suits	171
12	Equal Access to Justice	173
13	Common Criticisms	174
14	Cost of Regulation	174
REVIEW QUESTIONS		177

PART 3 CONTRACTS AND TORTS

8 Contract Law and Private Enterprise — 183

OVERVIEW — 183
1. Contract Law and Its Place in Private Enterprise — 184
2. Sources of Contract Law — 185
3. Classification of Contracts — 185
4. Remedies for Breach of Contract — 187
5. Offer to Contract — 188
6. Acceptance of Offer — 190
7. Voluntary Consent to Contracts — 191
8. Consideration in the Contract — 193
9. Capacity of Parties to Contract — 195
10. Illegal Contracts — 196
11. When Contracts Should Be in Writing — 198
12. The Parol Evidence Rule — 201
13. Interpretation of Contracts — 201
14. Assignment of Contracts — 203
15. Contracts Benefiting a Third Party — 204
16. Performance of Contracts — 206
17. Discharge of Contracts — 207
18. Trends in Contract Law — 208
REVIEW QUESTIONS — 209

9 Torts in the Business Environment — 212

OVERVIEW — 212
1. The Development of Tort Law — 213
INTENTIONAL TORTS — 214
2. Assault and Battery — 215
3. Intentional Infliction of Mental Distress — 215
4. Invasion of Privacy — 217
5. False Imprisonment and Malicious Prosecution — 217
6. Trespass — 218
7. Conversion — 218
8. Defamation — 219
9. Business Torts — 220
10. Trademarks and False Advertising: The Lanham Act — 223
11. Patents and Copyrights — 224
12. Constitutional Torts — 227
NEGLIGENCE — 227

	13 Duty of Care	227
	14 Unreasonable Behavior	228
	15 Cause in Fact	229
	16 Proximate Causation	231
	17 Defenses to Negligence	232
	STRICT LIABILITY IN TORT	234
	18 Respondeat Superior	234
	19 Other Strict Liability Torts	235
	20 Damages	236
	REVIEW QUESTIONS	239
10	**Products and Service Liability**	**242**
	OVERVIEW	242
	1 Historical Development of Products Liability	243
	THE BASIC THEORIES OF LIABILITY	245
	2 Introduction	245
	3 Duty Based Upon Conduct of the Seller: Negligence	246
	4 Duty Based Upon Quality of the Product	248
	IMPLIED WARRANTY OF MERCHANTABILITY	249
	5 Duty Based Upon Promises or Representations	251
	THE PLAINTIFF'S CASE	252
	6 Product Defect	252
	7 Defect in the Hands of the Defendant	254
	8 The Defect Must Have Caused the Harm	254
	9 Defect Must Make the Product Unreasonably Dangerous	255
	THE DEFENDANT'S CASE	257
	10 Parties	257
	11 Defendant's Defenses	259
	12 Industrial Accidents Involving Products	261
	13 Indemnification	261
	14 The Risk Retention Act	262
	15 Products Liability Trends	263
	16 Legislative Revision of Products Liability	264
	17 Management Planning for Products Liability	265
	SERVICE LIABILITY	268
	18 Overview	268
	19 Malpractice and the Accounting Profession	269
	REVIEW QUESTIONS	271

PART 4 CONDUCTING BUSINESS

11	**Forms of Business Organizations: Selection Process**	**275**
	OVERVIEW	275
	1 Alternatives of Organizational Forms	276

	2 Legal Capacity	277
GENERAL FACTORS		277
	3 Advantages and Disadvantages of Partnerships	277
	4 Advantages and Disadvantages of Corporations	278
GOING INTO BUSINESS		279
	5 Creating Partnerships	279
	6 Creating Corporations	281
	7 Creating Limited Partnerships	284
	8 Continuity of Organizations	285
LIABILITY FACTORS		288
	9 Liability Factors: Partnerships	288
	10 Liability Factors: Corporations	290
TAXATION FACTORS		292
	11 Taxation Factors: Partnerships	292
	12 Taxation Factors: Corporations	292
	13 Avoiding Double Taxation	293
CONTROL		295
	14 Control in Partnerships	295
	15 Control of Large Corporations	296
	16 Control of Closely Held Corporations	296
REVIEW QUESTIONS		299

12 Liability of Business Organizations and Managers — 302

OVERVIEW		302
	1 Terminology	302
LIABILITY BASED ON CONTRACT LAW		303
	2 Principals	303
	3 Agents	306
LIABILITY BASED ON TORT LAW		307
	4 Basic Concepts	307
	5 Illegal Conduct	310
LIABILITY BASED ON THE CRIMINAL LAW		312
	6 Business Organizations	312
	7 Corporate Executives	313
SPECIAL ASPECTS OF MANAGERIAL LIABILITY		315
	8 Partners	315
	9 Corporate Officers and Directors	316
	10 Liability of Agents to Principals	318
	11 Ethical Considerations	320
REVIEW QUESTIONS		321

13 International Transactions — 324

OVERVIEW		324
	1 Introduction	325
ALTERNATIVE METHODS OF CONDUCTING INTERNATIONAL BUSINESS		325
	2 Overview	325

3	Direct Sales Abroad	326
4	Use of Foreign Agents	326
5	Licensing of Technology	327
6	Foreign Subsidiaries	327
7	Joint Ventures	328
8	Risks of Direct Investment	329
LEGAL INSTITUTIONS AND AGREEMENTS		332
9	The United Nations (UN)	332
10	European Community (EC; or Common Market)	333
11	Other Organizations	333
12	General Agreement On Tariffs and Trade (GATT)	334
DOMESTIC LAWS HAVING SIGNIFICANT INTERNATIONAL TRADE CONSEQUENCES		334
13	Antidumping Laws	334
14	Antitrust	335
15	Foreign Corrupt Practices Act (FCPA)	336
16	Overseas Private Investment Corporation (OPIC)	338
17	Other Problem Areas	339
18	Arbitration	340
19	Conclusion	341
REVIEW QUESTIONS		341

PART 5 PROTECTING EMPLOYEES

14 Worker Protection — 345

OVERVIEW		345
1	The Occupational Safety and Health Act	346
2	Workers' Compensation Acts	349
3	Federal Compensation Acts	354
4	Wages and Hours of Work	355
5	Unemployment Compensation	358
6	Social Security	361
7	Private Pension Plans: Incentives and Protection	363
8	Trends in Worker Protection: Limitations on Employment-at-Will	367
REVIEW QUESTIONS		370

15 Discrimination in Employment — 372

OVERVIEW		372
1	Historical Development of Employment Discrimination Law	372
2	The Civil Rights Act: General Provisions	373
3	Enforcement Procedures	375
4	Discrimination On the Basis of Race or Color	378
5	Discrimination On the Basis of National Origin	379
6	Discrimination On the Basis of Religion	379
7	Discrimination On the Basis of Sex	380

EMPLOYMENT PRACTICES WHICH MAY BE CHALLENGED		383
8 Testing and Educational Requirements		383
9 Height and Weight Requirements		385
10 Appearance Requirements		386
11 Affirmative Action Programs and Reverse Discrimination		387
12 Seniority Systems		389
OTHER STATUTES AND DISCRIMINATION IN EMPLOYMENT		390
13 Civil Rights Act of 1866		390
14 Discrimination On the Basis of Age		392
15 Discrimination On the Basis of Handicaps		393
16 Other Federal Legislation		395
17 State Discrimination Laws		395
18 Avoiding Unfounded Discrimination Claims		395
REVIEW QUESTIONS		397

16 Right to Union Activity — 400

OVERVIEW		400
1 Introduction		400
FEDERAL LAWS BEFORE 1935		402
2 Clayton Act		402
3 Railway Labor Act		404
4 Norris-LaGuardia Act		406
THE WAGNER ACT		408
5 General Summary		408
6 The NLRB		409
7 NLRB Sanctions		410
8 NLRB Elections		411
THE TAFT-HARTLEY ACT		414
9 Major Provisions		414
10 Union Membership		415
11 Free Speech		416
12 Eighty-day Cooling-off Period		417
13 Suits Against Unions		418
THE LANDRUM-GRIFFIN ACT		418
14 As a "Bill of Rights"		418
15 Lmrda Reporting Requirements		421
16 Internal Union Activities		422
17 Labor Law and Government Employees		423
REVIEW QUESTIONS		424

17 Unfair Labor Practices — 427

OVERVIEW		427
1 Introduction		427
2 Interference with Efforts of Employees to Form or Join Labor Organizations		428
3 Interfering with Concerted Activities		432
4 Discharge and Other Forms of Retaliation		436

5 Domination of a Labor Organization	438
6 Discrimination for Union Affiliation	439
7 Discrimination: NLRB Proceedings	441
8 The Duty to Bargain Collectively in Good Faith	442
9 Agreeing With a Union to Engage in a Secondary Boycott	445
UNFAIR LABOR PRACTICES BY UNIONS	446
10 Introduction	446
11 Restraining or Coercing an Employee in Joining a Union	446
12 Causing an Employer to Discriminate Against a Nonunion Member	449
13 Secondary Boycotts and Other Illegal Strikes and Picketing	449
14 Requiring Employees to Pay Excessive Fees	452
15 Causing an Employer to Pay for Work Not Performed	453
16 Picketing When Not Certified	453
17 The Union's Duty of Fair Representation	454
REVIEW QUESTIONS	456

PART 6   PROTECTING PARTIES TO TRANSACTIONS

18 Investor Protection — 461

OVERVIEW	461
1 Definition of Security	462
2 Securities and Exchange Commission	463
FEDERAL SECURITIES ACT OF 1933: GOING PUBLIC	464
3 General Provisions	464
4 Parties Regulated	465
5 Documents Involved	466
6 Shelf Registration	467
7 Exemptions	468
8 Criminal Liability	469
9 Civil Liability	471
10 Defenses	474
FEDERAL SECURITIES EXCHANGE ACT OF 1934: BEING PUBLIC	476
11 General Coverage	476
12 Section 10(b) and Rule 10b-5	477
13 Insider Transactions	480
14 Nonpublic Information	481
15 Additional Civil Liability	484
16 Criminal Liability	485
CONSIDERATIONS BEYOND THE FEDERAL SECURITIES LAWS	486
17 State "Blue-Sky" Laws	486
18 Ethical Considerations	488
REVIEW QUESTIONS	489

19 Consumer Protection — 492

OVERVIEW — 492
    1 Who is a Consumer? — 493
FEDERAL CONSUMER PROTECTION — 494
    2 The Federal Trade Commission — 494
    3 FTC Penalties and Remedies — 496
    4 Traditional Trade Practice Regulation — 498
    5 Policy Trends At The FTC — 500
    6 Introduction to Federal Credit Regulations — 503
    7 Equal Credit Opportunity Act — 503
    8 The Fair Credit Reporting Act — 505
    9 The Truth-in-Lending Act — 508
    10 The Magnuson-Moss Warranty Act — 511
STATE CONSUMER PROTECTION — 512
    11 State Consumer Fraud Legislation — 512
CONSUMER PRIVACY ETHICS AND THE FUTURE OF CONSUMERISM — 514
    12 Consumer Privacy — 514
    13 Ethical Considerations — 515
    14 Policy Trends: the Future of Consumerism — 516
REVIEW QUESTIONS — 517

20 Creditor and Debtor Protection — 519

OVERVIEW — 519
CREDITOR PROTECTION — 520
    1 Introduction — 520
    2 Artisan's Liens — 520
    3 Mechanic's Liens — 521
    4 Bulk Transfers — 522
    5 Suretyship — 523
DEFENSES AVAILABLE TO SURETY — 525
    6 Secured Transactions in Personal Property — 528
    7 Secured Transactions in Real Property — 534
DEBTOR PROTECTION — 536
    8 Introduction — 536
    9 Usury — 537
    10 Debt Collection — 538
    11 Bankruptcy — 540
    12 Additional Protection for Consumer-Debtors — 544
REVIEW QUESTIONS — 546

PART 7 PROTECTING SOCIETY

21 Protecting Competition — 551

OVERVIEW — 551
    1 The Meaning of Antitrust — 552
    2 Statutes Involved — 552
    3 Exemptions to the Sherman Act — 554

4 The State Action Exemption	554
5 The Noerr-Pennington Doctrine	556
SANCTIONS	557
6 The Criminal Sanction	557
7 The Injunction	558
8 Triple Damages	560
9 The Illinois Brick Doctrine	562
10 Proof of Sherman Act Violations	564
11 The Rule of Reason and Per Se Illegality	565
12 Enforcement	567
REVIEW QUESTIONS	568

22 Sherman Act Enforcement — 570

OVERVIEW	570
1 Activities in Restraint of Trade	570
2 Price-Fixing	571
3 Resale Price Maintenance: Vertical Price-Fixing	573
4 Concerted Activities by Competitors	576
5 Joint Operations	579
6 Agreements Relating to Territory	580
MONOPOLY	581
7 Section 2: The Rationale	581
8 Section 2: The Approach	582
9 Ethical Considerations	587
10 Caterpillar Code of Competition	589
REVIEW QUESTIONS	590

23 Clayton Act and FTC ACT ENFORCEMENT — 592

OVERVIEW	592
1 Introduction	593
CLAYTON ACT—SECTION 2	594
2 Historical Perspective	594
3 Predatory Pricing	595
4 Price Discrimination	596
5 Proof Required	597
6 Levels of Competition	598
7 Defenses	600
8 Good-Faith Meeting-of-Competition Defense	601
9 The Future of Section 2	603
THE CLAYTON ACT—SECTION 3	603
10 Tying Arrangements—Generally	603
11 Reciprocal Dealings	605
12 Exclusive Dealings	605
13 Ethics and Section 3	607
THE CLAYTON ACT—SECTION 7	608
14 Introduction	608
15 General Principles	609
16 Special Doctrines	611

17 Enforcement	612
18 Tender Offers	613
19 FTC Premerger Notification	615
20 Justice Department Merger Guidelines	616
THE FEDERAL TRADE COMMISSION ACT	618
21 Introduction	618
22 Unfair Methods of Competition	619
REVIEW QUESTIONS	621

24 Environment Laws and Pollution Control 624

OVERVIEW	624
1 The National Environmental Policy Act	624
GOVERNMENT'S REGULATION OF BUSINESS	628
2 Introduction	628
3 The Environmental Protection Agency	628
4 The Clean Air Act: Basic Structure	628
5 The Clean Air Act: Policy Trends	631
6 The Clean Water Act	633
7 The Noise Control Act	635
8 The Pesticide Control Acts	636
9 The Solid Waste Disposal Act	637
10 Toxic and Hazardous Substances: Introduction	638
11 Toxic Substances Control Act	639
12 Natural Resource Conservation and Recovery Act	640
13 The Superfund	641
14 Radiation	641
SUITS BY PRIVATE INDIVIDUALS	642
15 Introduction	642
16 Tort Theories and Pollution	643
17 Trends	645
REVIEW QUESTIONS	647
APPENDIX: THE CONSTITUTION OF THE UNITED STATES OF AMERICA	649
GLOSSARY	669
INDEX	685

LIST OF CASES

Aaron v. Securities and Exchange Commission	473
Abel v. Eli Lilly and Co.	230
Allied Structural Steel Co. v. Spannaus	107
American Home Products Corp. v. F.T.C.	501
American Textile Manufacturers Institute, Inc. v. Donovan	176
Anderson v. City of Bessemer City, N.C.	89
Anderson v. Foothill Industrial Bank	493
Arkansas Writers' Project, Inc. v. Ragland	131
Armco Inc. v. Hardesty	123
Aspen Skiing Co. v. Aspen Highlands Skiing Corp.	584
AT&T Tech., Inc. v. Communications Workers	93
Attorney General of New York v. Soto-Lopez	150
Ayers v. Town of Jackson	644
Baltimore Gas & Electric v. Natural Resources Defense Council	170
Banco Nacionál de Cuba v. Sabbatino	330
Beckman v. Vassall-Dillworth Lincoln-Mercury	63
Bill Johnson's Restaurants, Inc. v. N.L.R.B.	429
Blue Shield of Virginia, et al. v. Mccready	563
Branti v. Finkel	137
Bridgman v. Curry	205
Brothers v. First Leasing	504
California Retail Liquor Dealers Assoc. v. Midcal Aluminum, Inc., et al.	555
Carey v. National Oil Corporation	331
Cargill, Inc. v. Monfort of Colorado, Inc.	559
Catalano, Inc. v. Target Sales, Inc.	567

LIST OF CASES

Case	Page
Chevron U.S.A. Inc. v. Natural Resources Defense Council	631
Chiarella v. United States	478
Citizen Publishing Co. et al. v. United States	579
Citizens St. Bank v. Timm Schmidt & Co.	270
Clayco Petroleum Corp. v. Occidental Petroleum Corp.	337
Connecticut v. Teal	384
Consol. Edison v. Public Service Com'n.	133
Continental T.V., Inc. v. GTE Sylvania, Inc.	580
Crandell v. Larkin and Jones Appliance Co.	259
Dirks v. Securities and Exchange Commission	481
Dixon v. Love	146
Donovan v. Trans World Airlines	356
Dothard v. Rawlinson	385
Dun & Bradstreet, Inc. v. Greenmoss Builders, Inc.	219
Dunaway v. Dept. of Labor	361
Eastex, Inc. v. N.L.R.B.	433
Edward J. Debartolo Corp. v. N.L.R.B. et al.	450
Eli Lilly and Company v. Sav-on-drugs, Inc.	282
Ellis v. Broth. of Ry., Airline and S.S. Clerks	404
Eppler, Guerin & Turner, Inc. v. Kasmir	306
Esquire Radio & Electronics, Inc. v. Montgomery Ward & Co.	195
F.C.C. v. Midwest Video	166
F.T.C. v. Indiana Federation of Dentists	620
Fall River Dyeing & Finishing Corp. v. National Labor Relations Board	401
First National Bank of Santa Fe v. Quintana	529
Ford Motor Co. v. Equal Employment Opportunity Comm.	376
Ford Motor Company v. N.L.R.B.	443
Ford v. Revlon, Inc.	216
Fortner Enterprises, Inc. v. United States Steel Corp. et al.	604
From the Nature of the Judicial Process	47
Garland Co., Inc. v. Roofco Co.	199
Germann v. F.L. Smithe Mach. Co.	247
Goldfarb Et Ux. v. Virginia State Bar et al.	572
Great Atlantic & Pacific Tea Co., Inc. v. F.T.C.	602
Greenman v. Yuba Power Products, Inc.	245
Hanson v. Funk Seeds International	250
Havens Realty Corp. v. Coleman	72
Herrera v. First Northern Savings & Loan Assn.	510
Hishon v. King & Spalding	374
Hobbie v. Unemployment Appeals Com'n of Florida	129
Hodel v. Indiana	115
Hofmann Corp. v. Superior Court (SMAYSTRLA)	81
Illinois Brick Co. v. Illinois	562
In Re Uranium Antitrust Litigation	335

LIST OF CASES

Insurance Company of North America v. Pasakarnis	232
J&K Computer Systems, Inc. v. Parrish	319
J. Truett Payne Co. v. Chrysler Motors Corp.	597
Jacksonville Bulk Terminals, Inc. v. International Longshoremen's Assoc.	407
Jacksonville State Bank v. Barnwell	539
Johnson v. Santa Clara County Transportation Agency	388
Junker v. Crory	465
Kassel v. Consolidated Freightways Corp., etc.	120
Kelly v. R. G. Industries, Inc.	236
Keystone Bank v. Flooring Specialists, Inc.	527
Kramer v. Mcdonald's System, Inc.	284
Land Management v. Department of Envir. Prot.	279
Libby, McNeil & Libby v. United Steelworkers	192
Linden Lumber Division, Summer & Co. v. NLRB	413
Local 3489 United Steelworkers of America v. Usery	419
Local Union No. 189, Amalgamated Meat Cutters, and Butcher Workmen of North America, AFL-CIO, et al. v. Jewel Tea Company, Inc.	403
Lupien v. Malsbenden	280
Maine v. Taylor	119
Mason v. Hosta	197
Matter of Tobin	543
Memphis Fire Dept. v. Shotts	390
Metropolitan Edison Co. v. People Against Nuclear Energy	626
Michelin Tire Corp. v. Wages	110
Mitsubishi Motors v. Soler Chrysler-Plymouth	340
Monsanto v. Spray-Rite Service Corporation	564
N.L.R.B. v. Action Automotive, Inc.	411
N.L.R.B. v. City Disposal Systems, Inc.	435
N.L.R.B. v. Intern. Broth. of Elec. Workers, Local 340	448
N.L.R.B. v. Retail Store Emp. Union, Etc.	450
N.L.R.B. v. Savair Manufacturing Co.	447
N.L.R.B. v. Sure-Tan, Inc.	436
N.L.R.B. v. Transportation Management Corp.	437
Nassau County School Board v. Arline	394
National Collegiate Athletic Association v. Board of Regents of the University of Oklahoma and University of Georgia Athletic Association	577
National Society of Professional Engineers v. U.S.	573
Navarro Savings Association v. Lee	57
New Hampshire Ins. Co. v. Gruhn	524
New York v. Burger	140
Newport News Shipbuilding and Dry Dock Co. v. EEOC	382
Palmateer v. International Harvester Co.	311

Case	Page
Pattern Makers' League of North America v. N.L.R.B.	416
Perkins v. Standard Oil Company of California	600
Phillips Petroleum Co. v. Shutts	74
Pioneer Realty and Land Company v. Mortgage Plus	189
Quivira Mining Co. v. EPA	634
Radford v. Community Mortgage and Investment Corp.	537
Reader v. Dertina & Associates Marketing	291
Reiter v. Sonotone Corp.	560
Renberg v. Zarrow	287
Rubin v. United States	471
Saint Francis College v. Al-Khazraji	391
Sampson v. Hunt	316
Sanford v. Kobey Bros. Const. Corp.	308
Santa Fe Industries, Inc. v. Green	477
Schreiber v. Burlington Northern, Inc.	484
Securities and Exchange Commission v. Lund	482
Securities and Exchange Commission v. W. J. Howey Co.	462
Shearson/American Express, Inc., and Mary Ann Mcnulty v. Eugene Mcmahon et al.	92
Siegal, et al. v. Chicken Delight, Inc., et al.	606
Simpson v. Union Oil Co.	575
Small v. Springs Industries, Inc.	368
Smith v. Jones	169
Sony Corporation of America v. Universal City Studios, Inc.	226
Southland Corp. v. Keating	104
Stanfield v. Laccoarce	309
State Farm Mutual Automobile Ins. Co. v. Queen	202
Supreme Court of N.H. v. Piper	112
Texas Industries, Inc. v. Radcliff Materials, Inc.	561
Textile Workers Union v. Darlington Manufacturing Co.	440
Toups v. Sears, Roebuck & Co.	256
Trans World Airlines, Inc. v. Hardison	379
Trans-Am Builders, Inc. v. Woods Mill Ltd.	289
Tudor Engineering Co. v. Mouw	64
Tuttle v. Raymond	238
Union Electric Co. v. EPA	630
United Parcel Service v. Fetterman	352
United States v. Container Corporation of America	576
United States v. Doe	142
United States v. Grinnell Corporation	583
United States v. Park	314
United States v. Reader's Digest Association, Inc.	496
United States v. Von's Grocery Co.	610
United States v. Yermian	159
United Steelworkers of America v. Sadlowski	420

Utah Pie Co. v. Continental Baking Co. et al.	598
Va. St. Bd. of Pharm. v. Va. Cit. Cons. Council	135
Vickers v. North Am. Land Development	304
Walker v. Armco Steel Corp.	60
Wardair Canada, Inc. v. Florida Dept. of Revenue	122
Welch v. Bancorp Management Advisors, Inc.	221
Whirlpool Corp. v. Marshall	347
William Inglis & Sons Baking Co., et al. v. ITT Continental Baking Co., Inc., et al.	586
Wimberly v. Labor and Industrial Relations Comm. of Missouri	360
Woodruff v. Georgia State University	51
World-Wide Volkswagen Corp. v. Woodson	76
Zamora v. Valley Federal Savings & Loan Association	507
Zapata Corporation v. Maldonado	297

PREFACE

An examination of the *Wall Street Journal* or any business magazine such as *Business Week* will reveal numerous articles covering the legal problems of the business community. For example, topics such as affirmative action, sexual harassment, insider trading, white-collar crime, product liability, professional malpractice and mergers dominate the information conveyed to the business community in such relevant publications. Television news also includes major coverage of legal issues affecting business and its environment. For example, television news during the summer of 1987 was dominated by congressional hearings on two nominations to the Supreme Court of the United States. The senate rejection of Judge Bork is still debated in both judicial and political circles. As a result of the TV hearings, the terms "judicial restraint" and "activist" have become part of the vocabulary of educated citizens. This text is designed to provide future business persons with the background needed to understand such matters and with the ability to use law-related information in making business decisions. It recognizes that today more than ever, students preparing for careers in business need to grasp the significance of law and its role in every business decision.

In the 1960s, the subject matter of law courses began to change significantly. New legal theories had brought expanded rights to employees, consumers, investors, and others. These new rights imposed corollary duties on business which were often enforced by regulatory agencies. In 1963 we wrote, along with Professor Robert L. Black of the University of Illinois, the first text that responded to these great changes taking place in the law. In it we developed an approach to law that has come generally to be recognized as the *legal environment of business*. This approach focuses on public law, the regulation of business and legal trends, rather than on the detailed private law rules of contracts, negotiable instruments, and business organizations. This approach emphasized relationships such as debtor-creditor, buyer-seller, and employer-employee, rather than transactions.

Although education in private-law subjects remains useful to many business persons, we believed that detailed coverage of them should be reserved for advanced, specialized courses which follow this general course about law and the legal system. The legal environment approach recognizes that for the basic law course business students now need to appreciate the legal relationships of government–business and business–society before they master the technical details of private law.

Fundamentals of the Legal Environment of Business continued this legal environment approach, which we have refined now for over almost three decades. The second edition, now called *The Legal Environment of Business: Briefed Case Edition,* updates and further refines this approach with content directed especially at lower-division students. The text is appropriate for use at any senior college or university where the legal environment of business is required as the basic course by the American Assembly of Collegiate Schools of Business (AACSB). Significantly, we also designed it for use at community colleges and other schools where business students may be transferring to an AACSB accredited senior college or university.

Guiding principle

In preparing these materials for an environmental course in law, a basic principle has guided us: the materials should actively prepare students for decision making in business rather than merely summarize for them the course content of various law school subjects. This is the heart of our instructional approach, and it means that we have treated law as an important institution of society and as a tool for generating policy. Only students who appreciate these dynamics of law will be able to go beyond the commonly held lay concept of law as a series of rules and to understand it most effectively for business decision making. They will also recognize that the law is only one influence on decisions. Ethical considerations also play a major role in defining appropriate business conduct.

Features

The Legal Environment of Business: Briefed Case Edition contains several noteworthy features. Among the more important are:

1 A clear, straight-forward writing style. We believe that the study of law is difficult enough without burdening students additionally by a complex writing style. The publisher has also aided readability by using color, large type, wide margins and numerous headings throughout the text.

2 Briefed cases. Each chapter contains many cases illustrating the text. These cases have been presented in a brief format. The 164 briefs contain all the essential facts and issues of the actual case opinions, lacking only the language of the judges themselves, who write opinions for lawyers instead of students. Note that special pains have been taken throughout the text to brief the most recent cases of interest to the business community. There are 69 cases new to this edition.

3 Text in seven distinct parts. The seven parts each consist of 3 or 4 chapters. The instructor is able to pick and choose those subjects to be covered and the order of coverage. The last three parts deal with the law in its role of protecting employees, the general public and society from harmful business activity.

4 International business. There is a new chapter, International Transactions, in the part dealing with conducting business. Education relating to conducting international business is of growing importance in business education and we are indebted to Professor Russell L. Welch of North Texas State University for preparing this chapter.

5 Appropriate private-law coverage. Although this text focuses on public law, part three contains appropriate private-law coverage as well. For instance, product liability and business-related accidents make it necessary for students to understand the tort system, which is the subject of two chapters. Since contracts form the basis for economic exchanges, and much government regulation affects contracts, one chapter is devoted to principles of contract law. This coverage also introduces contracts to students who will not take additional, specialized courses in private-law subjects. Agency and suretyship are also discussed in parts of chapters.

6 Treatment of ethical issues. Many chapters discuss ethical issues of public and social policy which underlie legal rules. The text contains several references to the Caterpillar Tractor Company Code of Worldwide Business Conduct and Operating Principles which are used to illustrate the approach of a major corporation to current ethical issues.

7 The chapter overview. Each chapter begins with an overview of the material covered in the chapter. We believe that this feature will prove very valuable in helping students relate their reading to key chapter concepts.

8 Other student study aids. At the end of each chapter are review questions - 341 in all. Of these, 150 are new to this edition. The text also includes a glossary that contains definitions of legal terms used in boldface throughout the text so that students will not require access to a legal dictionary while reading. The appendix includes the United States Constitution.

9 Following the preface, there is a special section addressed to students. In this section, we provide step-by-step instructions on how to study this textbook.

10 To supplement the text's coverage, a comprehensive instructor's manual and test bank are available to adoptors. For students there is a study guide. As a teaching tool, it should aid in understanding the more difficult subjects of the text.

Acknowledgements

The authors would like to thank the Caterpillar Tractor Company of Peoria, Illinois for permission to reprint excerpts from its Code of Worldwide Business Conduct and Operating Principles.

The authors would also like to acknowledge the assistance of the following professors who reviewed the manuscript and provided many helpful suggestions: Andy E. Hendrick, University of South Carolina, Coastal Carolina College; Stephen Kellogg, Fredonia State University College; Robert D. King, Stockton State College; Stephen L. Kroleski, Iona College; George McNary, Creighton University; William H. Ravenell, Florida A & M University and Lois Yoder, Kent State University.

Finally, we wish a special note of gratitude to Annette Bodzin who once again has been everything that any author could ask for in a production editor.

Robert N. Corley

O. Lee Reed

To the Student

How to Study the Legal Environment of Business

To gain the most from this textbook, you should learn how to study written material effectively. You can achieve effective study through use of the SQ3R method, a method widely taught by study-skills psychologists for learning textual material.

SQ3R stands for *survey, question, read, recite,* and *review.* As a study method, it has dramatically improved the grade-point averages of most students who have practiced it. It is based upon the concept that active study of written material improves memory and comprehension of information far better than passive reading. Unfortunately, many students have not recognized the difference between active study and mere passive reading.

Students often read a textbook chapter exactly as they would read a novel or a magazine article. They begin with the first sentence of the chapter and read straight through the material, pausing only to underline occasionally. This way of reading may be suitable for a novel, but it is quite inappropriate for a textbook. Psychologists insist that an active study method must begin with a *survey* of the material to be read. If you plan to spend two hours studying a thirty-page chapter, take three-to-five minutes in the beginning and survey the chapter. First, read the boldtype section headings (each chapter of this book is divided into numbered sections). Second, read a sentence or two from the text of each section. The purpose of this survey is to familiarize you with the topics covered in the chapter. Fight the tendency to stop your surveying process in order to comprehend all of the concepts you are surveying. Comprehension is not the goal of surveying.

Following the survey of all the sections, go back to the beginning of the chapter. Ask yourself a *question* before reading each section. Ask it aloud, if possible, but silently if circumstances demand. The important thing is actually to "talk to yourself." Normally, each section heading can easily be turned into a question. If the section heading reads *Stare Decisis,* ask yourself the question, "What does stare decisis mean?"

Only after asking a question are you finally ready to *read* a chapter section. In reading keep your question in mind. By so doing you will be reading for a purpose: to discover the answer to your question.

Upon finishing each section, stop and *recite* the answer to your question. An example is at the end of the section on stare decisis to say to yourself, "Stare decisis refers to the legal tradition that a judge in a given case will follow the precedent established in similar cases decided by courts in that jurisdiction." According to psychologists, to recite this way greatly aids memory. Recitation also lets you know whether or not you have understood the material just read.

The last step of the SQ3R method is *review*. When devoting two hours to the study of a chapter, take the final fifteen minutes of that time to review the material. Review the questions taken from the headings of each chapter section and recite the answers to them, rereading material if necessary to answer accurately.

SQ3R does not require you to study longer, but it does allow you to study more effectively. With practice and use SQ3R will become a very valuable tool in your academic life. Good study!

Robert N. Corley

O. Lee Reed

THE LEGAL ENVIRONMENT OF BUSINESS:
BRIEFED CASE EDITION

PART ONE

INTRODUCTION

1
Introduction To Law

2
The Powers and Functions of Courts

3
Court Systems

4
Litigation and Other Methods for Resolving Disputes

CHAPTER 1

INTRODUCTION TO LAW

OVERVIEW

This chapter introduces you to law, lawyers, and legal terminology. The various classifications of legal subjects, such as private law versus public law and substance versus procedure, are illustrated. Other influences on behavior, such as ethical considerations, are discussed. This text primarily deals with law that relates to the business environment and the ways in which it affects business decisions. The law is one of the means for controlling the conduct of businesses.

In reading this chapter, give special attention to the following legal terms: administrative law, felony, fixture, misdemeanor, negligence, procedural law, stare decisis, substantive law, tort, and white-collar crime.

1 THE LAW AND BUSINESS

The subject matter of this text is the law as it defines and prescribes the environment in which business is conducted in the United States. Since the focus of the book is law, much of the discussion concerns litigation and lawyers. In a real sense, litigation has replaced baseball as our national pastime. Today, our courts are filled with cases involving every conceivable controversy that may arise. Whenever people have a disagreement, there is a distinct possibility that they may resolve it with a lawsuit.

We are the most litigious society in history. We protect our rights by litigating. We change society through litigation. Every year several million lawsuits are filed. The issues include questions of broad public policy, such as the use of nuclear power or the right to life in the abortion cases. The range of cases includes such issues as liability for injuries caused by defective products or medical practice, and liability to a victim of discrimination in employment. Many cases, such as those dealing with couples seeking a divorce, involve issues of importance to the litigants only. Many cases are actually frivolous and of importance to no one. Thus, the range of litigation runs from the most serious and important issues to issues of no importance at all.

Whether it is a cause or an effect of our litigious society, a significant development in recent years is the explosion in the number of lawyers in this country. In 1970, there were about 350,000 lawyers. By the mid-1980s, there were 650,000, and in the 1990s the number will reach 1 million. Two-thirds of the world's lawyers practice in the United States, and more lawyers were admitted to practice in the 1970s than in the previous 100 years. Law and lawyers are involved in almost every aspect of our daily lives and in almost every business decision. An understanding of the law and the role of lawyers in conducting business is essential to an understanding of the legal environment of business.

The increase in litigation and in the number of lawyers is consistent with another trend in our society—increased regulation of business. Although enforcement varies from time to time, there has been increased regulation of business in the post-World-War-II-period. This has been in response to public demands for protection from an unhealthy environment, for safer products and workplaces, and for equal employment opportunity. This text discusses these regulatory laws as a major component of the legal environment of business.

The basic role of law in business decisions is readily apparent. It constrains business in its decisions and in its selection of alternative courses of action. Certain conduct is illegal, and individuals or businesses who commit acts or omissions declared to be illegal are subject to sanctions. There may be fines or imprisonment if the conduct is declared a crime. The sanctions may include liability for dollar damages if the conduct is tortious (involving a wrongful act) or a breach of contract. In addition, the law and legal sanctions may be used to prevent certain conduct or to require that certain things be done. Business decisions must be made within the law, or sanctions will be imposed. The law is the foundation for the regulation of all business conduct and decisions. Throughout this text, we will attempt to acquaint you with some of the more important laws controlling business decisions and individual behavior.

2 DEFINITIONS OF LAW

Before we classify various legal subjects, you should recognize several definitions of the word "law." No word of such common usage is so hard to define precisely or is used to express a variety of concepts so well as is the word "law." For example, "law" is used to describe specific statutory enactments and also to denote a general system of rules for governing conduct. Popular uses of the terms "law," "legal," and "illegal" are limitless. The meaning of these words in any particular situation must be determined from the context in which they are used. For example, the use of the word "illegal" to describe a forward pass in a football game differs significantly from the use of "illegal" to describe a contract. The force of the law generally is not involved in a football game, but since the game must be played by rules, the use of legal terminology is to be expected. An illegal contract is similar to an illegal forward pass in that both may result in penalties. However, the legality of a contract is determined by our courts and the legal system. To date, the legality of a forward pass is determined by the referees.

Law is often considered to be a command: You shall do this or you shall not do that. As a command, it is prescribed by a superior, and the inferior is bound to obey. Law is a rule of conduct commanding what is right and prohibiting what is wrong. The criminal law is essentially a body of commands flowing from the people as a whole to people as individuals telling them what they may or may not do.

Many areas of our law, such as those involving contracts and torts, do not "command compliance" in the technical sense. They are so constructed that an aggrieved party is given a remedy against one who violates accepted legal principles in these areas. Civil courts, except in unusual situations, do not require compliance but instead impose liability for noncompliance.

Law as Principles Used by Courts

Law has also been defined as the body of principles and rules which the courts apply in the decision of controversies. Law is made up of three elements: (1) formulated legislation, including constitutions, statutes, treaties, ordinances, and codes; (2) rules of law announced by the courts in deciding cases; and (3) the system of legal concepts and techniques which forms the basis of judicial action.

Justice Oliver Wendell Holmes said, "Law is a statement of the circumstances in which the public force will be brought to bear through courts." Law is simply what the courts will or will not order in any particular case.

Law as a Scheme of Social Control

Law is a scheme for controlling the conduct of people; it deals with social interests. Whereby social interests recognize a right in one person, courts create machinery to assist the person with this right in obtaining redress against the person with the duty or obligation, if the duty is not performed or if the obligation is unfulfilled. By this concept, law has four characteristics:

1 It is a scheme of social control.
2 It protects social interests.
3 It accomplishes its purpose by recognizing a capacity in persons to influence the conduct of others.
4 It provides courts and legal procedures to help a person with this capacity.

This definition of law supports the position of judges as social engineers. They function in this role when making decisions such as allowing abortions, prohibiting prayer in school, and requiring busing of school children to achieve racial balance in education.

Law as Justice

All the foregoing definitions convey the concept that law regulates human conduct and that through courts it resolves controversies. The goal of law is justice, but law and justice are not synonymous, just as legal justice and social justice are not synonymous. Justice has been defined as that which is founded in equity, honesty, and righteousness. It is the attempt of honorable persons to do that which is fair. Justice is the purpose and end of government and civil society. Apparently, the achievement of justice depends upon the concept of right and wrong in the society involved. The purpose of justice in our society, as stated in the Declaration of Independence, is to secure for all men "life, liberty, and the pursuit of happiness."

Social justice recognizes more rights and duties than does legal justice, although the trend of the law is toward equating these concepts. Perfect justice would require that all persons discharge all their obligations and duties so that all other persons may enjoy all their rights and privileges. Our society through law determines which rights and duties will be protected and strives through its judicial system for perfect justice. Of course, the law is incapable of perfect justice because it is in the hands of imperfect people and operates with imperfect procedures. As law approaches perfect justice, legal justice and social justice tend to merge.

Dean Roscoe Pound of the Harvard Law School attempted to define law in terms of justice when he said that the science of law is "that organized body of knowledge that has to do with the administration of justice by public or regular tribunals in accordance with principles or rules of general character and more or less uniform application."

3 SCHOOLS OF LEGAL THOUGHT

Closely allied to these definitions of law are schools of legal thought which help us understand the various uses of the words "law" and "illegal." They also identify the different influences which help to shape the development of legal principles. Among the more generally recognized schools of legal thought are the historical, the analytical, the natural, the sociological, and the realist.

The historical school gives great weight to custom and history as a source of law. Law comes from the habits and traditions of people. For example, conduct such as taking the life of another has traditionally been considered wrongful by all civilized peoples, and therefore we have laws relating to homicide. Similarly, the laws relating to business transactions have developed out of the manner of doing business and customary business practices. According to this school of legal thought, human actions and beliefs have formed the law, and not vice versa.

The analytical school of legal thought is based upon a belief and reliance on logic as the basis of law. Under this philosophy, law is conceived by reason and logic. Law comes from the sovereign or government because of the need for order and a system of known rules to follow. Social order logically requires definite rules for governing human conduct.

The natural school of legal thought gives great weight to the influence of religion and divine principles in developing the law. Law arises from right, reason, and the intelligence of man as derived from his Creator. Law distinguishes right from wrong. The natural law philosophy has given us courts of equity and, indeed, much of our constitutional theory. Such concepts as due process of law and equal protection of the laws have come from the natural law philosophy.

The sociological school of legal thought gives recognition to the law as a scheme of social control. It is consistent with the definition of law given on page 5. This legal philosophy considers the law to be the result of competing social forces and values. Law results from the purposes that are to be accomplished. The sociologist uses facts and economic and social theory in developing the law, and he or she views the law as the means of resolving disputes and conflicts between different groups and interests in society.

The realist school of legal thought is a development of this century. The realist takes a very pragmatic approach to law. Law comes from experience. Holmes's definition of law on page 5 is an example of realist reasoning. Realists are impressed with the role of facts and are willing to recognize exceptions to almost every general rule of law. Realists recognize that law is constantly changing.

These schools of legal thought further demonstrate the difficulty of defining "law" and of understanding its sources, uses, and development. It will be helpful to keep the various philosophies in mind as the subject matter of this text is studied.

4 THE RULE OF LAW

Justice Felix Frankfurter in his opinion in *United States v. Mine Workers,* 330 U.S. 258 (1947), began with these words: "The historic phrase 'a government of laws and not of men' epitomizes the distinguishing character of our political society. When John Adams put that phrase into the Massachusetts Declaration of Rights he was not indulging a rhetorical flourish. He was expressing the aim of those who, with him, framed the Declaration of Independence and founded the Republic." Adams's statement, which recognizes the role of the rule of law in our society, had its origin in England prior to the Magna Charta. The Magna Charta used the term "per legem terrae"—the law of the land. English history is filled with numerous statements proclaiming that even the royal power is subject to the rule of law.

The concept of the rule of law has been the cornerstone of our society and government from the beginning, and it is simply accepted as part of our heritage. As Lincoln said, it is the "political religion" of the country.

In our society, it is the law which is used to decide disputes, not the wishes or ideas of any mere mortal, irrespective of his or her position. Moreover, the parties for the most part accept the fact that the dispute will be decided by a rule of law and that the winner and the loser alike will accept the determination without resorting to another method of resolution, such as force.

The role of the rule of law as the basic ingredient in ordered liberty is obvious from even a cursory examination of the matters before the Supreme Court in any term. The issues presented involve due process of law, equal protection of the laws, and the power of the governors over the governed. To a substantial extent, the failures of our society can be directly attributed to the failure of people to accept and abide by application of rules of law. In a real sense, the subject matter of this text is the rule of law as it applies to business.

The study of law essentially concerns rules of law. A rule of law, using Holmes's definition, is a statement that if certain facts exist, then the judicial branch of government will take certain action or refuse to take certain action at the request of someone involved. In other words, a rule of law is a prediction as to what a court will or will not do in a given factual situation. It is then obvious that facts create legal issues which are resolved by using rules of law. You should therefore be aware of the tremendous importance of facts to the law. A majority of our legal procedures are designed to discover the facts. For instance, the function of the jury is fact finding.

5 LAWYERS

Before examining the various classifications of legal subjects, you should have some understanding about lawyers and the legal profession. As members of the legal profession, lawyers usually play a major role in the application of rules of law and legal principles. Liberty and justice are abstractions that can only be realized when individuals operate a system in such a manner as to achieve them. The law can only work through individuals; it is not self-enforcing. Although courts and juries constitute the decision makers in our judicial system, lawyers play an integral role in our legal system.

The practice of law is a profession. It involves a dedication to society in which the service performed is more important than any remuneration received for the service. The individual practitioner assumes duties and responsibilities which extend to the courts, to the public, and to the client.

A lawyer's first duty is to the administration of justice. As an officer of the court, he or she should see that proceedings are conducted in a dignified and orderly manner and that issues are tried on their merits only. The practice of law is not a game or mere battle of wits, but a means to promote justice. The lawyer's duties to each client require the highest degree of fidelity, loyalty, and integrity.

To engage in the practice of law is not a natural or constitutional right but a privilege conferred because one knows the law and possesses good moral character. The latter involves a proper conception of the nature and duties of the office of attorney and also of the ethics of the profession. It has sometimes been described as absolute obedience to the unenforceable. Absolute honesty and integrity are minimum standards for the profession.

Sometimes the conduct of some lawyers has not met the high professional standards of the profession. Conflicts of interest and activities such as "ambulance chasing" have occurred, contrary to professional ethics. The courts and bar associations try to eliminate such activities by disbarring or suspending such persons from the practice of law. The code of ethical standards for lawyers undergoes periodic review and updating in order that the profession may effectively serve the public interest.

A lawyer serves in essentially three capacities—counselor, advocate, and public servant. As a counselor, a lawyer by the very nature of the profession knows his or her client's most important secrets and affairs. A lawyer is often actively involved in the business and personal lives of clients, ranging from their business affairs and family matters such as divorce to their alleged violations of the criminal law. These relationships dictate that a lawyer meet the highest standards of professional and ethical conduct.

As an advocate, a lawyer is not only a "fighter" in court but a negotiator of compromise. Lawyers spend most of their efforts seeking solutions to differences between adversaries. Advocacy is practiced not only before courts and juries but before opposing counsel and with one's own client as well.

As public servants, lawyers serve in all capacities at all levels of organized society. Their formal education, training, and experience leave them better equipped than most to render valuable public service.

It is obvious that if a lawyer is to give competent advice and adequate representation, he or she must know to the fullest extent possible all the facts involved in any legal problem presented by the client. In attempting to ensure that a lawyer may be fully advised of a client's problems and all matters affecting them, the rules of evidence provide that confidential communications to a lawyer are privileged. The law does not permit a lawyer to reveal such facts and testify against a client, even if called to the stand to do so at a trial. This is called the attorney-client privilege, and it may extend to communications made to the lawyer's employees in certain cases. This is especially important today because law firms frequently use paralegals to gather facts and assist attorneys. This privilege extends to corporations as well as to individuals. The corporate privilege protects communications by corporate employees with corporate counsel.

6 GENERAL CLASSIFICATIONS OF LEGAL SUBJECTS

The law has often been described as "a seamless web" in which principles of law are hopelessly and endlessly intertwined with one another. For this reason, any attempted classification or description of the many and varied legal subjects is necessarily inaccurate.

One means of classifying the law is to divide it into matters of public law and matters of private law. *Public law* includes *constitutional law,* **administrative law,** and *criminal law.* In each of these areas, society or "the people" are directly involved. Their interests are represented by some governmental agency, officer, or official whose obligation it is to see that justice is accomplished and the ends of society fulfilled. Public law provides a major portion of the legal environment of business. For this reason, much of the material in subsequent chapters deals with constitutional and administrative areas of public law and their application to business.

Private law encompasses those legal problems and relationships which exist between individuals, as contrasted with those in which society is involved. Private law is traditionally separated into *the law of contracts, the law of* **torts,** and *the law of property*. There are many subdivisions, at least academically, in the law of contracts and in the law of property. Some of the more common subdivisions are set forth in Table 1-1.

Another important classification or distinction in law is the one between substance and procedure. **Substantive law** defines the legal relationship of people with other people, or as between them and the state. Thus, the rules

TABLE 1-1 SUBDIVISIONS OF THE CLASSIFICATIONS OF LEGAL SUBJECTS

The law of contracts	The law of property	Procedural law
Sales of goods	Real property	Pleadings
Commercial paper	Personal property	Evidence
Secured transactions	Leases	Trials
Bank deposits and collections	Bailments	Appeals
Creditors' rights	Wills	Civil procedure
Consumer protection	Trusts and estates	Criminal procedure
Debtor protection	Mortgages	Probate procedure

of contract law are substantive in nature. **Procedural law** deals with the method and means by which substantive law is made and administered. In other words, substantive rules of law define rights and duties, while procedural rules of law provide the machinery for enforcing those rights and duties. Every social institution has rules by which it conducts its affairs or "proceeds." There are rules of law relating to legislative procedure which govern the steps that must be taken for a statute to be valid. A typical rule of legislative procedure might require that all bills be read to the assembly twice before adoption. Failure to follow this rule of procedure might void the legislature's attempt to create rights or duties in the statute.

Judicial procedures involve the method of conducting lawsuits, appeals, and the enforcement of judgments. The rules for conducting civil trials are different from those for criminal trials. For example, each party may call the other party to the witness stand for cross-examination in a civil trial, but the defendant may not be required to testify in a criminal case. Procedural problems sometimes arise concerning papers filed in lawsuits, the admission of evidence, and various other techniques involved in trying the case. They are the rules of the game. Many rules classified as procedural in character might be just as easily classified as substantive because they actually affect rights and duties. Chapter 4 deals with the procedural aspects of law in greater depth. See Table 1-1 for some of the typical subject-matter breakdowns of procedural law.

A classification similar to that of public versus private contrasts civil law cases with criminal cases. For administrative purposes, courts usually separate criminal actions from other lawsuits, with the latter known as civil cases. Such cases include: (1) suits for breach of contract, (2) torts, and (3) other actions in which the remedy sought is not punishment of the defendant but a remedy such as dollar damages.

The sections that follow provide a brief introduction to four of the basic legal subjects. The first, criminal law, is a public law subject and the remainder are private law topics.

7 THE CRIMINAL LAW

A crime is a public wrong against society. Criminal cases are brought by the government on behalf of the people. When a person is convicted of a crime, the following punishments may be imposed by society: (1) death, (2) imprisonment, (3) fine, (4) removal from office, or (5) disqualification from holding and enjoying any office or from voting. Among the purposes of such punishment are to protect the public and to deter persons from wrongful conduct. Conduct involved in murder and kidnapping is considered criminal in order to protect individuals from harm. Arson and embezzlement are terms used to describe crimes relating to the protection of property. Some conduct is criminal in order to protect government and the public interest. For example, bribery of a public official is a wrong against society as is price-fixing or selling pornography. Punishment is also imposed simply for the sake of punishment, as well as the isolation and suppression of the criminal element of society.

Although criminal conduct often or usually involves acts of violence or the wrongful use of physical force, other criminal conduct involves nonviolent, illegal acts committed by guile, deceit, or concealment, or through simple contracts. Such wrongful conduct as obtaining money by false pretenses or obtaining a business advantage by agreeing with a competitor to fix the price of goods or services is criminal.

Although business crime does not depend on force or violence, physical injury and even death can be caused by it. Defective products sold in violation of applicable statutes frequently cause injuries. Building code violations may result in fire and injury to persons and property. Some businesses, to compete, buy stolen merchandise or employ illegal aliens. The maintenance of a dangerous workplace may be a crime. In one recent case, three executives of a corporation were sentenced to twenty-five years in prison because one of their employees died from work-connected cyanide poisoning.

Criminal law is generally subdivided into **felonies** and **misdemeanors**. This classification is based on the punishment imposed in the event of a conviction. Felonies are punishable by fine or imprisonment in a penitentiary for a period of one year or more, whereas misdemeanors are punishable by a fine or a jail sentence of less than one year. Table 1-2 lists typical offenses under each classification.

Violations of traffic ordinances, building codes, and similar municipal ordinances are sometimes called *petty offenses*. A person guilty of such an offense may be fined, put in jail, or both. Punishment is imposed for petty

TABLE 1-2   CRIMINAL LAW

Typical felonies (Imprisonment for more than one year and/or fine)	Typical misdemeanors (Jail for less than one year and/or fine)
Aggravated assault	Battery
Arson	Gambling
Bribery	Larceny (petty)
Burglary	Littering
Embezzlement	Prostitution
Forgery	Public disturbance
Kidnapping	Simple assault
Larceny (grand)	Traffic offenses
Manslaughter	Trespass
Mayhem	
Murder	
Price-fixing	
Rape	
Robbery	

offenses to deter others from similar conduct as well as punish the guilty party.

White-collar Crime

Criminal law includes many crimes that may be committed by business enterprises as well as those that may be committed by individuals. Some business crimes, such as violating antitrust laws and laws on insider trading of securities, will be discussed later in this book. These crimes are often referred to as **white-collar crimes.** The amount of white-collar crime greatly concerns the business community. Losses from embezzlement and employee theft, including theft through manipulation of computers, not only exceed losses from burglary and larceny but also are growing at an alarming rate.

Hundreds of millions of dollars were involved in illegal insider-trading cases in the mid-1980s. A recent study found that from 1976 to 1985 the number of women arrested for embezzlement increased 55 percent. Fraud arrests among women rose 84 percent during the same period. As the makeup of the work force has changed, it has become clear that white-collar crime is committed by both men and women and is a major problem facing business and society.

There is evidence that losses from shoplifting by employees exceed losses from shoplifting by customers. The cost of crime is a cost of doing business, which results in higher prices for consumers. Costs include higher insurance premiums as well as the cost of the property stolen. The total cost of business-related crime amounts to several billion dollars annually.

One reason sometimes advanced for the increase in white-collar crime is that historically the risk of being caught and sent to prison has been slight. For example, bribery of local officials frequently was considered a legitimate cost of doing business, especially overseas. In addition, employers are often hesitant to prosecute employees for crimes such as embezzlement because disclosure would adversely affect the image of the business. Discharge without prosecution has been a common action taken against employees committing such crimes.

Legal scholars are suggesting new approaches in an attempt to reverse the trend. The most common suggestion is to impose stiff penalties for white-collar crime. Another is to improve the internal controls of businesses so that internal theft and wrongdoing are more likely to be discovered. Finally, there is a trend toward punishing corporate officials for the crimes of their corporations. A corporate official who fixes prices with competitors in violation of the Sherman Antitrust Act is more likely to go to jail now than in the past, and the fine for such conduct has been greatly increased.

RICO

There is a growing tendency to combine suits for dollar damages with the criminal law, especially when the violations are considered to be white-collar crimes. In 1970, Congress enacted a statute entitled the Racketeer Influenced and Corrupt Organizations Act, commonly known as RICO. It was intended to combat organized crime by encouraging private parties to join the battle. It did so by giving private parties the right to file suits for triple damages and attorneys' fees when federal laws dealing with various forms of fraud have been violated by an individual or a business twice within a ten-year period. The illegal acts are any indictable federal crimes, including wire and mail fraud.

The law has not had its intended impact. Rather than encouraging suits against organized crime, RICO has encouraged suits against accounting firms, brokerage houses, banks, and other businesses. A recent survey found that over 75 percent of all RICO suits involve securities frauds or other types of business fraud and less than 10 percent involve criminal activity generally associated with organized crime. When you consider that RICO cases constitute almost 10 percent of the caseload in federal courts, the impact of the law is obvious.

RICO has converted cases where recovery was limited to actual damages to cases where triple damages may be collected. Under this law, two violations in a ten-year period establish racketeering even though there are no criminal convictions. The use of the mail or telephone makes access to RICO very easy for any plaintiff alleging fraud in a business transaction. A plaintiff need not prove a racketeering injury—only an injury resulting from the illegal act.

There are many threatened or filed RICO suits that lack merit. However, many defendants settle such suits and pay substantial sums to do so. The threat of triple damages and of being labeled a racketeer encourages settlement by people that are, in fact, innocent of criminal conduct.

RICO cases often involve routine commercial transactions and business disputes that generally are not considered to be criminal. For example, RICO has been used by the Federal Deposit Insurance Corporation (FDIC) to recover funds lost in a bank failure. RICO cases have arisen in landlord-tenant disputes, labor relations cases, the sale of land, and, of course, the sale of securities.

There are numerous proposals before Congress to change RICO. The sponsors want to require that a pattern of racketeering be evident before anyone can collect triple damages, and many would not allow a suit for damages in the absence of a criminal conviction. It is clear that in this important area of business criminal law new developments are likely. In the meantime, all business people should recognize the great risks inherent in RICO.

Problems

The criminal justice system is a subject of great debate today. For example, the acquittal of President Reagan's attempted assassin on the ground of temporary insanity has prompted a reexamination of the insanity defense.

The public attitude that "justice" was not achieved in so significant a case has fueled the continuing debate about an individual's responsibility for his or her conduct. In addition, the dockets of the criminal courts are overcrowded in many areas of the country. Many persons convicted of criminal conduct appeal their convictions to higher courts, which creates a heavy case load and congestion in those courts. Although the number of judges hearing criminal cases has been greatly increased in recent years, delay and the many problems associated with it still exist.

The criminal law system in this country often fails to provide swift and sure punishment of criminals. It has apparently failed to deter many criminal acts or to rehabilitate a significant portion of those persons convicted of crimes. We have overcrowded jails and unworkable probation systems. As a result, many experts are seeking changes in our criminal law system. For example, some people propose eliminating many offenses commonly regarded as victimless crimes. Alcoholism and drug addiction, for example, would no longer be considered wrongs against society if such people had their way. The same may be true of adultery, sodomy, and other sex crimes between consenting adults, as well as many forms of gambling. Those who propose these changes contend that far too much police effort is spent on these nonviolent crimes, which became part of criminal law in an earlier era when there were different views on morality.

In late 1981, a federal task force on violent crime made sixty-four recommendations to improve the criminal justice system. Among the more significant were to:

1. Permit judges to deny bail to persons rated a danger to the community.
2. Eliminate parole of federal inmates, forcing them to serve the entire sentence imposed.
3. Allow verdicts of "guilty but mentally ill," thus blocking release of many now considered not guilty because of insanity.
4. Make illegally seized evidence admissible in trials if police thought they were complying with the law.
5. Bar lawsuits challenging convictions unless they are filed within three years of a conviction.

As a result of these and other recommendations, there have been major changes in the criminal justice system in this decade.

For example, in 1987 the Supreme Court upheld the constitutionality of the Bail Reform Act of 1984, which permits judges to jail defendants awaiting trial if the defendants are found to be likely hazards to the community. Thus, preventive detention now is constitutional.

8 THE LAW OF CONTRACTS

Contract law concerns the legal relationships created between individuals by their own agreement. The purpose of contract law is to make promises enforceable by courts. Contract law contains several subbodies of law that are frequently treated as separate legal subjects. For example, there is a special body of law relating to contracts for the sale of goods, and there is another covering the subject of commercial paper such as checks and notes. Although the general principles of contract law are developed in the common law in case-by-case decisions, the specialized areas are usually covered to a substantial degree by a statute known as the Uniform Commercial Code.

The detailed subject matter of contracts is covered in Chapter 8. Throughout this book we refer to contracts and to contractual obligations. Many of the chapters contain discussions directly related to contracts. For example, most of the laws that protect consumers relate to the contractual obligations of consumers. Debtor protection, a part of contract law, protects debtors in their borrowing contracts. Much of the discussion about business organizations finds its basis in the law of contracts. The conduct of business primarily involves a series of contracts, and one of the major functions of lawyers is to assist with these contracts. Lawyers draft contracts and review those drafted by others prior to their execution. These duties are a part of the "preventive law" function of attorneys—to avoid disputes and controversies through legal advice. Large corporations usually retain "house counsel" to perform these functions, and other businesses frequently retain outside counsel for this purpose.

As we refer to contracts throughout this text, remember that the law of contracts provides the basis whereby persons can create legal rights and impose legal duties on themselves by their own agreement. Such agreements may be expressed orally or in writing, or they may be implied from the conduct of the parties. The force of organized society, exerted by the courts and the appropriate executive agencies, stands behind a valid contract and provides machinery for its enforcement. Whenever a contract is breached, the injured party can obtain money damages equivalent to the economic loss which he or she can prove was suffered because of the breach. If a breach by one party is serious enough, the other party may be permitted to rescind or cancel the contract. In some circumstances, the remedy of an injured party may be a decree of specific performance, an order of a court of equity commanding the defendant actually to perform the bargain as agreed.

9 THE LAW OF TORTS

A *tort* is a wrong other than a breach of contract committed against persons or their property for which the law gives a right to recover damages. It differs from a crime, which is a wrong against society, although the same act may be both a wrong against a person and a wrong against society, as for example, an assault.

Tort liability is based on two premises: that in a civilized society persons will not intentionally injure others or their property, and that all persons will exercise reasonable care and caution in their activities. The first premise has resulted in a group of torts usually labeled *intentional torts*. These include such traditional wrongs as assault and battery, false imprisonment, libel, slander, trespass, and conversion of personal property. It also includes relatively new torts such as interference with contractual relationships and invasion of privacy. The second premise has led to the general field of tort liability known as **negligence.** Negligence is frequently further broken down into degrees, depending on the extent of carelessness involved and the extent of the duty owed. For example, a grocery store's operator owes a higher standard of care to customers than to trespassers. Each of these premises creates liability for wrongful conduct because a party is at fault. Our legal system in effect says: "If you are at *fault* and cause injury to another person or his property, you shall compensate the injured party for the loss with money."

A major area of tort litigation today deals with malpractice suits against professionals such as physicians, dentists, accountants, lawyers, architects, and engineers. Malpractice actions are a special form of negligence action based on the alleged failure of the professional person to perform services in accordance with professional standards. The law of torts is covered in detail in Chapter 9.

For many years tort claims have been the single largest source of civil litigation in this country. Most of these controversies have resulted from automobile collisions. In addition to automobile accident and other negligence cases, business is often involved in tort actions arising out of the sale of a product which has caused harm. Product liability suits involve injuries such as those resulting from deleterious food or defective drugs. Although such suits have contractual aspects, they usually seek damages for injuries caused by the product. Therefore, product liability, a major subject of the law of torts, is covered in a separate chapter—Chapter 10.

10 THE LAW OF PROPERTY

The law of property concerns the rights and duties of ownership and possession of real estate and personal property. These rights and duties are frequently created by contract and enforced by the law of contracts and torts. Thus, some legal scholars do not consider property to be a separate classification. Perhaps no legal concept has been as important in American history, and as significant for our cultural and economic development, as that of private property. As one might expect, the vast majority of statutes and decisions rendered by both the courts and administrative agencies deals in some way with issues involving the ultimate determination of property rights.

Property is usually classified, according to the nature of the subject matter which is owned, as *real* or *personal property,* and the latter is further classified as *tangible* or *intangible*. Real property is land or any interest in land, and it includes things permanently attached thereto, such as timber and buildings, which are called **fixtures.** Personal property encompasses chattels or things such as livestock, an automobile, clothing, or a television set. These and real property are referred to as tangible property because the property owned has physical existence. Personal property also includes intangible property such as stocks, bonds, accounts receivable, and patent rights. Frequently, intangible property is associated with a document, such as a stock certificate. The document itself is not the property interest, or rights owned, but merely evidence of them. Even if the document is destroyed the property may still exist.

The concept of property is frequently described in terms of ownership, title to, and possession of corporeal objects. Ownership has to do with the extent of a person's rights in property and is usually synonymous with title. Title itself is a confusing term because it is frequently associated with a document of title, such as that to an automobile. Because of this, people frequently think of title in terms of a document labeled "title." Yet individuals usually have title to the clothes they wear and to their other property without a document of title. Possession is a term which often indicates physical control or dominion. However, in law, possession must be defined in terms of the assistance that the law gives a person in controlling property. For example, it is easy physically to possess a book, but impossible physically to possess a 1,000-acre tract of land. However, one may be in legal possession of a 1,000-acre tract because of sanctions provided by law to keep others out.

The term "ownership" includes, besides the right to possess objects, the right to dispose of them by sale, gift, or will; the right to use, possess, and enjoy them; the right to change their nature; and probably the right to destroy them. These rights are creatures of the law which are backed by legal sanctions. Thus, without law, property is nonexistent. Although most people tend to think of property as the thing owned itself, this approach is inaccurate. More correctly, it consists of a bundle of legal rights, such as those listed previously, with respect to a thing. This concept of property views it as a series of legal relationships between the owner and all other persons in which the owner has many rights, and the others, each individually, owe the owner many duties which are often negative in character. For example, there is a duty not to take or use the owner's property.

Ownership also encompasses a series of limitations imposed by law on the owner and often carries with it duties owed by the owner to other persons. Ownership does not include a complete bundle of rights. It is always subject to the rights of government to take private property for public purposes (eminent domain), to tax, and so on. When it is viewed in this manner, all property technically is intangible—it consists of specific legal rights and duties—that may exist *with regard to* a physical, tangible object. Nevertheless, it is generally acceptable in legal terminology to refer to the property rights associated with corporeal things as being tangible property.

Everyone knows the more common rights associated with ownership. Clearly, the owner of farmland generally has the right to sow crops on it, harvest and sell them, and keep the proceeds for personal use. (Unless, of course, the owner has contracted that right away by leasing the land to a tenant.) Also, the owner of a farm has the right, as a rule, to sell it and then use the proceeds of sale as he or she sees fit. And, by a properly executed will, the owner can, subject to some limitations, dispose of the farm at death as he or she wishes. Fundamental to the concept of property are the rights to exclude others from its possession and use.

11 SOURCES OF LAW

The total body of law by which we are governed comes from four basic sources: (1) constitutions, (2) legislation, (3) judicial decisions, and (4) the rules, regulations, and decisions of administrative agencies. If it is assumed that administrative agencies are part of the executive branch of government, then our body of law comes from all three branches.

Under our constitutional system, the constitution of the governmental unit is its basic and supreme law. All other laws, written or unwritten, must be in harmony with it, or they are void. By and large, state constitutions are modeled after the federal Constitution. As such, they provide the same general organization for government, dividing it into executive, legislative, and judicial branches, giving each branch checks and balances on the others. In addition to providing a government's organization, constitutions define the powers and functions of the various branches. Historically, there was a distinction in this respect between the federal and state constitutions. The federal Constitution when ratified was a delegation of authority from the states, which were the basic sovereigns, to the federal government. All powers not contained therein were retained by the states. In other words, the federal Constitution contains grants of power to the federal government, which was established by the states. On the other hand, state governments have all powers not denied them by the federal or their own constitution. State constitutions, therefore, generally contain limitations on the power of state government.

Most of our laws are found in some form of legislation. Legislative bodies exist at all levels of government, as the term includes not only Congress but also state general assemblies, city councils, and many other local government bodies that adopt or enact laws. The term "legislation" in its broad sense includes treaties entered into by the executive branch of government and ratified by the Senate.

Legislation enacted by Congress or a state legislature is usually referred to as a *statute*. Laws passed by local governments are frequently called *ordinances*. Compilations of legislation at all levels of government are called *codes*. For example, we have local traffic codes covering such matters as speed limits, and state laws such as the Uniform Commercial Code which covers all aspects of commercial transactions. The statutes of the United States are known as the U.S. Code.

Judicial decisions provide us with our third major source of laws, often referred to as the common law. Courts "make law" as part of the process of deciding cases and controversies before them. The case law created in this process is based on a doctrine known as **stare decisis,** the principle that prior decisions provide precedents which should be followed in subsequent cases involving the same question of law. In other words, where a rule of law has been announced and followed by courts so that the rule has become settled by judicial decision, a precedent is established for future cases. Judicial decisions create precedent where there is no legislation; they also create precedent by interpreting legislation. This precedent is found by studying cases.

When a court decides a case, particularly upon an appeal from a lower court decision, the court writes an opinion setting forth, among other things, the reasons for its decision. From these written opinions, rules of law can be deduced, and these make up the body of what is called case law or common law. The decisions set forth later in the text are cases that have been decided by courts of review. All cases that have been decided are available to interested persons for use in legal research, as are the statutory enactments of legislatures.

The common law system which originated in England is contrasted with civil law systems such as those in France and Spain. Civil law systems rely primarily on statutes for the law. Issues not covered by specific statutes are decided by courts on their merits in civil law systems without the use of precedent. With the exception of Louisiana, the states of the United States have used the common law system rather than the civil law system as a model. Many state constitutions specifically adopt the common law of England except where changed by statute.

Stare decisis arose from the desire of courts as well as society for certainty and predictability in the law. In addition, following precedent was expedient. The common law, through precedent, settled many legal issues and brought stability into many areas of the law, such as contracts. Individuals could then act in reliance upon prior decisions with reasonable certainty as the results of their conduct.

As you read further, remember that the judicial system has established a general priority among the various sources of law. Constitutions prevail over statutes, and statutes prevail over common law principles established in court decisions. Courts will not turn to case decisions for law if a statute is directly in point.

The fourth source of law is generally referred to as administrative law. This source gives us rules and regulations similar to statutes as well as case decisions. Chapter 7 discusses administrative law in detail. The role of courts in interpreting legislation and the problems associated with case law is discussed in the next chapter.

12 OTHER INFLUENCES ON BEHAVIOR

One definition of law noted in the previous section is a scheme of social control. Law is not the only method of controlling society, however. Factors other than law influence and regulate the behavior of individuals and business organizations. Among the more important are economic principles, individual and institutional ethical standards, and a company's or firm's view of its responsibility to society. The law interacts with economics, ethics, and social responsibility to influence decisions.

The forces or factors which influence business decisions and individual conduct are often compatible and consistent with one another. The law provides the foundation for ethical standards in that it often distinguishes right from wrong. However, the goals and principles of law and economics, of law and ethical standards, or of economics and ethical standards are sometimes in conflict. For example, the economics of a situation may indicate that a price-fixing agreement among competitors would be desirable, but the law and perhaps ethical values would dictate that such an agreement not be made. These factors have different weights at different times and under different conditions. The law is often said to provide the foundation for the operation of the other factors.

It is apparent that our competitive economic system provides both incentives and constraints on individual and business decisions and the conduct that flows from them. Indeed, most decisions to do or not to do a certain thing are based on the economic consequences of the contemplated course of action. The profit motive and cost considerations play as great a role in most decisions as do legal aspects. Our competitive economic system is based upon millions of people and thousands of businesses making numerous daily decisions in their own self-interest. Indeed, there are those who believe that economic considerations and the profit motive are the best means of regulating business conduct.

Ethical standards are also very important in business decision making and in controlling human behavior. Ethics has been defined as the name given to our concern for good behavior. It is our commitment to what is right and our rejection of what is wrong. Ethics provides a system of values beyond what the law requires or prohibits. Ethical values are required if people are to live together in a free society. It is not enough to have laws. People and businesses must have values because a free society depends upon the trust and confidence of people. High ethical standards are the foundation upon which trust and confidence are built.

Today, many business associations as well as professional groups such as the American Bar Association or the American Institute of Certified Public

Accountants have adopted ethics codes. In addition, many companies have established their own codes of ethics. There is also a federal ethics code for government service. Although these codes do not have the force of law, employees of these firms and members of the professions and government employees are expected to obey them. This "obedience to the legally unenforceable" in a real sense is the hallmark of a profession. If business persons desire professional status, a commitment to a positive code of ethical values is essential.

Although most of this book concerns laws and the legal environment in which business operates, it also deals with several aspects of economics and with business ethics and social responsibility. For example, the material on antitrust laws is the portion that deals most heavily with economic theory. The legal environment is so closely interconnected with our economic system that one of its major concerns is ensuring that our competitive economic system actually works. Materials on business ethics and businesses' responsibility to society are discussed throughout the text where appropriate because ethical standards which become generally accepted frequently are enacted into law. In a sense, the law follows society's view of what is right and wrong. Any examination of trends in the law requires reference to contemporary ethical standards that may become law.

13 LAW AND ETHICS

Defining ethics as "good behavior" and "a recognition of the rights and interests of others as well as society as a whole" means that ethical standards go beyond the law. It is often said that ethics leads the law and is ahead of or above the law. Morality must exist above the law if it is to advance. If the goal of the law is justice, including social justice, then the ethics of society plays a major role in the search for that goal.

The basis of most ethical standards is honesty. Honesty is also required in our legal system. Witnesses testify under oath and are cross-examined as a part of the search for truth. We assume that juries will be able to ascertain the truth. Thus, both the law and ethics are founded on the same fundamental principles and goals. Yet their standards are not always the same.

Although the law and ethics are not identical, each influences the other. Traditional ethical values have often changed the law as moral standards usually are developed and generally accepted prior to becoming law. The law also influences ethical values as it provides a sense of what is right and what is wrong. Ethical values are also affected by economic considerations. Economic principles and ethics are compatible most of the time. Profits cannot be considered unethical most of the time if our competitive system is to survive.

As previously noted, all professions, government, and many businesses have adopted codes of ethics. These value systems of the organizations serve as internal laws for persons subject to them. These codes of ethics are codes of conscience based on fairness, honesty, courtesy, self-restraint, and consideration for others. Such codes may only require disclosure of facts to superiors in certain situations. At other times they may dictate decisions and conduct. They are based on a collective sense of right and wrong. This, in turn, is influenced by the time frame and by the cultural background of society with special input from religions and philosophy. Many codes are general statements, because the more specific the code, the more difficult it is to obtain agreement to the principles. Most codes are written in positive rather than negative terms.

Ethical business conduct often requires behavior at a level well above the minimum required by law. Ethical conduct may be thought of as doing more than the law requires or less than it allows. An individual or society's sense of ethics may actually condemn that which the law allows. Ethical codes often recognize that the interests of society are paramount to those of the individual.

For purposes of illustrating a typical code of business conduct we have selected the one developed by the Caterpillar Tractor Company of Peoria, Illinois. Its code was selected because Caterpillar is a company conducting business worldwide in a basic industry employing thousands of people. The company has been very successful in obtaining acceptance and compliance with its operating principles and ethical standards. Excerpts from its Code of Worldwide Business Conduct and Operating Principles will be found throughout this text to demonstrate the close connection between law, ethics, and corporate responsibility.

Caterpillar's code recognizes that the company is subject to the law of many countries and that what is legal in some countries may be illegal in others. Its code requires adherence to local laws but goes further and contains a commitment to work for constructive change where desirable. The code states:

Observance of Local Laws

A basic requirement levied against any business enterprise is that it know and obey the law. This is rightfully required by those who govern; and it is well understood by business managers.

However, a corporation operating on a global scale will inevitably encounter laws which vary widely from country to country. They may even conflict with each other.

And laws in some countries may encourage or require business practices which—based on experience elsewhere in the world—we believe to be wasteful or unfair. Under such conditions it scarcely seems sufficient for a business manager merely to say; we obey the law, whatever it may be!

We are guided by the belief that the law is not an end but a means to an end—the end presumably being order, justice, and, not infrequently, strengthening of the governmental unit involved. If it is to achieve these ends in changing times and circumstances, law itself cannot be insusceptible to change or free of criticism. The law can benefit from both.

Therefore, in a world characterized by a multiplicity of divergent laws at international, national, state, and local levels, Caterpillar's intentions fall in two parts: (1) to obey the law; and (2) to offer, where appropriate, constructive ideas for change in the law.

The Caterpillar Code's Statement on Business Ethics also recognizes that complying with the law is only the beginning of what is necessary for ethical business conduct. Its comment on business ethics provides:

Business Ethics

The law is a floor. Ethical business conduct should normally exist at a level well above the minimum required by the law.

One of the company's most valuable assets is a reputation for integrity. If that be tarnished, customers, investors, suppliers, employees, and those who sell our products will seek affiliation with other, more attractive companies. We intend to hold to a single high standard of integrity everywhere. We will keep our word. We will not promise more than we can reasonably expect to deliver; nor will we make commitments we do not intend to keep.

The goal of corporate communication is the truth—well and persuasively told. In our advertising and other public communications, we will avoid not only untruths, but also exaggeration, overstatement, and boastfulness.

Caterpillar employees shall not accept costly entertainment or gifts (excepting mementos and novelties of nominal value) from dealers, suppliers, and others with whom we do business. And we will not tolerate circumstances that produce, or reasonably appear to produce, conflict between personal interests of an employee and interests of the company.

We seek long-lasting relationships—based on integrity—with all whose activities touch upon our own.

The ethical performance of the enterprise is the sum of the ethics of the men and women who work here. Thus, we are all expected to adhere to high standards of personal integrity. For example, perjury or any other illegal act ostensibly taken to "protect" the company is wrong. A sale made because of deception is wrong. A production quota achieved through questionable means or figures is wrong. The end doesn't justify the means.

Finally, the code acknowledges the importance of employee compliance by requiring regular reporting. Note the specific request that the reports go to the legal counsel:

Reporting Code Compliances

Each officer, subsidiary head, plant or parts department manager, and department head shall prepare a memorandum by the close of each year: (1) affirming a full knowledge and understanding of this Code; and (2) reporting any events or activities which might cause an impartial observer to conclude that the Code has not been fully followed. These reports should be sent directly to the company's General Counsel; General Offices; Peoria, Illinois.

REVIEW QUESTIONS

1. Name the five schools of legal thought discussed in section 3 of the text and give an example of a legal area or principle that was developed because of each school or philosophy.
2. Compare and contrast the following:
   a. Public law and private law
   b. Civil law and criminal law
   c. Tort and crime
   d. Felony and misdemeanor
   e. Substance and procedure
   f. Personal property and real property
   g. Title to property and possession of property
3. Which of the following are generally considered to be white-collar crimes?

   a. Arson
   b. Bribery
   c. Burglary
   d. Embezzlement
   e. Forgery
   f. Obstruction of justice
   g. Price-fixing
   h. Rape
   i. Robbery
   j. Securities fraud

4. A Belgian company believed that it was a victim of overbilling by a New York supplier of aviation parts. It sued for triple damages, alleging that the bills had been submitted by mail and were fraudulent. No criminal case had been brought against the supplier. Is the plaintiff entitled to triple damages? Explain.
5. Jones, a stockbroker, called two customers on the telephone and attempted to sell them stock. Assume that his statements constitute securities fraud. What action are the customers likely to take if the fraud is discovered? Explain.
6. List three of the changes in the criminal law system that have been proposed by the federal task force on violent crime and give the common thread of each proposal.
7. Which body of civil law results in the most litigation in the United States? What is the usual legal theory asserted in such cases? Why did the law develop this theory?
8. Ranch owners in West Texas brought suit against the owners and operators of airplanes and equipment used in a "weather modification program" by which they engaged in cloud seeding. The trial court issued an injunction commanding the defendants to refrain from seeding the clouds or in any way interfering with the natural conditions of the air, atmosphere, and air space over and in the area of plaintiff's lands, and to refrain from affecting or modifying the weather conditions on or about said lands in any degree or way. What theory of property was used by the court?

9 In which of the following events is a successful lawsuit likely? What theory would be used by the plaintiff? Explain.
   a A man attempted suicide by jumping in front of a subway train.
   b A burglar fell through a skylight while attempting to steal lights from the roof of a public school.
   c An overweight man had a heart attack while starting his lawn mower.
   d A man was injured in a telephone booth when a drunken driver rammed the booth.
10 Different terminology is used to describe legislation. List three terms which describe the product of the legislative process.
11 Name four factors other than the law which have significant influence on individual and business behavior.
12 A worker was killed when a trench collapsed. An investigation revealed that the trench was 27-feet deep and was without shoring, which is in violation of safety standards. The president of the corporation was charged with negligent homicide. Is a finding of guilty possible? Explain.

CHAPTER 2

THE POWERS AND FUNCTIONS OF COURTS

OVERVIEW

This chapter discusses the powers and functions of courts. There are three basic powers: (1) judicial review, (2) interpretation of the Constitution and legislation, and (3) the making of law in the process of deciding cases (stare decisis). Judicial review is the power to decide if a statute passed by the legislative branch or an action by the executive branch violates the Constitution. Those involved in the process of interpretation apply the general language of a statute to a specific controversy. Judicial interpretation helps "fill-out" legislation, and thus courts have a "legislative" function to perform. Case law gives us our common law system and all of the problems inherent in it. The chapter will also discuss the fact-finding function of the jury in our court system.

The following legal terms and concepts are of special importance in this chapter: conflict-of-laws principles, dicta, judicial activism, judicial restraint, judicial review, legislative history, precedent, procedural law, remedial statutes, and substantive law.

1 INTRODUCTION

As was noted in Chapter 1, law comes from constitutions, legislation, decided cases, and administrative rulings. Courts play a major role in the development of the law as it comes from each of these sources. Courts not only have the function to interpret the Constitution but also have the power of judicial review.

When legislation is enacted, courts are frequently called upon to interpret its language and to apply it to a specific controversy. Statutes usually are written in general language. Since cases deal with specific problems, interpretation is necessary to fill in the gaps of the legislation and to eliminate the ambiguities caused by the general language used in statutes. Judicial interpretation gives much of the substance to legislation, and thus courts have a "legislative" function to perform.

The common law system has several aspects which tend to increase the cost of litigation and which fail to give it the desired level of certainty and predictability. Case law is sometimes difficult to find, and it is not always followed. As you study this chapter, keep in mind the distinction between questions of law and questions of fact.

2 JUDGES AND JUSTICES

Before we look at the powers and functions of courts, some background and understanding of the people who operate our courts are helpful. The people who operate our courts are usually called judges. In some reviewing courts, such as the U.S. Supreme Court, jurists are called justices. In this discussion, we will refer to trial court persons as judges and reviewing court persons as justices.

In all cases being tried before a judge, the function of the court is to determine the applicable rules of law to be used to decide the case before it. In cases tried without a jury, the court is also responsible for finding the facts. In cases tried before a jury, the function of the jury is to decide questions of fact.

Trial judges are the main link between the law and the citizens it serves. The trial judge renders decisions which deal directly with people in conflict. These judges bear the burden of upholding the dignity of the courts and maintaining respect for the law. They have the primary duty to observe and apply constitutional limitations and guarantees. Trial judges are responsible for conducting the "search for truth."

The roles of justice and judge differ substantially. Whereas a trial judge has direct contact with the litigation and litigants, a justice rarely has any contact with them. Justices do more than simply decide an appeal—they give reasons for their decisions in written form so that they will become precedent and a part of our body of law. Thus, decisions by justices may affect society as a whole as well as the litigants. In deciding cases before them, justices must consider not only the result between the parties but also the total effect of the decision on the law. In this sense, their role is similar to that of legislators. On review, justices are essentially concerned with issues of *law*. Issues of *fact* are resolved at the trial court level.

For the foregoing reasons, the personal characteristics required for a justice are somewhat different from those of a trial judge. The manner of performing duties and the methodology also vary between trial and reviewing courts. A trial judge who has observed the witnesses is able to use knowledge gained from participation as an essential ingredient in his or her decision. A justice must spend most of the time in the library studying the briefs, the record of proceedings, and the law in reaching decisions.

The judicial power is perhaps the most extensive power possessed by any branch of government. Lower-court judges may be reviewed by a reviewing court, but they have almost total personal immunity from legal actions against them based on their judicial acts. Judicial immunity extends to court personnel such as prosecutors and police officers who testify, as well. The system works only if such people can act without fear of reprisal. The judicial immunity of judges applies even when the judge acts maliciously, exceeds his or her authority, or commits grave procedural errors. A judge can be sued only if he or she acts in clear absence of jurisdiction or is to be prevented from doing so. For example, the Supreme Court in 1984 held that a judge may be enjoined by another court from doing an illegal act, but even then he or she has no liability for damages flowing from the illegal act. In such cases, the only liability is for the attorney's fees and court costs involved in the injunction suit.

3 THE JURY

Before we turn to a discussion of the judicial functions, we should understand the role of the jury as a fact-finding body. Since litigation involves questions of law and fact, the distinction between such questions and the limited role of the courts in cases tried before a jury must be recognized.

The function of the jury in criminal cases is to prevent government oppression and, in both criminal and civil cases, to ascertain the facts. This contrasts with the function of the court, which is to ascertain the law applicable to a case. Remember that in cases tried without a jury, the court also is the finder of the facts.

The jury system was adopted as a matter of right in the Constitution of the United States. The Sixth and Seventh Amendments to the United States Constitution guarantee the right of trial by jury in both criminal and civil cases. The Fifth Amendment provides for indictment by a grand jury for capital offenses and infamous crimes. A grand jury differs from a petit jury. A *grand jury* determines whether there is sufficient evidence of guilt to warrant a trial. The *petit jury* is the jury that determines actual guilt or innocence. Indictment is the term used to describe the decision of a grand jury. In civil cases the right to trial by a jury is preserved in suits at common law when the amount in controversy exceeds $20. State constitutions have like provisions guaranteeing the right of trial by jury in state courts.

Historically, a jury consisted of twelve persons. Today many states and some federal courts have rules of procedure which provide for smaller juries in both criminal and civil cases. Such provisions are constitutional since the Constitution does not specify the *number* of jurors—only the *types* of cases which may be brought to trial before a jury at common law. There is no discernible difference in results reached by a six-person jury from those reached by a twelve-person jury. As a result, many cases are tried before six-person juries today.

In most states, a jury's decision must be unanimous, or a total assertion. It is believed that the truth is more nearly to be found and justice rendered if the jury acts only on one common conscience. Statutes and constitutions specify the number of jurors who must concur for a verdict. In some states less than a unanimous verdict is constitutionally permissible for a jury of twelve. However, less-than-unanimous verdicts are not permissible for six-person juries.

Recognizing that a jury's function is to determine the facts, a relatively new technique of a "mock" trial is being used by attorneys in very significant cases.

The jury system has been subject to much criticism. It has been contended that many jurors are not qualified to distinguish fact from fiction, that they vote their prejudices, and that their emotions are too easily swayed by skillful trial lawyers. However, most members of the bench and bar feel the "right to be tried by a jury of his peers" in criminal cases is as fair and effective a method of ascertaining the truth and giving an accused his or her "day in court" as has been devised.

As Jeremiah Black, the attorney for the defendant in the famous case of *Ex Parte Milligan,* said:

> I do not assert that the jury trial is an infallible mode of ascertaining truth. Like everything human, it has its imperfection. I only say, that it is the best protection for innocence and the surest mode of punishing guilt that has yet been discovered. It has borne the test of longer experience, and borne it better than any other legal institution that ever existed among men.

Many people attempt to avoid jury duty. Some lose money because of time away from a job or profession. As a result of people avoiding jury duty, many juries are made up primarily of the unemployed and the retired. Because of their desire to have juries that are a cross-section of society, many courts are refusing most excuses that are advanced to avoid jury duty.

To alleviate problems associated with jury service, many states are expanding the rolls of people eligible for service and are reducing the list of occupations that exempt a person from jury duty. For example, lawyers and the police are exempt in most states, but firefighters are usually not exempt. In addition, some states are limiting the service of each juror to one case, and if a juror is called for duty and not assigned to a case, that juror is excused for at least one year. Today there is a strong trend toward requiring jury duty of all citizens, irrespective of any hardship that such service may entail.

4 JUDICIAL REVIEW

The most significant of the powers of the judiciary is known as **judicial review**. The doctrine of judicial review empowers courts to review laws passed by the legislative body and to declare them to be unconstitutional and thus void. It also allows the courts to review actions taken by the executive branch and to declare them to be unconstitutional. Although the Constitution does not expressly provide that the judiciary shall be the overseer of the government, the net effect of this doctrine is to make it so. Chief Justice John Marshall in *Marbury v. Madison*[1] announced the doctrine of judicial review, using the following language and reasoning:

> The question, whether an act, repugnant to the constitution, can become the law of the land, is a question deeply interesting to the United States; but, happily, not of an intricacy proportioned to its interest....
>
> It is a proposition too plain to be contested, that the constitution controls any legislative act repugnant to it; or that the legislature may not alter the constitution by an ordinary act....
>
> Certainly, all those who have framed written constitutions contemplate them as forming the fundamental and paramount law of the nation, and consequently, the theory of every such government must be, that an act of the legislature, repugnant to the constitution, is void....
>
> If an act of the legislature, repugnant to the constitution, is void, does it, notwithstanding its invalidity, bind the courts, and oblige them to give it effect? Or, in other words, though it be not law, does it constitute a rule as operative as if it was a law? This would be to overthrow, in fact, what was established in theory; and would seem, at first view, an absurdity too gross to be insisted on. It shall, however, receive a more attentive consideration.
>
> It is, emphatically, the province and duty of the judicial department, to say what the law is. Those who apply the rule to particular cases, must of necessity expound and interpret that rule. If two laws conflict with each other, the courts must decide on the operation of each. So, if a law be in opposition to the constitution; if both the law and the constitution apply to a particular case, so that the court must either decide that case, conformable to the law, disregarding the constitution; or conformable to the constitution, disregarding the law; the court must determine which of these conflicting rules governs the case: this is of the very essence of judicial duty. If then, the courts are to regard the constitution, and the constitution is superior to any ordinary act of the legislature, the constitution, and not such ordinary act, must govern the case to which they both apply.

The doctrine of judicial review as a component part of the concept of separation of powers was subjected to a severe test during the mid-1970s. As a part of the so-called "Watergate affair," a special prosecutor sought to subpoena certain documents and tape recordings from the President of the United States. The President claimed executive privilege and stated that he was the final authority on the issue. The application of judicial review to

---

[1] U.S. (1 Cranch) 137 (1803).

the executive branch was the basic issue in this historic confrontation. Chief Justice Warren Burger, in speaking for a unanimous court in the case of *United States v. Nixon,* stated in part:[2]

> ...[W]e turn to the claim that the subpoena should be quashed because it demands "confidential conversations between a President and his close advisors that it would be inconsistent with the public interest to produce." The first contention is a broad claim that the separation of powers doctrine precludes judicial review of a President's claim of privilege....
>
> In the performance of assigned constitutional duties each branch of the Government must initially interpret the Constitution, and the interpretation of its powers by any branch is due great respect from the others. The President's counsel...reads the Constitution as providing an absolute privilege of confidentiality for all presidential communications. Many decisions of this Court, however, have unequivocally reaffirmed the holding of *Marbury v. Madison,* that "it is emphatically the province and duty of the judicial department to say what the law is."...
>
> Our system of government "requires that federal courts on occasion interpret the Constitution in a manner at variance with the construction given the document by another branch."...Notwithstanding the deference each branch must accord the others, the "judicial power of the United States" vested in the federal courts by Art. III, § 1 of the Constitution can no more be shared with the Executive Branch than the Chief Executive, for example, can share with the Judiciary the veto power, or the Congress share with the Judiciary the power to override a presidential veto. Any other conclusion would be contrary to the basic concept of separation of powers and the checks and balances that flow from the scheme of a tripartite government. We therefore reaffirm that it is "emphatically the province and the duty" of this Court "to say what the law is" with respect to the claim of privilege presented in this case.

The most recent demonstration of the Supreme Court's power to settle disputes between the other two branches of government occurred in 1983. Congress had given itself a legislative veto over acts of the executive and rules and regulations of many administrative agencies. The court held that legislative vetoes are unconstitutional, a violation of separation of powers. The decision prevented Congress from countermanding presidential decisions and thereby affected the political balance in the nation.

5 ATTITUDES TOWARD JUDICIAL REVIEW

As individual jurists exercise the power of judicial review, they do so with varying attitudes and philosophies. Some judges believe that the power should be used very sparingly, while others are willing to use it more often. Those who believe that the power should not be used except in unusual cases are said to believe in **judicial restraint**. Those who think that the

---

[2] 94 S.Ct. 3090 (1974).

power should be used whenever the needs of society justify its use believe in **judicial activism**. All members of the judiciary believe in judicial restraint, and all are activists to some extent. Often a jurist may be an activist in one area of the law and a firm believer in judicial restraint in another. Both judicial restraint and judicial activism describe attitudes or tendencies by matters of degree. Both terms also are used to describe general attitudes toward the exercise of the power of judicial review.

Judicial Restraint

The philosophy of judicial restraint developed naturally from the recognition that, in exercising the power of judicial review, the courts are overseeing their co-equal branches of government. When the power of judicial review is used to set aside decisions by the other branches of government, the courts are wielding great power. Logic and a commitment to the constitutional system dictate that this almost unlimited power be exercised with great restraint, say those jurists who follow the judicial restraint philosophy.

Those who believe in such a philosophy think that constitutional issues are too important to be decided unless absolutely necessary and are to be avoided if there is another legal basis for a decision. They believe that the proper use of judicial power demands that courts refrain from determining the constitutionality of an act of Congress unless it is absolutely necessary to a decision of a case. This modest view of the role of the judiciary is based upon the belief that litigation is not the appropriate technique for bringing about social, political, and economic change.

The philosophy of judicial restraint is sometimes referred to as *judicial abstention* or *strict construction*. Strict constructionists believe that the Constitution should be interpreted in light of what the founding fathers intended. They place great weight on the debates of the constitutional convention and in the language of the Constitution. "Judicial abstention" means that courts will decide only those matters which they must to resolve actual cases and controversies before them. Courts should abstain from deciding issues whenever possible, and doubts about the constitutionality of legislation should be resolved in favor of the statute. Cases should be decided on the facts if possible and on the narrowest possible grounds.

Those who believe in judicial restraint feel that social, political, and economic change in society should result from the political process rather than from court action. Justice John Marshall Harlan in *Reynolds v. Sims*, 84 S.Ct. 1362 (1964), epitomized this philosophy when, in dissenting from a reapportionment decision, he stated in part:

> The vitality of our political system, on which in the last analysis all else depends, is weakened by reliance on the judiciary for political reform....These decisions give support to a current mistaken view of the Constitution and the constitutional function of this court. This view, in a nutshell, is that every major social ill in the country can find its cure in some constitutional 'principle,' and that this

Court should 'take the lead' in promoting reform when other branches of government fail to act. The Constitution is not a panacea for every blot upon the public welfare, nor should this Court, ordained as a judicial body, be thought of as a general haven for reform movements. The Constitution is an instrument of government, fundamental to which is the premise that in a diffusion of governmental authority lies the greatest promise that this nation will realize liberty for all its citizens. This Court, limited in function in accordance with that premise, does not serve its high purpose when it exceeds its authority, even to satisfy justified impatience with the slow working of the political process.

Judges who identify with judicial restraint give great deference to the political process and to the other branches of government. They believe that the courts, especially the federal courts, ought to defer to the actions of the states and of the coordinate branches of government unless these actions are clearly unconstitutional. They allow the states and the federal legislative and executive branches wide latitude in finding solutions to the nation's problems.

Judicial restraint jurists have a deep commitment to precedent. They overrule cases only when the prior decision is clearly wrong. Persons who follow this belief do not feel that they should attempt to write their own personal convictions into the law. They do not view the role of the lawyer and the practice of law as that of social reform. To them, this is the function of the political process.

Followers of judicial restraint often take a pragmatic approach to litigation. Whenever possible, decisions are based on the facts rather than a principle of law. Reviewing courts exercising judicial restraint tend to accept the trial court decisions unless they are clearly wrong in the facts or the law. If there is any reasonable basis for the lower court decision, it will not be reversed if the judicial restraint philosophy dominates the thinking of the reviewing court. Such courts often engage in a balancing approach to their decisions. They weigh competing interests. For example, justices who adhere to judicial restraint often weigh the rights of the person accused of crime with the interests of the victim and of society in determining the extent of the rights of the accused in criminal cases.

Judicial Activism

Throughout most of our history, judicial restraint has been the dominant philosophy. Today, a majority of the justices of the United States Supreme Court usually follow this philosophy, but all courts to some degree are activists. Indeed, many argue that today's Supreme Court is significantly activist. They point to decisions such as those allowing abortions to prove their point.

Those who believe in the philosophy of judicial activism believe that courts have a major role to play in correcting wrongs in our society. To them, courts must provide leadership in bringing about social, political, and economic change because the political system is often too slow or unable to bring about those changes which are necessary to improve society. Activists tend to be innovative and less dependent on precedent for their decisions. They are value-oriented and policy-directed. Activist jurists believe that constitutional issues must be decided within the context of contemporary society and that the meaning of the Constitution is relative to the times in which it is being interpreted. To activists, the courts, and especially the Supreme Court, sit as a continuing constitutional convention to meet the needs of today.

During the 1950s and 1960s, there was an activist majority on the Supreme Court. This activist majority brought about substantial changes in the law, especially in such areas as civil rights, reapportionment, and the criminal law. For example, the activist court of this period ordered desegregation of public schools and gave us the one-man, one-vote concept in the distributing of legislative bodies. Earl Warren, Chief Justice during this period, used to request that lawyers appearing before the Court address themselves to the effect of their clients' positions on society. "Tell me why your position is 'right' and that of your opponent is 'wrong' from the standpoint of society," was a common request to lawyers arguing cases before him.

Activist courts tend to be more result-conscious and place less reliance on precedent. Activists are often referred to as liberals, but that description is too narrow to explain their belief in the role of the judiciary as an instrument of change. They also believe that justices must examine for themselves the great issues facing society and then decide them in light of contemporary standards. Otherwise, we are governed by the dead or by people who were not aware of all of the complexities of today's problems.

Tables 2-1 and 2-2 illustrate typical activist and judicial restraint decisions. Those labeled "judicial restraint" have left the decision to other branches of government and to the political process. Those labeled "activist" are examples of the judiciary imposing its will on society.

TABLE 2-1 TYPICAL JUDICIAL RESTRAINT DECISIONS

1 Male-only draft is not a denial of equal protection of the law.
2 States can regulate nuclear power.
3 States can tax the foreign income of multinational corporations.
4 Prayer in the legislature does not violate the First Amendment.
5 Unanimous verdicts are not required, and juries may consist of fewer than twelve persons.
6 Communal living may be prohibited.
7 Homosexuality can be a crime.
8 Class action suits require actual notice to members of the class.
9 Plaintiffs must have direct interest in a lawsuit to have standing to sue.
10 Seniority has preference over affirmative action in layoffs.
11 A city-erected Nativity scene does not violate the First Amendment.
12 State and local employees are subject to the Federal Fair Labor Standards Act.

TABLE 2-2 TYPICAL ACTIVIST DECISIONS

1. Busing is a valid technique to achieve school desegregation.
2. Legislative apportionment must be based on population and not area.
3. No prayer is to be permitted in school.
4. The Miranda warning shall be given to all criminal suspects prior to interrogation.
5. Abortion is not a crime.
6. Female pensions must be the same as male pensions, even though females live longer.
7. Sexual harassment is sex discrimination prohibited by the Fourteenth Amendment.
8. Legislative veto of decisions of governmental agencies is unconstitutional.
9. Residency requirement for public assistance violates equal protection.
10. OSHA inspectors must have a search warrant if a business objects to inspection.
11. Aliens are entitled to be notaries public.
12. Certain public employees, such as a public defender, cannot be fired because of political affiliation.

The importance of judicial philosophy and ideology was never more apparent than in the 1987 hearings on the nomination of Judge Robert H. Bork of the Washington, D.C., Court of Appeals to be a member of the Supreme Court. Judge Bork had been confirmed unanimously by the Senate to serve on the Court of Appeals. Yet as soon as his nomination was announced, violent opposition to the appointment surfaced. Few, if any, challenged his impressive legal credentials, which included a professorship in constitutional law at Yale University and numerous scholarly articles.

Why was there so much opposition to Judge Bork? It was simply because the Supreme Court in 1987 was closely divided between advocates of judicial restraint and advocates of judicial activism. Many people believed that four of the sitting justices could qualify as followers of judicial restraint and the other four could correctly be labeled as activists. Some court watchers found three activists (Brennan, Marshall, and Blackman), three strong followers of judicial restraint (Rehnquist, O'Connor, and Scalia), and two swing votes (Stevens tending toward judicial activism and White toward judicial restraint). In any event, it was believed by many Senators that Judge Bork would certainly tilt the court toward conservatism. It was assumed that he might vote to reverse the decisions legalizing abortion and would favor free markets over government regulation of business. As a result, Senators who agreed with his perceived views strongly backed his appointment and those with differing views sought to prevent his confirmation. Although Bork did not receive Senate approval, the country as a whole became aware of the importance of the judicial philosophy of each member of the Supreme Court.

6 THE INTERPRETATION OF LEGISLATION

The second major function of the courts is to interpret legislation. Most legislation is by its very nature stated in general language. It usually purports to cover a multitude of factual situations and is often ambiguous and imprecise. It is up to the judiciary to find the meaning of general language in a statute and apply it to the limited facts of a case. The purpose of statutory construction is to determine the intent of the legislature when the statute was enacted.

One technique of statutory interpretation is to examine the **legislative history** of an act to determine the purpose of the legislation, or the evil it was designed to correct. Courts try to find the legislative intent by examining the debates of the legislative body, the committee reports, amendments that were rejected, and other matters that transpired prior to the adoption of the statute. Legislative history may supply the legislative intent, but many of the questions of interpretation which confront courts were never even visualized by the legislature. The real problem often is to determine what the legislature *would have* intended had it considered the question.

Resort to legislative history is not the only means for ascertaining the legislative intent. Courts have developed rules of statutory construction which are frequently followed in determining the legislative intent. These rules, in effect, recognize that the courts do not actually know what the legislature intended. Therefore, by following the rule of construction it is assumed that the legislature intended a certain meaning. Many of these rules are based on the type of law being interpreted. For example:

1 Taxing laws shall be *strictly* construed.
2 Criminal laws shall be *strictly* construed.
3 Statutes in derogation of the common law shall be *strictly* construed.
4 Remedial statutes shall be *liberally* construed.

The first two rules mean that doubts about the applicability of a taxing law or criminal law *will be resolved* in favor of the taxpayer or the defendant, respectively. The third rule means that statutes which change the common law will be interpreted as doing so only to the extent that the lawmakers intended and specified. Such a statute will change the common law only to the extent necessary to carry out legislative intent. The fourth rule recognizes that many laws provide a legal remedy for victims of a violation of the law. Such statutes *are described* as remedial because of the remedy given. As a general rule, a **remedial statute** is given a broad or liberal *interpretation*. Doubts about meaning *are* usually *resolved* in favor of the remedy created for the injured party. What happens if a remedial statute is in derogation of the common law? Courts have an obvious choice of alternative rules that allow the desired interpretation.

There are rules of law which aid in finding the meaning of words used in statutes. Some words are simply given their plain or usual meaning. Technical words *are* usually *given* their technical meaning. Others *are interpreted* by the context in which they are used. For example, if a general word in a statute follows particular and specific words of the same nature, the general words take their meaning from the specific words and are presumed to be restricted to the same genus as those words. For example, a statute that said that indigent persons were not required to pay filing fees, sheriff's fees, or "other court costs" was construed to include the cost of publishing notice of a lawsuit in the newspaper. The language "other court costs" takes its meaning from the words preceding it.

There are other rules of statutory construction that are not based on the type of statute or the words used. For example, if a statute contains both specific and general provisions, the specific provisions control. However, courts also attempt to give effect to all the provisions of a statute, if possible, so the purpose of the act will be accomplished. Exemptions from statutes are construed strictly against the party claiming the exemption. Repeal by implication is not favored. If two statutes purport to cover the same topic, they will be construed as consistent with each other if possible, and effect will be given to both. However, if two statutes so clearly conflict that they cannot stand together upon any reasonable construction of both, the legislature is presumed to have repealed the earlier statute while it enacted the later one.

A frequently cited rule provides: "A thing may be within the letter of the statute and yet not within the statute because not within its spirit nor within the intention of the makers." This rule allows a court to have a great deal of flexibility and to give an interpretation contrary to the plain meaning.

The meaning of a statute may also be established indirectly. A legislative body may fail to act in an area in which the meaning of a law has already been established. The meaning may have been based on judicial decision or on interpretation by the executive branch of government charged with its administration. When an established interpretation is present and not changed, it becomes the accepted one because presumably the legislature would pass a new law if the meaning were not correct. Many people question the validity of this reasoning.

The role of courts in interpreting statutes is very important. The power of courts to interpret legislation means that, in the final analysis, it is what the court says a statute means that determines its effect.

7 UNIFORM STATUTES

Each state has its own constitution, statutes, and body of case law. As a result, there are substantial differences in the law among the various states. In many cases, it does not matter that the law is not uniform. If the parties to a dispute are citizens of the same state and if the controversy has all of its contacts with that state, the law of that state is used to resolve the dispute. However, if citizens of different states are involved in a transaction (perhaps a buyer in one state contracts with a seller in another), many difficult questions may arise if the law in one state differs from the law in another. Although a body of law called "conflict of laws" (see page 43) has been developed to cover such cases, more uniformity may be desirable.

Uniformity in the law may be achieved either by federal legislation or by the enactment of the same law by all states. The latter method has been attempted by a legislative drafting group known as the National Conference of Commissioners on Uniform State Laws. These commissioners endeavor to promote uniformity by drafting model acts. When approved by the National Conference, proposed uniform acts are recommended to the state legislatures for adoption.

More than 100 uniform laws have been drafted and presented to the various state legislatures. Most of these relate to business; the response has varied. A few of the uniform laws have been adopted by all the states. Sometimes a state adopts the uniform law in principle but changes some of the provisions to meet local needs. As a result, we often have "nonuniform uniform state laws."

The most significant uniform law for business is the Uniform Commercial Code. It was prepared for the stated purpose of collecting in one body the law that "deals with all the phases which may ordinarily arise in the handling of a commercial transaction from start to finish...." Thus, it covers the law as it relates to the sale of goods, the use of commercial paper to pay for them, and the giving of security to ensure that the purchase price will be paid. The Uniform Commercial Code is not applicable to contracts for the sale of real estate or to contracts for personal services. It is limited to commercial transactions involving personal property.

CASE LAW

8 INHERENT PROBLEMS

The third major function of courts is to create law when deciding cases and controversies. Precedent is a byproduct of judicial decisions. Several aspects of case law must be understood if we are to understand the role of law and lawyers in the decision-making process. First, notwithstanding the fact that common law arose out of a desire for certainty and is designed to create it, common law creates a great deal of uncertainty in the law. The sheer volume of judicial decisions, each possibly creating precedent, makes "the law" beyond the comprehension of lawyers and judges, let alone the rest of us. Large law firms employ lawyers whose sole task is to search the case reports for "the law" to be used in lawsuits and in advising their clients. Access to hundreds of volumes of cases is required. Since the total body of ruling case law is beyond the grasp of lawyers, it is obvious that laypersons who are supposed to know the law and govern their conduct accordingly do not know the law and are somewhat bewildered by it. Case law does not give the level of certainty and predictability intended by its creators. Moreover, in many cases the law is not clear. It is not found by searching cases. The law used to decide many cases is being made in the process. Many years ago a legal scholar in discussing this aspect of case law observed:

> It is the judges that make the common law. Do you know how they make it? Just as a man makes laws for his dog. When your dog does anything you want to break him of, you wait till he does it, and then beat him for it. This is the way you make laws for your dog: and this is the way the judges make laws for you and me. They won't tell a man beforehand what it is he should not do—they won't so much as allow of his being told: they lie by till he has done something which they say he should not have done, and then they hang him for it. What way, then, has any man of coming at this dog-law? Only by watching their proceedings: by observing in what cases they have hanged a man, in what cases they have sent him to jail, in what cases they have seized his goods, and so forth.[3]

The common law system of reliance on precedent is not very efficient. Conflicting precedents are frequently cited to a court by the parties to litigation. One of the major tasks of the courts in such cases is to determine which of the precedents cited is applicable. In addition, even today, many questions of law arise on which there has been no prior decision, or in areas where the only authority is by implication.

The problem of finding the law in a case law system is compounded in a country which consists of fifty sovereign states, because each of these creates its own body of common law. The law as it develops on a case-by-case basis in different states varies from state to state. Moreover, the federal legal system is superimposed on the state systems, thus creating additional bodies of judge-made laws. The methods of determining the applicable precedent where conflicts exist between the laws of different jurisdictions are discussed later in Section 10.

There is an important distinction between **precedent** and mere **dicta**. A judicial decision, as authority for future cases, is limited by the facts upon which it is founded and the rules of law upon which the decision actually is based. Frequently courts make comments on matters not necessary to the decision reached. Such expressions, called "dicta," lack the force of a judicial settlement; they, strictly speaking, are not precedent which courts will be required to follow within the rule of stare decisis. However, dicta may be followed if sound and just, and dicta which have been repeated frequently are often given the force of precedent. Moreover, even though a statement by a court is not pure precedent, it does express the court's opinion, and to the extent that the court is knowledgeable about the subject matter, the court's opinion is entitled to some weight.

One of the major reasons that the case law system leads to uncertainty is

---

[3] 5 Bentham, *Works* 235, quoted in 1 Steffen and Levi, *Cases and Materials on the Elements of the Law* 207 (3d ed., 1946).

that a precedent may be changed or reversed. Since case law is susceptible to change, absolute reliance on it is not possible. This problem is discussed further in the next section.

9 THE WEIGHT TO BE GIVEN PRECEDENT

Case law created by the judiciary can be changed by the judiciary. The common law is not set in stone to be left unchanged for decades and centuries. As Justice William O. Douglas observed:

> Inherent in the common law is a dynamic principle which allows it to grow and to tailor itself to meet changing needs within the doctrine of stare decisis, which, if correctly understood, was not static and did not forever prevent the courts from reversing themselves or from applying principles of common law to new situations as the need arose. If this were not so, we must succumb to a rule that a judge should let others "long dead and unaware of the problems of the age in which he lives, do his thinking for him."

Courts usually hesitate to reject a precedent or to change case law. The assumption is made that a principle or rule of law announced in a former judicial decision, if unfair or contrary to public policy, will be changed by legislation. Precedent has more force in trial courts than in courts of review, which have the power to make precedent in the first instance. However, stare decisis does not mean that former decisions *always* will be followed, even by trial courts. A former ruling may have been erroneous, or the conditions upon which it was based may have changed or may no longer exist. The doctrine does not require courts to multiply their errors by using former mistakes as authority and support for new errors. Thus, just as legislatures change the law by new legislation, so also do courts change the law, from time to time, by reversing or modifying former precedents.

Justice White, in a dissent in one of the cases subsequent to *Roe v. Wade*, 93 S.Ct. 705 (1973), which legalized abortions, had occasion to discuss the rule of stare decisis and the deference which ought to be given precedent. He observed:

> The rule of *stare decisis* is essential if case-by-case judicial decisionmaking is to be reconciled with the principle of the rule of law, for when governing legal standards are open to revision in every case, deciding cases becomes a mere exercise of judicial will, with arbitrary and unpredictable results. But *stare decisis* is not the only constraint upon judicial decisionmaking. Cases—like this one—that involve our assumed power to set aside on grounds of unconstitutionality a State or federal statute representing the democratically expressed will of the people call other considerations into play. Because the Constitution itself is ordained and established by the people of the United States, constitutional adjudication by this Court does not, in theory at any rate, frustrate the authority of the people to govern themselves through institutions of their own devising and in accordance with principles of their own choosing. But decisions that find in the Constitution principles or values that cannot fairly be read into that document usurp the people's

authority, for such decisions represent choices that the people have never made and that they cannot disavow through corrective legislation. For this reason, it is essential that this Court maintain the power to restore authority to its proper possessors by correcting constitutional decisions that, on reconsideration, are found to be mistaken.

The Court has therefore adhered to the rule that *stare decisis* is not rigidly applied in cases involving constitutional issues, and has not hesitated to overrule decisions, or even whole lines of cases, where experience, scholarship, and reflection demonstrated that their fundamental premises were not to be found in the Constitution. *Stare decisis* did not stand in the way of the Justices who, in the late 1930s, swept away constitutional doctrines that had placed unwarranted restrictions on the power of the State and Federal Governments to enact social and economic legislation. Nor did *stare decisis* deter a different set of Justices, some fifteen years later, from rejecting the theretofore prevailing view that the Fourteenth Amendment permitted the States to maintain the system of racial segregation. In both instances, history has been far kinder to those who departed from precedent than to those who would have blindly followed the rule of *stare decisis*.[4]

Justice Stevens, in response to Justice White, wrote:

Justice White...is of course correct in pointing out that the Court "has not hesitated to overrule decisions, or even whole lines of cases, where experience, scholarship, and reflection demonstrated that their fundamental premises were not to be found in the Constitution." But Justice White has not disavowed the "fundamental premises" on which the decision in *Roe v. Wade* rests. He has not disavowed the Court's prior approach to the interpretation of the word "liberty" or, more narrowly, the line of cases that culminated in the unequivocal holding, applied to unmarried persons and married persons alike, "that the Constitution protects individual decisions in matters of childbearing from unjustified intrusion by the State."

Nor does the fact that the doctrine of *stare decisis* is not an absolute bar to the reexamination of past interpretations of the Constitution mean that the values underlying that doctrine may be summarily put to one side. There is a strong public interest in stability, and in the orderly conduct of our affairs, that is served by a consistent course of constitutional adjudication.

Thus, it can be seen that the amount of deference to be given stare decisis often depends on the conclusion that a justice may desire to reach. Justices agree on the abstract principle of commitment to precedent except where the rule of law is wrong. Disagreement is likely to arise, however, on the issue of correctness of a legal rule or principle and whether it should continue to be followed.

Judges are subject to social forces and changing circumstances just as are legislatures. The personnel of courts changes, and each new generation of judges has a responsibility to reexamine precedents and to adapt them to changing conditions. This responsibility is especially present in cases in-

---

[4] *Thornburgh v. American College of Obstetricians*, 106 S.Ct. 2169, 2192 (1986).

volving constitutional issues. A doctrine known as "constitutional relativity" stands for the proposition that the meaning of the language found in the Constitution is relative to the time in which it is being interpreted. The doctrine has been used rather frequently by the Supreme Court to give effect to society's attitudes. Under this concept, great weight is attached to social forces and needs, as the court sees them, in formulating judicial decisions. As the attitudes and problems of society change, precedent changes.

Some quotes from justices indicate their attitude toward precedent. For example, Justice Wanamaker in the case of *Adams Express Co. v. Beckwith*, 100 Ohio St. 348, said: "A decided case is worth as much as it weighs in reason and righteousness, and no more. It is not enough to say 'thus saith the court.' It must prove its right to control in any given situation by the degree in which it supports the rights of a party violated and serves the cause of justice as to all parties concerned." Or, as Justice Musmanno stated in the case of *Bosley v. Andrews*, 393 Pa. 161 (1958):

> Stare decisis is the viaduct over which the law travels in transporting the precious cargo of justice. Prudence and a sense of safety dictate that the piers of that viaduct should be examined and tested from time to time to make certain that they are sound, strong and capable of supporting the weight above.... A precedent, in law, in order to be binding, should appeal to logic and a genuine sense of justice. What lends dignity to the law founded on precedent is that, if analyzed, the particularly cited case wields authority by the sheer force of its self-integrated honesty, integrity, and rationale. A precedent cannot, and should not, control, if its strength depends alone on the fact that it is old, but may crumble at the slightest probing touch of instinctive reason and natural justice.

The extent to which precedent is followed varies a great deal depending on the subject matter of the litigation. If the dispute involves subject areas of private law, such as torts, contracts, or property, there is much greater deference to precedent than if the subject area is constitutional law. The fact that precedent is to be given great weight in the areas of private law does not mean that courts will continue to follow a rule of private law where the reasoning behind the rule no longer exists. Even here, precedents are reversed as the needs of society change. The belief that the meaning of the Constitution is relative to the times in which it is being interpreted results in less deference to precedent in constitutional law cases. To the extent that courts provide leadership in bringing about social, political, and economic change, they are likely to give less weight to precedent and more weight to other factors which influence judicial decisions.

10 SELECTING THE APPLICABLE CASE LAW

Each state has its own statutory laws and its own body of judge-made precedent. These laws cover both matters of substance and matters of procedure. Generally, the decisions of one state are considered to be applicable precedent only in that state. The decisions of other states, however, may be considered by way of analogy when there are no previous decisions on the point in question in the state where a case is being heard. For example, precedent of other states is frequently referred to in cases involving the construction of statutes such as the Uniform Acts, where each state has adopted the same statute. Where there is no precedent, a case is one of "first impression." In such cases, each state is free to decide for itself questions concerning its common law and interpretation of its own constitution and statutes.

In addition to this system of fifty distinct bodies of state precedent, there is the federal legal system. The federal courts have their own body of procedural law and substantive law on questions arising under the federal Constitution, codes, statutes, or treaties. Decisions of the federal courts are binding on state courts in federal question cases. In federal court suits based on diversity of citizenship, the federal courts use the substantive law of the states in which they are sitting to determine the rights and duties of the parties. However, in such cases, the federal courts use their own rules of procedure. Thus, just as state courts are bound by federal precedent in certain situations, so also are federal courts bound by state precedent in others.

The problem of determining the applicable case law is sometimes difficult because of conflicting precedents within the same court system. When a case or controversy involves more than one state, the difficulty is compounded when the precedents of each state differ. Differences in case law between the states are quite common. The law of torts varies from state to state as does the law of contracts. For example, in some states the plaintiff in an auto accident case must allege and prove freedom from negligence that contributed to the accident. In other states, a defendant must prove that the accident was the fault of the plaintiff if liability is to be avoided. Similar differences exist in every area of the law because there is no uniformity in case law.

In cases involving transactions or occurrences with contact with more than one state, the question must always be asked: Which state law applies? To answer this question a body of law has developed primarily through judicial decisions, which is generally referred to as **conflict of laws**. The decisions that comprise this body of law simply determine which state's substantive law is applicable to any given question when more than one state is involved. This usually arises where all or some of the facts occur in one state and the trial is held in another. For example, the conflict-of-laws rules for tort actions are, in most cases, that the law of the place of injury is applicable. Thus, if a car accident occurred in Missouri but suit was brought in an Illinois state court, the judge would apply the law of Missouri in determining the rights of the parties. There are several different views held by courts about which law to select in resolving issues involving contracts. Some favor the law of the state where the contract was made, others the law of the place of performance, and still others have adopted the "grouping of contacts" theory which uses the law of the state with the most substantial contact with the contract. This latter theory has also been applied in a few tort cases. In the criminal law, the law of the place of the crime is the applicable substantive law. Table 2-3 illustrates typical conflict-of-laws principles.

In a multistate situation, the first problem confronting the court is, therefore, to select the appropriate state to turn to for legal precedent on substantive issues. Once a determination has been made of which state is appropriate, the court's business then is to review the citations of authority advanced by the opposing attorneys to determine which of that state's case decisions to apply in following the doctrine of stare decisis.

Therefore, it must be recognized that there is a body of law used to decide conflicts between the precedent of the various states. This is especially significant in our modern society, with its ease of communication and transportation. The trend toward uniform statutes and codes has tended to decrease these conflicts, but many of them still exist. So long as we have a federal system and fifty separate state bodies of substantive law, the area of conflict of laws will continue to be of substantial importance in the application of the doctrine of stare decisis.

11 THE JUDICIAL PROCESS

In deciding cases and in examining the powers discussed in the prior sections, courts are often faced with several alternatives. They may decide the case by use of existing statutes and precedents. This will often be the case,

TABLE 2-3 SAMPLE CONFLICT-OF-LAWS PRINCIPLES

Substantive law issue	Law to be applied
1 Liability for injury caused by tortious conduct	1 State in which injury was inflicted
2 Validity of a contract	2 State in which contract was made or State in which it is to be performed or State with most significant contacts with the contract or State specified in the contract
3 Inheritance of real property	3 State of situs of real property
4 Inheritance of tangible personal property	4 State of domicile of deceased
5 Validity of a marriage	5 State of celebration
6 Child custody	6 State of domicile of child
7 Workers' compensation	7 State of employment or State in which injury was received

as courts must have a deep commitment to the common law system. However, as previously noted, they may refuse to apply existing case law or may declare a statute to be void as unconstitutional. Also, if there is no statute or case law, the court may decide the case and create law in the process. However, case law as a basis for deciding controversies often provides only the point of departure from which the difficult labor of the courts begins. Courts must examine and compare cases cited as authority to them to determine not only which is correct but whether the principles or rules of law contained there should be followed or rejected as no longer valid. In reaching and preparing its decision, the court must consider whether the law as announced will provide justice in the particular case and whether it will establish sound precedent for future cases involving similar issues.

The foregoing alternatives raise several questions: Why do courts reach one conclusion rather than another in any given case? What formula, if any, is used in deciding cases and in determining the direction of the law? What forces tend to influence judicial decisions when the public interest is involved?

There is, obviously, no simple answer to these questions. Many persons assume that logic is the basic tool of the judicial decision. But Justice Holmes stated: "the life of the law has not been logic; it has been experience."[5] Other persons argue that courts merely reflect the predominant attitude of the times and that they simply follow the more popular course in decisions where the public is involved.

Justice Benjamin Cardozo, in a series of lectures on the judicial process, discussed the sources of information judges utilize in deciding cases. He stated that if the answer were not clearly established by statute or by unquestioned precedent, the problem was twofold: "He [the judge] must first extract from the precedents the underlying principle, the *ratio decidendi;* he must then determine the path or direction along which the principle is to work and develop, if it is not to wither and die."[6] The first part of the problem is separating legal principles from dicta so that the actual precedent is clear. Commenting on the second aspect of the problem, Cardozo said: "The directive force of a principle may be exerted along the line of logical progression; this I will call the rule of analogy or the method of philosophy; along the line of historical development; this I will call the method of evolution; along the lines of the customs of the community; this I will call the method of tradition; along the lines of justice, morals and social welfare, the *mores* of the day; and this I will call the method of sociology."

In Cardozo's judgment, the rule of analogy was entitled to certain presumptions and should be followed if possible. He believed that the judge

---

[5] Holmes, *The Common Law* 1 (1938).
[6] Cardozo, *The Nature of the Judicial Process* (1921). Excerpts are used by permission from the Yale University Press.

who molds the law by the method of philosophy is satisfying humanity's deep-seated desire for certainty. History, in indicating the direction of precedent, often illuminates the path of logic and plays an important part in decisions in areas such as real property. Custom or trade practice has supplied much of the direction of the law in the area of business. All judicial decisions are at least in part directed by the judge's viewpoint on the welfare of society. The end served by law must dictate the administration of justice, and ethical considerations, if ignored, will ultimately overturn a principle of law.

Noting the psychological aspects of judges' decisions, Cardozo observed that it is the subconscious forces which keep judges consistent with one another. In so recognizing that all persons, including judges, have a philosophy which gives coherence and direction to their thought and actions, whether they admit it or not, he stated:

> All their lives, forces which they do not recognize and cannot name, have been tugging at them—inherited instincts, traditional beliefs, acquired conviction; and the resultant is an outlook on life, a conception of social needs,...which when reasons are nicely balanced, must determine where choice shall fall. In this mental background every problem finds its setting. We may try to see things as objectively as we please. None the less, we can never see them with any eyes except our own. To that test they are all brought—a form of pleading or an act of parliament, the wrongs of paupers or the rights of princes, a village ordinance or a nation's charter.

In the following comments, Cardozo summarized his view of the judicial process.

FROM THE NATURE OF THE JUDICIAL PROCESS
Benjamin N. Cardozo

...My analysis of the judicial process comes then to this, and little more: logic, and history, and custom, and utility, and the accepted standards of right conduct, are the forces which singly or in combination shape the progress of the law. Which of these forces shall dominate in any case, must depend largely upon the comparative importance or value of the social interests that will be thereby promoted or impaired. One of the most fundamental social interests is that law shall be uniform and impartial. There must be nothing in its action that savors of prejudice or favor or even arbitrary whim or fitfulness. Therefore in the main there shall be adherence to precedent. There shall be symmetrical development, consistently with history or custom when history or custom has been the motive force, or the chief one, in giving shape to existing rules, and with logic or philosophy when the motive power has been theirs. But symmetrical development may be bought at too high a price. Uniformity ceases to be a good when it becomes uniformity of oppression. The social interest served by symmetry or certainty must then be balanced against the social interest served by equity and fairness or other elements of social welfare. These may enjoin upon the judge the duty of drawing the line at another angle, or staking the path along new courses, of marking a new point of departure from which others who come after him will set out upon their journey.

    If you ask how he is to know when one interest outweighs another, I can only answer that he must get his knowledge just as the legislator gets it, from experience and study and reflection; in brief, from life itself. Here, indeed, is the point of contact between the legislator's work and his. The choice of methods, the appraisement of values, must in the end be guided by like considerations for the one as for the other. Each indeed is legislating within the limits of his competence. No doubt the limits for the judge are narrower. He legislates only between gaps. He fills the open spaces in the law. How far he can go without traveling beyond the walls of the interstices cannot be staked out for him upon a chart. He must learn it for himself as he gains the sense of fitness and proportion that comes with years of habitude in the practice of an art. Even within the gaps, restrictions not easy to define, but felt, however impalpable they may be, by every judge and lawyer, hedge and circumscribe his action. They are established by the traditions of the centuries, by the example of other judges, his predecessors and his colleagues, by the collective judgment of the profession, and by the duty of adherence to the pervading spirit of the law....None the less, within the confines of these open spaces and those of precedent and tradition, choice moves with a freedom which stamps its action as creative. The law which is the resulting product is not found, but made. The process, being legislative, demands the legislator's wisdom....

REVIEW QUESTIONS

1. Contrast the functions of the following:
   a. A trial judge and a reviewing court justice
   b. A grand jury and a petit jury
   c. Judge and jury
   d. Uniform statutes and federal laws
2. The Supreme Court held that the Selective Service law is constitutional, notwithstanding the fact that only males are subject to the draft. It also allowed courts in the state of Florida to televise criminal proceedings, over the objection of defendants. What judicial philosophy is reflected in these decisions? Explain.
3. The jury system is frequently criticized by litigants and jurists. List four reasons for much of the criticism.
4. A government employee who had been fired by the President of the United States sued the President for wrongful discharge. The defendant contended that he could not be sued for actions performed as part of his official duties. Who decides this issue? Why?
5. At the hearings on his confirmation, one Supreme Court Justice laid out his judicial philosophy as follows:

It is the business of a judge to decide cases on the narrowest grounds possible and not to reach out for constitutional questions. As a judge, you can't have the freedom to substitute your own views for the law.

    A judge should try to obey and not go beyond the intent of Congress in interpreting federal laws. A judge must be most reluctant to depart from prior precedent. A judge is not a legislator and the Supreme Court should not be used as an instrument of policy.

Which judicial philosophy is expressed by the foregoing summary?

6 In recent years, courts have halted construction of a dam to preserve an endangered species of fish, ruled that females must be allowed to compete with males in athletics, banned school dress codes, and blocked suspension of public school students without a hearing. Courts have operated the schools in Boston, Massachusetts, and the prisons in Alabama. Which judicial philosophy is present in these decisions? Explain.

7 Courts are frequently called upon to interpret the Constitution and legislation. This function is performed in the context of applying legislation to a factual situation. Answer the following questions relative to statutory interpretation.
  a Why is it necessary for courts to interpret legislation?
  b List two techniques that are used to perform this function.
  c List three rules of statutory construction based on the type of law involved.
  d List two rules of statutory construction based on the words used in the statute.

8 A state statute provided that "every person who, at the request of the owner of any real property...rents, leases or otherwise supplies equipment...for clearing, grading, filling in, or otherwise improving any real property...has a lien upon such real property for the value of the services rendered for such purposes."

  A wrecking company supplied trucks and drivers for removal of debris, which resulted from the demolition of a building on certain premises. The owner failed to pay the cost of removal, and the wrecking company filed a lien under the statute mentioned above. There was no such lien at common law. What rules of statutory construction could be used by a court to decide the validity of the lien?

9 What are some of the advantages of a precedent-oriented legal system? What are some of the disadvantages?

10 Ann, a resident of Iowa, purchased some auto parts by mail from RST Company in Illinois. The contract called for the seller to deliver the parts to Ann. Ann wishes to return some of the parts she received, but RST refuses to accept returns. Iowa has a law requiring sellers of consumer goods to refund the purchase price if the goods are returned within ten days. Illinois has no such law. What law will be applied regarding the return of the merchandise? Explain.

11 George was on a coast-to-coast trip by automobile. While passing through Ohio, he had a flat tire. It was fixed by Al's Turnpike Service Station, and later, while George was driving in Indiana, the tire came off and George was injured. George was hospitalized in Indiana, so he sued Al in Indiana for his injuries. What rules of substantive law will the Indiana court use to determine if Al is at fault? Explain.

12 Justice Cardozo, in his comments about the judicial process, described four forces which, singly or in combination, shaped the progress of the law. Name or describe these four forces, and give an example of each.

13 Stare decisis is less likely to be followed in the area of public law than in the area of private law. Why?

CHAPTER 3

COURT SYSTEMS

OVERVIEW

This chapter examines the state and federal court systems. It demonstrates the difference between trial courts and reviewing courts. It also distinguishes between courts of law and courts of equity. Finally, it identifies some of the problems with the court systems.

The following terms are introduced: clean-hands doctrine, certiorari, chancery, diversity of citizenship, doctrine of abstention, equity, federal questions jurisdiction, small-claims court.

1 INTRODUCTION

The court system at the federal level and in most states contains three levels—trial courts, intermediate reviewing courts, and final reviewing courts. Lawsuits are commenced at the trial court level, and the results are reviewed at the other two levels.

For a court to hear and decide a case at any level it must have **jurisdiction**. Jurisdiction is power over the subject matter of the case and over the parties. Some state trial courts have general jurisdiction; others have limited jurisdiction. They may be limited as to subject matter, amount in controversy, or area in which the parties live. For example, small-claims courts have jurisdiction only if the amount in controversy does not exceed a certain sum. Even a court of general jurisdiction has geographical limitations. As we shall see in this chapter, all federal courts have limited jurisdiction.

Courts, especially those of limited jurisdiction, may be named according to the subject matter with which they deal. Probate courts deal with wills and the estates of deceased people; juvenile courts with juvenile crime and dependent children; criminal and police courts with violators of state laws and municipal ordinances; and traffic courts with traffic violations. For an accurate classification of the courts of any state, the statutes of that state must be examined.

Even courts of general jurisdiction cannot attempt to resolve every dispute or controversy that may arise. Some issues are simply nonjusticiable, as the following case illustrates.

WOODRUFF v. GEORGIA STATE UNIVERSITY

394 S.E.2d 697 (Ga. 1983)

FACTS

Woodruff sued Georgia State University and certain professors. She had received a master's degree even though she had been accused of plagiarism. The professors refused to recommend her to a Ph.D. program.

ISSUE

Is a dispute concerning academic decisions of a public educational institution a justiciable controversy?

DECISION

No.

REASONS

1. Courts traditionally have been reluctant to embark upon courses of judicial action that would require continuing supervision of the official conduct of public officers.
2. Courts cannot review a teacher's academic assessment of a student's work. Courts have confidence that school authorities are able to discharge their academic duties in fairness and with competence.
3. Teachers are protected from the cost and agony of litigation initiated by pupils and their parents who would rely upon the legal process rather than the learning process.

---

2 THE STATE COURT SYSTEM

Government in the United States is based on dual sovereignty; that is, the judicial branch is an essential element of government at both the state and federal levels. Both the state and federal court systems are created and

FIGURE 3-1 The typical state court system.

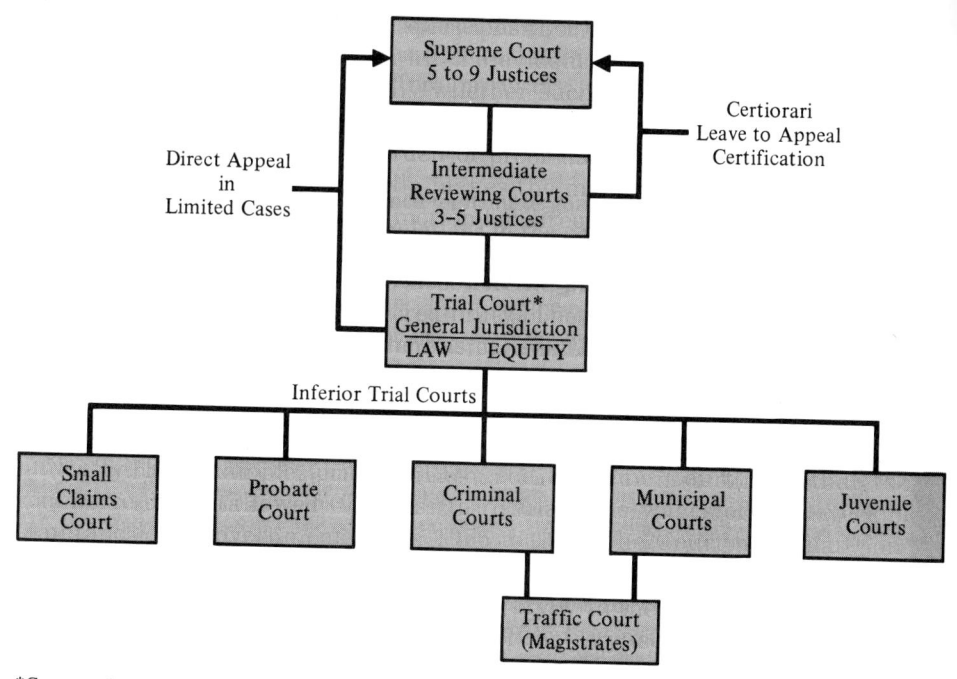

*Commonly called Circuit Court, District Court or Superior Court in many states.

[Diagram description: Supreme Court (5 to 9 Justices) → Intermediate Reviewing Courts (3-5 Justices) → Trial Court* General Jurisdiction LAW EQUITY. Direct Appeal in Limited Cases on left; Certiorari, Leave to Appeal, Certification on right. Inferior Trial Courts: Small Claims Court, Probate Court, Criminal Courts, Municipal Courts, Juvenile Courts; Traffic Court (Magistrates) under Criminal Courts.]

their operations governed from three sources. First of all, constitutions provide the general framework for the court system. Second, the legislature, pursuant to constitutional authority, enacts statutes which add body to the framework. This legislation provides for various courts; establishes their **jurisdiction,** or an area of authority; and deals with such problems as the tenure, selection, and duties of judges. Other legislation may establish the general rules of procedure to be used by these courts. Finally, each court sets forth its own rules of procedure within the statutory bounds set. These rules are detailed and may specify, for example, the form of a summons or the times when various documents must be filed with the court clerk. Thus, a study of the court system for any particular state must refer to its constitution, such legislation as Civil Practice Acts, and the rules of the various courts. Each state has its own terminology and arrangement for its courts. Figure 3-1 is representative of the courts of a typical state.

Trial Courts

The general jurisdiction trial court is frequently known as the "circuit court," deriving its name from earlier times when the judge "rode the circuit," or in other words traveled from town to town in a certain territory over which his court had jurisdiction, hearing and deciding cases. Some states call the basic trial court the "superior court," while others call it the "district court" or "court of common pleas." In New York it is known as the "supreme court." The term "general jurisdiction" means that the court has the power to hear any type of case. The courts below this trial court in Figure 3-1 are limited to certain types of cases which they may hear and thus are referred to as "inferior courts" or courts of limited jurisdiction. For example, probate courts are involved with the administration of the estates of deceased persons or those of incompetents. Juvenile courts deal with criminal offenses committed by children below a stated age.

At one time the basic trial courts were divided into two branches, one known as a "court of law" and the other a "court of chancery, or equity," but this is no longer the case in most states. The distinction between law and equity is discussed in section 9 of this chapter.

Some states do not have intermediate reviewing courts between the trial court and the court of final resort; however, intermediate reviewing courts are usually found in the more heavily populated states. Some states call their court of last resort "Supreme Court of Appeals" or "Court of Appeals."

Reviewing Courts

In states with two levels of reviewing courts, most appeals are taken to the lower of the two courts, and the highest court of the state reviews only very important cases. Courts of review are essentially concerned with questions of law. While a party is entitled to one trial and one appeal, he or she may obtain a second review if the higher reviewing court, in the exercise of its discretion, agrees to such a review. The procedure for requesting a second review is to file what is called a "petition for leave to appeal" in some states and a "petition for a writ of certiorari" in others.

Since this request for a second review must be acted upon by the higher court, the party requesting it actually obtains a second review, although it is a limited one. The case is examined to see whether it is one that the highest court wishes to hear. Deciding such requests is a major function of the Supreme Court of the United States and of the highest court in each state. As a practical matter, less than 5 percent of all such requests are granted.

3 SMALL-CLAIMS COURTS

One court of limited jurisdiction is especially important to the business community. This court, usually known as **small-claims court,** handles the majority of litigation between business and its customers. Small-claims courts are used by businesses to collect accounts and by customers to settle disputes with the business community that are relatively minor from a financial standpoint. Such suits are often quite important from the standpoint of principle, however. For example, many people use small-claims courts to sue for damages caused by defective merchandise or services poorly performed. Landlord-tenant disputes are another example of controversies decided in these courts.

Small-claims courts have low court costs and simplified procedures. The informality of the proceedings speeds up the flow of cases. The services of a lawyer are not usually required, but if one side uses a lawyer, the other side probably needs one also. Some states do not allow lawyers to participate in these proceedings. Such courts usually are subject to a dollar limitation over the suits which may be filed. In some states, this amount may be as low as $500, whereas in others it may be as high as $5,000. A typical jurisdictional amount is $2,000. Most states have raised this jurisdictional limitation, as inflation has taken its toll here also.

As small-claims courts have grown in number and as their case loads have expanded, numerous problems have arisen. In large cities, there is often a need for a bilingual court. In addition, night sessions are frequently required so that litigants need not miss work. As a practical matter, the judge often serves as mediator of the dispute, and many cases are settled by agreement with the court. For many people, the chance to complain to some third party is all they really seek in filing a lawsuit. Any financial recovery is secondary. One continuing problem, however, is that many successful litigants are unable to collect their judgments because the decision of the small-claims court is not self-enforcing. A recent study in New York City found that 44 percent of successful litigants in small-claims court did not collect any money.

4 THE FEDERAL COURT SYSTEM

Article III of the Constitution (see Appendix 1) provides that judicial power be vested in the Supreme Court and such lower courts as Congress may create. These courts are described in Figure 3-2. The judicial power of the federal courts is limited. Essentially, it extends to matters involving questions of federal law (**federal question cases**), to matters in which the United States is a party, to controversies among the states, and to cases involving **diversity of citizenship** (suits between citizens of different states). The federal judicial power does not extend to cases involving a state law between citizens of the same state. Such cases will be dismissed by federal courts because they lack the power to hear them.

In order for a claim to arise under the Constitution, laws, or treaties of the United States, a right or immunity created by said Constitution or laws must be an essential element of the plaintiff's cause of action. Thus, federal question cases may be based on issues arising out of the United States Constitution or out of federal statutes. Any amount of money may be involved in such a case, and it need not be a suit for damages. For example, a suit to

CHAPTER 3: COURT SYSTEMS 55

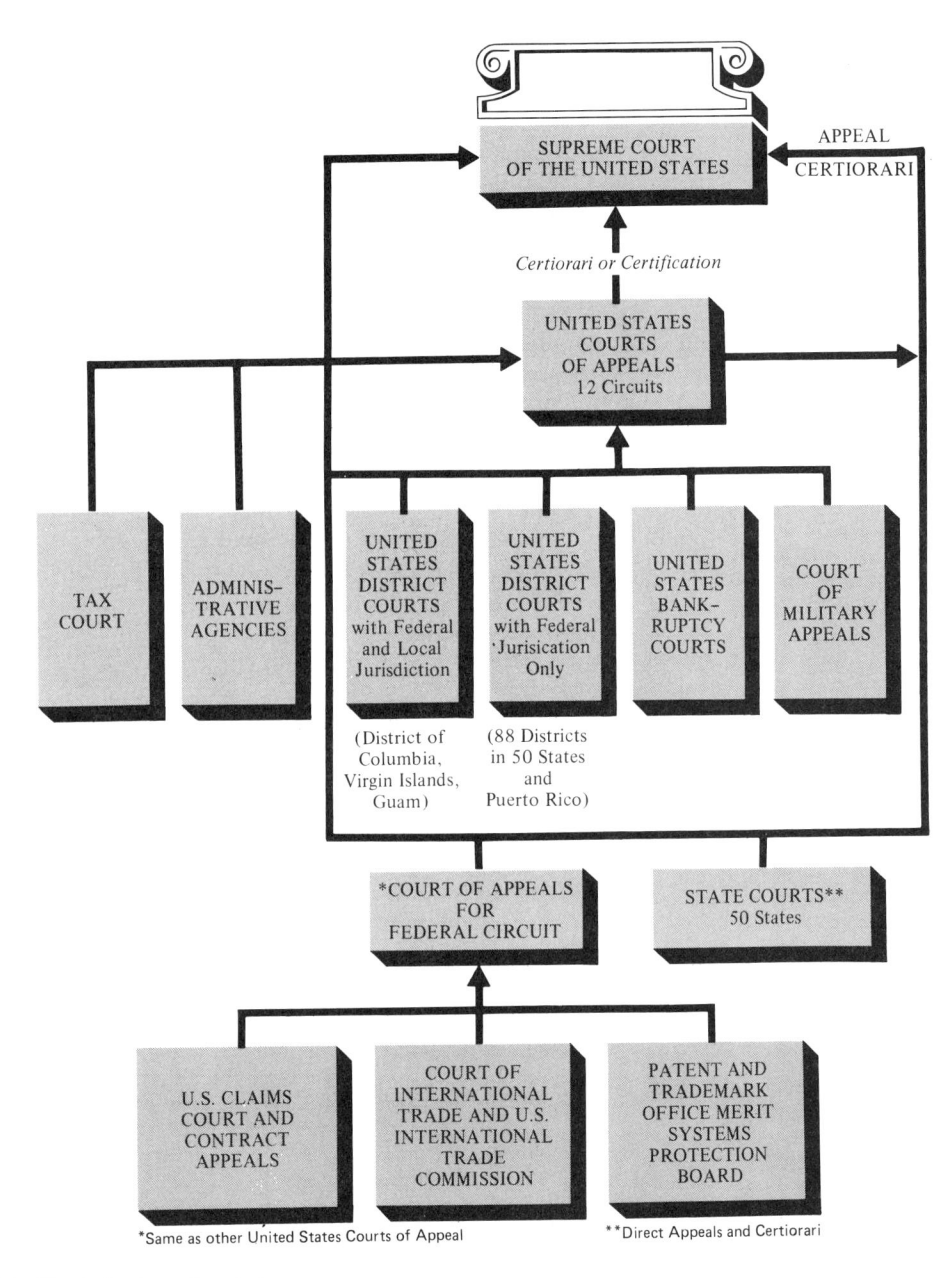

FIGURE 3-2 The federal court system.

enjoin a violation of a constitutional right can be filed in the federal courts as a federal question case.

These civil actions may involve matters such as bankruptcy or suits based on patents, copyrights, trademarks, taxes, elections, the rights guaranteed by the Bill of Rights, and those rights secured to individual citizens by the Fourteenth Amendment. In addition, by statute the federal district courts have original jurisdiction to try tort cases involving citizens who suffer damages caused by officers or agents of the federal government.

The district courts are the trial courts of the federal judicial system. They have original jurisdiction, exclusive of the courts of the states, over all federal crimes, that is, all offenses against the laws of the United States. The accused is entitled to a trial by jury in the state and district where the crime was committed.

If a case affects ambassadors or other public ministers and consuls, or if it is one in which a state is a party, the Supreme Court has original jurisdiction. In all other cases, the Supreme Court has appellate jurisdiction unless Congress creates an exception.

Under its constitutional authorization, Congress has enacted legislation providing for various inferior federal courts and defined their jurisdiction. Congress has created twelve U.S. courts of appeals plus a special court of appeals for the Federal Circuit. This special reviewing court, located in Washington, D.C., hears appeals from special courts such as the U.S. Claims Court and Contract Appeals, as well as from administrative decisions such as those by the Patent and Trademark Office. Congress has also created the U.S. district courts (at least one in each state) and other courts, such as the Court of Military Appeals, to handle special subject matter. Figure 3-2 illustrates the federal court system and shows the relationship of state courts and administrative agencies for review purposes. The U.S. Code also contains provisions concerning such matters as appellate procedure and the review of actions by administrative agencies. The Federal Rules of Civil Procedure provide the details concerning procedures to be followed in federal court litigation.

5 DIVERSITY-OF-CITIZENSHIP CASES

There are several problems related to the jurisdiction of federal courts based on diversity of citizenship. Diversity of citizenship does not extend to domestic relations cases. The fact that a husband and wife may live in different states does not justify the federal courts to hear their divorce cases. In addition, diversity of citizenship requires that all plaintiffs be citizens of different states from all defendants. If a case involves several parties on one or more sides, and if a party on one side is a citizen of the same state as a party on the other, there will be then no diversity of citizenship and thus no federal jurisdiction. In some types of cases where some parties actually represent others, deciding if total diversity exists is difficult.

NAVARRO SAVINGS ASSOCIATION v. LEE
100 S.Ct. 1779 (1980)

FACTS

Plaintiff, trustees of a business trust organized under Massachusetts law, brought a diversity of citizenship action in a Texas federal court against the defendant, a citizen of Texas, for his failure to pay an outstanding loan. None of the trustees were Texas citizens, but several of the beneficiaries were citizens of Texas. The terms of the trust gave plaintiff exclusive authority over the trust assets, free from any power and control of the shareholders and provided that the trustee could sue or be sued in the name of the trust. The defendant asserted that there was no diversity of citizenship because of Texas beneficiaries.

ISSUE

Whose citizenship is used for diversity purposes, the trustees or the beneficiaries?

DECISION

Trustees.

REASONS:

1. A federal court must disregard nominal parties and rest jurisdiction only upon the citizenship of real parties to the controversy.
2. A trustee is a real party to the controversy for purposes of diversity jurisdiction when he or she possesses certain customary powers to hold, manage, and dispose of assets for the benefit of others.
3. The trustees have legal title; they manage assets; they control litigation. In short, they are real parties to the controversy.

The fact that business corporations are frequently incorporated in one state and have their principal place of business in another state also causes problems in determining when diversity of citizenship exists. A corporation is a citizen of the state of incorporation and also a citizen of the state in which it has its principal place of business, for purposes of diversity jurisdiction. Thus, a Delaware corporation with its principal place of business in Illinois is a citizen of both Delaware and Illinois for purposes of diversity. If any party on the other side of a lawsuit with such a corporation is a citizen of either Illinois or Delaware, there is then no diversity and no federal jurisdiction. Questions as to the state in which a corporation has its principal place of business often arise. The total activity of the corporation is examined to determine its principal place of business. This test incorporates both the "place of activities" and the "nerve center" tests. The nerve center test places general emphasis on the locus of the managerial and policy-making functions of the corporations. The place of activities test focuses on production or sales activities. The "total activity" test is not an equation that can provide a simple answer to the question of a corporation's principal place of business. Each case necessarily involves somewhat subjective analysis.

In diversity-of-citizenship cases, the federal courts also have a jurisdictional amount of more than $50,000. If a case involves multiple plaintiffs with separate and distinct claims, *each* claim must satisfy the jurisdictional amount. Thus, in a class action suit, the claim of each plaintiff must meet the $50,000 minimum unless changed by statute.

6 FEDERAL REVIEWING COURTS

Direct appeals from the district courts to the U.S. Supreme Court may be taken in three situations: (1) in criminal cases when the district court holds invalid the statute upon which the indictment or information was based, (2) when the district court holds an act of Congress unconstitutional in a case in which a government agency is a party, and (3) when the district court consisting of three judges has either granted or denied an injunction. In most cases appeals are taken from the U.S. district court to the courts of appeals. Since litigants are entitled to one review as a matter of right, parties may obtain additional review of decisions only if the court of appeals holds a state statute to be unconstitutional or contrary to federal law, or upon the granting of a writ of **certiorari** by the Supreme Court.

A petition for a writ of certiorari is a request by the losing party to a higher court for permission to file an additional appeal. In such cases, the Supreme Court has discretion as to whether or not it will grant the petition and allow another review. The review is not a matter of right. Writs of certiorari are granted only in cases of substantial federal importance or where there is an obvious conflict between decisions of two or more circuit courts of appeals in an area of the law which needs clarification. Certiorari may be granted before or after the decision of the circuit court of appeals. When the Supreme Court of the United States reviews petitions for a writ of certiorari, the writ is granted if four of the nine justices vote to take the case. The net result of this procedure is that the Supreme Court spends a great deal of time and effort in deciding which cases it will hear. It is able to pick and choose those issues with which it will be involved.

In addition to cases on appeal and accepted by writ of certiorari, the Supreme Court will review questions of law certified to it for decision by the court of appeals. The federal court system is thus limited in the types of cases it decides.

The U.S. district courts and the courts of appeals cannot review, retry, or correct the judicial errors charged against a state court. Final judgments or decrees rendered by the highest court of a state are reviewed only by the Supreme Court of the United States. State cases appealed to the U.S. Supreme Court must concern the validity of a treaty or statute of the United States or must present a question involving the validity of a state statute on the grounds that the statute is repugnant to the Constitution, treaties, or laws of the United States and that the state decision is in favor of the statute's validity. When a case involves the constitutionality of a state statute or treaty, or when a citizen's rights, privileges, or immunities under the constitution or laws are impaired, the case may be brought to the Supreme Court by writ of certiorari. In all other cases, the decision of the highest state court is not subject to review.

7 TRANSFER FROM THE STATES TO THE FEDERAL SYSTEM

It is possible to transfer a case from the state court system to the federal court system under three circumstances. First, a defendant sued in a state court may have the case removed to the federal system if it meets the requirements of those cases which first could have been brought into the federal system. In other words, if the case involves a *federal question,* or if there is diversity of citizenship and the requisite amount is involved, the case may be transferred by a defendant to the federal district court.

In addition, there is a special statute dealing with civil rights cases. If a defendant is denied or cannot enforce in the courts of a state a right under any law providing for the equal civil rights of citizens of the United States, the case may be removed from the state courts to the appropriate federal district court.

Whenever a separate and independent claim or cause of action, which would be removable if sued upon alone, is joined with one or more otherwise nonremovable claims or causes of action, the entire case may be removed. The district court may determine all issues in the case, or, in its discretion, may send all matters not otherwise within its original jurisdiction back to the state court.

Second, a party has the right to appeal a decision of the highest court of a state to the Supreme Court of the United States if: (1) the case involves the validity of a treaty or statute of the United States, and the decision is against its validity; or (2) the case involves the validity of a state statute which allegedly violates the United States Constitution, and the decision is in favor of its validity.

Third, a party may seek review of the decision of a state's highest court by writ of certiorari where a federal question is involved. Each year there are several thousand such petitions filed. Almost all of them are denied.

8 THE LAW IN THE FEDERAL COURTS

Generally speaking, each court system uses its own rules of procedure. Thus, in the federal courts, the Federal Rules of Procedure (both civil and criminal) are followed. For state court proceedings, each state has adopted applicable rules of procedure.

The problem as to the applicable substantive law is far more complex. In federal question cases, the controlling statutes and judicial decisions are those of the federal courts. However, if the case is in the federal courts because of diversity of citizenship, the applicable substantive law is that of the state in which the court sits. In a diversity-of-citizenship case, a federal court is just another court of the state insofar as the applicable substantive law is concerned. As a result, there is no general federal common law.

In following the law of the state where the court sits in diversity-of-citizenship cases, the federal court will examine the total body of law of the state in which it is sitting, *including the state's conflict-of-laws principles*. Thus, in using the law of state X the court may, in turn, examine the law of some other state for actual precedent. For example, assume that a citizen of Illinois sues a citizen of Indiana in federal district court in Indiana for personal injuries received in an automobile accident which occurred in Kentucky. The federal district court sitting in Indiana will use federal procedure and the substantive law of the state of Indiana. The substantive law of Indiana includes the conflict-of-laws principle that the applicable tort law is the law of the place of injury. The federal court in Indiana will use the Kentucky tort law since that is the law which would be used by an Indiana state court.

Since federal courts use federal procedures and state substantive law in diversity cases, many decisions are concerned with whether a given issue is one of substantive law or one of procedure. If the state rule of law, whether created by statute or case decision, will affect the *result* of the controversy, the rule is treated as substantive and will be followed by the federal court in diversity cases. The case which follows illustrates that even a rule of procedure may be treated as substantive for this purpose.

WALKER v. ARMCO STEEL CORP.
100 S.Ct. 1978 (1980)

FACTS

Walker, a carpenter and resident of Oklahoma, was injured on August 22, 1975, in Oklahoma City, Oklahoma, while pounding a sheffield nail into a cement wall. Defendant, a nonresident of Oklahoma, was the manufacturer of the nail. Walker claimed that the nail contained a defect which caused its head to shatter and strike him in the right eye, resulting in permanent injuries.

The complaint was filed on August 19, 1977. Although a summons was issued that same day, service of process was not made until December 1, 1977. Defendant contended that the action was barred by the Oklahoma two-year statute of limitations. Oklahoma does not deem an action "commenced" until service of the summons on the defendant. However, if the complaint is filed within the limitations period, the action is not barred if the defendant is served within sixty days. Plaintiff admitted that his case would be foreclosed in state court, but he argued that Rule 3 of the Federal Rules of Civil Procedure governs the manner in which an action is commenced in federal court for all purposes, including whether the state statute of limitations continues to run or not. Under this federal rule, the filing of the complaint tolled the statute of limitations.

ISSUE

In a diversity action, should the federal court follow state law or, alternatively, Rule 3 of the Federal Rules of Civil Procedure in determining when an action is commenced for the purpose of tolling the state statute of limitations?

DECISION

State law.

REASONS

1. Except in matters governed by the federal Constitution or by acts of Congress, the law to be applied in any diversity case is the law of the state.
2. In all cases where a federal court is exercising jurisdiction solely because of the diversity of citizenship of the parties, the outcome of the litigation in the federal court should be substantially the same, so far as legal rules determine the outcome of a litigation, as it would be if tried in a state court.
3. A state statute of limitations bars recovery in a state court, and federal courts cannot give a cause of action longer life in the federal court than it would have had in the state court without adding something to it.
4. A state statute on the service of a summons is an integral part of the statute of limitations.

Federal courts sometimes face a dilemma when there is no state decision or statute on the issue involved in a diversity case. In such situations, the federal court, under a **doctrine of abstention,** may hold its case in abeyance and direct the litigants to try their case in the state court. This is also true if a federal question is involved with a question of state law. The doctrine of abstention is invoked to allow the state to decide state issues before the federal court decides federal issues, especially where the state decision may end the litigation. The doctrine of abstention allows federal courts to eliminate guesswork on the meaning of local laws and is designed to further harmonious relations between state and federal courts. The state court may decide the federal question if the parties so desire, or it may leave the federal question to the federal courts. If the state court decides the federal question, the losing party may then appeal to the United States Supreme Court.

9 LAW AND EQUITY

Courts having general jurisdiction in the United States have traditionally been divided into courts of law and courts of equity. Some states historically had two separate courts, and others simply had one court with one side known as law and the other side known as **equity**, or **chancery**.

Courts of law were developed early in English jurisprudence to handle cases such as the various forms of trespass, other torts, and breach of contract. These courts dealt with legal disputes where one party was seeking money damages from another. Courts of law were not equipped to give remedies such as requiring a person to do or not to do something.

When courts of law were inadequate to furnish the desired relief, a practice developed of petitioning the king of England for such relief. As the number of such petitions grew, the king delegated his authority in granting or denying petitions to his chancellor. The name "chancery" is derived from this practice. Since the action taken was originally taken by the king, results were not a matter of right but in each case rested in the grace and favor of the king; or, by modern terminology, the decisions were strictly discretionary.

The concept of equity did not originate in England, however. Aristotle had defined equity as the "correction of the law, where, by reason of its universality, it is deficient." The purpose of equity has always been to remedy defects in the law. As courts of chancery grew and developed in England, the need for supplemental legal procedures where courts of law were inadequate assisted the steady growth of equity, although the courts of law strenuously objected.

Courts of chancery or equity were firmly entrenched in English jurisprudence by the time the American court system was developed. Those who established our courts recognized the need for resort to natural principles to define and interpret positive law and to remedy its defects, and they therefore provided for equity jurisprudence.

In recent years, federal law and many state laws have attempted to abolish the distinctions between law and equity. These attempts have affected procedural aspects of the distinction but have not changed its substantive aspects. These attempts have combined the procedures of law and equity into one action known as a "civil action." In civil actions, equitable concepts have been generally utilized and adopted for actions at law. The influence of equity has predominated over law where the procedures have been combined.

Notwithstanding statements that the distinctions between law and equity have been abolished, since the historical substantive distinctions are still important, it is usually necessary to decide whether an action would have been "at law" or "in chancery." Many states require that the pleading so indicate.

Many matters depend on whether an action is legal or equitable in nature. For example, cases in chancery, with a few exceptions such as will contests, are not tried before a jury. The court, or in a few states a person appointed by it, known as a "master in chancery," serves as the trier and finder of the facts. Thus, whether a party has a right to a trial by jury depends on the nature of the action.

Equity jurisdiction is used in cases where the remedy at law is deemed inadequate. That is, where dollar damages are not an adequate remedy, a court of chancery will hear the case. Such cases as suits for an accounting; cancellation, rescission, or reformation of a contract; injunctions; partition suits; suits to quiet title; and suits for specific performance are litigated in chancery. If a case is filed in equity and if the remedy at law, such as dollar damages for breach of contract, is an adequate remedy, the suit in equity will be dismissed, as occurred in the following case.

BECKMAN v. VASSALL-DILLWORTH LINCOLN-MERCURY
468 A.2d 784 (Pa. Super. 1983)

FACTS

Beckman signed a contract with the Vassall-Dillworth Lincoln-Mercury dealership for the purchase of a 1979 Lincoln Continental. The purchase-order agreement was lost, and no car was ordered. The dealer offered to order a 1979 Lincoln Continental, but at a price higher than the price originally agreed upon. Beckman sued the dealership for specific performance.

ISSUE

Is he entitled to specific performance?

DECISION

No.

REASONS

1. Specific performance is inappropriate when the moving party has an adequate remedy at law.
2. Specific performance is a proper remedy when the subject matter of an agreement is an asset that is unique or one that its equivalent cannot be purchased on the open market.
3. The remedy is damages for any difference between the original order price and the actual purchase price he paid.

---

10 EQUITABLE PROCEDURES

Courts of equity use *maxims* instead of rules of law. Strictly speaking, there are no legal rights in equity, for the decision is based on moral rights and natural justice. A court of equity is a court of conscience in which precedent is secondary to natural justice.

Some of the typical maxims of equity are:

1. "Equity will not suffer a right to exist without a remedy."
2. "Equity regards as done that which ought to be done."
3. "Where there is equal equity, the law must prevail."
4. "He who comes into equity must do so with clean hands."
5. "He who seeks equity must do equity."
6. "Equity aids the vigilant."
7. "Equality is equity."

These maxims serve as guides for the chancellor to use in exercising his or her discretion. For example the **clean-hands doctrine** (no. 4) prohibits a party who is guilty of misconduct in the matter in litigation from receiving the aid of a court of equity. Many cases simply involve a balancing of the equities in order to achieve justice. Notice how obvious the equities are in the case which follows.

TUDOR ENGINEERING CO. v. MOUW
709 P.2d 146 (Idaho 1985)

FACTS

Plaintiff, Tudor Engineering Company, obtained a judgment against defendant, Mouw, for $304.22 for professional land-surveying services. When Mouw failed to pay the judgment, plaintiff had defendant's home sold at a judicial sale. Mouw was not served with actual notice of the sale. Plaintiff was the only bidder at the sale and purchased the home for $385.65. After the statutory period during which the defendant could pay off the debt and regain his home (period of redemption) had expired, plaintiff was given a sheriff's deed.

Upon receipt of the deed, plaintiff advertised the property for sale for the price of $49,000. The defendant then petitioned the court that he be allowed to redeem the property.

ISSUE

Should the defendant be allowed to redeem his property?

DECISION

Yes.

REASONS

1. Courts of equity may, upon a proper bill declaring fraud, mistake, or other circumstances appealing to the discretion of the chancellor, relieve a debtor whose property has been sold from failure to redeem within the statutory period.
2. A granting of an equitable right of redemption is, in effect, a balancing of the equities that exist on either side of the dispute. The trial court must

weigh the various equitable considerations and determine whether, in its discretion, the debtor is entitled to an equitable right of redemption.
3. Here, equitable relief was proper because of the inadequacy of the purchase price and because the plaintiff failed to provide the defendant with actual notice of the execution sale.

The decision of the court of equity is called a decree, as contrasted with a judgment in a court of law which is measured in damages. A decree of a court of equity is said to be in personam; that is, it directs the defendant to do or not to do some specific thing.

Decrees are either final or interlocutory. A decree is final when it disposes of the issues in the case, reserving no question to be decided in the future. A decree is interlocutory when it reserves some question to be determined in the future. A decree granting a temporary injunction would be interlocutory.

Failure of the defendant to obey a decree of a court of equity is contempt of court. Any person in contempt of court may be placed in jail or fined.

Equity has played a significant role in our system of jurisprudence, and it will continue to do so. In moving toward social justice, the courts will rely more on equitable maxims and less on rigid rules of law. This will also contribute further to the decay of the doctrine of stare decisis.

11 CONTEMPORARY PROBLEMS

A recent headline in *The Wall Street Journal* read "Too Much Law, Too Many Lawyers, Not Enough Justice." The president of Harvard, Derek Bok, observed that "there is far too much law for those who can afford it and far too little for those who cannot." Such articles and observations are strong evidence that there are numerous problems facing the court system. Delay and the high cost of operating the system are two major problems. Court dockets have expanded with resultant delays in recent years because of the litigious nature of our society and increases in population. The high cost of litigation has priced most minor disputes either out of the court system or to small-claims court, where the matter can be resolved without legal counsel. It is no longer economically feasible to litigate with the aid of an attorney such matters as consumer claims for shoddy merchandise or poor services. The costs of transmitting property on death are unsatisfactorily high for many Americans. It has been estimated that it costs up to 100 times as much to transfer property on death in this country as it does in England. Probate costs often run 2½ to 3 times funeral expenses.

"Justice delayed is justice denied." That often-quoted cliché sums up the most obvious defect in our court system—court congestion and the delay that results therefrom. In many large cities, the backlog of civil cases is so great that a period of five or more years elapses between the transaction or occurrence in question and a jury trial. Such delays tend to force unsatisfactory settlements upon many plaintiffs. They also cause other serious problems for the parties and adversely affect the search for truth. The thousands of criminal cases awaiting trials or pending on appeal at all times raise many serious consequences for society. Not the least of these is that an accused person free on bond is free to commit more crimes while the case is awaiting trial.

The high cost of legal services, especially of litigation, greatly concerns clients and the organized bar. Litigation is expensive, not only for the parties to the dispute, but for society as a whole. Society pays the cost of providing judges, court officials, and juries. The current trend is to have more and longer jury trials, thus greatly increasing the cost of the system. Much of jurors' time is unproductively spent, since they must frequently wait for the lawyers and the court to proceed. Since jurors are paid by the day, inefficiency adds to society's costs.

Adequate legal advice is priced out of the reach of many low- and middle-income persons. The wealthy can afford the best legal talent. Public defender programs provide free legal service to indigents charged with crime, and legal aid projects have generally made legal service available to poor persons with civil problems. However, the cost of legal services for the average person is often prohibitive. As a result, many people either do not have legal advice when it is needed or often turn to other laypersons for legal advice. Although the increase in the number of lawyers and the resulting competition have helped alleviate this problem, the cost of adequate legal assistance has made it unavailable to many Americans.

Adequate legal services are usually available to personal-injury and other damage claim litigants, irrespective of the client's ability to pay. The poorest person in the country can obtain the best legal talent in a personal-injury case because of a method of compensation known as the *contingent fee system*. In cases handled under the contingent fee arrangement, the attorney's fee is a fixed percentage of the total recovery. In a typical case, the attorney receives one-third of the net amount collected for the client.

The contingent fee system gives everyone equal access to the courts and to legal talent. However, it often does so at a high cost to the client. Assume that a person loses both legs as the result of the negligent conduct of another, and that the issue of negligence is not debatable. Assume that the jury awards the victim $3 million as damages. It is difficult to believe that the attorney earned a fee of $1 million in such a case. Of course, if the liability or the extent of injury is not clear, then the attorney certainly would "earn" more of the fee for his or her efforts.

12 DELAY: SOME SOLUTIONS

Many state legislatures and court authorities are implementing several changes designed to eliminate and reduce court congestion and the backlog of court cases. Among the changes to reduce court congestion which have partial acceptance to date are: (1) six-person juries instead of twelve; (2) requiring only majority verdicts instead of unanimous ones; (3) elimination of oral argument on appeal whenever possible; (4) application of management techniques to the system by designating someone other than a judge to assign cases, court rooms, and juries so that all judicial personnel are utilized more effectively; and (5) elimination of jury trials in certain types of cases. In addition, the number of judges has been expanded in many jurisdictions.

Several suggestions have been made to reduce the case load of the federal courts. Perhaps the most radical idea is to abolish diversity of citizenship jurisdiction in the federal courts or to deny jurisdiction if the plaintiff is from the same state as the court in which the case is filed. It is argued that there is no rational basis today for putting an automobile accident case in a federal court simply because litigants are citizens of different states, especially if the plaintiff is from the state from which the jury will be selected. A similar proposal would raise the jurisdictional amount to $50,000. This would mean that only substantial cases are in the federal courts.

It has also been proposed that a special court be created to hear petitions for writs of certiorari. This would free the Supreme Court to spend its time deciding cases before it rather than requiring it to spend a significant portion of its time deciding which cases it wants to hear. Each year the Supreme Court must review over 5,000 petitions for writs of certiorari. This new court would probably consist of courts of appeals justices on a rotating basis.

REVIEW QUESTIONS

1 An attorney filed a $10 million class action suit against the National Football League for allowing the 1987 players' strike. He alleged a denial of the pursuit of happiness. Discuss whether or not this suit is proper.
2 Answer the following questions about the jurisdiction of federal courts:
   a Over what type of cases do federal courts have jurisdiction?
   b What is the jurisdictional amount in the federal courts?
   c For diversity-of-citizenship purposes, a corporation is a citizen of two states. Name them.
3 Pat sues Mike in a state court, seeking damages for breach of contract. The trial court finds for Mike. Pat announces that she will appeal "all the way to the Supreme Court of the United States if necessary" to change the decision. Assuming that Pat has the money to do so, will she be able to obtain review by the Supreme Court of the United States? Explain.
4 Paula, a citizen of Georgia, was crossing a street in New Orleans when she was struck by a car driven by David, a citizen of Texas. The car was owned by David's employer, a Delaware corporation, which has its principal place of business in Atlanta, Georgia. Paula sues both David and the corporation in the federal district court in New Orleans. Paula's complaint alleges damages in the amount of $100,000. Does this court have jurisdiction? Why, or why not?
5 Henry, a citizen of Illinois, was driving in downtown Keokuk, Iowa, when

his automobile was struck by a truck owned by XYZ Corporation and operated by Daniel, an employee of XYZ. XYZ is a Delaware corporation with its principal place of business in Madison, Wisconsin. Daniel resides in Green Bay, Wisconsin. Henry suffered serious injuries resulting in damages of approximately $95,000. Henry sues Daniel and XYZ Corporation in the federal district court in Keokuk, Iowa. Does the court have jurisdiction? Why?

6 Use the same facts as in question 5, except assume that XYZ's principal place of business is Moline, Illinois. Does the federal district court have jurisdiction? Why?

7 Peter agreed to sell the Blackacre property to Paul. Prior to closing the transaction, oil was discovered on Blackacre, and Peter refused to complete the contract. Paul sues Peter to require performance of the contract. Is he entitled to a jury trial? Explain.

8 Adam and Eve were not married. By contract they had agreed to live together and to divide all property evenly on death of either party or on separation. They separated and began to live in separate states. Adam sued Eve in federal court to collect all of the proceeds of the sale of their apartment. Eve moved to dismiss, alleging it was a domestic relations suit and thus an exception to diversity jurisdiction. What was the result? Why?

9 A tort action was filed in the state court of Illinois by an Illinois limited partnership. The general partner was a citizen of Illinois, and the limited partners were citizens of Illinois and a Delaware corporation. The defendant was a Delaware corporation. The defendant requests that the case be removed from the Illinois court to a federal district court. Should it be? Explain.

10 Joe College deposited $300 with his landlord to secure his lease and pay for any damages to the apartment which he had rented. At the end of the school year, he vacated the apartment and requested the return of his deposit. Although the landlord admitted that the apartment was in good shape, she refused to return the deposit. What should Joe College do? Explain.

11 Plaintiff, a shareholder of Defendant Corporation, sought dissolution of the corporation. He alleged that the acts of those in control of the corporation were illegal, fraudulent, or both, and corporation assets were being misapplied. Plaintiff admitted to participating in some of the illegal acts. Is plaintiff entitled to equitable relief? Why, or why not?

12 Plaintiff, a Pennsylvania citizen, filed suit for personal injuries against defendant, a Delaware corporation. After the state statute of limitations had run out, the defendant filed a motion to dismiss and proved that its principal place of business is Pennsylvania. Will plaintiff's case be dismissed? Explain.

CHAPTER 4

LITIGATION AND OTHER METHODS FOR RESOLVING DISPUTES

OVERVIEW

This chapter is primarily concerned with litigation as the most important means of finally resolving disputes. It traces a lawsuit through its four stages—pleading, discovery, the trial, and review. It also describes mediation and arbitration as alternatives to litigation in settling controversies.

The following legal terms are introduced in this chapter: appellant, appellee, brief, burden of proof, class action suit, clear and convincing proof, deposition, directed verdict, forum non conveniens, hearsay rule, in personam, in rem, jury instruction, long-arm statute, mediation, motion, peremptory challenge, pleadings, preponderance of evidence, privilege, res judicata, standing to sue, submission, summary judgment, summons, venue, and voir dire.

1 INTRODUCTION

The law as a means to an ordered and civilized society seeks to avoid controversy and disputes. It also provides techniques for resolving them when they arise. Although a judicial decision ending litigation among parties to a controversy is the most obvious legal technique for resolving disputes, other methods exist which have their basis in law. These legal methods have replaced naked force as a solution to controversy.

Although statistics are not kept which would prove the point, it is generally accepted that most disputes in our society are resolved by mutual agreement without resort to litigation. In addition, more than 90 percent of all lawsuits filed are settled by the parties and their attorneys without a court decision.

The law plays a major role in encouraging such settlements. It is the framework within which the parties evaluate their positions and contains many procedures designed to encourage settlement. The high cost of litigation both financially and in time is a major force in many settlements. Since both parties are usually required to pay their own attorneys (the losing party usually pays court costs only), financial considerations weigh heavily even for wealthy parties and large corporations. The high cost of litigation often results in payments to plaintiffs with very weak cases because such cases have nuisance value. The amount of the nuisance value is often the cost of a successful defense.

2 PARTIES TO LITIGATION

In a criminal case, the people of the state or the people of the United States, depending on whether or not the alleged crime is a state offense or a federal offense, bring action against the named defendant. Whereas most civil cases use the term "plaintiff" to describe the party bringing the lawsuit, and the term "defendant" to describe the party against whom it is brought, there are some cases, especially in courts of equity, in which the parties are described as the *petitioner* and the *respondent*. When a counterclaim is filed, most jurisdictions use the terms *counter-plaintiff* and *counter-defendant* to describe the parties to the counterclaim. Thus, the plaintiff also becomes a counter-defendant and the defendant also becomes a counter-plaintiff when a counterclaim is filed.

When the result at the trial court level is appealed, the party appealing is usually referred to as the **appellant**, and the successful party in the trial court is called the **appellee.** Most jurisdictions, in publishing decisions of reviewing courts, list the appellant first and the appellee second, even though the appellant may have been the defendant in the trial court. As a result, the names used in a case are somewhat misleading. Since the party first named is not always the plaintiff, in studying cases in this text it should be recognized that the first-named party in the case title may be the defendant-appellant.

In most state jurisdictions and in federal courts, the law allows all persons to join in one lawsuit as plaintiffs if their causes of action arise out of the same transaction or series of transactions and involve common questions of law or fact. In addition, plaintiffs may join as defendants all persons who are necessary to a complete determination or settlement of the questions involved. Each defendant does not have to be interested in every claim. In addition, if a defendant alleges that there cannot be a complete determination of a controversy without the presence of other parties, such a defendant may bring in new third parties as third-party defendants. This procedure is usually followed when there is someone who may have liability to a defendant if the defendant has liability to the plaintiff.

There are two problem areas or issues relating to the parties to a lawsuit which frequently arise in litigation. The first of these issues is generally described as "standing to sue," which is discussed in the next section. The second problem area relating to the parties is class action suits. These suits, which involve one or more individuals suing on behalf of all who may have the same grounds for suit, are discussed more fully in section 4.

3 STANDING TO SUE

The question in **standing to sue** is whether a litigant is entitled to have the court decide the dispute. This issue has two aspects: (1) Does the court have jurisdiction, and (2) if the answer is yes, should the court in the exercise of its discretion assume jurisdiction? Both questions recognize the limited role of courts in our society.

The Constitution requires that a plaintiff must allege a case or controversy between himself or herself and the defendant if the court is to have jurisdiction. The "standing" question is whether the plaintiff has alleged such a personal stake in the outcome of the controversy to warrant his or her invocation of the court's jurisdiction and to justify its exercise in his or her behalf.

Standing requires an allegation of a present or immediate injury in fact; the party requesting standing must allege such a personal stake in the outcome of the controversy as to assure concrete adverseness, which sharpens the presentation of issues. There must be some causal connection between the asserted injury and the challenged action, and the injury must be of the type likely to be redressed by a favorable decision.

Additional limitations on standing may exist even though the foregoing requirements are met, because the judiciary seeks to avoid deciding questions of broad social import where no individual rights would be vindicated; it also seeks to limit access to the federal courts to those litigants best suited to assert a particular claim. One of these limits on standing is that a litigant must normally assert her or his own legal interests rather than those of third parties. Without the requirement of standing, courts would be called upon to decide abstract questions of wide public significance. Such questions are best resolved by the political process.

When the asserted harm is a generalized grievance shared in substantially equal measure by all or a large class of citizens, that harm alone normally does not warrant the exercise of jurisdiction by a court. For example, individual radio listeners do not have standing to obtain review of a decision canceling a radio station's license. Likewise, a plaintiff must assert her or his own legal rights and not those of a third party. For example, a citizen objected to surveillance of civilians by the Army. The case was dismissed without a showing that the plaintiff was one of the civilians under surveillance.

Standing to sue is often an issue in cases brought by organizations on behalf of their members. An association may have standing to assert claims for its members even if it suffers no injury. Representational standing requires that: (1) the association have members with standing to sue in their own right; (2) the interest the association seeks to protect must be fundamental to the organization's purpose; and (3) the claim asserted and the relief requested must not require individual participation in the litigation. This last requirement was used to prevent a college-student organization from challenging the constitutionality of the Selective Service Act provision making students who failed to register for the draft ineligible for federal financial assistance. The court held that there was no organizational standing because individual participation is required. It held that it is in the financial interests of many students to defend the constitutionality of the statute and that their individual participation is required.

Standing to sue does not depend upon the merits of the plaintiff's contention that particular conduct is illegal. The presence of standing is determined by the nature and source of the plaintiff's claim. The basic question in such a case is whether the constitutional or statutory provision on which the claim rests can be understood as granting the plaintiff a right to judicial relief. Congress may grant an express right of action to people who otherwise would lack standing if the plaintiff has sustained a personal injury, even if the injury is shared by a large class.

As a general rule, "standing" requires that a complaining party have a very personal stake in the outcome of the controversy to ensure adversity in the proceedings; that will result in all aspects of the issues being presented for decision. A complainant must present facts showing that his or her individual needs require the remedy being sought. A plaintiff must show that he or she has sustained or is immediately in danger of sustaining a direct injury as a result of a governmental action involved in the lawsuit. In civil rights cases and in cases involving environmental threats, the courts have been rather liberal in finding a personal stake in a plaintiff bringing an action. In such cases, standing to sue still requires a specific injury in fact to the plaintiff.

HAVENS REALTY CORP. v. COLEMAN
102 S.Ct. 1114 (1982)

FACTS

The Fair Housing Act of 1968 outlaws discrimination in housing and authorizes civil suits to enforce the law. Suit was filed against the defendant operator of two apartment complexes alleging "racial steering" in violation of the law. Suit was filed by a black tester (Coleman) and a white tester (Willis). Coleman was told that no apartments were available, but Willis was told that there were vacancies. Neither intended to rent the apartment. The District Court held that the plaintiffs lacked standing and dismissed the suit because neither intended to rent.

ISSUE

Did either party have standing to sue under the Fair Housing Act?

DECISION

Yes—Coleman. No—Willis.

REASONS

1. The black tester has standing to sue, but since the white tester received no false information, he lacks standing.
2. Congress intended standing to extend to the full limits of Article III, and therefore the sole requirement is injury in fact, that is, that a plaintiff allege that as a result of a defendant's actions he has suffered distinct and palpable injury.
3. Despite the fact that the "testers" had no intent to rent the apartments, Congress prohibited misrepresentation to "*any* person," and therefore all people have a legal right to truthful information.

4 CLASS ACTION SUITS

A **class action suit** is one in which a person files suit on his or her own behalf and on behalf of all other persons who may have a similar claim. For example, all sellers of real estate through a broker were certified as a class in an antitrust suit against Atlanta, Georgia, realtors. All persons suing a drug company, alleging injuries from a product, also were considered a class in that case. Class action suits may also be filed on behalf of all shareholders of a named corporation. The number of people comprising a class is frequently large. Class action suits are popular because they often involve matters in which no one member of the class would have a sufficient financial interest to warrant litigation. However, the combined interest of all members of the class not only makes litigation feasible, it quite often makes it very profitable for the lawyer who brings the suit. In addition, such litigation avoids a multiplicity of suits involving the same issue, especially when the issues are complex and the cost of preparation and defense is very substantial. Many of the cases involve millions of dollars. In one recent case, the recovery was $310 million and the attorney's fees were $25 million.

Class action suits are often considered a form of harrassment by many defendants. It has been alleged that some lawyers have on occasion sought out a member of a class and encouraged him or her to file suit. Courts cannot prevent lawyers for a class from contacting members of the class even though this increases the danger of abuse.

At the federal level, the Supreme Court has tended to discourage class action suits. First, federal cases require that all members of the class be given actual notice of the pendency of the lawsuit—individual notice and not merely public notice. This notice must be given to all members of the class whose names and addresses can be found through reasonable efforts. In addition, those plaintiffs seeking to bring the class action suit must pay all court costs of the action, including the cost of compiling the names and addresses of those in the class. If the trial court denies the plaintiff a right to represent the class, that decision cannot be appealed until a final decision in the lawsuit itself. Denial of class action status making it impractical to continue the litigation does not give grounds for an immediate appeal of the denial.

If a class action suit is in federal court because of diversity of citizenship, the claim of each member of the class must meet the jurisdictional amount of $10,000. This requirement, together with the requirement of notice to each member of the class, has greatly reduced the number of class action suits in federal courts. However, the practice of consumers' and plaintiffs' lawyers of combining a single grievance into a lawsuit on behalf of every possible litigant is quite common in state courts. There are numerous state class action statutes which allow consumers and others to file suit in state courts on behalf of all citizens of that state. For some claims suitable to class action, there may be as many as fifty class action suits at once. Although the Supreme Court has attempted to reduce class action cases, it is apparent that public companies are still subject to this type of claim.

The notice in class action suits typically includes a form for persons to sign indicating that they desire to be a part of the class. However, some state procedures are "opt-out" rather than "opt-in." In these states, a person is a member of the class unless affirmative action is taken to be excluded. Either procedure satisfies due process, as the case which follows illustrates.

PHILLIPS PETROLEUM CO. v. SHUTTS
105 S.Ct. 2965 (1985)

FACTS

Phillips Petroleum Co. (Phillips) produced natural gas from leased land located in eleven states. Royalty owners possessing rights to leases from which Phillips produced the gas brought a class action suit in a Kansas state court; they sought to recover interest on delayed royalty payments. The trial court certified a class consisting of 33,000 royalty owners. Each class member was sent a notice by first-class mail describing the action and informing each that he could appear in person or by counsel, that otherwise he would be included in the class and bound by any decision unless they "opted out" of the action by returning a "request for exclusion." The final class consisted of some 28,000 members, who reside in all fifty states, the District of Columbia, and several foreign countries. The average claim of each member of the class was $100. Phillips objected to including the claims of those that did not opt out.

ISSUE

Did the trial court have jurisdiction over class action plaintiffs that did not opt out?

Yes.

REASONS

1. The class action was an invention of equity to enable it to proceed to a decree in suits where the number of those interested in the litigation was too great to permit joinder. The absent parties would be bound by the decree so long as the named parties adequately represented the absent class and the prosecution of the litigation was within the common interest.
2. Unlike a defendant in a normal civil suit, an absent class action plaintiff is not required to do anything. He may sit back and allow the litigation to run its course, content in knowing that there are safeguards provided for his protection.
3. A forum state may exercise jurisdiction over the claim of an absent class action plaintiff, even though that plaintiff may not possess the minimum contacts with the forum which would support personal jurisdiction over a defendant. The plaintiff must receive notice and an opportunity to remove himself from the class by executing and an "opt out" or "request for exclusion" form and returning it to the court.

5 JURISDICTION OF COURTS

Jurisdiction refers to the power of a court to hear a case. To have the power to hear a case, the court must have jurisdiction over the subject matter of the case and the parties to the case. Jurisdiction over the subject matter exists if the case is of the type which the court is authorized to hear. This is not a problem with state courts of general jurisdiction. It may be in cases before the inferior state courts and can be an issue in all federal cases, because, as previously noted, all federal courts are courts of limited jurisdiction. For example, a federal court would not have jurisdiction over a breach of contract suit for $5,000 damages between citizens of different states because it does not meet the jurisdictional amount. If the amount were $15,000 and the parties were citizens of the same state, the federal court would still have no power to hear the case because of lack of diversity of citizenship. Similarly, a state probate court would lack the power to hear a murder case.

Jurisdiction over the plaintiff is obtained by plaintiff's filing the suit. Such action indicates voluntary submission to the power of the court. Jurisdiction over the defendant is usually obtained by the service of a **summons**, or notice to appear in court, although in some cases it is obtained by the publication of notice and mailing a summons to the last known address. Service of summons on the defendant usually is valid if it is served upon any member of the household above a specified age, and if another copy addressed to the defendant is mailed to the home. This procedure recognizes the practical difficulties which may exist in finding the defendant, and at the same time accomplishes the goal of the summons, which is simply to give the defendant fair notice of the suit.

For many years, it was felt that a summons could not be properly served beyond the borders of the state in which it was issued. However, this concept has changed, and most states now have **long-arm statutes** which provide for the service of process beyond their boundaries. Such statutes are valid and constitutional if they provide a defendant with due process of law. Due process requires only that if a defendant is not present within the forum state, he or she must have certain minimum contacts with it so that maintenance of the suit does not offend "traditional notions of fair play and substantial justice."

The typical long-arm statute allows a court to obtain jurisdiction over a defendant even though the process is served beyond its borders if the defendant has: (1) committed a tort within the state; (2) owns property within the state, which property is the subject matter of the lawsuit; or (3) entered into a contract within the state or transacted the business which is the subject matter of the lawsuit within the state.

Long-arm statutes do not authorize extraterritorial service of process in all cases. It is only where requiring a defendant to appear and defend does not violate due process that jurisdiction is obtained under long-arm statutes. The case which follows illustrates the extent of constitutional limitations on modern long-arm statutes which allow extraterritorial service of process to obtain jurisdiction.

WORLD-WIDE VOLKSWAGEN CORP. v. WOODSON
100 S.Ct. 559 (1980)

FACTS

Plaintiff filed a product liability suit in a state court of Oklahoma to recover for personal injuries sustained in an automobile accident in Oklahoma. The automobile had been purchased from the defendant retailer in the state of New York. The retailer in turn, had purchased it from a wholesaler in New York. The defendants were New York corporations that did no business in Oklahoma. They were served under the Oklahoma long-arm statute, and they objected to the court's jurisdiction.

ISSUE

Does due process allow the Oklahoma court to assert jurisdiction over these nonresident defendants?

DECISION

No. There was no contact, connection, or conduct in the forum state.

REASONS

1. A state court may exercise personal jurisdiction over a nonresident defendant only so long as there exist "minimum contacts" between the defendant and the forum state.
2. The concept of minimum contacts performs two related but distinguishable functions. It protects the defendant against the burdens of litigating in a distant or inconvenient forum. It also acts to ensure that the states through their courts do not reach out beyond the limits imposed on them by their status as co-equal sovereigns in a federal system.
3. The defendant's contacts with the forum state must be such that maintenance of the suit "does not offend 'traditional notions of fair play and substantial justice.'" The relationship between the defendant and the forum must be such that it is reasonable to require the corporation to defend the particular suit which is brought there.
4. The due process clause does not contemplate that a state may make binding a judgment in personam [against the person] against an individual or corporate defendant with which the state has no contacts, ties, or relations.

Occasionally, process may be served upon a defendant who has no minimum contacts with the state in which a court sits. For example, a bankruptcy court may order process served nationwide. It may be required to do so to settle the affairs of a bankrupt corporation such as Braniff Airlines. All citizens of the United States have sufficient contact to justify this jurisdiction by United States courts.

It was previously noted that jurisdiction may sometimes be obtained by publication of notice of the suit in a general circulation newspaper and by mailing a copy of the summons to the defendant. This method is often used in cases involving title to real estate and in divorce actions. Such cases proceed **in rem** (against the thing) rather than **in personam** (against the person). The judgments or decrees in such cases affect the property involved or the status (marriage) but do not operate against the defendant individually. Martial status or title to property may be changed, but no personal liability results. Service by publication must also meet due process standards. For example, a Kentucky law which authorized posting of a notice of eviction of a tenant on the premises rather than by mail was held to be a denial of due process. Notice by publication must be reasonably calculated to ensure that the defendant learns of the suit.

The foregoing discussion of jurisdiction related to civil suits. In criminal suits, the crime must have been committed within the state for the court to have jurisdiction of the case. Jurisdiction of the person of the defendant is obtained by arrest. In the event of arrest in a state other than that in which the crime was committed, extradition is necessary. This is obtained by the governor of the state of arrest voluntarily turning the prisoner over to the governor of the requesting state.

6 VENUE

A question similar to jurisdiction refers to the place or court in which the lawsuit should be brought, or what is the proper **venue.** Although jurisdiction determines if a court has the *power* to hear a case, venue determines whether a court *should* hear the case when any one of several courts technically might have jurisdiction. A typical venue statute specifies that suit must be brought in the county of residence of any defendant who is joined in good faith and not solely for the purpose of fixing venue in that county. Suits may also be brought in the county where the transaction or some part thereof occurred out of which the cause of action arose. Actions against nonresidents can usually be commenced in any county which has jurisdiction, with jurisdiction being obtained under a long-arm statute. Corporations are usually considered to be residents of any county in which they have a registered office or are doing business. Corporations not authorized to do business in a state are usually treated as nonresidents. Similar rules usually exist for partnerships. They are generally considered to be residents of any county in which a partner resides, in which there is a partnership office, or in which the partnership does business. Thus, venue statutes provide, as one of two possibilities for the proper forum for a lawsuit, the place of residence of the defendant, and they define where this is.

Most venue statutes have special provisions for suits involving real estate which require the suit to be brought in the county where the real estate is located. Special provisions frequently allow suits against insurance companies in the county where the plaintiff resides.

A defendant may object to the venue for several reasons. First of all, he or she may complain that the requirements of the venue statute as discussed above are not met. This will not usually be the case because, as noted, the statutes are specific and relatively clear. Venue may also be objected to because of prejudice of either the judge or, in some cases, the probable jury to be selected. The latter objection is frequently made in a criminal trial which has had substantial publicity. Motions for a change of venue based on the prejudice of the trial judge must usually be supported by affidavit but are granted as a matter of right if in proper form. Failure to object to the venue is a *waiver,* and the trial may proceed if the court where the suit was brought has jurisdiction, in spite of the provisions of the venue statute, or constitutional requirements of due process.

Another ground for a change of venue is the doctrine of **forum non conveniens,** which literally means that the place of trial is not convenient. The defendant may attempt to invoke this principle in cases in which the plaintiff has attempted to have the suit tried in a county which produces juries known for large verdicts. For example, a plane crash killed a citizen of Scotland. The crash was in Scotland. When suit was filed in the United States, the case was dismissed for being brought in the wrong venue. The plaintiff had filed in the United States expecting a larger verdict.

7 PLEADINGS

Most lawsuits begin by a plaintiff's filing a pleading called a "complaint" with the court clerk. (In this section, for convenience, we refer to the judge, plaintiff, and defendant as if they are male; obviously, however, both sexes may be represented by these terms.) The complaint contains allegations by the plaintiff and a statement of the relief sought. The clerk issues a summons which, together with a copy of the complaint, is served on the defendant by leaving it either with him personally or with some member of his family, if the law so provides. The summons notifies the defendant of the date he is required to file his **pleading,** usually called an "answer," or his appearance in the suit. Failure to file an appearance is considered a default, which may result in the court's awarding the plaintiff the relief sought. The defendant's answer will either admit or deny each allegation of the plaintiff's complaint and may contain affirmative defenses, such as payment of the obligation, which will defeat the plaintiff's claim. The answer may also contain causes of action the defendant has against the plaintiff, called "counterclaims." After receiving the defendant's answer, the plaintiff will, unless the applicable rules of procedure do not so require, file a reply which specifically admits or denies each allegation of the defendant's answer. The factual issues of a lawsuit are thus formed by one party making an allegation and the other party either admitting it or denying it. Pleadings give notice of each party's contentions and serve to set the boundary lines of the litigation.

8 MOTIONS

Not all lawsuits involve questions of fact. In many cases, the parties may be in complete agreement as to the facts, in which case the issue to be decided is the legal effect of these facts. Such cases involve only questions of law. Questions of law may be raised at several stages of the lawsuit.

First of all, the defendant may, instead of filing an answer, file a pleading which at common law was called a "general demurrer." Today we usually call this a "**motion** to dismiss for failure to state a cause of action or a claim for relief." By this pleading the defendant, in effect, says to the court: "Even if everything the plaintiff says in his complaint is true, he is not entitled to the relief he seeks." For example, in a state where mental cruelty is not a ground for divorce, a complaint seeking a divorce on such grounds would be dismissed. The litigation would end unless the plaintiff then filed an amended complaint. It would have to properly allege a ground on which a divorce might be granted.

In addition, a defendant may also move to dismiss a suit for reasons which as a matter of law prevent the plaintiff from winning his suit. Such matters as a discharge in bankruptcy, lack of jurisdiction of the court to hear the suit, or expiration of the time limit during which the defendant is subject to suit may be raised by such a motion. This latter ground is usually referred to as the "statute of limitations." Each state has proscribed a time limit after which you cannot file suit. For example, suits for breach of a contract for the sale of goods must be filed within four years of the breach. These are matters of a technical nature which raise questions of law for the court's decision.

Most states and the federal courts will allow either party to submit a case for final decision through procedures known as "motions for **summary judgment**" or "motions for judgment on the pleadings." In such hearings, the court examines all papers on file in the case, including affidavits that may have been filed with the motion or in opposition to it, to see if a genuine material issue of fact remains. If there is no such question of fact, the court will then decide the legal question raised by the facts and find for one party or the other.

Remember that the above discussion refers to matters occurring prior to any trial of the case. As the trial itself proceeds, questions of fact raised by the pleadings may be resolved, leaving only questions of law. If the case is being tried by a jury, a party moves to take the case from the jury by asking the judge to **direct a verdict**. The court can only direct a verdict for one party if the evidence taken in the light most favorable to the other party establishes as a matter of law that the party moving is entitled to a verdict. Either party may make such a motion, although it is usually used by defendants to argue that the plaintiff has failed to prove each allegation of his complaint. Just as a plaintiff must *allege* certain facts or have the complaint dismissed by motion to dismiss, he must have some *proof* of each essential allegation, or lose the case on a motion for a directed verdict.

In cases tried without a jury, either party may move for a finding in his favor. Such a motion will be allowed during the course of the trial if the result is not in doubt. While judges on such motions weigh the evidence, they may end the trial only if there is no room for a fair difference of opinion as to the result.

Finally, questions of law may be raised after the trial is completed by motions seeking a new trial or a judgment notwithstanding the verdict of the jury. A motion seeking a new trial may be granted if the judge feels that the jury's verdict is contrary to the manifest weight of the evidence. The court may enter a judgment opposite to that of the jury verdict if the judge finds that the jury verdict is, as a matter of law, erroneous. To reach such a conclusion, the court must find that reasonable people viewing the evidence could not have reached the jury verdict returned. For example, a verdict for the plaintiff may be based on sympathy instead of evidence. Thus, the results of lawsuits may turn on procedural questions of law raised by the pleadings or evidence. These issues of law are the sole province of the court to resolve.

9 DISCOVERY PROCEDURES

Modern law has procedures commonly referred to as "discovery procedures." These are used when the parties are filing their pleadings and before the trial itself. These procedures are designed to take the "sporting aspect" out of litigation and ensure that the results of lawsuits are based on the merits of the controversy and not on the ability, skill, or cunning of counsel. Historically, an attorney who had no case on the facts or law could win a lawsuit through surprise by keeping silent about a fact or by concealing his or her true case until the trial. Lawsuits should not be based on the skill or lack thereof of counsel, but on the relative merits of the controversy. Discovery practice is designed to ensure that each side is fully aware of all the facts involved in the case and of the intentions of the parties, prior to trial. One of its purposes is to encourage settlement of suits, avoiding actual trial.

Discovery practices include the taking of the **deposition** of other parties and witnesses; the serving of written questions, called interrogatories, to be answered under oath by the opposite party; compulsory physical examinations by doctors chosen by the other party; orders requiring the production of exhibits, documents, maps, photographs, and so on; and the serving by one party on another of demands to admit facts under oath. (Some courts, those of Illinois for example, have even allowed the discovery of the amount of insurance coverage possessed by the defendant in a personal injury case.) These procedures allow a party to learn not only about matters that may be used as evidence but also about matters that may lead to the discovery of evidence.

Just prior to the trial, a pretrial conference between the lawyers and the judge will be held in states with modern rules of procedure. At this conference the pleadings, results of the discovery process, and probable evidence are reviewed in an attempt to settle the suit. The issues may be further narrowed, and the judge may even predict the outcome to encourage settlement.

On occasion, a party may fail to comply with the discovery rules. When this occurs, a party may actually lose a case or facts sought may be considered proved because of the noncompliance with discovery rules.

The fact that evidence is relevant does not always mean that it is subject to discovery. Courts may deny discovery when other interests, such as trade secrets, may outweigh the needs of a party to litigation. In the case which follows, a plaintiff was denied discovery that could lead to irreparable damage to the defendant.

HOFMANN CORP. v. SUPERIOR COURT (SMAYSTRLA)
218 Cal. Rptr. 355 (Cal.App. 1 Dist. 1985)

FACTS

A products liability suit for personal injuries was filed in which it was alleged that a carlift manufactured by the defendant was defective. Plaintiffs sought a complete list of the defendant's customers so that each of them could be contacted to determine if any other carlifts had failed to function properly. The trial court ordered the defendant to produce the customer list.

ISSUE

Is this proper discovery?

DECISION

No

REASONS

1. Ordinarily, information that is relevant to the subject matter of a lawsuit and not privileged is discoverable. However, a limited protection is given to sensitive information that people may wish to keep confidential, such as their financial dealings.
2. Defendant's customer list is clearly information falling within this sensitive category, as evidenced by the fact that a confidential customer list is protected by the courts in the context of a trade secret.
3. Plaintiffs have other means of obtaining the information besides a query to all of the petitioner's customers who have purchased a lift. They can ask the defendant for its records of complaints.

10 CONDUCT OF A TRIAL

In addition to questions of law, most lawsuits involve questions of fact. Such cases as automobile negligence actions and criminal proceedings are essentially questions of fact. Suits at law and criminal actions have traditionally been tried before a jury, while suits in equity have been considered too complicated for juries, and as a general rule the questions of fact have been found by the courts. It should be noted that juries are sometimes used in chancery cases to serve as the trier of the facts.

Jury Selection

For purposes of examining a trial, we shall assume a typical suit for dollar damages either in tort or contract being tried before a jury. As the case is called, the first order of business is to select a jury. Prior to the calling of the case, the court clerk will have summoned prospective jurors. Their names will be drawn at random from lists of eligible citizens, and the number of jurors required, usually twelve, will be selected or called into the jury box for the conduct of **voir dire** examination. Voir dire examination is simply a method by which the court and the attorneys for each party examine jurors as to their qualifications and ability to hear the case. A party to a lawsuit is entitled to fair and impartial jurors in both civil and criminal cases. Due process requires that a party be allowed to inquire into a prospective juror's biases and prejudices.

Each side in the lawsuit may challenge or excuse a prospective juror for cause. In addition, each side will be given a certain number of challenges known as **peremptory challenges** for which no cause need be given. Each side has an opportunity to examine the jurors and either to accept them or to reject them until the challenges are exhausted. Prospective jurors are sworn to give truthful answers to the questions on voir dire. The processes continue until the full jury is selected.

Opening Statements

After selecting jurors to hear the case, the attorneys then make their opening statements. An opening statement is not evidence but is only used to familiarize the jury with the essential facts in the case which each side expects to prove. It is similar to the prologue of a book. So that the jury may understand the overall picture of the case and the relevancy of each bit of evidence as presented, each side informs the jury of the facts she or he expects to prove and of the witnesses she or he expects to call to make such proof. After the opening statements are made, the party with the burden of proof, which is usually the plaintiff, presents his or her evidence. The term "burden of proof" is explained more fully in the next section.

Introducing Evidence

Evidence is normally presented in open court by examination of witnesses and production of documents and other exhibits. The person calling a witness has a right to examine that witness and ask questions to establish the facts with which the witness is familiar about the case. As a general rule, a party calling a witness is not permitted to ask "leading questions." After the party calling the witness has completed direct examination, the other party is given the opportunity to cross-examine the witness. Matters inquired into on cross-examination are limited to those matters raised on direct examination. Cross-examination is an art, and the well-prepared lawyer will usually not ask a question on cross-examination to which he or she does not already know the answer.

After the cross-examination, the party calling the witness again has the opportunity of examining the witness. This examination is called "redirect examination." It is limited to those matters gone into on cross-examination and is used to clarify matters raised on cross-examination. After redirect examination, the opposing party is allowed recross-examination, with the corresponding limitation as to scope of the questions. Witnesses may be asked to identify exhibits. Expert witnesses may be asked to give their opinion, within certain limitations, about the case. Sometimes, experts are allowed to answer hypothetical questions. For example, a doctor in a personal injury case may be given all the evidence surrounding the accident and then be asked hypothetically whether such an occurrence might have or could have caused the injury which the plaintiff suffers.

After the party with the burden of proof has presented his or her evidence, the opposing party usually makes the motion for a directed verdict, as heretofore mentioned. If the motion for directed verdict is overruled, the defendant then presents his or her evidence. The order of examination of these witnesses is the same as those for the plaintiff. The party calling a witness vouches for his or her credibility. The party is not allowed to impeach witnesses whom he or she has called. After the defendant has presented all his or her evidence, the original party may bring in rebuttal evidence. When neither party has any additional evidence, the attorneys and the judge retire for a conference to consider the instructions to be given the jury.

Jury Instructions

Jury instructions serve to acquaint the jury with the law applicable to the case. As previously stated, the function of the jury is to find the facts, and the function of the court is to determine the applicable law. The purpose of jury instructions is to bring these two together in an orderly manner that will result in a decision. At the conference, each attorney submits to the court instructions which he or she feels should be given to the jury. The court examines these instructions and confers with the attorneys, then decides which instructions will be given to the jury. A typical jury instruction follows:

> The plaintiff in his complaint has alleged that he was injured as the proximate cause of the negligence of the defendant. If you find from the evidence that the defendant was guilty of negligence, which proximately caused plaintiff's injuries, then your verdict should be for the plaintiff.

In this instruction, the court is, in effect, saying that the plaintiff must prove that the defendant was at fault. Thus, the jury is instructed as to the result to be returned if they find certain facts.

Closing Argument

After the conference on jury instructions, the attorneys argue the case to the jury. The party with the burden of proof, usually the plaintiff, is given an opportunity to open the argument and to close it. The defendant's attorney is only allowed to argue after the plaintiff's argument and is only allowed to argue once. After the arguments are completed, the court reads the instructions to the jury, and the jury retires to deliberate. Upon reaching a verdict, the jury returns from the jury room and announces its verdict, and judgment is entered. Thereafter, the losing party starts the procedure of posttrial motions and appeals. Any final decision of the court, whether on a motion made before trial, during the trial, or after the trial, or on the court's judgment or decree, may be appealed within certain prescribed time limits. If the appeal is perfected according to law, the right of review is absolute.

11 THE BURDEN OF PROOF

The term **burden of proof** has two distinct meanings, depending on the context in which it is used. It may describe the person with the burden of coming forward with evidence on a particular issue. The party alleging the existence of a certain fact usually has the burden of coming forward with evidence to establish the fact.

The more common usage of the term is to identify the party with the *burden of persuasion*. The party with this burden must convince the trier of fact on the issue involved. If a party with the burden of persuasion fails to do so, that party loses the lawsuit.

The extent of proof required to satisfy the burden of persuasion varies, depending upon the issue and the type of case. There are three distinct levels of proof recognized by the law. For criminal cases, the burden of proof is described as "beyond a reasonable doubt." This means that the prosecution in a criminal case has the burden of convincing the trier of fact, usually a jury, that the defendant is guilty of the crime charged and that the jury has no reasonable doubt about the defendant's guilt. This burden of proof does not require evidence beyond any doubt, but only beyond a reasonable doubt. A reasonable doubt is one that a reasonable person viewing the evidence might reasonably entertain. This standard is not used in civil cases.

In civil cases the party with the burden of proof will be subject to one of two standards—the **clear and convincing proof** standard, or the **preponderance of the evidence** standard. The latter standard is used most frequently. It requires that a party convince the jury by a preponderance of evidence that the facts are as he or she contends. By preponderance of evidence we mean there is greater weight of evidence in support of the proposition than there is against it. In terms of the scales of justice, it means that they tilt more one way than the other.

The clear and convincing proof requirement is used in certain situations where the law requires more than a simple preponderance of the evidence but less than proof beyond a reasonable doubt. For example, in a securities law case, proof of fraud usually requires clear and convincing evidence if a plaintiff is to succeed. The scales of justice must tilt heavily one way. A slight preponderance of evidence in favor of the party asserting the truth of a proposition is not enough. Unless the evidence clearly establishes the proposition, the party with the burden of proof fails to sustain it and loses the lawsuit.

12 RULES OF EVIDENCE

In the conduct of a trial, the rules of evidence govern the admissibility of testimony and exhibits and establish which facts may be presented to the jury and which facts may not. The lawyer is concerned with specific rules of evidence, but an understanding of the areas in which these rules operate will give us some insight into the workings of our judicial system.

Privileged Communications

One of the major rules for excluding evidence is based on what the law calls "privileged communications," or **privilege**. Nearly everyone is aware that the Fifth Amendment contains a privilege against compulsory self-incrimination. In addition, communications between an attorney and client are considered privileged by the law so that such communications can be made without fear of their subsequent use against the client. Fair play requires that an attorney not be required to testify as to matters told in confidence by a client. Some matters are privileged, such as the existence of insurance coverage of a party, because of the great effect that knowledge of the existence of insurance would have on a jury. Matters which are privileged are matters which by the rules of fair play should not be admitted into evidence.

Hearsay Rule

Another basic concept of our judicial system is the right of confrontation, or the right to be confronted by the witnesses against you and to cross-examine them about their allegations or contentions. Cross-examination in open court, as a fundamental right, provides the background for the rule of evidence known as the **hearsay rule.** Hearsay is an out-of-court statement which is being offered to prove the truth of the matter contained in the statement. For example, if the issue of the case were whether certain stock had been purchased, the testimony of a witness that her broker had *told* her the stock had been purchased would be hearsay. The statement is offered to prove the purchase of the stock when the *broker* is not available for cross-examination. The lack of cross-examination establishes that hearsay evidence should not be admitted. There are many exceptions to the hearsay rule. For example, if the party *himself* had made the statement, he could hardly object to the fact that he was not able to cross-examine himself, and thus we have the exception for admissions against interest by a party to the suit. Testimony at a former trial at which the party was able to cross-examine and subsequent unavailability of the witness create another exception to the hearsay rule. Business entries made in the ordinary course of business constitute still another exception. They may be introduced as evidence of the facts they represent. In a criminal case, a dying declaration by the victim of murder is an exception, because the effect of impending death is considered by the courts to give sufficient credibility to the truthfulness of the testimony to eliminate the need for cross-examination. There are many other exceptions to the hearsay rule, but each of them is based on the fact that cross-examination has either been had at a former time or is not required for a fair trial in the present case.

Relevancy

There are other rules of evidence, such as the rule requiring that all evidence be relevant to the matter involved in the litigation. If a person is involved in a suit for breach of contract for the sale of goods, wares, or merchandise, the fact that he has been divorced five times should have no effect on the litigation and would not be admissible evidence. It might, if presented, influence some member of the jury who particularly disliked divorced persons. In cases where direct testimony as to what happened is not available, evidence of habit or practice is sometimes admitted to show what probably happened, and this is considered relevant.

Documents

Another rule of evidence concerns the requirement of producing the best evidence available as proof in a lawsuit. The "best evidence rule," as it is commonly called, pertains only to written documents. There are many other rules of evidence concerning written documents, such as the "parol evidence rule," which prevents the proof of modification or change of a written document by the use of oral evidence.

It can be seen from this short examination of these elementary rules of evidence that they specify the rules of the game, so to speak, to ensure a fair trial and that each party has ample opportunity to present his or her contentions and case without unduly taking advantage of the other party. These rules were not created to serve as a stumbling block to meritorious litigants or to create unwarranted roadblocks to justice. On the contrary, the rules of evidence were created and should be applied to ensure fair play and to aid in the goal of having controversies determined on their merits.

Federal Rules

In order to reduce the cost of litigation and to speed up the search for truth, the Supreme Court has adopted rules of evidence for civil and criminal trials in the federal courts which greatly expand the admissibility of evidence and eliminate many of the traditional technical rules of evidence. For example, (1) cross-examination of a witness is not limited to the scope of direct examination; (2) a lawyer calling a witness does not vouch for the witness's credibility, which may be attacked by any party, including the party calling the witness; (3) expert testimony requires much less groundwork in that the facts or data upon which an expert bases his or her opinion need not be admissible in evidence; (4) opinion testimony on the ultimate issue to be decided by the jury is admissible; and (5) an expanded list of exceptions may be applied to the hearsay rule. This list of hearsay exceptions includes any statement having some inherent guarantee of trustworthiness if the statement has more bearing on the point for which it is offered than the other evidence reasonably available.

These rules of evidence have reduced the expense of litigation and also have sped up the trial process. In addition, more evidence is presented to juries for their factual determination. As a result of these rules, evidence is often admissible in federal cases that would not be admissible if the case were tried in state courts.

13 APPELLATE PROCEDURE

The previous chapter discussed the structure of the court system, including courts of review. Each state prescribes its own appellate procedure and determines the jurisdiction of its various reviewing courts. Although the procedure followed in an appeal is essentially a problem for the lawyer, certain aspects of this procedure assist us in understanding our judicial system.

Courts of review deal with the record of the proceedings in lower court. All the pleadings, testimony, and motions are reduced to a written record, which is filed with the court of review. The court of review studies the issues, testimony, and proceedings to determine whether prejudicial errors occurred or whether the lower court reached an erroneous result. In addition to the record, each party files a **brief** (the appellant may file a reply brief on receipt of the appellee's brief), which contains a short description of the nature of the case, the factual situation, the points and authorities on which the party relies, and his or her argument for reversing or affirming the decision of the lower court, depending on whether the party is an appellant or appellee. The points and authorities contain the statutes and judicial decisions relied upon as precedent in the argument.

In addition to the brief, the reviewing court is often given the benefit of oral argument in deciding the case. The attorneys are given a specified amount of time to explain orally to the court their position in the case. This also gives the court of review an opportunity to question the attorneys about various aspects of the case.

After oral argument, an impression vote is usually taken, and the case is assigned to one justice to prepare an opinion. Each justice has a staff of clerks assisting in the preparation of opinions. The intellectual backgrounds of these clerks have some influence on the decisions. The opinion as prepared by the clerks and the justice may not follow the impression vote. After the opinion is prepared, it will be circulated among the other members of the court. If a majority approve the opinion, it is adopted. Those who disagree may prepare a dissenting opinion. Thereafter the opinion is announced, and the losing party may ask for a rehearing on points stated in the opinion which he or she believes to be erroneous. Such rehearings are rarely granted. If the rehearing is denied or none is requested, the decision then becomes final. The mandate of the reviewing court is then forwarded to the trial court for appropriate proceedings either by way of enforcement of the decision or new proceedings, if required.

Courts of review are essentially concerned with questions of law. However, a reviewing court may be asked to grant a new trial on the ground that the decision in the lower court is contrary to the manifest weight of the evidence found in the record. Thus, questions of fact may be examined. In the federal courts and in many states, reviewing courts are not allowed to disturb factual findings unless they are clearly erroneous. This limitation recognizes the unique opportunity afforded the trial judge in evaluating the credibility of witnesses and weighing the evidence. Because of the deference due the trial judge, unless an appellate court is left with the "definite and firm conviction that a mistake has been committed," the reviewing court must accept the trial court's findings of fact. Determining the weight and credibility of the evidence is the special province of the trial court. An appellate court cannot substitute its interpretation of the evidence for that of the trial court simply because the reviewing court might give the facts another construction or resolve the ambiguities differently.

The case which follows illustrates the deference that must be given the trial judge by appellate courts. This deference is especially important when a decision rests heavily on the credibility of the witnesses, because only the trial judge can be aware of the variations in demeanor and tone of voice that bear so heavily on the listener's understanding of and belief in what is said.

ANDERSON v. CITY OF BESSEMER CITY, N.C.
105 S.Ct. 1504 (1985)

FACTS

Bessemer City decided to hire a new recreation director. A committee of four men and one woman was responsible for choosing the director. Eight persons applied for the position, including Anderson, the only woman applicant. She was a thirty-nine-year-old schoolteacher with college degrees in social studies and education. The committee chose a twenty-four-year-old male applicant, who had recently graduated from college with a degree in physical education. The four men voted to offer the job to him, and only the woman voted for Anderson. The trial court found that Anderson had been denied the position because of her sex, that she was the most qualified candidate, that she had been asked questions during her interview that other applicants were not asked regarding one's spouse's feelings about the application, and that the male committee members were biased against hiring a woman. The court of appeals reversed, holding that the district court's findings were clearly erroneous.

ISSUE

Did the court of appeals err in holding the finding of discrimination to be clearly erroneous?

DECISION

Yes.

REASONS

1. A finding is "clearly erroneous" when, although there is evidence to support it, the reviewing court on the entire evidence is left with the definite and firm conviction that a mistake has been committed.
2. This standard plainly does not entitle a reviewing court to reverse the finding of the trier of fact simply because it is convinced that it would have decided the case differently.
3. In applying the clearly erroneous standard to the findings of a district court sitting without a jury, appellate courts must constantly have in mind that their function is not to decide factual issues de novo. If the district court's account of the evidence is plausible in light of the record viewed in its entirety, the court of appeals may not reverse it. It may not do so even though convinced that had it been sitting as the trier of fact, it would have weighed the evidence differently. Where there are two permissible views of the evidence, the fact finder's choice between them cannot be clearly erroneous.
4. When the record is examined in light of the appropriately deferential standard, it is apparent that it contains nothing that mandates a finding that the district court's conclusion was clearly erroneous.

14 ENFORCEMENT OF JUDGMENTS AND DECREES

After a judgment in a court of law or a decree in a court of equity has become final, either because the decision is on appeal or because the losing party failed to perfect an appeal within the proper time, it may become necessary for the successful party to obtain judicial assistance in enforcing the court decision. For example, the judgment debtor may not voluntarily pay the amount of the judgment to the judgment creditor.

In such a case, the judgment creditor may levy execution on the property of the judgment debtor, cause any property which is not exempt from execution by statute to be sold at public sale, and have the proceeds applied on the judgment. The judgment creditor may also garnishee the wages of the judgment debtor, subject to the amount that is exempt, or attach any property which may be due him or her. Modern statutes give the judgment creditor the right to question the judgment debtor in open court to discover assets that might be applied to the debt. All states allow a debtor to keep certain items of property and a certain amount of wages free from his or her debts. In addition, the federal bankruptcy law provides exemptions. The debtor may exempt significant amounts of property from the proceedings. The net effect of this law is to allow bankrupt judgment debtors to avoid the judgment and at the same time retain many of their assets.

15 RES JUDICATA

Once a decision of the court has become final, it is **res judicata**—"the thing has been decided"—meaning that a final decision is conclusive on all issues between the parties whether raised in the litigation or not. Res judicata means that a cause of action finally determined by a competent court cannot be litigated by the parties in a new proceeding by the same court or in any other court. By final decision, we mean that either the case has been finally decided on appeal or that the time for appeal has expired. This prevents successive suits involving the same question between the same parties and brings disputes to a final conclusion. A matter once litigated and legally determined is conclusive between the parties in all subsequent proceedings.

16 MEDIATION AND ARBITRATION

The term **mediation** describes a process in which a third party is brought into a controversy to help settle the dispute. The mediator brings to the discussions an unbiased viewpoint and skill in effecting compromise. Although a mediator cannot impose a solution upon the parties, her or his viewpoint as to what would constitute a fair and reasonable settlement is usually given significant weight. This is especially true in labor-management disputes, because the public usually accepts the mediator's viewpoint as a reasonable solution.

Arbitration proceedings are a nonjudicial means for submitting a controversy to a third person or persons for a binding decision. Arbitration may result either from agreement of the parties to the controversy or from legislation which requires that certain disputes be decided by that process.

Arbitration has several advantages over litigation as a means for resolving disputes. Arbitration procedures generally are much quicker and less expensive than litigation. The arbitrators selected do not have a crowded docket and other disputes to decide, and thus there is little or no delay. In most arbitration proceedings, formal pleadings and other procedural steps which tend to prolong litigation are not required.

Arbitration also has the advantage of submitting many disputes to experts for solution. For example, if the issue involves whether or not a building has been properly constructed, the matter could be submitted to an architect for resolution. If it involves a technical accounting problem, it could be submitted to a certified public accountant. The Securities and Exchange Commission (SEC) has approved an arrangement where investors with complaints against securities dealers may submit them for arbitration. The arbitration is handled by arbitrators assigned by the various stock exchanges and the National Association of Securities Dealers. They possess the special knowledge required to determine if a customer of a brokerage house has a legitimate complaint. As a result, most contracts with brokerage firms contain an agreement to submit all disputes to arbitration. The Supreme Court recently held that such agreements preclude litigation between customers of brokerage firms and the firms even if statutory rights are involved. Note in the case which follows that RICO was one of the statutes involved.

SHEARSON/AMERICAN EXPRESS, INC., AND MARY ANN McNULTY v. EUGENE McMAHON ET AL.
107 S.Ct. 2332 (1987)

FACTS

Customers of a stock brokerage firm filed suit in the federal courts, alleging violations of the antifraud provisions of the Securities Exchange Act of 1934 and the Racketeer Influenced and Corrupt Organization Act (RICO). Their contracts with the brokerage firm provided for arbitration of any controversy relating to their accounts. The brokerage firm moved to compel arbitration of the claims pursuant to Section 3 of the Federal Arbitration Act, which requires a court to stay its proceedings if it is satisfied that an issue before it is arbitrable under an arbitration agreement.

ISSUE

Must these disputes be submitted to arbitration rather than to litigation?

DECISION

Yes.

REASONS

1. The Arbitration Act establishes a federal policy favoring arbitration, which requires that the courts rigorously enforce arbitration agreements. This duty is not diminished when a party bound by an agreement raises a claim founded on statutory rights.
2. Respondents' Exchange Act claims are arbitrable under the provisions of the Arbitration Act. Nothing in the statute requires that antifraud issues only be decided in the courts.
3. The RICO claim is also arbitrable under the Arbitration Act. Nothing in RICO's text or legislative history even arguably evinces congressional intent to exclude civil RICO claims for treble damages from the Arbitration Act. The public interest in the enforcement of RICO does not preclude submission of such claims to arbitration.

Arbitration as a substitute for litigation is very important to business, especially in international business transactions. It is used not only in labor-management relations but also to solve disputes in many contracts. In international business transactions, it avoids turning a dispute over to the courts of any one country and allows the parties in advance to agree upon the person or persons to resolve any controversies that may arise.

17 ARBITRATION PROCEEDINGS

Arbitration almost always results from an agreement of the parties, but it may result from legislation. Agreement may come before the dispute or controversy, or it may come after the controversy has developed. In other words, the parties by contract may agree to submit all issues that may arise in the future, or they may agree to submit a particular dispute to arbitration after it has arisen. The term **submission** is used to describe the act of referring a matter to the arbitration process.

The decision in arbitration is known as an *award*. It is final on all issues submitted, and it will be enforced by the courts just as if it were a judgment of a court. Awards are not subject to judicial review on the merits of the decision.

Arbitrators are the final judges of both the facts and the law, and mistakes of either will not justify a court to change the decision. Arbitration is viewed favorably by the law, and every doubt is resolved in favor of the award. However, a court may review whether there was, in fact, a submission of the issue to arbitration or whether the arbitrator exceeded his or her authority. Arbitrators must act within the authority conferred by the submission. In addition, a party may obtain judicial review of allegations of fraud or other misconduct by the arbitrator amounting to corruption. Short of fraud or other gross errors, courts do not reexamine the facts and substitute their view for that of the arbitrator.

Sometimes a dispute arises as to whether or not the parties have agreed to submit an issue to arbitration. In such a case, one party refuses to arbitrate and the other files suit to compel arbitration. The court hearing the case decides the issue of arbitrability but does not decide the basic issue between the parties. The case which follows explains the role of courts when the issue of arbitrability arises.

AT&T TECH., INC. v. COMMUNICATIONS WORKERS
106 S.Ct. 1415 (1986)

FACTS

A collective-bargaining agreement covering telephone equipment installation workers provided for arbitration of differences arising over interpretation of the agreement. Article 9 provided that the employer was free to exercise certain management functions, including the hiring, placement, and termination of employees. Such issues were excluded from the arbitration clause, but Article 20 prescribed the order in which employees would be laid off when lack of work necessitated layoff.

The employer laid off seventy-nine installers, and the union filed a grievance claiming that there was no lack of work and, therefore, that the layoffs violated Article 20. The employer refused to submit the grievance to arbitration on the ground that under Article 9 the layoffs were not arbitrable. The union then sought to compel arbitration by filing suit in federal district court. That court found that the union's interpretation of Article 20 was at least "arguable" and that it was for the arbitrator, not the court, to decide whether that interpretation had merit; accordingly, it ordered the petitioner to arbitrate. The court of appeals affirmed.

ISSUE

If a court has been asked to order arbitration of a grievance filed under a collective-bargaining agreement, must it first determine that the parties intended to arbitrate the dispute? Or is that determination properly left to the arbitrator?

DECISION

The court and not the arbitrator must decide if the issue is subject to arbitration.

REASONS

1. Arbitration is a matter of contract, and a party cannot be required to submit to arbitration any dispute that he has not agreed so to submit.
2. The question of arbitrability—whether a collective-bargaining agreement creates a duty for the parties to arbitrate the particular grievance—is undeniably an issue for judicial determination. Unless the parties clearly and unmistakably provide otherwise, the question of whether the parties agreed to arbitrate is to be decided by the court, not the arbitrator.
3. In deciding whether the parties have agreed to submit a particular grievance to arbitration, a court is not to rule on the potential merits of the underlying claims. The courts, therefore, have no business weighing the merits of the grievance, considering whether there is equity in a particular claim, or determining whether there is particular language in the written instrument that will support the claim.
4. Where the contract contains an arbitration clause, there is a presumption of arbitrability. One presumes that an order to arbitrate the particular grievance should not be denied unless the arbitration clause is not susceptible of an interpretation that covers the asserted dispute. Doubts should be resolved in favor of coverage.
5. The lower courts erred in ordering the parties to arbitrate the arbitrability question. It is the court's duty to interpret the agreement and determine whether the parties intended to arbitrate grievances concerning layoffs predicated on the company's "lack of work" determination. If the court determines that the agreement so provides, then it is for the arbitrator to determine the relative merits of the parties' substantive interpretations of the agreement.

Generally, arbitrators are under no obligation to explain the reasons for their award or findings of fact and conclusions of law on which that award is premised. However, disclosure of findings and the reasons therefor must be given if the applicable statute, arbitration agreement, or submission so requires. In addition, it should always be recognized by those agreeing to arbitration that in so doing, a party necessarily accepts the more summary, informal, and less structured procedures which characterize arbitration as compared with judicial litigation.

Most states have enacted statutes covering arbitration procedures, and these statutes have changed the common law. Most statutes cover all aspects of the submission, the award, and its enforcement. Under statutory arbitration, an agreement to submit an issue to arbitration is irrevocable, and a party who senses that the process is not going as well as expected cannot withdraw and resort to litigation. Most arbitration statutes require a written agreement to arbitrate.

If a party who has agreed to submit an issue to arbitration refuses to do so, the court will order the parties to proceed with arbitration according to the agreement. After the award is made by the arbitrator, it is usually filed with the clerk of an appropriate court. If no objections to the award are filed within a statutory period, it becomes final and enforced as if a judgment of the court.

Although many arbitration proceedings are conducted by an arbitrator, it is common to use three. In such a case, the parties to the dispute each select one arbitrator and the two arbitrators so selected name a third. Since the parties themselves are selecting two of the arbitrators, it is not a ground to remove an arbitrator that the arbitrator is biased or has an interest in the subject matter of the dispute. Many arbitrators are not lawyers. They are not required to use the usual rules of evidence and are not bound by the rules of substantive law. Arbitrators are free to fashion their own rules of procedure and to determine the facts of the dispute as they see them.

REVIEW QUESTIONS

1 For each term in the left-hand column, match the most appropriate description in the right-hand column:

   (1) Best evidence rule
   (2) Beyond a reasonable doubt
   (3) Brief
   (4) Opening statement
   (5) Attorney-client privilege
   (6) Preponderance of the evidence

   (a) The burden-of-proof standard in criminal cases
   (b) The usual burden-of-proof standard in civil cases
   (c) A rule of evidence which prevents lawyers from testifying against their clients
   (d) A method of collecting a judgment
   (e) A document used in the appeal process to set forth the grounds on which the appeal is based
   (f) A factual summary as to what each party expects to prove in a jury trial

(7) Garnishment

(g) A rule of evidence that requires that a document be presented as evidence; it does not permit oral testimony as to the contents of the document

(8) Hearsay

(h) A principle that gives finality to legal disputes

(9) Voir dire examination

(i) The removal of a prospective juror for which no cause need be given

(10) Res judicata

(j) Questioning a witness under oath by the attorney on the opposing side

(11) Peremptory challenge

(k) An out-of-court statement offered to prove a point which is not subject to cross-examination

(12) Clear-and-convincing proof standard

(l) A process in which a third party attempts to help settle a dispute

(13) Cross-examination

(m) The questioning of prospective jurors as to their qualifications to be fair and impartial

(14) Mediation

(n) A method of informing the jury as to the law applicable to the case

(15) Jury instruction

(o) A burden-of-proof standard used in limited situations in which the law requires more proof than usual

2 Kay was injured when a pool table collapsed on her foot. The manufacturer was a Missouri corporation which sold the pool table to a wholesaler in Nebraska. The wholesaler sold to an Iowa pool hall where the injury occurred. Kay sued the manufacturer in Iowa, and summons was served on the manufacturer in Missouri. The defendant challenged the jurisdiction of the court. Decide the challenge. Give reasons for your answer.

3 The Minnesota Public Interest Research Group is a college-student-directed, nonprofit corporation; it purports to represent the interests of college students on issues of public importance. This group filed suit to challenge the constitutionality of the Selective Service Act provision that makes students who failed to register for the draft ineligible for federal financial assistance. The government moved to have the suit dismissed. Rule on the motion, and give reasons for your ruling.

4 A class action suit was filed on behalf of certain odd-lot traders against brokerage firms and a stock exchange for alleged violations of the antitrust and securities laws. Plaintiffs asked the court to order defendants to furnish the names and addresses of all members of the class because defendants could easily gather the information and because plaintiffs had limited funds. Should the court grant the plaintiffs' request? Explain.

5 The plaintiff alleged that the defendant caused pharmacists to mislabel drugs by marketing drugs with the similar appearance to those sold by the plaintiff. The trial court found for the defendant. It found that a technical violation of federal law had occurred, but it found no proof of intent. The court of appeals reversed, holding that the trial court failed to give sufficient weight to the evidence of a violation.

Did the reviewing court act within its proper role? Explain.

6 An action was brought in federal court by a realtor against the Real Estate Commission challenging a regulation relating to advertising by real estate dealers. The court found for the defendants. A subsequent action was brought in state court by the same plaintiff against the same defendants. They moved to dismiss the suit. How should the court rule on the motion? Explain.

7 A paving contractor, incorporated in Delaware with the principal place of business in Georgia, was hired to oil and chip streets in a mobile-home park located in Florida. Heavy winds developed during the spraying of oil on the street and a light film of oil was sprayed on thirty-six mobile homes, doing approximately $500 damage to each. A class action suit was filed in federal court seeking $18,000 damages. Does the court have jurisdiction? Explain.

8 A New York resident sued *Hustler* magazine for libel in the federal courts of New Hampshire. The defendant is an Ohio corporation with its principal place of business in California. The magazine was sold in every state, and at least ten thousand copies were sold in New Hampshire. Service was obtained by use of a long-arm statute. Did the court have jurisdiction? Explain.

9 Geraldine's car had been illegally repossessed in Texas by the Baker Bank, a federally chartered national bank located in the state of Tennessee. The National Bank Act requires that suits against national banks be brought in the county in which the bank is located. Geraldine sued the bank in Texas, and it moved to dismiss. What was the result? Why?

10 Mincey was injured by a steel drum which he was cutting with a circular saw. He sued the manufacturer, and it served interrogatories upon the plaintiff. The interrogatories requested information about the defendant's medical history, work history, and educational background. In addition, the defendant requested the identities of expert witnesses to be called by the plaintiff and the substance of their testimony. Must the plaintiff answer the questions? Why, or why not?

11 A Japanese manufacturer of valve stems for tires sold its product to a Taiwan company; the Taiwan company assembled the valve stems into its tires, which were sold worldwide. Twenty percent of the tires were sold in California. In that state, an accident occurred in which a motorcycle tire blew out, injuring the rider. Is the Japanese manufacturer subject to suit in California by the Taiwan manufacturer that settled the product liability suit? Why, or why not?

12 Burger King, a Florida corporation, granted a twenty-year franchise to a Michigan franchisee. The franchisee provides that it is established in Miami and governed by Florida law. All payments of fees and reports are to be made in Florida. The franchisor sued the franchisee in Florida and sought jurisdiction under Florida's long-arm statute. Must the franchisee defend the case in Florida? Explain.

PART TWO

CONSTITUTIONAL AND ADMINISTRATIVE LAW

5
The Constitution and Business

6
The Bill of Rights and Business

7
Administrative Law

CHAPTER 5

THE CONSTITUTION AND BUSINESS

OVERVIEW

The Constitution of the United States provides the foundation for the legal system. This chapter covers some of the provisions of the original Constitution which are of special significance to the business community. The next chapter is devoted to amendments to the Constitution and their role in the legal environment of business.

This chapter gives special attention to the commerce clause. As interpreted, this clause grants certain powers to the federal government and also limits the regulatory powers of state and local governments. Since taxation is a form of regulation, the commerce clause has a significant impact on state and local taxation of business.

In addition to the commerce clause, this chapter introduces the supremacy clause, the import-export clause, the contract clause, and the privileges and immunities clause. The complete United States Constitution is given in Appendix 1 on page 649. Refer to it as this chapter and the next one are studied.

The following terms are important in this chapter: apportionment, commerce clause, contract clause, federalism, full faith and credit clause, import-export clause, nexus, police power, preemption, privileges and immunities clause, separation of powers, and supremacy clause.

1 ORGANIZATION

The Constitution, as originally enacted, contained seven articles and a preamble. The preamble sets forth the purposes of the Constitution, which include such general goals as the establishment of justice and the promotion of general welfare.

Article I establishes the legislative branch of government and defines its functions, powers, method of conducting business, and limitations on its powers, as well as the manner of election and removal of its members. Section 8 of Article I grants Congress numerous powers, including the power to tax and the power to regulate commerce. These powers will be discussed later in this chapter. Some of the other enumerated powers relate to external affairs and the power to wage war. Of special importance to business is the power to enact uniform laws on the subject of bankruptcy and make laws that promote the progress of science and useful arts. The latter secure for limited times to authors and inventors the exclusive right to their writings and discoveries.

Article II vests the executive power in the President. It defines his term of office, qualifications for office, and manner of election. This latter provision, together with the Twelfth Amendment, which concerns the electoral college, is currently the subject of much criticism, with many people advocating election by popular vote. Article II also makes the President the Commander in Chief of the Armed Forces and authorizes him to enter into treaties with the advice and consent of the Senate. It is this article that requires the annual State of the Union message by the President.

Article III creates the judicial branch of government. It defines the original jurisdiction of the Supreme Court and authorizes Congress to create other federal court systems, as discussed in Chapter 3. This provision underlies recent attempts to deny courts the power to decide cases involving abortions, school prayer, and busing to achieve integration. Article III also defines treason.

Article IV contains several provisions dealing with relationships between the states. It is often referred to as "the states' relation article," and is discussed in section 8 of this chapter.

Article V sets forth methods for amending the Constitution. To date, there have been twenty-six amendments approved by one of the authorized methods. A proposed equal rights for women amendment was adopted by Congress and ratified by thirty-five states before the time for ratification expired. Proposed amendments on abortion and school busing are also pending.

Article VI contains the supremacy clause, which states that federal laws and treaties are the supreme law of the land. The supremacy clause frequently comes into play when states attempt to regulate a business activity that the federal government also regulates. It will be discussed further in section 3 of this chapter.

2 SEPARATION OF POWERS

One of the most important of our constitutional law concepts is the doctrine of **separation of powers**. It arose out of the strong fear the founders of this country had that too much power might be concentrated in one branch of government. This doctrine has both horizontal and vertical aspects. First, the horizontal aspect describes the theory that each of three branches of government (executive, legislative, and judicial) has a separate function to perform. Each is not to perform the functions of the others because no one person may exercise the powers of more than one branch at the same time. As the Supreme Court has stated in several cases:

> Each branch shall by the law of its creation be limited to the exercise of the powers appropriate to its own department and no other.... As a general rule...the powers confided by the Constitution to one of these departments cannot be exercised by another.

One facet of this functional aspect of separation of powers is that each branch has the capacity or power to limit the other branches in the performance of their respective functions. For example, courts exercising the power of judicial review may limit the actions of the executive and the legislative branches of government. The legislative branch may determine the jurisdiction of federal courts and may limit the powers of the executive. The executive appoints the judiciary with the advice and consent of the Senate. Therefore, although each branch of government has a separate function to perform, these branches are closely inter-related and each has some control over the others. No branch of government is free to act with total independence of the others. Although the separation of powers concept admits that each branch has some control and influence over the others, it should be recognized that each branch of government is to be free from the *coercive* influence of the others. Congress should not interfere with the President as he carries out his duty to "take care that the Laws be faithfully executed." The converse is also true. The President should not interfere with Congress as it performs its constitutional responsibilities.

The vertical aspect of separation of powers is **federalism** or dual federalism. This aspect recognizes that we have two levels of government—a federal level and a state and local level. Each has a separate and distinct role to play. The federal government must recognize that it was created by the states and that states have some sovereignty. The Tenth Amendment reserves some powers to the states and to the people. Congress may not impair the ability of state government to function in the federal system. Likewise, state government may not curtail in any substantial manner the exercise of powers granted by states to the federal government. Thus, the doctrine of separation of powers has both vertical and horizontal aspects.

Former Justice John M. Harlan, in discussing the reasons for our government of divided powers, concluded that in such a government lay the best promise for realizing a free society. In explaining the doctrine of separation of powers he observed:

> The matter has a double aspect: *first,* the division of governmental authority between the states and the central government; *second,* the distribution of power within the federal establishment itself. The former, doubtless born not so much

of political principle as of the necessity for achieving a more perfect union than had proved possible under the Articles of Confederation, was solved by making the authority of the Federal Government supreme within the sphere of powers expressly or impliedly delegated to it and reserving to the states all other powers—a reservation which subsequently found express protection in the Bill of Rights through the provisions of the Tenth Amendment. The second aspect of the governmental structure was solved, purely as a matter of political theory, by distributing the totality of federal power among the legislative, executive and judicial branches of the government, each having defined functions. Thus eventuated the two great constitutional doctrines of federalism—often inaccurately referred to as the doctrine of states' rights—and separation of powers.

3 THE SUPREMACY CLAUSE

Closely related to the doctrine of separation of powers is the **supremacy clause**. This clause makes the federal law supreme over a state law if the two are in conflict. This specific clause guarantees federal supremacy even though the states created the federal government.

When courts are called upon to decide if a state law is invalid under the supremacy clause because it conflicts with a federal law, they must construe or interpret the two laws to see if they are in conflict. A conflict exists if the state statute would prevent the accomplishment and execution of the full purposes and objectives of Congress. It is immaterial that a state did not intend to frustrate the federal law if the state law in fact does so. In the case which follows, keep in mind that arbitration is a procedure for submitting controversies to a person or persons other than a court for a binding decision.

SOUTHLAND CORP. v. KEATING
104 S.Ct. 852 (1984)

FACTS

A franchisor had as part of its franchise agreement a clause that required arbitration of all disputes between the franchisor and the franchisee. The state of California enacted a law covering franchises. It authorized courts to hear claims brought by franchisees against franchisors that arose out of the franchise agreement. Several franchisees filed suit against a franchisor of convenience stores, alleging fraud and breach of contract. The franchisor asked to have the cases dismissed. The franchisor argued that the state law was unconstitutional, as it was in conflict with the United States Arbitration Act.

ISSUE

Is the state law constitutional?

DECISION

No.

> **REASON**
>
> The California law violated the supremacy clause. The federal statute declares a national policy favoring arbitration. States have no power to require a judicial decision. Such a law defeats the announced national policy.

Sometimes a federal law is said to **preempt** an area of law. If a federal law preempts a subject, then any state law is unconstitutional under the supremacy clause. The conflict is apparent, and the evidence of it is conclusive. This is true of federal statutes, but it also applies to the rules and regulations of federal administrative agencies.

The first question in preemption cases is whether Congress intended to displace state law. Congress sometimes specifically provides for preemption. If it does not do so, a state statute is preempted only where compliance with both the federal law and the state law is a physical impossibility or where the state law stands as an obstacle to the accomplishment and execution of the full purposes and objectives of Congress. Where there is no actual conflict between a federal law and a state law, there must be provable congressional intent to preempt. In evaluating the impact of a state law, courts usually examine the purposes of both laws. If the objectives are virtually identical, then the courts attempt to reconcile the laws and enforce both. If the purposes are in conflict, chances are that the state law cannot be enforced and the court will find an intent to preempt. Table 5-1 lists several examples of cases in which the preemption issue has been litigated in recent years.

Many of the cases involving preemption and the supremacy clause involve conflicts that are not readily apparent. Arizona had a statute which provided for the suspension of licenses of drivers who could not satisfy judgments arising out of auto accidents, even if the driver was bankrupt. The statute was unconstitutional since it was in conflict with the federal law on bankruptcy. The purpose of the Bankruptcy Act is to give debtors new opportunity unhampered by the pressure and discouragement of pre-existing debt. The challenged state statute hampers the accomplishment and execution of the full purposes and objectives of the Bankruptcy Act enacted by Congress.

4 EXTERNAL AFFAIRS

The President has the power to make treaties, with the advice and consent of the Senate, in Article II, Section 2, of the Constitution. This power has grown in its importance to the economic life and defense of the nation as the United States has become a leader in world affairs.

The treaties of most countries affect only their external relations with other countries. The United States is unique in that its treaties are part of the "supreme Law of the Land," and thus have the internal force of the

TABLE 5-1 EXAMPLES OF STATE LAWS CHALLENGED AS PREEMPTED BY FEDERAL LAW

	State or local law	Federal law	Preemption Yes	Preemption No
1	A state law conditions the construction of nuclear power plants on the existence of adequate storage facilities and the means of disposal.	Atomic Energy Act		X
2	A city conditions renewal of taxicab franchise on settlement of labor dispute.	National Labor Relations Act	X	
3	A state statute provides that employee is ineligible for unemployment compensation if employee is provided "financing," by means other than payment of regular union dues, for strike that has caused his unemployment. (Financing of strike by national union prevents unemployment compensation.)	National Labor Relations Act		X
4	A state statute permits indirect purchasers to collect damages for overcharges resulting from price-fixing conspiracies.	Sherman Antitrust Act	X	
5	A state law authorizes a tort claim by workers that a union has breached its duty to insure a safe workplace.	Labor-Management Relations Act (Landrum-Griffin)	X	
6	A state statute requires employers to allow up to four months unpaid pregnancy leave and reinstatement.	Pregnancy Discrimination Act		X
7	A state imposes permit requirements on mining operations located on federal forest lands.	Forest Service Statutes and Regulations		X
8	A state law prohibits repeat violators of labor laws from doing business with the state.	National Labor Relations Act	X	
9	The New Jersey Casino Control Act requires annual registration of unions representing people employed in casinos or casino hotels. It also provides that a union may be prohibited from receiving dues from such employees and from administering any pension or welfare funds if any union officer is disqualified under the law.	National Labor Relations Act		X
10	A suit for breach of contract against an employer is brought in state court by strike replacements. They have been displaced by reinstated strikers after having been offered and accepted jobs on a permanent basis. They were assured that they would not be fired to accommodate returning strikers.	National Labor Relations Act		X
11	A state statute attempts to control share acquisitions in state companies. The statute withholds voting rights from an acquiror of a controlling share of an Indiana corporation until a majority of the company's pre-existing, disinterested shareholders approves the acquisition.	Williams Act (Governs hostile corporate stock tender-offers)		X

Constitution and laws enacted by Congress. Article VI of the Constitution provides in part: "This Constitution, and the Laws of the United States which shall be made in Pursuance thereof; and all Treaties made, or which shall be made, under the Authority of the United States, shall be the supreme Law of the Land; and the Judges in every State shall be bound thereby, any Thing in the Constitution or Laws of any State to the Contrary notwithstanding." Note that the language employed makes the laws enacted by Congress binding only if made within the limitations of the Constitution. It apparently provides no such restriction on the effect of treaties made "under the Authority of the United States." Therefore, business is subject to the provisions of all treaties entered into by the President which are ratified by the Senate. They are the supreme Law of the Land.

5 THE CONTRACT CLAUSE

Section 10 of Article I of the United States Constitution says, in part, that no state shall pass any law impairing the obligation of contracts. This provision does not apply to the federal government, which does, in fact, frequently enact laws and adopt regulations that affect existing contracts. For example, the Department of Agriculture sometimes embargoes grain sales to foreign countries, usually as a result of problems in foreign affairs.

The limitation on state action impairing contracts has not been given a literal application. As a result of judicial interpretation, some state laws which affect existing contracts have been approved, especially when the law is passed to deal with a specific emergency situation. On the other hand, this constitutional provision does generally limit alternatives available to state government and prevents the enactment of legislation that changes vested contract rights. The case that follows, while declaring a state statute unconstitutional for violating the **contract clause**, does indicate those areas in which a literal application will not result.

ALLIED STRUCTURAL STEEL CO. v. SPANNAUS
98 S.Ct. 2716 (1978)

FACTS

Plaintiff, an Illinois corporation, maintained an office in Minnesota with thirty employees. It adopted a pension plan in 1963, qualified under Section 401 of the Internal Revenue Code (I.R.C.), but retained the right to amend the plan or terminate it at any time and for any reason. The plan did not obligate the company to pay anything into the plan. Any voluntary payments were simply subject to its terms. In 1974, Minnesota enacted the Private Pension Benefits Protection Act. Under this act, a private employer of 100 employees or more (at least one of whom was a Minnesota resident) who provided pension benefits under a plan which met the qualification of Section 401 of the I.R.C. was subject to a "pension funding charge" if she or he terminated the plan or closed a Minnesota office. Shortly thereafter, plaintiff closed its Minnesota office. Several discharged employees then sought to collect a pension funding charge of $185,000 under the act. Plaintiff brought suit, claiming that the act unconstitutionally impaired its contractual obligations to its employees under its pension plan.

ISSUE

Does Minnesota's Private Pension Benefits Protection Act violate the contract clause of the United States Constitution?

DECISION

Yes.

REASONS

1. The contract clause, as it must be understood, imposes some limits upon the power of a state to abridge existing contractual relationships, even in the exercise of its otherwise legitimate police power.
2. There was no showing that the severe disruption of contractual expectations was necessary to meet an important social problem.
3. There was a severe, permanent, immediate, and retroactive change in the affected contractual relationships.

6 THE TAXING POWER

The taxing power is the power by which government raises revenue to defray its expenses. It apportions the cost of government among those who receive its benefits. The purpose of taxation and the purposes and function of government are coextensive, in that the taxing power, in the broad sense, includes all charges and burdens imposed by government upon persons or property for the use and support of government.

The taxing power can be exercised only for public purposes. A tax is not a contract based on assent but is a statutory liability based on force and authority. A tax is not a debt in the usual sense of the word, and the constitutional prohibitions against imprisonment for debt are not applicable.

The theory supporting taxation is that since governmental functions are a necessity, the government has the right to compel persons and property within its jurisdiction to defray the costs of these functions. The payment of taxes gives no right to the taxpayer. The privilege of enjoying the protection and services of government is not based on taxes paid. As a matter of fact, there are many examples which illustrate that those who receive the most from the government pay the fewest taxes.

Taxes are paid by those able to do so, so that all persons may share in the general benefits resulting from government. Thus, property can be taxed without an obvious personal benefit to the property owner.

The power of taxation is, in theory, exclusively exercised by the legislative branch of the government. The only limitations on the exercise of the taxing power are found in federal and state constitutions and the political power of the electorate to replace the legislators. Since the power of taxation is a legislative function, statutes dealing with taxation must be complete as to both the method of ascertaining the tax and its collection. The fact that a tax may destroy a business or the value of property is no basis for a judicial determination that the tax is unconstitutional. The court must find that the tax violates some specific provision of the Constitution before it can be held invalid. The decision as to the wisdom or propriety of the tax is left to the legislature.

The taxing power is used to accomplish many goals other than raising revenue. Taxation is a very important form of regulation. Tax policy is a major ingredient in government efforts to regulate the economy. Tax laws are also used by the federal government to equalize competition among different businesses. For example, the gasoline tax is an important part of the equalization of costs between truckers and other forms of transportation. The taxing power has been used to encourage uniform legislation among the states. States were encouraged to adopt unemployment compensation benefits because the federal tax allows, as a credit, a certain portion of the tax paid to states.

The federal taxing power is also used to implement social policies. For example, the federal estate tax and the graduated income tax were in part adopted to break up large accumulations of wealth. In addition, the federal government pays money to the states to encourage certain activities such as education, road building, and raising the drinking age. Persons in one part of the country may pay for social improvements in another as a direct result of the exercise of the taxing and spending power of the federal government. An examination of the implementation policies of the federal government will reveal that many of them are tied directly to taxation.

Few questions are raised today concerning the *validity* of a federally imposed tax. The Sixteenth Amendment to the Constitution and the broad scope of the federal taxing power which has been approved by the courts eliminates most such issues. Of course, there is a considerable amount of litigation involving the *interpretation* and *application* of the federal tax laws and regulations. Great deference is given to the position taken by the Commissioner of Internal Revenue in such cases. Courts tend to hold that federal taxing laws are valid unless there is some clear constitutional infirmity in them.

7 THE IMPORT-EXPORT CLAUSE

A provision closely connected with the taxing power is the **import-export clause**. This clause prohibits states from taxing imports. It prohibits both the federal and state governments from directly taxing exports. Difficult questions often arise regarding when property ceases to be an import or becomes an export and comes within the protection of the constitutional guarantee. At one time it was thought that goods remained imports so long as they were in their original package. Today, the original-package doctrine is not followed. If goods have lost their status as imports, the clause does not prevent state taxation of them. The case that follows discusses the reasons for the constitutional provision and indicates the narrow scope of its application today.

MICHELIN TIRE CORP. v. WAGES
96 S.Ct. 535 (1976)

FACTS

The state of Georgia assessed a nondiscriminatory ad valorem (value) property tax against Michelin's inventory of imported tire and tubes. The tires were in a Georgia warehouse from which petitioner as a wholesaler sold them to franchised dealers in six southeastern states.

Approximately 25 percent of the tires and tubes were manufactured in and imported from Nova Scotia. They were brought to the United States in tractor-driven over-the-road trailers packed and sealed at the Nova Scotia factory. The remaining 75 percent of the imported tires and tubes were brought to the United States by sea from France and Nova Scotia in sea vans packed and sealed at the foreign factories. Upon arrival of the ship at the United States port of entry, the vans were unloaded, the wheels replaced, and the vans tractor-hauled to the petitioner's distribution warehouse.

The imported tires were sorted by size and style; stacked on wooden pallets, each bearing four stacks of five tires of the same size and style; and stored in pallet stacks of three each. This is the only processing required or performed to ready the tires for sale and delivery to the franchised dealers.

Michelin filed suit to have the assessment declared to be unconstitutional under the import-export clause which provides: "No state shall, without the consent of the Congress, lay any Imposts or Duties on Imports or Exports, except what may be absolutely necessary for executing its inspection laws...."

ISSUE

Is the nondiscriminatory, ad valorem property tax assessment against these imports constitutional?

DECISION

Yes.

REASONS

1. The import-export clause of the Constitution sought to alleviate three main concerns by committing sole power to lay imposts and duties on import in the federal government, with no concurrent state power: (a) the federal government must speak with one voice when regulating commercial relations with foreign governments, and tariffs, which might affect foreign relations, could not be implemented by the states consistently with that

exclusive power; (b) import revenues were to be the major source of revenue of the federal government and should not be diverted to the states; and (c) harmony among the states might be disturbed unless seaboard states, with their crucial ports of entry, were prohibited from levying taxes on citizens of other states by taxing goods merely flowing through their ports to the inland states not situated as favorably geographically.
2. A nondiscriminatory ad valorem property tax constitutes no danger to those three federal concerns when imposed on goods no longer in transit. The tax has no impact on foreign commerce.
3. Taxation is a fair exchange for benefits covered by the taxing state.
4. The import-export clause clearly prohibits state taxation based on the foreign origin of the imported goods. However, it cannot be read to give imported goods preferential treatment that would permit them to escape from uniform taxes imposed without regard to foreign origin for services which the state supplies.

8 STATES' RELATION ARTICLE

Article IV is sometimes referred to as the states' relation article. It contains provisions for the admission of new states and authorizes Congress to make rules governing territories and property of the United States. Section 4 of the article guarantees every state a republican form of government and imposes upon the federal government the duty to protect the states from invasion. It also guarantees each state protection against domestic violence.

Section 2 of Article IV contains the so-called **privileges and immunities clause**. This clause provides that "the Citizens of each State shall be entitled to all Privileges and Immunities of Citizens in the several States." This clause assures equality of treatment for all citizens. The clause places the citizens of each state on the same footing as citizens of other states concerning the advantages of citizenship. It relieves them from the disabilities of alienage in other states. It inhibits discriminating legislation against them by other states; it gives them the right of free ingress into other states, and egress from them; it ensures to them while in other states the same freedom possessed by the citizens of those states in acquisition and enjoyment of property and in the pursuit of happiness; and it secures to them while in other states equal protection of their laws. No provision in the Constitution tends so strongly to constitute the citizens of the United States as one people as this provision, because it prevents a state from discriminating against citizens of other states in favor of its own. A municipality is a subdivision of the state, and municipal ordinances may be challenged as a violation of the privileges and immunities clause.

Many attempts to favor local citizens over citizens of other states arise from attempts to benefit local residents economically. For example, Alaska passed a local hire act that required that oil and gas leases to which the state was a party contain a provision requiring the employment of qualified Alaskan residents in preference to nonresidents. The act violated the privileges and immunities clause. Alaska's ownership of the oil and gas was insufficient justification for the discrimination.

The case which follows is typical of those which deal with attempts to aid local citizens. Notice that in this case, the courts attempted to do so.

SUPREME COURT OF N.H. v. PIPER
105 S.Ct. 1272 (1985)

FACTS

The rules of the Supreme Court of New Hampshire limit bar admission to state residents. Piper lives about 400 yards from the New Hampshire border. The New Hampshire Board of Bar Examiners found that Piper was of good moral character and allowed her to take the bar exam, which she passed. She was informed by the Board that she would have to establish a home address in New Hampshire prior to being sworn in as an attorney.

ISSUE

Does this restriction violate the privileges and immunities clause of the United States Constitution, Article IV, Section 2?

DECISION

Yes.

REASONS

1. It is only with respect to those privileges and immunities bearing on the vitality of the nation as a single entity that a state must accord residents and nonresidents equal treatment.
   The clause does not preclude discrimination against nonresidents when: (1) there is a substantial reason for the difference in treatment; and (2) the discrimination practiced against nonresidents bears a substantial relationship to the state's objective.
2. One of the privileges which the clause guarantees to citizens of state A is that of doing business in state B on terms of substantial equality with the citizens of that state.
3. The lawyer's role in the national economy is not the only reason that the opportunity to practice law should be considered a "fundamental right." The legal profession has a noncommercial role and duty. Because of this, the practice of law is seen as falling within the scope of the privileges and immunities clause. Out-of-state lawyers may—and often do—represent people who raise unpopular federal claims. In some cases, representation by nonresident counsel may be the only means available for the vindication of federal rights.

The clause does not prevent state citizenship from being used to distinguish among people, however. A state may limit the right to vote and to hold office to its citizens. The same is true of the right to pay resident tuition to a state university. It is only with respect to those privileges and immunities bearing upon the vitality of the nation as a single entity that the state must treat all citizens, resident and nonresident, equally.

Article IV also contains the so-called **full faith and credit clause**. It provides that "Full Faith and Credit shall be given in each State to the public Acts, Records, and judicial proceedings of every other State...." This does not mean that the precedent in one state is binding in other states but only that final decisions or judgments rendered in any given state shall be enforced as between the original parties in other states. Full faith and credit applies to a specific decision as it affects the rights of the parties, and not to the reasons or principles upon which it was based. A court judgment in one state is conclusive upon the merits of the issues in another state only if the court in the first state had power to pass on the merits—that is, had jurisdiction over the subject matter and the relevant parties. The first court's decision on jurisdiction, if that is an issue, is res judicata if the issue of jurisdiction was fully considered by the first court deciding the controversy. A party with a judgment or decree from the courts of one state may obtain enforcement through proper proceedings in other states without relitigating the issues of the original case.

Finally, the states' relation article provides for extradition of those accused of crime from one state to another. This is accomplished by judicial proceedings with the consent of the governor of the surrendering state.

THE COMMERCE CLAUSE

9 INTRODUCTION

The power of the federal government to regulate business activity is found in the so-called **commerce clause** of the Constitution. The commerce clause states: "Congress shall have power...to regulate Commerce with foreign Nations, and among the several States, and with the Indian Tribes...." This grant of power has been broadly interpreted to give the federal government broad power to regulate business. This power to regulate is the power to prescribe the rules by which commerce is to be conducted. The actual extent of this power will be discussed in subsequent sections.

The commerce clause has been interpreted as imposing limitations on the power of state government to regulate business under the state police power. The **police power** of state and local governments is the inherent power to control persons and property within the jurisdiction of the state to promote the general welfare. General welfare includes the public health, safety, and morals. The inherent police power of the states was reserved to them by the Constitution. The effect of the commerce clause on the police power will be discussed in section 12 of this chapter.

10 FOREIGN COMMERCE

The commerce clause has three parts. The first grants the federal government power to regulate foreign commerce. The power to regulate foreign commerce is vested exclusively in the federal government, and it extends to all aspects of foreign trade. In other words, the power to regulate foreign commerce is total. The federal government can prohibit foreign commerce entirely. For example, in recent years the federal government has imposed trade embargoes on countries such as the Soviet Union. It can also allow commerce with restrictions.

To state that federal power to regulate foreign commerce is exclusive means that state and local governments may not regulate such commerce. However, state and local governments sometimes attempt directly or indirectly to regulate imports or exports to some degree. Such attempts are unconstitutional. State or local laws which regulate or interfere with federal regulation of commerce with foreign nations are invalid as violations of the commerce and supremacy clauses.

The right to import includes the right to sell goods imported. States may not prohibit sale of imported goods any more than can prohibit their import. The exclusive federal power over imported goods continues until the goods are mingled with and become a part of the general property of the country, so that for all purposes the imported product is given similar treatment with other property. In most cases, imported goods become a part of internal commerce when the importer or wholesaler disposes of them to retail dealers in local communities. However, if a state or local law tends to continue to distinguish the goods from a point of origin, the foreign-commerce aspect continues, and the law is invalid. For example, a city required that all goods sold at retail originating behind the Iron Curtain be so labeled. This law was unconstitutional.

11 INTERSTATE COMMERCE

The second component of the commerce clause is the power to regulate commerce "among the several states." At first, this phrase was interpreted to mean interstate commerce as contrasted with intrastate commerce. Later, a long series of judicial decisions expanded the interpretation of power to include not only the channels and instrumentalities of interstate commerce but also activities affecting interstate commerce.

The power of Congress over commerce is complete, or plenary. Labeling an activity a "local" or "intrastate" activity does not mean that Congress may not regulate it under the commerce clause. The commerce power extends to those intrastate activities which so affect interstate commerce, or the exertion of the power of Congress over it, that regulation of them is appropriate. Regulation is appropriate if it helps to effectively control interstate commerce. Even activity that is purely intrastate in character may be regulated by Congress when the activity, combined with like conduct by others similarly situated, affects commerce among the states or with foreign nations. Interstate commerce may be affected positively or negatively in the sense that regulated economic activity may encourage commerce or hinder it. The nature of the activity itself and its effect on interstate commerce may warrant the application of federal law. Such activity need not result from a violation of the law. The unlawful conduct itself need not have an effect on interstate commerce.

Today, legislative acts adjusting the benefits and burdens of economic life we presume to be constitutional. A court may invalidate legislation enacted under the commerce clause only if there is clearly no rational basis for a congressional finding that the regulated activity affects interstate commerce, or if there is no reasonable connection between the regulatory means selected and the asserted ends. The judicial task ends once the court determines that Congress acted rationally in adopting a particular regulatory scheme. The case which follows is typical of those which review laws passed by Congress under the power to regulate commerce among the several states.

HODEL v. INDIANA
101 S.Ct. 2376 (1981)

FACTS

Several coal companies filed suit, alleging that the provisions of the Surface Mining and Reclamation Control Act of 1977 violated the commerce clause. The district court ruled that the challenged provisions were unconstitutional and permanently enjoined their enforcement. The district court was persuaded that surface coal mining on prime farmland has "an infinitesimal effect or trivial impact on interstate commerce"; therefore, the provisions go beyond the congressional power to regulate interstate commerce.

ISSUE

Is the act a permissible exercise of congressional power under the commerce clause?

DECISION

Yes.

REASONS

1. A court may invalidate legislation enacted under the commerce clause only if there is no rational basis for a congressional finding that the regulated activity affects interstate commerce, or if there is no reasonable connection

> between the regulatory means selected and the ends asserted. Congress could rationally conclude that surface coal mining on prime farmland affects interstate commerce in agricultural products.
> 2. The court will not substitute its judgment for that of Congress unless the relation of the subject to interstate commerce and its effect upon it are clearly nonexistent.
> 3. The statutory provisions advance legitimate goals, and Congress acted reasonably in adopting the regulations in the act.

The power of Congress under the commerce clause is subject to other constitutional limitations such as those contained in the Bill of Rights. The effect of the commerce clause on the rights of state and local government as protected by the Tenth Amendment has caused the courts a great deal of difficulty. For example, prior to 1976, the Supreme Court held that the commerce clause allowed Congress to regulate the wages of employees of state and local government. From 1976 to 1985, the Court held that Congress could not regulate employees that were engaged in areas of traditional governmental functions. This later decision was reversed in 1985 when the court recognized the inherent difficulty in separating traditional functions from nontraditional ones.

The commerce clause by its specific language does not provide any special limitation on Congress' action with respect to the states. However, the Constitution precludes the national government from devouring the essentials of state sovereignty. There is general reliance on the political process to protect the states from such action by the federal government. The judicial process is used only as a last resort to protect the states as states.

In summary, the states occupy a special and specific position in our constitutional system. The scope of Congress' authority under the commerce clause must reflect that position. But the principal and basic limit on the federal commerce power is that inherent in all congressional action—the built-in restraints that our system provides through state participation in federal governmental action. The political process ensures that laws that unduly burden the states will not be promulgated. If laws are passed under the commerce clause that apply to state government, they are presumed to be constitutional.

Keep in mind that although Congress has the power to regulate certain activities, it may decide not to exercise it. There are activities that the federal government could regulate but has chosen not to. Also keep in mind that not all business or commercial activity is commerce. For example, it has been held that the activity of accrediting institutions of higher learning is not commerce. Professional baseball has repeatedly been held to be a "sport" and not a business. As a practical matter, the trend is to consider that almost every business activity is a part of commerce, but there are still some noncommercial pursuits.

12 THE COMMERCE CLAUSE AND THE STATE POLICE POWER

The grant of power to Congress over commerce does not contain any provision which expressly excludes states from exercising authority over commerce. The Supreme Court in *Cooley v. The Board of Wardens of Port of Philadelphia*[1] held that the nature of the commerce power did not *by implication* prohibit state action and that some state power over commerce is compatible with the federal power. Nevertheless, there are definite limitations on the state powers over commerce because of the commerce clause. This is sometimes called the dominant commerce clause concept.

The decisions of the Supreme Court have established three distinct subject areas of governmental regulation of commerce, as shown in Table 5-2.

TABLE 5-2 POSSIBLE SUBJECTS FOR GOVERNMENT REGULATION

Exclusively federal subjects	Possible dual regulation subjects	Exclusively local subjects

I.
Any state regulatory law is unconstitutional under supremacy and commerce clauses.
	II.
	Federal law preempts the field—moves the subject matter to area No. I.
	
	III.
	Federal law does not preempt the field.
	A state law is unconstitutional if it:
	  1 Is in irreconcilable conflict with federal law
	  2 Constitutes an *undue* burden on interstate commerce
	  3 Discriminates against interstate commerce in favor of intrastate commerce
	
	IV.
	No federal law—state law is unconstitutional if it:
	  1 Constitutes an undue burden on interstate commerce
	  2 Discriminates against interstate commerce in favor of intrastate commerce
		V.
		The impact on state and local government of laws based on the commerce clause is very limited. Very few subjects are exclusively local.

[1] 53 U.S. 299 (1851)

Some areas are exclusively federal, some are said to be exclusively local, and still others are such that regulation of them may be dual.

The subject area which is exclusively federal, in addition to foreign commerce, concerns those internal matters where uniformity on a nationwide basis is essential. Any state regulation of such subjects is void, whether Congress has entered the field or not.

In theory, those matters which are exclusively within the states' power are intrastate activities that do not have a substantial effect on interstate commerce. As noted in the previous section, it is becoming more and more difficult, if not impossible, to find a subject matter which is truly exclusively local in the sense that it does not affect interstate commerce.

The third subject area between the above two extremes, where joint regulation is permissible, can be divided into three subparts. The first concerns those subjects over which the federal government has preempted the field. By express language or by comprehensive regulation Congress has shown that it intends to exercise exclusive dominion over the subject matter. When a federal statute has thus preempted the field, *any* state or local law pertaining to the same subject matter is unconstitutional under the commerce clause and the supremacy clause, and the state regulation is void. The net effect of a law that preempts the field makes the subject matter of the law exclusively federal. The subject of preemption was discussed in section 3 under "The Supremacy Clause."

The second division of the area of possible joint regulation includes situations in which the federal regulation of a subject matter is not comprehensive enough to preempt the field. Here state regulation is permitted, but when state law is inconsistent or conflicts irreconcilably with the federal statute, it is unconstitutional and void. Irreconcilable conflicts exist when it is not possible for a business to comply with both statutes. If compliance with both is not possible, the state law must fall under the supremacy clause and the commerce clause. If compliance with both is reasonably possible, dual compliance is required. This usually has the effect of forcing business to meet the requirements of the law with the greatest burden. For example, if the state minimum wage is $4.00 per hour and the federal is $3.35, employers would be required to pay $4.00 since the conflict can be reconciled.

The commerce clause also invalidates state laws imposing an undue burden on interstate commerce. The commerce clause does not prohibit the imposing of burdens on interstate commerce—only the imposition of undue burdens. The states have the authority under the police power to regulate matters of legitimate local concern, even though interstate commerce may be affected. The case which follows is typical of those in which state regulation that significantly impacts interstate commerce is approved.

MAINE v. TAYLOR
106 S.Ct. 2440 (1986)

FACTS

Taylor arranged to have golden shiners, a species of minnow commonly used as live bait in sport fishing, imported into Maine, despite a Maine statute prohibiting such importation. He was indicted under a federal statute which made it a federal crime to transport fish in interstate commerce in violation of state law. He contended that the Maine statute unconstitutionally burdened interstate commerce. Maine intervened to defend the validity of its statute, contending that its fisheries are unique and unusually fragile. The district court held the statute constitutional. The court of appeals reversed, concluding that the state statute was unconstitutional.

ISSUES

Does the state statute violate the commerce clause?

DECISION

No.

REASONS

1. The limitation imposed by the commerce clause on state regulatory power is by no means absolute; states retain authority under their general police powers to regulate matters of legitimate local concern even though interstate commerce may be affected.
2. In determining whether a state has overstepped its role in regulating interstate commerce, a distinction is made between state statutes that burden interstate transactions only incidentally and those that affirmatively discriminate against such transactions.
3. Statutes in the first group violate the commerce clause only if the burdens they impose on interstate trade are clearly excessive in relation to the putative local benefits. Statutes in the second group are subject to more demanding scrutiny—the state must demonstrate both that the statute serves legitimate local purpose and that such purpose could not be served as well by available nondiscrimatory means.
4. Under commerce clause analysis, shielding in-state industries from out-of-state competition is almost never a legitimate local purpose; state laws that amount to simple economic protectionism are subject to a virtual per se rule of invalidity.
5. Maine had a legitimate interest in guarding against imperfectly understood environmental risks, that is, parasites and nonnative species, despite possibility that they might ultimately prove to be negligible. It was shown that such purposes could not adequately be served by available nondiscriminatory alternatives.
6. As long as a state does not needlessly obstruct interstate trade or attempt to place itself in a position of economic isolation, it retains broad authority under the commerce clause to protect the health and safety of its citizens and the integrity of its natural resources.

The preceding case pointed out that state statutes fall into two categories: those that burden interstate commerce only incidentally, and those that affirmatively discriminate against such transactions. For cases in the first category, courts weigh the burdens against the benefits and find undue burdens only if they clearly exceed the local benefits. Cases in the second category are subject to more-demanding scrutiny. If a state law either in substance or in practical effect discriminates against interstate commerce, the state must not only prove that the law has a legitimate purpose but also that the purpose cannot be achieved by a nondiscriminatory means. If a state law is pure economic protectionism, the courts apply a virtual per se rule of invalidity.

In deciding cases that are concerned with state legislation that may or may not burden interstate commerce without discrimination against it the courts are involved in a "weighing" process, or a balancing of competing interests. However, in many cases incomparables exist that cannot be weighed. In the weighing process, the court examines the goal of the state legislation and weighs it against the burden imposed on business. Although doubts are resolved in favor of state laws, many are held to be unconstitutional, such as the one in the case which follows.

KASSEL v. CONSOLIDATED FREIGHTWAYS CORP., ETC.
101 S.Ct. 1309 (1981)

FACTS

An Iowa statute prohibited the use of 65-foot double-trailer trucks within its borders, while allowing the use of 55-foot single-trailer trucks and 60-foot double-trailer trucks. Plaintiff, a common carrier trucking company, was forced to discontinue use of its 65-foot doubles in order to move goods through Iowa. Doubles have larger capacities than the shorter authorized truck combinations and can be detached and routed separately if necessary. Plaintiff had to divert its 65-foot doubles around Iowa or use shorter truck units. It challenged the constitutionality of the statute burdening interstate commerce while the state of Iowa defended the statute as being a reasonable safety measure.

ISSUE

Does the Iowa safety interest justify the burden on the interstate commerce?

DECISION

No.

REASONS

1. The commerce clause is a limitation upon state power even without congressional action on the subject being regulated.
2. If safety justifications are not illusory, the court will not second-guess legislative judgment about their importance in comparison with related

burdens on interstate commerce. Those who would challenge bona fide safety regulations must overcome a strong presumption of validity.
3. Where the state's safety interest is illusory and its regulations impair significantly the federal interest in efficient and safe interstate transportation, the state law cannot be harmonized with the commerce clause. The record shows that Iowa's law added about $12.6 million each year to the costs of trucking companies. Plaintiff alone incurred about $2 million per year in increased costs.

Among examples of state laws found to be constitutional through the balancing or weighing process are: (1) a Minnesota law which banned retail sale of milk in plastic, nonreturnable, and nonrefillable containers but permitted such sale in other nonreturnable, nonrefillable containers such as paperboard milk cartons; (2) a New Hampshire law requiring aircraft used for hunting to display large registration numbers; and (3) a Virginia statute which required all stockbrokers to register with the state. In all three cases, the court held that the burden was not excessive in relation to the local benefits.

Finally, as noted above, the commerce clause has been construed as prohibiting discrimination against interstate commerce in favor of intrastate commerce. State and local governments frequently attempt by legislation to aid local business in its competition with interstate business. The commerce clause requires that all taxes and regulations be the same for local businesses as for businesses engaged in interstate commerce. Although interstate commerce is required to pay its fair share of all taxes, it must be placed on a plane of equality with local trade or commerce. A state may not place itself in a position of economic isolation from other states.

The third area of possible joint regulation exists where there is no federal law at all. When there is no federal regulation of a subject, state regulation of interstate commerce is permissible, providing, of course, that it does not discriminate against interstate commerce in favor of local business and does not impose an undue burden on interstate commerce.

13 THE COMMERCE CLAUSE AND TAXATION

Taxation is a primary form of regulation. Therefore, taxes imposed by state and local governments are subject to the limitations imposed by the commerce clause. The commerce clause limits property taxes, income taxes, and sales or use taxes levied by state and local governments on interstate commerce. Since taxation distributes the cost of government among those who receive its benefits, interstate commerce is not exempt from state and local taxes. The commerce clause ensures that it only pays its fair share.

Several distinct constitutional problems exist when a state seeks to tax businesses engaged in interstate commerce. These issues are: (1) Is the tax properly apportioned? (2) Is there a sufficient minimum connection (**nexus**) between the activity being taxed and the tax to satisfy due process? (3) Does the tax discriminate against interstate commerce? And (4) does the tax impose an unconstitutional burden on interstate commerce? This latter issue goes to the question as to whether the tax is fairly related to services provided by the state.

When the issue also involves taxation of foreign commerce, two additional issues are raised, as they were in the following case.

WARDAIR CANADA, INC. v. FLORIDA DEPT. OF REVENUE
106 S.Ct. 2369 (1986)

FACTS

Florida taxes the sale of fuel to airlines within the state. Prior to 1983, the tax was prorated on mileage within Florida to total worldwide mileage. Florida then imposed a 5-percent tax on all aviation fuel sold within the state to airlines, regardless of whether the fuel was used to fly within or without the state, or whether the airline engaged in a substantial or a nominal amount of business within the state. A Canadian airline that operates charter flights to and from the United States filed suit, attacking the law's validity insofar as it authorized assessment of a tax on fuel used by foreign airlines exclusively in foreign commerce. The Florida Supreme Court held that the Florida tax was not invalid under the foreign commerce clause of the federal Constitution.

ISSUE

Is the Florida law constitutional?

DECISION

Yes.

REASONS

1. Even if the federal government has not specifically disapproved of a state regulation, a state regulation may be invalid under the unexercised commerce clause if it works to the detriment of the nation as a whole and thus ultimately to all of the states.
2. In international relations and with respect to foreign intercourse and trade, the people of the United States act through a single government with unified and adequate national power.
3. The concern in foreign commerce clause cases is not with an actual conflict between state and federal law but with the policy of uniformity.
4. When a state tax is challenged as violative of the dormant interstate commerce clause, courts ask four questions: Is the tax applied to an activity with a substantial nexus with the taxing state? Is the tax fairly apportioned? Does the tax discriminate against interstate commerce? Is the tax fairly related to the services provided by the state?
5. When the state tax allegedly interferes with the federal government's authority to regulate foreign commerce, two additional questions must be asked: Does the tax create a substantial risk of international multiple

taxation? Does the tax prevent the federal government from speaking with one voice when regulating commercial relations with foreign governments?
6. The Florida tax clearly satisfies the four questions, and there is no threat of multiple taxation because the only sale was in Florida.
7. There is no federal policy to prevent such taxation. Rather, the facts presented by this case (70 bilateral agreements that do not mention sales taxes) show that the federal government has affirmatively decided to permit the states to impose these sales taxes on aviation fuel.

The concept of **apportionment** is used to prevent multiple taxation of the same property or income of interstate businesses. Apportionment formulas are used to allocate the tax burden of an interstate business among the states entitled to tax it. The commerce clause requires states to use reasonable formulas when more than one state is taxing the same thing.

The term **nexus** describes the requirement of some sufficient contact, connection, tie, or link to the taxing state to justify the tax. In other words, there must be sufficient local activities to justify the tax in a constitutional sense. A business operating in a state directly benefits from its police and fire protection, use of its roads, and the like. Indirectly, it will be able to recruit employees more easily if they have easy access to good schools, parks, and civic centers. If the state gives anything for which it can reasonably expect payment, then the tax has a sufficient nexus. In cases involving property taxes, the term *taxable situs* is used in place of nexus, but each is concerned with the adequacy of local activities to support the tax.

The concepts of undue burdens against interstate commerce and discrimination against interstate commerce through taxation are the same as these concepts as applied to other forms of regulation. Taxes which differ from those levied on intrastate commerce cannot be levied on interstate commerce. The case which follows is typical of those finding a state tax unconstitutional under the commerce clause.

ARMCO INC. v. HARDESTY
104 S.Ct. 2620 (1984)

FACTS

Armco Inc. is an Ohio corporation qualified to do business in West Virginia. It manufactures and sells steel products. It conducts business in West Virginia through five divisions. Two of these had facilities and employees in the state, while the other three sold various products to customers in the state only through franchisees or nonresident traveling salespeople. West Virginia imposes a gross receipts tax on people engaged in the business of selling tangible property at wholesale. Armco contends that the gross receipts tax could not be imposed on the sales it made through franchisees and nonresident salespeople because local manufacturers were exempt from the tax, even though they paid a separate manufacturing tax.

> **ISSUE**
>
> Does the West Virginia tax violate the commerce clause?
>
> **DECISION**
>
> Yes.
>
> **REASONS**
>
> 1. The commerce clause of its own force protects free trade among the states. One aspect of this protection is that a state "may not discriminate between transactions on the basis of some interstate element." That is, a state may not tax a transaction or incident more heavily when it crosses state lines than when it occurs entirely within the state.
> 2. On its face, the gross receipts tax provides that two companies selling tangible property at wholesale in West Virginia will be treated differently, depending on whether the taxpayer conducts manufacturing in the state or out of it. Thus, if the property were manufactured in the state, no tax on the sale would be imposed. If the property were manufactured out of the state and imported for sale, a tax of 0.27 percent would be imposed on the sale price.
> 3. The gross sales tax imposed on Armco cannot be deemed a compensating tax for the manufacturing tax imposed on its West Virginia competitors. Manufacturing and wholesaling are not substantially equivalent events. The heavy tax on in-state manufacturers cannot be said to compensate for the admittedly lighter burden placed on wholesalers from out of state.

REVIEW QUESTIONS

1. Goldkist had entered into a contract to sell 50 million chickens to Russia. When the Russians invaded Afghanistan, President Carter imposed an embargo on the sale of food to Russia. Did his action violate the contract clause? Explain.
2. A class action suit was filed that charged two real estate trade associations and six named real estate firms with violating the federal antitrust laws. It alleged a conspiracy to fix prices in the purchase and sale of residential real estate by the systematic use of fixed commission rates, widespread fee splitting, and the suppression of market information from buyers and sellers. The defendants contended that the law could not cover their activities, which were local and not in interstate commerce. Does the power of the federal government extend to this local activity? Explain.
3. The federal government enacted a statute requiring all automobiles sold in interstate commerce to be equipped with "air bags" in the front passenger compartment. A state has a statute requiring all motor vehicles sold in the state to be equipped with three sets of seat belts in the front seat. The auto manufacturers indicate that they can comply with both laws, but only at extra expense to the manufacturer. Are both laws enforceable? Explain.
4. A Florida statute prohibits out-of-state banks from owning or controlling a business in Florida that sells investment advisory services. Another statute prohib

its all corporations except state-chartered banks and national banks located in Florida from performing certain trusts and fiduciary functions. An Illinois bank sought to operate an investment management subsidiary in Florida. It challenged the constitutionality of these statutes. What was the result? Why?

5 Illinois enacted a statute which prohibited transporting into the state for purposes of disposal or storage spent nuclear fuel that was used by out-of-state electric utilities. Illinois has the only away-from-site facility in the U.S. that is accepting spent fuel for storage. Is this statute constitutional? Why, or why not?

6 A Maine statute imposed a truck tax. The tax required owners and operators of foreign-based (out-of-state) trucks using Maine highways to purchase either an annual highway-use permit or a one-trip permit. Trucks based in-state were exempt. An out-of-state trucker challenged the constitutionality of the statute. What was the result? Why?

7 A manufacturer of rope, in filing its Ohio personal-property tax return, deducted from the total value of its inventory the value of imported fibers. These were stored in their original packages for future use in the manufacturing process. Are goods exempt from state taxation so long as they remain in the original package? Explain.

8 A federal savings and loan association attempted to foreclose a mortgage under a due-on-sale clause. Enforcing the due-on-sale clause violated California law. The Federal Home Loan Bank board regulations permitted such clauses governing federal savings and loans. Does the Federal Bank board's due-on-sale regulation preempt the state law? Explain.

9 A Virginia statute prohibited nonresidents of Virginia from catching certain fish in the Virginia portion of Chesapeake Bay and obtaining commercial fishing licenses. There was a federal enrollment and licensing law which authorized federal licensing of fishing boats. Is the Virginia law constitutional? Why, or why not?

10 North Carolina imposed an ad valorem tax on imported tobacco held in custom-bonded warehouses prior to domestic manufacture and sale. The tobacco was usually held for two years as part of the aging process. Customs duties were paid the federal government when the tobacco was taken from the warehouse. Does the North Carolina tax violate the import-export clause? Why, or why not?

11 The city of Camden, New Jersey, adopted an ordinance requiring that at least 40 percent of the employees of contractors working on city construction projects be Camden residents. The constitutionality of the ordinance was challenged under the privileges and immunities clause of Article IV of the United States Constitution. The city contended that the clause only applies to state laws and not to local ordinances. Is the city correct? Explain.

12 The Montana statutory elk-hunting-license scheme imposed substantially higher (seven-and-a-half times) license fees on nonresidents of the state than on residents. It also required nonresidents, but not residents, to purchase a "combination" license to be able to obtain any number of elks, even one. Out-of-state hunters challenged the constitutionality of the Montana hunting license law. What was the result? Why?

13 A Rhode Island statute defined debt collection as the practice of law; it limited the activity to licensed attorneys. A nationwide debt-collection corporation challenged the constitutionality of the state statute, pointing out that debt collection includes activities that fall short of court proceedings. Is the state law constitutional? Why, or why not?

14 A private landfill for solid waste in New Jersey was prohibited by court order from accepting waste from Philadelphia, Pennsylvania. The landfill was almost full, but New Jersey communities were allowed to continue its use. Did the court decision violate the commerce clause? Explain.

15 New York's Alcoholic Beverage Control Law required every distiller selling to wholesalers in the state to affirm that they will sell liquor at a price that is no higher than the lowest price they will charge wholesalers anywhere else in the United States during the next month. Is this law constitutional? Why, or why not?

16 Perez was convicted of loan-sharking activities in violation of the Consumer Credit Protection Act. He contended that Congress has no power to control the local activity of lending money, even at illegal rates of interest. Is he correct? Why, or why not?

CHAPTER 6

THE BILL OF RIGHTS AND BUSINESS

OVERVIEW

This chapter discusses the protections of the Bill of Rights as they relate to business. It also covers the Fourteenth Amendment to the United States Constitution. Courts use this amendment to make the provisions of the Bill of Rights applicable to state and local governments. Special attention is given to the protection of commercial speech. As you study the material, keep in mind that even our basic constitutional rights are limited and that they change over time.

The following legal terms are introduced in this chapter: commercial speech, double jeopardy, procedural and substantive due process, equal protection clause, establishment clause, free exercise clause, grand jury, libel, malice, and prior restraint.

1 Introduction

Perhaps no part of the United States Constitution is so well known or held as sacred as the so-called Bill of Rights, the first ten amendments to the Constitution. Most of us are acquainted to some degree with the freedoms of speech, press, religion, and assembly. Usually we do not think of these matters in a business context but more as dealing with personal rights of individuals in a free society. There are, however, very important aspects of these freedoms relating to economic opportunity and business activity.

As the materials dealing with the Bill of Rights are studied, four important aspects should be noted. First, constitutional rights are not absolutes. They are limited to some degree. Justice Hugo Black, dissenting in *Tinker v. Des Moines Independent Community School Dist.*, 89 S.Ct. 733 (1969), noted this fact when he stated:

> The truth is that a teacher of kindergarten, grammar school, or high school pupils no more carries into a school with him a complete right to freedom of speech and expression than an anti-Catholic or anti-Semitic carries with him a complete freedom of speech and religion into a Catholic church or Jewish synagogue. Nor does a person carry with him into the United States Senate or House, or to the Supreme Court, or any other court, a complete constitutional right to go into those places contrary to their rules and speak his mind on any subject he pleases. It is a myth to say that any person has a constitutional right to say what he pleases, where he pleases, and when he pleases.

The same sense of limitation applies to all basic constitutional protections, although certain people (including some Supreme Court justices) from time to time contend to the contrary.

Second, the extent of any limitation on a basic constitutional guarantee depends upon the nature of the competing public policy in a given case. Cases involving the Bill of Rights almost always require courts to strike a balance either between some goal or policy of society and the constitutional protection involved or between competing constitutional guarantees. For example, such cases may involve conflict between the goal of deterring or preventing crime and the rights of the accused, or between freedom of the press and the rights of one on trial. The courts are continually involved in a weighing process to determine the extent of constitutional protections.

Third, constitutional guarantees exist to remove certain issues from the political process and the ballot box. They exist to protect the minority from the majority. Freedom of expression (press and speech) protects the unpopular idea or viewpoint. Freedom of assembly allows groups with ideologies foreign to most of us to meet and express their philosophy. Even the most dangerous criminal is entitled to an attorney and is protected from illegal searches and seizures of evidence. The Bill of Rights protects the "worst" among us even more than it does the "best."

Finally, as previously noted, constitutional rights vary from time to time. The doctrine of constitutional relativity especially applies to the Bill of Rights. Not only do the rights change, they are affected by emergencies such as war or civil strife. Constitutional principles are constantly reapplied and reexamined.

THE FIRST AMENDMENT
2 FREEDOM OF RELIGION

The First Amendment gives us our basic freedoms, commonly known as: (1) freedom of religion, (2) freedom of speech, (3) freedom of the press, (4) freedom of assembly, and (5) the right to petition the government for a redress of grievances. These freedoms are intimately connected with the conduct of business as well as with all other aspects of our daily lives.

Freedom of religion is sometimes referred to as the separation of church and state. The First Amendment provisions on freedom of religion have two aspects or are based on two clauses. The First Amendment bans any law "respecting an establishment of religion" (the **establishment clause**), or prohibiting the free exercise thereof (the **free exercise clause**). Cases involving school prayer and tax aid to parochial schools are examples of cases arising under the establishment clause. Cases under this clause usually involve aid to religious organizations or the intrusion of religion into government activities.

Most business-related freedom-of-religion cases involve the free exercise clause. Religious principles are cited in attempts to prevent the application of a state law or regulation to religious organizations; thus, religion is often asserted as the basis for an exemption to a law. In such cases, courts are called upon to weigh the free exercise of religion against a compelling state interest. A burden upon religion exists where the state conditions receipt of an important benefit upon conduct proscribed by a religious belief, or where it denies such a benefit because of conduct mandated by religious belief, thereby putting substantial pressure on an adherent to modify his or her behavior and to violate his or her beliefs. The state may justify an inroad on religious liberty by showing that it is the least restrictive means of achieving a compelling state interest. However, only those interests of the highest order can overbalance legitimate claims to the free exercise of religion. For example, a Jehovah's Witness could not be denied unemployment compensation when he quit his factory job because it started making turrets for army tanks. His religious beliefs were a good cause for quitting. In the case which follows, notice that the person asserting religious beliefs acquired these beliefs after being employed.

HOBBIE v. UNEMPLOYMENT APPEALS COM'N OF FLORIDA
107 S.Ct. 1046 (1987)

FACTS

After working over two years, Hobbie informed her employer that she was joining the Seventh-Day Adventist Church and that, for religious reasons, she would no longer be able to work at the employer's jewelry store on her Sabbath. When she refused to work scheduled shifts on Friday evenings and Saturdays, she was discharged. She then filed a claim for unemployment compensation, which was denied for "misconduct connected with [her] work" under the applicable Florida statute.

ISSUE

Does Florida's refusal to award unemployment compensation benefits violate the free exercise clause of the First Amendment?

DECISION

Yes.

REASONS

1. When a state denies receipt of a benefit because of conduct mandated by religious belief, thereby putting substantial pressure on an adherent to modify her behavior and violate her beliefs, that denial must be subjected to strict scrutiny. It can be justified only by proof of a compelling state interest.
2. The denial of benefits cannot be upheld, on the ground that the conflict between work and religious belief was not caused by the employer's alteration of the conditions of employment after appellant was hired. It was caused, instead, by appellant's conversion during the course of her employment.

Freedom of religion has been used to challenge legislation requiring the closing of business establishments on Sunday. Although the motive for such legislation may be, in part, religious, there are also economic reasons for such legislation. As a result, if law is based on economic considerations, it may be upheld if its classifications are reasonable and in the public interest. However, many such laws have been held invalid as a violation of the First Amendment.

There are other examples of freedom-of-religion cases that concern business. Some of them are summarized in Table 6-1.

TABLE 6-1 EXAMPLES OF FREEDOM-OF-RELIGION ISSUES AFFECTING BUSINESS

		Yes	No
1	Is it constitutional to apply the Fair Labor Standards Act (minimum-wage law) to a nonprofit religious organization?	X	
2	Is it constitutional to apply the labor laws relating to union elections to parochial school teachers?		X
3	Is a state law constitutional which provides Sabbath observers with an absolute and unqualified right not to work on their Sabbath?		X
4	Is religious belief justification for refusing to participate in the Social Security system?		X
5	Does the 1964 Civil Rights Act, which obligates employers to make reasonable accommodations of employees' religious beliefs, violate the First Amendment's establishment clause?		X
6	A provision of the Civil Rights Act exempts religious organizations from the provisions against discrimination based on religion; does it cover secular, nonprofit activities as well as religious ones?	X	

3 FREEDOM OF THE PRESS

The publishing business is the only organized private business given explicit constitutional protection. Freedom of the press as guaranteed by the First Amendment authorizes a private business to provide organized scrutiny of government.

Freedom of the press means more than just the right to print and to publish. It essentially means that this right must exist without governmental interference. Interference may take many forms, including taxation, as the case which follows illustrates.

ARKANSAS WRITERS' PROJECT, INC. v. RAGLAND
107 S.Ct. 1722 (1987)

FACTS

The Arkansas sales tax covers general-interest magazines, but the law exempts newspapers and certain magazines that qualify as "religious, professional, trade and sports journals." A publisher of a general-interest magazine filed for a sales tax refund, contending that the law was a violation of the First Amendment's freedom-of-the-press protection.

ISSUE

Is the sales tax constitutional?

DECISION

No.

REASONS

1. Even though there is no evidence of an improper censorial motive, the Arkansas tax burdens rights protected by the First Amendment. It discriminates against a small group of magazines, including plaintiff's, which are the only magazines that pay the tax.
2. The law requires official scrutiny of publications' content as the basis for imposing a tax. This is incompatible with the First Amendment. The amendment's requirements are not avoided merely because the statute does not burden the expression of particular views expressed by specific magazines. The law also exempts other members of the media who might publish discussions of the various subjects contained in appellant's magazine.
3. The state has not satisfied its heavy burden; it has not shown that its discriminatory tax scheme is necessary to serve a compelling state interest and is narrowly drawn to achieve that end. The state's general interest in raising revenue does not justify selective imposition of the sales tax on some magazines and not others, based solely on their content. Revenues could be raised simply by taxing businesses generally.

Freedom of the press is not absolute. The press is not free to print anything it wants without liability. Rather, freedom of the press is usually construed to prohibit **prior restraints** on publications. If the press publishes that which is illegal or libelous, it has liability for doing so. This liability for damages may be either criminal or civil.

There are many examples of limitations on freedom of the press. For example, courts have allowed the Federal Communications Commission to censor "filthy" words on television. The power of the Commission extends to upholding the public's interest in responsible broadcasting. Freedom of the press does not create an absolute right to know and a concomitant governmental duty to disclose. Thus, the press may not always have access to government records in the absence of a statute such as the Freedom of Information Act.

Do members of the media have rights greater than other citizens? The press frequently asserts that it does. For example, members of the press frequently assert the existence of privileged communications between themselves and informants. They contend that there is a constitutional right to protect the confidential identity of sources of information. The courts have held that no such privileged communication exists. The Constitution does not create such a privileged communication. Unless a statute creates a "shield" for reporters, none exists. There is no federal "shield" law, but some states have enacted them. Even where a statute creates such a privilege, the rights of the press must be balanced with the rights of others, and the shield law may or may not protect reporters who wish to keep their sources confidential.

A major area of litigation involving freedom of the press is defamation. The tort theory known as **libel** is used to recover damages as a result of printed defamation of character. Libel cases compensate individuals for harm inflicted by defamatory printed falsehoods. Since the threat of a libel suit could have a chilling effect on freedom of the press and on the public's rights to information, the law has a different standard for imposing liability when the printed matter concerns an issue of public interest and concern. In such cases, if the person involved is a public official or public figure, a plaintiff seeking damages must prove actual **malice** in order to recover. "Actual malice" includes knowledge that the printed statements were false or circumstances showing a reckless disregard for whether they were true or not. If the plaintiff is not a public figure or public official, there is liability for libelous statements without a proof of malice.

The gist of a libel suit is a false statement. At common law, there was a presumption that a defamatory statement was false. This presumption has been changed in most states. Even if it has not been changed, the Supreme Court has held that a plaintiff who is a public figure must always prove falsity of the media's statements. Also, a plaintiff who is a private figure must prove falsity if the subject matter of the statement is of public concern. When the statement is of public concern, the constitutional protections of free speech and free press supplant the common-law presumption.

4 FREEDOM OF SPEECH

Freedom of speech is sometimes referred to as freedom of expression. This freedom covers both verbal and written communications. In addition, it covers conduct or actions considered symbolic speech. Although freedom of speech is not absolute, it is as close to being absolute as any constitutional guarantee. It exists to protect the minority from the majority. It means freedom to express ideas antagonistic to those of the majority. Freedom of speech exists for thoughts many of us hate and for ideas that may be foreign to us. It means freedom to express the unorthodox, and it recognizes that there is no such thing as a false idea.

Freedom of speech protects corporations as well as individuals. The public interests served by freedom of expression protect the listener as well as the speaker. Freedom of expression includes freedom of information or the rights of the public to be informed. Since corporations may add to the public's knowledge and information, they also have the right to free speech. Although it may not be coextensive with the right of an individual, it may not be limited without a compelling state interest in doing so. State regulatory commissions often seek to limit the activities of public utilities. Such attempts may run afoul of the First Amendment, as occurred in the following case.

CONSOL. EDISON v. PUBLIC SERVICE COM'N.
100 S.Ct. 2326 (1980)

FACTS

The Consolidated Edison Company of New York placed written material entitled "Independence Is Still a Goal, and Nuclear Power Is Needed To Win the Battle" in its billing envelopes. The bill inserts stated that the benefits of nuclear power far outweighed any potential risk, and that nuclear power plants are safe, economical, and clean. The Public Service Commission of New York issued an order prohibiting utilities from using bill inserts to discuss political matters, including the desirability of future development of nuclear power.

ISSUE

Is the order a violation of the First Amendment?

DECISION

Yes.

REASONS

1. A restriction that regulates only the time, place, or manner of speech may be imposed so long as it is reasonable. But when regulation is based on the content of speech, governmental action must be scrutinized more carefully to ensure that communication has not been prohibited merely because public officials disapprove of the speaker's view.

> 2. Here the speech of Consolidated Edison does not invade substantial privacy interests in an unacceptable manner. The customer of Consolidated Edison may escape exposure to objectionable material simply by transferring the bill insert from envelope to wastebasket.

The issue of freedom of speech arises in many business situations. For example, cases involving picketing, especially with unions, often are concerned with this issue. The right to picket peacefully for a lawful purpose is well-recognized. A state or local law that prohibits all picketing would be unconstitutional since picketing per se is a valuable form of communication. However, a state law that limits picketing or other First Amendment freedoms may be constitutional if: (1) the regulation is within the constitutional power of government, (2) it furthers an important or substantial governmental interest, (3) it is unrelated to suppression of free expression, and (4) the incidental restriction on First Amendment freedoms is no greater than is essential to further the government's interest. Under these principles, laws that prevent pickets from obstructing traffic and those designed to prevent violence would be constitutional. For example, a Texas statute that prohibits "mass picketing," defined as picketing by more than two persons within 50 feet of any entrance or of one another, does not violate the First Amendment. Courts may limit the number of pickets to preserve order and promote safety, but they will not deny pickets the right to express opinions in a picket line. For example, a court order preventing a client from picketing her lawyer was held to be a violation of the First Amendment. Freedom of speech even extends to boycotts of a business for a valid public purpose such as the elimination of discrimination.

Freedom of expression does not protect obscene materials. In the case of pornography involving children, the material is not protected by the First Amendment, even if it is not legally obscene. The community's interest in banning such material outweighs any First Amendment interests. People who sell obscene materials or child pornography are frequently prosecuted for doing so. The difficult issues in obscenity cases are defining obscenity and determining whether or not items involved are obscene.

A movie, book, or magazine is obscene and subject to state regulation if it violates a three-part test: (1) if it, taken as a whole, appeals to a prurient interest in sex; (2) if it portrays, in a patently offensive way, sexual conduct specifically defined by the applicable state law; and (3) if it, taken as a whole, does not have serious literary, artistic, political, or scientific value. In deciding whether allegedly obscene work has "literary, artistic, political, or scientific value," a court must determine not whether an ordinary member of any given community would find serious literary, artistic, political, or scientific value in a work, but whether a reasonable person would find such value in the material taken as whole. The mere fact that a minority of a population believes that a work has serious value does not mean that the "reasonable person" would not find that a work has such value, for purpose of obscenity prosecution. At one time, if a work had any redeeming social value or if it were of social importance, it was not obscene. This test of obscenity has been rejected.

Obscenity cases based on past conduct are much less difficult than those involving a prior restraint. Although freedom of speech does not protect obscenity, it does prevent most attempts to censor speech in advance. Prior restraints, while not illegal per se, must have safeguards to protect First Amendment rights. Courts will seldom enjoin obscenity and will leave law enforcement to deal with actual violations.

In some free-speech cases, an individual whose own speech or conduct may be prohibited is nevertheless permitted to challenge a statute limiting speech because it also threatens other people not before the court. The person is allowed to challenge the statute because others who may desire to engage in legally protected expression may refrain from doing so. They may fear the risk of prosecution, or they may not want to risk having a law declared to be only partially invalid. This is known as the *overbreadth doctrine*. It means that the legislators have gone too far in seeking to achieve a goal.

5 COMMERCIAL SPEECH

Historically, **commercial speech** was not protected by the First Amendment. However, in the 1970s the Supreme Court began to recognize that free commercial speech is essential to the public's right to know. Several cases have established that commercial speech is protected.

VA. ST. BD. OF PHARM. v. VA. CIT. CONS. COUNCIL
96 S.Ct. 1817 (1976)

FACTS

The consumers of prescription drugs brought suit against the Virginia State Board of Pharmacy and its individual members. They challenged under the First Amendment a Virginia statute which declared that it was unprofessional conduct for a licensed pharmacist to advertise the prices of prescription drugs. The defendant contended that advertising was not protected by the First Amendment and that it was in the public interest to prevent such advertising.

ISSUE

Is commercial speech protected by the First Amendment?

DECISION

Yes.

> **REASONS**
> 1. Any First Amendment protection enjoyed by advertisers is also enjoyed, and thus may be asserted, by the recipients of such information. "Commercial speech" is not wholly outside the protection of the First and Fourteenth Amendments.
> 2. The fact that the advertiser's interest is purely economic does not disqualify him from the protection under the First Amendment. Society has a strong interest in the free flow of commercial information, particularly where prescription drugs are concerned.
> 3. This interest must be balanced against the state's interest in maintaining a high degree of professionalism on the part of licensed pharmacists. Here, the First Amendment interest outweighs the state interest.

Commercial speech is not protected to the same extent as noncommercial speech. In a case involving a billboard ordinance which banned all billboards, the Supreme Court held the law unconstitutional because it banned noncommercial billboards. The court stated that the Constitution accords a lesser protection to commercial speech than to other forms of speech. Commercial speech is protected only if it concerns a lawful activity and is not misleading. A restriction on commercial speech is valid if it seeks to implement a substantial governmental interest, directly advances that interest, and reaches no farther than necessary to accomplish the objective. For example, a state may restrict some advertising that is designed to promote products that, though legal, are considered undesirable by the legislature. Such limitations might cover prostitution, gambling, alcohol, smoking, or chewing tobacco. It is up to the states to decide how best to regulate legal but potentially harmful businesses.

In commercial speech cases, the courts are involved in the weighing process previously noted. "For sale" signs cannot be banned in residential areas, but "adult entertainment" businesses may be restricted to certain areas. Universities may ban sales by outsiders in residence halls, but all live entertainment may not be banned from a community. Many commercial speech cases involve attempts by government to regulate morality. These attempts often fail in the weighing process because of the overwhelming importance of freedom of speech, but some are successful, as previously noted.

6 OTHER FIRST AMENDMENT FREEDOMS

First Amendment freedoms also include the right to assemble and associate, and the right to petition the government for a redress of grievances. In addition, the specifics of the Bill of Rights have additional implied rights, such as the right of privacy, the right to knowledge, and the right to one's beliefs. These rights were derived from the others actually specified. For example, the right of freedom of speech and press has been held to include not only the right to utter or to print but the right to distribute, the right to receive, and the right to read. Freedom of expression includes freedom of inquiry, freedom of thought, and freedom to teach. Moreover, the right of association is more than the right to attend a meeting. It includes the right to express an attitude or philosophy by group membership. It also includes the right *not* to join a group. For example, lack of political party affiliation may not be a ground for discharging certain employees.

BRANTI v. FINKEL
100 S.Ct. 1287 (1980)

FACTS

After the control of the county legislature had shifted to the Democratic Party, the newly appointed county public defender, a Democrat, notified the assistant public defenders, both Republicans, that their employment was to be terminated. The discharged public defenders brought this civil rights action based on the allegation that they were discharged solely because they were Republicans. The trial court found the allegations to be true.

ISSUE

Do the First and Fourteenth Amendments protect those who are satisfactorily performing their jobs from discharge solely because of their political beliefs and party affiliation?

DECISION

Yes.

REASONS

1. If the First Amendment protects a public employee from discharge based on what he has said, it must also protect him from discharge based on what he believes. Unless the government can demonstrate an overriding interest of vital importance requiring that a person's private beliefs conform to those of the hiring authority, his beliefs cannot be the sole basis for depriving him of continued public employment.
2. If an employee's private political beliefs would interfere with the discharge of his public duties, his First Amendment rights may be required to yield to the state's vital interest in maintaining governmental effectiveness and efficiency.
3. Party affiliation is not necessarily relevant to every policy-making or confidential position. The hiring authority must demonstrate that party affiliation is an appropriate requirement for the effective performance of the public office involved.
4. The continued employment of an assistant public defender cannot be properly conditioned upon his allegiance to the political party in control of the county government. The primary, if not the only, responsibility of an assistant public defender is to represent individual citizens in controversy with the state.

The freedom of assembly and association protection is relevant to many cases involving unpopular groups such as Nazis and Communists. For example, some cases concern the issuance of passports to Communists, and others involve laws prohibiting Communists from holding certain positions, such as officers in labor unions or jobs in defense plants. Such laws have been held as unconstitutional as a result of the First Amendment. On the other hand, the First Amendment has been held not to prevent laws designed to change the conduct of traditional mainstream groups such as the International Rotary or the United States Jaycees. The Constitution is no bar to state laws requiring that these organizations admit women to membership. While such organizations and their members have a First Amendment right of expressive association, there is not evidence to suggest that admitting women will affect in any significant way the existing members' ability to carry out their various purposes. Thus, it can be seen that the Constitution is designed to protect minorities more than the majority.

The guarantee of freedom of assembly and association prevents guilt by association. It also ensures privacy in one's association. For example, it has been held that state law may not compel the disclosure of membership lists of a constitutionally valid association. Such a disclosure implies likelihood of a substantial restraint upon the member's right to freedom of association. Protection also extends to forms of association that are not political, such as the social, legal, and economic benefits of membership in groups. For example, the First Amendment right to associate and to assemble prevents a state from denying a license to practice law to a Communist. It also prevents a state from denying a group such as the South African rugby team the right to play a match in the United States.

The right to assemble extends to all people irrespective of their race or ideology. The right of "association," like the right of belief, includes the right to express one's attitudes or philosophies by membership in a group, or by affiliation with it, or by other lawful means. Association is a form of expression of opinion. However, keep in mind that the right to associate and to express collective opinions does not mean that government or anyone else must follow those opinions.

OTHER AMENDMENTS

7 THE FOURTH AMENDMENT

The Fourth Amendment protects individuals and corporations from unreasonable searches and seizures. It primarily protects persons from unwarranted intrusions into their individual privacy.

Fourth Amendment issues usually arise in criminal cases. Among typical issues are: (1) the validity of searches incident to an arrest, (2) the validity of search warrants—the presence of probable cause to issue the warrant, (3) the validity of consents to searches, and (4) the extent to which property such as automobiles may be searched without a warrant. In addition, electronic surveilance often raises Fourth Amendment issues. For example, the Omnibus Crime Control and Safe Streets Act authorizes the electronic interception of communications pursuant to a court-authorized order. A "bug" was placed in a building by covert entry. The Supreme Court held that such surveillance does not violate the Fourth Amendment.

In recent years, the protection of the Fourth Amendment often has been narrowed by court decisions. To protect police officers, it has been held that they may search someone being arrested and the immediate area around him or her for weapons. Officers searching an automobile are given far more latitude than when searching a person, a home, or a building. Persons lawfully arrested may be convicted of other crimes with evidence obtained as the result of valid searches which are an incident of a lawful arrest. The right to search for evidence extends to the premises of persons not suspected of criminal conduct. Such premises may include offices of operating newspapers and attorneys. In addition, one who does not own a vehicle may not object to its search even if the person has property physically present in the vehicle. In 1987, the court continued to narrow the protection of the Fourth Amendment. It held that public employers may search a government worker's office without a search warrant if they have reason to suspect wrongdoing. Only a reasonable suspicion of wrongdoing is required, not probable cause. Government employees do have some expectation of privacy, and this issue will be litigated further as government attempts to deal with problems such as drug abuse and AIDS.

Fourth Amendment protection extends to civil matters as well as to criminal cases. For example, in a case involving the right of a counselor to visit the home of a welfare recipient, it was held that such home visits did not violate the Fourth Amendment. In another case, it was held that building inspectors do not have the right to inspect for building code violations without a warrant, if the owner of the premises objects. The Fourth Amendment has been used to prevent the Securities and Exchange Commission (SEC) from using confidential reports obtained in the course of its function to establish a violation of federal law. The reports cannot be required for one purpose and then used for another without running afoul of the Fourth Amendment.

Legislative bodies frequently provide for inspections of businesses without a search warrant. For example, the Occupational Safety and Health Act (OSHA) authorizes agents of the secretary of labor to conduct unannounced searches of the work area of any employment facility to inspect for safety hazards and violations of OSHA regulations. The Supreme Court in 1978 held this federal law to be unconstitutional under the Fourth Amendment. If an owner of a business objects to an inspection, inspectors must go to court and obtain a search warrant. Probable cause is not required for a warrant, only a showing that the standards for conducting an inspection are satisfied.

In 1987, the Supreme Court reviewed a state law that authorizes warrantless searches of junkyards. A divided court (5 to 4) in the case which follows said that warrantless searches of junkyards are constitutional.

> **NEW YORK v. BURGER**
> 107 S.Ct. 2636 (1987)
>
> **FACTS**
>
> Burger's junkyard business consists of dismantling automobiles and selling their parts. A New York statute authorized warrantless inspections of automobile junkyards. Police officers entered his junkyard and asked to see his license and records as to automobiles and vehicle parts in his possession. He replied that he did not have such documents, which are required by the statute. After announcing their intention to conduct an inspection of the junkyard pursuant to the statute, the officers, without objection by respondent, conducted the inspection and discovered stolen vehicles and parts. Burger, who was charged with possession of stolen property, moved to suppress the evidence obtained as a result of the inspection. He contended that the administrative inspection statute is unconstitutional when it authorizes warrantless searches.
>
> **ISSUE**
>
> Is this warrantless search a violation of the Fourth Amendment?
>
> **DECISION**
>
> No.
>
> **REASONS**
>
> 1. A business owner's expectation of privacy in commercial property is reduced with respect to commercial property employed in a "closely regulated" industry.
> 2. Where the owner's privacy interests are weakened and the government's interests in regulating particular businesses are heightened, a warrantless inspection of commercial premises, if it meets certain criteria, is reasonable within the meaning of the Fourth Amendment.
> 3. Junkyards are a closely regulated industry, and the state has a substantial interest in regulating it because of automobile theft. Warrantless searches are necessary to further the regulatory scheme. Owners are aware that regular inspections will be made.

8 THE FIFTH AMENDMENT

The Fifth Amendment is best known for its protection against compulsory self-incrimination. People frequently plead "the Fifth," and almost everyone knows they are exercising their right to its protection. The Fifth Amendment goes much further, however. It contains other protections, and, more specifically, it: (1) requires indictment by a **grand jury** for a capital offense or infamous crime, (2) prohibits **double jeopardy**, (3) requires just compensation in eminent domain proceedings, and (4) contains a due process clause.

A grand jury must decide whether there is sufficient evidence of guilt to justify the accused's standing trial. Grand juries are usually made up of twenty-three persons, and it takes a majority vote to indict a defendant. It takes less proof to indict a person and to require him or her to stand trial than it does to convict. The grand jury provision contains an exception for court-martial proceedings.

Proper functioning of the grand jury system depends upon secrecy of the proceedings. This secrecy protects the innocent accused from disclosure of the accusations made against him or her before the grand jury. However, transcripts of grand jury proceedings may be obtained if necessary to avoid possible injustice in judicial proceedings. For example, a litigant may use a grand jury transcript at a trial to impeach a witness, to refresh the witness's recollection, to test his or her credibility, and the like. The disclosure of a grand jury transcript is appropriate only in those cases where the need for it outweighs the public interest in secrecy, and the burden of demonstrating this balance rests upon a private party seeking disclosure.

Protection against double jeopardy means that a person cannot be tried twice by the same governmental body for the same offense. The double jeopardy clause protects corporations as well as individuals.

"Eminent domain" is used by governmental bodies to acquire real property for public purposes. The Fifth Amendment requires just compensation. This is a question of fact for a jury if the property owner and the condemning governmental unit cannot agree on a fair market value of the property taken.

In 1987, the Supreme Court gave new vigor to the rights of property owners. For several decades, the courts had approved land-use regulations and held that they did not constitute a taking which required just compensation. In two cases that year, the court retreated from this proposition. In the first case, it held that any temporary taking of property required just compensation. If the state occupies your property, even for a short period, it must pay rental. The case involved a church summer camp whose buildings were destroyed by a flood. The state restricted all use of the land because it was in a flood plain. A state court lifted the restriction but denied compensation to the owners for the loss of use prior to the decision. The Supreme Court said that the state had to pay for the time the restriction was in effect. According to the Fifth Amendment, any governmental action that even temporarily denies a landowner use of land is a taking. The fact that it lessens government flexibility in land-use regulation is immaterial.

The second case involved access to public beaches. A landowner sought a building permit. The state conditioned granting it on the owners granting an easement to the public to pass across their beach. This condition was held by the Supreme Court to be a taking and unconstitutional without just compensation. If state and local governments attach conditions to building permits that are unrelated to the purpose of the development or to problems created by them, the result is a taking for which the government must compensate the landowners. The issuance of building permits cannot be used for other goals. It should be recognized that the government's power to forbid a particular land use includes the power to condition such use on some concession by the owner; however, the condition must further the same governmental purpose advanced as justification for prohibiting the use.

The Fifth Amendment protects life, liberty, and property from deprivation by the federal government without due process of law. The Fourteenth Amendment contains an identical provision which applies to the states. Although due process is difficult to define, it basically amounts to "fundamental fairness." Since interpretations of the due process clauses of the Fifth and Fourteenth Amendments are, for all practical purposes, identical, the discussion of due process later in this chapter under the Fourteenth Amendment and the cases included there also illustrate due process under the Fifth Amendment.

Protection against compulsory self-incrimination is subject to several limitations. It does not apply to corporations. Although corporations are citizens for most purposes, they are not citizens for this purpose. However, corporate officials retain their personal privilege against compulsory self-incrimination. As a result, corporate officials cannot be required to testify, but they may be required to deliver all corporate records since they are not privileged.

The privilege against compulsory self-incrimination is to protect individuals against compelled self-incrimination. It does not protect against voluntary acts such as the preparation of records in the ordinary course of business. Since the production of records does not compel oral testimony, the Fifth Amendment does not prevent the use of evidence including documents in the hands of an accused or in the hands of someone else such as an accountant. All that is protected is extortion of information from the accused. However, as the case which follows shows, the act of producing the document may be privileged. If the act of producing a business document has testimonial aspects which may have an incriminating effect, the Fifth Amendment protection may be asserted.

UNITED STATES v. DOE
104 S.Ct. 1237 (1984)

FACTS

Doe is the owner of several sole proprietorships. A grand jury, during the course of an investigation of corruption in the awarding of county and municipal contracts, served five subpoenas on respondent. They sought his business records, including telephone calls, bank accounts, and checks.

ISSUE

To what extent does the Fifth Amendment privilege against compelled self-incrimination apply to the business records of a sole proprietorship?

DECISION

The records are not privileged, but their production is.

REASONS

1. An individual may not assert the Fifth Amendment privilege on behalf of a corporation, partnership, or other collective entity.
2. Where the preparation of business records is voluntary, no compulsion is present. A subpoena that demands production of documents does not compel oral testimony; nor would it ordinarily compel the taxpayer to restate, repeat, or affirm the truth of the contents of the documents sought. The contents are not privileged.
3. Although the contents of a document may not be privileged, the act of producing the document may be. A government subpoena compels the holder of the document to perform an act that may have testimonial aspects and an incriminating effect. Compliance with the subpoena tacitly concedes the existence of the papers demanded and their possession or control by the taxpayer. It also would indicate the taxpayer's belief that the papers are those described in the subpoena.

9   THE SIXTH AMENDMENT

The Sixth Amendment, like the Fifth, provides multiple protection in criminal cases. Essentially, its protections give one the right: (1) to a speedy and public trial, (2) to a trial by jury, (3) to be informed of the charge against him or her, (4) to confront one's accuser, (5) to subpoena witnesses in one's favor, and (6) to have the assistance of an attorney.

The American concept of a jury trial contemplates a jury drawn from a fair cross-section of the community. The jury guards against the exercise of arbitrary power by using the commonsense judgment of the community as a hedge against the overzealous or mistaken prosecutor. The jury's perspective of facts is used in preference to the professional or perhaps overconditioned or biased response of a judge.

Community participation in administering criminal law is not only consistent with our democratic heritage, it is also critical to public confidence in the fairness of the criminal justice system. Therefore, a state may not restrict jury service only to special groups or exclude identifiable segments playing major roles in the community. For example, a Missouri law which excluded females who requested an automatic exemption from jury duty was unconstitutional; it violated the cross-section concept. Likewise, minorities may not be systematically excluded from jury duty.

The right to a trial by jury does not require twelve-person juries nor does it require unanimous verdicts. However, if the jury is less than twelve, the verdict must be unanimous. A person may not be convicted by a nonunanimous six-person jury.

The right to a jury trial does not extend to state juvenile court delinquency proceedings because they are not criminal prosecutions. However, juveniles do have the right to counsel, to confront the witnesses against them, and to cross-examine them.

The right to an attorney exists in any cases where incarceration is a possible punishment. It exists at every stage of the proceeding, commencing with an investigation that centers on a person as the accused. Thus, it can be seen that there are many technical aspects to the Sixth Amendment, and numerous cases still arise concerning it.

10 THE SEVENTH AMENDMENT

The Seventh Amendment guarantees the right to a trial by jury in suits at common law where the amount in controversy exceeds $20. (This amount obviously has not been changed to keep up with inflation.) There is no right to a trial by jury in suits in equity or chancery. Likewise, there is no right to a trial by jury when the proceedings did not exist at common law but where they have been created by legislation. For example, in suits against the United States where Congress has waived governmental immunity, there is no right to a trial by jury unless the statute waiving the immunity specifically grants it. This concept was recently reaffirmed in a suit by a government employee alleging age discrimination. There is a right to trial by jury in age discrimination cases against private employers, but no such right exists in cases against the government because the Seventh Amendment does not apply in suits against the government.

There is also no right to a jury trial in cases brought before administrative agencies. These agencies did not exist at common law. The Seventh Amendment does not prohibit Congress from assigning the fact-finding function and initial judicial decision to an administrative forum. The jury would be incompatible with this. Fact finding was never the exclusive province of the jury. The Seventh Amendment does not make the jury the exclusive mechanism for fact finding. Much of it is done by administrative agencies such as the National Labor Relations Board, the Equal Employment Opportunity Commission, and the Occupational Health and Safety Administration.

THE FOURTEENTH AMENDMENT

11 INTRODUCTION

Section 1 of the Fourteenth Amendment contains four provisions. First, it establishes that all people born or naturalized in the United States are citizens of both the United States and of the state in which they reside. This provision was designed to establish state citizenship as well as United States citizenship for the slaves freed by the Emancipation Proclamation and by the Thirteenth Amendment.

To further establish rights of all citizens including freed slaves, the Fourteenth Amendment contains three clauses commonly referred to as: (1) the privileges and immunities clause, (2) the due process clause, and (3) the equal protection clause. The exact language is as follows:

> No State shall make or enforce any law which shall abridge the privileges or immunities of citizens of the United States; nor shall any State deprive any person of life, liberty or property, without due process of law, nor deny to any person within its jurisdiction the equal protection of the laws.

While all three clauses play a significant role in constitutional law, the due process clause and the equal protection clause have been involved in more significant litigation than has the privileges and immunities clause. The due process clause has played a unique role in constitutional development—one that was probably not anticipated at the time of its ratification. This significant role has been to make most of the provisions of the Bill of Rights applicable to the states. The first phrase of Article I of the Bill of Rights commences: "*Congress* shall make no law...." How then are state and local governments prohibited from making such a law? Some jurists have argued that the due process clause of the Fourteenth Amendment "incorporates" or "carries over" the Bill of Rights and makes its provisions applicable to the states. Starting in 1925, a majority of the Supreme Court started applying various portions of the first eight amendments to the states using the due process clause of the Fourteenth Amendment as the vehicle establishing applicability.

Some justices have argued that all the provisions of the Bill of Rights are incorporated, while others have strongly rejected the incorporation theory. In 1937, Justice Benjamin Cardozo contended that those basic human rights "implicit in the concept of ordered liberty" were incorporated by the due process clause, but all other rights were not. In the latter group at this time were such protections as the Fifth Amendment's safeguard against double jeopardy. As time went by, piecemeal incorporation or absorption of the Bill of Rights continued. For example, the doctrine of separation of church and state was picked up in 1947; the requirement of public trials in 1948; the Fourth Amendment protection against unreasonable searches and seizures in 1961; the Eighth Amendment's guarantee against cruel and unusual punishment in 1962; the Sixth Amendment's right to counsel in 1963; and the Fifth Amendment's safeguard against compulsory self-incrimination in 1964. Although justices used different theories and argued about the wisdom of allowing federal courts to use the due process clause to invalidate any state legislative act which they found offensive, the steady march of incorporation continued in the 1960s and 1970s. Cases have held that the Fourteenth Amendment incorporated the right to trial by an impartial jury, the right to a speedy trial, and the protection against double jeopardy. Only a few provisions of the first ten amendments, such as a grand jury indictment, a jury trial in civil cases, and excessive bail, are not yet picked up or incorporated by the due process clause.

The following sections discuss the other aspects of due process and the meaning of the equal protection clause.

12 DUE PROCESS OF LAW

The term "due process of law," which is probably involved in more litigation than any other constitutional phrase, cannot be narrowly defined. The term describes fundamental principles of liberty and justice. Simply stated, due process means "fundamental fairness and decency." It means that *government* may not act in a manner that is arbitrary, capricious, or unreasonable. The clause does not prevent private individuals or corporations, including public utilities, from acting in an arbitrary or unreasonable manner. The due process clause only applies to state action.

The issues in due process cases are usually divided into questions of **procedural due process** and **substantive due process**. Substantive due process issues arise when property or other rights are directly affected by governmental action. Procedural due process cases often are concerned with whether proper notice has been given and a proper hearing has been conducted. Such cases frequently involve procedures established by state statute. However, many cases involve procedures which are not created by statute. For example, the due process clause has been used to challenge the procedure used in the dismissal of a student from a university medical school.

Due process issues have been discussed previously in other chapters. For example, the validity of long-arm statutes and the minimum contact required is a due process issue. The clause is invoked any time procedures are questioned. The case which follows typifies those challenging state procedures as a denial of due process of law.

DIXON v. LOVE
97 S.Ct. 1723 (1977)

FACTS

Love, a truck driver, had his Illinois driver's license revoked after he was convicted of three traffic offenses within twelve months. The revocation was based on administrative regulations which did not require a hearing prior to revocation. But they did make a hearing available after revocation. Love challenged this as a denial of due process, and the lower court upheld the challenge.

ISSUE

Has Illinois provided constitutionally adequate procedures for suspending or revoking the license of a driver repeatedly convicted for traffic offenses?

DECISION

Yes.

REASONS

1. Although the due process clause applies to the deprivation of a driver's license by the state, the analysis must balance several factors: (a) the private interest that will be affected; (b) the risk of an erroneous deprivation of such interest through the procedures used, and probable value, if any, of additional or substitute procedural safeguards; and (c) the government's interest, both in the function itself and the burdens of additional procedural safeguards.
2. In this case, a driver's license is probably not a vital or essential interest. Moreover, the Illinois statute makes special provision for hardship cases. The risk of an erroneous deprivation is slight, since revocations are largely automatic.
3. Finally, public interest demands the swift removal of safety hazards from the highways. Procedural due process in the administrative setting does not require application of the judicial model.

During the early part of this century, the due process clauses of the Fifth and the Fourteenth Amendments were used by the Supreme Court to guard the sanctity of private property. Legislative attempts to regulate the economy by laws such as those imposing minimum wages or maximum hours for women and children were held to be unconstitutional, a denial of "substantive due process of law." During this period, if the substance of a law deprived persons of property, the law usually would be declared unconstitutional by the courts as a denial of "due process." If a federal law were under attack, the Fifth Amendment was cited as the ground; and if a state law were involved, the protection of the Fourteenth was invoked.

After the mid-1930s and President Roosevelt's attempt to pack the Supreme Court, the judicial attitude toward the application of the due process clause to economic legislation changed dramatically. The Supreme Court refused to find such legislation unconstitutional on the ground of infringement of substantive due process, and substantive due process as a bar to economic legislation tended to pass into oblivion.

After the 1930s, the due process clause was most frequently invoked in cases involving individual liberties and civil rights. In the latter area, it was used by courts in seeking a balance between the basic civil rights of individuals and the interests of society as a whole. These cases frequently dealt with *procedural* issues rather than with *substantive* issues. Many of the noneconomic issues were raised in criminal cases, while others concerned state action that affected such basic rights as freedom of speech, press, and religion.

Since the change of attitude by at least a majority of the court toward the due process clause, there is in effect a double standard in the application of the clause. Legislation in the economic sector is presumed to be constitutional, and few challenges on the due process ground can expect to be successful. On the other hand, when basic human freedoms are involved, the courts regard any legislation tending to curb or limit them to be suspect. As a result, courts do not hesitate to declare legislation dealing with fundamental human rights—those such as freedom of speech, press, assembly, worship, or petition—to be unconstitutional as a denial of due process of law. In other words, today there is a presumption of constitutionality of economic legislation, but legislation which tends to restrict fundamental rights is suspect and subject to more exacting judicial scrutiny under the Fourteenth Amendment. This double standard is often justified because of the crucial importance of these basic freedoms, which must be protected by the judiciary from the "vicissitudes" of political action. As a result, the due process clause prohibits experimentation with the basic fundamental liberties by the legislative and executive branches of government. It places the judiciary in the role of guarding these rights. Courts are thus the guardians of fundamental liberty; but, at least today, they are not part of the administration of our economic system.

13 EQUAL PROTECTION

Almost no law treats all persons equally. Laws draw lines and treat people differently. Therefore, almost any state or local law imaginable can be challenged under the equal protection clause. It is obvious that the equal protection clause does not always deny states the power to treat different persons in different ways. Yet the equal protection clause embodies the ethical idea that law should not treat people differently without a satisfactory reason making such treatment fair under the circumstances. In deciding cases using that clause to challenge state and local laws, courts use two distinct approaches. One is the traditional, or "minimum rationality" approach, and the other is called the "strict scrutiny" approach (See Table 6-2). Whether the approach determines the result of a case or whether the desired result dictates the approach to be used is not always clear. As a practical matter, if the traditional (minimum rationality) approach is used, the challenged law and its classifications are usually found *not* to be a violation of equal protection. On the other hand, if the "strict scrutiny" test is used, the classifications are usually found to be unconstitutional under the equal protection clause.

Under the minimum rationality approach, a classification will survive an equal protection challenge if it has a *rational* connection to a *permissible* state end. A permissible state end is one that is not prohibited by another

TABLE 6-2 EQUAL PROTECTION ANALYSIS

Standard	Minimum rationality	Quasi-strict scrutiny	Strict scrutiny
Classifications must be	Rationally connected to a permissible or legitimate government objective	Substantially related to an important government interest	Necessary to a compelling state interest
Examples	**Presumed valid** Height Weight Age Testing School desegregation Veteran's preference Marriage	**Quasi-suspect classes** Sex Gender Legitimacy Affirmative Action	**Suspect classes** Race National origin Alienage **Fundamental rights** To vote To travel

provision of the Constitution. It qualifies as a legitimate goal of government. The classification must have a reasonable basis (not wholly arbitrary), and the courts will assume any state of facts that can be used to justify the classification. These laws often involve economic issues such as mandatory retirement ages or social legislation such as welfare laws.

Such laws are presumed to be constitutional because courts recognize that the legislature must draw lines creating distinctions and that such tasks cannot be avoided. Further, courts in applying this standard admit that perfection in making classifications is neither possible nor necessary. Only when no rational basis for the classification exists is it unconstitutional under the equal protection clause. A classification judged by this standard must be rationally related to the state's objectives. The classification may be imperfect and may not be the best to accomplish the purpose. Yet it is still constitutional if there is a rational basis for the classification. For example, a state law imposing mandatory retirement of police at age fifty was held valid when the rational basis test was applied to it.

Under the strict scrutiny test, a classification will be a denial of equal protection unless the classification is necessary to a *compelling* state end. It is not enough that a classification be rational, it must be necessary. It is not enough that a classification be permissible to a state end, it must be a compelling state objective. To withstand constitutional challenge when this test is used, the law must serve important governmental objectives and the classification must be substantially related to achieving these objectives.

The strict scrutiny test is used if the classification involves either: (1) a suspect class or (2) a fundamental constitutional right. A suspect class is one that has such disabilities, has been subjected to such a history of purposeful unequal treatment, or has been relegated to such a position of political powerlessness that it commands extraordinary protection from the political process of the majority. For example, classifications directed at race, national origin, and alienage are clearly suspect. As a result, the judiciary strictly scrutinizes laws directed at them. Unless the state can prove that its statutory classifications have a compelling state interest as a basis, the classifications will be considered a denial of equal protection. Classifications that are subject to strict judicial scrutiny are presumed to be unconstitutional. The state must convince the court that the classification is fair, reasonable, and necessary to accomplish the objective of legislation that is compelling to a state interest.

Strict judicial scrutiny is applied to a second group of cases, those which involve classifications directed at fundamental rights. If a classification unduly burdens or penalizes the exercise of a constitutional right, it will be stricken unless it is found to be necessary to a compelling state interest. Among such rights are the right to vote and the right to travel. Doubts about such laws result in their being stricken by the courts as a denial of equal protection, as occurred in the case which follows.

ATTORNEY GENERAL OF NEW YORK v. SOTO-LOPEZ
106 S.Ct.2317 (1986)

FACTS

The New York Constitution and Civil Service Law grant a civil service employment preference to certain veterans in the form of points added to examination scores. To qualify, they must: (1) be New York residents who are honorably discharged veterans of the armed forces, (2) have served during time of war, and (3) have been New York residents when they entered military service. Some Army veterans, long-time New York residents, passed the New York City civil service examinations but were denied the veterans' preference because they were not New York residents when they joined the Army.

ISSUE

Does the New York veterans' preference system violate the equal protection clause of the Fourteenth Amendment?

DECISION

Yes. (It also violates their right to travel.)

REASONS

1. The laws create different classes of citizens—veterans and nonveterans—and thus there is an equal protection issue.
2. Whenever a state law infringes a constitutionally protected right (the right to travel in this case), the court uses strict scrutiny to determine constitutionality and the state must come forward with a compelling justification.
3. The New York law favors New York residents at a fixed point over those

who were not New York residents at the same point in their lives. There is no compelling justification for this distinction.
4. Once veterans establish bona fide residence in a state, they become the state's own and may not be discriminated against on the basis of the date of their arrival in the state.

Some cases actually fall between the two tests previously discussed. These cases use what is sometimes called the *quasi-strict scrutiny test* because the classifications are only partially suspect or the rights involved are not quite fundamental. For example, classifications directed at sex and legitimacy are partially suspect. In cases involving classifications based on sex or gender, the courts have taken this position between the two tests or at least have modified the strict scrutiny approach. Such classifications are unconstitutional unless they are *substantially* related to an *important* government objective. This modified version of strict scrutiny has resulted in holdings which find laws to be valid as well as unconstitutional.

Equal protection cases run the whole spectrum of legislative attempts to solve society's problems. For example, a major use of the equal protection clause by courts has been to require the integration of public schools. In addition, the meaning and application of the equal protection clause have been central issues in cases involving: (1) apportionment of legislative bodies, (2) racial segregation in the sale and rental of real estate, (3) laws distinguishing between the rights of legitimates and illegitimates, (4) the makeup of juries, (5) voting requirements, (6) welfare residency requirements, (7) rights of aliens, and (8) the use of property taxes as the means of financing public schools. The equal protection clause is the means to the end, or goal, of equality of opportunity. As such, it may be utilized by anyone claiming unequal treatment in any case. To be successful, a party alleging discrimination must not only prove unequal treatment, it must prove discriminatory intent by a governmental body if the minimum rationality standard is used.

REVIEW QUESTIONS

1 A restaurant was refused a liquor license because of opposition by a church located within 10 feet of the restaurant. A state statute gives churches and schools veto power over liquor licenses if the church is within 100 feet of the establishment seeking the license. Is the state law constitutional? Why, or why not?

2 Charges were filed against a judge by a commission on judicial conduct. The judge sought to take the deposition of a newspaper reporter to question him about persons he had interviewed and the information obtained. The newspaper reporter claimed a privilege of confidential communications to a reporter and refused to reveal his sources. He was held in contempt on appeal. What was the result? Why?

3. A Florida statute required newspapers that assail the character of political candidates to afford free space to the candidate for reply. Is the law constitutional? Why, or why not?

4. A Maine statute has prohibited roadside billboards except for signs announcing the time and place of religious or civic events, election campaign signs, and signs erected by historic and cultural institutions. A suit is filed challenging the constitutionality of the statute. What will be the result? Why?

5. A Pennsylvania Bar Association rule prohibited direct-mail solicitation by attorneys. A Pennsylvania attorney who was a certified pilot with a master's degree in computer science used direct mail to solicit clients among aircraft owners and computer users. When the bar association sought to discipline the attorney, he contended that the rule was unconstitutional. What was the result? Why?

6. A promoter of theatrical productions applied to a municipal board charged with managing a city-leased theater for a license to stage the play *Hair*. Relying on outside reports that because of nudity the production would not be in the best interests of the community, the board rejected the application. Were the promoter's First Amendment rights abridged? Why, or why not?

7. A federal statute prohibits the mailing of unsolicited advertisements for contraceptives. When the manufacturer of contraceptives proposed to mail to the public unsolicited advertisements including informational pamphlets discussing family planning and venereal disease, the United States Postal Service claimed that the mailings would violate the statute. The company contended that the law violated the First Amendment. Is the law constitutional? Why, or why not?

8. OSHA inspectors arrived at Barlow's Factory to conduct a safety inspection. Barlow's refused to allow them to enter the plant and then filed suit for an injunction to prevent any inspections without a search warrant. Section 8(a) of the Occupational Safety and Health Act empowers agents of the secretary of labor to conduct unannounced searches of the work area of any employment facility for safety hazards and violations of OSHA regulations. Is Barlow's entitled to the injunction? Why, or why not?

9. An Indiana statute requires government officials to post notice at the courthouse of the sale of real property for nonpayment of taxes. In addition, notice must be posted in a newspaper, and notice by certified mail must be given the property owner. Notice to mortgagees is not required. After the tax sale, the owner has two years in which to redeem the property. If there is no redemption, the purchaser at the tax sale may apply for a deed, provided notice is once again given to the property owner. Notice need not be given the mortgagee. A mortgagee contends that the statute is unconstitutional. Is he correct? Explain.

10. Thornton, a manager of a department store, refused to work on Sundays. A state statute provided Sabbath observers with an absolute and unqualified right not to work on their Sabbath. Is the state law constitutional? Why, or why not?

11. P brought suit against D, a privately owned and operated public utility, for damages. D had terminated P's electric service because she failed to pay her bills. P alleged that she had not been given any notice and that there was no hearing before her service was discontinued; therefore, she contended, there was a denial of property without due process of law, contrary to the Fourteenth Amendment. D contended that its action was not "state action," and therefore the traditional requirements of due process did not need to be met. What was the result? Why?

12 A village passed a zoning ordinance which prohibited all live entertainment, including nonobscene nude dancing, in any business establishment in the village. The owners of an adult book store that contained coin-operated devices for showing adult films challenged the constitutionality of the ordinance. What was the result? Why?

13 Under a state workers' compensation law, a widower is denied benefits for his wife's work-related death unless he is mentally or physically incapacitated or proves dependence on his wife's earnings. However, the statute grants death benefits to a widow without such restrictions. When Wengler's wife died in a work-related accident, a claim for death benefits was denied. He contended that the statute was unconstitutional. What was the result? Why?

14 The state of Connecticut enacted a statute, under which, for tuition purposes, the status of state university students as nonresidents at time of application for admission was, in effect, conclusively and irrebuttably presumed to continue for the entire period of attendance. A suit was filed challenging the statute under the due process clause of the Fourteenth Amendment. What was the result? Why?

15 The state of Virginia followed the common law doctrine of necessaries under which a husband was liable for necessaries such as food, lodging, and medical care furnished the wife, but a wife did not have a similar obligation on behalf of the husband. A hospital sought to collect from a husband for his wife's hospital bill. He contended that the doctrine violated the equal protection clause of the Fourteenth Amendment. Was he correct? Why, or why not?

CHAPTER 7

ADMINISTRATIVE LAW

OVERVIEW

This chapter concerns the legal principles and problems relating to what is sometimes called the fourth branch of government—the regulatory agencies, bureaus, and commissions. The fourth branch of government creates laws when it adopts rules and regulations to regulate business activity. It investigates business to determine if laws have been violated, and it prosecutes violations. Finally, it holds hearings to determine questions of fact and of law. The direct day-to-day legal impact on business of the rules and regulations adopted and enforced by these agencies is probably greater than the impact of the courts or other branches of government. Administrative agencies create and enforce the majority of all laws constituting the legal environment of business. Almost every business activity is regulated to some degree by the administrative process at either the state or federal level.

This chapter will discuss administrative powers and those situations in which courts will set regulatory decisions or the rules aside. It will also discuss regulations adopted by agencies. Special emphasis will be placed on the problems that business encounters as a result of the administrative process.

The following terms are of special importance in this chapter: administrative law judge, cease and desist order, consent order, exhaustion of remedies, general counsel, immunity, Peter principle, quasi-judicial function, and quasi-legislative function.

1 INTRODUCTION

As our industrial society grows and becomes more complex, the social and economic problems that confront society multiply fantastically. Not only do these issues increase in number, but interrelationships and conflicting social goals complicate their solution. Also, advances in technology require special training and experience for us to attempt an intelligent solution of problems in many areas.

To solve these problems, our society turns to the methodology referred to as the *administrative process*. This administrative process relies upon independent regulatory agencies, bureaus, and commissions to develop laws and enforce them. In a real sense, these independent regulatory agencies constitute a fourth branch of government.

Table 7-1 lists several of the more important federal agencies and briefly describes their functions. Many of these agencies will be discussed in detail in later chapters. For example, the Equal Employment Opportunity Commission is discussed in Chapter 15, the National Labor Relations Board in Chapters 16 and 17, the Securities and Exchange Commission in Chapter 18, the Federal Trade Commission in Chapters 21 to 23, and the Enviromental Protection Agency in Chapter 24.

Although we focus on federal agencies in this chapter, keep in mind that state and local governments also have many agencies. For example, cases involving industrial accidents and injuries to employees are heard by state workers' compensation boards, and most local governments have zoning boards which make recommendations on zoning laws. State governments usually license and regulate intrastate transportation in a manner similar to the Interstate Commerce Commission's (ICC) regulation of interstate ground transportation. In addition, state boards usually get rates for local utilities supplying gas and electricity. The principles and problems discussed in this chapter generally apply to the state and local administrative process as well as to the federal. It is clear that almost every aspect of our daily lives is regulated to a substantial degree by the administrative process.

2 REASONS FOR THE USE OF ADMINISTRATIVE AGENCIES

Early in our history it was necessary to create a fourth branch of government possessing the powers and functions of the other three branches. There are many reasons why we needed to create administrative agencies to have a more effective government. First, the legislative branch apparently could not legislate in sufficient detail to cover all aspects of a problem. Congress cannot possibly legislate in minute detail and, as a consequence, it uses more and more general language in stating its regulatory aims and purposes. For example, Congress cannot enact a tax law that would cover every possible issue that might arise. Therefore, it delegates to the Internal Revenue Service (IRS) the power to make rules and regulations to fill in the

TABLE 7-1   MAJOR FEDERAL AGENCIES

Name	Functions
Consumer Product Safety Commission (CPSC)	Protects the public against unreasonable risks of injury associated with consumer products
Environmental Protection Agency (EPA)	Administers all laws relating to the environment, including laws on water pollution, air pollution, solid wastes, pesticides, toxic substances, etc.
Federal Aviation Administration (FAA) (part of the Dept. of Transportation)	Regulates civil aviation to provide safe and efficient use of airspace
Federal Communications Commission (FCC)	Regulates interstate and foreign communications by means of radio, television, wire, cable, and satellite
Federal Reserve Board (FRB)	Regulates the availability of and the cost of money and credit; the nation's central bank
Federal Trade Commission (FTC)	Protects the public from anticompetitive behavior and unfair and deceptive business practices; law-enforcement agency
Food and Drug Administration (FDA)	Administers laws to prohibit distribution of adulterated, misbranded, or unsafe food and drugs
Equal Employment Opportunity Commission (EEOC)	Seeks to prevent discrimination in employment based on race, color, religion, sex, or national origin and other unlawful employment practices
Interstate Commerce Commission (ICC)	Regulates interstate surface transportation
National Labor Relations Board (NLRB)	Conducts union certification elections and holds hearings on unfair labor practice complaints
Nuclear Regulatory Commission (NRC)	Licenses and regulates the nuclear energy industry
Occupational Safety and Health Administration (OSHA)	Ensures all workers a safe and healthy work environment
Securities and Exchange Commission (SEC)	Enforces the federal securities laws which regulate sale of securities to the investing public

gaps and create the necessary details to make tax laws workable. In many areas an agency has had to develop detailed rules and regulations to carry out a legislative policy.

Courts also cannot handle all disputes and controversies that may arise. For example, each year tens of thousands of industrial accidents cause injury or death to workers. If each of these industrial accidents results in traditional litigation, the courts simply would not have the time nor the personnel to handle the multitude of cases. Therefore, workers' compensation boards decide such claims. Likewise, most cases involving alleged discrimination in employment are turned over to agencies for decision.

Another reason many agencies are created is to refer a problem or area to experts for solution and management. The Federal Reserve Board, the Nuclear Regulatory Commission, and the Food and Drug Administration are examples of agencies with expertise beyond that of Congress or the executive branch. The development of sound policies and proper decisions in many areas requires expertise, and thus we tend to resort to administrative agencies for this expertise. Similarly, administrative agencies are often desirable because they provide needed continuity and consistency in the formulation, application, and enforcement of rules and regulations governing business.

Many governmental agencies exist to protect the public, especially from the business community. Business has often failed to regulate itself, and the lack of self-regulation has often been contrary to the public interest. For example, the failure of business to voluntarily refrain from polluting many streams and rivers as well as the air led to the creation of the Enviromental Protection Agency (EPA). The sale of worthless securities to the investing public was a major force behind the creation of the Securities and Exchange Commission (SEC). The manufacture and the sale of dangerous products led to the creation of the Consumer Product Safety Commission (CPSC). It is our practice to turn to a governmental agency for assistance whenever a business or business practice may injure significant numbers of the general public. The prevailing attitude is that the government's duty is to protect the public from harm.

Agencies are often created to replace competition with regulation. When a firm is given monopoly power, it loses its freedom of contact and a governmental body is given the power to determine the provisions of its contracts. For example, electric utility companies are usually given a monopoly in the geographic area in which they serve. A state agency such as a public service commission then has the power to set the rate structure for the utility. Similar agencies have regulated transportation and banking because of the disparity of bargaining power between the business and the public. Regulation is often a substitute for competition.

Of course, many agencies were created simply out of necessity. If we are to have a mail service, a post office is necessary. Welfare programs require governmental personnel to administer them. The Social Security concept dictates that there be a federal agency to determine eligibility and pay benefits. The mere existence of most government programs automatically creates a new agency or expands the functions of an existing one.

Almost every governmental agency has been created because of a recognized problem in society and from the belief that an agency may be able to help solve the problem. Governmental agencies usually have laudable goals and noble purposes, such as the elimination of discrimination, the providing of a safe and healthy workplace, or the protection of consumers. These agencies allow other branches of government to determine policy while giving those carrying out the policy a significant degree of flexibility and discretion.

3 FUNCTIONS

As previously noted, administrative agencies often possess functions of the other three branches of government. These functions are generally described as: (1) rule making, (2) adjudicating, (3) prosecuting, (4) advising, (5) supervising, and (6) investigating. These functions do not concern all administrative agencies to the same degree. Some agencies are primarily adjudicating bodies, such as industrial commissions that rule on workers' compensation claims. Others are primarily supervisory, such as the Securities and Exchange Commission (SEC), which oversees the issue and sale of investment securities. To be sure, most agencies perform all the foregoing functions to some degree in carrying out their responsibilities. Figure 7-2 explains how these functions have been delegated to these agencies.

Agencies perform their **quasi-legislative function** by issuing rules and regulations that have the force and effect of law. These rules and regulations may be used to resolve an issue if they are relevant to any issue involved in an adjudicative proceeding. Before rules and regulations are adopted, interested parties are given an opportunity to be heard on the desirability and legality of the proposals.

Guidelines are also issued by agencies to supplement rules. Guidelines are administrative interpretations of the statutes which a commission is responsible for enforcing, and they provide guidance in evaluating the legal-

FIGURE 7-1 Administrative agencies.

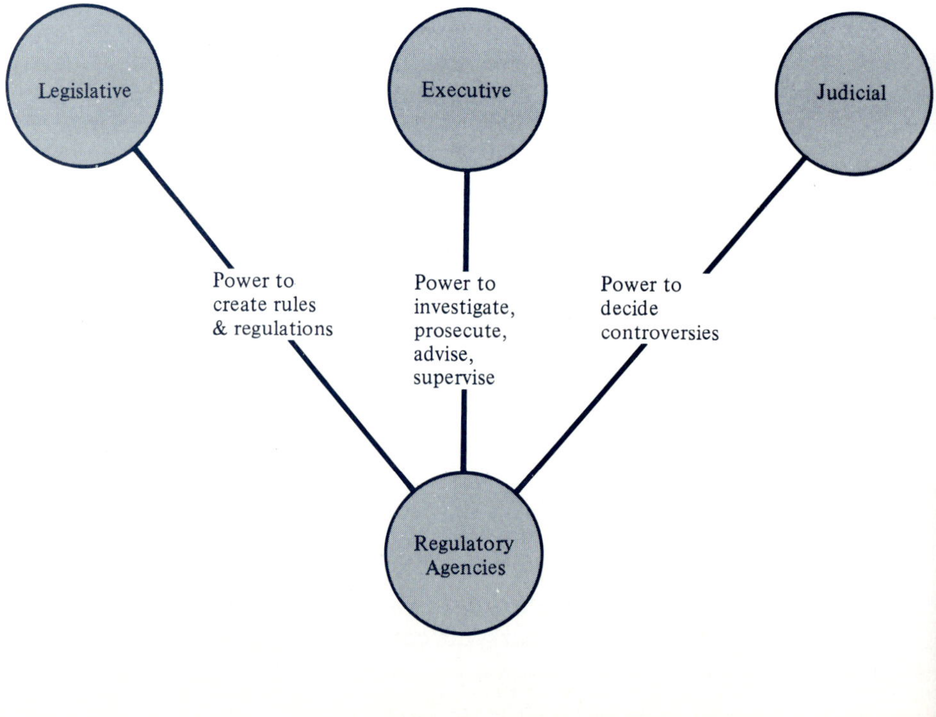

ity of certain practices. They deal with a particular practice and may cut across industry lines.

Rules and regulations may apply to a business practice irrespective of the industry involved or they may apply only to an industry. For example, the Occupational Safety and Health Administration (OSHA) rules may cover anyone using certain equipment, or a rule may be drafted so that its coverage is limited to an industry such as drug manufacturing.

The advisory function may be accomplished by making reports to the President or to Congress. For example, the FTC may propose new legislation to Congress, or it may inform the attorney general of the need for judicial action because of violations of the law. Agencies also report information to the general public that should be known in the public interest, and they publish advisory opinions. For example, a commission may give advice as to whether a firm's proposed course of action might violate any of the laws which that commission administers. Advisory opinions are not as binding as formal rulings, but they do give a business an indication of the view an agency would take if the practice in question were challenged formally. The advisory opinion is a unique device generally not available in the judicial system, as courts deal only with actual cases and controversies.

One of the major functions of all agencies is to investigate activities and practices that may be illegal. Because of this investigative power, agencies can gather and compile information concerning the organization and business practices of any corporation or industry engaged in commerce to determine whether there has been a violation of any law. In exercising their investigative functions, agencies may utilize the subpoena power and require reports, examine witnesses under oath, and examine and copy documents, or they may obtain information from other governmental offices. This power of investigation complements the exercise of the other powers such as giving advice, prosecuting violations, issuing rules, and entering cease and desist orders.

There is a federal law which makes it a crime to make any false or fraudulent statement in any matter within the jurisdiction of a federal agency. A person may be guilty of a violation without proof that he or she had knowledge that the matter was within the jurisdiction of a federal agency, as happened in the following case.

UNITED STATES v. YERMIAN
104 S.Ct. 2936 (1984)

FACTS

Yermian was convicted on three counts of making false statements, in violation of federal law which makes it a crime to make any false or fraudulent statement in any matter within the jurisdiction of a federal agency. The convictions were based on false statements he supplied his private employer in connection with a

Department of Defense security questionnaire. The information was supplied to the Defense Industrial Security Clearance Office by his employer, a defense contractor. Yermian failed to disclose that he had been convicted of mail fraud, and he also falsely reported that he had been employed by two companies that had not actually employed him. Yermian's defense was that he had no actual knowledge that the false statements he made would be transmitted to a federal agency by his employer.

ISSUE

Do the terms "knowingly" and "willfully" in the law require the government to prove that false statements were made with actual knowledge of federal agency jurisdiction?

DECISION

No.

REASONS

1. The statute requires that knowingly false statements be made "in any matter within the jurisdiction of any department or agency of the United States."
2. The terms "knowingly" and "willfully" modify only the making of "false, fictitious or fraudulent statements," and not the predicate circumstance that those statements be made in a matter within the jurisdiction of a federal agency.

The quasi-judicial function involves both fact finding and applying law to the facts. If violations of the law are found, sanctions, such as a fine or other penalty, may be imposed. In addition, an agency may issue a cease and desist order to prevent further violations. Violations of cease and desist orders are punishable by fine.

Quasi-judicial proceedings usually begin with a complaint filed by the agency. The complaint contains allegations of fact concerning the alleged illegal conduct. After the formal complaint is served, the respondent files an answer to the charges and allegations. The case is then assigned to an administrative law judge. At the hearing, counsel for the agency and the respondent produce evidence to prove or disprove the allegations of fact in the complaint and answer. The judge rules on the admissibility of evidence, rules on motions made by counsel, and renders an initial decision that includes a statement of findings and conclusions, along with reasons for them, as to all material issues of fact and law. The ruling also includes an order the judge deems appropriate in view of the evidence in the record. This order becomes final if not challenged within thirty days after it is filed. On the appeal, the agency, board, or commission reviews the record of the initial decision and has all the powers it could have exercised if it had rendered that decision itself.

In reviewing the evidence, the agency uses the preponderance of the evidence standard rather than the clear and convincing proof or beyond a reasonable doubt standard of the criminal law. (Refer to the discussions of burden of proof in Chapter 4.)

Many cases before agencies are settled by agreement before a final decision, just as most lawsuits are settled. Such a settlement results in the issuance of a *consent order* which states that the respondent admits to the jurisdiction of the agency and waives all rights to seek a judicial review. However, a respondent does not have to admit it has been guilty of a violation of the law; but it does agree that it will not engage in the business activities which were the subject of the complaint. A consent order has the same legal force and effect as a final cease and desist order issued after a full hearing. Consent orders save considerable expense; the business involved is not found guilty but only agrees that it will not do the act in the future.

4 ORGANIZATION

Administrative agencies, boards, or commissions usually have a chairperson and four other members. Laws creating the regulatory body usually specify that no more than three of the five members may belong to the same political party. Appointments require Senate confirmation, and appointees are not permitted to engage in any other business or employment during their terms. They may be removed from office by the President only for inefficiency, neglect of duty, or malfeasance in office.

Regulatory agencies require staffs to carry out their duties. Although each agency has its own distinctive organizational structure to meet its responsibilities, most agencies have persons performing certain functions common to all agencies. Most agencies have quasi-legislative and **quasi-judicial functions** as well as the usual executive ones. Therefore, the organizational chart of an agency usually contains all the usual duties of government. Figure 7-3 shows an organizational chart outlining the usual functions and duties of most agencies.

The chairperson is designated by the President and is the presiding officer at agency meetings. The chairperson usually belongs to the same political party as the President. She or he, while an equal in voting, is somewhat more important than the other members because of visibility and the power to appoint staff. For example, the chairperson of the Federal Reserve Board is often in the news while the other members are relatively unknown.

The secretary is responsible for the minutes of agency meetings and is legal custodian of its records. The secretary usually signs orders and official correspondence and is responsible for publication of all actions in the *Fed-*

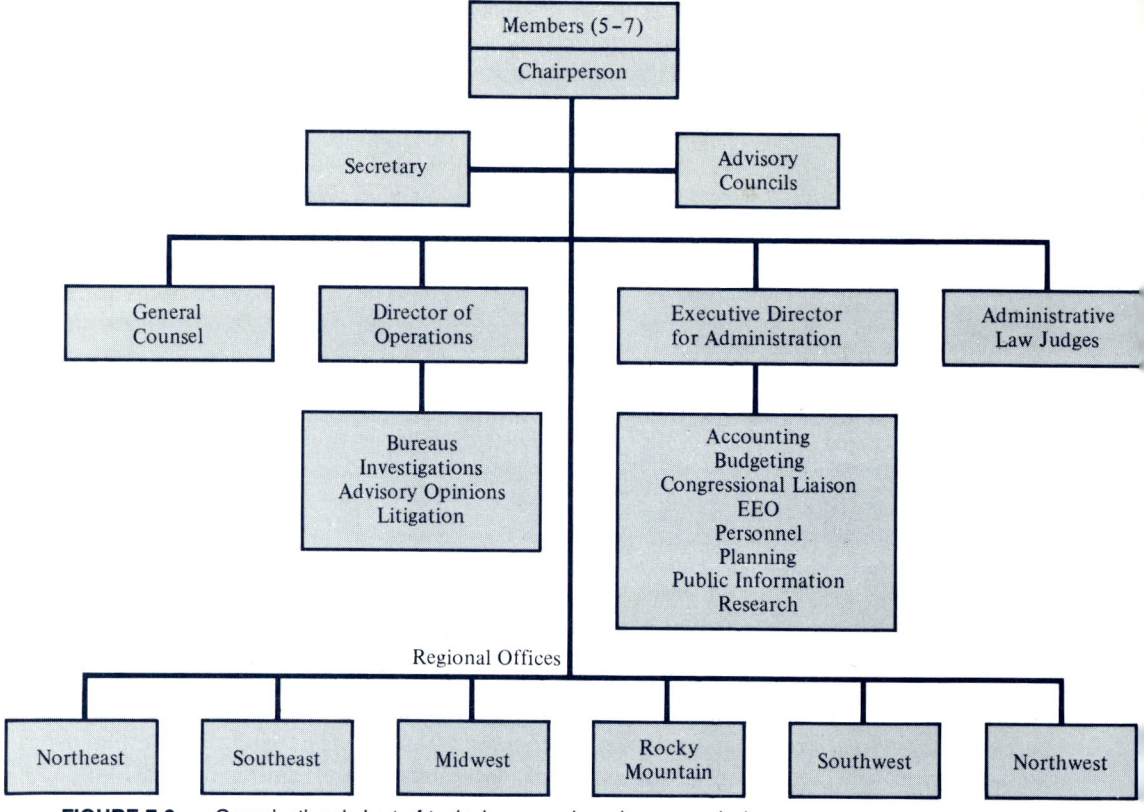

FIGURE 7-2 Organizational chart of typical agency, board, or commission.

eral Register. The secretary also coordinates the activities of the agency with others involved in the regulatory process.

Advisory counsels consist of people who are not employed by an agency but who are interested in its mission. Persons serving on councils are usually selected because of their expertise. For example, the Consumer Product Safety Commission has an advisory council in poison prevention packaging and another on flammable fabrics. These councils provide for interaction between regulators and regulatees.

The office of **general counsel** is so important in many agencies that the appointment usually requires Senate approval. The general counsel is the chief law officer and legal adviser. He or she represents the agency in court and often makes the decision as to whether or not a suit will be filed, or what other remedies will be pursued. The general counsel has a significant impact on policy and is often as powerful as a commissioner or board member.

The executive director for administration is the chief operating official of an agency who supervises usual administrative functions such as accounting, budgeting, and personnel. Research and planning are usually supervised by the executive director, also. Since agencies spend a great deal of time lobbying with Congress, most agencies have a legislative liaison which is under the executive director for administration.

Administrative law judges perform the adjudicative fact-finding functions. They hear cases of alleged law violations and apply the law to the facts. The members of the agency board or commission only hear appeals from the decisions of the administrative law judges. These judges are organizationally separate from the rest of the agency so that the quasi-judicial function will be performed impartially. Administrative law judges use prior decisions as precedent. In addition, they must follow the procedural rules of the agency as well as its policy directives.

The duties and suborganization of the director of operations vary greatly from agency to agency. These operating bureaus are assigned specific areas of activity. For example, at the EPA, one group will be concerned with clean air and another with water problems.

Regional offices investigate alleged violations of the law. In addition, they usually have an educational function. Many regional offices have their own administrative law judges and special legal counsel.

5 INFLUENCING AGENCY DECISIONS

As discussed in section 3, agencies adopt rules and regulations as part of their quasi-legislative function and decide controversies in the performance of the quasi-judicial function. Due process of law requires that before a rule or regulation may be adopted by an agency, interested parties be given notice of the proposed rules and an opportunity to express their views on them. Statutes require that agencies give public notice of proposed rules and that they hold public hearings on them.

At public hearings, interested parties are allowed to present evidence in support of, or in opposition to, a proposed rule or regulation. As a result, the best means of influencing a quasi-legislative decision of an administrative agency is to participate in the adoption process.

What alternatives are available to a party unhappy with either rules and regulations that have been adopted or with the quasi-judicial decisions? What are the powers of courts in reviewing decisions of administrative agencies? What chance does one aggrieved by an agency's decision have in obtaining a reversal of the decision? How much deference is given to an agency's decisions? Answers to these questions must be clearly understood if one is to really appreciate the role of administrative agencies in our system. The principles and issues are somewhat different, depending upon whether the court is reviewing either a rule or a regulation or a quasi-judicial decision. Judicial review of agency decisions is discussed in the sections that follow. However, it should be recognized that judicial review may sometimes be available even in cases where there was no hearing before the administrative agency. A federal statute known as the Hobbs Act grants judicial review in the courts of appeal from all final orders of federal administrative agencies.

In addition to the direct court-imposed constraints on agency action, more subtle ones exist. These include potential lawsuits against individual administrators, and political pressures. The subject of lawsuits against agency personnel is discussed in section 11.

Agencies are not politically responsible, in the sense that they are elected by the people. However, it is clear that they react, sometimes dramatically, to the force of public opinion. For example, in the late 1970s OSHA changed much of its emphasis and efforts from nit-picking safety concerns to major health problems because of public criticism.

Letters designed to obtain action or a change in policy to agencies from citizens may be effective. These are probably even more effective if directed to a member of Congress, who, in turn, asks the agency for an official response or explanation. At various times, a given agency may find itself bombarded with official congressional hearings inquiring into its activities. Such investigations may actually result in a budget cutback or change in the agency's authority. Just the threat of such a proceeding is often sufficient to cause a review of administrative policy. Finally, even without hearings, it is evident that agencies have often reevaluated policies and changed their posture because of adverse criticism from the media.

JUDICIAL REVIEW OF AGENCY DECISIONS

6 INTRODUCTION

Each branch of government has some control over the administrative process. The executive branch normally appoints the top officials of an agency with the advice and consent of the legislative branch. In addition, the executive branch makes budget recommendations to the legislature and has veto power over its statutes. The legislature can review and control administrative activity by abolishing the agency, enacting specific legislation contrary to rules adopted by the agency, more explicitly defining limitations on agency activities, providing additional procedural requirements for the agency's adjudications, or limiting appropriations of funds to the agency.

The courts also check on administrative bodies by using judicial review of their actions. Just as laws enacted by the legislature must be within its power as established by the Constitution or be void, rules and regulations promulgated by an administrative body must be within the confines of its grant of power from the legislature or a court will find them void. However, once having determined that an act of the legislature is constitutional or a rule of an agency is authorized, the courts will not inquire into its wisdom or effectiveness. An unwise or ineffectual law may be corrected by political action at the polls; an unwise rule or regulation adopted by an agency may be corrected by the legislature that gave the agency power to make the rule in the first place. In the sections which follow, court functions in reviewing agency activities will be discussed in more detail. Keep in mind that the principles and issues differ somewhat, depending upon whether the court reviews a rule or regulation on one hand or a quasi-judicial decision on the other.

7 JUDICIAL REVIEW OF AGENCY RULE MAKING

The rule-making function in the administrative process is essentially legislative in character. Administrative agencies are usually created by enactments of the legislature in which that branch delegates certain responsibility or quasi-legislative power to the agency. Some courts view the legislature as unable to delegate its lawmaking function at all, but they conclude that authorizing an administrative agency to "fill in the details" of legislation is not an exercise of the legislative power. Other courts have stated that the legislature can delegate part of its function to an agency as long as certain constitutional safeguards are met. The difference is largely a matter of semantics.

There are two basic issues in litigation challenging the validity of a rule made by an administrative agency. First, is the delegation valid, and second, has the agency exceeded its authority? Delegations of quasi-legislative authority to administrative agencies are subject to two constitutional limitations. First, a delegation must be definite, or it will violate due process. Definiteness means that the delegation must be set forth with sufficient clarity so that all concerned, and especially reviewing courts, will be able to ascertain the extent of the agency's authority. For many reasons, broad language has been held sufficiently definite to meet this test. For example, the term "unfair methods of competition" has been held to be sufficiently definite to meet the requirements of due process.

A very similar limitation to the definiteness requirement on the exercise of quasi-legislative authority is the requirement that the power of administrative agencies to make rules be limited. The limited-power concept means that delegations must contain standards by which a court can determine whether the limitations have been exceeded. The standards set must meet certain minimum requirements before the agency in question is validly empowered to act in a certain area, and the rules promulgated by the agency must follow these standards and limitations imposed by the law establishing the agency, if they are to be upheld. Also, procedural safeguards must exist to control arbitrary administrative action and any administrative abuse of discretionary power.

Just as broad language has been approved as being sufficiently definite for a delegation to be valid under the due process clause, so also have broad standards been approved to meet the limited-power test since the 1930s. Today, it is generally agreed that delegations of authority to make rules may be in very broad language. For example, the delegation of authority to make such rules as the "public interest, convenience and necessity" may require is subject to a valid standard. Delegations that include criteria that are as concrete as the field and factors involved permit will be held valid, since the law now recognizes that practical considerations often make definite standards impossible. In fact, some cases have held that on a challenge of unconstitutional delegation of legislative authority, the court's inquiry should focus on procedural safeguards rather than on statutory standards.

Although it is highly unlikely that a court would hold a delegation invalid because of indefiniteness or lack of standards, courts find that agencies have exceeded their authority from time to time. Delegation of quasi-legislative power usually involves grants of substantial discretion to the board or agency involved. Keep in mind that the delegation of discretion is to the agency and not to the courts. Therefore, courts cannot interfere with the discretion given to the agency and cannot substitute their judgment for that of the agency. Courts will hold that an agency has exceeded its authority if an analysis of legislative intent confirms the view that the agency has gone beyond that intent.

F.C.C. v. MIDWEST VIDEO
99 S. Ct. 1434 (1979)

FACTS

The Federal Communications Commission (FCC) promulgated rules that required cable television systems that have 3,500 or more subscribers and carry broadcast signals to develop, at a minimum, a twenty-channel capacity by 1986 to make available certain channels for access by public, educational, local governmental, and leased access users. Cable operators were deprived of all discretion in such programming. The statute on cable television specifically prohibited the FCC from treating cable operators as common carriers. During the rule-making proceedings, the FCC rejected arguments that it was treating cable television operators as common carriers.

ISSUE

Are these rules within the delegation of authority?

DECISION

No, the Commission exceeded its authority.

REASONS

1. The access rules have effectively given the cable system a common carrier status, which the law prohibits.
2. Though the court has in the past tended to defer to the Commission's judgment regarding the source of its authority, there are strong indications that agency flexibility was to be sharply limited in this area.

8 REVIEW OF ADJUDICATIONS: PROCEDURAL ASPECTS

The exercise of quasi-judicial functions by administrative agencies is very common. Critics say that an agency acts as prosecutor, finder of facts, and judge. However, similar to the current attitude on delegation of legislative power, judicial power may be generally granted to an administrative agency if the power is restricted by procedural safeguards preventing its abuse. The right to a jury trial does not exist in either formal or informal hearings conducted by administrative bodies. Judicial review of agency adjudications, by its very nature, is quite limited. Legislatures have delegated authority to agencies because of their expertise, and courts usually exercise restraint and resolve doubtful issues in favor of the agency. For example, courts reviewing administrative interpretations of law do not always decide questions of law for themselves. It is not unusual for a court to accept an administrative interpretation of law as final if it in the record is warranted and has a rational basis in law. Administrative agencies are frequently called upon to interpret the statute governing the agency, and the agency's construction is persuasive to courts. However, courts frequently replace administrative holdings with their own interpretations of law.

Administrative agencies develop their own rules of procedure unless mandated otherwise by an act of the legislature. These procedures are far less formal than judicial procedures because one of the functions of the administrative process is to decide issues expeditiously. To proceed expeditiously usually means, for example, that administrative agencies are not restricted by the strict rules of evidence used by courts. Such agencies cannot ignore all rules, but they can use some leeway. They cannot, for example, refuse to permit any cross-examination or unduly limit it. Because the agency "is frequently the accuser, the prosecutor, the judge and the jury," it must remain alert to observe accepted standards of fairness. Reviewing courts are, therefore, alert to ensure that the true substance of a fair hearing is not denied to a party to an administrative hearing. However, the inordinate delay common in administrative hearings is a legitimate cause of public concern.

In reviewing the procedures of administrative agencies, courts are not empowered to substitute their judgment or their own procedures for those of the agency. Judicial responsibility is limited to ensuring consistency with statutes and compliance with the demands of the Constitution for a fair hearing. The latter is based on the due process clause. Due process usually requires a hearing by the agency, but on occasion sanctions may be imposed prior to the hearing.

The principle that federal administrative agencies should be free to fashion their own rules of procedure and pursue methods of inquiry permitting them to discharge their duties grows out of the view that administrative agencies and administrators will be familiar with the industries they regulate. Thus, they will be in a better position than courts or legislative bodies to design procedural rules adapted to the peculiarities of the industry and the tasks of the agency involved.

Important procedural aspects of the broad area of judicial review of administrative action are those of standing to sue and exhaustion of remedies. Standing to sue involves two important issues. First, is the action or decision of the agency subject to judicial review? Not all administrative decisions are reviewable. The Federal Administrative Procedure Act provides for judicial review except where (1) statutes preclude judicial review or (2) agency action is committed to agency discretion by law. Few statutes actually preclude judicial review, and preclusion of judicial review by inference is rare. It is most likely to occur when an agency decides not to undertake action to enforce a statute. For example, prison inmates asked the Food and Drug Administration (FDA) to ban the use of lethal injections to carry out the death penalty. It refused to do so. The Supreme Court held that this decision of the FDA was not subject to judicial review. Congress may commit an issue only to an agency's discretion by failing to include a meaningful standard against which courts may judge the agency's exercise of discretion.

The second issue is whether or not the plaintiff in any particular case is able to obtain judicial review. It is generally required that the plaintiff be "an aggrieved party" before he or she is allowed judicial review. This subject was discussed as a part of Chapter 4 on page 71. It is clear that persons who may suffer economic loss because of agency action have standing to sue. Recent decisions have expanded the group of persons with standing to sue to include those who have noneconomic interests such as First Amendment rights. The second procedural aspect, exhaustion of remedies, is discussed in the next section.

9 EXHAUSTION OF REMEDIES

The doctrine of **exhaustion of remedies** recognizes that in reviewing administrative decisions courts should not decide in advance of a hearing that it will not be conducted fairly by the agency in question. In general (although there are exceptions), courts refuse to review administrative actions until a complaining party has exhausted all the administrative remedies and procedures available to him or her for redress. Judicial review is only available for final agency actions. Preliminary orders, such as a decision to file a complaint, are not reviewable. Otherwise, the administrative system would be denied important opportunities to make a factual record, to exercise its discretion, or to apply its expertise in its decision making. Also, exhaustion allows an agency to discover and correct its own errors, and thus helps to dispense with any reason for judicial review. Exhaustion clearly should be required in those cases involving an area of the agency's expertise or specialization; it should require no unusual expense. It should also be required when the administrative remedy is just as likely as the judicial one to provide appropriate relief. The doctrine of exhaustion of remedies avoids the premature interruption of the administrative process. In general, it is probably more efficient for that purpose to go forward without interruption.

However, when there is nothing to be gained from the exhaustion of administrative remedies, and when the harm from the continued existence of the administrative ruling is great, the courts have not been reluctant to discard this doctrine. This is especially true when very fundamental constitutional guarantees such as freedom of speech or press are involved, or when the administrative remedy is likely to be inadequate. Also, probably no court would insist upon exhaustion where the agency is clearly acting beyond its jurisdiction (because its action is not authorized by statute, or the statute authorizing it is unconstitutional), or where it would result in irreparable injury (such as great expense) to the petitioner. Finally, an exception to the doctrine is a lawsuit based on the theory of fraud.

SMITH v. JONES
474 N.E.2d 415 (Ill. App. 3 Dist. 1985)

FACTS

Plaintiffs purchased state lottery tickets and were winners along with seventy-six others. The state had advertised that $1,750,000 would be the prize, but it only distributed $744,471. Plaintiff sued the lottery director, alledging fraud in the conduct of the lottery. The Illinois Lottery law provides for administrative hearings upon complaints charging violations of the lottery law or of regulations thereunder. It also allows any party adversely affected by a final order or determination of the administrative agency to seek judicial review.

ISSUE

Must the plaintiffs exhaust their administrative remedies?

DECISION

No.

REASONS

1. The general rule is that judicial review of an administrative decision may not be had until the aggrieved party has exhausted all administrative remedies.
2. The purpose of the doctrine of exhaustion of administrative remedies is to allow administrative agencies to correct their own errors, clarify policies, and reconcile conflicts before resorting to judicial relief.
3. An exception to the doctrine of exhaustion of administrative remedies is a suit based on the theory of fraud by the administrative agency or its personnel.

A doctrine similar to exhaustion of remedies is known as *primary jurisdiction*. "Exhaustion" applies where a claim is cognizable in the first instance by an administrative agency alone. "Primary jurisdiction" applies where a claim is originally cognizable in the courts. It comes into play whenever enforcement of the claim requires the resolution of issues which, under a regulatory scheme, have been placed within the special competence of an administrative body. In such a case, the judicial process is suspended pending referral of such issues to the administrative body for its views. Primary jurisdiction ensures uniformity and consistency in dealing with matters entrusted to an administrative body. The doctrine is invoked when referral to the agency is preferable because of its specialized knowledge or expertise in dealing with the matter in controversy. Statutes, such as those guaranteeing equal employment opportunity, that create a private remedy for dollar damages sometimes require resort to an administrative agency as a condition precedent to filing suit. Some of these are federal statutes which require referral to state agencies. In these cases, referral must occur, but the right to sue is not limited by the results of the administrative decision.

10 REVIEW OF AGENCY'S DETERMINATION OF FACTS

When it reviews the findings of fact made by an administrative body, a court presumes them to be correct. A court of review examines the evidence by analyzing the record of the agency's proceedings. It upholds the agency's findings and conclusions on questions of fact if they are supported by substantial evidence in the record. In other words, the record must contain material evidence from which a reasonable person might reach the same conclusion as did the agency. If substantial evidence in support of the decision is present, the court will not disturb the agency's findings, even though the court itself might have reached a different conclusion on the basis of other conflicting evidence also in the record. The determination of credibility of the witnesses who testify in quasi-judicial proceedings is for the agency to determine and not the courts.

Thus, it is apparent that, on review, courts do not: (1) reweigh the evidence, (2) make independent determinations of fact, and (3) substitute their view of the evidence for that of the agency. However, courts do determine if there is substantial evidence to support the action taken. But in their examination of the evidence, all that is required is evidence sufficient to convince a reasonable mind to a fair degree of certainty. Thus, substantial evidence is that which a reasonable mind might accept as adequate to support the conclusion. When a case involves the special expertise of the agency, even more deference is paid to the agency decisions.

BALTIMORE GAS & ELECTRIC v. NATURAL RESOURCES DEFENSE COUNCIL
103 S.Ct. 2246 (1983)

FACTS

The National Environmental Policy Act (NEPA) requires federal agencies to consider the environmental impact of any major federal action. This impact must be included in an environmental impact statement. The dispute in this case concerns the adoption by the Nuclear Regulatory Commission (NRC) of a series of rules to evaluate the environmental effects of a nuclear power plant's fuel cycle. The rules were challenged as arbitrary and capricious and inconsistent with the NEPA. The challenge was made because the NRC had not factored into its rules and considered the uncertainties surrounding its assumptions made in the licensing process of power plants.

ISSUE

Will a court change the rules of the NRC?

DECISION

No.

REASON

1. The NRC complied with NEPA, and its decision was not arbitrary or capricious.
2. It is not the task of the court to determine what decision it would have reached if it had been the NRC. The court's only task is to determine whether the NRC had considered the relevant factors and articulated a rational connection between the facts found and the choice made.
3. When examining an agency's prediction within its area of special expertise, a reviewing court must generally be at its most deferential.

The findings of an administrative body are not set aside unless the record clearly precludes the decision of the administrative body. The decision of the agency will be affirmed even if the court believes it to be erroneous, if a reasonable person could have reached the conclusion stated. It is the function of the agency to pass upon the weight to be accorded to the evidence and to make the choice, if necessary, between varying inferences which might be drawn therefrom. The possibility of drawing either of two inconsistent inferences from the evidence does not prevent the agency from drawing one of them. Courts, however, do not always agree with the administrative determination, and sometimes they set aside a finding because it is not supported by substantial evidence.

For the courts to exercise their function of limited review, the agency must provide a record which sets forth the reasons and basis for its decision. If this record shows that the agency did not examine all relevant data and that it ignored issues before it, a court may set aside an agency decision because such a decision is arbitrary and capricious. Agencies cannot assume their decisions. They must be based on evidence, and the record must support the decision.

11 AGENCY PERSONNEL AND DAMAGE SUITS

In a litigious society such as ours, it is not surprising that often administrators are sued for dollar damages by parties subject to administrative rules, regulations, and decisions. Such suits may involve allegations that government officials have violated the constitutional rights of citizens. For example, it has been held that a violation of the Fourth Amendment by federal agents gives rise to a cause of action for damages because of the unconstitutional conduct. However, it should be recognized that government officials are not liable for mere mistakes in judgment, whether the mistake is one of fact or one of law. Damage suits cannot be used as a means to review agency decisions.

Government officials faced with damage suits usually assert the defense of **immunity** or contend that they cannot be sued. The courts have recognized that in certain situations some government officials are absolutely immune from suit. They have no liability even if an act performed is unconstitutional. In other cases, the courts have held that there is only a limited or qualified immunity. The immunity defense is usually limited because government officials should not with immunity ignore the limitations which controlling law places on their powers. Immunity only protects officials from conduct that is within the scope of their duties and responsibilities. In most cases, if a government official does an unconstitutional act or one that is clearly beyond his or her legal authority, there is no defense of immunity from suit. If an act is constitutional and is authorized, the defense of immunity is available irrespective of the motive of the official doing the act. Even proof of malice will not overcome the immunity defense for authorized acts.

Immunity is granted to public officials for two reasons: (1) It would be an injustice, particularly in the absence of bad faith, to subject a public official to liability for discretion poorly exercised if his or her position requires exercising discretion, and (2) the threat of liability would deter public officials in the performance of their duties, and they would not act with the decisiveness required by the public. The law recognizes that public officials must often act swiftly and on the basis of information supplied by others. The extent to which an immunity is qualified or limited is determined by the extent to which the aforesaid reasons apply. In certain cases, they dictate that the immunity be absolute; in others they dictate that it be limited. Officials who seek immunity have the burden of proving that public policy requires it.

As a general rule, executive officials are entitled only to qualified immunity. An important exception exists for hearing examiners and administrative law judges. Judges and justices in our judicial system have almost absolute immunity because of the special nature of their responsibilities. (The only exception is that judges have been held liable for the attorney's fees of persons clearly wronged by them. There is no liability for damages.) Hearing examiners and administrative judges serve a similar function. They exercise independent judgment on the evidence, and they must be free from pressures from the parties. Therefore, persons performing in adjudicatory functions within a government agency are entitled to immunity from damage suit liabilities.

Public prosecutors also have been granted absolute immunity because of the importance of their function and the need to prevent harassment of them by persons charged with crime. The prosecutor's role would likely provoke retaliation unless the immunity were absolute. Therefore, the courts have concluded that agency officials who perform functions analogous to those of a prosecutor and who are responsible for the decision to initiate or to continue a proceeding are also entitled to absolute immunity from damage claims. In addition, an agency attorney who presents evidence in an agency hearing has absolute immunity from suits based on the introduction of such evidence. Legal remedies are available within the agency and within the courts to provide a sufficient check on the activities of such agency officials. The quasi-judicial function of governmental agencies shares enough of the characteristics of the judicial process so that those who participate in it have the same immunity as their counterparts in the judicial process. The risk of an unconstitutional act by those involved in such agency proceedings is clearly outweighed by the importance of preserving the independent judgment of those involved.

12 EQUAL ACCESS TO JUSTICE

The Equal Access to Justice Act, which took effect October 1, 1982, requires Uncle Sam to pay the legal costs of small businesses, nonprofit groups, and most individuals who can show they were unjustly treated by the federal government. Prior to the enactment of this law, small companies often were reluctant to take on the United States government because of litigation costs. The government was at a great advantage because of the number of attorneys and other resources it has. The law enables the "little guy" to fight the bureaucracy. It should be recognized that awards for legal expenses aren't available to just anyone. Congress limited eligibility to persons whose net worth doesn't exceed $1 million and businesses with no more than $5 million net worth and 500 employees. Charitable and religious tax-exempt organizations qualify if they have 500 or fewer employees. Also, the law grants legal fees only to parties that overcome the government position in court, administrative proceedings, or a settlement. Even then, the governmental agency isn't required to pay if it can show that the United States position was substantially justified. The substantially justified standard is separate and distinct from the legal standards that decide the merits of the case. The court assessing an Equal Access to Justice Act application must deny costs and fees if, on the basis of this independent perspective, it concludes that the government acted slightly more than reasonably, even though not in compliance with substantive legal standards applied in the merits phase.

The Equal Access to Justice Act is not being used very extensively. During the first nineteen months under the law, the government lost 12,000 lawsuits, but there were only 30 applications for legal fees. Under the law, courts may order the federal government to pay attorneys' fees and other legal costs if the agency has acted without "substantial justification." Most of the time, the government's position usually meets this test.

13 COMMON CRITICISMS

The independent regulatory agencies and the administrative process are subjected to a great deal of criticism. (See Table 7-2, which summarizes many of the common criticisms.) They are often charged with being inefficient and ineffective. Many complaints about the administrative process are directly related to its vastness and size. This vastness permeates all levels of government—federal, state, and local. In a real sense, bureaucracy and bureaucrats are the actual rulers of the country.

Of course, one of the major criticisms of the fourth branch of government is its high cost. This is discussed in the next section.

14 COST OF REGULATION

Regulation is a form of taxation. It directly increases the cost of government. But these direct costs of regulation are only a small fraction of the indirect costs. Regulation significantly adds to the cost of doing business, and these costs are passed on to the taxpaying, consuming public. The consumer, for whose protection many regulations are adopted, pays both the direct cost of regulation (in taxes) and the indirect cost (when purchasing products and services).

The existence of a governmental agency usually forces a business subject to the agency's jurisdiction to create a similar bureaucracy within its own organization to deal with the agency. For example, the existence of EEOC has caused most large corporations to designate affirmative action employees; they assist the company in complying with the laws, rules, and regulations enforced by EEOC. Whenever a bureaucracy exists, firms dealing with it must have internal groups with responsibilities that are the mirror image of the agency.

Other costs the public must absorb result from agency regulations that inhibit competition and innovation. Regulation has protected existing companies by creating a barrier to entry into a market. Regulation tends to protect "cozy competition" to the extent that, quite often, the parties that object the most to deregulation are the businesses being regulated.

Perhaps the most disturbing additional cost to the business community is the cost of paperwork. The burden of the paperwork involved in filing applications, returns, reports, and forms is overwhelming and a major cost of doing business. In a recent year, it was estimated that 2 billion forms had to be filled out and filed by business because of bureaucratic red tape—at a cost in excess of $20 billion.

TABLE 7-2 COMMON CRITICISMS OF ADMINISTRATIVE AGENCIES

Relating to personnel

1. Government has difficulty in hiring and retaining the best-qualified people. Salaries are often not competitive, and advancement is often slower than in the private sector. Also, some people are overqualified for their positions.
2. The reward system usually doesn't make a significant distinction between excellent, mediocre, and poor performances. There are few incentives to improve productivity and job performance.
3. It is very difficult, if not impossible, to discharge unsatisfactory employees. Transfers of employees are easier to accomplish than discharges.
4. The "Peter principle," which holds that people are promoted to their level of incompetence, is obviously present in many administrative agencies.
5. Personnel in many top positions are selected for political reasons. They often lack the necessary expertise to run an effective organization.

Relating to procedures

1. Delay in the decision-making process is quite common. There often is no reason to expedite decisions, and a huge backlog of cases is common in agencies such as EEOC.
2. The administrative process is overwhelmed with paperwork and with meetings.
3. Rules and regulations are often written in complex legal language—"legalese"—which laypeople cannot understand.
4. There is often a lack of enforcement procedures to follow up actions taken to insure compliance.
5. The administrative process can be dictatorial; there may be too much discretionary power, often unstructured and unchecked, placed in many bureaucratic hands. Formal as well as informal administrative action can amount to an abuse of power.

Relating to substance

1. There are so many agencies making rules and regulations directed at the business community that the rules and regulations often overlap and are in conflict.
2. Some agencies are accused of "sweetheart regulations," or favoring the industry or industries they regulate over the public interest. This may arise as a result of the "revolving door" relationship. Regulators are often persons who had former high executive positions in the industries they regulate. The reverse is also true: people in high-paying jobs in certain industries often had been regulators in those very industries.
3. Many actions for illegal conduct end with only consent orders. A business accused of a violation agrees not to violate the law in the future without admitting any past violation. Such actions have little deterrent effect on others, and no punishment is imposed for illegal conduct.
4. The volume of rules adopted by agencies is beyond the ability of the business community to absorb. In 1987, the *Federal Register* contained over 40,000 pages—down from 80,000 in 1980, but still extremely high.
5. Enforcement of some laws varies over time. For example, OSHA, as a part of its reversal of a deregulatory trend, recently fined Chrysler $1.6 million. The vascillation can be seen in the following:

OSHA PENALTIES

Penalties set by OSHA for record-keeping violations

Fiscal year		Fiscal year	
1980	$22,826	1984	$ 21,950
1981	14,166	1985	23,061
1982	15,990	1986	1,445,915
1983	9,561	1987*	1,681,000

* 6 months
Source: Occupational Safety and Health Administration

Historically, there was little or no cost-benefit analysis when new rules and regulations were proposed. Government has tended only to assess the benefits accruing from a cleaner environment, safer products, healthier working conditions, and so on, in deciding to embark upon vast new regulatory programs. The primary focus of policy making by way of such social regulation has not been on balancing the costs of the programs with their potential benefits. The public, and especially consumers, have frequently been forced to pay for many things they did not want or need in the sense that the cost far exceeded the benefits. Moreover, the law does not generally require cost-benefit analysis, as the case which follows illustrates.

AMERICAN TEXTILE MANUFACTURERS INSTITUTE, INC. v. DONOVAN
101 S.Ct. 2478 (1981)

FACTS

To prevent "brown lung" disease, OSHA promulgated a strict standard limiting the level of exposure to cotton dust for the cotton manufacturing industry. Representatives of the industry appealed the validity of the "cotton dust standard," contending that the cost of compliance greatly exceeded any benefit that would result from the rule. The court of appeals upheld the standard.

ISSUE

Does the Occupational Safety and Health Act require OSHA to demonstrate that the benefits of the standard bear a reasonable relationship to the costs?

DECISION

No.

REASONS

1. Section 6(b)(5) of the act, which deals with toxic materials, requires standards that assure "to the extent feasible" that no employee will suffer material impairment of health. By using this language, Congress defined the costs and benefits, placing the benefit of employee health above all other considerations.
2. The legislative history supports the agreement that Congress meant "feasible" and not "cost-benefit" analysis. Congress, through the passage of the act, chose to place the highest value of assuring employees a safe and healthful working environment, limited only by the feasibility of achieving such an environment.

At first glance, the application of cost-benefit analysis to the administrative process would seem to make sense. However, on closer examination, it is obvious that in many cases it is not possible to weigh the costs against the benefits of regulation.

How do you apply cost-benefit analysis to a rule dealing with human life? How much dollar benefit is to be assigned to a life in measuring it against the cost? Assume that a Department of Transportation rule requiring air bags in all new automobiles sold adds a cost of $800 to each car. Assume also that it saves 50,000 lives per year. Is the cost worth the benefit? Your answer may depend on whether you are one of the 50,000 or not. Cost-benefit analysis becomes ethically awkward when there is an attempt to place a dollar value on things not usually bought and sold, such as life, health, or mobility.

REVIEW QUESTIONS

1 For each term in the left-hand column, match the most appropriate description in the right-hand column:

(1)	CPSC	(a)	Protects the public from anticompetitive behavior and unfair and deceptive business practices; a law enforcement agency
(2)	EPA	(b)	Licenses and regulates the nuclear energy industry
(3)	FCC	(c)	Protects the public against unreasonable risks of injury associated with consumer products
(4)	FTC	(d)	Seeks to prevent discrimination in employment based on race, color, religion, sex, or national orgin, and other unlawful employment practices
(5)	FDA	(e)	Regulates interstate and foreign communications by means of radio, television, wire, cable, and satellite
(6)	EEOC	(f)	Ensures all workers a safe and healthy work environment
(7)	NLRB	(g)	Enforces the federal securities laws which regulate sale of securities to the investing public
(8)	NRC	(h)	Administers laws to prohibit distribution of adulterated, misbranded, or unsafe food and drugs
(9)	OSHA	(i)	Conducts union certification elections and holds hearings on unfair labor practice complaints
(10)	SEC	(j)	Administers all laws relating to the environment, including laws on water pollution, air pollution, solid wastes, pesticides, toxic substances, etc.

2 A liquor control board suspended a liquor license because a clerk sold a twelve-pack of beer to a twenty-year-old. The customer looked "old," and the drinking age was twenty-one. There was no evidence of previous violations. Will a court reverse the decision? Why, or why not?

3 The EPA discovered that a chemical company was dumping toxic waste into a local river. The agency conducted a hearing, first giving proper notice to the chemical company, and found the company to be in violation of EPA's regulations. A heavy fine was imposed. The company appealed to the court, contending that the hearing had denied it its right to a trial by jury. Is it correct? Why, or why not?

4 The statute creating the EPA states that its purpose is to establish rules and regulations to "promote a healthful environment." Using this delegation of authority, the agency adopted a rule that made it unlawful to utilize power plant equipment that allowed emissions "detrimental to the atmosphere." A power company, charged with violating the rule, challenged its constitutionality. What was the result? Why?

5 The Reagan administration, when it took office, rescinded the requirement by the National Highway Traffic Safety Administration that all new cars sold after September 1982 include air bags. Several automobile insurance companies filed suit, challenging the rescission of the air-bag rule. The rule had been rescinded on the belief that it was an example of excessive governmental regulation. Once the air-bag order was issued, was its rescission proper? Why, or why not?

6 To bring destabilizing competition among dairy farmers under control, a federal law authorizes the secretary of agriculture to issue milk market orders setting the minimum prices that handlers (those who process dairy products) must pay to producers (dairy farmers) for their milk products. Ultimate consumers of milk brought suit, challenging milk market orders. Should the case be dismissed? Why, or why not?

7 A congressman filed an administrative complaint with the Federal Election Commission, alleging various violations of the Federal Election Campaign Act by several different groups that made campaign contributions. Dissatisfied with the progress of the FEC's investigation, he filed suit against the FEC in federal district court, seeking to compel agency action. The court found that the agency action was "arbitrary and capricious." Does this entitle him to an award of attorney's fees under the Equal Access to Justice Act? Why, or why not?

8 Lawyers and legally trained persons are highly visible and important in most administrative agencies. Why do these agencies require so many legally trained personnel to accomplish their goals? Explain.

9 Dooley Company was charged with violating a rule of an administrative agency, and a hearing was conducted by an administrative law judge. The judge found the company guilty. The rules of the agency provided for a review by the full commission, but rather than seek such a review, Dooley Company filed a case in the courts to enjoin further agency action. What was the result? Why?

10 Joe owned a tract of real estate across the street from a major shopping center. The lot was at an intersection of a main road leading to the shopping center, and Joe wanted to build a service station on the property. The property was zoned for single-family residences. Joe filed a request to have the zoning classification changed to commercial. The zoning board denied the request, and Joe filed suit. He contended that the present and best use of the property was for commercial purposes. The zoning board contended that there needed to be a buffer between the shopping center and the residential area, and the only appropriate buffer was the street. What was the decision? Why?

11 Hershel filed a claim for workers' compensation, alleging that he received a knee injury which arose out of and in the course of his employment. The employer contended that Hershel's knee had been hurt in a touch football game. The hearing examiner denied the claim. Hershel then filed suit against the employer and the hearing examiner, contending that there was collusion between

them in the denial of his claim. The hearing examiner moved to dismiss the lawsuit. What was the result? Why?

12. The Federal Trade Commission issued an administrative complaint against several major oil companies, alleging unfair methods of competition. After failing to get the FTC to dismiss the complaint, the oil companies brought a separate action against it in federal court. They asserted that the FTC had issued the complaint without having reason to believe that the companies were violating the law. They sought an order to require the FTC to withdraw the complaint. The gist was that political pressure for a public explanation of the gasoline shortages forced the FTC to issue the complaint despite insufficient investigation. Should the case be dismissed? Why, or why not?

PART THREE

CONTRACTS AND TORTS

8
Contract Law and Private Enterprise

9
Torts in the Business Environment

10
Products and Service Liability

CHAPTER 8

CONTRACT LAW AND PRIVATE ENTERPRISE

OVERVIEW

Millions of new contracts are formed daily in the United States. Both businesspeople and consumers alike make contractual agreements. Over the years, no other area of the law has been as important as the law of contracts in supporting the private enterprise system.

The making of contracts is basic to the understanding of the legal environment of business. Labor unions and managers make collective bargaining agreements, which are contracts (Chapter 16). Antitrust law prohibits contracts that restrain trade (Chapters 21 to 23). Corporations can act only through contracts made by their agents (Chapters 11 to 13). In securities law (Chapter 18), consumer protection (Chapter 19), and debtor protection (Chapter 20), the government regulates the contractual process. Security agreements that protect creditors are contracts (Chapter 20). A major cause of action in product liability cases is breach of contract (Chapter 10). Even the Constitution has a clause that prohibits the states from "impairing the Obligation of Contracts" (Chapter 5).

There are five basic elements of a contract: offer, acceptance, consideration, capacity of parties, and legality of purpose. A substantial part of this chapter focuses on these elements and how they come together to form contracts. However, before discussing the formation of contracts, we must develop the role of contract law in the private enterprise system and consider various classifications of contracts.

Sections of this chapter also discuss other contract law topics, such as the significance of written contracts, the interpretation of contracts, the rights of third parties to contracts, and the performance of contracts. The concluding section outlines trends in contract law.

A special area of contract law covers the sale of goods. *Goods* are tangible, movable personal property, a category that covers everything from airplanes to flea collars. It does not, however, include services and real estate. Contracts for the sale of goods are covered by the Uniform Commercial Code, a special body of law adopted in every state except Louisiana. This chapter recognizes many instances in which the law treats sales of goods differently from other types of contracts.

Important contract terms include accord and satisfaction, assignment, bilateral contract, capacity, consideration, duress, executory contract, firm offer, fraud, implied contract, parol evidence rule, promissory estoppel, quasi-contract, rescission, specific performance, statute of frauds, third-party beneficiary, and voidable contract.

1 CONTRACT LAW AND ITS PLACE IN PRIVATE ENTERPRISE

When is the last time you entered a contract? Was it last month when you signed an apartment or dorm lease? If so, you must be very hungry. This is because one enters a contract when buying a meal or a snack from the vending machine. Actually, most people contract daily for a great variety of goods and services that they purchase or lease. The rules of contract law underlie the private enterprise system at every turn.

A **contract** is a *legally enforceable promise*. It need not usually be a formal, written document, and those who make a contract do not have to use the word "contract" nor recognize that they have made a legally enforceable promise. Still, the rules of contract law apply. If the expectations of the parties to a contract are not met, these rules affect legal negotiations or a lawsuit. For instance, contract law says that a restaurant "promises" that its food is fit to eat. Should the restaurant serve a meal that gives the buyer food poisoning, it would now be liable for the injury caused by breaking its promise.

Contract law enables people to make private agreements legally enforceable. Enforceability of agreements is desirable because it gives people the certainty they need to rely on promises contained in agreements. For instance, a shirt manufacturer in Los Angeles must know that it can rely on the promise of a store in Boston to pay for a thousand specially manufactured shirts. The manufacturer is more likely to agree to sew the shirts if it can enforce payment from the buyer, if necessary, under the law of contracts.

In an important sense, then, the law of contracts is vital for our private enterprise economy. It helps make buyers and sellers willing to do business together. Contract law is not as needed in the economy of the Soviet Union, where the state controls all buying and selling relationships. It is also less needed in countries such as Japan, where centuries of tradition regulate business arrangements. But in the United States the law of contracts promotes certainty that agreements will be kept and permits reliance on promises. It encourages the flow of commerce.

2 SOURCES OF CONTRACT LAW

Most of the contract law outlined in this chapter is common law (see Chapter 1). The courts have developed principles controlling contract formation, performance, breach, and remedies in countless cases that come to us today in the form of precedents. This judge-made law affects many types of contracts, including real property, service, employment, and general business contracts.

Another source of contract law is legislation. Various states have enacted parts of the common law, sometimes modifying it. The Uniform Commercial Code's coverage of the sale of goods is an example of how the legislation may modify the common law of contracts. The making of contracts in specific industries, such as the insurance industry, is also often controlled by legislation.

3 CLASSIFICATION OF CONTRACTS

Executory and Executed Contracts

We use a number of terms to help classify contracts. Mastery of these terms provides an important basis for further understanding of the topic. For instance, an **executory contract** (or term of a contract) is one which the contracting parties have not yet performed. An **executed contract** (or term) is one which the parties have performed.

Express and Implied Contracts

Many contracts arise from discussions in which parties actually discuss the promised terms of their agreement. These are called **express contracts.** A negotiated purchase of land for construction of a manufacturing plant is an example of an express contract. There are also **implied contracts** which arise from the conduct or actions of the parties, rather than by words. For instance, seeking professional services at a doctor's office implies a contractual agreement to pay the going rate for services even though no express promise to pay is made.

Unilateral and Bilateral Contracts

One classification of contracts concerns those that are unilateral and those that are bilateral. A **unilateral contract** involves a present act given in

186   PART 3:   CONTRACTS AND TORTS

return for a promise of future performance. A loan of money in return for a promise to repay at interest illustrates the unilateral contract. Another example is catching a bank robber in return for the promise of a reward. In **bilateral contracts** each party makes a promise to perform for the other: Greshman promises to deliver a deed to the land on October 31; Gomez promises to pay Greshman $50,000 for the land on that date. When it is unclear whether the parties to an agreement intend a unilateral or a bilateral contract, courts usually presume that the contract is bilateral.

Void Contracts

Void contracts are really not contracts at all. They are agreements which lack an essential contractual element. Often this element is legality of purpose. For example, in states where gambling is illegal, a bet on a football game is void. This usually means that a court will take no action when parties do not live up to the betting agreement. The opposite of a void contract is a **valid** one, which contains all the proper elements of a contract.

Voidable Contracts

A **voidable contract** binds one of the parties to the agreement but gives the other party the option of withdrawing from it. Contracts based on fraud or misrepresentation are voidable. **Fraud** involves an intentional misstatement of material (important) fact which induces one to rely justifiably to his or her injury. Intentionally calling a zircon a diamond and persuading someone to purchase it on that basis is a fraud. The defrauded party can withdraw from the contract. **Misrepresentation** is simply a misstatement without intent to mislead. However, a contract entered into through misrepresentation is still voidable by the innocent party.

Other examples of voidable contracts are those induced by duress or undue influence. **Duress** means force or threat of force. The force may be physical or, in some instances, economic. **Undue influence** occurs when one is taken advantage of unfairly through a contract by a party who misuses a position of relationship or legal confidence. Contracts voidable because of undue influence often arise when persons weakened by age or illness are persuaded to enter into a disadvantageous contract by a family member or other person.

Quasi-Contract

When one party is unjustly enriched at the expense of another, the law may imply a duty on the first party to pay the second, even though there is no contract between the two parties. The doctrine which requires this result is **quasi-contract**.

If a debtor overpays a creditor $5,000, the debtor can force the creditor to return that amount by suing under quasi-contract. It would be an unjust enrichment to allow the creditor to keep the $5,000. Likewise, when John has paid taxes on land, thinking that he owns it, and Mary comes along with a superior title (ownership) to the land and has John evicted, quasi-contract requires that Mary reimburse John for the taxes paid.

Note that quasi-contract is not an answer to every situation in which no contract exists. Over the years, courts have come to apply quasi-contract in a fairly limited number of cases based on unjust enrichment.

4 REMEDIES FOR BREACH OF CONTRACT

A party that does not live up to the obligation of contractual performance is said to **breach** the contract. There are several remedies available for a breach of contract. Figure 8-1 summarizes these remedies, which include negotiated settlement, arbitration, various damage awards, specific performance, and rescission.

The victim of a contract breach must *mitigate* compensatory and consequential damages when possible. To mitigate damages requires the victim to take reasonable steps to reduce them. Example: when a tenant breaches a house lease by moving away before the lease expires, the landlord must mitigate damages by renting the house to another willing and suitable tenant if such a person is available.

Trial litigation for breach of contract is fairly rare. By far the most common remedy for breach of contract is the *negotiated settlement*. The parties voluntarily reach an agreement to resolve the breach of contract. There are several reasons for this fact. First, trial litigation is time-consuming and very expensive. No matter who ultimately wins a lawsuit, both sides will lose the valuable productive effort of employees required to participate in the litigation. If at all possible, it is better to reach a mutual settlement of a breach of contract and to avoid trial litigation. Second, litigation inevitably causes hard feelings between parties and can destroy valuable business relationships. Since the parties may need to continue to do business with each other, it is best to settle a breach of contract rather than litigate it. Finally, in a trial situation one party wins and the other loses. When millions of dollars are at stake, it may be better to compromise and settle a breach of contract rather than risk losing everything in a trial. The wisdom of compromise and settlement in such situations is emphasized by the fact that juries are often ignorant of business practices, which tends to make their verdicts in business matters unpredictable.

In the mid-1970s, Westinghouse Electric Corp. failed to honor contracts calling for it to deliver uranium to a number of utility companies operating nuclear reactors. A sudden, worldwide tripling of prices by uranium producers caused Westinghouse to be unable to afford uranium to supply to the utility companies. When more than fifteen companies sued Westinghouse,

REMEDY
Negotiated Settlement
(A satisfactory solution to most breaches of contract is resolved by the parties themselves through voluntary negotiated settlements.)

REMEDY
Arbitration
(The parties agree to abide by the decision of a neutral third party or parties. See Chapter 4.)

REMEDY
Compensatory Damages
(Court-awarded damages to put the plaintiff in the same position as if the contract had been perfomed. Includes lost profits on the contract and cost of getting a substitute performance.)

REMEDY
Specific Performance
(Court-ordered remedy when subject matter of the contract is unique. Example: If seller does not convey contracted-for land to buyer, buyer can get court to order seller to convey the land.)

REMEDY
Consequential Damages
(Court-awarded damages arising from unusual losses which the parties knew would result from breach of the contract. Example Plaintiff's losses due to closing of business when defendant knew that failure to deliver ordered equipment would cause the losses.)

BREACH OF CONTRACT

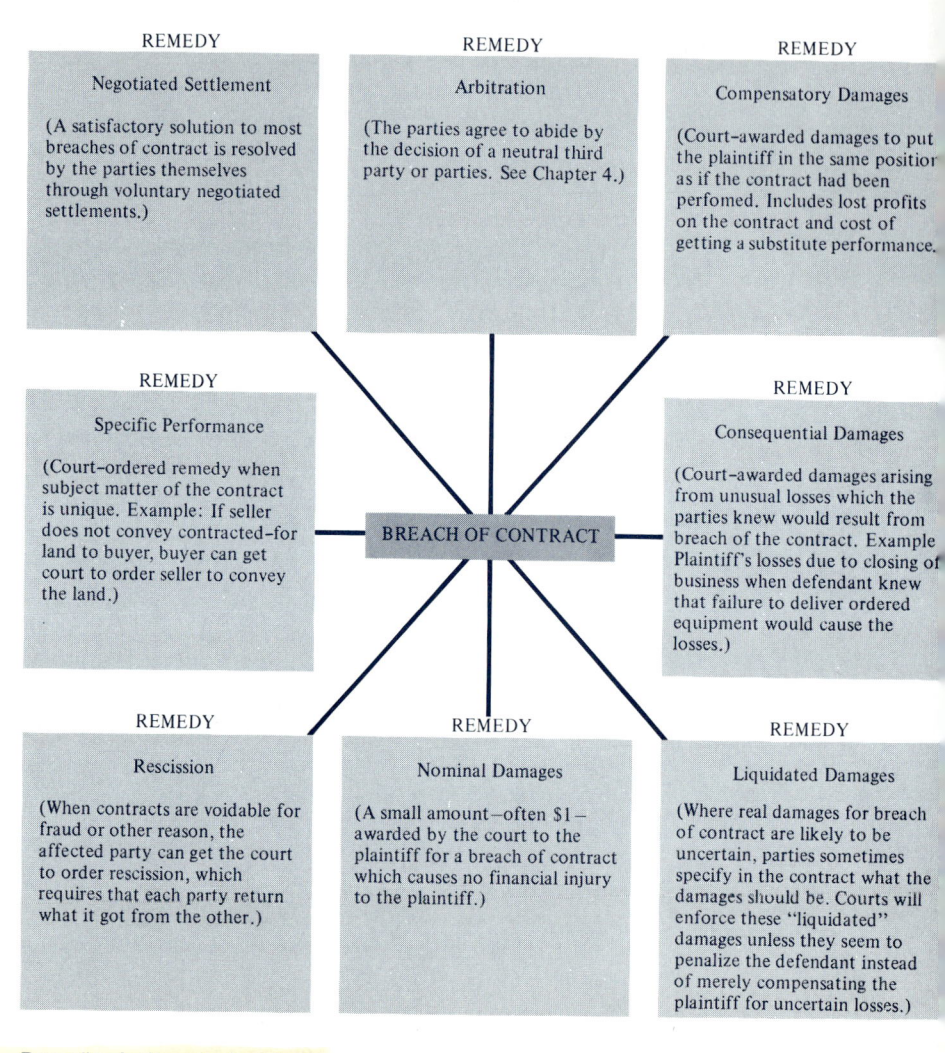

REMEDY
Rescission
(When contracts are voidable for fraud or other reason, the affected party can get the court to order rescission, which requires that each party return what it got from the other.)

REMEDY
Nominal Damages
(A small amount—often $1— awarded by the court to the plaintiff for a breach of contract which causes no financial injury to the plaintiff.)

REMEDY
Liquidated Damages
(Where real damages for breach of contract are likely to be uncertain, parties sometimes specify in the contract what the damages should be. Courts will enforce these "liquidated" damages unless they seem to penalize the defendant instead of merely compensating the plaintiff for uncertain losses.)

FIGURE 8-1 Remedies for breach of contract.

Westinghouse reached settlements totaling over $700 million. Not one of the cases ever went to trial.

5 OFFER TO CONTRACT

The contractual agreement begins with an offer made to an offeree (the person to whom the offer is made). An **offer** contains a specific promise and a specific demand. "I will pay $15,000 for that electrical transformer" promises $15,000 and demands a specific transformer in return. An offeror (person making the offer) must intend to make the offer, but courts measure intent objectively, that is, by how others reasonably see it rather than by what the offeror thinks he or she means. Still, as the following case illustrates, there can be confusion over what is and what is not an offer.

PIONEER REALTY AND LAND COMPANY v. MORTGAGE PLUS
346 N.W.2d 286 (N.D. 1984)

FACTS

Prospective home buyers applied for mortgages with Mortgage Plus. At the time of application, Mortgage Plus told the home buyers that its interest rate was 11½ percent. While the applications were being processed, Mortgage Plus raised its rate and refused to honor the 11½ percent rate. The home buyers then got their loans elsewhere and had to pay more than 11½ percent. They sued Mortgage Plus, claiming that Mortgage Plus breached its offer to lend money to qualified buyers at 11½ percent.

ISSUE

Did Mortgage Plus offer to lend money to these home buyers at 11½ percent interest?

DECISION

No.

REASONS

1. An offer requires a willingness to be legally bound.
2. Mortgage Plus did not display a willingness to be bound to provide a loan at 11½ percent following approval of home buyers' applications. It simply informed potential borrowers of the rate it was demanding at the time they filled out their applications. Mortgage Plus did not promise that the rate would remain at 11½ percent until the loans were approved.

Definiteness of Terms

Under the common law of contracts, contractual terms must be definite and specific. An offer to employ at a "reasonable salary" cannot be the basis for a contract because of *indefiniteness*. Most advertisements and catalog price quotes are considered too indefinite to form the basis for a contract unless they are specific about the quantity of goods being offered.

However, under the Uniform Commercial Code (UCC), contracts for the sale of goods can leave open nonquantity terms to be decided at a future time. An agreement for the sale of 500 cameras will bind the parties even though they leave open the price to be decided on delivery in six months.

Termination of Offer

Once an offer is made, when does it terminate if the offeree does not accept it? Table 8-1 lists several common instances showing when an offer may terminate.

6 ACCEPTANCE OF OFFER

Acceptance of an offer is necessary to a binding contract. An offer to enter into a bilateral contract is accepted by the offeree's making the required promise. When Toni offers Aaron certain widgets for $2,500 to be delivered by November 30 on ninety-day credit terms, and Aaron accepts, Aaron is promising to pay $2,500 on ninety-day credit terms.

Unilateral contracts are accepted by performing a requested act, not by making a promise. A company's offer of a $2,500 reward for information leading to the conviction of anyone vandalizing company property is not accepted by promising to provide the information. Only the act of providing information accepts such an offer.

Deposited Acceptance Rule

When does the acceptance become binding on the offeror? Unless the offer itself specifies a particular moment, the acceptance usually binds the parties when the offeree dispatches it. Since the offeree frequently mails the acceptance, the acceptance becomes binding when it is "deposited" with the postal service—hence, the *deposited acceptance rule*.

The importance of the deposited acceptance rule is that the offeror cannot revoke the offer once the offeree has accepted it. An added significance is that an offeror's revocation is not effective until the offeree actually re-

---

TABLE 8-1 WHEN AN OFFER TERMINATES

1. By provision in the offer: "This offer terminates at noon Friday."
2. By lapse of a reasonable period of time if the offer fails to specify a time: What is "reasonable" depends on the circumstances.
3. By rejection of the offer: "Thank you, but I do not want the widgets you are offering." A *counteroffer* is also a rejection: "Your offer of $10,000 for the land is too low. I will sell it to you for $12,500."
4. By revocation of the offer: "I regret to inform you that I am withdrawing my offer."
5. By destruction of the subject matter: The widgets are destroyed by fire before the offer of their sale has been accepted.
6. By the offeror's death or insanity: Offeror dies before the offer has been accepted.
7. By the contractual performance becoming illegal: The State Department declares that sales of certain computers to the Soviet Union are illegal. This terminates an offer to sell the computers to a Soviet trading company.

ceives it. Thus, a deposited acceptance creates a binding contract even though a revocation is also in the mail.

Mirror Image Rule

For an acceptance to create a binding contract, standard contract law requires that the acceptance must "mirror" the offer, that is, must match it exactly. If the acceptance changes the terms of the offer or adds new terms, it is not really an acceptance. It is a counteroffer.

The UCC has changed the **mirror image rule** with regard to merchants contracting for the sale of goods. An acceptance between merchants creates a binding contract even though it proposes new or different terms. The new or different terms become part of the contract unless: (1) the offer expressly limits acceptance to the original terms; (2) the proposed terms materially (importantly) alter the contract; or (3) the offeror rejects the proposed terms.

Silence Not Acceptance

In general, an offeror's failure to reject an offer does not imply acceptance. Another way to say this is that silence is not acceptance. The offeree has no usual duty to reply to the offer, even if the offer states that the offeror will treat silence as acceptance.

There are major exceptions to this rule. For instance, parties may have a contract that specifies that future shipments of goods be made automatically unless the offeree expressly rejects them. Many book- and record-club contracts operate in this manner.

A related doctrine looks at the parties' prior *course of dealing*—the way they have done business in the past. Silence may well imply acceptance if the parties previously dealt with each other by having the buyer take shipments from the seller unless the buyer notified the seller in advance not to ship.

Finally, the UCC says that a contract may arise from the *conduct* of a buyer and seller of goods. Emphasis is placed on how the parties act rather than on a formal offer and acceptance of terms.

7 VOLUNTARY CONSENT TO CONTRACTS

To be enforceable, a contract must be voluntarily made. The previously discussed doctrines of fraud, misrepresentation, duress, and undue influence show that a contract is voidable when both parties do not reach it through a voluntary, knowing consent.

What happens when each party misunderstands something very basic and material about a contract? Such a situation goes right to the heart of whether there has been a "voluntary" consent to a contract. When there is *mutual mistake* as to a material fact inducing a contract, rescission is appropriate. The test of materiality is whether the parties would have contracted had they been aware of the mistake. If they would not have contracted, the mistaken fact is material.

There is a difference between a mutual or bilateral mistake and a unilateral mistake. A **unilateral mistake** arises when only one of the parties to a contract is wrong about a material fact. Suppose that Royal Carpet Co. bids $8.70 per yard for certain carpet material instead of $7.80 per yard as it had intended. If the seller accepts Royal Carpet's bid, a contract results even though there was a unilateral mistake. As the following case shows, a party who has made a contractual promise because of a unilateral mistake cannot in most instances withdraw from it.

LIBBY, McNEIL & LIBBY v. UNITED STEELWORKERS
809 F.2d 1432 (9th Cir. 1987)

FACTS

The United Steelworkers Union represented employees at the Sacramento, California, plant of Libby, McNeil & Libby, Inc. (Libby), from 1974 until the plant closed in 1983. Every three years, the union negotiated collective-bargaining agreements with Libby. In 1974, Libby agreed to "duplicate" the pension plan the union had previously negotiated with American Can Company. In 1977, Libby agreed to modify its pension plan "in a similar manner" to that negotiated between the union and American Can. Libby agreed in 1980 to adopt the "same modifications" to its pension plan as those put into effect by American Can.

After its Sacramento plant closed in 1983, Libby filed suit, asking the court to declare that it did not owe early retirement benefits to certain employees whose jobs were discontinued because of the plant closing. When the union countered that these benefits were part of its collective-bargaining agreement with American Can, Libby responded that it had entered negotiations with the union under the mistaken belief that these benefits were not part of the collective-bargaining agreement.

ISSUE

Does Libby's mistaken belief excuse it from having to provide early retirement benefits to certain employees?

DECISION

No.

REASONS

1. Under California law, the unilateral mistake of one party does not excuse it from performance of its promise unless the other party "knew or had reason to know" of the mistake.
2. The evidence shows that the union reasonably believed Libby knew of the

early retirement benefits provided for in the agreement with American Can. Libby is not excused from paying these benefits by reason of its unilateral mistake.

8 CONSIDERATION IN THE CONTRACT

Courts will not enforce contractual promises unless they are supported by **consideration.** Before Robert can enforce a promise made by Peter, Robert must have given consideration, that is, assumed a legal obligation to Peter or surrendered a legal right. In a bilateral contract, each party promises something to the other. The binding promises are the consideration. In a unilateral contract, the consideration of one party is a promise; the consideration of the other party is performance of an act. When it is not clear whether there is consideration to support a promise, a court will often examine a transaction as a whole.

Consideration Must Be Bargained For

An important part of consideration is that it must be *bargained for*. Sometimes the parties to an agreement specify an insignificant consideration in return for a great one, for example, a promise of $1 in return for a promise to convey 40 acres of land. In such situations a court must decide whether the party promising to convey the land really bargained for the $1 or merely promised to make a gift. Promises to make gifts are not binding, because no bargained-for consideration supports the promise.

Similarly, *prior consideration* is no consideration. For instance, after many years of working at Acme Co., Bigman retires as vice-president for financial planning. The company's board of directors votes him a lifetime pension of $3,000 per month "for services rendered." One year later the board terminates his pension. If Bigman sues for breach of contract, he will lose. He gave no consideration to support the promise of a pension. The past years of service were not "bargained for" by the company's board when they granted the pension. The board merely promised to give an unenforceable gift to Bigman.

Agreement Not to Sue Is Consideration

Where reasonable grounds for a lawsuit exist, an agreement not to sue is consideration to support a promise. If First Bank agrees not to sue Maria, who has failed to repay a student loan, in return for the promise of Maria's parents to repay the loan, First Bank has given consideration. It has promised to surrender its legal right to sue Maria.

Likewise, suppose that a consulting firm bills a client $5,000 for fifty hours' work at $100 per hour. The client disputes the bill and contends that the consulting firm worked only twenty-five hours and should get only $2,500. If the two parties compromise the bill at $3,500 for thirty-five hours, this agreement binds them both. Each has surrendered the right to have a court determine exactly what amount is owed. Such an agreement and the payment of the $3,500 is an **accord and satisfaction.**

Performance of Pre-existing Obligation Is Not Consideration

A party to an agreement does not give consideration by promising to do something which he or she is already obligated to do. For example, suppose a warehouse owner contracts to have certain repairs done for $20,000. In the middle of construction, the building contractor demands an additional $5,000 to complete the work. The owner agrees, but when the work is finished he gives the contractor only $20,000. If the contractor sues, he will lose. The owner's promise to pay an extra $5,000 is not supported by consideration. The contractor is under a pre-existing obligation to do the work for which the owner promises an additional $5,000.

If the contractor promised to do something he was not already obligated to do, there would be consideration to support the promise of the additional $5,000. Promising to modify the repair plans illustrates such new consideration.

When No Consideration Is Necessary

The pre-existing obligation rule discussed above does not apply to a sale-of-goods contract. The UCC states that parties to a sale-of-goods contract may make binding modifications to it without both parties giving new consideration. If a buyer of widgets agrees to pay a seller an additional $5,000 over and above the amount already promised, the buyer is bound, although the seller gives only the consideration (widgets) that she is already obligated to give.

Under the UCC, the rules of consideration also do not apply to a **firm offer.** A firm offer exists when a merchant offering goods promises in writing that the offer will not be revoked for a period not to exceed three months. This promise binds the merchant, although the offeree buyer gives no consideration to support it. With offers not involving sales of goods by a merchant, a promise not to revoke an offer must be supported by the offeree's consideration to be binding. Such an arrangement is called an *option.*

An important exception to the rule requiring consideration to support a promise is the doctrine of **promissory estoppel.** This doctrine arises when a promisee justifiably relies on a promisor's promise to his or her economic injury. The promisor must know that the promisee is likely to rely on the promise. As the next case illustrates, promissory estoppel is becoming an increasingly used doctrine when the facts of a business relationship do not amount to an express or implied contract.

ESQUIRE RADIO & ELECTRONICS, INC. v. MONTGOMERY WARD & CO.
804 F.2d 787 (2d Cir. 1986)

FACTS

Esquire Radio & Electronics (Esquire) helped develop and import consumer electronics products for Montgomery Ward & Co. (Ward). Ward issued import orders to foreign manufacturers for products and spare parts. The orders were shipped to Esquire, which inventoried both products and spare parts for Ward's buy back. Although this arrangement continued for many years, the buy back terms were never expressly set forth. On several occasions, Esquire became concerned about its large inventories of spare parts. Each time Esquire was assured that Ward would buy the parts, and Ward urged Esquire to inventory even more. In 1984, Ward terminated its relationship with Esquire and refused to buy Esquire's existing spare parts inventory. Esquire sued.

ISSUE

Must Ward pay for the spare parts that Esquire has in inventory?

DECISION

Yes.

REASONS

1. The doctrine of promissory estoppel applies to the facts of this case.
2. Promissory estoppel has three principal requirements: "a clear and unambiguous promise; a reasonable and foreseeable reliance by the party to whom the promise is made; and an injury sustained by the party...by reason of his reliance."
3. Based on the evidence, the jury properly concluded that, over the years, Ward induced Esquire to accumulate spare parts by promising that the parts would be repurchased. Esquire reasonably and foreseeably relied on such promises and was injured.

Note in the *Montgomery Ward* case that the court apparently did not believe that Ward's assurances that it would buy the spare parts amounted to an implied-in-fact contract. Promissory estoppel usually arises when there is no contract.

9 CAPACITY OF PARTIES TO CONTRACT

Capacity refers to a person's ability to be bound by a contract. Courts have traditionally held three classes of persons to lack capacity to be bound by contractual promises: minors (also called "infants"), intoxicated persons, and mentally incompetent persons.

Minors

In most states, a minor is anyone under age 18. Minors usually cannot be legally bound to contractual promises unless those promises involve *necessaries of life* such as food, clothing, shelter, medical care, and—in some states—education. Even for necessaries, minors often cannot be sued for the contract price, only for a "reasonable" value. In a number of states, courts will hold a minor who has misrepresented his or her age to contractual promises.

A contract into which a minor has entered is voidable at the election of the minor. The minor can *disaffirm* the contract and legally recover any consideration which has been given an adult, even if the minor cannot return the adult's consideration. On the other hand, the adult is bound by the contract unless the minor elects to disaffirm it.

A minor may disaffirm a contract anytime before reaching the age of majority (usually 18) and for a reasonable time after reaching majority. If the minor fails to disaffirm within a reasonable time after reaching majority, the minor is said to *ratify* the contract. Upon ratification, the minor loses the right to disaffirm.

Intoxicated and Mentally Incompetent Persons

Except when a court has judged an adult to be mentally incompetent, she or he does not lose capacity to contract simply because of intoxication or mental impairment. In most cases involving adult capacity to contract, courts measure capacity by whether the adult was capable of understanding the nature and purpose of the contract. Obviously, the more complex a contractual transaction gets, the more likely a court is to decide that an intoxicated or mentally impaired person lacks capacity to contract.

10 ILLEGAL CONTRACTS

A basic requirement of a valid contract is legality of purpose. A "contract" to murder someone is hardly enforceable in a court of law. Contracts which require commission of a crime or tort or which violate accepted standards of behavior (*public policy*) are void. Table 8-2 gives common examples of illegal contracts.

Effect of Illegality on a Contract

Illegality makes a contract void. Courts will generally take no action on a void contract, and they will leave the parties to the contract where they

TABLE 8-2 EXAMPLES OF ILLEGAL CONTRACT

1. Gambling agreements (except where permitted)
2. Certain contracts made on Sunday (in about half the states)
3. Contracts for usurious interest (see Chapter 20)
4. Professional contracts made by unlicensed persons in which a regulatory statute requires licensing
5. Contracts which unreasonably restrain trade (see Chapters 21 to 23)
6. Many contracts which attempt to limit negligence liability of a seller of goods or services to the public (called *exculpatory contracts*)
7. Unconscionable contracts involving a sale of goods under the UCC (usually applied when a difference in bargaining power or education leads a merchant to take unreasonable advantage of a consumer)
8. Other contracts prohibited by statute or against public policy

have put themselves. As the next case shows, this fact means that a plaintiff can get no damages for breach of an illegal contract.

MASON v. HOSTA
199 Cal. Rptr. 859 (1984)

FACTS

A doctor who provided emergency physician services for various hospitals contracted with an administrator of one of the hospitals. The contract provided that the doctor would pay the administrator for each other hospital that the administrator could convince to use the doctor's services. The doctor was later advised by his attorney that it was illegal for him to pay for anyone to solicit business for him. The doctor quit paying the administrator under the contract. The administrator sued for breach of contract.

ISSUE

Was the contract void, since it was illegal for the doctor to pay for the solicitation?

DECISION

Yes.

REASONS

1. A contract that requires the performance of an unlawful act is illegal and void.
2. A court generally will take no action for breach of a void contract.

There are several exceptions to the general rule that courts will take no action on an illegal contract. A contract may have both legal and illegal provisions to it. In such a case, courts will often enforce the legal provisions and refuse to enforce the illegal ones. For instance, a contract providing services or leasing goods sometimes contains a provision excusing the service provider or lessor from liability for negligently caused injury. Courts usually will not enforce this provision but will enforce the rest of the contract.

Often, courts will allow an innocent party to recover payment made to a party who knows (or should know) that a contract is illegal. For example, courts will allow recovery of a payment for professional services made by an innocent person to a person who is unlicensed to provide such services.

Finally, in some cases courts may allow a person to recover compensation under quasi-contract for services performed on an illegal contract. Recovery may be allowed where an otherwise qualified professional lets his or her license expire and provides services to a client before renewing the license.

11 WHEN CONTRACTS SHOULD BE IN WRITING

Some people have the impression that contracts have to be in writing to be enforceable. In most instances, this is not so. However, it is true that certain contracts must be in writing (or at least evidenced by writing) to be enforceable.

The law requiring that certain contracts be in writing is the **statute of frauds.** Designed to prevent frauds arising from oral contracts, the original English statute is more than 300 years old. Today, every state has its own statute of frauds. Business-related provisions require the following contracts to be in writing: (1) contracts for the sale of an interest in land, (2) collateral contracts to pay the debt of another person, (3) contracts which cannot be performed within one year, and (4) sale-of-goods contracts for $500 or more.

Contracts for the Sale of an Interest in Land

Sales of interests in land are common contracts covered by the statute of frauds. Although "sales of interests in land" covers a contract to sell land, it includes much more. Interests in land include contracts for mortgages (see Chapter 20), mining rights, easements (rights to use another's land, such as the right to cross it with electrical power wires), and leases of longer than one year. However, a contract to insure land or to erect a building is not an interest in land.

The doctrine of *part performance* creates an exception to the requirement that sales of interests in land must be in writing. When a buyer of land has made valuable improvements in it, or where the buyer is in possession of it and has paid part of the purchase price, even an oral contract to sell is enforceable.

Collateral Contracts to Pay the Debt of Another

A collateral promise is a secondary one. For example, it is not Janet's promise to pay Joan's debt, which is an original or primary promise. A collateral contract arises only from Janet's promise to pay Joan's debt if Joan does not. Under the statute of frauds only collateral contracts must be in writing. The following case illustrates the difference between a collateral and an original promise.

GARLAND CO., INC. v. ROOFCO CO.
809 F.2d 546 (8th Cir. 1987)

FACTS

Garland Co. sold $48,517 worth of roofing materials to Roofco Co. Roofco failed to pay. In conversations between George Rasor, president and principal shareholder of Roofco, and agents of Garland Co., Rasor personally guaranteed that he would pay the debt. When after some nine months the debt remained unpaid, Garland Co. sued to enforce the oral promise. Rasor asserted the statute of frauds as a defense.

ISSUE

Is the statute of frauds a defense against Garland Co.'s action to collect the debt from Rasor?

DECISION

No.

REASONS

1. Enforcement of an original oral promise between a promisee and a promisor is not barred by the statute of frauds.
2. The tests to determine an original promise are the following: (1) benefit must be given by the promisee to the promisor alone, (2) the main purpose of the promisor in making the promise must be to benefit himself or herself, and (3) the promise must be supported by a consideration beneficial to the promisor.
3. In this case, benefit was given by the promisee (Garland) to the promisor (Rasor) alone. Garland delayed in filing suit against Roofco, which allowed Roofco to continue operations and realize profit from several jobs. As president and principal shareholder, Rasor received consideration from the delay. This consideration was Rasor's main purpose in making the oral promise to pay Roofco's debt.

> 4. The oral promise is thus original, not collateral, and the statute of frauds does not bar its enforcement.

Contracts Which Cannot Be Performed within One Year

The statute of frauds applies to a contract which the parties cannot perform within one year after its making. Courts usually interpret the one-year requirement to mean that the contract must specify a period of performance longer than one year. Thus, an oral contract for services which last twenty months is not enforceable. But an oral contract for services to be completed "by" a date twenty months away is enforceable. The difference is that the latter contract can be performed within one year, even if it actually takes longer than that to perform it.

As interpreted by the courts, the statute of frauds applies only to executory contracts which the parties cannot perform within a year. Once one of the parties has executed her performance for the other, she can enforce an oral multiyear contract.

Sale of Goods of $500 or More

Under the UCC, the statute of frauds covers sales of goods of $500 or more. Modifications to such contracts are also included. Table 8-3 lists exceptions to the writing requirement for sale-of-goods contracts.

Other Contracts Required to Be in Writing

In addition to the basic contracts covered by the statute of frauds, other contracts must be in writing in various states. Most states require insurance

TABLE 8-3 EXCEPTIONS TO STATUE-OF-FRAUDS REQUIREMENT FOR ORAL SALE-OF-GOODS CONTRACTS

1. Contract for goods specially manufactured for the buyer on which the seller had begun performance
2. Contract for goods for which payment has been made and accepted or which have been received and accepted
3. Contract for goods in which the party being sued admits in court or pleadings that the contract has been made
4. Contract for goods between merchants in which the merchant sued has received a written notice from the other merchant confirming the contract and in which merchant sued does not object to the confirmation within ten days

policies to be written. Several states demand written estimates in contracts for automobile repair.

Nature of the Required Writing

In some states, the statute of frauds requires that the actual contract between the parties must be in writing. However, most states merely require that the contract be *evidenced* by writing and be signed by the party to be held. This requirement means that the party being sued must have signed a note, memorandum, or another written form short of a formal contract which describes with reasonable certainty the terms of the oral agreement. As Table 8-3 indicates with regard to a sale of goods between merchants, the writing need not always be by the party sued. Under certain circumstances, it may be by the suing party.

12 THE PAROL EVIDENCE RULE

Like the statute of frauds, the **parol evidence rule** influences the form of contracts. This rule states that parties to a complete and final written contract cannot introduce oral evidence in court which changes the intended meaning of the written terms.

The parol evidence rule applies only to evidence of oral agreements made at the time of or prior to the written contract. It does not apply to oral modifications coming after the parties have made the written contract (although the statute of frauds may apply).

Suppose that Chris Consumer wants to testify in court that a merchant of an Ultima Washing Machine gave him an oral six-month warranty on the machine, even though the $450 written contract specified "no warranties." If the warranty was made after Chris signed the contract, he may testify about its existence. Otherwise, the parol evidence rule prevents him from testifying about an oral agreement which changes the terms of the written contract.

An exception to the parol evidence rule allows evidence of oral agreement which merely explains the meaning of written terms without changing the terms. Also, oral evidence which changes the meaning of written terms can be given if necessary to prevent fraud.

13 INTERPRETATION OF CONTRACTS

If each party is satisfied with the other's performance under a contract, there is no problem with interpreting the contract's terms. But when disagreement about contractual performance exists, often interpretation of the terms becomes necessary. Courts have devised several rules to assist in interpreting contracts.

Common words are given their usual meaning. "A rose is a rose is a rose," said the poet, and a court will interpret this common word to refer to a flower. However, if the word has a particular *trade usage,* courts will give it that meaning. In a contract in the wine trade, the term "rose" would not refer to a flower at all but to a type of wine.

Some words have special legal meanings. A party to a contract had best appreciate that courts give legal terms their legal meaning. The buyer of radios may think that a contractual phrase calling for "delivery to the buyer on November 20" means that the seller will take the radios to the buyer's place of business, but it does not.

"Delivery" is a legal term referring to the transfer of possession from the seller to the buyer. It does not make the seller responsible for "shipping" the radios to the buyer. Furthermore, the UCC says that when the contract states no place for delivery, the place of delivery is the seller's place of business. The buyer will have to take delivery of the radios at the seller's place of business on November 20. Because some terms have both common and legal meanings, a person should have an attorney examine contracts drawn up by others.

Many businesses today use printed form contracts. Sometimes the parties to one of these printed contracts type or handwrite additional terms. What happens when the typed or handwritten terms contradict the printed terms? What if the printed terms of a contract state "no warranties" but the parties have written in a ninety-day warranty? In such a case, courts interpret handwritten terms to control typed terms and typed terms to control printed ones. The written warranty will be enforced since the writing is the best evidence of the parties' true intention.

Another rule is that when only one of the parties drafts (draws up) a contract, courts will interpret ambiguous or vague terms against the party that drafts them. As the following case shows, courts often apply this rule to insurance contracts.

STATE FARM MUTUAL AUTOMOBILE INS. CO. v. QUEEN
685 P.2d 935 (Mont. 1984)

FACTS

Rhonda R. Queen was sued for injuries caused when she was driving an automobile that she did not own. She demanded that State Farm Insurance Co. defend her under a liability insurance policy written on another automobile. That policy provided that only the first person named on the insurance policy was to be insured for liability while driving a vehicle owned by someone else.

The policy in question listed the people insured as follows: "Queen, Gary A. and Rhonda R." State Farm argued that Gary A. Queen was the first named insured and, accordingly, Rhonda Queen was not insured while driving someone else's car.

ISSUE

Was Rhonda R. Queen insured while driving someone else's car?

DECISION

Yes.

REASONS

1. Since the last name of both insured parties is "Queen," the insurance policy contract is ambiguous as to who is the first named insured.
2. Ambiguity is interpreted against the drafter of a contract.
3. State Farm drafted the insurance policy contract.

14 ASSIGNMENT OF CONTRACTS

Electronics, Inc., sells 250 radios on credit at $20 apiece to Radio Land Retail. Electronics then sells its rights under the contract to Manufacturers' Credit Co. When payment is due, can Manufacturers' Credit legally collect the $5,000 owed to Electronics by Radio Land? This transaction is controlled by the law of **assignment,** which is a transfer (generally a sale) of rights under a contract. Figure 8-2 shows the transaction and introduces important terms.

There is an important exception to the rule that assignees are subject to assignors' defenses. Under the UCC, an assignee, called a *holder in due course* who takes an assignment of rights through a *negotiable instrument* or *document*, will not be subject to the personal contract defenses of an assignor. To be negotiable, an instrument or document must be signed by the

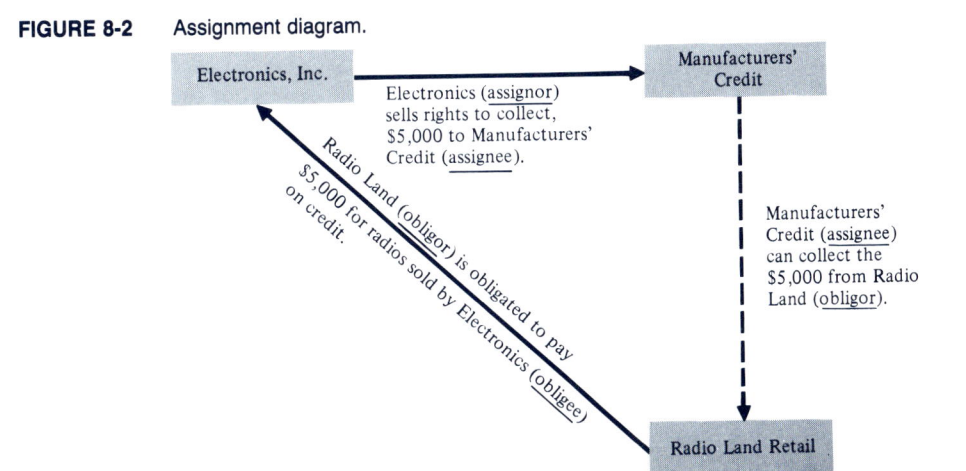

FIGURE 8-2 Assignment diagram.

Electronics, Inc.

Electronics (assignor) sells rights to collect, $5,000 to Manufacturers' Credit (assignee).

Radio Land (obligor) is obligated to pay $5,000 for radios sold by Electronics (obligee) on credit.

Manufacturers' Credit

Manufacturers' Credit (assignee) can collect the $5,000 from Radio Land (obligor).

Radio Land Retail

obligor (the party bound by legal obligation) and must contain certain language.

When an assignor assigns rights, he or she makes an implied warranty that the rights are valid. If the assignee is unable to enforce the rights against the obligor because of illegality, incapacity, or breach of contract, the assignee can sue the assignor. But the assignor does not guarantee that the obligor is able to pay the claim.

Notice of Assignment

When an assignment is made, an assignee should notify the obligor immediately. Otherwise, the obligor may perform for the obligee-assignor. If Radio Land pays Electronics before being notified of the assignment by Manufacturers' Credit, Radio Land cannot be held liable to Manufacturers' Credit.

A dishonest or careless assignor may assign the same contract rights to two different assignees. Notification of the obligor is especially important in this situation. In most states, the law says that the first assignee to notify the obligor has priority no matter which assignee receives the first assignment of rights.

Contracts Which Cannot Be Assigned

Although most contracts can be assigned, certain ones cannot. An assignment that increases the burden of performance to the obligor cannot be assigned. For instance, a right to have goods shipped to the buyer's place of business cannot be assigned by an Atlanta buyer to a Miami buyer if a New York seller has to ship the goods to Miami instead of Atlanta. Similarly, a *requirements contract* to supply a retail buyer with all the radios needed cannot be assigned because it depends upon the buyer's personal situation.

Most states regulate the assignment of wages. They limit the amount of wages which a wage earner can assign. This protects wage earners and their families.

A party to a contract cannot assign (delegate) performance of duties under a contract when performance depends on the character, skill, or training of that party. Otherwise, duties under a contract can be assigned as well as rights.

15 CONTRACTS BENEFITING A THIRD PARTY

The performance of a contract may benefit persons who are not parties to the contract. Such persons are called **third-party beneficiaries.** In general, persons who are not parties to a contract have no rights to sue to enforce the contract or to obtain damages for breach of contract. As the next case illustrates, however, a third-party beneficiary can sue if the parties to the contract intended to benefit that person.

BRIDGMAN v. CURRY
398 N.W.2d 167 (Iowa 1986)

FACTS

Plaintiffs Thomas and Ann Bridgman sold their farm to John and Edna Curry. The contract of sale obligated the Currys to make annual payments to the plaintiffs. The Currys later assigned four-sixths of the farm to the four defendants. The assignment contract stated that the defendants agreed "to be bound by the terms of the Bridgman contract." When the Currys failed to pay the Bridgmans and filed for bankruptcy, the plaintiffs sued the defendants.

ISSUE

Are the plaintiffs third-party beneficiaries of the assignment contract between the Currys and the defendants?

DECISION

Yes.

REASONS

1. The chief factor in determining whether a party may bring an action to enforce a contract between other parties is the intent of the contracting parties.
2. The facts of this case show that the plaintiffs are intended beneficiaries who have the right to enforce the promises the defendants made to the Currys.

Creditor, Donee, and Incidental Beneficiaries

If Susan owes Bob $1,000 and she performs services for Frank, she may contract to have Frank pay Bob $1,000. In such an instance, Bob is a third-party **creditor beneficiary** of the contract between Susan and Frank. Bob can sue Frank if there is a breach of the contract and can also sue Susan, since she still owes him $1,000.

When the performance under a contract is meant as a gift to a third party, that person is a **donee beneficiary.** Donee beneficiaries can sue the party that owes them a performance under a breached contract, but they cannot sue the party that contracted to make them a gift. The beneficiary of a life insurance policy is usually a donee beneficiary.

An **incidental beneficiary** is a third party that unintentionally benefits from a contract. The incidental beneficiary has no rights under a contract.

16 PERFORMANCE OF CONTRACTS

At the time parties reach agreement under a contract, the *duty of performance* becomes binding. Each party must perform the consideration promised to the other. Failure to perform breaches the contract.

Conditions in Contracts

Parties often put **conditions** in a contract that affect its performance. If something must take place in the future before a party has a duty to perform, it is called a *condition precedent.* For example, a building developer may contract to buy certain land "when the city of Euphoria annexes it." The annexation is a condition precedent to the developer's duty to purchase the land.

A *condition subsequent* excuses contractual performance if some future event takes place. A marine insurance policy that terminates shipping loss coverage "if war is declared" contains a condition subsequent.

Under *concurrent conditions* each party's contractual performance is triggered by the other party's tendering (offering) performance. In a contract for the purchase of land, the performing obligations of the seller and buyer are concurrent conditions. The significance of a concurrent condition is that a party must offer to perform before legally holding the other party for nonperformance. The land buyer must offer to pay for the land before suing the seller for failing to perform.

The conditions discussed above may be express or implied. Express conditions are set forth in the contract. Implied conditions do not appear in the contract but are implied by law.

Levels of Contract Performance

A party to a contract may not always perfectly perform duties under it. The more complex a contract is, the more difficult it is for a party to complete every aspect of performance. Courts generally recognize three levels of **specific performance.**

Complete performance recognizes that a contracting party has fulfilled every duty required by the contract. Payment of money, for example, is a contractual duty of performance which a party can perform completely. A party that performs completely is entitled to a complete performance by the other party and may sue to enforce this right.

Substantial performance represents a less-than-complete performance. A contracting party has honestly attempted to perform but has fallen short. Because of the complexity of building contractors' work, they often are able to reach substantial performance but not complete performance. One who substantially performs is entitled to the price promised by the other less that party's damages.

Material breach is a level of performance below what is reasonably acceptable. A party that has materially breached a contract cannot sue the other party for performance and is liable for damages arising from the breach.

17 DISCHARGE OF CONTRACTS

A party to a contract is *discharged* when the party is released from all further obligation of performance. Of course, complete performance discharges a party to a contract. Table 8-4 lists other events which create discharge.

Impossibility of Performance

One event which discharges a party's obligation of performance deserves special attention. A party is discharged because of *impossibility of performance*.

If the subject matter of the contract is destroyed, the contract becomes impossible to perform. When a contract exists for the sale of a building, and the building burns, the seller is discharged from performance. Likewise, when there is a contract for personal services, and the party promising the services becomes ill or dies, the party receives discharge from performance.

The party that promised performance which becomes illegal is also discharged because of impossibility of performance. Mere increased difficulty or reduced profitability, however, does not constitute impossibility of performance.

Finally, under the UCC a party to a sale-of-goods contract receives discharge from performance because of **commercial impracticability.** The "impracticability" standard is not as difficult to meet as the "impossibility" standard. What constitutes impracticability of performance depends upon the circumstances of the situation. For instance, a manufacturer may be discharged from an obligation to make goods for a buyer when the manufacturer's major source of raw materials is unexpectedly interrupted. But if

TABLE 8-4   EVENTS WHICH DISCHARGE A PARTY TO A CONTRACT

1 Complete performance
2 Occurrence of a condition subsequent
3 Nonoccurrence of a condition precedent
4 Material breach by the other party
5 Legal surrender of the right to enforce performance (waiver)
6 Mutual agreement to rescind
7 Expiration of the statute of limitations for enforceability
8 Novation (the substitution by agreement of one party for another on a contract)
9 Impossibility of performance

the raw materials are reasonably available from another supplier, the manufacturer may not receive discharge because of impracticability.

18 TRENDS IN CONTRACT LAW

This chapter has given you an appreciation of the influence of contract law on private commercial transactions. To this end, the discussion has centered on the rules of contract law. Legal enforceability of contractual agreements provides an important framework for promoting certainty and efficiency in commercial dealings.

In general, however, trends in contract law do not affect the basic rules discussed in this chapter. Other chapters in the book develop many of the trends that affect contract law today. They deal with specific types of contracts or the use of contracts in particular situations. Still, several trends which are not mentioned elsewhere deserve attention here.

Trends Affecting Contractual Relationships between Businesses

As commercial transactions have grown increasingly complex, courts and legislatures have created more and more exceptions to traditional, fairly inflexible requirements of contract formation. These exceptions reflect an attempt to accommodate law to the actual reality of business dealings. For instance, UCC provisions on modification of contracts without consideration, opened-ended contract terms, and contract formation by course of dealing are exceptions to traditional rules.

Similarly, courts have demonstrated greater willingness in recent years to grant damages based on one party's reasonable reliance on another's promises instead of merely on the party's expectations under a formal contract. This development reflects attempts to conform law to actual behavior in a complicated business world.

Finally, as previously mentioned, many contracting parties do not seek legal enforcement of breached agreements. With ever greater frequency, parties use arbitration, mediation, and negotiation when business problems arise under contracts. They avoid the time-consuming, expensive, and uncertain litigation process.

Trends Affecting Contractual Relationships between Businesses and Employees

A recent statistic asserts that more than half of the country's biggest corporations now have employment contracts for top management. This figure represents a 50 percent increase since 1982. Contract negotiation is becoming increasingly important for many executives.

Most lower-level workers still do not have express contracts with their employers. Employers may terminate the employment of these workers at will (see Chapter 14). However, courts in growing numbers have been willing to take statements made by employers in personnel manuals and other documents and use them as a basis for implying contract rights for employees.

Trends Affecting Contractual Relationships between Businesses and Consumers

A major trend in contract law has been the passage of many statutes affecting contracts between businesses and consumers. Government has stepped in at both the federal and state levels to protect consumers as they make contracts with businesses. Chapters 19 and 20 discuss protection of consumers and debtors.

One recent development affecting business and consumer contracts has been enactment of "plain English" statutes in several states. These statutes require that standard business and consumer form contracts be written in a clearly understandable way. Drafters of such contracts must avoid legal expressions not ordinarily comprehended by consumers. More than thirty states have related statutes directed specifically at insurance contracts. A number of federal laws affecting readability also apply to specific types of contracts.

REVIEW QUESTIONS

1 For each term in the left-hand corner column, match the most appropriate description in the right-hand column:

(1) Accord and satisfaction
(2) Assignment
(3) Bilateral contract
(4) Condition precedent
(5) Executory contract
(6) Firm offer
(7) Material breach
(8) Parol evidence rule

(a) A recovery based on unjust enrichment
(b) A merchant's written promise to hold open an offer
(c) A contract which binds one party but which allows the other party to withdraw legally
(d) A future uncertain event which must occur before performance is due
(e) A level of contractual performance which is below what is reasonably acceptable
(f) Settlement and payment of a disputed debt by mutual agreement
(g) The doctrine that prohibits use of oral evidence to alter or vary the terms of certain written contracts
(h) A contract the consideration for which is a binding promise given by each party

(9) Quasi-contract
(10) Rescission
(11) Voidable contract

(i) A remedy which requires that each party return what it got from the other
(j) A transfer of contractual rights
(k) A contract which the parties have not yet performed

2 Why is the law of contracts vital to the private enterprise system?
3 Gustavson contracts with Sanders to buy 51 percent of the stock of Gimlet Corporation. When Sanders breaches the contract, Gustavson sues for specific performance. Is specific performance an appropriate remedy under these circumstances? Explain.
4 Most contractual disputes are resolved by negotiated settlement. Explain why.
5 Condor Equipment Company offers to sell Snappy Jack Biscuits, Inc., a dough-cutting machine. The offer states: "This offer expires Friday noon." On Thursday morning, the sales manager for Condor calls the president of Snappy Jack and explains that the machine has been sold to another purchaser. Discuss whether Condor has legally revoked its offer to Snappy Jack.
6 Fielding Bros. offers to ship six furnaces to Central City Heating and Cooling Co. for $4,500 cash. Central City accepts on the condition that Fielding give 120 days' credit. Has a contract resulted? Explain.
7 Goldman, an appliance wholesaler, signs an agreement with the Cool-It Corporation for 250 air-conditioners. The order price is left open and is to be decided in three months when the air-conditioners are delivered. Has a binding contract resulted? Would your answer be different if the parties specified the price but left open the quantity term until delivery?
8 Hunt signs an equipment lease contract with Edwards Rental. The contract contains a clause stating: "Lessor disclaims all liability arising from injuries caused by use of this equipment." Because the equipment has been improperly serviced by Edwards Rental, Hunt is injured while using it. If Hunt sues, will the disclaimer clause likely be enforced? Explain.
9 Elegante Haberdashery telephones an order to Nordic Mills for 500 men's shirts at $15 each. Each shirt will carry the Elegante label and have the Elegante trademark over the pocket. After the shirts are manufactured, Elegante refuses to accept delivery of them and raises the statute of frauds as a defense. Discuss whether this defense applies to these facts.
10 Gus contracts to buy a used car from Cars Galore, Inc. The printed contract specifies "no warranties." But Gus and the sales manager of Cars handwrite into the contract a ninety-day guarantee on the transmission. If the transmission fails after sixty days, is there a warranty protecting Gus or not?
11 Franchetti Rifle Distributors assigns a $20,000 claim against Top Gun, Inc., to the Zenith Collection Agency. When Zenith sues Top Gun, Top Gun asserts that it rejected a shipment of rifles from Franchetti, out of which the claim arose, because they had defective trigger guards. Explain whether Top Gun can properly assert its defense against plaintiff Zenith.
12 The Store Owners Association at the Clearcreek Mall hires City Security Service to patrol the mall's parking lot after dark. Nancy Boggins, owner of the Shoe Attic at the mall, is mugged one night while the security guard is making an unauthorized visit to a friend's house. Can Nancy successfully sue City Security? Does it change your answer if Nancy is not a member of the Store Owners Association?
13 Bryan Developers signs a contract to purchase certain real estate for $256,000

"if the property is annexed by the city of Carnesville within one year." What type of condition is the quoted language? What is its legal effect?

14 Ace Contracting constructs an office building for Realty Enterprises. Realty's tenants quickly find a number of minor problems with the plumbing and insulation of the new building. When Realty contacts Ace about bringing its work up to standard, Ace promises to correct the problems, but never does. Can Realty rescind the contract? What are Realty's legal remedies?

15 In the mid-1970s, a tripling of prices by an illegal cartel of uranium producers caused Westinghouse Electric Corp. to default on uranium delivery contracts to a number of utility companies. The companies sued, and Westinghouse settled. If the case had gone to trial, what defense might Westinghouse have raised to excuse its nonperformance under the contracts?

CHAPTER 9

TORTS IN THE BUSINESS ENVIRONMENT

OVERVIEW

The word "tort" means "wrong." Legally, a tort is a civil wrong other than a breach of contract. Most torts involve injuries to persons or property. These injuries may be crimes as well as torts, but the doctrine of tort itself is civil rather than criminal. The usual remedy for a tort is court-granted damages. Behavior which constitutes a tort is called *tortious* behavior. One who commits a tort is a *tortfeasor*.

This chapter divides torts into three main categories: intentional torts, negligence torts, and strict liability torts. Intentional torts involve deliberate actions which cause injury. Negligence torts involve injury following a failure to use "reasonable care." Strict liability torts impose legal responsibility for injury even though a liable party neither intentionally nor negligently causes the injury.

Important to torts are the concepts of duty and causation. One is not liable for another's injury unless he or she has a *duty* toward the person injured. And, of course, there is usually no liability for injury unless one has *caused* the injury. We explain these concepts under the discussion of negligence, where they are most relevant.

This chapter also covers the topic of damages. The topic concerns the business community because the size of damage awards, frequently against businesses, has risen greatly in recent years. The chapter concludes with consideration of policy trends which are developing in tort law.

There are a great number of significant terms in this chapter. They include assault and battery, assumption of risk, cause in fact, comparative responsibility, contributory negligence, conversion, copyright, defamation, duty, false imprisonment, infliction of mental distress, intentional interference with contractual relations, invasion of privacy, patent, proximate causation, punitive damages, respondeat superior, strict liability, trademark, trade secret, and trespass.

1 THE DEVELOPMENT OF TORT LAW

Nineteenth Century

Prior to 1800, much of the law of personal-property injury was founded on the doctrine of **trespass.** When we think of trespass now, we think mainly of trespass to land. In the past, however, the doctrine was used by any plaintiff who had sustained an injury to person or property due to the act of the defendant. And the trespass doctrine was a strict liability one. The fact that the defendant was not at fault nor could have reasonably avoided the accident was usually irrelevant.

The trespass doctrine as applied to personal injury, however, was the doctrine of an uncomplicated age and of a simple people. At that time, any injury done by another invited swift revenge if the law did not impose itself between the actor and the injured. But in the 1800s, as populations expanded and social and economic life became more complex, values and attitudes grew more sophisticated. The law changed to meet these changing conditions, and the doctrine of **negligence** emerged. No longer was one liable for reasonably unavoidable injury inflicted upon the person of another. Instead, liability would be imposed only where the actor was at fault and had failed to act as a "reasonable man."

Economic realities in the 1800s help explain the widespread acceptance of the new negligence doctrine. Many judges apparently considered that the strict liability of trespass would threaten the struggling infant industries of the time, putting an end to the socially valuable production of machined goods. The courts thus extended negligence law and defenses into areas of employer-employee relations, products liability, and accidents arising from business activity.

Nineteenth-century negligence doctrine is sometimes viewed as achieving a type of distributive justice that removed legal liability from nonnegligent business persons. It left the risk of injury from nonnegligent behavior on the victims of such behavior, providing a type of "subsidy" for business development. Although this view prevails today among legal scholars, it is not the only one. Many economics-inclined scholars disagree. They argue that in cases developing negligence doctrine the courts simply were allocating accident losses and property rights in the most economically efficient manner possible.

Whichever view is most accurate, it remains undeniable that courts in the 1800s fashioned numerous tort principles which left injury losses on accident victims. In addition to negligence doctrine, the courts created the defense of **contributory negligence**, which barred plaintiffs from any recovery if their own fault contributed to their injuries. Another court-created doctrine, the **assumption-of-risk** defense, barred plaintiffs from recovery when they knowingly submitted themselves to hazardous conditions created by the carelessness of others.

Another barrier courts placed in the way of plaintiff recovery was the doctrine of *proximate causation*. Not only did plaintiffs have to prove that their injuries actually were caused by negligence, they also had to establish that their injuries "foreseeably" arose from (were proximately caused by) the negligence (see section 16). Courts regarded questions of proximate cause as "matters of law." Judges dismissed many negligence claims upon the basis that the alleged facts showed no proximate cause.

Twentieth Century

Beginning in the twentieth century, the pendulum started to swing back. The courts (and legislatures) acted in many situations to distribute accident losses away from injured victims. In the workplace, the passage of workers' compensation statutes accomplished this goal (see Chapter 14). In product-related accidents, the courts arrived at tort reform through a series of developments which culminated in strict tort liability—which requires no proof of fault—for the sale of defective products (see Chapter 10). Also, the harsh application of contributory negligence has been eased (see section 17).

Even the application of negligence doctrine has changed. Today, many courts consider questions of proximate cause as issues which plaintiff-sympathetic juries, rather than judges, should resolve. Also, in recent years courts have expanded the scope of "duty," which defines those to whom one owes reasonable care (nonnegligence) (see section 13).

What has caused these changes in tort law in the twentieth century? Economic conditions are chiefly responsible. The infant industries of the nineteenth century have grown into healthy maturity. Business no longer needs the liability protection it required a hundred years ago. Courts and legislatures also follow the mood of the country. To a significant extent, the public has demanded that tort laws be reformed to relieve injured individuals of potentially catastrophic accident losses.

Note that the rapid development of tort law has chiefly concerned negligence and strict liability. Changes in intentional tort law have been more gradual, although they have also taken place.

INTENTIONAL TORTS

An important element in the following torts is *intent,* as we are dealing with *intentional* torts. "Intent" is usually defined as the desire to bring about certain results. But in some circumstances the meaning is even broader, including not only desired results but also results which are "substantially likely" to result from an action. Recently, employers who knowingly exposed employees to toxic substances without warning them of the dangers have been sued for committing the intentional tort of battery. The employers did not desire their employees' injuries, but these injuries were "substantially likely" to result from the failure to warn.

The following sections explain the basic types of intentional torts. Table 9-1 lists these torts.

2 ASSAULT AND BATTERY

An **assault** is the placing of another in immediate apprehension for his or her physical safety. "Apprehension" has a broader meaning than "fear." It includes the expectation that one is about to be physically injured. The person who intentionally creates such apprehension in another is guilty of the tort of assault. Many times a battery follows an assault. A **battery** is an illegal touching of another. As used here, "illegal" means that the touching is done without justification and without the consent of the person touched. The touching need not cause injury.

A store manager who threatens an unpleasant customer with a wrench is probably guilty of assault. Actually hitting the customer with the wrench would constitute battery.

3 INTENTIONAL INFLICTION OF MENTAL DISTRESS

Intentional **infliction of mental distress** is a battery to the emotions. It arises from outrageous, intentional conduct which carries a strong probability of causing mental distress to the person at whom it is directed. Usually, one who sues on the basis of an intentional infliction of mental distress must prove that the defendant's outrageous behavior caused not only mental distress, but also physical symptoms, such as headaches or sleepless-

TABLE 9-1 TYPES OF INTENTIONAL TORTS

Assault and battery
Intentional infliction of mental distress
Invasion of privacy
False imprisonment
Trespass
Conversion
Defamation
Common law business torts
Statutory competitive torts
Constitutional torts

ness. The following case shows how this tort can occur in the employment relationship.

FORD v. REVLON, INC.
734 P.2d 580 (Ariz. 1987)

FACTS

A supervisor made repeated sexual advances toward an employee. The employee complained to management, but she was advised "to forget the matter." Nine months later, the employee filed an official charge of sexual harassment and asked protection against her supervisor. She was told the supervisor would be "closely monitored." Finally, thirteen months after the initial harassment, the employer issued a letter of censure to the supervisor. Four months later, the employee, who had developed high blood pressure and chest pains, attempted suicide. That same month, the employer fired the supervisor. The employee then sued the supervisor and the employer.

ISSUE

Did the employer's conduct amount to intentional infliction of mental distress?

DECISION

Yes.

REASONS

1. The employer's failure to investigate promptly the employee's complaint, which violated the employer's own guidelines, was a tort, independent of the supervisor's harassment of the employee.
2. The employer's conduct meets the requirements of intentional infliction of mental distress. First, it was outrageous and extreme. Second, even if the employer did not intend to cause distress, its reckless disregard of its supervisor's behavior made it nearly certain that emotional distress would occur. Third, both physical and other evidence indicates that emotional distress did occur.

In the business world, many examples of infliction of mental distress come about from the efforts of creditors to extract payment from their debtors. Frequent, abusive, threatening phone calls by creditors might provide the basis for a claim of intentional infliction of mental distress. As torts go, this one is of fairly recent origin. It is a judge-made tort, which furnishes a good example of how the courts are becoming increasingly sensitive to the range of injuries for which compensation is appropriate. In some states, courts have gone so far as to establish liability for carelessly inflicted mental distress, such as the distress of a mother who sees her child negligently run down by a delivery truck.

4 INVASION OF PRIVACY

The tort of **invasion of privacy** is one that is still in the early stages of legal development. As the statutes and court cases recognize it, the tort at present comprises three principal invasions of personal interest. An invasion of any one of these areas of interest is sufficient to trigger liability.

Most commonly, liability will be imposed on a defendant who appropriates the plaintiff's name or likeness for his or her own use. Many advertisers and marketers have been required to pay damages to individuals when pictures of them have been used without authorization to promote products, or when their names and identities have been used without permission for promotional purposes. Before using anyone's picture or name, an advertiser must obtain a proper release from that person to avoid possible liability. Appropriating another's name and identity in order to secure credit is an additional example of this invasion-of-privacy tort.

A second invasion of privacy is the defendant's intrusion upon the plaintiff's physical solitude. Illegal searches or invasions of home or possessions, illegal wiretapping, and persistent and unwanted telephoning can provide the basis for this invasion-of-privacy tort. In one case, a woman even recovered damages against a photographer who entered her sickroom and snapped a picture of her. Employers who enter their employees' homes without permission have also been sued successfully for invasions of privacy. If the invasion of privacy continues, it may be enjoined by the court. Jacqueline Kennedy Onassis sought and obtained an injunction which forbade a certain photographer from getting too close to her and her children. Under this tort, the invasion of physical solitude must be highly objectionable to a reasonable person.

The third invasion of personal interest which gives rise to the invasion-of-privacy tort is the defendant's public disclosure of highly objectionable, private information about the plaintiff. A showing of such facts can be the basis for a cause of action, even if the information is true. Thus, publishing in a newspaper that the plaintiff does not pay his or her debts has been ruled to create liability for the defendant creditor. Communicating the same facts to a credit reporting agency or the plaintiff's employer usually does not impose liability, however. In these cases, there has been no disclosure to the public in general. Also, the news media are protected under the First Amendment when they publish information about public officials and other public figures.

5 FALSE IMPRISONMENT AND MALICIOUS PROSECUTION

Claims of **false imprisonment** stem most frequently in business from instances of shoplifting. This tort is the intentional unjustified confinement of a nonconsenting person. Although most states have statutes which permit merchants or their employees to detain customers suspected of shoplifting, this detention must be a reasonable one. The unnecessary use of force, lack of reasonable suspicion of shoplifting, or an unreasonable length of confinement can cause the merchant to lose the statutory privilege. The improperly detained customer is then able to sue for false imprisonment. Allegations of battery are also usually made if the customer has been touched.

The tort of **malicious prosecution** is often called "false arrest." Malicious prosecution arises from causing someone to be arrested criminally without proper grounds. It occurs, for instance, when the arrest is accomplished simply to harass someone. In 1984 in Albany, New York, a jury awarded a man $200,000 for malicious prosecution. His zipper had broken, leaving open his fly, and a store security guard had him arrested for indecent exposure even after he explained that he had not noticed the problem.

6 TRESPASS

To enter another's land without consent or to remain there after being asked to leave constitutes the tort of **trespass**. A variation on the trespass tort arises when something (such as particles of pollution) is placed on another's land without consent. Although the usual civil action for trespass asks for an injunction to restrain the trespasser, the action may also ask for damages.

Union pickets walking on company property (in most instances), customers refusing to leave a store after being asked to do so, and unauthorized persons entering restricted areas are all examples of trespass. Note that trespass is often a crime as well as a tort. Intentional wrongdoing is frequently criminal.

7 CONVERSION

Conversion is the wrongful and unlawful exercise of dominion (power) and control over the personal property of another. Conversion deprives the proper owner of lawful rights in the property. The deprivation may be either temporary or permanent, but it must constitute a serious invasion of the owner's rights. Abraham Lincoln once convinced an Illinois court that a defendant's action in riding the plaintiff's horse for fifteen miles was not sufficiently serious to be a conversion since the defendant had returned the horse in good condition. The plaintiff had left the horse with the defendant to be stabled and fed.

Conversion arises often in business situations. Stealing property or purchasing stolen property (even innocently) is a conversion. Failing to return properly acquired property at the designated time, delivering property to the wrong party, and destruction and alteration of property are all conversions if the deprivation of ownership rights is serious or long-lasting. Even if she or he intends to return it, one who converts is absolutely liable for any damage done to property. A warehouse operator who improperly transfers stored goods from a designated to a nondesignated warehouse is absolutely liable when a tornado destroys the goods, or when a thief steals them.

8 DEFAMATION

Defamation is the publication of untrue statements about another which hold up that individual's character or reputation to contempt and ridicule. "Publication" means that the untruth must be made known to third parties. If defamation is oral, it is called **slander.** Written defamation, or defamation published over radio or television, is termed **libel.**

False accusations of dishonesty or inability to pay debts frequently bring on defamation suits in business relationships. Sometimes, such accusations arise during the course of a takeover attempt by one company of another through an offering to buy stock. In a recent instance, the chairman of one company called the chairman of a rival business "lying, deceitful, and treacherous" and charged that he "violated the standards by which decent men do business." If untrue, these remarks provide a good example of defamation of character. Punitive or punishment damages, as well as actual damages, may be assessed in defamation cases.

Individuals are not the only ones who can sue for defamation. A corporation can also sue for defamation if untrue remarks discredit the way the corporation conducts its business. Untruthfully implying that a company's entire management is dishonest or incompetent defames the corporation.

Because of the First Amendment, special rules regarding defamation apply to the news media. These media are not liable for the defamatory untruths they print about public officials and public figures unless plaintiffs can prove that the untruths were published with "malice" (evil intent, that is, the deliberate intent to injure) or with "reckless disregard for the truth." Public figures are those who have consciously brought themselves to public attention.

Despite the difficulty of proving malice or reckless disregard, defamed persons can successfully sue news media. In 1984, *The Wall Street Journal* agreed to pay two federal prosecutors $800,000 after the prosecutors sued the newspaper. The paper alleged that the prosecutors improperly harassed a prisoner to force his cooperation with an investigation they were conducting.

Does the malice standard apply to nonmedia as well as to media defendants? The Supreme Court faced this issue in the following case.

DUN & BRADSTREET, INC. v. GREENMOSS BUILDERS, INC.
105 S.Ct. 2939 (1985)

FACTS

Dun & Bradstreet issued a false credit report to plaintiff's creditors, indicating that the plaintiff had filed a voluntary petition for bankruptcy. The report grossly misrepresented plaintiff's assets and liabilities. Dun & Bradstreet thereafter issued a corrective notice, but the plaintiff was dissatisfied with the notice.

Plaintiff then filed a defamation suit in Vermont State Court, alleging injury to reputation. When the jury awarded compensatory and punitive damages to the plaintiff, the trial court granted Dun & Bradstreet's motion for a new trial. The Vermont Supreme Court reversed the trial court. The United States Supreme Court granted certiorari.

ISSUE

Does the Constitution require a showing of "actual malice" before damages can be awarded against a nonmedia defamation defendant?

DECISION

No.

REASONS

1. Not all speech is of equal First Amendment importance.
2. The speech in this case does not involve significant issues of public concern. Only in such cases must a defamation plaintiff prove "actual malice" in the defendant's publication of untrue statements.
3. State interest in preventing defamation in this case supports awards of presumed and punitive damages—even without a showing of "actual malice."

Plaintiffs' verdicts in defamation cases are often overturned by appellate courts. Because of the constitutional protection given to speech and the media, appellate judges reexamine trial evidence very closely to determine whether the necessary elements of defamation had been proven.

There are two basic defenses to a claim of defamation. One defense is that the statements made were true. *Truth* is an absolute defense. The second defense is that the statements arose from *privileged communications*. For example, statements made by legislators, judges, attorneys, and those involved in lawsuits are privileged under many circumstances.

Nearly one-third of all defamation suits are currently brought by employees against present and former employers. Often these suits arise when employers give job references on former employees who have been discharged for dishonesty. As a result, many employers will now not give job references, or will only say that former employees did work for them.

9 BUSINESS TORTS

The label *business torts* is admittedly a vague one. It embraces several different kinds of torts which involve intentional interference with business relations.

Injurious Falsehood

Injurious falsehood, sometimes called **trade disparagement,** is a common business tort. It consists of the publication of untrue statements which disparage the plaintiff's ownership of property or its quality. General disparagement of the plaintiff's business may also provide basis for liability. As a cause of action, injurious falsehood is similar to defamation of character. It differs, however, in that it usually applies to the plaintiff's property or business rather than character or reputation. The requirements of proof are also somewhat different. Defamatory remarks are presumed false unless the defendant can prove their truth. But in disparagement cases the plaintiff must establish the falsity of the defendant's statements. In disparagement cases, the plaintiff must also show actual damages arising from the untrue statements.

As an example of injurious falsehood, consider the cases filed by a major home products company. The complaints alleged that the defendants had distributed handouts which associated the company's familiar emblem of moon and stars with satanism—the worship of the devil. At the heart of this tort is the interference with the company's future sales.

Intentional Interference with Contractual Relations

A second type of business tort is intentional **interference with contractual relations.** Inducing employees to breach contracts with their employers can bring liability to third parties. Recently, a brokerage firm in New Orleans sued a competitor and obtained a judgment for several hundred thousand dollars because the competitor had induced a number of the firm's employees to break their employment contracts. In another suit, a jury awarded Pennzoil over $10 billion against Texaco for persuading Getty Oil to breach an agreement of merger with Pennzoil. After Texaco filed for bankruptcy, Pennzoil accepted a settlement of around $3 billion.

Lawsuits for interfering with contractual relations are not limited to those involving employee contracts. As the following case shows, however, suits to recover damages for such interference are not always successful.

WELCH v. BANCORP MANAGEMENT ADVISORS, INC.
675 P.2d 172 (Or. 1984)

FACTS

Plaintiff Welch was a real estate developer. He contracted to borrow money from an investment trust. The trust hired the defendant Bancorp as an investment advisor on the contract. Bancorp was comprised of key employees of the banks from which the investment trust ultimately got its funds.

After the plaintiff and the trust contracted for the trust to invest its money with the plaintiff, the defendant Bancorp advised the trust to breach the contract. Consequently, the trust refused to invest. Plaintiff Welch sued Bancorp in tort for intentional interference with the contractual relations between plaintiff and the trust. The facts showed that the advisor Bancorp had mixed motives in recommending that the trust breach the contract. It wanted to protect the interest of the banks as well as the interest of the trust.

> **ISSUE**
>
> Is Bancorp liable for intentionally interfering with the contract between plaintiff Welch and the trust?
>
> **DECISION**
>
> No.
>
> **REASON**
>
> An advisor's interference is privileged as long as it is within the scope of employment and is intended to further the best interests of the one advised. This rule holds even if the interference also advances the interest of the advisor or others.

Obtaining Trade Secrets

Another variety of business tort arises from wrongfully obtaining a rival's trade secrets. The Fifth Circuit Court of Appeals has defined a **trade secret** as "any formula, pattern, device, or compilation of information which is used in one's business, and which gives him an opportunity to obtain an advantage over competitors who do not know or use it." Information which is general knowledge cannot be a trade secret.

Many times employees who leave their employment to go into competition with their employers are accused of misappropriating trade secrets. An employee may draw upon the general knowledge, skills, and experience he or she has gained in working for a former employer, but it is a tort for the employee to use specific customer lists, documents, or other trade secrets gained through previous employment. In addition to obtaining provable damages, someone whose trade secrets have been misappropriated will usually ask the court to enjoin the defendant from using trade secrets in competition with the plaintiff.

For a trade secret to remain a trade secret, a business must take active steps to keep the information confidential. A major soft-drink manufacturer once withdrew from a consumer market of 400 million people in India rather than reveal the secret of its cola-based mixture, as demanded by the Indian government.

A final common law business tort involves *unfair competition*. It includes "palming off" a competitor's goods as one's own, and misappropriating trademarks. In addition to being a common law tort, unfair competition also includes several statutory torts. A statutory tort, of course is, one created by statute. For instance, violation of the antitrust laws is a tort under the Clayton Act (see Chapter 23). The next two sections discuss statutory torts of unfair competition involving trademarks, false advertising, patents, and copyrights.

10 TRADEMARKS AND FALSE ADVERTISING: THE LANHAM ACT

Trademarks

The law of trademarks covers trademarks, service marks, certification marks, and collective marks. A **trademark** is any mark, word, picture, or design which attaches to goods to indicate their source. If the mark is associated with a service, it is a *service mark*. A *certification mark* is used by someone other than its owner to certify the quality, point of origin, or other characteristic of goods or services. Use of a *collective mark* represents membership in a certain organization or association. McDonald's golden arches, the words and design of Coca-Cola, the Good Housekeeping Seal of Approval, the prancing horse of Ferrari, and the "union label" are all marks of one kind or another. In the discussion which follows, all marks are termed trademarks.

The common law protects the use of trademarks, but since the *Lanham Act* of 1946, the principal protection has come from federal law. Trademark law recognizes that property rights extend beyond ownership of actual goods to the intangible aspects of goodwill which trademarks represent. In forbidding misappropriation of trademarks, the law prevents misappropriation of a company's goodwill and reputation. It protects both the company that owns the mark and the buyer of goods or services who relies upon it.

To acquire the protection of the Lanham Act, a trademark must be registered on the Principal Register. Only a mark in current use on goods and services in interstate commerce may be registered. In addition, the mark must be uniquely distinctive and nondescriptive. A mark which merely describes a use or characteristic of the product cannot generally be registered. A quick-order restaurant could not register the trademark "Fast Food."

Unauthorized use of a registered trademark constitutes the competitive tort of **infringement**. Infringement exists not only when the exact trademark is copied but also when the mark used resembles the protected trademark enough to confuse the public. The Lanham Act provides that any person who infringes on another's registered trademark in selling or advertising goods or services is liable for damages and subject to injunction. In instances of willful infringement, a court may award triple damages. Wendy's International, Inc. forced dozens of retailers to remove thousands of "Where's the beef?" t-shirts from their shelves. The shirts' manufacturer lacked the fast-food chain's permission to use the trademarked slogan.

A growing problem in recent years has been the deliberate counterfeiting of products. Levi jeans, Rolex watches, and other well-known brand products have been copied and sold. The U.S. International Trade Commission estimated that the volume of counterfeiting tripled between 1978 and 1983.

Now Congress has made deliberate counterfeiting a felony, punishable by jail terms and substantial fines. It is also a federal crime to traffic knowingly in goods containing a counterfeit mark.

To maintain a trademark, the owner must prevent its misuse and unauthorized use. If the public comes to think that a registered trademark represents a general class of goods, rather than a single brand, registration and the right to sue for trademark infringement may be lost. For instance, employees of a popular cola beverage have been instructed always to ask for it at a restaurant by its famous trademarked name. If the restaurant brings a competitor's cola beverage instead of the one ordered, the employees are instructed to object strenuously to the substitution for the trademarked brand. It is all part of the attempt to preserve the uniqueness of the trademark. Table 9-2 gives examples of trademarks which have lost their uniqueness due to general use.

False Advertising

A tort related to but different from trademark infringement is the competitive tort of **false advertising.** Section 43(a) of the Lanham Act establishes an action for civil damages for any false description or representation of one's goods or services which may damage a competitor. This action need not involve trademark infringement.

There are many different kinds of false advertising which are actionable under the Lanham Act. For an advertiser to represent its product as "California redwood" when the wood is actually red oak might invite a tort action by anyone legitimately associated with the redwood industry. To portray a picture of a competitor's product as one's own, as in an advertisement, is actionably false if the two products are not identical.

Section 43(a) applies only to false representations made about the defendant's own goods or services. It does not apply to false statements made about the plaintiff's goods or services. Falsehoods of the latter kind are actionable under the common law tort of disparagement.

11 PATENTS AND COPYRIGHTS

Patents

In the last century, a government official urged that the Patent Office be closed because there was nothing left to invent. Today, however, inventors

TABLE 9-2 TRADEMARKS LOST DUE TO GENERAL USE

Aspirin
Cellophane
Thermos
Monopoly (the game)
Escalator

file approximately 100,000 new patent applications every year. When granted, **patents** give their holders a seventeen-year legal monopoly over the use and licensing of new processes, products, machines, and other combinations of matter. Design patents can be obtained for shorter time periods. Underlying the grant of patents is the belief that the law should encourage invention by granting inventors exclusive rights for a limited duration to the profits of their efforts.

To be patentable, inventions must be *nonobvious, novel,* and *useful.* They also must be tangible applications of an idea. Discovery of a new fact about the universe does not in itself allow the discoverer to patent all future uses of that fact. Only when that fact is specifically applied through design of a new machine or process may it be patented.

Federal patent law permits the holder of a patent to bring a statutory tort action against anyone who infringes on the patent. The principal issues in most patent cases are: (1) whether or not the patent is valid and (2) whether or not the defendant has infringed the patent. The plaintiff in patent cases usually seeks remedies of injunction and damages. Interestingly, having a patent properly registered with the Patent Office does not conclusively establish its validity. It creates only a presumption of validity. In over half the cases involving patents, courts find the patents either invalid or otherwise unenforceable.

New technologies lead to new issues of patent law. Of especial current concern is the patentability of computer programs. In the 1981 case of *Diamond v. Diehr and Lutton,* the Supreme Court held that a process for curing rubber did not become unpatentable simply because it incorporated a computer program. On the other hand, computer applications of mathematical formulas are not patentable. Another issue of present significance to patent law involves the extent to which new "genetically engineered" life forms can be patented. The Supreme Court has ruled that under some circumstances patent law does apply to protect the inventors of such life forms.

Copyrights

Copyright law protects authors rather than inventors. An author creates works of a literary, dramatic, musical, graphic, choreographic, audio, or visual nature. Ranging from printed material to photographs to records and motion pictures, these works receive automatic federal protection under the Copyright Act of 1976 from the moment the author creates them. The copyright allows the holder to control the reproduction, display, distribution, and performance of a protected work. The copyright runs for the author's lifetime, plus fifty additional years.

Although copyright protection is automatic, a tort action for copyright infringement cannot be begun unless the author has properly filed copies of the protected work with the Copyright Office. And one who infringes on a copyright cannot be held liable for actual or statutory damages unless a copyright symbol or notice accompanies the protected work. When the author has observed the proper formalities, however, she or he may recover actual or statutory damages, attorney's fees, and any profits which the infringer has made. Illegally reproduced copies may also be seized, and willful copyright violations are criminal offenses.

The law permits a fair use of copyrighted work for teaching, research, and reporting purposes. In the next case, the Supreme Court considers whether videotaping television programs for home use violates the copyright laws.

SONY CORPORATION OF AMERICA v. UNIVERSAL CITY STUDIOS, INC.
104 S.Ct. 774 (1984)

FACTS

Sony Corporation manufactures home videotape recorders (VTRs). Universal City Studios brought an action against Sony, alleging that VTR owners were recording some of Universal's copyrighted television shows aired on commercial television. Universal claimed that Sony was liable for copyright infringement because Sony manufactured VTRs.

ISSUE

Does noncommercial home use of VTRs to record copyrighted television programs constitute copyright infringement?

DECISION

No.

REASONS

1. Private viewers use VTRs mainly to record and watch programs at times more convenient for them than the broadcast times.
2. Many copyright holders do not object to such time-shifting, and it is unlikely that time-shifting harms the potential market for Universal's copyrighted works.
3. The law permits reproduction of copyrighted works for a "fair use."
4. Unauthorized noncommercial time-shifting of Universal's programs is a proper fair use.

Recently, Congress has granted copyright protection to the designs of integrated circuits. These circuits are designed into silicon chips used in computers and other electronic equipment. The new law gives ten years of copyright protection to any chips designed since July 1, 1983.

12 CONSTITUTIONAL TORTS

Section 1983 of the Civil Rights Act of 1871 creates tort liability for any public official or employee who injures a person by depriving him or her of constitutionally guaranteed rights. Through interpretation, the Supreme Court has extended this liability to municipal (city) governments that support such behavior by "custom, practice, or policy." An example of constitutionally guaranteed rights—called "civil rights"—is the Fourteenth Amendment's right not to be deprived of life, liberty, or property without due process.

Most Section 1983 cases have involved police misconduct—usually false arrest, physical abuse, or failure to protect prisoners in custody. However, other areas of potential liability exist (see Table 9-3). Injured persons may sue municipal governments and their employees for actual damages and attorneys' fees. Employees may have to pay *punitive* (punishment) *damages* as well.

As with many other types of tort cases, the number of cases filed annually doubled. Even judges are not immune from the reach of Section 1983. In 1984, the Supreme Court ruled that it applied to a judge who wrongfully jailed two men who were unable to post bond for misdemeanors which were not jailable offenses.

NEGLIGENCE

The second major field of tort liability involves behavior which causes an unreasonably great risk of injury. This field of tort is called *negligence*. In the United States, more lawsuits allege negligence than any other single cause of action.

A complaint for negligence must show four elements (see Table 9-4). The following sections discuss these elements.

13 DUTY OF CARE

A critical element of the negligence tort is **duty.** Without a duty to another person, one does not owe that person reasonable care. Accidental injuries

TABLE 9-3 AREAS OF POTENTIAL LIABILITY INVOLVING SECTION 1983

1 Unfavorable recommendations of former government employees
2 Use of zoning for political or discriminatory purposes
3 Failure to award contracts to lowest bidders (in some instances)
4 Discharge of government employees
5 Failure to train and supervise public employees
6 Use of permit, inspection, or licensing procedures for political, harassing, or discriminatory purposes

TABLE 9-4 ELEMENTS OF NEGLIGENCE

1. Existence of a duty of care owed by the defendant to the plaintiff
2. Unreasonable behavior which breaches the duty
3. Causation of the plaintiff's injury by the defendant's behavior:
   a. Cause in fact
   b. Proximate causation
4. An actual injury

occur daily for which people other than the victim have no responsibility, legally or otherwise.

Duty usually arises out of a person's conduct or activity. A person doing something has a duty to use reasonable care and skill around others to avoid injuring them. Whether one is driving a car or manufacturing a product, she or he has a duty not to injure others by unreasonable conduct.

Usually, a person has no duty to avoid injuring others through nonconduct. There is no general duty requiring a sunbather at the beach to warn a would-be surfer that a great white shark is lurking offshore, even if the sunbather has seen the fin. There is moral responsibility, but no legal duty present.

Where there is a special relationship between persons, the situation changes. A person in a special relationship with another may have a duty to avoid unreasonable nonconduct. A business renting surfboards at the beach would probably be liable for renting a board to a customer who was attacked by a shark if it knew the shark was nearby and failed to warn the customer. The "special business relationship" between the two parties creates a duty to warn and makes the business potentially liable for nonconduct (failing to warn).

In recent years, negligence cases against business for nonconduct have grown dramatically. Most of these cases have involved failure to protect customers from crimes. The National Crime Prevention Institute estimates that such cases have increased tenfold since the mid-1970s. In probably the most famous case to date, singer Connie Francis settled with a Long Island motel for $1,475,000. She alleged that the motel was negligent for failing to protect her from an attack she suffered in her room.

14 UNREASONABLE BEHAVIOR

At the core of negligence is the unreasonable behavior which breaches the duty of care that the defendant owes to the plaintiff. The problem is how do we separate reasonable behavior which causes accidental injury from unreasonable behavior which causes injury? Usually a jury determines this issue, but negligence is a mixed question of law and fact. Despite the trend for judges to let juries decide what the standard of reasonable care is, judges also continue to be involved in the definition of negligence. A well-known definition by Judge Learned Hand states that negligence is determined by "the likelihood that the defendant's conduct will injure others, taken with the seriousness of the injury if it happens, and balanced against the interest which he must sacrifice to avoid the risk."

In some negligence cases, there is a strong suspicion that the defendant failed to use reasonable care, but the plaintiff may have great difficulty in proving exactly what the defendant did. Suppose that a barrel rolled off an upper story of the defendant's warehouse and struck the plaintiff on the head. No one seems to know how the barrel came to fall from the warehouse. A negligence doctrine which aids a plaintiff in situations such as these is called **res ipsa loquitur.** Meaning "the thing speaks for itself," res ipsa loquitur applies when a plaintiff can show that the item which caused the injury was within the sole control of the defendant and that the injury typically would not have occurred unless the defendant were negligent.

When the plaintiff's case shows these circumstances, the burden of proof shifts from the plaintiff to the defendant. Instead of the plaintiff having to prove that the defendant's conduct was unreasonable, the defendant must now prove that he or she followed reasonable standards. In our hypothetical case, the barrel was in the sole control of the defendant, and barrels do not normally roll off buildings unless someone is negligent. Res ipsa loquitur is appropriate for this case.

A special type of aggravated negligence is "willful and wanton" negligence. Although this negligence does not reveal intent, it does show an extreme lack of due care. Negligent injuries inflicted by drunk drivers show willful and wanton negligence. The significance of this type of negligence is that the injured plaintiff can recover punitive damages as well as actual damages.

15 CAUSE IN FACT

Before a person is liable to another for negligent injury, the person's failure to use reasonable care must actually have "caused" the injury. This observation is not so obvious as it first appears. A motorist stops by the roadside to change a tire. Another motorist drives past carelessly and sideswipes the first as he changes the tire. What caused the accident? Was it the inattention of the second motorist, or the fact that the first motorist had a flat tire? Did the argument that the second motorist had with her boss before getting in the car cause the accident, or was it the decision of the first motorist to visit one more client that afternoon? In a real sense, all these things caused the accident. Chains of causation stretch out infinitely.

Still, in a negligence suit the plaintiff must prove that the defendant actually caused the injury. The courts term this **cause in fact.** In light of the many possible ways to attribute accident causation, how do courts determine if a plaintiff's lack of care, in fact, caused a certain injury? They do so very practically. Courts leave questions of cause in fact almost entirely to juries as long as the evidence reveals that a defendant's alleged carelessness could have been a substantial, material factor in bringing about an injury. Juries then make judgments about whether a defendant's behavior in fact caused the harm.

A particular problem of causation arises where the carelessness of two or more tortfeasors contributes to cause the plaintiff's injury, as when two persons are wrestling over control of the car which strikes the plaintiff. Tort law handles such cases by making each tortfeasor *jointly and severally* liable for the entire judgment. The plaintiff can recover only the amount of the judgment, but she or he may recover it wholly from either of the tortfeasors, or get a portion of the judgment from each.

A variation of the joint tortfeasor situation occurs when one of two or more persons is guilty of negligence and the plaintiff cannot identify the specific tortfeasor. In the next case, the Michigan Supreme Court faces this problem.

ABEL v. ELI LILLY AND CO.
343 N.W.2d 164 (Mich. 1984)

FACTS

Plaintiff Gail Abel brought suit against several companies which had previously manufactured the drug diethylstilbestrol (DES). She alleged that she had developed cancer because of her mother's use of the drug to prevent miscarriage while pregnant with plaintiff. She also contended that the defendants knew or should have known that the drugs which they marketed were both dangerous and ineffective in preventing miscarriages. She could not identify which of the defendants actually manufactured the DES her mother took.

ISSUE

May an injured plaintiff sue all manufacturers of a drug even though no one manufacturer is identifiable as the supplier of a particular prescription?

DECISION

Yes.

REASONS

1. There are at least two traditional tort theories which allow for liability in this case.
2. Under the theory of *alternative liability*, the defendants are liable jointly and severally (a) if all have acted unreasonably, (b) if the plaintiff has been injured by the conduct of one of the defendants, and (c) if the plaintiff, through no fault of her own, cannot identify which specific defendant caused the harm. Individual defendants can escape liability by proving they were not guilty.
3. Under the *concert of action* theory, the defendants will each be liable for the

> entire damages if they acted tortiously according to a "common design" in testing and promoting DES. The plaintiff need not identify the specific defendant who caused the injury in fact.

Other courts have handled DES cases differently. In *Sindell v. Abbott Laboratories,* the California Supreme Court adopted what it called the "*market share theory.*" When the plaintiff could not identify which defendant in fact manufactured the DES which injured her, the court held all defendants liable, according to the percentage of the market they had at the time the plaintiff's mother took the drug.

16 PROXIMATE CAUSATION

It is not enough that a plaintiff suing for negligence prove that the defendant caused an injury in fact. The plaintiff also must establish **proximate causation.** "Proximate cause" is, perhaps, more accurately termed "legal cause." It represents the proposition that those engaged in activity are legally liable only for the *foreseeable* risk which they cause.

Defining proximate causation in terms of foreseeable risk creates further problems about the meaning of the word *foreseeable*. In its application, foreseeability has come to mean that the plaintiff must have been one whom the defendant could reasonably expect to be injured by a negligent act. For example, it is reasonable to expect, thus foreseeable, that a collapsing hotel walkway should injure those on or under it. But many courts would rule as unforeseeable that someone a block away, startled upon hearing the loud crash of the walkway, should trip and stumble into the path of an oncoming car. The court would likely dismiss that person's complaint against the hotel as failing to show proximate causation.

Another application of proximate cause doctrine requires the injury to be caused *directly* by the defendant's negligence. Causes of injury which intervene between the defendant's negligence and the plaintiff's injury can destroy the necessary proximate causation. Some courts, for instance, would hold that it is not foreseeable that an owner's negligence in leaving keys in a parked car should result in an intoxicated thief who steals the car, crashing and injuring another motorist. These courts would dismiss for lack of proximate cause a case brought by the motorist against the car's owner.

The torts scholar William Prosser urges that we not try to force the doctrine of proximate causation into a rigid logical structure. He says that at the basis of the doctrine is "social policy": the view of nineteenth-century courts that economic activity was valuable and that those engaged in it required insulation from liability for all but the most direct and immediate consequences of their negligence.

Although tort law still requires that the plaintiff prove proximate causation, courts today treat the doctrine somewhat differently than they did a hundred years ago. Today the trend is for courts not to dismiss cases on the basis of lack of proximate cause. The trend is to let plaintiff-sympathetic juries determine this issue.

17 DEFENSES TO NEGLIGENCE

There are two principal defenses to an allegation of negligence: contributory negligence and assumption of risk. Both these defenses are *affirmative defenses,* which means that the defendant must specifically raise these defenses to take advantage of them. When properly raised and proved, these defenses limit or bar the plaintiff's recovery against the defendant. The defenses are valid even though the defendant has actually been negligent.

Contributory Negligence

As orginally applied, the **contributory negligence** defense absolutely barred the plaintiff from recovery if the plaintiff's own fault contributed to the injury "in any degree, however slight." The trend today, however, in the great majority of states is to offset the harsh rule of contributory negligence with the doctrine of comparative responsibility (also called comparative negligence and comparative fault). Under comparative principles, the plaintiff's contributory negligence does not bar recovery. It merely compares the plaintiff's fault with the defendant's and reduces the damage award proportionally. Under comparative responsibility, injury damages of $100,000 would be reduced by the jury to $80,000 if the jury determined that the plaintiff's own fault contributed 20 percent to the injury.

The following case illustrates contributory negligence and comparative responsibility. Can you tell from the Florida Supreme Court's decision why contributory negligence is an affirmative defense?

INSURANCE COMPANY OF NORTH AMERICA v. PASAKARNIS
451 So.2d 447 (Fla. 1984)

FACTS

The plaintiff was driving a jeep when the jeep was struck by an automobile driven by one of the defendants. The collision was the fault of the defendant. The plaintiff was thrown from the jeep and sustained injuries. Though an operational seat belt was available to the plaintiff, he did not wear it.

ISSUE

May the damages awarded the plaintiff be reduced if the injuries were caused, at least in part, by his failure to use available operational seat belts?

DECISION

Yes.

REASONS

1. It is foreseeable that collisions will frequently occur.
2. Seat belts are installed for the specific purpose of reducing or preventing injury.
3. Fastening a seat belt requires minimal effort.
4. "The defendant has the burden of pleading and proving that the plaintiff did not use an available and operational seat belt, that the plaintiff's failure to use the seat belt was unreasonable under the circumstances, and that there was a causal relationship between the injuries sustained by the plaintiff and plaintiff's failure to buckle up."

Assumption of Risk

If contributory negligence involves failure to use proper care for one's own safety, the **assumption-of-the-risk** defense arises from the plaintiff's knowing and willing undertaking of an activity made dangerous by the negligence of another. When professional hockey first came to this country, many spectators injured by flying hockey pucks sued and recovered for negligence. But as time went on and spectators came to realize that attending a hockey game meant that one might occasionally be exposed to flying hockey pucks, courts began to allow the defendant owners of hockey teams to assert that injured spectators had assumed the risk of injury from a speeding puck.

Assumption of the risk may be implied from the circumstances, or it can arise from an express agreement. Many businesses attempt to relieve themselves of potential liability by having employees or customers agree contractually not to sue for negligence, that is, to assume the risk. Some of these contractual agreements are legally enforceable, but many will be struck down by the courts as being against public policy, especially where a business possesses a vastly more powerful bargaining position than does its employee or customer.

It is important to a successful assumption-of-the-risk defense that the assumption was voluntary. Entering a hockey arena while knowing the risk of flying pucks is a voluntary assumption of the risk. Courts have often ruled, however, that people who imperil themselves while attempting to rescue their own or others' property from a risk created by the defendant have not assumed the risk voluntarily. A plaintiff who is injured while attempting to save his possessions from a fire negligently caused by the defendant is not subject to the assumption-of-the-risk defense.

A voluntary assumption of risk usually bars the plaintiff from any recovery for the defendant's negligence. Contrast this with the situation in many states where the plaintiff's contributory negligence merely reduces the recovery for negligent injury. Because assumption-of-the-risk and contributory negligence defenses in practical application frequently are very similar, this result appears unfair.

STRICT LIABILITY IN TORT

Strict liability is a catchall phrase for the legal responsibility for injury-causing behavior which is neither intentional nor negligent. There are various types of strict liability torts, some of which are more "strict" than others. What ties them together is that they all impose legal liability, regardless of the intent or fault of the defendant. The next two sections discuss these torts and tort doctrines.

18 RESPONDEAT SUPERIOR

Any time an employee is liable for tortious acts in the "scope of employment," the employer is also liable. This is because of the tort doctrine of **respondeat superior** ("let the master reply").

The reason for respondeat superior is that the employee is advancing the interests of the employer when the tortious act occurs. If the employee were not doing the work, the employer would have to do it. Therefore, the employer is just as liable as the employee when the employee acts tortiously in carrying out the work. In a sense, the employer has set the employee in motion and is responsible for the employee's acts.

Most respondeat superior cases involve employee negligence. Note, however, that the employer is strictly liable once the employee's fault is established. And it does not matter that the employer warned the employee against the tortious behavior. Because Mary's employer told her to be careful while delivering pizzas does not prevent him from being liable when Mary runs a red light and has an accident.

Some respondeat superior cases involve an employee's intentional tort. If a store's service representative strikes a customer during an argument over the return of merchandise, the store will be liable under respondeat superior. But if the argument concerns football instead of the return of merchandise, the store will not be liable. The difference is that the argument over football is not within the scope of employment.

Usually, the only defense the employer has to the strict liability of respondeat superior is that the employee was outside the scope of employment. Sometimes this defense is made using the language **frolic and detour**. An employee who is on a frolic or detour is no longer acting for the employer. If Mary has delivered her employer's pizzas and is driving to see a friend when an accident occurs, the employer is not liable.

An employer who must pay for an employee's tort under respondeat superior may legally sue the employee for reimbursement. In practice, this seldom happens because the employer carries insurance. Occasionally, an insurer who has paid a respondeat superior claim will sue the employee who caused the claim.

19 OTHER STRICT LIABILITY TORTS

In most states, the courts impose strict liability in tort for types of activities they call "ultrahazardous." Transporting and using explosives and poisons fall under this category, as does keeping dangerous wild animals. Injuries caused from artificial storage of large quantities of liquid also can bring strict liability on the one who stores. In one unfortunate instance, a 2-million-gallon vat of molasses burst and drowned a number of passersby in a nearby street. Regardless of whose fault or intent it was, the vat owner is strictly liable in this situation because of ultrahazardous activity.

The majority of states impose strict liability upon tavern owners for injuries to third parties caused by their intoxicated patrons. The acts imposing this liability are called *dram shop acts*. Because of the public attention given in recent years to intoxicated drivers, there has been a tremendous increase in dram shop act cases.

Common carriers, transportation companies licensed to serve the public, are also strictly liable for damage to goods being transported by them. Common carriers, however, can limit their liability in certain instances through contractual agreement, and they are not liable for: (1) acts of God, such as natural catastrophies; (2) action of an alien enemy; (3) order of public authority, such as authorities of one state barring potentially diseased fruit shipments from another state from entering their state; (4) the inherent nature of the goods, such as perishable vegetables; and (5) misconduct of the shipper, such as improper packaging.

A major area today of strict liability law is **strict tort liability** for defective products. Sellers of such products are liable without fault to any injured user. Chapter 10 covers product liability in detail. Note that many scholars do not consider this liability as being *strict,* in the truest legal sense of the word.

Under workers' compensation statutes, employers are strictly liable for accidental injuries their employees suffer which arise "out of and in the course of employment." Chapter 14 discusses the workers' compensation system.

In the following case, the Maryland Supreme Court became the first court in the nation to apply strict liability against manufacturers for a criminal's use of cheap handguns. Although several other state courts have refused to apply liability in similar situations, the *Kelly* case could start a trend. Think of this case in terms of deterrence, distributive justice, and judicial creation of new law.

> **KELLEY v. R. G. INDUSTRIES, INC.**
> 497 A.2d 1143 (Md. 1985)
>
> **FACTS**
>
> The plaintiff Kelley was injured when an armed robber shot him in the chest at the grocery store where he worked. The robber used a handgun, known as a "Saturday night special," manufactured by Rohm Gesellschaft and designed and marketed by R. G. Industries. Kelley sued both these parties.
>
> **ISSUE**
>
> May a handgun manufacturer or marketer be held liable under principles of strict liability for gunshot injuries resulting from a criminal's use of its product?
>
> **DECISION**
>
> Yes.
>
> **REASONS**
>
> 1. The common law is not static. It must constantly search for just solutions to pressing societal problems.
> 2. It is not against the policy of any state statutory law to impose strict liability upon the manufacture and marketing of handguns that are too inaccurate and unreliable for legitimate use but that are particularly attractive for criminal use.
> 3. When a "Saturday night special" injures a victim while in criminal use, the manufacturer or any marketer shall be liable for all resulting damages.

20 DAMAGES

A noted legal scholar concludes that "the crucial controversy in personal injury torts today" is in the area of damages. This is because the average personal injury award has been increasing at nearly double the rate of inflation. For dramatic examples of the size of awards or settlements in some recent cases, take note of Table 9-5. The size of damage awards is largely determined by juries, but judges also play a role in damages, especially in damage instructions to the jury and in deciding whether to approve substantial damage awards.

Compensatory Damages

Most damages awarded in tort cases compensate the plaintiff for injuries suffered. The purpose of damages is to make the plaintiff whole again, at least financially. There are three major types of loss which potentially follow tort injury and which are called "compensatory damages." They are: (1) past and future medical expenses, (2) past and future economic loss (in-

TABLE 9-5 RECENT DAMAGE AWARDS OR SETTLEMENTS IN TORT CASES

Defendant company	Event causing injury	Award or settlement in millions of dollars
A. H. Robins	Product (Dalkon Shield)	233
Arco	Ship sinking	51
Cargill Inc.	Interference with contractual relations	16
Cessna Aircraft Corp.	Product (airplane)	29
Chevron	Toxic fumes	15
Dow Chemical	Product (Bendectine)	120
Hyatt Corp.	Skywalk collapse	120
MGM	Hotel fire	75
Seven chemical companies	Product (Agent Orange)	180
Stouffer Corp.	Hotel fire	48
Texaco	Interference with contractual relations	10,530
Wyeth Laboratories	Drug (suppository)	22

cluding property damage and loss of earning power), and (3) past and future pain and suffering. Compensatory damages may also be awarded for loss of limb, loss of consortium (the marriage relationship), and mental distress.

Calculation of damage awards creates significant problems. Juries frequently use state-adopted life expectancy tables and present-value discount tables to help them determine the amount of damages to award. But uncertainty about the life expectancy of injured plaintiffs and the impact of inflation often makes these tables misleading. Also, awarding damages for pain and suffering is an art rather than a science. These awards measure jury sympathy as much as they calculate compensation for any financial loss. The recent dramatic increases in the size of damage awards helps underline the problems in their calculation. One result is that many individuals and businesses are underinsured for major tort liability.

Punitive Damages

Compensatory damages are not the only kind of damages. There are also **punitive damages**. By awarding punitive damages, courts or juries punish defendants for committing intentional torts and for negligent behavior considered "gross" or "willful and wanton." The key to the award of punitive damages is the defendant's motive. Usually the motive must be "malicious," "fraudulent," or "evil." Increasingly, punitive damages are also awarded for dangerously negligent conduct which shows a conscious disregard for the interests of others. These damages punish those who commit aggravated torts, and act to deter future wrongdoing. Because they make an example out of the defendant, punitive damages are sometimes called *exemplary damages*.

Presently, there is much controversy about how appropriate it is to award punitive damages against corporations for their economic activities. Especially when companies fail to warn of known danger created by their activities, or when cost-benefit decisions are made at the risk of substantial human injury, courts are upholding substantial punitive damage awards against companies. Yet, consider that these damages are a windfall to the injured plaintiff who has already received compensatory damages. And instead of punishing guilty management for wrongdoing, punitive damages may end up punishing innocent shareholders by reducing their dividends.

In the next case, however, the Maine Supreme Court upholds the remedy of punitive damages yet increases the plaintiff's burden of proof in obtaining them.

TUTTLE v. RAYMOND
494 A.2d 1353 (M. 1985)

FACTS

On July 6, 1977, the plaintiff, Hattie Tuttle, was seriously injured when a Lincoln driven by the defendant, Ralph Raymond III, struck the Plymouth in which she was a passenger. The force of the impact sheared the Plymouth in half. Based on the evidence presented at trial, the jury could have found that the defendant was driving at an excessive speed in a 25-mile-per-hour zone when he struck the Plymouth and that the defendant went through a red light just before the impact. The defendant conceded liability at trial. The jury awarded $22,000 in punitive damages.

ISSUES

1. Should the law of Maine recognize punitive damages?
2. Are punitive damages justified in the present case?

DECISIONS

1. Yes.
2. No.

REASONS

1. Punitive damages provide an incentive for private civil enforcement of society's rules against serious misconduct.
2. A plaintiff may recover punitive damages only if she or he can prove by clear and convincing evidence that the defendant acted with malice. The defendant's reckless driving in this case did not meet the malice standard.

The *Tuttle* decision overlooks a very important consideration about punitive damages. Most companies carry liability insurance policies which reimburse them for "all sums which the insured might become legally obligated to pay." This includes reimbursement for punitive damages. Instead of punishing guilty companies, punitive damages may punish other companies who have to pay increased insurance premiums, and may punish consumers, who ultimately pay higher prices. As a matter of public policy, several states prohibit insurance from covering punitive damages, but the great majority of states permit such coverage. This fact severely undermines arguments for awarding punitive damages against companies for their economic activities.

Consider also that an award of punitive damages greatly resembles a criminal fine. Yet the defendant who is subject to these criminal-type damages lacks the right to be indicted by a grand jury and cannot assert the right against self-incrimination. In addition, the defendant is subject to a lower standard of proof than in a criminal case. Might a defendant in a tort suit challenge an award of punitive damages on a constitutional basis?

Finally, note that the United States is the only country in the world where punitive damages are regularly awarded.

Structured Settlements

A major response to the growing size of damage awards is the rapid spread of **structured settlements** of damages in personal-injury cases. For example, in 1980 a Florida court awarded two children $18 million. Negligent derailment of several tank cars had released poisonous gases which injured the children and killed their parents. Instead of paying the children a lump sum, the railroad negotiated a structured settlement for them. Also known as a periodic payment or protected settlement, the structured settlement usually takes the form of a guaranteed annuity for the plaintiff's lifetime. The annuity purchased for the children in the Florida case could be worth as much as $52 million during their lives, although it only cost the railroad $11.5 million.

Already a tort reform movement in this country has persuaded many states to change some tort doctrines. These states have eliminated (or modified) joint and several liability, limited damages for the pain and suffering of personal injury, and significantly reduced the circumstances that warrant punitive damages. Many business lobbying groups are also urging Congress to federalize tort reform.

Much of the pressure to reform tort law arises because of business concern over product liability. Specific tort reforms being urged in product liability are discussed in the next chapter.

REVIEW QUESTIONS

1 For each term in the left-hand column, match the most appropriate description in the right-hand column:

(1) Assumption of risk (a) The liability of an employer for an employee's torts
(2) Comparative negligence (b) Damages which punish a defendant for wrongdoing
(3) Copyright (c) Knowingly encountering a dangerous condition caused by another
(4) Defamation (d) The legal cause of an injury, which is determined by the "foreseeability" test
(5) Duty (e) Reduction of plaintiff's damages by the amount that plaintiff's own carelessness caused the injury
(6) Proximate causation (f) The legal right of an author to control reproduction or performance of a literary, musical, or graphic work
(7) Punitive damages (g) Publication of harmful, untrue statements about another
(8) Respondeat superior (h) The legal responsibility of a person, which arises out of conduct, to act (or not act) in a certain way toward others
(9) Trademark (i) The tort of entering another's land without consent
(10) Trespass (j) A mark, word, picture, or design which attaches to goods to indicate their source

2 Discuss the basic change in accident loss distribution in the twentieth century.
3 In recent months, homeowners downwind from International Cement Company have had clouds of cement dust settle on their property. Trees, shrubbery, and flowers have all been killed. The paint on houses has also been affected. Explain what tort cause of action these homeowners might pursue against International.
4 You are concerned because several of your employees have recently broken their employment contracts and left town. Investigation reveals that your competitor in a nearby city has paid bonuses to your former employees to persuade them to break their contracts. Discuss what legal steps you can take against your competitor.
5 Acme Airlines attempts to get control of Free Fall Airways by making a public offer to buy its stock from shareholders. Free Fall's president advises the shareholders in a letter that Acme's president is "little better than a crook" and "can't even control his own company." Analyze the potential liability of Free Fall's president for these remarks.
6 The Stillwater Record Corporation discovers that a number of retail stores are selling counterfeit copies of its popular line of environmental records and tapes. Discuss Stillwater's legal rights against the retailers and the counterfeiter.
7 Total Truck Renter, Inc., ran advertising that showed both its trucks and the trucks of its biggest competitor. Tricks of photography were used to make Total's trucks appear larger than the competitor's. Actually, the trucks were all of similar size. Is what Total has done legally acceptable? Discuss.
8 Bartley signs a storage contract with Universal Warehouses. The contract specifies that Bartley's household goods will be stored at Universal's midtown storage facility while he is out of the country on business. Later, without contacting

Bartley, Universal transfers his goods to a suburban warehouse. Two days after the move, a freak flood wipes out the suburban warehouse and Bartley's goods. Is Universal liable to Bartley? Explain.

9. Carlos delivers pizza for Mama Mia's Pizza Parlor. One of his employer's rules is that delivery employees are never to violate posted speed limits. While traveling 50 miles per hour in a 30-mile-per-hour speed zone, Carlos negligently crashes into a city bus. Is Mama Mia's liable for the injuries caused by Carlos? Discuss.

10. Through no one's fault, a sludge dam of the Phillps Phosphate Company breaks. Millions of gallons of sludge run off into a nearby river that empties into Pico Bay. The fishing industry in the bay area is ruined. Is Phillips Phosphate liable to the fishing industry? Explain.

11. An equipment manufacturer learns that a former employee has begun a competing business. Many of the same processes used by the manufacturer are also being used by the new business. Further, many of the manufacturer's customers are being contacted by the former employee. The manufacturer desires to sue its former employee. What must it prove in order to maintain a successful suit? Discuss.

12. State Realty owns a large apartment complex. One if its tenants has been robbed and badly beaten in the unlighted parking lot of the complex. The tenant now sues State Realty for negligently failing to maintain adequate security. Describe the basic elements of negligence and discuss how they might apply to these facts.

13. A jury finds liable the defendant in a tort case. It determines that the plaintiff has suffered $200,000 in damages. The jury also finds that the plaintiff's own fault contributed 25 percent to his injuries. Under a comparative negligence instruction, what amount of damages will the jury award the plaintiff?

14. How does the "market share" theory modify traditional rules of tort causation?

15. Discuss the pros and cons of punitive damage awards against corporations.

CHAPTER 10

PRODUCTS AND SERVICE LIABILITY

OVERVIEW

Products and service liability are of special importance to managers, marketers, product designers, insurers, engineers, attorneys, accountants, health care specialists, and many other members of the business and professional communities. Chapter 10 explains the legal theories out of which this liability arises.

After briefly covering the historical development of products liability, the chapter discusses current liability theories based on seller conduct, product quality, and promises or representations. Next, it examines product defect and injury causation, which the plaintiff must prove to win a case. Then it identifies the various defendants whom the plaintiff may sue and what their defenses are. Then it examines legislative reform, management planning for products liability, and trends.

Closely related to products liability is service liability. The final sections of this chapter focus on liability concerns of the professional and of other service providers. Malpractice and the accounting profession are highlighted.

The previous chapter on torts explained many of the significant terms used in this chapter. Important terms introduced in this chapter include caveat emptor, defect, implied warranty of merchantability, indemnification, malpractice, merchant, privity, state-of-the-art defense, statute of repose, and subrogation.

1 HISTORICAL DEVELOPMENT OF PRODUCTS LIABILITY

Negligence

Chapter 9 discussed how tort law moved away from strict liability to embrace negligence in the 1800s. This movement was significant for the developing law of liability for injury because of defective products.

The new doctrine of negligence almost totally insulated manufacturers and retailers from being sued successfully. This result occurred because judges ruled that sellers of products owed the "reasonable man" duty only to persons with whom they had actually dealt. For a manufacturer to be liable, the manufacturer must have sold the defective product directly to the injured party. If the injured party were not the purchaser, or if the injured party had purchased the product from a retailer, the manufacturer would not have been liable for the defects. This aspect of negligence, which limited liability of sellers to those persons with whom they had entered into a contract, was called the privity doctrine. Although the doctrine originally arose out of contract law, it now came to be applied as well in tort cases.

Privity

The **privity** doctrine protected retailers in addition to manufacturers. Even if the injured party had purchased the product directly from the retailer, the retailer could seldom be found negligent. The defective product, which was frequently packaged, was the fault not of the retailer but of the manufacturer. The retailer had therefore acted as a "reasonable man." And so moral attitudes and economic conditions became embodied in law which assisted the growing industries of the nineteenth century. With the exception of cases involving "inherently dangerous" products (guns, drugs, and so on), the law placed the risk of loss upon the injured party in most instances. It was truly a time of **caveat emptor,** "let the buyer beware."

In the twentieth century, the pendulum began to swing slowly back toward strict liability. As infant industries grew into healthy maturity, as the country became economically prosperous, and as products became increasingly more numerous and complex, the courts began dismantling the legal structure of products liability which had been raised in the preceding century. In its place rose the condition of **caveat venditor,** "let the seller beware."

Abolition of Privity

First to go was the privity doctrine as applied to negligence law. In the famous case of *MacPherson v. Buick* in 1916, Justice Benjamin Cardozo ruled that a plaintiff could sue an automobile company even though the plaintiff had not purchased the defective automobile from the company and was not in privity of contract. Cardozo noted that the automobile company knew that the buyer (the retailer) would resell the automobile to someone like the plaintiff. He argued that "precedents drawn from the days of travel by stagecoach" must not control the "needs of life in a developing civilization."

It took nearly fifty years following the *MacPherson* case for the privity doctrine as used in negligence to collapse completely. But today no state applies privity in negligence law.

Rise of Implied Warranty

Around the time of *MacPherson,* state courts across the country also began to abandon the concepts of "fault" and the "reasonable man" and to find sellers strictly liable when defective food and drink damaged consumers. Rather than use a strict liability in tort, the courts used a type of strict liability based on an "implied" warranty or guarantee which manufacturers and sellers supposedly made to those who might be affected by the food and drink. Although "warranty" and "guarantee" are words based in contract law, the courts generally did not require the presence of privity of contract between plaintiff and defendant in these cases. Instead, the courts, and in some instances the legislatures, imposed such warranties by law.

During the next half century, as the privity doctrine collapsed in negligence law, it collapsed as well in implied warranty cases involving food, drink, and drugs, imposing strict liability for defects in these products in increasing numbers of states. Finally, in the late 1950s and early 1960s the implied warranty doctrine expanded to cover all types of products. And in the famous case of *Henningsen v. Bloomfield Motors* in 1960, the New Jersey Supreme Court made it clear that the implied warranty could not be disclaimed by the manufacturer in an express contract where the manufacturer's bargaining power was so much greater than the purchaser's that the disclaimer could be presented on a take-it-or-leave-it basis. Other states swiftly followed this reasoning, and throughout the cases the courts continually made reference to "modern marketing conditions" and "the needs of the community."

Return to Strict Liability in Tort

Still, the close connection of implied warranty to contract law prevented many plaintiffs from suing successfully. The difficulty of meeting various technical requirements of contract law kept many product-injured plaintiffs out of the courts. One last step remained before the full circle of products liability could be completed. The law would have to return to strict liability in tort. Then came the following case.

> **GREENMAN v. YUBA POWER PRODUCTS, INC.**
> 377 P.2d 897 (Calif. 1963)
>
> **FACTS**
>
> Plaintiff received the present of a power tool, which he used as a lathe. A piece of wood flew out of the lathe and hit him in the head. The plaintiff sued the manufacturer.
>
> **ISSUE**
>
> Does the success of the plaintiff's action depend on the showing of a breach of warranty by the manufacturer?
>
> **DECISION**
>
> No.
>
> **REASONS**
>
> 1. The remedies of product-injured parties should not depend on the complexities of contract law.
> 2. The plaintiff states a strict liability cause of action in tort if he shows that the lathe was defective and injured him while he was using it in an intended manner.

With Justice Roger Traynor's decision in the *Greenman* case, the law in California returned to strict tort liability. State after state has followed the reasoning of this case. Today, strict tort liability is nearly universal in its application to product-related injuries. And underlying the widespread adoption of strict liability are social and economic considerations. (See Table 10-1.)

THE BASIC THEORIES OF LIABILITY

2 INTRODUCTION

To many sellers of products, it must seem as though they are liable anytime someone is injured by one of their products. This, however, is untrue. Sell-

TABLE 10-1 ARGUMENTS MADE FOR ADOPTION OF STRICT TORT LIABILITY

1. Where sellers promote mass consumption, injured product users should not have to bear financial losses caused by defective products.
2. Sellers are better able than injured product users to spread liability losses by raising the price of products and obtaining insurance.
3. Strict tort liability will provide manufacturers with incentives for more careful product design and quality control.

ers are not insurers in the sense that they guarantee no injury will befall those who come into contact with the seller's products. Another way of putting it is to say that sellers are not absolutely responsible for all harm which follows the use of their products. Instead, they are liable only when they have breached some *legal duty* which is owed to any injured party. Such legal duties may arise: (1) because of the conduct of the seller, especially that of the manufacturer; (2) because of the quality of the product; and (3) because of promises or representations the seller has made.

3 DUTY BASED UPON CONDUCT OF THE SELLER: NEGLIGENCE

The concepts of negligence discussed in the torts chapter apply in products liability cases. The conduct of sellers must fulfill the duty of "ordinary and reasonable" care. Otherwise, sellers must answer in damages for negligence to those injured by their conduct.

Duty of Reasonable Care

In products liability law, sellers owe the duty of reasonable care to all those who may come in contact with the sellers' products. The duty exists because of the sellers' act in placing their products into the stream of commerce. It is the legal reflection of society's judgment that those who make a profit by selling products must bear the expense of harm when by fault of their conduct they cause injury.

Under negligence law, however, not every sale of a defective product, or of one capable of causing injury, constitutes a failure to use reasonable care. For instance, in today's era of prepackaged goods, a retail seller of a defective product can usually not be found liable for negligence. It is not legally "reasonable" to expect that a retailer will open every can of peas to discover whether or not there is a nail in them. Nor can the manufacturing seller always be held liable for negligence for placing a defective product into the stream of commerce. An injured plaintiff must show how the manufacturer was at fault for using unreasonable design, production, or inspection standards. In light of the complexity of modern production processes, it is frequently difficult for the plaintiff actually to show this unreasonableness.

Res Ipsa Loquitur

Over the years, plaintiffs have used the negligence doctrine of res ipsa loquitur in appropriate circumstances to assist them in establishing breach of the duty of reasonable care. Recall that this doctrine applies when a plaintiff can prove that the "thing" causing harm was within the sole control of the defendant and that the injury would not typically have happened unless the defendant were negligent (see Chapter 9). In products liability cases, which apply res ipsa loquitur, the plaintiff must show that the product defect occurred while the product was within a defendant's sole control. This may not be difficult to show if the defect is a mouse in a soft-drink bottle. But if the defect is a crack in the bottle, a specific defendant's sole control may be harder to prove. For example, did the crack in the soft-drink bottle which exploded occur during the manufacturing process or the bottling process? Or did the retailer drop the bottle on the floor prior to shelving it?

Proximate Causation

Proximate causation is also important in products liability cases. Negligent products sellers (and those who are strictly liable) are liable only for injuries that are "foreseeable." Thus, when a defective soft-drink bottle explodes in a grocery store and puts out the eye of the shopper who has just picked it up, the bottler, if at fault, will be liable, since such an injury is foreseeable. But as to the store manager who was also injured by the same explosion when the loud noise caused him to slip from a chair in which he was standing to replace a light bulb on the other side of the store, he will not likely recover from the bottler. The court will probably rule that his injury was not foreseeable and therefore that there was no proximate cause between the negligent conduct and the injury. As the next case indicates, proximate causation also applies in cases when a product user has misused a product.

GERMANN v. F.L. SMITHE MACH. CO.
395 N.W.2d 922 (Minn. 1986)

FACTS

The defendant, Smithe, sold Germann's employer an hydraulic press with a detachable safety bar. During routine maintenance of the press, the safety bar was removed and not reattached. Germann, who did not know about the safety bar, sustained serious injury to his left leg when it became caught in the press. He sued the defendant.

ISSUE

Was Germann's misuse of the press without its safety bar foreseeable, giving rise to a duty to warn?

DECISION

Yes.

REASONS

1. So that the press might be serviced, it was designed with a detachable safety bar.
2. If the safety bar were not reattached following service work, the user-

> operator would be in danger of injury of the type the safety bar was supposed to prevent.
> 3. Misuse of the press without its safety bar was foreseeable, not remote, and danger of injury to a user because of the misuse was also foreseeable.
> 4. Smithe had a legal duty to warn of the peril of running the press without a properly attached safety bar. Failure to warn supports liability.

4 DUTY BASED UPON QUALITY OF THE PRODUCT

If negligence law in products liability is founded upon fault in the conduct of the seller, then strict liability principles come from defects in the quality of the product. The focus in negligence is upon the behavior of the seller; in strict liability, it is upon the behavior of the product in the environment of its use. Because it is far easier to prove a product defect than it is to establish unreasonable human behavior, the enormous explosion in products liability suits during recent times can be explained in large part by the development of strict liability doctrines.

In strict products liability, the duty of the commercial seller is to avoid placing defective products into the stream of commerce. As it is currently expressed, such liability can be imposed in virtually every state under tort law or through breach of the implied warranty of merchantability, a contract doctrine.

Strict Liability in Tort

Since the *Greenman* decision in 1963, strict products liability in tort has swept the country. In many states, the courts have declared this doctrine to be law. In other states, the legislatures have imposed strict tort liability on sellers. There is considerable variation in the manner and extent of application of the doctrine from state to state, but the majority of states have applied strict tort liability as it is found in the Second Restatement of Torts. Students should recall that the restatement was prepared by the American Law Institute, a national body of lawyers, judges, and legal scholars whose pronouncements of the law are very influential, even though they have no official legal weight until courts or legislatures decide to apply them.

Section 402A of the Second Restatement of Torts says that anyone engaged in the business of selling a product who sells it in a "*defective condition unreasonably dangerous* to the user or consumer or to his property" is liable for injuries caused to the user or his property by the defect. The section emphasizes that such liability results even if "the seller has exercised all possible care" and despite the fact that the injured party is not in privity of contract with the seller.

The effect of 402A is to open up all sellers in the distribution chain—manufacturer, wholesaler, distributor, and retailer—to liability to the injured user or consumer. No longer can the retailer successfully defend the suit involving the nail in the can of peas by asserting the reasonableness of his or her behavior. Any seller in the chain of distribution is liable without fault for sale of a defective product causing injury.

The restatement does not take a position, however, on whether or not strict tort liability extends to protect parties other than consumers or users. Does strict liability act to protect an injured pedestrian who is hit by a car which is out of control due to a defective steering column? The definite trend among the states is to extend strict liability in tort to such *bystanders*, but several states have chosen not to protect these individuals through strict liability. In states which have not so extended strict liability, bystanders are covered only by negligence law.

Once the plaintiff establishes strict products liability in tort, the question arises as to the extent to which the plaintiff can recover damages. Presently, the majority of states permit injured parties to recover personal damages, which compensate for bodily harm, and property damages, which compensate for property other than the defective product itself, but they do not allow injured parties to recover for *economic damages* such as harm to profits or loss of goodwill. Thus, in most states a restaurant owner cannot recover from a food supplier in strict tort liability when restaurant customers suffer food poisoning from spoiled fish, even though the incident deprives the restaurant of goodwill and future profits.

IMPLIED WARRANTY OF MERCHANTABILITY

Another theory of strict products liability arises from the **implied warranty of merchantability** which accompanies every sale of *goods* by a **merchant**. This warranty is implied by law into every contract for the sale of goods by one who is in the business of selling such goods, and it is imposed on sellers by Section 2-314 of the Uniform Commercial Code (UCC). Every state has adopted the UCC with the exception of Louisiana, and Louisiana recognizes law similar to Section 2-314.

Under the implied warranty of merchantability, it is the seller's duty to provide the buyer with a product which is "*fit for the ordinary purposes for which such goods are used.*" If the product is not fit for its ordinary use, the seller is strictly liable for injury to person, property, or the product itself. This warranty also guarantees that the goods sold are properly packaged and conform to the class of goods (Grade A, Grade B, and so on) of which they are members. Such guarantees are especially important to commercial buyers who purchase for industrial use or resale. Products liability law is by no means limited only to consumer application.

The UCC permits sellers to disclaim the implied warranty of merchantability. In a written contract, for the disclaimer to be binding, the seller must either use the term "merchantability," that is, "seller disclaims all warranties of merchantability," or else use language such as "with all faults" or "as is." Language which recites merely that the seller disclaims "all warranties" does not exclude the implied warranty of merchantability.

It is important, also, to note that presently under federal law a seller cannot disclaim the implied warranty of merchantability as to the product itself in any written consumer warranty or service contract made by the seller. The disclaimer permitted by the UCC still applies in the commercial setting and in consumer transactions in which the seller is not offering a written warranty or a service contract. The UCC, however, does not permit disclaimers to limit damages for personal injuries. Nor does it allow disclaimer of damages in any situation where the court decides the disclaimer is *unconscionable*. In reading the following case, note the similarity between the doctrine of unconscionability and the doctrine of contractual illegality discussed in Chapter 8.

HANSON v. FUNK SEEDS INTERNATIONAL
373 N.W.2d 30 (S.D. 1985)

FACTS

Larry Hanson purchased seed corn from Funk Seeds International. Hanson's agent took delivery of the fifty-five bags of corn and signed a delivery receipt that stated in part: "By acceptance and use of the seed, Buyer agrees that the company's liability and the buyer's exclusive remedy for breach of any warranty...shall be limited in all events to a return of the purchase price of the seed." This provision was also contained on a tag attached to each bag of corn. When some of the fields planted with corn failed to grow properly, Hanson sued Funk.

ISSUE

Is the provision limiting the buyer's remedy to a return of the purchase price unconscionable?

DECISION

Yes.

REASONS

1. The plaintiff was not in a position to bargain with the defendant.
2. To enforce the provision would effectively leave the plaintiff without a remedy for the defendant's breach.
3. The trial court's determination that the provision was unconscionable under the UCC is not in error.

The implied warranty of merchantability applies only to sales of *goods*, that is, tangible, movable personal property. In recent years, however, many courts have applied the implied warranty concept by analogy to home builders who are sued by home buyers. The courts call the new legal theory the *implied warranty of habitability*. Under this theory, buyers can sue commercial builder-sellers who sell houses with major construction defects.

Of the jurisdictions adopting the warranty, the majority have ruled that it applies only to sales of new housing. Most courts have also imposed privity-of-contract requirements on the enforceability of the warranty. Thus, only the original buyer may hold the builder-seller to the warranty.

5 DUTY BASED UPON PROMISES OR REPRESENTATIONS

A seller has an absolute duty of performance for any promises or representations he or she makes about a product when such statements become part of the basis for the bargain with the buyer. Several theories of law apply to this duty, which is of particular significance in commercial dealings.

Express Warranty

Section 2-313 of the UCC creates an **express warranty** for any promises the seller makes about a product's performance, such as: "The transmission of this tractor is guaranteed against mechanical defect for five years." This UCC section also establishes an express warranty for any factual statements describing the product. ("All moving parts are made of stainless steel.") Similarly, the seller is held to warrant expressly that a final shipment of goods will conform to any sample or model that has been furnished the buyer. None of these express warranties need use the words "warranty" or "guarantee," and express warranties cannot be disclaimed by the seller. Special federal law applies to the making of written warranties to consumers. This law is covered in Chapter 19.

Note that an express warranty places upon the seller an absolute duty of performance. That he or she has acted reasonably or that the product is fit for its ordinary use and is not defective does not protect the maker of an express warranty. If the product is not as described or if it does not perform as promised, the seller is liable.

Misrepresentation

A duty of performance which overlaps that of express warranty places tort liability on anyone who misrepresents to the public a material fact about the character or quality of a product through advertising or labeling. This doctrine of **misrepresentation** also imposes a duty of absolute performance upon the seller. A good example of this absolute duty involves a pharmaceutical laboratory. The laboratory advertised its painkilling product as being "nonaddictive." When a patient, whose doctor prescribed the drug freely, became addicted and later died, his widow sued the drug maker. Although the court found that the laboratory was not negligent, that the product was neither defective nor unreasonably dangerous, and that the laboratory honestly believed the drug to be nonaddictive, it held the laboratory liable. The description of the drug contained the misrepresentation of a material fact and created absolute liability for the manufacturer. The doctrines of express warranty and misrepresentation warn manufacturers not to oversell products by describing them beyond their capabilities of performance.

Implied Warranty of Fitness for a Particular Purpose

In addition to the doctrines of express warranty and misrepresentation, the law imposes absolute liability on sellers through the **implied warranty of fitness for a particular purpose.** Under UCC Section 2-315, if a purchaser relies upon a seller's skill and judgment to select a product to serve a particular mentioned purpose, the seller is liable if the product fails the purpose. At the basis of this doctrine is the purchaser's describing the purpose to the seller and the subsequent reliance upon the seller to select the proper product. Thus, if a contractor asks a manufacturer to furnish a digging machine which is capable of digging through a certain rocky soil, the manufacturer who supplies a digger is liable if it fails to cleave the soil. This is true even though the machine is not defective and is capable of digging in other kinds of softer soil. To avoid problems in which a piece of equipment is required for a particular purpose, however, the purchaser must make sure that the seller does not disclaim the implied warranty of fitness. The UCC permits such disclaimer.

THE PLAINTIFF'S CASE

In most instances, a plaintiff must prove certain things to hold the defendant liable for products that injure. (See Table 10-2.) The plaintiff must prove these things whether the case involves negligence, strict tort liability, or the implied warranty of merchantability.

6 PRODUCT DEFECT

Except where there is an absolute duty of performance (such as in express warranty), the plaintiff must establish that the product causing in-

TABLE 10-2 NECESSARY ELEMENTS OF THE PLAINTIFF'S PRODUCTS LIABILITY CASE

1. Defect must be in production or design.
2. Defect must be in the hands of the defendant.
3. Defect must have caused the harm.
4. Defect must make the product unreasonably dangerous.

jury is defective before recovery is permitted. Since the great majority of plaintiffs in product liability suits cannot rely upon express warranties or similar legal theories, they must prove that the product contains a **defect.** Such proof is required whether the lawsuit focuses upon the unreasonableness of the defendant's conduct (negligence), the unreasonable dangerousness of a defect (strict tort liability), or the lack of fitness for ordinary use (implied warranty of merchantability). How the law identifies a defect assumes considerable significance to both plaintiff and defendant.

Determination of Defect

A number of factors enter into the determination of a defect. Probably the best way to summarize these factors is to say that a *product becomes defective when it does not meet the standard of safety society expects.* That the blade of a kitchen knife may slice a person's thumb, even in normal use, is to be expected, and the law does not regard the knife as defective for doing so. On the other hand, for the sharp blades of a self-propelled power mower to slice the foot of a user is a different matter. If such injury could have been avoided by adding a safety guard, the law may regard lack of the guard as a defect in the mower.

Production Defects

For convenience, product defects can be divided into two categories: production defects and design defects. *Production defects* are generally easy to identify. The product does not meet the manufacturer's own internal production standards. Although the manufacturer may not be negligent simply because there is a production defect, such a defect usually allows the plaintiff to rely upon strict tort or implied warranty of merchantability theories of liability.

Design Defects

In contrast to the case of production defect, the *design defect* case does not involve a deviation from the manufacturer's own standards. Indeed, the product acts just as the manufacturer intended it should. Still, it has injured a plaintiff who sues. In such a case, might the manufacturer be liable because of the product's design? Here the expectations of the user and society become important.

One significant cause of products liability suits is the breakdown of products toward the end of their useful lives. Products, especially complex machinery, are hardly expected to last forever, yet when older products break down, causing injury, they are frequently considered "defective" by those injured. Lawsuits ensue.

The issue of whether product breakdown after long use means the product is defective is presently of primary concern to manufacturers. Obviously, if the breakdown, even after long product life, is due to a production flaw, the manufacturer is likely to be found liable for injuries which arise. Many manufacturers, however, have also been held liable in cases of breakdown for design defects. Courts and juries usually determine such cases on the basis of whether or not the breakdown has been premature. The prematurity question relates directly back to the reasonable expectations users have for products they purchase.

Manufacturers can often protect themselves in cases involving the performance life of products by issuing appropriate warnings; warnings should cover both the expected duration of product use and proper maintenance procedures. In some states, the legislatures have set *statutes of limitations* for the bringing of products liability suits which permit a suit to be filed, for example, only within six years following purchase. After six years, the manufacturer is not liable for injuries arising out of product use. Such statutes eliminate the long "tail" of many tort statutes of limitation which run, not from the time of purchase, but from the time of injury.

7 DEFECT IN THE HANDS OF THE DEFENDANT

Just because a product user has been injured by a defect in the product does not mean that the manufacturer, or any particular party in the chain of distribution, is liable. A vital fact which the plaintiff must prove to win a products liability case is that the defect occurred or existed while in the hands of the defendant. As we previously mentioned, a defective crack in a beverage bottle may have occurred during manufacture or distribution, while being shelved, or when the injured user placed the warm bottle in the freezer to chill.

Engineering consultants and other expert witnesses can frequently provide testimony which will fix at what point the product became defective. Sometimes, however, expert witnesses for the plaintiff and for the defendant disagree and contradict one another. In such cases, the jury must decide whom to believe, bearing in mind that it is the obligation of the plaintiff to prove his or her case by the preponderance of the evidence.

8 THE DEFECT MUST HAVE CAUSED THE HARM

Chapter 9 discussed the requirement of proof of causation in a successful tort action. The same requirement applies in products liability cases based either on tort or in contract. To win a products liability case, the plaintiff must do more than establish merely that a defect in the product existed at the time of the accident. To win, the plaintiff must show a causal link between the defect and the harm. An inability to do so will usually defeat the claim. For instance, an automobile crash can hardly be attributed to a defective transmission when the automobile turned over after hitting a pothole in the road, even though the defect may have been present when the accident occurred.

In more subtle cases, however, the causation issue can be extremely difficult to unravel. A dramatic example of this was the tragic crash in 1979 of a DC-10 jetliner immediately after takeoff. Authorities initially assigned responsibility for the accident to a sheared wing-mounting bolt found in the grass near the runway. Only after several days had passed did they change their minds and place the cause for the crash elsewhere. Instead of being defective, the bolt had merely broken under the great pressure put upon it by another mechanical failure.

As among manufacturers, parts makers, and various subcontractors, it is extremely important to place causation for an accident like the DC-10 crash as precisely as possible. Tens of millions of dollars may be involved. Even experts, however, often disagree on whether a particular defect has caused a particular harm.

9 DEFECT MUST MAKE THE PRODUCT UNREASONABLY DANGEROUS

Closely tied to the concept of product defect is that the defect must make the product *unreasonably dangerous*. This "unreasonably dangerous" element of the plaintiff's proof in strict liability cases merges completely with the proof of defect when a production flaw causes the injury. The defectively produced product *is* unreasonably dangerous if the defect causes injury.

In cases which involve charges of unsafe design, however, the "unreasonably dangerous" doctrine becomes important. Since the injury-causing item contains no production defect, it will create liability for the manufacturer only if the court determines that the design is unreasonably dangerous. To this extent, strict liability and negligence liability for defectively designed products are very similar. Both theories focus on whether or not it is unreasonable for a product to be sold in the marketplace.

Warnings

Proper warnings which accompany a potentially dangerous product can go far toward reducing the possibility that a court might find the product unreasonably dangerous. Although many products, such as drugs, can be dangerous under certain conditions or to certain groups, these products are often useful and valuable to society. Hence, when accompanied by a warning, they can be used without risk of unreasonable danger. Consider the need for a product warning in the following case.

> **TOUPS v. SEARS, ROEBUCK & CO.**
> 15 PSLR 437 (La. 1987)
>
> **FACTS**
>
> Fuel vapors from a gas-powered lawn mower traveled along a floor and were ignited by the pilot flame of a water heater. The three-year-old plaintiff was badly burned.
>
> **ISSUE**
>
> Did the failure to warn about the dangers of gasoline vapors make the mower an unreasonably dangerous product?
>
> **DECISION**
>
> Yes.
>
> **REASONS**
>
> 1. A product not otherwise defective may still be unreasonably dangerous if its manufacturer fails adequately to warn about a danger related to the product's design.
> 2. That gasoline vapors travel along the floor or ground is not generally well known. Sears knew of this fact because of a Consumer Product Safety Commission report. Sears breached its duty to warn about its unreasonably dangerous product.

The *Germann* case in section 3 also emphasizes the importance of adequate product warnings.

In deciding whether or not a warning is necessary or how to word a warning, manufacturers often face two undesirable alternatives. The dramatic impact of a warning may affect product marketability. On the other hand, the failure to warn may subject the manufacturer to multimillion-dollar products liability suits. A company's legal staff, as well as its marketing division, must be consulted in weighing these alternatives.

When a manufacturer does decide to warn about product features or side effects, the statement must be worded precisely, or the manufacturer may be held liable even though a warning has been made. In one noted case, the label of a cleaning solvent cautioned users not to breathe the solvent's fumes and to make sure that the place of use was adequately ventilated. Nonetheless, a court held the manufacturer liable when several people were injured by the fumes. The court stated that the warning should have said explicitly that the fumes must be vented to the outside air. The people had been injured because the ventilating system was a closed circulation system which had recycled fumes back into the room.

In planning for product safety, manufacturers frequently seek to avoid products liability problems by ensuring that their products meet all relevant government standards and industry practices. Although courts will take such steps into their deliberations, many courts have ruled that the meeting of standards and industry practices by no means will bar the courts from determining products to be unreasonably dangerous. The likelihood of a product being called unreasonably dangerous is, of course, substantially less when the product meets relevant standards than when it does not.

THE DEFENDANT'S CASE

10 PARTIES

In today's highly complex marketplace, seldom does a single firm or company bear complete responsibility for the manufacture, distribution, and sale of a product to the ultimate user. As a result, when someone's person or property is injured through use of a defective product, the damage will usually create potential liability for a number of parties (see Figure 10-1). The plaintiff in these cases usually sues all such parties to increase the chances

FIGURE 10-1 Possible defendants in product liability.

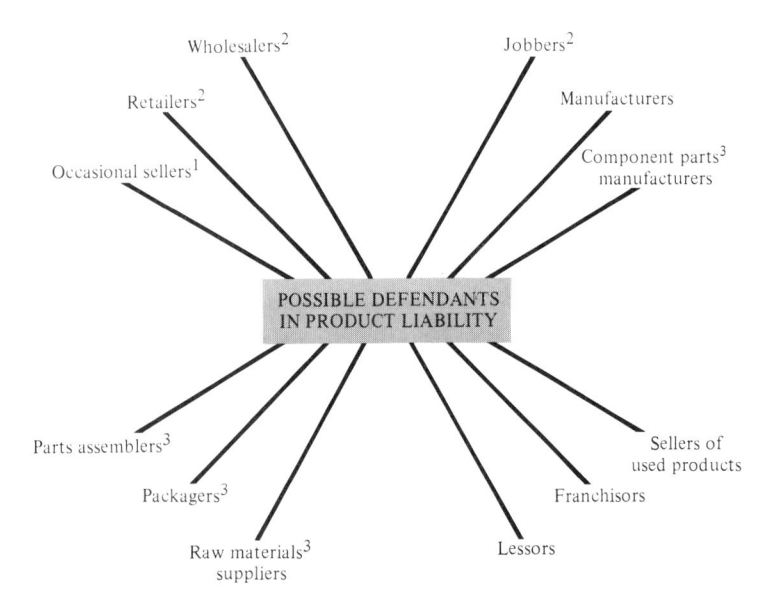

- Wholesalers[2]
- Retailers[2]
- Occasional sellers[1]
- Jobbers[2]
- Manufacturers
- Component parts[3] manufacturers
- Parts assemblers[3]
- Packagers[3]
- Raw materials[3] suppliers
- Lessors
- Franchisors
- Sellers of used products

POSSIBLE DEFENDANTS IN PRODUCT LIABILITY

of recovery against a guilty party that is financially able to pay the judgment. It becomes important, then, to know who may be a defendant in a products liability lawsuit.

Lessors

The principles of products liability had their beginnings in regular sales transactions. Conditions of the modern marketplace, however, have now led other groups besides those in the normal distribution chain of sale to be pulled within the controlling influence of these principles. Commercial lessors are one such group.

Using the rules of strict tort and warranties of merchantability or fitness for a particular purpose, courts in most jurisdictions presently impose strict liability on commercial lessors of defective products. In 1982, the Supreme Court of Rhode Island imposed strict liability on a commercial lessor. The court noted that such lessors "stand in a far better financial and technical position than lessees to insure against, prevent, or spread the costs of product-related injuries."

Note that in a technical sense both Section 402A of the Restatement and the warranty sections of the UCC apply only to the *sale* of products. In extending strict liability to commercial lessors, the courts have analogized to these rules rather than relied upon them in any absolute fashion. Thus, courts make new law, stretch old rules, and fill in existing legal gaps and ambiguities to meet what they see as changing needs of society.

Franchisors

One of the most significant developments in marketing during the past twenty-five years has been the growth of franchising. The franchisor grants the franchisee the right to manufacture, distribute, or sell a product using the trademark and name of the franchisor. As a result, almost inevitably, franchisors have become the target of products liability suits based on theories of strict tort and implied warranty. Although franchisors may not manufacture, handle, design, or require the use of a product, they frequently do retain the right to control or approve the design, and they may specify quality-control standards and conduct advertising for the trademark.

Sellers of Used Products

Sellers of used products are liable for negligence when they fail to use reasonable care in selling defective products that cause injury. However, it is not clear that they may be held strictly liable. Courts in some states favor strict liability for injury-causing, defective used products. Courts in other states do not.

As the following case illustrates, courts are more likely to impose strict liability on a seller of a used product when the product has been rebuilt or reconditioned.

CRANDELL v. LARKIN AND JONES APPLIANCE CO.
334 N.W.2d 31 (S.D. 1983)

FACTS

Gloria Crandell purchased a used clothes dryer from the Larkin and Jones Appliance Co. The dryer was described as a "Quality Reconditioned Unit." Within two weeks after purchase, the dryer overheated, started a fire, and caused $25,000 damage to Crandell's house.

ISSUE

Does strict liability apply in this instance?

DECISION

Yes.

REASONS

1. "The application of strict liability to sellers of used products, who rebuild or recondition those products, helps to protect the reasonable expectations of consumers."
2. The implied warranty of merchantability also operates to protect the plaintiff.

Whether or not courts apply strict tort liability or implied warranties of merchantability in used-product cases, sellers of such products will quickly be held liable if a used product does not live up to an express warranty. For example, in the *Crandell* case the court also found that the defendant had given the plaintiff a ninety-day express warranty on the clothes dryer.

11 DEFENDANT'S DEFENSES

As we mentioned previously, the defendant in products liability cases usually will not be held absolutely liable for injuries caused to the plaintiff. There are still certain burdens of proof, such as "defect," "unreasonable dangerousness," or "fault," which the plaintiff must meet to win the lawsuit. Also, the defendant can raise and prove various defenses, which will defeat a plaintiff's recovery. (See Table 10-3.). Some of the defenses can be

TABLE 10-3 DEFENDANT'S PRODUCT LIABILITY DEFENSES

1. Contributory negligence (comparative fault type)
2. Assumption of risk
3. State-of-the-art
4. Misuse

raised only to defeat causes of action based on negligence. Other defenses also apply in strict liability cases.

Contributory Negligence

As it is modified by comparative fault principles, *contributory negligence* can be a defense in a products liability negligence action. Chapter 9 discusses this defense in its general tort context. Specifically, products liability defendants are concerned with whether or not they can raise this defense when the plaintiff attempts to hold them strictly liable. Some states do not recognize contributory negligence as a defense to strict tort or warranty liability. However, the trend is to allow defendants to raise comparative fault versions of the contributory negligence defense in products liability actions.

Assumption of Risk

Although states disagree over whether or not carelessness may bar a plaintiff's recovery in strict liability cases, most states permit defendants to claim that the plaintiff voluntarily assumed the risk of a defective product or that injury resulted from the plaintiff's misuse of the product. These defenses are available to defendants in negligence, strict tort, and warranty cases. For the defense of *assumption of risk* to succeed, the defendant must show that the plaintiff understood the nature of the risk and voluntarily and unreasonably assumed it. This defense is frequently used in industrial accident cases in which the plaintiff argues defective design (for example, lack of a safety guard on a machine) and the defendant can prove that the plaintiff knew the risk and assumed it.

State-of-the-Art

A final defense is the so-called **state-of-the-art defense.** Product manufacturers, especially machine makers, frequently find themselves sued for injuries which occur during the use of a product which is twenty years old or more. Since the time an older product has been manufactured, the state of technological art may have progressed until it is now possible to manufacture a product considerably safer than the older product. Products liability defendants in situations involving older products raise the state-of-the-art defense usually when the plaintiff has alleged a defective design. The state-of-the-art defense requires that juries judge defendants by the technology feasible at the time the defendants manufactured the products in question.

Misuse

The defendant may also avoid liability by showing that the plaintiff deliberately misused the product. The **misuse** defense might apply when a plaintiff is injured while using a frying pan as a hammer or a power lawnmower as a hedge trimmer. As the *Germann* case in section 3 indicates, courts have been reluctant to bar the plaintiff's recovery when the manufacturer should have foreseen specific misuse. However, even when misuse is foreseeable, some states permit the defendant to raise it as an absolute defense.

12 INDUSTRIAL ACCIDENTS INVOLVING PRODUCTS

When workers suffer job-related injuries, they receive workers' compensation from their employers. Chapter 14 discusses this workers' compensation law in detail. This chapter, however, stresses that workers' compensation is the only amount which an injured employee can get from an employer. Usually, it is only a small fraction of what a jury may have given an employee for the same injury.

As might be expected, injured employees often look to parties other than the employer in an attempt to escape the limitations of workers' compensation. Since many employees are injured while using industrial machinery, they turn to the manufacturers and sellers of this equipment for legal satisfaction of their injury claims. Products liability suits are the result.

Claims by injured employees against the manufacturers and sellers of industrial equipment now constitute a significant portion of total products liability costs. Work-related accidents account for almost half the amount paid to satisfy products liability claims. Furthermore, in many states the employer who has paid workers' compensation to an employee because of a product-related injury has the right to recover the entire amount from the manufacturer or seller if a products liability claim can be made. This right is the right of **subrogation.** Under the principles of subrogation, the employer stands in the place of the employee for the purposes of exercising the legal claim.

13 INDEMNIFICATION

As we discussed previously, a large group of defendants may be potentially liable in products liability cases. This group ranges from the retail seller all the way back to the manufacturer or even to the raw materials supplier. To establish the basis for liability, however, the plaintiff must be able to prove that the defect existed while the product was in the hands of a particular seller. Because several sellers in the chain of distribution may be liable to the plaintiff, what is their relationship to one another? If one seller pays the entire claim, can that seller seek recovery from other sellers in the distribution chain?

The law answers these questions through the principles of **indemnification.** As they are applied in products liability, these principles permit any seller who is compelled to pay the injured plaintiff to obtain full recovery from the party that sold the defective product to him or her. For instance, a retailer who is held liable can get indemnification from the manufacturer, provided that the defect can be traced back to the manufacturer and the retailer is without fault for failing to conduct a reasonable inspection of the product.

14 THE RISK RETENTION ACT

The passage of the *Risk Retention Act of 1981* shows closer federal involvement in current problems created by products liability laws. This act makes easier the formation of "captive" insurance companies and also permits group purchase of standard products liability insurance.

During times of rapid change in products liability law, it is difficult for insurers to predict the timing and amount of the liability for which they may bear responsibility. Hence, they sometimes overrate the risks. As premium costs soar, manufacturers and other product sellers search for alternatives to standard liability insurance. One alternative is self-insurance. There are advantages to this approach, namely that the self-insured firm pays only for its actual liabilities, and it can earn income from reserves which it sets aside. Drawbacks, however, are that reserve contributions are not deductible for tax purposes, and that failure to keep adequate reserves invites potentially serious impacts on earnings and cash flow when liability losses occur.

Another alternative to purchasing standard liability insurance is participating in the risk retention program of a captive insurer. A captive insurer is one formed by a large company or a group of companies to insure against certain risks (in this case, products liability risks). Advantages in using captive insurers are: (1) that members are frequently able to evaluate their risks better than are underwriters of standard insurers; (2) that through a captive insurer an insured company can control the defense of a products liability action; and (3) that the insured company can participate in profits realized by the captive insurer.

The Risk Retention Act advances the formation of captive insurers by legislating that only the state which charters a captive insurer can regulate its formation and operations. This act limits other states to imposing minimal requirements on captives, such as assessing nondiscriminatory premium taxes and requiring the submission of certain reports. Although large standard insurers are subjected to different admission, qualification, and regulatory requirements for each state in which they do business, such a burden would be fatal to small captive insurers.

A number of states have passed the necessary enabling legislation for formation of captive insurers. Major independent insurance brokerage firms usually assist in organizing captive insurers for the risk retention group members.

A second provision of the Risk Retention Act permits manufacturers and other product sellers to group for the purpose of acquiring standard products liability insurance. Before passage of the act, approximately forty-five states had laws limiting or prohibiting the formation of such groups. Now, not only must states allow the formation of these groups but also they can neither impose group size requirements nor prohibit insurers from offering discounts to the groups.

One potential problem faced by members of risk retention and insurance purchase groups involves possible violations of antitrust law. Members of these groups must be aware that exchange of sensitive pricing data among members could lead to unreasonable restraints on competition. Members should arrange for an independent third party to collect sensitive data, or take some other step to minimize antitrust difficulties.

In 1986, the Risk Retention Act was amended. It now allows captive insurers to purchase almost all types of liability insurance, except for workers' compensation insurance. Previously, captive insurers could purchase only products liability insurance.

15 PRODUCTS LIABILITY TRENDS

The Litigation Explosion

In the past twenty years, the number of lawsuits brought against businesses has exploded. No area of the law is more responsible for this explosion than products and service liability. Between 1978 and 1983, for example, the number of products liability cases filed in federal courts more than doubled. Malpractice suits against those who provide services have increased in a similar dramatic fashion.

Responsibility for the present situation cannot be attributed to any single cause. Many factors have led to it. Among them has been the increase in the number of suits brought due to the growing public awareness of the right to sue for injuries arising from defective products and carelessly rendered services. This awareness is likely related to certain changes in the law, which have made it easier for injured parties to recover, and to the resulting widespread coverage in the media of extraordinarily large recoveries received by plaintiffs in some lawsuits.

The Federal Interagency Task Force on Product Liability has also pinpointed the growth in number and complexity of products on the market as a reason for the increase in products liability suits. Uninformed use of such products frequently causes injury, which, in turn, leads to litigation. An estimated 33 million persons are injured and 28,000 killed each year by consumer products.

A major problem created by the litigation explosion is due to the litigation system itself. Litigation costs take up the largest part of every insurance dollar—nearly 40 percent. The lengthy formal proceedings required by the traditional adversarial process help create this situation. The eroding of many products liability defenses in recent years and the knowledge of the jury that most corporations carry liability insurance have also contributed to higher jury verdicts and greater overall costs in that area.

Magnuson-Moss Act and Attorneys' Fees

One products liability trend of recent years has developed after passage of the Magnuson-Moss Act, which is discussed in detail in Chapter 19. One provision of the act allows a prevailing consumer to recover attorneys' fees and costs from a defendant in a products liability case. The case must arise from the defendant's breach of an express warranty or implied warranty or of a service contract.

This provision permits consumers to sue product sellers when otherwise they could not because of high legal costs. Remember that usually plaintiffs must pay their own attorneys' fees and costs. This means that in cases involving only a few hundred (or even a few thousand) dollars, it is hardly worthwhile for a plaintiff to file a lawsuit because of the expense involved.

Now under Magnuson-Moss, consumers are much more willing to bring certain lawsuits because they can recover attorneys' fees and costs. These lawsuits usually involve automobiles or major appliances which consumers have purchased and find unsatisfactory.

16 LEGISLATIVE REVISION OF PRODUCTS LIABILITY

Traditionally, products liability law has been largely judge-made. It emerged out of common law in a case-by-case process over the last 150 years. Since the early 1950s, the pace of its development has accelerated. There has been much "judicial activism" as courts have evolved products liability law to accommodate what they believe are changing needs in society. Many commentators applaud this evolutionary process and view the judicial system as a "laboratory of ideas" where courts can develop new concepts and modify old ones in the best interests of society.

However, this case-by-case development imposes costs on manufacturers, insurers, and consumers. Manufacturers face uncertainty about products design and safety standards. Uncertainty also deters new products development. For insurance companies, it makes difficult rate-setting for products liability insurance. Ultimately, the costs arising from uncertainty are passed on to consumers.

State Reform

Responding to rapidly changing judge-made law and the uncertainty it creates, approximately half the states have enacted statutes revising products liability laws. From the viewpoint of the business community, however, these revisions have not produced satisfactory results. The problem is that product manufacturers and sellers often do business in many states. Even where states have revised products liability laws, their revisions have not been uniform on a state-by-state basis. Moreover, much reform has been on a piecemeal basis. Uncertainty still results, and businesses frequently find themselves forced to set marketing policies or insurance rates on a "worst case" basis, that is, on what the current law is in the strictest jurisdiction. But since the law is still evolving, even that approach cannot always be depended upon for long.

Federal Reform

As of this writing, many trade association groups are lobbying Congress to enact a federal products liability law to help bring uniformity and certainty to this area. Some consumer groups and most attorney associations oppose federal enactment as an attempt to roll back the rights of injured parties, kill the "laboratory of ideas," and deprive the states of their traditional role in setting products liability policies.

We can identify several key areas of products liability revision that proponents and opponents of federal adoption are debating. (See Table 10-4.) In these areas, some state revision has already occurred and other state revision is possible if federal reform efforts fail.

17 MANAGEMENT PLANNING FOR PRODUCTS LIABILITY

The best solution for a company's anxieties concerning products liability is not in legislative reform of existing laws. It lies in placing concern for products liability prevention into every phase of manufacturing, from initial design through production and final sale. (See Table 10-5.) Until recently, few companies formally evaluated the dangers of products liability and then followed procedures to lessen them. A Conference Board study concluded that fewer than 30 percent of nearly 300 companies surveyed had full-time products liability managers at the corporate level. Yet, management plan-

TABLE 10-4 POSSIBLE PRODUCTS LIABILITY REFORMS

1. Reduce the various products liability theories that apply against manufacturers to one theory similar to strict liability.
2. Permit only negligence actions against retailers and wholesalers unless the product manufacturer is insolvent.
3. Eliminate strict liability recovery for defective product design.
4. Establish comparative negligence (fault) principles in all products liability actions.
5. Bar products liability claims against sellers if products have been modified or altered by a user.
6. Provide for the presumption of defense in product-design cases in which the product meets the "state-of-the-art," that is, the prevailing industry standards, at the time of product manufacture.
7. Create a **statute of repose** which would specify a period (such as twenty-five years) following product sale after which plaintiffs would lose their rights to bring suits for product-related injuries.
8. Reduce or eliminate punitive damage awards in most products liability cases.
9. Reduce products liability awards by the amount of workers' compensation the product-injured employees have received.
10. Create a no-fault alternative to litigation for injured product users who do not wish to sue.

ning is one of the most crucial components in reducing a manufacturer's products liability.

Although all departments of a company, especially marketing and engineering, should share an interest in the problems of potential products liability, management ultimately is one to deal effectively with these problems. For instance, a company's engineers may bear the responsibility for designing a product and developing standards for its parts, but management should decide whether to incorporate certain safety features into the product or rely upon warnings about possible product hazards. This evaluation and decision-making process must not be too informal. A formally constituted committee or products safety officer who reports to top management is desirable.

Many potential product defects can be eliminated prior to the time actual production builds up sales inventories. Thus, management must consider the extent to which preproduction testing is necessary. Lack of proper test-

TABLE 10-5 PRODUCTS LIABILITY PREVENTION

1. Management involvement at all levels of planning and production
2. Formal product-safety policies
3. Product-safety officers or committees
4. Preproduction safety testing
5. Production quality controls and safety audits
6. Thorough legal review of product documents, such as labeling, warranties, and advertising
7. Product monitoring of actual consumer use
8. Product recall plans

ing as well as faulty design contributes to the creation of defective products. Also, before production begins, management should be aware of what dangers may arise from product use and of how purchasers will be safeguarded from or warned about them.

Of course, quality control during production is central to preventing product defects, but merely setting standards is not enough. Management must make sure it constantly audits production to determine that standards are being observed. The key to products safety is supervision.

Before a product is released into the marketplace, management must carefully review all support documents related to the product. Such documents include buyer instructions, labeling, warranties, and even advertising. Legal advice is particularly important at this step. Leaving the review to the marketing department is risky, since that department may be more concerned with sales than with liability prevention.

People in management must realize that products liability prevention does not stop with sale of the product. Buyer experience with the product must be monitored. To this end, consumers might be provided with a toll-free number to call if they encounter problems in product use. Sales representatives should be instructed to forward complaints concerning product defects directly to the products safety committee or officer. The company should also make plans for product recall in case that becomes necessary.

Finally, from the beginning to the end of the manufacturing and sales processes, management must convey to all departments that the high quality of company products is a primary company objective. One way to convey this is through a formal statement of company policy, as the following excerpt from the Caterpillar Code of Ethics illustrates:

Product Quality

A major Caterpillar objective is to design, manufacture, and market products of superior quality. We aim at a level of quality which, in particular, offers superiority for demanding applications....

Products are engineered to exacting standards to meet users' expectations for performance, reliability, and life. Throughout the world, products are manufactured to the highest quality level commensurate with value....

Product quality is constantly monitored. Our policy is to offer continuing product improvements in response to needs of customers and requirements of the marketplace.

Products liability prevention efforts should represent more than a practical business response to dealing with the cost of products liability and its effect on the profitability of the business. By satisfying society's ethical expectation that marketed products will be safe, a business can demonstrate that it also cares about human life and safety.

SERVICE LIABILITY

18 OVERVIEW

Another component of the liability explosion in the business and professional communities is service liability. Providers of services frequently become defendants in lawsuits when the services they render cause personal or property injuries. Unlike defective products cases, however, strict liability does not generally reach cases that involve only the sale of services. For instance, the South Carolina Supreme Court ruled that strict liability did not apply in a case in which the defendant failed to remove a deteriorating valve stem from an automobile tire he installed. And an Illinois court held that an injured plaintiff could not sue in strict liability an installer of an elevator furnished by another company.

Most defective service cases are tried under negligence concepts of ordinary and reasonable care. But there are some instances in which courts have found defendants strictly liable when they sell a product and a service together. Plaintiffs have successfully sued under strict liability hairdressers who sell, then apply a hair product which causes injury. Such cases resemble those in the food preparation area where restauranteurs are subject to strict liability for injuries arising from the food they prepare and serve.

Lawyers, accountants, doctors, dentists, hospital administrators, realtors, engineers, and other professionals are held to special standards for defective services. Instead of the duty of the "reasonable person," providers of professional services must observe a higher duty—the duty of the "reasonable professional." Those who breach this duty are guilty of **malpractice.** The chief concept of malpractice, then, is professional negligence, although it also encompasses breach of contract (including the breach of confidential relationship) and even fraud.

Who determines the nature of the duty owed by professionals? Although standards of professional practice set or followed by professional groups are persuasive in determining this duty, the courts ultimately define its nature and extent. In several instances, courts have imposed liability even when the conduct of defendants was acceptable by professional standards.

The number of malpractice suits filed has grown rapidly in recent years. Many of the same factors discussed before are responsible for the rise in litigation in each area, principally the heightened awareness of potential plaintiffs of their rights to sue and the increased willingness of such parties to sue. Because of the lobbying pressure of various professional groups, several states have taken steps to limit the effects of excessive numbers of malpractice suits against one profession or another. Usually, these steps center upon submitting malpractice claims to arbitration rather than to the formal courtroom process. Some professional organizations have taken internal steps to understand the causes of and reduce the numbers of malpractice suits. For instance, the American Bar Association funded a multiyear project to study legal malpractice insurance claims. Other professional organizations present seminars aimed at reducing malpractice claims.

The next section considers what constitutes malpractice in one particular profession.

19 MALPRACTICE AND THE ACCOUNTING PROFESSION

The federal securities laws are the source of much potential liability for the accounting profession. Chapter 18 examines these laws. What follows here is a discussion of the common law liability of the accountant for malpractice.

In the conduct of their profession, accountants must exercise that degree of care and competence reasonably expected of members of their profession. Failure to exercise this care renders them liable for malpractice. As Table 10-6 shows, malpractice can cost accounting firms dearly. When they are guilty of malpractice against their clients, accountants are liable either for breach of contract or, in tort, for negligence or fraud. All such actions, however, are based on the injury-causing failure of proper professional care.

Accounting malpractice toward a client can arise, for instance, when accountants present a negligently prepared financial statement to the client, and the client relies on it and is injured. Malpractice also results during an audit when accountants fail to pursue evidence that a client's employee is defrauding the client.

A frequent issue in accounting malpractice cases involves the accountants' liability to parties other than their clients for breach of the duty of professional care. The starting point from which to consider this issue is the famous decision in *Ultramares Corp. v. Touche*. In that case, Justice Cardozo ruled that an accountant did not owe a duty to all parties that might foreseeably rely upon the accountant's negligent work. To hold otherwise would be to expose accountants "to a liability in an indeterminate amount for an indeterminate time to an indeterminate class."

Most jurisdictions, however, impose liability on an accountant for negligence when the accountant "knows specifically" that a certain third party will be relying on the work prepared by the accountant for the client. An

TABLE 10-6 OUT-OF-COURT MALPRACTICE SETTLEMENTS BY "BIG EIGHT" ACCOUNTING FIRMS, 1980–1985

Firm	Settlement total
Arthur Andersen	$137,089,359
Peat Marwick Mitchell	19,400,000
Ernst & Whinney	6,020,500
Deloitte Haskins & Sells	4,997,585
Coopers & Lybrand	4,375,850
Price Waterhouse	3,500,000
Touche Ross	2,250,000
Arthur Young	1,490,000

example would be the accountant negligently preparing a financial statement when she knows that the client will use it in obtaining a loan at the bank. Some jurisdictions go a step further and extend an accountant's liability for negligence to parties who, although not known, are members of a "limited class" whose reliance on the accountant's work is "specifically foreseen." Suppliers who sell inventory on credit to a retailer fit the definition of a limited class. Finally, as the next case shows, a growing number of jurisdictions impose malpractice liability on accountants with regard to third parties under general negligence standards. Accountants are held liable for all "foreseeable injuries."

CITIZENS ST. BANK v. TIMM SCHMIDT & CO.
335 N.W.2d 361 (Wis. 1983)

FACTS

Timm is an accounting firm. For the years 1973 to 1976, Timm prepared financial statements for Clinton Fire Apparatus, Inc. (CFA). Each year Timm sent a letter to CFA stating that the financial statements fairly presented the financial condition of CFA and were prepared in accordance with generally accepted accounting principles. In 1975, Citizens Bank made several loans to CFA after reviewing the financial statements which Timm had prepared. By the end of 1976, CFA owed Citizens approximately $380,000. In 1977, Timm discovered that CFA's 1974 and 1975 financial statements contained a number of material errors totaling over $400,000. Timm informed Citizens of the errors, and Citizens called all its loans due. As a result, CFA went out of business still owing Citizens $152,214.44. Citizens sued Timm and its malpractice insurance company for this amount.

ISSUE

May an accountant be held liable for the negligent preparation of an audit report to a third party not in privity who relies on the report?

DECISION

Yes.

REASONS

1. Imposing liability will make accountants more careful in carrying out their responsibilities to their clients.
2. If third parties, such as creditors, who rely on audit reports are not allowed to recover against negligent accountants, the cost of credit to the general public will increase.
3. Accountants may spread the risk of negligence liability through the use of liability insurance.
4. Accountants will be held liable for all foreseeable injuries resulting from their acts.

If they have been hesitant to expose accountants to the possibility of third-party liability for negligence, many courts have been willing to allow *any* injured third party, foreseen or not, to sue accountants who are party to a *fraud*. Moreover, some courts do not require a showing of *intentional* misrepresentation before assessing fraud liability. They hold that gross negligence or even "blindness to the obvious" may provide sufficient evidence upon which to sustain a finding of fraud. This blurring of the distinction between professional negligence and fraud in accounting malpractice cases has helped further extend accountant malpractice liability to third parties.

Frauds can involve not only misrepresentation of facts but also, under certain circumstances, the failure to disclose facts. In one instance, an accounting firm was held liable in fraud for failing to disclose newly learned information which changed the implications of a previously released financial statement. Highly controversial at present is whether accounting firms must disclose the problems of one client to another client who does business with the first client.

REVIEW QUESTIONS

1 For each term in the left-hand column, match the most appropriate description in the right-hand column:

(1) Caveat emptor
(2) Production defect
(3) Merchant
(4) Implied warranty of merchantability
(5) Indemnification
(6) Malpractice
(7) Privity
(8) State-of-the-art defense
(9) Subrogation
(10) Statute of repose

(a) Professional negligence
(b) A contractual connection
(c) Let the buyer beware
(d) Legislation establishing a legal date after which no lawsuit may be begun
(e) A difference between the way a manufacturer intended a product to be and the way it actually is
(f) One who ordinarily sells goods in the course of business
(g) An insurer's right to be put into the legal position of an insured to whom it has paid benefits
(h) The right to recover from someone based on payment of that person's legal obligation
(i) Requires that juries judge products by the technology feasible at the time of manufacture
(j) The guarantee that a product is fit for ordinary use

2 Products liability law has gone from caveat emptor to caveat venditor. Discuss the legal developments that have made this statement true.

3 Why is negligence a more difficult standard than strict liability for plaintiffs to prove?
4 Acme Tiller Company sells a tiller to Whole Earth Wholesalers, which resells the tiller to Ralph's Retail. Ralph's Retail sells the tiller to Mr. Smith. While using the tiller, Mr. Smith's assistant is injured when a defective blade bolt breaks. Discuss the potential liability of the various sellers to the assistant.
5 Assume that when the defective blade bolt in question 4 breaks, the tiller blade flies through the window of a passing car, injuring its driver, Ms. Jones. The car then runs off the road and hits Billy Bystander. Under these facts, who will be liable to whom and under what legal theories?
6 To what extent does the law allow a seller to disclaim an implied warranty of merchantability?
7 A manufacturer describes its personal computer as "the best in the world." Does this description amount to an express warranty? Explain why or why not.
8 While driving under the influence of alcohol, Joe College runs off the road and wrecks his car. As the car turns over, the protruding door latch hits the ground and the door flies open. Joe, who is not wearing his seat belt, is thrown from the car and badly hurt. Joe sues the car manufacturer, asserting that the door latch was defectively designed. Discuss the legal issues raised by these facts.
9 An injured worker sues the Darrell Brothers Forklift Company, alleging that she was injured because the forklift she was driving lacked certain safety features. Is the plaintiff alleging a production defect or a design defect? Explain the difference between these two types of defects.
10 While using a skinning knife, a hunter accidentally slices his leg and severs a nerve. He sues the manufacturer of the knife, alleging that the blade was defective because it was too sharp. Discuss whether or not the court is likely to hold the manufacturer liable.
11 A new car purchaser has returned her car twelve times to the dealer for warranty work on the drive train. Still, the car does not drive properly. The purchaser wants the dealer to replace the car or grant her rescission of the purchase contract. Explain how federal law has made it more likely that the purchaser will sue the dealer under these circumstances.
12 Your company is being sued by an injured plaintiff who alleges that the company's widget is defectively designed. Your company is able to prove that the widget meets all current government standards for widgets. The widget is also as well-designed as any other company's widget. Will your company likely win the lawsuit? Discuss.
13 Does strict liability apply to the selling of services? Explain.
14 What steps have been taken in recent years to help control the effects of rising numbers of malpractice suits?
15 As president of the City National Bank, you are notified that a major borrower has defaulted on repayment of a $5 million loan and is declaring bankruptcy. Investigation uncovers that the borrower's certified financial statement, upon which City National relied in extending the loan, contains a major misstatement as to both assets and liabilities of the borrower. You now consider the possibility of a lawsuit against the accounting firm which certified the financial statement. Discuss the theories upon which such a suit might be based, and indicate what proof is needed to support each theory.

PART **Four**

CONDUCTING BUSINESS

11

Forms of Business Organizations: Selection Process

12

Liability of Business Organizations and Managers

13

International Transactions

CHAPTER 11

FORMS OF BUSINESS ORGANIZATIONS: SELECTION PROCESS

OVERVIEW

As we continue to focus on the law and business portion of the legal environment of business, it is appropriate that we examine some of the fundamental legal aspects of business organizations. These aspects fall into two categories: (1) legal issues relating to setting up various forms of business organizations, and (2) issues of liability. The liability of the business organization and its owners will be discussed in the next chapter. In this chapter, we will discuss the types of business organizations, their operational advantages and disadvantages, and the factors to consider when selecting one of these organizational forms.

This question of selecting the best-suited organization for a business's purpose is of vital importance when a business is being started or when it encounters a substantial change, such as rapid growth. Therefore, the factors used to select a form of organization need to be reviewed periodically. This review should be in consultation with close advisers, such as attorneys, accountants, and bankers. These people weigh the factors and costs involved and then select the organizational form deemed most suitable to the business's needs at that time. Because this selection process balances advantages against disadvantages, the decision often is to choose the least objectionable form of organization.

Prior to examining this chapter in depth, you should understand that the discussion throughout this chapter is based on the presumption that the business being analyzed is closely held. In other words, a limited number of owners of the business are involved in this selection decision. When a business is publicly held by an unlimited number of owners, the form of organization almost always is a corporation. The reason for this corporate form being utilized is that shareholders can transfer their ownership interests without interfering with the organization's management.

After having completed your study of this chapter, you should be familiar with the meaning and application of the following terms: corporation, derivative action suit, dissolution, general partnership, incorporators, joint and several liability, limited partnership, sole proprietorship, Subchapter S corporation.

1 ALTERNATIVES OF ORGANIZATIONAL FORMS

Business is conducted under a variety of legal forms. The three basic forms are sole proprietorships, partnerships, and corporations. Many hybrid forms take on the form of both a partnership and a corporation. These forms include the limited partnership, the professional corporation, and the Subchapter S corporation.

As the name implies, a **sole proprietorship** is a business owned by only one person. The business's property belongs to the proprietor, and any income or losses are added to or deducted from that individual's personal income for tax purposes. Any debts incurred by the organization actually are obligations of the proprietor. Because of its inherent limitation to one owner, a sole proprietorship cannot be a possible choice when more than one person wants to co-own a business.

In general, a **partnership** is created by an agreement between two or more persons to operate a business and to share profit and losses. A **corporation** is an artificial, intangible person or being which is created under the authority of a state's law. When a partnership allows some of the partners to be treated like corporate shareholders for liability purposes, these partners are said to have limited liability. They are limited partners in a **limited partnership.** The law also allows shareholders of a corporation to elect to have their organization taxed like a partnership. Such an election creates a **Subchapter S corporation.** The law also permits the formation of **professional corporations** when the owners are performing professional services such as practicing law, medicine, and dentistry.

When considering which of these organizational alternatives is best suited for your new or changing business, the following factors must be studied: (1) legal capacity, (2) creation, (3) continuity, (4) liability, (5) taxation, and (6) operation. The relative importance of each of these independent factors will vary greatly depending on the size of the business. As we have mentioned, the determination of which organization is best is a weighing or balancing process that should be discussed with competent advisers.

The factor of legal capacity is discussed below; discussion of these other factors makes up this chapter.

2 LEGAL CAPACITY

"Legal capacity" refers to the capacity of the organization to sue and be sued in its own name. It also refers to the organization's power to own and dispose of property as well as to enter into contracts in its own name. When an organization lacks this legal capacity, it must act through its owners as representatives of the organization rather than as a legal entity itself.

In early law, a corporation was considered a legal entity, but a partnership was not. Being a legal entity usually meant that capacity was present to sue and be sued and to hold title to and convey real and personal property in the name of the business instead of the names of the individual owners. Modern statutes on procedure allow suits by and against a partnership in the firm name. They also allow a partnership to own and dispose of real estate and personal property in the firm name. To this extent, a partnership is treated as a legal entity. Because of this modern view of partnerships, the importance of considering this factor has diminished.

GENERAL FACTORS

3 ADVANTAGES AND DISADVANTAGES OF PARTNERSHIPS

The basic law relating to partnerships is found in the Uniform Partnership Act, which has been adopted by every state except Louisiana. According to this statute, the partnership form of organization generally has the following advantages:

1. A partnership is easily formed because it is based on a contract among persons.
2. Costs of formation are not significant.
3. Partnerships are not a tax-paying entity.
4. Each partner has an equal voice in management, unless there is a contrary agreement.
5. A partnership may operate in more than one state without obtaining a license to do business.
6. Partnerships generally are subject to less regulation and less governmental supervision than are corporations.

Offsetting these advantages, the following aspects of partnerships have been called disadvantages:

1 For practical reasons, only a limited number of people can be partners.
2 A partnership is dissolved any time a partner ceases to be a partner, regardless of whether the reason is withdrawal or death.
3 Each partner's personal liability is unlimited, contrasted with the limited liability of a corporate shareholder.
4 Partners are taxed on their share of the partnership's profits, whether the profits are distributed or not. In other words, partners often are required to pay income tax on money they do not receive.
5 In a limited partnership, the limited partners are not entitled to participate in management.

4 ADVANTAGES AND DISADVANTAGES OF CORPORATIONS

The usual advantages of the corporate form of organization include the following:

1 This form is the best practical means of bringing together a large number of investors.
2 Control can be vested in those with a minority of the investment.
3 Ownership may be divided into many unequal shares.
4 Shareholders' liabilities are limited to their investments.
5 This organization can have perpetual existence.
6 In addition to being owners, shareholders may be employees entitled to benefits such as workers' compensation.

Among the frequently cited disadvantages of the corporate organization are the following:

1 The cost of forming and maintaining a corporation, with its formal procedural requirements, is significant.
2 License fees and franchise taxes often are assessed against corporations but not partnerships.
3 Corporate income may be subject to double taxation.
4 A corporation must be qualified in all states where it is conducting local or intrastate business.
5 Generally, corporations are subject to more governmental regulation at all levels than are other forms of business.
6 A corporation, as a legal entity, is required to be represented by an attorney in any litigation.

The case that follows provides the reasoning behind the requirement that corporations must be represented by an attorney-at-law in litigation.

LAND MANAGEMENT v. DEPARTMENT OF ENVIR. PROT.
368 A.2d 602 (Me. 1977)

FACTS

Plaintiff is incorporated to do business in the state of Maine, where the parties to any legal proceeding must be represented by an attorney authorized to practice law in the state. An exception exists for a person pleading or managing his own cause of action. The plaintiff corporation filed a lawsuit and was represented in court by its president, who concededly was not authorized to practice law in the state. The defendant moved for dismissal on the ground that the plaintiff was not properly represented. The corporation contended that it could appear on its own behalf by an agent such as its president.

ISSUE

May a corporation designate a non-attorney agent to represent it in a legal proceeding?

DECISION

No.

REASONS

1. Although an individual may represent himself in court, state law prohibits a corporation from being represented by a nonattorney.
2. A corporation is an artificial entity created by law, and as such it can neither practice law nor appear or act in person. To allow a corporation to be represented by its officer would allow persons not qualified to practice law and unamenable to the general discipline of the court to maintain litigation.

GOING INTO BUSINESS

5 CREATING PARTNERSHIPS

A partnership, which is an association of two or more persons who co-own a business for profit, is created by an agreement of the parties who are to be the owners and managers. This agreement, usually known as *Articles of Copartnership,* creates the partnership as between the partners. A partnership may also arise by implication from the conduct of the parties. Conduct may create a partnership even though the parties do not call themselves partners or understand the consequences of their conduct.

LUPIEN v. MALSBENDEN
477 A.2d 746 (Me. 1984)

FACTS

Lupien entered into an agreement with Cragin, doing business as York Motor Mart, to construct a Bradley automobile from a kit. Lupien was to pay $8,020, and he paid a down payment of $4,450. During weekly visits to the Motor Mart, Lupien dealt with Malsbenden because of Cragin's absence. Malsbenden had Cragin sign over the ownership of his pickup truck for sale so that the proceeds could be used to complete construction of the car. Malsbenden also provided Lupien with a "demo" model of the Bradley and a rental car. When Lupien did not receive the car he had contracted for, he sued Malsbenden for the purchase price. Malsbenden asserted that his interest in the operation of the business was only that of a banker. He had made an $85,000 interest-free loan to Cragin to finance the Bradley portion of the business. Kits for the Bradley automobiles were purchased by Malsbenden with personal checks. Malsbenden retained control of the premises of the business after Cragin disappeared, and Malsbenden disposed of assets until the trial of 1983.

ISSUE

Was Malsbenden a partner with Lupien?

DECISION

Yes.

REASONS

1. The Uniform Partnership Act provides that parties can be partners even though they did not intend to form such a relationship. If the business relationship meets the requisites of a partnership, it will be deemed a partnership even though this is not what the parties intended.
2. Malsbenden's "total involvement" in the business was in the capacity of a partner. This was supported by the form of payment and the fact that he participated in day-to-day operations.
3. Malsbenden had the right to participate in the control of the business and did so on a regular basis. Even though Malsbenden and Cragin may have seen their relationship to be that of creditor-debtor, the trial court did not err in finding that it was a partnership.

The sharing of the net profits of a business enterprise by two persons gives rise to a presumption that a partnership exists between them, except when the share of profits is received by one of them for a special reason such as for wages of an employee, for rent to a landlord, or as interest on a loan. A partnership may be considered to be between the partners and third persons when a person by his or her conduct leads third persons to believe a partnership exists and the third person acts in reliance on this conduct (partnership by estoppel). This is true even though there is in fact no partnership between the alleged partners.

A partnership is easily formed, since all that is required is an agreement between partners. The cost of formation is minimal, and the business need not qualify to do business in foreign states. One problem which frequently is a major concern in the creation of a business entity is the name to be used. Since a partnership is created by an agreement, the parties select the name. This right of selection is subject to two limitations in many states. First, a partnership may not use any word in the name, such as "company," that would imply the existence of a corporation. Second, if the name is other than that of the partners, they must give notice as to the actual identity of the partners. Failure to comply with a state's assumed-name statutes may result in the partnership's being denied access to courts, or it may result in criminal actions being brought against those operating under the assumed name.

6 CREATING CORPORATIONS

A corporation is created by a state issuing a charter upon the application of individuals known as **incorporators.** In comparison with partnerships, corporations are more costly to form. Among the costs of incorporation are: filing fees, license fees, franchise taxes, attorneys' fees, and the cost of supplies, such as minute books, corporate seals, and stock certificates. In addition to these costs of creation, there also are annual costs in continuing a corporation's operation. These recurring expenses include annual reporting fees and taxes, the cost of annual shareholders' meeting, and ongoing legal-related expenses. For example, a corporation involved in litigation must be represented by an attorney, whereas individuals and partners may represent themselves.

The application for corporate charter, which is called the "Articles of Incorporation," must contain the proposed name of the corporation. So that persons dealing with a business will know that it is a corporation, the law requires that the corporate name include one of the following words or end with an abbreviation of them: "corporation," "company," "incorporated," or "limited." In addition, a corporate name must not be the same as, or deceptively similar to, the name of any domestic corporation or that of a foreign corporation authorized to do business in the state to which the application is made. Courts of equity may enjoin the use of deceptively similar names, and charters will be refused if the state believes that the names are deceptively similar. The corporate name is an asset and a part of goodwill. As such, it is legally protected.

In addition to the proposed corporate name, the Articles of Incorporation usually will include the proposed corporation's period of duration, the purpose for which it is formed, the number of authorized shares, and information about the initial corporate officials. Typically, a corporation will apply for a perpetual duration; however, a corporation can legally be created for a stated number of years. The corporate purpose stated in the Articles of Incorporation usually is very broad. For example, it would be better to say that a corporation is in the business of selling goods, rather than to limit this activity to either the retail or wholesale level. Stating the purpose very specifically may prohibit a growing corporation from expanding into related areas of operations.

With respect to authorized shares of stock, these Articles of Incorporation must indicate the class and value of stock and the number of shares of each class that will be sold. For example, incorporators may request that the state authorize 250,000 shares of $5 par value common stock, of which 100,000 shares will be sold during the first year of operation. A corporation must pay taxes on the shares actually sold rather than on the shares authorized. If additional stock is sold after these initial 100,000 shares, the corporation must file a report and pay the extra taxes or fees.

Finally, the Articles of Incorporation must indicate the names and addresses of the initial board of directors. In other words, these directors are appointed by the incorporators until such time as the shareholders can elect a board. Also appointed and specifically named in the application is the person serving as the corporation's agent to whom legal papers, such as complaints in lawsuits, may be served. Usually, the names and addresses of those persons acting as incorporators also must be included in the Articles of Incorporation.

Once drafted, these papers are sent to the appropriate state official (usually the secretary of state) who approves them and issues a corporate charter. Notice of this incorporation usually has to be advertised in the local newspaper to inform the public that a new corporation has been created. The initial board of directors then meets, adopts the corporate bylaws, and approves the sale of stock. At this point, the corporation becomes operational. Sections 15 and 16 discuss issues relating to operating a corporation.

If a corporation wishes to conduct business in states other than the state of incorporation, that corporation must be licensed in these foreign states. The process of qualification usually requires payment of license fees and franchise taxes above and beyond those paid during the initial incorporation process. If a corporation fails to qualify in states where it is conducting business, the corporation may be denied access to the courts as a means of enforcing its contracts. The following case is a landmark one which illustrates this point.

ELI LILLY AND COMPANY v. SAV-ON-DRUGS, INC.
366 U.S. 276 (1961)

FACTS

Eli Lilly and Company is an Indiana corporation which manufactures and sells pharmaceutical products. In New Jersey, Eli Lilly conducts business through both interstate and intrastate channels. Interstate sales are made to New Jersey wholesalers who then sell the Eli Lilly products in intrastate commerce to New Jersey hospitals, physicians, and retail drugstores. These retail stores then sell the Eli Lilly products, in intrastate commerce, to the general public.

In addition to its Indiana sales staff, Eli Lilly employs eighteen "detailmen" who work out of a big office in Newark, New Jersey. This office has Eli Lilly's name on the door and in the lobby of the building. Eli Lilly has a district manager and a secretary in charge of this office. Among the duties of these detailmen is calling on New Jersey hospitals, doctors, and retail stores to promote Eli Lilly's products. However, actual sales are always made by one of the New Jersey wholesalers.

Sav-On-Drugs, which was one of these wholesalers, was sued by Eli Lilly for failing to follow directions given by Eli Lilly. Sav-On moved to dismiss this complaint on the grounds that Eli Lilly had not qualified to do business with the New Jersey secretary of state. Indeed, Eli Lilly had not qualified because it claimed to be engaged only in interstate business activities.

ISSUE

Is Eli Lilly allowed to file this suit in New Jersey?

DECISION

No.

REASONS

1. The eighteen "detailmen" have been traveling throughout New Jersey promoting the sales of Eli Lilly's products not to the wholesalers, which are Eli Lilly's interstate customers, but to the physicians, hospitals, and retailers, who buy those products in intrastate commerce from the wholesalers. To this end, they have provided these hospitals, physicians, and retailers with up-to-date knowledge of Eli Lilly's products and with free advertising and promotional material designed to encourage the general public to make more intrastate purchases of these products. They sometimes even directly participate in the intrastate sales themselves by transmitting orders from the hospitals, physicians, and drugstores they service to the New Jersey wholesalers.
2. It is reasonable to conclude that Eli Lilly is engaged in intrastate as well as interstate aspects of the New Jersey drug business. Therefore, the state can require it to get a certificate of authority to do business. In this situation, Eli Lilly cannot escape state regulation merely because it is also engaged in interstate commerce.
3. A New Jersey statute denies a foreign corporation transacting business in the state the right to bring any action in New Jersey upon any contract made there unless and until the corporation does two things: (1) files with the New Jersey secretary of state a copy of its charter together with a limited amount of information about its operations, and (2) obtains from the secretary a certificate authorizing the corporation to do business in the state.

7 CREATING LIMITED PARTNERSHIPS

A limited partnership is a hybrid between a general partnership and a corporation. This special organization has at least one general partner with unlimited liability and one or more limited partners who are comparable to shareholders of a corporation. The general partners manage the daily operations of the organization, and they are personally liable for the business's debts. The limited partners also contribute capital and share in the profits or losses, but they are not allowed to control the organization's operations. In return for foregoing this control, these limited partners incur no personal liability beyond their capital contribution with respect to the partnership's debts. It is from this limited liability of the limited partners that the organization gets its name.

Like a general partnership, a limited partnership is created by agreement. However, as in the case of a corporation, state law requires that the contents of a certificate must be recorded in a public office so that everyone may be fully advised as to the details of the organization. This certificate contains, among other matters, the following information: the name of the partnership, the character of the business, its location, the name and place of residence of each member, those who are to be the general partners and those who are to be the limited partners, the length of time the partnership is to exist, the amount of cash or the agreed value of property to be contributed by each partner, and the share of profit or compensation each limited partner shall receive.

The limited-partnership certificate is required to be recorded in the county where the partnership has its principal place of business. An additional copy has to be filed in every community where the partnership conducts business or has an office. Whenever there is a change in the information contained in the filed certificate, a new certificate must be prepared and recorded. If an accurate certificate is not on record and if the limited partnership continues its operation, the limited partners become liable as general partners. Substantial compliance with all the technical requirements of the limited-partnership law is essential if the limited partners are to be assured of their limited liability. Moreover, a limited partner may not seek to protect her or his investment through devices such as security agreements, as the following case makes clear.

KRAMER v. MCDONALD'S SYSTEM, INC.
396 N.E.2d 504 (Ill. 1979)

FACTS

Kramer, a limited partner in a McDonald's franchise, invested $90,000 in the limited partnership. To secure his investment, he took a security agreement from the franchisee which covered all of its equipment, inventory, and receivables. When the business failed, another creditor caused a public sale of the assets. McDonald's bought them at the public sale. Kramer then sued McDonald's, the franchisor, for conversion of his property.

ISSUE

May a limited partner obtain a security interest in the partnership's assets to protect his capital contribution?

DECISION

No.

REASONS

1. A limited partner is prohibited from taking collateral to secure repayment of his or her capital contribution. To do so would give him or her an unfair priority over the creditors of the partnership.
2. The statute provides that a limited partner shall not receive any part of his or her contribution until all liabilities of the partnership have been paid or there remains property of the partnership sufficient to pay them.
3. A limited partnership interest is an investment. The limited partner becomes entitled to share in the profits and losses of the partnership, although his share of the losses will not exceed the amount of capital initially contributed to the enterprise.
4. When the limited partner makes the contribution, he is placing that amount at risk. He is not permitted to insure that risk or to guarantee a return to himself by taking some form of security. He may not vie with creditors for the assets available to pay the partnership's obligations.

8 CONTINUITY OF ORGANIZATIONS

One factor that should be considered when selecting the best form of organization for your business purpose is the degree to which an organization's existence is tied to its owners. In essence, this factor concerns how stable is an organization's independent continuity. In this section, the dissolution of organizations is examined. This term **dissolution** refers to the legal existence of the organizational form. The following paragraphs include general principles about dissolutions and statements about the impact of a dissolution on a business.

A general partnership is dissolved any time there is a change in the partners. For example, if a partner dies, retires, or otherwise withdraws from the organization, the partnership is dissolved. Likewise, if a person is added as a new partner, there is a technical dissolution of the organization. Therefore, it generally is said that the partnership organization is easily dissolved. Even if the partnership agreement provides that the partnership will continue for a stated number of years, any partner still retains the power to dissolve the organization. In other words, although liability may be imposed on the former partner for wrongful dissolution in violation of the agreement, the partnership nevertheless is dissolved. [Note: The principles stated in this paragraph are applicable to limited partnerships if there is a change in the general partners. A limited partner may assign his interest to another without dissolving the limited partnership.]

In contrast to the easily dissolved nature of a partnership, a corporation usually is formed to have perpetual existence. The law treats a corporation's existence as distinct from its owners' status as shareholders. Thus, a shareholder's death or sale of her or his stock does not affect the organizational structure of a corporation. This ability to separate management from ownership is an often cited advantage of the corporation.

To rely on the general principles of a partnership's continuity being much more unstable than a corporation's is to be short-sighted. The more important question is: How will a dissolution of an organization affect the business of that organization? A dissolution does not necessarily destroy the business of a partnership. Dissolution is not the equivalent of terminating an organization's business activity. Termination involves the winding up or liquidating of a business; dissolution simply means the legal form of organization no longer exists. Likewise, the death of a major shareholder of a corporation has no impact on the organization's existence. However, such an event may have an adverse influence on that corporation's ability to keep old customers or attract new ones.

The solution to problems arising when a partner dies or withdraws from a partnership, or when a shareholder dies or desires to withdraw from a closely held corporation, is a "buy and sell" agreement. These agreements, which need to be entered into when the business entity is *created,* provide for the amount and manner of compensation for the interest of the deceased or withdrawing owner. In a partnership, the buy and sell provisions are usually contained in the Articles of Copartnership. In a corporation, the agreement may be between shareholders or between shareholders and the corporation itself. In the latter case, the corporation redeems the stock of the withdrawing or deceased shareholder. Buy and sell agreements frequently use formulas to compute the value of the withdrawing owner's interest and provide for the time and method of payment. In the case of death, the liquidity needed is often provided by the cash proceeds from life insurance which was taken out on the life of the deceased and made payable to the business or to the surviving partner or shareholder. Upon payment of the amount required by the buy and sell agreement to the estate of the deceased, the interest of the deceased ends, and the surviving owners continue the business. A buy and sell agreement should specify whether the agreement is a right of first refusal or whether the surviving or remaining owners must purchase the interest of the deceased or withdrawing owner.

RENBERG v. ZARROW
667 P.2d 465 (Okla. 1983)

FACTS

Sam, Rose, Jack, and Henry Zarrow and Dorothy Renberg were stockholders in Sooner Pipe & Supply Corporation. In 1963, the Sooner shareholders executed a stock purchase agreement which provided that upon the death of any shareholder the survivors had an option, to be exercised within one year of the date of death, to buy the deceased parties' shares at a price set by the majority shareholders each year. If no price were to be established for a given year, the most recently set price would prevail.

Dorothy Renberg died April 22, 1978. During April of 1979, the Zarrows, as the surviving shareholders of Sooner, notified Dorothy's husband that they wished to purchase her shares pursuant to the 1963 buy and sell agreement. Dorothy's husband refused to sell. Instead, he initiated this suit to prevent the transfer of stock at a price far below its value.

ISSUE

Is this buy and sell agreement, whereby, upon the death of any shareholder in a closely held corporation, the survivors are granted an option to purchase the deceased party's shares, valid?

DECISION

Yes.

REASONS

1. The purpose of such buy and sell agreements is to prevent transfers of stock to outsiders without first providing an opportunity for the existing shareholders to acquire the stock. These agreements assure the purchase by persons most likely to act in harmony with other stockholders.
2. A basic reason for buy and sell agreements is to provide a way to determine the value of stock. This is important because stock in a closely held corporation is not publicly traded, and, therefore, the value cannot be readily ascertained.
3. Courts must give great deference to a buy and sell agreement when it is unambiguous, when the intent of the drafters is clear, and when there is no indication of fraud or bad faith. Mere disparity between the price specified and the actual value of the stock is not enough to invalidate the agreement.
4. Dorothy throughout her life stood to benefit the most from the buy and sell agreement because she was the youngest shareholder. Furthermore, she was consistently advised as to the value of the stock, and she had access to the corporation's records and could have called a meeting of the shareholders to reassess the value of the stock had she so desired.

LIABILITY FACTORS

9 LIABILITY FACTORS: PARTNERSHIPS

All partners in a general partnership and the general partners in a limited partnership are treated the same for liability purposes. These partners have unlimited liability for their organization's debts. In other words, these partners' personal assets, which are not associated with the partnership, may be claimed by the partnership's creditors. From a creditor's perspective, this personal liability of each partner extends to the organization's entire debt, not just to a pro rata share. These partners are **jointly and severally liable** for the partnership's obligations. For example, assume that a general partnership has three partners and that it owes a creditor $300,000. If it is necessary to collect the debt, this creditor can sue all three partners jointly for the $300,000. As an alternative, the creditor can sue any one partner or any combination of two for the entire $300,000. Between the partners, anyone who has to pay the creditor more than her or his pro rata share of the liability usually can seek contribution from the remaining partners.

A more in-depth discussion of partners' liability is presented in the next chapter. There you will see that personal liability may arise from: (1) breach of a contract, (2) commitment of a tort, (3) failure to perform a public duty, or (4) violation of a statute. The degree of liability placed on the individual partner may vary, depending on the occurrence of each of these events.

The limited partnership as a hybrid for liability purposes has been mentioned previously. The Uniform Limited Partnership Act, which has been adopted or revised by every state except Louisiana, governs the rights and duties of the general and limited partners. Under this statute, a limited partner is viewed as one who lends money to the business organization for a percentage of the profits rather than for a fixed return such as interest. Because the limited partner is treated as a creditor, there are several restrictions placed on the activities of this party. For example, contributions to the firm may be in cash or property but not in services. Surnames of the limited partner may not be used in the partnership's name unless there is a general partner with the same name. If a limited partner's name is used in the firm's name, that partner will become personally liable to unsuspecting creditors. Also, limited partners may not participate in management without incurring unlimited liability. In some states, this participation may not even be indirect, as by managing the partnership through a corporate general partner. However, limited partners do not lose their limited liability by showing an interest in the firm or by making suggestions.

TRANS-AM BUILDERS, INC. v. WOODS MILL LTD.
210 S.E.2d 866 (Ga. 1974)

FACTS

Defendants were limited partners in a real estate venture. After the business was in financial difficulty, the limited partners had two meetings with the general partners to discuss the problems of the venture. In addition, one limited partner visited the construction site and "obnoxiously" complained of the way the work was being conducted.

ISSUE

Do these actions constitute taking part in the control of the business, enough to make the limited partners liable as general partners?

DECISION

No.

REASONS

1. It is well-established that just because a person is a limited partner in an enterprise, he or she is not by reason of that status precluded from continuing to have an interest in the affairs of the partnership, from giving advice and suggestions to the general partner or to nominees, and from interesting himself or herself in specific aspects of the business.
2. The casual advice the limited partners may have given in this case can hardly be said to be interference in day-to-day management. Certainly, common sense dictates that in times of severe financial crisis all partners in such an enterprise, limited or general, will become actively interested in any effort to keep the enterprise afloat, and many abnormal problems will arise that are not, under any stretch of the imagination, mere day-to-day matters of managing the partnership business.
3. It would be unreasonable to hold that a limited partner may not advise with the general partner and may not visit the partnership business, especially in times of severe financial crisis.

In an attempt to modernize and clarify the law of limited partnership, a Revised Uniform Limited Partnership Act has been prepared and proposed to the states for adoption. At least ten states (Arkansas, Colorado, Connecticut, Maryland, Minnesota, Montana, Nebraska, Washington, West Virginia, and Wyoming) have adopted this revised act. In these states, there is a substantial change in the liability of a limited partner who participates in control of the business. The liability of a general partner is imposed on a limited partner who participates in the control of the business only if the third party has had knowledge of the participation. In addition, this revised act clarifies that a limited partner does not participate in the control of the business by: (1) being an agent or employee of the business, (2) consulting with or advising a partner with respect to the partnership, (3) acting as surety of the limited partnership, (4) approving or disapproving of an amendment to the certificate, and (5) voting on matters such as dissolution, sale of assets, or a change of name.

10 LIABILITY FACTORS: CORPORATIONS

Traditionally, it has been said that the investors in a corporation have limited liability and those in a partnership have unlimited liability. This generalization is too broad and needs qualification. To be sure, someone investing in a company listed on the New York Stock Exchange will incur no risk greater than the investment, and the concept of limited liability certainly applies. However, if the company is a small, closely held corporation with limited assets and capital, it will be difficult for it to obtain credit on the strength of its own net worth standing alone. As a practical matter, shareholders will usually be required to add their own individual liability as security for debts. For example, if the XYZ Company seeks a loan at a local bank, the bank often will require the owners, X, Y, and Z, to personally guarantee repayment of the loan. This is not to say that shareholders in closely held corporations do not have some degree of limited liability. Shareholders have limited liability for contractlike obligations which are imposed as a matter of law (such as taxes). Liability also is limited when the corporate obligation results from torts committed by company employees while doing company business.

Even in these situations, the mere fact of corporate existence does not mean the shareholders will have liability limited to their investment. When courts find that the corporate organization is being misused, the corporate entity can be disregarded. This event has been called "piercing the corporate veil." When this veil of protection has been pierced, the shareholders are treated like partners who have unlimited liability for their organization's debts.

Courts have identified several situations in which the corporate veil can be pierced. First, the corporate entity may be used to defraud or avoid an otherwise valid obligation. For example, if A sold B a business and A agreed not to compete with B for two years, but if, in violation of the contract, A organized a corporation and competed with B, the contract would have been breached. Second, the corporation may be used to evade a statute. For example, if a state law provides that a person may not hold more than one liquor license at a time, this law cannot be circumvented by forming multiple corporations. Third, the corporate entity may be disregarded when one corporation is organized, controlled, and conducted in a manner that makes it an instrument of another corporation. In such circumstances, one corporation is said to be the "alter ego" of another. It must be recognized that the mere relationship of a parent corporation with a subsidiary is not enough by itself to justify piercing the corporate veil. Subsidiaries are often formed to limit the liability of the parent corporation. The alter-ego theory, by which the corporate veil can be pierced, may also be used to impose personal liability upon corporate officers and stockholders. If the corporate entity is disregarded by the principals themselves, so that there is such a unity of ownership and interest that separateness of the corporation has ceased to exist, the alter-ego doctrine will be followed and the corporate veil will be pierced. The following case illustrates that courts are not limited to these three factors when they decide whether or not to disregard a corporation's separate identity. If there is, in fact, no separate personality for the corporation, the corporate veil may be pierced.

READER v. DERTINA & ASSOCIATES MARKETING
693 P.2d 398 (Colo. App. 1984)

FACTS

As a sole proprietor, Dertina hired Adamson, Reader, and Kruse to perform services. Later, the business was incorporated, with Dertina as the sole stockholder. After being discharged, plaintiffs sued Dertina individually for commissions and bonuses.

ISSUE

Is the sole shareholder individually liable?

DECISION

Yes.

REASONS

1. If the corporate veil is pierced by application of the alter-ego doctrine, a stockholder may be held personally liable for corporate obligations. This doctrine arises in cases where the corporate entity has been used to defeat public convenience; to justify or protect wrong, fraud, or crime; or in other similar situations where equity requires.
2. The business had been incorporated as a mere formality for IRS purposes: no directors' meetings were held, Dertina retained total control of company operations, he set the commission structures, and took money from the corporate account for personal purchases.
3. Dertina used the corporate entity principally as an instrumentality for the transaction of his own affairs. There was a unity of interest in ownership such that separate personalities of the corporation and Dertina himself did not exist. Adherence to the corporate entity would promote injustice.

TAXATION FACTORS

11 TAXATION FACTORS: PARTNERSHIPS

A partnership, whether of a general or limited nature, is not a taxable entity. The fact that this type of organization pays no income tax does not mean that the profits of the partnership are free of income tax. A partnership files an information return, which allocates to each individual partner his or her proportionate share of profits or losses from operations, dividend income, capital gains or losses, and other items which would affect the income tax owed by a partner. Partners then report their share of such items on their individual income tax returns, irrespective of whether they have actually received the items.

This aspect of a partnership becomes advantageous to the partners if the organization suffers a net loss. The pro rata share of this loss is allocated to each partner, and it can be used to reduce these partners' personal taxable income. However, by this same reasoning, the partnership organization becomes disadvantageous if any profits made are retained by the organization for expansion purposes. Suppose a partnership which has three equal partners has $30,000 in net income. If this money is kept by the partnership, there still is a constructive distribution of $10,000 to each partner for tax purposes. Assuming that these partners are in a 28 percent personal income tax bracket, they each would have to pay $2,800 in taxes even though they actually received nothing from the partnership.

12 TAXATION FACTORS: CORPORATIONS

Unlike partnerships, corporations must pay income taxes on their earnings. The corporate tax rates may be changed by Congress. These changes relate to the condition of our economy and the impact desired on employment and economic growth. In August 1986, Congress enacted a tax-reform law, which lowered both individual and corporate tax rates. The lower rates were offset by the elimination of certain deductions and credits, such as the investment tax credit. The following table sets forth these tax rates, beginning in 1987:

CORPORATE TAX RATES

$ of income	Tax rate
0–50,000	15 percent
25–75,000	25 percent
Over 75,000	34 percent

An additional 5 percent tax, up to $11,750, is imposed on corporate taxable income over $100,000. Corporations with taxable income of at least $335,000 will pay a flat rate of 34 percent.

The fact that there is a separate corporate income tax may work as an advantage or disadvantage. If the corporation makes a profit that is to be retained by the corporation for growth needs, no income is allocated to the shareholders. In other words, these shareholders will not have their personal taxable income increased as would a partner in a similar situation. Also, the corporate rate on the first $75,000 of corporate taxable income is lower than the individual rate, which for most shareholders is 28 percent. The corporate tax also creates the advantage of having health insurance and other medical expenses paid by the corporation for its employees' benefit become 100 percent tax deductible. As an individual, a partner in a partnership can deduct only those medical expenses that exceed 5 percent of his or her adjusted income.

In the past, the most often cited advantage of the corporate organizational form was the sheltering of taxable income in pension and profit-sharing plans. In general, the employees of a corporation could defer from taxes much more income than could employees of a proprietorship, partnership, or limited partnership. Therefore, whenever a business became very successful, there were strong incentives to become a corporation. As of 1984, these incentives have been removed by Congress. Indeed, for the purposes of sheltering income from taxes for retirement-plan purposes, all business organizations are treated essentially equally. Thus, the factor of the amount that can be paid into profit-sharing and pension plans is no longer of major importance when deciding which organization is the best for a particular business.

Now we turn to some tax disadvantages of the corporation. Suppose a corporation suffers a loss during a given tax year. The existence of the corporate tax works as a disadvantage, since this loss cannot be distributed to the shareholders to reduce their personal tax liability. Indeed, a net operating loss to a corporation can be used only to offset corporate income earned in other years. And the allocation of such a loss can be carried back only for three years and carried forward only fifteen years. [Note: There are many different rules concerning specialized carryover situations. The Internal Revenue Code should be examined prior to relying on the general rule just stated.] Perhaps a greater disadvantage of the corporate tax occurs when a profit is made and the corporation wishes to pay a dividend to its shareholders. The money used to pay this dividend will have been taxed at the corporate level. It is then taxed again, because the shareholder must take the amount of the dividend into his or her own personal income. The rate of this second tax depends on the personal tax rate of the shareholder receiving the dividend. This situation has been called the "double tax" on corporate income. A similar situation of "double taxation" occurs when a corporation is dissolved and its assets are distributed to shareholders as capital gains. This next section presents a discussion which indicates that the double tax may not be as big a disadvantage as it first seems.

13 AVOIDING DOUBLE TAXATION

There are at least five techniques for avoiding at least part of the problem caused by the double taxation of corporate income. First of all, reasonable salaries paid to corporate officials may be deducted in computing the taxable income of the business. Thus, in a closely held corporation in which all or most shareholders are officers or employees, this technique may avoid double taxation of substantial portions of income. As might be suspected, the Internal Revenue Code disallows a deduction for excessive or unreasonable compensation and treats such payments as dividends. Therefore, the determination of the reasonableness of corporate salaries is often a tax problem in that form of organization.

Second, corporations provide expense accounts for many employees including shareholder-employees. These are used to purchase travel, food, and entertainment. When so used, the employee, to some extent, has compensation which is not taxed. In an attempt to close this tax loophole, the law limits deductions for business meals and entertainment to 80 percent of the cost. Meal expenses and entertainment are deductible only if the expenses are directly related to or associated with the active conduct of a trade or business. For a deduction, business must be discussed directly before, during, or directly after the meal. Additionally, meal expenses are not deductible to the extent the meal is lavish or extravagant. Thus, it is apparent that the use of the expense account to avoid taxation of corporate income is subject to numerous technical rules and limitations.

Third, the capital structure of the corporation may include both common stock and interest-bearing loans from shareholders. For example, assume that a company needs $100,000 cash to go into business. If $100,000 of stock is issued, no expense will be deducted. However, assume that $50,000 worth of stock is purchased by the owners, and $50,000 is lent to the company by them at 10 percent interest. In this case, $5,000 interest each year is deductible as an expense of the company and thus subject to only one tax as interest income to the owners. Just as in the case of salaries, the Internal Revenue Code has a counteracting rule relating to corporations that are undercapitalized. If the corporation is undercapitalized, interest payments will be treated as dividends and disallowed as deductible expenses.

The fourth technique for avoiding double taxation, at least in part, is simply not to pay dividends and to accumulate the earnings. The Internal Revenue Service seeks to compel corporations to distribute those profits not needed for a business purpose, such as growth. When a corporation retains earnings in excess of $250,000, there is a presumption that these earnings are being accumulated to avoid a second tax on dividends. If the corporation cannot rebut this presumption, an additional tax of 27½ percent is imposed on the first $100,000 unreasonably accumulated in excess of $250,000. For undistributed earnings above this amount, the penalty tax equals 38½ percent of the unreasonable accumulation.

Fifth, there is a special provision in the Internal Revenue Code that allows small, closely held business corporations to be treated as partnerships for income tax purposes and thereby avoid having a tax assessed on the corporate income itself. These Subchapter S corporations cannot have over thirty-five shareholders, each of whom must elect to be taxed as a partnership, that is, to have the corporate income allocated to the shareholders annually in computing their income for tax purposes, whether actually paid out or not. The permissible number of shareholders has been increased in recent years from ten to thirty-five to encourage greater use of the Subchapter S election. There are many technical rules of tax law involved in Subchapter S corporations, but as a rule of thumb, this method of organization has distinct advantages for a business operating at a loss because the loss is shared and immediately deductible on the returns of the shareholders. It is also advantageous for businesses capable of paying out net profits as earned. In the latter case, the corporate tax is avoided. If net profits must be retained in the business, Subchapter S tax treatment is disadvantageous because income tax is paid on earnings not received, and there is a danger of double taxation to the individual because undistributed earnings which have been taxed once are taxed again in the event of the death of a shareholder. Thus, it is evident that the theoretical advantage of using the Subchapter S corporation to avoid double taxation of corporate income must be heavily qualified.

CONTROL

14 CONTROL IN PARTNERSHIPS

In every business organization, some individual or group of people will make decisions or possess control of the business. In a general partnership, unless the agreement provides to the contrary, each partner has an equal voice in the firm's affairs, with an equal right to possess partnership property for business purposes. In a limited partnership, the general partner or partners with unlimited liability are in control. Limited partners have no right to participate in management.

Partners are liable for all transactions entered into by any partner in the scope of the partnership business and are similarly liable for any partner's torts committed while she or he is acting in the course of the firm's business. Each partner is, in effect, both an agent of the partnership and a principal, being capable of creating both contract and tort liability for the firm and for her or his co-partners, and likewise being responsible for her or his own acts. There are many technical rules concerning what acts of a partner are within the scope or course of the partnership. One such special rule is worthy of mention. A partner in a trading partnership, that is, one engaged in the business of buying and selling commodities, has the implied authority to borrow money in the usual course of business and to pledge the credit of the firm; but a partner in a nontrading partnership, such as an accounting firm, has no implied power to borrow money. In the latter case, such authority must be actual before the firm will be bound. A further discussion of the partnership's operation and liability of the partners is presented in the next chapter.

15 CONTROL OF LARGE CORPORATIONS

In the corporate form of organization, legal problems created by persons in control and those seeking control are quite numerous. In very large corporations, control by management is maintained with a very small percentage of stock ownership through the utilization of corporate records and funds to solicit proxies. Management can, at corporate expense, solicit the right to vote the stock of shareholders unable to attend the meetings at which the directors of the company are elected. An outsider must either own sufficient stock to elect the directors or must solicit proxies at his or her own expense. Although there are a few proxy fights, the management of a large corporation usually can maintain control with only a small minority of actual stock ownership.

In corporations having several hundred shareholders or more, a number of techniques are used to gain control without having a majority of the total investment. One technique is to issue classes of stock. In some states, there can be nonvoting stock—the group seeking to keep control will buy voting stock while selling nonvoting stock to others. Preferred stock may be used to increase capital without losing control. For example, a group may invest $100,000 in common stock of $1 par value each. Then they will sell another $100,000 of the same common stock, requiring that for each share of common stock purchased, a $5 share of nonvoting preferred stock must be purchased. Thus, the corporation would raise $700,000, and the $100,000 original investment made by the organizing individuals would have 50 percent of the voting power. There are other schemes which can be used, such as selling some stock to the organizers for 10 cents per share and selling later shares for $1 to outsiders. Another method of gaining and keeping control is to pool the stock of several shareholders into a voting trust so that one person gains the power, by contract, to vote all the shares in the trust.

Once again, other issues concerning corporate operations are discussed in the next chapter on liability and in Chapter 18 on securities regulation. An understanding of these securities laws really is essential when a corporation's stock is being publicly traded.

16 CONTROL OF CLOSELY HELD CORPORATIONS

Unlike the situation with a large, publicly held corporation, one shareholder (or at least a small group of shareholders) may be able to control a closely held corporation. This can result because this individual (or the group) can own an actual majority of the issued shares. This majority can control the election of a board of directors. In fact, the shareholders with the largest amount of stock often are elected to this board of directors. The directors, in turn, elect officers, who again may be the shareholders with the largest interests. The directors also establish important corporate policies such as declaring dividends and amending the bylaws. In a very real sense those who own a majority of a closely held corporation can rule with near absolute authority.

What then are the rights of those who do not possess control in a closely held corporation—the so-called "minority interest?" To a very large degree, the owners of the minority interest are subject to the whim or caprice of the majority. The majority may pay themselves salaries which use up profits and may never declare a dividend. However, the minority interest is not without some rights, because the directors and officers stand in a fiduciary relation to the corporation and to the minority shareholders if the corporation is closely held. This relation imposes a duty on directors to act for the best interests of the corporation rather than for themselves individually.

If the majority shareholders are acting illegally or are oppressive of the rights of the minority shareholders, a lawsuit known as a **derivative action** may be brought by a minority shareholder on behalf of the corporation. Such suits may seek to enjoin the unlawful activity or to collect damages for the corporation. For example, contracts made between the corporation and an interested director or officer may be challenged. The burden is on the director or officer (who may be the majority shareholder) to prove good faith and inherent fairness in such transactions if a suit is commenced.

A derivative suit cannot be used as a means of harassing management. Therefore, these actions generally cannot begin until all possible means to solve the problem within the corporate organization have been exhausted. Generally, a minority shareholder must first demand that the board of directors institute a suit to protect the corporation. However, a formal demand on the board is excused if the demand would be futile, such as when the directors are accused of the wrongdoing. In these situations, companies may appoint a disinterested committee to decide when a derivative suit filed on behalf of the company is in the organization's best interest. The following case illustrates that an independent committee balancing between the rights of the aggrieved shareholders and the needs of management is subject to judicial review.

ZAPATA CORPORATION v. MALDONADO
430 A.2d 779 (Del. 1981)

FACTS

William Maldonado instituted a shareholder's derivative suit against ten officers and/or directors of Zapata Corporation (Zapata), alleging breaches of fiduciary duty. Maldonado did *not* first demand that the board of directors sue. He argued that such a demand would be futile because all directors were named as defendants and had participated in the alleged wrongful acts. While this litigation was pending, Zapata's board of directors lost four of the defendant-directors. The remaining directors appointed two new *outside* directors to the board. The board then created an "Independent Investigation Committee" composed of these two new members. This committee's job was to determine whether the corporation should continue the litigation pending on its behalf. After an investigation, the committee concluded that Maldonado's action should be dismissed because it was not in the best interest of the corporation. The trial court granted the corporation's motion to dismiss, and Maldonado appealed.

ISSUE

Can an authorized board committee be permitted to dismiss derivative litigation which has been properly initiated by a stockholder?

DECISION

Perhaps, if the court's standards are satisfied. (In this case, the court returns this question to the lower court for factual findings consistent with the reasoning below.)

REASONS

1. To ensure that corporations are able to rid themselves of harmful litigation, while at the same time ensuring that legitimate derivative claims are allowed to proceed, Delaware courts use a two-step analysis.
2. First, the court must inquire into the independence and good faith of the committee. If the court is satisfied that the committee is independent and acting in good faith, the court proceeds to step two.
3. This second step involves the court's applying its own independent business judgment as to whether the motion should be granted. In other words, a corporation could satisfy step one but still lose its motion for dismissal in this step two if the court concludes the committee's recommendation is not in the organization's best interest.

The basic difficulty of owning a minority interest in a closely held corporation is the fact that there is no ready market for the stock should the shareholder desire to dispose of it. Of course, if there is a valid buy and sell agreement, then there is a market for the stock. Thus, buy and sell agreements are absolutely essential in closely held corporations. Although shareholders have the right to attend meetings and vote for directors, they may be constantly outvoted. They have a right to any dividends that are declared, but no right to have them declared. They also have a preemptive right, which is to purchase their proportionate share of any new stock issue, but they may not be interested in investing more money when no dividends are being paid. Therefore, as a practical matter, the majority may be able to increase their percentage of ownership further.

The minority shareholder has a right to inspect the books and records of the company, but at a proper time and place; and the books may not have much meaning without entries and account balances being analyzed by an expert.

Finally, minority shareholders have the right to their proportionate share of assets on dissolution, but they have no right to dissolution, except that they may seek it in a court of equity under circumstances that will cause a court to step in to protect creditors and the corporation.

REVIEW QUESTIONS

1 Identify the terms in the left-hand column by matching each with the appropriate statement in the right-hand column.

(1) Partnership
(2) Proprietorship
(3) Limited partnership
(4) Corporation
(5) Legal capacity
(6) Buy and sell agreement
(7) Subchapter S corporation
(8) Accumulated earnings tax

(a) A business owned by one person who is personally liable for all losses
(b) An artificial being created by a state
(c) Imposed when a corporation fails to justify not paying dividends from earnings
(d) Created when shareholders elect to be treated as partners for tax purposes
(e) Created by an agreement between two or more persons who agree to share profits and losses
(f) Provides for compensation to a deceased or withdrawing owner of a business in return for that owner's interest
(g) The ability of an organization to sue or to own property
(h) Exists when some partners are treated like shareholders for liability purposes

2 The You-Can-Be-Rich Corporation sells products for resale to citizens in Texas. You-Can-Be-Rich is a Delaware corporation with its principal place of business in Chicago, Illinois. Although it is not licensed to do business in Texas, it has sold its products through sales representatives who have operated out of their own homes. One customer in Texas has failed to pay the money owed, and the corporation has filed suit to collect the debt. What defense, if any, is available to the customer? Explain.

3 Curtis sold feed to a corporation. He was given a corporate check that was returned by the bank for insufficient funds. When the corporation failed to cover the check, he sued the directors and sought to hold them personally liable for the check. Give examples of factors that would justify a decision for the plaintiff.

4 Beck and Kirk entered into a "land development agreement" that provided that Beck would contribute land and Kirk would furnish her expertise to create a residential housing development to be called "Beckhaven Estates." Beck and Kirk agreed to divide any profits. Kirk employed the plaintiff, Indiana Surveying, to plot the development. When Kirk failed to pay for the survey, a suit was instituted against Beck and Kirk as partners to collect. Beck denied liability. What was the result? Why?

5 Lewis and Tabor signed a written agreement to operate a dairy farm. This contract required Tabor to furnish the cows and the labor and Lewis to provide the land and the milking equipment. These parties also agreed to share the proceeds or losses equally. Their agreement specifically stated that these parties were not partners, but that Tabor was leasing Lewis's land and equipment. Are these parties actually partners? Why, or why not?

6 You and a friend are considering forming a business organization to manufacture and sell widgets. You suspect that the company will show a loss during its first two years of operation. You also know that another manufacturer of widgets has suffered three product liability lawsuits totaling $300,000 within the past year. What form of business organization should be selected under these circumstances? Why?

7 Libby and Gloria have formed a limited partnership, with Gloria agreeing to be the general partner. This partnership has purchased supplies from Carl. Carl has received a promissory note signed on behalf of the partnership as payment. If the partnership is unable to pay this note, can Carl hold Gloria personally liable? Explain.

8 An injured worker filed for unemployment compensation. His former corporate employer challenged the claim before the appropriate state agency. The president of the corporation and its sole shareholder attended the proceedings and sought to cross-examine the claimant and argue the case. The agency refused to allow him to do so, since he was not a licensed attorney. Was the agency action correct? Explain.

9 Sam was employed by George to sell and service boilers. He was paid 50 percent of the net profit of each sale. Are Sam and George partners? Why, or why not?

10 List and explain four techniques used to avoid the double taxation of corporate income in closely held corporations.

11 X, Y, and Z wish to go into the television sale and repair business. X will contribute $20,000 and work in the business as the chief repairperson. Y will contribute $30,000. She will be employed as manager in charge of buying and selling new television sets. Z will contribute $60,000. Whereas Z will not actively engage in the operations of the business, before he contributes any money he wants to be assured that he will have the final say on all matters other than the day-to-day operations of the business. What form of business organization should be selected to accomplish these objectives? Explain.

12 Albert Anderson and Barbara Brinson wish to enter into the business of manufacturing fine furniture. Which form of business organization would you recommend in each of the following situations? Explain each of your answers.

   a Brinson is a furniture expert, but she has no funds. Anderson knows nothing about such production, but he is willing to contribute all the money needed to start the business.

   b The furniture manufacturing process requires more capital than either Anderson or Brinson can raise together. However, they wish to maintain control of the business.

   c The production process can be very dangerous, and a large tort judgment against the business is foreseeable.

   d Sales will be nationwide.

   e A loss is expected for the first several years.

13 Michal, Walter, Olga, and Harold executed and recorded a certificate to establish the River Bend Limited Partnership. One was listed as general partner, and the others were listed as limited partners. This certificate was signed and acknowledged by all the partners before a notary. It was not sworn to, however. Are all partners liable as general partners? Why, or why not?

14 Richard and his son Robert each raised potatoes on their own land. The potatoes are stored together, and the parties advertised together under the name Richard and Son. The profit from the sale of the potatoes was split evenly. A major loss was incurred by Robert as a result of spraying the potatoes with the wrong spray. Must Richard share in the loss? Why, or why not?

CHAPTER 12

LIABILITY OF BUSINESS ORGANIZATIONS AND MANAGERS

OVERVIEW

When a contract is breached, a tort is committed, or a law is violated, issues of liability immediately arise. Is the business entity liable? Is the person involved liable? If there is liability, to whom? If payment is made to one person, is there a right of contribution or indemnity from another? These issues are, in part, answered by the law of agency. Other answers are found in the law of partnerships and corporations. Still others are found in various statutes and in case law. The sections which follow will discuss some of the more important legal theories used to impose liability on various kinds of businesses and those who operate them. You should understand the meaning and application of the following terms: actual authority, agency, agent, apparent authority, master, principal, ratification, respondeat superior, and servant.

1 TERMINOLOGY

Because individuals by themselves cannot accomplish all they desire, each of us asks for help from others and is asked by others for help from us. From the perspective of operating business organizations, partnerships and corporations must act through others—the partners, owners, and employees. This nature of our increasing interdependency makes the law of agency very important today. The term **agency** is applicable to those situations in which one person acts on behalf of another. A **principal** is the person or organization who controls the activities of an **agent** who is the person or organization acting on behalf of the principal. These parties may be individuals, partnerships, corporations, or other types of organizations.

The relationship between a principal and agent is fiduciary in nature. Fiduciaries occupy a special position of trust and confidence. Therefore, principals and agents owe to one another the duty of loyalty and honesty. This fiduciary concept of the agency is of major importance when examining the liability of business organization managers.

Typically the terms "principal" and "agent" are used whenever the factual situation involves the negotiation or performance of a contract. If the circumstances involve a tort or personal injury, the term **master** is technically more correct than "principal" and the term **servant** is more accurate than "agent." In either case, the agent or servant usually will have encountered a **third party,** who often raises questions about holding the principal (master) or agent (servant) or both liable.

In general, the third party, who has signed a contract with an agent, wants the principal bound to the contract. In other words, the third party wants to have the principal liable instead of the agent. Likewise, when a third party is injured by a servant, that third party usually wants to recover from the master because the master has a "deeper pocket." For contractual liability to pass from the agent to the principal, the law requires the agent to act within the scope of authority. Similarly, the master becomes liable for a servant's torts only when the servant is acting within the scope of employment.

Although contract and tort liability are discussed in more detail throughout this chapter, the next three sections give further background on the concept of authority.

LIABILITY BASED ON CONTRACT LAW

2 PRINCIPALS

Businesses obviously have liability on authorized contracts entered into on their behalf. However, questions of contractual liability often arise when an alleged agent enters into a contract with a third party on behalf of a purported principal. The general rule is that a principal has liability on all contracts entered into by the agent within the scope of the actual or apparent authority of the agent. **Actual authority** includes that expressly given and all that is necessarily implied to carry out the express authority. The principal may be a corporation, a partnership, or a sole proprietorship. Before the person dealing with the agent can hold the principal to the contract, he or she must prove the existence of this authority of the agent, although such factors as trade custom and emergencies may be used to establish it. Actual authority is that which is expressly given and all that is necessarily incidental to or implied in the express authority.

Apparent Authority

The term **apparent authority,** sometimes called "ostensible authority," refers to situations in which no actual authority exists, but in which the law binds the principal as if it did. The law does so if the principal by his or her conduct, has led third persons to believe that the agent has authority and that they should rely on the belief. Ostensible authority is when a principal, intentionally or through carelessness, causes or allows another to believe the agent possesses authority. Liability of the principal for the ostensible agent's acts rests on the doctrine of estoppel. Its essential elements are representation by the principal, justifiable reliance thereon by the third party, and change of position or injury resulting from such reliance.

VICKERS v. NORTH AM. LAND DEVELOPMENT
607 P.2d 603 (N.M. 1980)

FACTS

Plaintiff sued to enforce a land sales contract. It provided that the plaintiff would be allowed to trade one purchased lot for a 2-acre parcel of the plaintiff's choice as soon as the property was developed for sale. Defendant contended that its salesperson, Walsh, lacked authority to agree to trade commercial property for residential property.

ISSUE

Is the principal bound by this contract term agreed to by its agent?

DECISION

Yes.

REASONS

1. Where there was no actual authority, Walsh had apparent authority.
2. A principal is bound by the apparent authority of his agent, irrespective of whether he has actual authority, if the agent is placed in a position which would lead a reasonably prudent person to believe that the agent did indeed possess that apparent authority.
3. If a principal knowingly permits another to occupy a position in which it is usual for the occupant to have authority of a particular kind, anyone having occasion to deal with the person in that position is justified in inferring that he or she possesses such authority, unless the contrary is then made known.
4. The doctrine of apparent authority is based upon an estoppel theory: The principal will not be permitted to establish that the agent's authority was

> less than what was apparent from the course of dealing, for when one of two innocent parties must suffer, the loss must fall upon the party who created the enabling circumstances.

In addition to being the basis of liability when an agent lacks actual authority, apparent authority can expand an actual agent's authority beyond that granted by the principal. In other words, apparent authority may exist in a person who is not an agent, or it may increase the actual authority of an agent. In either of these situations, an agent cannot create her or his own apparent authority. This type of authority must be based on the principal's words or conduct; it cannot be based on anything the agent says or does.

Probably the typical situation in which apparent authority is found to exist is when the actual authority is terminated, but notice of this fact is not given to third parties. Cancellation of actual authority does not automatically terminate the apparent authority created by prior transactions. Because apparent authority may survive the termination of an agency relationship, the principal should give notice of termination to third parties.

Ratification

A principal is also liable for unauthorized contracts if he or she is found to have ratified the contract. Conduct that indicates an intention to adopt an unauthorized transaction will constitute **ratification.** For example, an expression of approval to the agent or performance of the contract will constitute a ratification. For a valid ratification to occur, the principal must: (1) have capacity to do what the agent has done, (2) be known to the third party, and (3) have full knowledge of the facts.

First, since ratification relates to the time of the agent's actions, both the principal and agent must be capable of that action at that time. Furthermore, they must maintain their capacity until the ratification actually occurs.

Second, an agent's act may be ratified only when the agent has acted as an agent. A person who professes to act for himself in his own name does nothing that can be ratified, even though he intends at the time to let another have the benefit of his acts. In other words, the third party has to have known about the existence of the principal at the time the unauthorized actions have occurred.

Third, in general, a principal cannot be held to have ratified an agent's unauthorized acts if he lacks full knowledge of all the material facts associated with the agent's actions. When the principal expressly ratifies unauthorized acts and shows no desire to learn all the facts, he may not deny liability on the ground that he has been ignorant of all important information. However, when ratification is implied from the principal's conduct, a lack of full knowledge may become a defense against liability.

A ratification may be expressed by the principal, or it may be implied from the principal's conduct. Any conduct that clearly indicates the principal's intention to approve the agent's actions will be a ratification. Accepting the benefits of the unauthorized acts definitely is a ratification. If the principal knows what the agent has done, and if she or he makes no objection within a reasonable time, a ratification results by operation of law. The issue of what is a reasonable time is a factual one for a jury to resolve.

3 AGENTS

In contractual situations, the ultimate purpose of an agency is to have the agent negotiate and reach an agreement with the third party. Although the contract is made by these two parties, typically they each desire to have the liability run between the principal and third party. That is, in general it is desirable and the expectation of all parties involved for the principal to be substituted for the agent. In other words, if everything works according to plan, the principal and third party become liable to each other, and the agent is not liable on the contract.

EPPLER, GUERIN & TURNER, INC. v. KASMIR
685 S.W. 2d 737 (Tex. App. 5th Dist. 1985)

FACTS

Plaintiff, an investment banking firm, was hired by defendants to render an opinion on the value of certain securities. The securities were the subject of a suit between defendants' client, Intercontinental Industries, Inc., and the Internal Revenue Service. It is undisputed that plaintiff knew at the time it was hired by defendants that defendants were attorneys representing Intercontinental Industries in the pending suit. A letter between the parties stated that billings were to be rendered to the defendants' firm.

ISSUE

Are the agents personally liable on the contract?

DECISION

No.

REASONS

1. Except in the case of negotiable instruments, the general rule is that when an agent contracts for the benefit of a disclosed principal, the agent is not liable on the contracts he makes.
2. The parties to a contract can alter this general rule by agreement so that the agent will be liable on the contract. The agent may bind himself to such

> a contract by expressly or impliedly agreeing either to substitute his own responsibility for that of his principal or to add his personal responsibility.
> 3. When an attorney contracts with a third party for the benefit of a client for goods or services to be used in connection with the attorney's representation of a particular client, and when the third party is aware of these facts, the attorney is not liable on the contract unless he either expressly or impliedly assumes some type of special liability.

As the foregoing case illustrates, the general rule is that agents do not become personally liable to third parties, since with regard to liability the principal is substituted for the agent. However, there are three situations in which an agent and third party are contractually bound to one another. First, if the agent fails to disclose the identity of the principal, the agent is personally liable. A person who fails to identify the principal and the fact of the agency relationship is liable as a principal on the contract. This rule seems logical, since the third party has no one other than the agent to hold liable. The agent remains liable to the third party until that time when the principal is disclosed and the third party elects to hold the principal, and not the agent, liable.

The second situation involving the agent's liability to third parties arises whenever the agent agrees to be personally liable or when the agent has failed to sign a document in a representative capacity. When an agent works for a truly undisclosed principal, no representative capacity will be indicated. However, if the agent for a disclosed or partially disclosed principal fails to indicate clearly his agency apacity, that agent becomes personally liable to the third party.

A third instance of an agent's becoming personally bound to a third party occurs when the agent has exceeded actual and apparent authority. In essence, whenever a person as an agent negotiates with a third party, that agent implicitly promises she or he has authority to make the contract involved. If that promise is breached, the agent is liable to the third party.

LIABILITY BASED ON TORT LAW

4 BASIC CONCEPTS

The typical situation involving tort liability occurs when an employment arrangement results in injury to a third party. The issue usually involves determining who is liable for the third party's injury—the employee (servant) or the employer (master). The following general statements present the guidelines used in determining tort liability:

1 The party committing the tort (wrong) is liable for the damage done.

2 A master is liable for the torts of servants who were acting within the scope of their employment.
3 The party hiring an independent contractor usually is not liable for the torts of that independent contractor.

An employee is always liable for his or her own torts. The fact that the employer may also be liable does not excuse the employee.

SANFORD v. KOBEY BROS. CONST. CORP.
689 P.2d 724 (Colo. App. 1984)

FACTS

Kobey Brothers Construction Corporation (Kobey Brothers) constructed a house for the plaintiffs. For various reasons, the foundation was incompatible with the soil, resulting in heaving and damage to the house. Plaintiffs sued both Harris Kobey as an individual and Kobey Brothers as a corporation for negligent construction. The trial court found no individual liability on the part of Harris Kobey, even though he supervised the construction and made all decisions, but found Kobey Brothers liable for damages arising from the negligent reduction of the "void space" between the foundation and interior basement walls.

ISSUE

Does the fact that a defendant is acting in a representative capacity bar tort liability?

DECISION

No.

REASONS

1. Neither the doctrine of respondeat superior nor the fiction of corporate existence bars imposition of individual liability for individual acts of negligence, even when the individual is acting in a representative capacity.
2. Rather, a servant may be held personally liable for his individual acts of negligence, as also may an officer, director, or agent of a corporation for his or her tortious acts, regardless of the fact that the master or corporation also may be vicariously liable.

Respondeat Superior

A principal is vicariously liable for the torts of an agent, and an employer is liable for the torts of an employee if the agent or employee acts within the scope of his or her employment or is working for the employer. Likewise, a partnership and the individual parties have tort liability for torts of a partner or of an employee of the partnership committed within the scope of the partnership business. This liability is created by a doctrine known as **respondeat superior.**

The doctrine of respondeat superior imposes vicarious liability on those (masters) who actually have not committed any tort. This concept of vicarious liability is based on the public policy of placing responsibility on the party who is most capable of paying for the damage done. This principle has been referred to as the *deep pocket* theory of liability. In essence, the doctrine of respondeat superior provides that the cost of doing business should include liability for injuries to persons and property which are caused by employees within the scope of employment. Thus, the business, rather than just the injured victim or the employee, bears the cost of these injuries.

The concept of vicarious liability is an expanding one. In the twentieth century, juries and courts have enlarged the definition of scope of employment and thus have increased the total risk of businesses of all types. This is especially true now that the automobile and truck play a major role in the conduct of business.

STANFIELD v. LACCOARCE
588 P.2d 1271 (Ore. 1978)

FACTS

Roy Laccoarce was driving his truck on his return home from Roseburg when it went out of control and injured Stanfield. Roy worked for his parents, and consequently Stanfield sued both Roy and his parents. Although the evidence as to the primary purpose for Roy's trip to Roseburg was conflicting, the jury could reasonably conclude that at least one purpose was to pick up supplies for various businesses owned by Roy's parents. The jury returned a verdict for Stanfield.

ISSUE

Was Roy acting within the scope of his employment?

DECISION

Yes.

REASONS

1. In deciding whether an employee was acting within the scope of his employment, the factors to be considered are whether the act in question is of a kind the employee was hired to perform, whether the act occurred substantially within the authorized limits of time and space, and whether the employee was motivated, at least in part, by a purpose to serve the employer.
2. The standard that an employee be within the scope of employment is designed to ensure that employers will be held liable only for harm resulting from activities from which benefits are received.
3. The ultimate issue is whether or not it is just that the loss resulting from

> the employee's acts should be considered one of the normal risks to be borne by the business in which the servant is employed.
> 4. There was evidence from which the jury could conclude that Roy was within the scope of his parents' employment when the accident occurred.

Principals may also have tort liability based on apparent authority. For example, a trade association was held to have liability under the antitrust laws if its personnel were involved in the violations. Likewise, a principal is liable for an agent's fraud, even though the agent acts solely to benefit himself or herself, if the agent has apparent authority.

Under the apparent authority theory, liability is based upon the fact that the agent's position facilitates the consummation of the fraud, in that from the point of view of the third person the transaction seems regular on its face and the agent appears to be acting in the ordinary course of business.

It should be noted that everyone performing a service is not necessarily a servant or agent of an employer. Work is sometimes performed by an independent contractor. Whether a person is a servant or an independent contractor is determined by the degree of control the employing party exercises. More control indicates a master-servant relationship. Less control is associated with a proprietor-independent contractor relationship. In essence, an independent contractor has the power to control the details of the work performed.

As a general rule, the person hiring an independent contractor is not personally liable for the contracts or torts of the independent contractor. In other words, general agency principles, including the doctrine of respondeat superior, are not applicable in the typical situation involving an independent contractor.

Liability based on tort theories is so important that it was the subject matter of Chapter 9.

5   ILLEGAL CONDUCT

A business may owe dollar damages to injured parties because of illegal conduct by its officers, agents, or other employees. Conduct may be illegal either because it violates a statute or because it is contrary to public policy. Many statutes provide legal rights to injured parties to recover the damages caused by a business organization. In a civil action, investors can seek to recover their investment when the organization has violated any of the securities laws (Chapter 18), labor laws (Chapters 16 and 17), or antitrust laws (Chapters 22 and 23). The law of employment also provides for civil remedies if a worker is discharged in violation of equal employment opportunities (Chapter 15). Indeed, a breach of any contract by a business can result in the wronged party seeking monetary damages.

In recent years, courts increasingly have imposed liability upon a business even though the organization has not violated a statute. The basis of this liability is the fact that a business may have acted contrary to public policy. For example, such issues have arisen in cases concerned with the right of an employer to discharge an employee. Public-policy considerations are very important when an employee is not protected by either a collective-bargaining agreement or another contract that provides a stated term of employment. Employees who lack these protections traditionally have been called *employees at will,* since the employer can terminate the employment relationship at any time for any reason.

Although the employment-at-will doctrine still exists today, there is a growing movement by courts to vest workers with certain rights and to require business organizations to justify firing a worker. This justification requirement is especially important when the discharge appears to deny an employee the opportunity to exercise a legal right. Such rights may include: (1) serving on a jury, (2) filing a workers' compensation claim, (3) refusing to give perjured testimony, (4) refusing to commit an illegal or unethical act, and (5) assisting in the investigation of the organization's wrongful acts.

PALMATEER v. INTERNATIONAL HARVESTER CO.
421 N.E.2d 876 (Ill. 1981)

FACTS

Ray Palmateer worked for International Harvester (IH) as a manager. He informed local law-enforcement authorities that an IH employee may have engaged in criminal activity. Palmateer also agreed to assist in any investigation of this employee. When Palmateer's superiors learned of his actions, he was fired. Palmateer sued for damages, claiming he had been wrongfully discharged. IH argued that Palmateer's employment was terminable at will. Palmateer contended his dismissal was contrary to the public policy of encouraging assistance to law-enforcement agencies.

ISSUES

Are there public-policy reasons to support a finding that Palmateer was wrongfully discharged?

DECISION

Yes.

REASONS

1. A proper balance must be maintained among the employer's interest in operating a business efficiently and profitably, the employee's interest in earning a livelihood, and society's interest in seeking to have its public policies carried out.
2. Although an employer has the right to fire employees at will when no public policy is involved, the employer commits a legal wrong when a discharge contravenes or impedes public-policy goals.
3. An employee who in good faith believes a crime has been committed should

> not be deterred from reporting it by the fear that he or she may lose his or her employment. Therefore, Palmateer should be allowed to recover for the company's improper action in discharging him.

LIABILITY BASED ON THE CRIMINAL LAW

6 BUSINESS ORGANIZATIONS

Most statutes provide for penalties to be imposed upon those who violate their provisions. If a statute imposes fines or incarceration as a penalty, the law is criminal, and for a court to find a violation there must be proof beyond a reasonable doubt.

In addition to criminal sanctions, many statutes impose civil liability upon wrongdoers as a result of illegal conduct. For example, the antitrust laws allow victims of price-fixing to collect triple damages from those violating the law. These damages are to deter wrongful conduct as well as to compensate the injured parties.

The fiction of the corporate entity creates some difficult problems insofar as criminal law is concerned. A corporation cannot be imprisoned, although in theory a death penalty of sorts could be imposed simply by the domiciliary state's dissolving it. Corporations act only through agents, and while it is possible to imprison the agents in many instances, this would not be satisfactory punishment for the corporate entity. It is, of course, possible to punish a corporation by imposing a fine.

Proving the commission of a crime by a corporation is often as difficult as imposing a meaningful penalty. "Crime" is usually defined in terms of intentional commission of some prohibited act, often with the *specific* intent to do so. How can an artificial being with no mind have criminal intent? The law has generally resolved this problem by imputing to the corporation the guilty intent of an agent, if the agent was authorized and acting within the scope of his or her employment at the time he or she committed the crime. Many cases have equated "acquiescence" by the company in the wrongful conduct with authority to commit the illegal act.

One of the more important laws imposing criminal liability on business is the Foreign Corrupt Practices Act of 1977. This act makes it a criminal offense for any United States business enterprise—whether or not incorporated or publicly held—to offer a bribe to a foreign official, foreign political party, party official, or candidate for foreign political office to obtain, retain, or direct business to any person. Companies violating the act can be fined up to $1 million. Individuals convicted of violating the law may be fined up to $10,000 and imprisoned for up to five years. The act prohibits the fine imposed on the individual from being paid directly or indirectly by the company on whose behalf he or she acted.

The Foreign Corrupt Practices Act also establishes certain standards for business records and internal controls for businesses subject to the reporting requirements of the Securities Exchange Act of 1934. As a practical matter, companies doing business in foreign countries must have corporate codes of conduct which prevent bribery of foreign officials and maintain adequate internal controls to monitor and enforce codes of conduct. They must maintain reasonably detailed, complete, and accurate books and records which will reveal any bribery or attempted bribery. Businesses subject to the act must devise sufficient systems of internal accounting control to provide reasonable assurances that the following four objectives have been met:

1. All transactions must be executed in accordance with management's authorization.
2. All transactions are recorded as necessary: (a) to permit preparation of financial statements in conformity with generally accepted accounting principles, and (b) to maintain accountability for assets.
3. Access to assets is permitted only to those authorized.
4. The recorded accountability for assets is compared with existing assets at reasonable intervals and appropriate action taken with respect to any differences.

Accountants have a high degree of responsibility to monitor compliance with the law. A firm's accountants must evaluate the internal controls used to safeguard assets and assure the reliability of financial records. These internal controls must be designed to both prevent violations and detect any that may occur. Prevention techniques permit only valid transactions to be processed, and detection techniques identify errors and irregularities. Accountants must report to their clients any weaknesses in either aspect of internal control.

7 CORPORATE EXECUTIVES

Just as employees are liable for their own torts, they are responsible for their own crimes. And, as employers are liable for torts committed while employees are acting in the course of their employment, employers may also be held culpable for the business-related crimes of their employees. For example, suppose that the chief of marketing of ABC, Inc., enters into a price-fixing arrangement with two major competitors of ABC. Clearly both the chief and ABC are guilty of a violation of the Sherman Act, discussed in Chapter 20, and both could be fined. The chief also could be imprisoned. But what about the officers of ABC who are superiors of the chief of marketing, who have no knowledge of the chief's wrongdoing, and who are only indirectly connected to it by reason of their executive position and overall company responsibilities? Are they also guilty? Technically, such persons are not the employer of the chief of marketing—ABC is. Therefore, it would appear that the doctrine of respondeat superior would not apply to such top officials. However, they sometimes are prosecuted criminally. The issue in the following case was whether the chief executive officer of a corporation was properly convicted of a crime when he had no direct connection with its commission.

UNITED STATES v. PARK
95 S.Ct. 1903 (1975)

FACTS

Acme Markets, Inc., and Park, its chief executive officer, were charged with violating the Federal Food, Drug and Cosmetic Act (FFDCA). They allegedly allowed interstate food shipments to be contaminated by rodents. Park pleaded not guilty to these charges. He contended that the responsibility for sanitation had been delegated and that he had checked on these procedures through a company vice president. In essence, Park argued that he could not have done anything more constructively than what was being done. The trial court instructed the jury that to convict him, it was not necessary to find that Park personally had participated in the situation if he had "a responsible relationship to the issue." Park was convicted, and he appealed.

ISSUE

Under the Federal Food, Drug and Cosmetic Act, can an executive be liable for the company's violation?

DECISION

Yes.

REASONS

1. The FFDCA imposes not only a positive duty to seek out and remedy violations when they occur, but it also requires executives to implement measures that will ensure that violations will not occur.
2. The requirements of foresight and vigilance imposed on responsible corporate officials are not more stringent than the public has a right to expect of those who voluntarily assume positions of authority in business organizations whose products affect the health and well-being of the public.
3. By virtue of his position, Park had the authority and responsibility to deal with the situation and to correct the FFDCA violations.

In one recent case, the officers of a corporation were convicted of murder. The company used cyanide in its processes, and steps had not been taken to protect workers from cyanide poisoning. From these cases, it is clear there is a trend toward holding top company officials responsible for crimes, even though they are only indirectly involved. This is particularly true when public-welfare statutes are violated, making certain acts criminal because they endanger the public health, safety, or general welfare. Conviction of such crimes usually does not require proof of an intent to commit the acts outlawed.

SPECIAL ASPECTS OF MANAGERIAL LIABILITY

8 PARTNERS

The general laws of agency apply to partnerships. Each partner, in effect, is an agent of the organization and both a principal and an agent with respect to all fellow partners. As such, every partner owes the duty of loyalty to the partnership and to the other partners. When conducting business, each partner is obligated to exercise good faith and to contemplate the well-being of the organization and the partners. Any time one partner tries to take advantage of a business opportunity for her own personal benefit, she becomes personally liable for damages, since she has broken her fiduciary duty.

With respect to contractual liability, the principles of authority and ratification are applicable to both the partnership and its partners. In general, the implied authority of a partner is greater than that of a general agent. Among the common implied powers are the following: to compromise, adjust, and settle claims or debts owed by or to the partnership; to sell goods in the regular course of business and to make warranties; to buy property within the scope of the business for cash or upon credit; to buy insurance; to hire employees; to make admissions against interest; to enter into contracts within the scope of the partnership; and to receive notices. A partner in a trading partnership—that is, one engaged in buying and selling commodities—has the implied authority to borrow money in the usual course of business and to pledge the credit of the firm; but a partner in a nontrading partnership, such as an accounting firm, has no implied power to borrow money. In the latter case, such authority must be actual before the firm will be bound. A partner entering into such a contract is personally liable on it.

With respect to torts, a partner has the power to impose liability on the partnership through the doctrine of respondeat superior. As we discussed in the previous chapter, partners are jointly and severally liable for the debts of their partnership. Therefore, each partner potentially is liable for the torts of every other partner. If a partnership has liability because of a tort of a partner, the organization has the right to collect its losses from the partner at fault. Likewise, any partner who has liability due to another partner's tort can seek contribution from the partner at fault. However, if the injured third party collects directly from the guilty partner, that partner cannot seek contribution from the other partners.

In addition to the agency principles, creating contract and tort liability on partners, an act in violation of a statute or an act contrary to public policy, may make the partners liable for monetary damages to third parties. Criminal liability may be imposed on the individual partners as well.

9 CORPORATE OFFICERS AND DIRECTORS

The officers and directors of a corporation may have personal liability both in tort and in contract. Liability is based on common law theories and is also created by statutes. The liability is usually to the corporation. It may also extend to shareholders and to third parties. The tort liability of corporate officers and directors is predicated upon basic principles of fault. For example, a director who participates in fraudulent conduct by the corporation has personal liability to the third party on the usual common law tort theories, just as does any other agent or servant. Moreover, the director need not personally commit fraud. He or she is liable if the director sanctions or approves it.

The liability of corporate directors is most frequently based on a violation of the fiduciary duty of loyalty owed to the corporation. A director occupies a position of trust and confidence in the corporation and cannot, by reason of his or her position, directly or indirectly derive any personal benefits not enjoyed by the corporation or the shareholders. The duty of loyalty and the duty to act in good faith prohibit directors from acting with a conflict of interest. The most common violation of this duty occurs when a director enters into a contract with, or personally deals with, the corporation. Since all officers enter into contracts of employment, alleged violations of this duty are quite common. In all circumstances, the director or officer must fully disclose his or her conflict of interest to the corporation. If he or she fails to do so, the contract may be rescinded.

At common law, such a contract was voidable unless it was shown to be: (1) approved by a disinterested board, and (2) "fair" to the corporation, in that its terms were as favorable as those available from any other person. Under some modern statutes, the transaction is valid if: (1) it is approved, with knowledge of the material facts, by a vote of disinterested directors or shareholders; and (2) the director can show it to be "fair."

The good-faith requirement is also lacking when a director or officer takes an opportunity for him or herself that the corporation should have had. A director is required to first present all possible corporate opportunities to the corporation. Only after an informed determination by the disinterested directors that the corporation should not pursue such opportunities can a director pursue them for personal benefit. In a closely held corporation, this fiduciary duty of loyalty and good faith extends to the other shareholders and even to the other officers, as the case that follows illustrates.

SAMPSON v. HUNT
564 P.2d 489 (Kan. 1977)

FACTS

The two shareholders of Bonanza, Inc., which operated a shopping center, each owned 50 percent of the stock. The defendant president managed the business.

The plaintiff was secretary, but inactive. The defendant purchased the plaintiff's stock for $75,000. At the time of the sale, the defendant did not inform the plaintiff of: (1) additional leases that had been obtained, (2) a commitment for financing of a third phase of the development, and (3) the sale of part of the stock to three doctors. When the plaintiff learned these facts, he sued to recover the difference between the selling price and the fair market value of the stock at the time of the sale.

ISSUE

Was there a breach of fiduciary duties?

DECISION

Yes.

REASONS

1. A director of a corporation owes a high fiduciary duty to the other stockholders of the corporation.
2. When two parties occupy to each other a confidential, or fiduciary, relation, and a sale is made by one to the other, equity raises a presumption against the validity of the transaction.
3. In a closely held corporation where one director or officer has a superior knowledge of corporate affairs because he is intimately involved in the daily operations of the corporation while the other director or officer has only a limited role in corporate management, the fiduciary duty is the same as if the latter were a stockholder not actively engaged in corporate affairs.

Directors are also liable for failure to exercise due care. In its simplest terms, the duty of care is synonymous with a duty not to be negligent. The standard may be stated in a variety of ways, but the most common says that a director must exercise that degree of care that an ordinarily prudent person would exercise in managing his or her own personal affairs.

Since many directors are not actively engaged in the day-to-day operation of the business, the law recognizes that they must rely on others for much of the information used in decision making. In performing duties, a director is entitled to rely on information, opinions, reports, and statements of others. These include officers and employees whom the director reasonably believes to be reliable and competent in the matters presented. A director may also rely on legal counsel, public accountants, and other expert professionals. Finally, a director may also rely on committees of the board if they act within the designated authority and if he or she reasonably believes they merit confidence. A director does not fulfill his or her duties and does not act in good faith if he or she has knowledge that would cause the reliance to be unwarranted.

These requirements allow directors to use their best business judgment without incurring liability for honest mistakes. Directors must make difficult policy decisions, and they should not have liability if their decisions are based on information that later turns out to be false.

The liability of directors for negligence in the management of the corporation is to the corporation. Since no duty runs to third-party creditors, there is no liability to them or to shareholders. Of course, a shareholder may enforce this liability through a derivative suit—one brought by a shareholder on behalf of the corporation.

The Caterpillar code recognizes that the duties owed by the board of directors is to the company and to shareholders. However, all decisions are to take the public interest into account. The code provides:

Board Stewardship

Law and logic support the notion that boards of directors are constituted to represent shareholders—the owners of the enterprise. We have long held the view that Caterpillar board members can best meet their responsibilities of stewardship to shareholders if they are elected solely by them—and not appointed by governments, labor unions, or other nonowner groups.

Board composition and board deliberations should be highly reflective of the public interest. We believe that is a basic, inseparable part of stewardship to shareholders.

There are several statutes that impose liability on directors and officers. For example, directors or officers may be liable for failure to pay federal withholding and Social Security taxes for corporation employees if they have responsibility in that area. Likewise, a director or officer is subject to third-party liability for aiding a corporation in such acts as patent, copyright, or trademark infringements, unfair competition, antitrust violations, violation of laws relating to discrimination, or violations of securities laws. Many of these matters are covered in subsequent chapters.

10 LIABILITY OF AGENTS TO PRINCIPALS

Agents owe various duties to their principals. Many of these duties are based on the contract of employment, and others are implied by law from the nature of the relationship. Since the relationship is a fiduciary one, there is an implied duty of loyalty to the principal. This duty of loyalty requires that agents avoid conflicts of interest. A conflict of interest exists if an agent undertakes a business venture that competes or interferes in any manner with the business of the employer. In addition, an agent may not make a contract for himself or herself that should have been made for the principal. Agents cannot enter into contracts on behalf of the principal with themselves as the other party. Agents may deal with themselves only if they obtain permission of the principal, after full disclosure of all facts materially influencing the situation. Transactions violating the duty of loyalty may always be rescinded by the principal, even if the agent acted for the best interests of his or her principal and the contract was as favorable as could be obtained elsewhere. If an agent violates this duty of loyalty through a conflict of interest, the principal may rescind the contract. Moreover, a principal is entitled to treat any profit realized by the agent in violation of this duty as belonging to the principal. Such profits include rebates, bonuses, commissions, or divisions of profits received by the agent.

Violations of the duty of loyalty often involve improper use of confidential information. Confidential information or trade secrets may include formulas, customer lists, processes, and business data. Trade secrets are known only to a few persons, and efforts to protect them are required if they are to be protected by law. The law prohibits employees from using trade secrets in competition with the employer or from making them public. Industrial espionage is a major problem for high-technology industries. The law in all its aspects is available to assist employers in protecting these trade secrets. Theft of them is a crime. Courts will enjoin the improper use of them and may award damages for violations of the duty of loyalty. Of course, many important property interests are also protected by laws on patents and copyrights. Infringement suits are common, and there is extensive litigation to protect property rights based on the creation of new products and ideas.

J&K COMPUTER SYSTEMS, INC. v. PARRISH
642 P.2d 732 (Utah 1982)

FACTS

Plaintiff, J&K Computer Systems, Inc., sued to recover damages and enjoin its former employees from using or disclosing certain of plaintiff's confidential computer programs.

ISSUE

Are computer programs trade secrets?

DECISION

Yes.

REASONS

1. A trade secret includes any formula, patent, device, plan, or compilation of information which is used in one's business and which gives him or her an opportunity to obtain an advantage over competitors who do not know it.
2. Defendants were not enjoined from using their general knowledge, skills, memory, or experience. They were, however, enjoined from using the proprietary accounts receivable program which the plaintiff had developed.

11 ETHICAL CONSIDERATIONS

The fiduciary duties which the director, officer, or other employee owes the corporation—especially the duty of loyalty—can often present difficult ethical as well as legal questions. In the past, it has been all too common for corporate officers to engage in bribery, price-fixing, illegal campaign contributions, tax evasion, fraud, kickbacks, and bid rigging to further their business interests. Obviously, such blatant illegality could not hide behind any "duty of loyalty," for it violates not only the law but also contemporary ethical ideas of what is "right" and "good." True loyalty to a corporation would entail seeing that the corporation operates within the law. Often, ethical standards are embodied in the law, thus ensuring that the principled corporation is not put at a disadvantage in competing with less scrupulous corporations. For example, every United States firm doing business in a foreign country is prohibited from bribing public officials. Each corporate management has a responsibility under the Foreign Corrupt Practices Act, as discussed in section 6 to ensure adequate internal controls to prevent business bribes to foreign officials. Further, management must take corrective action if violations are discovered. Various laws prohibit bribes and kickbacks in the United States. Caterpillar's Code of Ethics regarding these matters is consistent with both the statutes and generally accepted ethical norms.

Relationships with Public Officials

In dealing with public officials, as with private business associates, Caterpillar will utilize only ethical commercial practices, We won't seek to influence sales of our products (or other events impacting on the company) by payments of bribes, kickbacks, or other questionable inducements.

   Caterpillar employees will take care to avoid involving the company in any such activities engaged in by others. We won't advise or assist any purchaser of Caterpillar products, including dealers, in making or arranging such payments. We will discourage dealers from engaging in such practices.

   Payments of any size to induce public officials to fail to perform their duties—or to perform them in an incorrect manner—are prohibited. Company employees are also required to make good faith efforts to avoid payment of gratuities or "tips" to certain public officials, even where such practices are customary. Where these payments are as a practical matter unavoidable, they must be limited to customary amounts; and they may be made only to facilitate correct performance of the officials' duties.

A more difficult ethical problem to come to grips with is any subtle form of self-dealing by corporate executives. Is an executive being "loyal" to the corporation and its shareholders by negotiating a lavish salary or extravagant employment guarantees (often called "golden parachutes")? It is argued that the executive has the right to demand what he or she is worth and that the corporation has to pay "good money" to get the best people. But consider the so-called golden parachute. This is a special employment contract protecting key executives if corporate control changes hands. The "protection" requires that hefty sums of money be paid to executives, usually over a period of years. In an era of mergers, golden parachutes to protect corporate managers are becoming more common.

Without doubt, golden parachutes arranged in the heat of corporate takeover attempts raise serious ethical questions. During the Bendix–Martin Marietta merger battle, sixteen Bendix officers arranged for the company to pay $4.7 million annually should they be fired or demoted after a takeover. Martin Marietta followed suit, securing agreements covering twenty-eight executives, ensuring employment or compensation if Bendix was successful in its tender offer for Martin Marietta. One respected business publication editorialized that this practice amounted "to an outrageous misuse of stockholders' assets and an abuse of management prerogatives." Although approved by the corporations' boards of directors, golden parachutes were compared ethically to an executive stuffing a suitcase of company money under the bed as an insurance policy against losing the job in a takeover (clearly an outright theft). Golden parachutes arranged at the time of employment, rather than in the heat of battle, may not be subject to the same strong criticism. Yet the nagging problem of overcompensation remains. As is often the case, the courts will soon have the opportunity to decide the legal question of whether (or when) a golden parachute is a waste of corporate assets.

REVIEW QUESTIONS

1 Test your knowledge and understanding by matching the term in the left-hand column with the appropriate statement in the right-hand column.

(1) Implied authority
(2) Apparent authority
(3) Ratification
(4) Undisclosed principal
(5) Respondeat superior
(6) Fiduciary
(7) Business judgment rule
(8) Duty of loyalty

(a) Approval of an agent's unauthorized acts
(b) Doctrine that creates vicarious liability on the master
(c) Standard by which managers' decisions are judged
(d) A type of actual authority
(e) The fundamental obligation owed by all agents to their principals
(f) The authority that is created by the principal from the third party's perspective
(g) Exists when a third party does not know of a principal's existence
(h) Type of relationship based on trust and confidence

2 Plaintiffs, residents of a housing development built by Milzoco Builders, Inc., sued the president, vice president, and secretary of the corporation as individuals. The plaintiffs allege that due to faulty planning, their homes were built in an area that is often flooded by the drainage of the other areas of the develop-

ment and that the defendants were negligent in constructing the development. Can these officers be held personally liable? Why, or why not?

3 Klepp Wood Flooring is a contractor engaged in the business of installing wood floors in gymnasiums. Butterfield, an architect, invited Klepp to bid on a job. After the bid was received, Butterfield accepted the bid, but no formal contract was signed. Klepp completed the work and billed Butterfield. Butterfield refused to pay and told Klepp for the first time that the gym was owned by an undisclosed principal. Klepp sued Butterfield for the work performed. What was the result? Why?

4 Taylor and Terry agreed to operate a business called the Christian Book Center, Inc. Each owned 50 percent of the corporate stock. From the business' inception, Taylor was the corporate president. An argument occurred over the operations of the business. Thereafter, Taylor told Terry that he was "out of business." A short time later, a promissory note that the corporation owed became due. Rather than discussing a possible extension of this note with Terry, Taylor allowed the corporation to default. At a foreclosure sale, Taylor purchased the assets of the corporation and continued the operation in his own name. Terry was not informed of the default or foreclosure sale. When he learned of Taylor's actions, he sued. What was the result? Why?

5 Ann wanted automobile insurance and contacted the Wills Insurance Agency. It was an independent insurance agent and broker for several companies. Mr. Wills told Ann that she had full coverage with the defendant insurance company and accepted her premium check. Later, she had an accident, and the defendant company denied that she was insured. Wills had never applied for the insurance and had kept the premium. Is the defendant company liable? Why, or why not?

6 David purchased a new car and called the Prestige Insurance Company's main office to transfer the insurance from his old car to his new one. He spoke to several employees before being transferred to Agnes. Although she had no actual authority to do so, Agnes told David, "Okay, your new car is covered." David had an accident the next day. The insurance company denied the existence of any coverage. If David sues Prestige, should he win? Explain.

7 Agatha, Alicia, and Hilary operated the AAH Family Health Spa. Agatha and Hilary paid themselves salaries of $18,000 a year, but they paid Alicia only $5,000 annually. Agatha and Hilary sold spa membership to their families at below the normal rate. They also refused to discuss partnership affairs with Alicia. Does Alicia have a cause of action against Agatha and Hilary? Explain.

8 A patient sued Dr. Flynn for medical malpractice. Dr. Flynn, who is a partner in a medical partnership, sought contributions from his partners. He contended that his negligence, if any, occurred in the course of the partnership's business. Is Dr. Flynn entitled to contributions from his partners? Why, or why not?

9 Phil sued the Dallas Company for breach of contract. He was director of the company, and his presence and vote were necessary to the approval of the contract with him. Dallas Company contends that the contract is not binding. Is the company correct? Explain.

10 R. J. owned a majority of the stock of U-Wing Oil Company, and he ran the corporation by himself. The balance of the stock was owned by R. J.'s brother and sister, who agreed to sell their stock to him. At the time of the purchase, R. J. was negotiating a sale of the company, but he did not reveal this fact to his brother and sister. The sale of the company resulted in a great profit to R. J. The

brother and sister brought suit to recover the difference. Should the brother and sister succeed? Why?

11 Scott, a truck driver for Matthew Co., decided to detour seven blocks and stop by his sister's house for a visit. Twenty minutes later, Scott headed back to the Matthew Co.'s garage. He was driving faster than the speed limit when he struck and injured Theresa.

   a What are Theresa's rights, if any, against Scott?

   b Assuming Matthew Co. had instructed its drivers to obey all traffic laws, what are Theresa's rights, if any, against the company?

12 Tammy was shopping in Save-a-Lot Grocery Store when Stewart, an employee, brushed Tammy's ankle with a grocery cart. A short time later, while still shopping, Tammy told Stewart that he should say "Excuse me," and then people would get out of his way. Stewart then punched Tammy in the face, knocking her to the floor. If Tammy sues Save-a-Lot, should she collect for her injuries? Explain.

13 Carr, the president of D Corp., entered into a contract to purchase the stock of P Corp. from Ostrich, its sole shareholder, and to hire Ostrich at a compensation exceeding $100,000. On learning of the transaction, D Corp.'s board of directors discharged Carr as president and renounced the contract. D Corp. contended that Carr lacked authority to make the contract. Did Carr have any authority to make the contract? Why, or why not?

14 One of several owners of a parcel of real estate granted an option to Bell to buy the land. The party granting the option claimed to be the sole owner and did not purport to be the agent of anyone. The other owners refused to go along with the sale when Bell exercised the option. The option consideration had benefited all the owners in that it had been used to pay expenses connected with the land. Are the other owners bound to the contract? Why, or why not?

15 Parents of a deceased child brought a wrongful death action against a company whose employee collided with the deceased when the employee was driving home in an intoxicated condition from the employer's Christmas party. Is the employer liable under the doctrine of respondeat superior? Why, or why not?

16 An injured workman brought an action to enforce a worker's compensation award against a bankrupt corporation. The corporation failed to carry workers' compensation insurance. Since the employee was unable to recover from the bankrupt corporation, he brought an action against the officers and directors of the corporation. What was the result? Why?

CHAPTER **13**

INTERNATIONAL TRANSACTIONS

OVERVIEW

Some understanding of the international legal environment is essential for students of business. The legal issues involved in transactions which involve more than one country are appreciably different than those for transactions occurring entirely within a single country. The need for businesses to know and obey local law was discussed in Chapter 1. This need is even more important when companies conduct business internationally. Domestically, there may be significant differences in the laws among states. Internationally, not only may the law of one country differ from the law of another, but there are fundamental variations in the basic structure of legal systems. Common law, civil (or code) law, socialist law, Muslim law, and tribal law systems exist throughout the world. Most countries' legal systems are not purely one or another of these, but involve mixtures of two or more. Therefore, obtaining knowledge of the legal environment in which one is conducting business will often be extraordinarily difficult. Yet, the need to know and comply with foreign legal requirements is of paramount importance.

The relevant international legal environment does not consist of a cohesive body of uniform principles. It contains elements of United States domestic law, the law of other countries, bilateral and regional agreements or conventions (treaties), and "customary international law." The entire international legal environment is not summarized here; instead, selected aspects of important issues for firms engaging in international business transactions are presented. These issues include: (1) alternative methods of conducting international business, (2) the legal institutions and agreements affecting international business, and (3) domestic laws having international trade consequences.

This chapter will introduce the terms and concepts of letters of credit, choice-of-law, expropriation, confiscation, nationalization, the act-of-state doctrine, sovereign immunity, most-favored nation, dumping, and sovereign compulsion. In addition, several international organizations and agreements will be explained.

1 INTRODUCTION

More than one-third of the United States, gross national product is generated from international business activities. Over 3,500 U.S. firms have more than 25,000 direct investments in other countries, to say nothing of less complex involvement abroad. The worldwide impact of international business activities is also impressive. More than two hundred multinational businesses have sales exceeding $1 billion per year.

Several factors have contributed to the increased levels of international involvement by United States firms during the last few decades. The recognition of markets in other countries for a firm's goods and services, better availability of raw materials for manufacturing, the willingness of workers in other countries to accept lower wages, and regulatory standards which are not as strict as those in the United States have all contributed. In addition, many countries offer incentives to businesses for locating their operations within the country. These incentives can be in the form of grants or loans on favorable terms, relief from tax obligations, exclusive rights to a particular market, or other attractive provisions. Our consideration of the international legal environment will be primarily from the viewpoint of a United States firm which is considering expanding its operations into other countries.

ALTERNATIVE METHODS OF CONDUCTING INTERNATIONAL BUSINESS

2 OVERVIEW

A United States firm that wants to engage in business activities abroad is presented with an almost limitless array of possibilities regarding the manner in which it can do business. Choosing a method of doing business in other countries requires considering not only the factors involved in operating domestically (such as who is in control and what the income tax consequences are), but also other factors. Determining the most appropriate form for conducting international operations involves assessing marketing and finance factors as well as international law issues.

3 DIRECT SALES ABROAD

The simplest, least risky approach for a manufacturer to use when trying to penetrate foreign markets is to sell goods directly to buyers located in other countries. However, with foreign sales, increased uncertainty over the ability to enforce the buyer's promise to pay for goods often requires that more complex arrangements for payment be made than with the usual domestic sale. Often, the parties to an international transaction use an **irrevocable letter of credit** to reduce this uncertainty. In such a transaction an **issuing bank** in the buyer's country issues a commitment to pay a specified amount (that is, the price of the goods) to a **confirming bank** in the United States; it does so when it receives a **bill of lading** from the carrier, indicating that the goods have been shipped. The seller obtains payment from the confirming bank, which is reimbursed by the issuing bank in the buyer's country. The bill of lading is issued by the carrier to the confirming bank, which pays the seller. The confirming bank then forwards the bill of lading to the issuing bank in exchange for reimbursement. The issuing bank provides the bill of lading to the buyer after it is paid, and the buyer uses the bill of lading to obtain the goods from the carrier. Use of a letter of credit in the transaction thus reduces the uncertainties involved. The buyer need not pay the seller for goods prior to shipment, and the seller can obtain payment for the goods immediately upon shipment.

Relatively few risks are involved in direct sales abroad. The exports may be subject to tariffs or other fees, but there is no foreign presence by the domestic firm, so the transaction does not usually subject the seller to foreign taxation. Note that both United States laws and the laws of other countries may prohibit the sale (export) of certain types of goods. For example, the **Export Administration Act** authorizes the President to prohibit the export of certain goods or technology. In 1980, the export of computer parts and technology to the Soviet Union was prohibited. The **Trading with the Enemy Act** prohibits exports to certain specified countries.

4 USE OF FOREIGN AGENTS

Domestic sellers of goods may be better able to locate potential buyers in other countries by using representatives or **agents** within those countries. Designation of agents with contractual authority is considered by most countries to constitute "doing business" within the country, thus subjecting a selling firm to taxation, fees for doing business, and potential lawsuits in foreign courts. Further, principles of agency law in many foreign countries are significantly different from principles of agency law in the United States. In some some countries, an agency's relationships may be irrevocable, regardless of the principal's dissatisfaction with performance rendered by an agent. In other countries, especially Middle Eastern ones, a company's appointment of a local agent may be possible only if it uses an approved "model contract of agency," which includes provisions giving exclusive distribution rights to the agent. It is extremely important for local companies to retain counsel when dealing with unfamiliar legal systems.

5 LICENSING OF TECHNOLOGY

In appropriate circumstances, a domestic firm may choose to grant a foreign firm the rights to produce and sell a product. **Licensing** concerns the transfer of intangible property rights, such as patents, trademarks, or manufacturing processes, in exchange for the payment of royalties, which are usually based upon the quantity of goods manufactured or sold. Licensing is often used as a transitional technique for firms expanding international operations, since the risks are greater than with exporting but considerably less than with direct investment abroad. A variation of licensing which is becoming an increasingly favored technique for firms entering foreign markets is franchising of trademarks, trade names, or copyrights. The McDonald's restaurants located in Paris are illustrative of this practice.

The international licensing of intangible intellectual property rights presents the need for international protection of these rights. Under national law, owners are provided with exclusive rights to patents, copyrights, trademarks, and trade names after they are registered in the United States. Foreign violations cannot be prohibited unless these rights are also registered in other countries, many of which have differing attitudes toward providing protection. International counterfeiting and piracy of intellectual property have become, during the last decade or so, a monumental problem. Cartier watches, Apple computers, designer jeans, books, movies, videotapes, computer software, and many other products are being produced and sold in violation of the patent, trademark, or copyright owner's rights. Three major **conventions** (agreements) exist that provide some copyright protection on an international scale, but major gaps in protection still exist. The United States is actively seeking diplomatic and political resolution of these serious deficiencies.

6 FOREIGN SUBSIDIARIES

As their level of involvement in foreign activities increases, domestic firms may find that creation of foreign subsidiaries is necessary. Most countries will permit a foreign firm to conduct business only if a national (individual or firm) of the host country is designated as its legal representative. This designation may create difficulties in control and result in unnecessary expense, so the usual practice for multinational corporations is to create a foreign subsidiary in the host country. Most countries have legal provisions for the creation of an entity closely resembling a United States corporation, although the names and formalities necessary to form such a legal entity vary. Other forms of subsidiaries may also exist; they have characteristics of limited liability of the owners and fewer formalities in their creation and operation. Local legal counsel or an attorney familiar with the law of the host country must be consulted.

Creation of a foreign subsidiary may pose considerable risk to the domestic parent firm. The 1983 incident in Bhopal, India, whereby three thousand people were killed and thousands more injured as a result of toxic gas leaks from a chemical plant, resulted in lawsuits against both the Indian subsidiary corporation and the parent firm in the United States, Union Carbide. The questions of liability in this tragedy are still unresolved as of late 1987.

As with all forms of international activities, the establishment of contractual provisions between the parties in a licensing arrangement is critically important. Some aspects of all agreements between parties from different countries that merit consideration include:

1 *Language:* Language and translation problems are especially important in the international legal environment. In addition to the usual difficulties associated with all translation, the translation of legal terms often creates additional uncertainty because many terms do not have precise counterparts in other languages. Many legal terms also convey concepts or principles much broader than the words themselves. The language used in contracts and other legal instruments, as well as the interpretation given to the words in all relevant languages, should be agreed upon before the documents are finalized.

2 *Choice of law:* Disputes are inevitable. The parties in an international transaction may be able to reduce time, expense, and delay in resolving disputes by providing a clause in the contract which designates the law that will be used to determine their rights and obligations. Such a provision is known as a **choice-of-law clause.** Commonly, the law of New York is used, but the law, say, of Sri Lanka, Nebraska, or France may be as appropriate. The important thing is that the parties agree in advance which law will be controlling.

3 *Arbitration:* Increasingly, parties in international transactions recognize the advantages that arbitration of disputes has over litigation. The International Chamber of Commerce and other organizations have well-developed rules for arbitration of international disputes. A contractual provision calling for arbitration under these (or other) rules should be considered.

7 JOINT VENTURES

In many instances, the only legally or politically feasible means a firm has to directly invest in a foreign country is to engage in a joint venture with a "partner" from the host country. A host country's participant may be a private enterprise or, especially in developing countries, a government agency or government-owned corporation. In many countries, for example, mineral resources are considered to be owned by the state; thus, extraction or production of these resources depends upon participation of a state agency.

Among industrialized countries, Japan most notably restricts foreign investment in joint ventures. Indeed, in many industries in Japan the foreign partner may participate only as minority owner. In developing countries such as India and most countries of South America, joint venture participation is also increasingly required.

8 RISKS OF DIRECT INVESTMENT

If a domestic firm is involved in a foreign country to the extent of locating assets there (whether through branches, subsidiaries, joint ventures, or otherwise), it may be subject to the ultimate legal and political risk of international business activity—expropriation. **Expropriation,** as used in the context of international law, is the seizure of foreign-owned property by a government. When the owners are not fairly compensated, the expropriation is also considered to be a **confiscation** of property. Usually, the expropriating government also assumes ownership of the property, so the process includes **nationalization** as well. In the United States, the counterpart of expropriation is called the power of **eminent domain.** This power of all governments to take private property is regarded as inherent, yet it is subject to restraints upon its exercise. The United States Constitution (as well as the constitutions of most states) prohibits the government from seizing private property except for "public purposes" and upon the payment of "just compensation." These constitutional safeguards are limited, however, to the taking of property by the states or the federal government. Questions arise, then, as to the legal recourse against a foreign government that has taken over ownership of property within its jurisdiction.

Of course, constitutional or statutory safeguards against expropriation may exist in other countries as well as in the United States. However, the extent of such protection varies widely. Treaties (or other agreements) between the United States and other countries may provide some additional protection against uncompensated takings of property. It is customary for international law to recognize the right of governments to expropriate the property of foreigners only when accompanied by prompt, adequate, and effective compensation. This standard is followed by most industrialized countries; however, developing countries and socialist countries have increasingly rejected this standard in favor of a *national* standard whereby absolute supremacy is asserted with regard to nationalizations in general and compensation in particular.

Nationalization of United States firms accompanied by unsatisfactory offers of compensation have led companies to file lawsuits in United States courts that seek more satisfactory compensation. Two distinct but related doctrines pose serious obstacles for recovery in these situations: the act-of-state doctrine and the sovereign immunities doctrine.

Act-of-State Doctrine

The classic statement of the **act-of-state doctrine** provides that, "the courts of one country will not sit in judgment on...the acts of the government of another." Thus, if one accepts this doctrine on an absolute basis, claims that an expropriation by one country violates United States or international law simply cannot be adjudicated in United States courts.

Several exceptions to the doctrine have been recognized. The Restatement (2d) of Foreign Relations law of the United States implies that the doctrine applies only when the foreign state has acted "to give effect to its public interest." This interpretation recognizes that governments may act not only in a governmental capacity, but in a private or commercial capacity as well. When a government acts in its commercial (as opposed to governmental) capacity, its actions will be subject to the same rules of law as are applicable to private individuals. Of course, a nationalization of assets will almost certainly be considered an act in the "public interest."

Congress expressed its interpretation of the doctrine in an amendment to the **Foreign Assistance Act of 1964.** This act directs that the act-of-state doctrine shall *not* be applied by the courts in cases when property is confiscated in violation of international law unless the President advises that application of the doctrine is required. Federal courts, however, have narrowly construed this provision and applied it only in cases when the property has somehow found its way back into the United States. This amendment was enacted in response to the following case, which also illustrates that the doctrine is not found directly in the Constitution but is based on the separation of powers concept.

BANCO NACIONÁL DE CUBA v. SABBATINO
84 S.Ct. 923 (1964)

FACTS

Shortly after Castro came to power in Cuba, the United States reduced the import quota for Cuban sugar into this country. In retaliation, Cuba nationalized many companies in which Americans held interests, including Compañía Azucarera Vertientes-Camaguey (CAV), which had contracted to sell a shipload of sugar to a buyer in the United States. After the nationalization, the United States buyer paid CAV for the sugar instead of Cuba, and Banco Nacionál sued in New York to obtain the proceeds. The United States buyer defended on the basis that title to the sugar did not pass to Cuba because the expropriation violated international law. The district court granted and the Court of Appeals for the Second Circuit upheld summary judgment against Banco Nacionál.

ISSUE

Should the act-of-state doctrine apply to Cuba's nationalization of these companies?

DECISION

Yes.

REASONS

1. The act-of-state doctrine is not compelled by international law or the Constitution; instead it reflects the "proper distribution of functions between the judicial and political branches of the Government on matters bearing upon foreign affairs."
2. The conduct of foreign relations may be hindered if the judicial branch passes on the validity of acts of foreign governments.

Soverign Immunity Doctrine

The judicially developed doctrine of **sovereign immunity** provides that a foreign sovereign is immune from suit in the United States. Until approximately 1952, this notion was absolute. From 1952 until 1976, United States courts adhered to a "restrictive theory" under which immunity existed with regard to sovereign or public acts but not with regard to private or commercial acts. In 1976, Congress enacted the **Foreign Sovereign Immunities Act,** which codifies this restrictive theory and rejects immunity for commercial acts either carried on in the United States or having direct effects in this country. The case which follows illustrates the application of a foreign sovereign's immunity from suit in this country.

CAREY v. NATIONAL OIL CORPORATION
453 F.Supp. 1097 (USDC, SDNY 1978)

FACTS

Plaintiffs brought suit against both the Libyan Arab Republic and National Oil Corporation (NOC), the latter a corporation wholly owned by the Libyan government, to recover $1.6 billion in damages for alleged breach of contract to supply them with oil. NOC had entered into contracts to sell oil to plaintiffs, but in 1973 oil-producing nations of the Middle East, including Libya, imposed an embargo on petroleum exports to the United States. NOC was ordered by the government of Libya not to fulfill its contractual obligations.

ISSUE

Does the doctrine of sovereign immunity apply?

DECISION

Yes.

> **REASONS**
>
> Jurisdictional immunity to suit applies to foreign states in all cases except for those set out in the Foreign Sovereign Immunities Act. The only exception which might even arguably apply is the one for commercial activities. Here, however, the order not to fulfill the contract was a matter of foreign policy, and not a commercial undertaking.

It is often difficult to distinguish between governmental and commercial acts and to determine whether such acts have direct effects in this country. With regard to nationalization, however, one court has stated flatly: "nationalization is the quintessentially sovereign act, never viewed as having a commercial character."

These two doctrines of judicial restraint present serious obstacles to recovery by a domestic owner of nationalized property. Before concluding that the risks are too great for direct investment abroad, however, refer to the section discussing the **Overseas Private Investment Corporation (OPIC).**

LEGAL INSTITUTIONS AND AGREEMENTS

9 THE UNITED NATIONS (UN)

The **United Nations** (UN) is the paramount international political organization in terms of representation and scope of activities.

The **International Court of Justice** (ICJ), or World Court, is the judicial branch of the UN. It sits at The Hague in the Netherlands and consists of fifteen judges who represent all of the world's major legal systems. The judges are elected by the UN's General Assembly and the Security Council after having been nominated by national groups, not governments. No more than one judge may be a national of any country. Since it began functioning in 1946, the ICJ has rendered, on average, only one contested decision per year and one advisory opinion every two years. Obviously, there has been widespread reluctance to resort to the ICJ as a forum for resolving international disputes. An often misunderstood aspect of the ICJ's jurisdiction to hear and decide disputes is the provision that only *countries* have access to the court. Private persons or corporations may not directly present claims before the court. Further, only countries that have submitted to the jurisdiction of the court may be parties.

In some instances, countries have presented claims to the ICJ on behalf of their aggrieved nationals, but no device exists in United States law by which a firm or individual can compel the United States government to press a claim on its behalf before the ICJ.

The **United Nations Commission on International Trade Law**

(UNCITRAL) was created 1966 in an effort to develop standardized commercial practices and agreements. It has achieved moderate success in a limited number of areas which involve international trade, such as sale of goods, shipping, commercial arbitration, and payments. UNCITRAL has drafted a **Convention on the International Sale of Goods** (CISG), which, when widely adopted, will eliminate much of the uncertainty associated with international sales. The CISG applies to international transactions, much as Article 2 of the Uniform Commercial Code applies to domestic transactions.

The **United Nations Conference on Trade and Development** (UNCTAD) is a permanent organ of the General Assembly. It was created in 1964 to deal with international trade reform and redistribution of income through trade. It works primarily on behalf of developing countries. To date, UNCTAD has achieved little notable success.

10 EUROPEAN COMMUNITY (EC; OR COMMON MARKET)

In 1957, the **Treaty of Rome** created the **European Economic Community** (EEC), later renamed the **European Community** (EC, or Common Market.) Membership now includes Belgium, Denmark, France, West Germany, Greece, Ireland, Italy, Luxembourg, the Netherlands, Portugal, Spain, and the United Kingdom. The EC has proven to be an unrivaled international organization for promoting and achieving economic unity.

In seeking to achieve its goal of political as well as economic integration, the EC has, in its treaty, provided for the implementation of free flow of goods, persons, services, and capital among its members; the establishment of common commercial policies toward third-world countries; and the inauguration of common agricultural and transport policies. Further, the treaty calls for enactment of a system to ensure that competition shall not be distorted in the Community. This latter objective is achieved under Articles 85 and 86 of the treaty, which are roughly equivalent to Sections 1 and 2 of the Sherman Act. The EC has the equivalent of its own legislative, executive, and judiciary branches. EC law, when conflicting with national law of a member state, is supreme; the courts of member states are expected to enforce the Community's law. This is a remarkable provision. Sovereign states rarely concede sovereignty, yet the members of the EC have done so.

11 OTHER ORGANIZATIONS

The **Council for Mutual Economic Aid** (COMECON) is the Soviet-bloc counterpart to the EC. COMECON members include Bulgaria, Cuba, Czechoslovakia, East Germany, Hungary, Poland, Rumania, and the Soviet Union. The stated purpose of COMECON is to coordinate the development efforts of, and further economic cooperation among, its members. Dominated by the Soviet Union, COMECON has been weakened in its supranational structure by the increasing unwillingness of some member countries to accept the roles delegated to them.

A number of other regional organizations exist that have not achieved the degree of success of the EC or COMECON. They include the Latin American Free Trade Association, the Central American Common Market, the East African Economic Community, and the Economic Community of West African States. In addition, many narrowly based international organizations exist, such as the International Labour Organization, the International Monetary Fund, the International Civil Aviation Organization, and the Organization of Petroleum Exporting Countries.

12 GENERAL AGREEMENT ON TARIFFS AND TRADE (GATT)

The **General Agreement on Tariffs and Trade** (GATT) is a series of over one hundred international agreements and protocols, subscribed to by approximately ninety countries, including the United States, that attempts to prohibit discrimination in import regulations and prevent the establishment of import quotas. GATT seeks to implement these goals through the mechanism of **most-favored nation** status. Under this provision, each member of GATT is obligated to treat all other GATT members at least as well as it treats the country that receives the most favorable treatment regarding imports or exports. In other words, no country is to give special trading advantages to others. An additional provision specifies that imports will be treated no worse than domestic products with regard to internal taxation or regulation. Under special circumstances, exceptions to these principles may be allowed; they may apply to regional trading organizations such as the EC or to developing countries. Such exceptions may involve temporary restraints being imposed on imports when they are causing serious injury to a domestic industry or quotas being implemented in the event of a domestic balance-of-payments crisis.

DOMESTIC LAWS HAVING SIGNIFICANT INTERNATIONAL TRADE CONSEQUENCES

13 ANTIDUMPING LAWS

Dumping is the practice of selling foreign goods in one country at less than the comparable price in the country from which the goods are being exported. Since the practice of dumping may potentially create an unfair economic advantage (especially when a foreign market may be protected against reciprocal competition from domestic firms), Congress has limited it through several antidumping statutes. Current antidumping legislation is found in the **Trade Agreements Act of 1979.** This statute establishes a two-part test for triggering additional import duties on the goods being dumped. First, the secretary of the Treasury must determine that a class or kind of merchandise is being or is likely to be sold in the United States at **less than fair value** (LTFV). In LTFV determinations, the price for which the goods are being sold in the United States is compared with the price for which the goods are being sold in the country of origin. The second provision requires that the International Trade Commission (part of the Department of Commerce) determine that a domestic industry is being materially injured or threatened, or that establishment of domestic industry is being materially retarded. When both determinations prove affirmative, an additional duty will be imposed upon the goods in an amount by which their foreign value exceeds the domestic price. Obviously, the question of what is a "material" injury or threat is crucial to these determinations, but the statute does not define the term.

14 ANTITRUST

Perhaps no other aspect of our legal system has generated as much recent controversy and ill will abroad as the application of our antitrust law to conduct occurring beyond the borders of the United States. Such activity seems to interfere with the general international agreement that countries are free to regulate economic conduct within their borders. However, economic activities which are prohibited in the United States, such as price-fixing, may actually be encouraged in foreign countries. The United States attitude toward the extraterritorial application of domestic antitrust law is that conduct that has a direct, substantial, and forseeable effect on domestic trade or commerce, no matter where it occurs, will be subject to scrutiny. In other words, domestic firms, foreign subsidiaries of domestic firms, and foreign firms that violate domestic antitrust law in the United States or abroad may be subject to antitrust enforcement actions. In instances in which the required effect on domestic commerce is found but a foreign state also has an interest in regulating the conduct, a **jurisdictional rule of reason** may be applied. This rule involves balancing the interests of the United States along with those of the foreign state to determine whether application of our law is warranted. The elements to be considered include the relative significance of the domestic and foreign effects, the nationality or allegiance of the parties involved, the locations of the parties' principal places of business, and the extent to which enforcement by either nation can be expected to achieve compliance.

IN RE URANIUM ANTITRUST LITIGATION
617 F.2d 1248 (7th Cir. 1980)

FACTS

In 1976, Westinghouse filed a complaint, alleging antitrust violations against twenty-nine foreign and domestic uranium producers. All of the defendants were served with process; however, nine foreign defendants chose not to appear. Default judgments were entered against those defendants. On subsequent appeals,

> briefs were filed by the governments of several countries where the alleged violations occurred, as *amici curiae* (friends of the court) contended that the courts of the United States have no jurisdiction over conduct occurring outside this country.
>
> **ISSUE**
>
> 1. Does jurisdiction exist?
> 2. If so, should it be exercised?
>
> **DECISION**
>
> 1. Yes.
> 2. Yes.
>
> **REASONS**
>
> 1. In *United States v. Aluminum Company of America (Alcoa),* the "intended effects" doctrine was enunciated. Since *Alcoa,* United States courts have exercised jurisdiction over antitrust activity outside the United States so long as there is an intended effect on American commerce.
> 2. *Timberlane Lumber Company v. Bank of America* added the "jurisdictional rule of reason" that, in addition to the effect on American commerce, a further determination based on comity and fairness should be made before jurisdiction is exercised. Here, the district court did consider additional factors and did not abuse its discretion in determining to exercise jurisdiction.

The extraterritorial application of United States antitrust law can be defended by the act-of-state and sovereign immunity doctrines, discussed previously, and the **doctrine of sovereign compulsion.** This latter doctrine allows the defendant in an antitrust action to assert, in its defense, that its conduct was compelled by a foreign country.

To enable domestic exporters to compete better on an international level, the **Webb-Pomerene Act** exempts from application of the Sherman Act conduct by associations of export traders that would otherwise violate antitrust law. However, the conduct must not restrain trade within the United States or with domestic competitors of the export associations. Anticompetitive conduct such as price-fixing or dividing markets may thus be allowed.

15 FOREIGN CORRUPT PRACTICES ACT (FCPA)

In 1977, following widespread disclosure of scandalous payments by domestic firms to officials of foreign governments, Congress enacted the **Foreign Corrupt Practices Act** (FCPA). This statute has two main provisions: (1) financial records and accounts must be kept "which, in reasonable detail, accurately and fairly reflect the transactions and disposition of assets" of the firm, and (2) firms must "devise and maintain a system of internal accounting controls sufficient to provide reasonable assurances" that transactions are being carried out in accordance with management's authorization. The general language of these "accounting provisions" has resulted in some uncertainty as to the requirements for compliance. These provisions are intended to correct the previously widespread practice of accounting for bribes as commission payments, payments for services, or other normal business expenses, and illegally deducting the payments on income tax returns. Further, they state that investors or potential investors are deemed entitled to disclosure of the financial information. Cynics have referred to the accounting provisions of the FCPA as the "Accountants Full Employment Act," and some domestic criticism of the provisions has occurred, but these features of the FCPA have generated little international comment.

Much more international controversy has arisen over the so-called antibribery provisions of the FCPA. These provisions declare that it shall be unlawful for any "domestic concern" (that is, *any* business) or its officers, directors, employees, or agents to give or pay "anything of value" to "any foreign official for the purpose of influencing any act or decision of such foreign official." Payments to foreign officials who will use their influence to assist firms in obtaining business in their countries are also prohibited, as are payments to "any person" when the payer knows or has reason to know that all or part of the payments will be given to a foreign official. Firms are subject to fines of up to $1 million, and individuals may be fined up to $10,000 and imprisoned up to five years for violations. In the statute, foreign officials are defined as employees of foreign governments except for those whose duties are "essentially ministerial or clerical."

The controversy over the antibribery provisions stems from two main considerations. First, in many parts of the world, under-the-table payments to government officials are an accepted practice. Indeed, civil servants may be expected to supplement their salaries in this manner. The United States prohibition of such payments is perceived as an attempt to impose American standards of morality in other parts of the world, and it has caused resentment or discrimination against our businesses. A second objection to the FCPA comes from domestic firms that contend that the prohibition of bribes, especially in countries where they are expected, puts United States firms at a competitive disadvantage. Competitors from other countries are not likely to be operating under similar restrictions. The following case is one of the very few appellate decisions which discusses the FCPA. Note the overlap with the act-of-state doctrine.

CLAYCO PETROLEUM CORP. v. OCCIDENTAL PETROLEUM CORP.
712 F.2d 404 (9th Cir. 1983)

FACTS

Defendant allegedly made secret payments to the Oil Minister of Umm al Qaiwain, a sheikdom which is part of the United Arab Emirates, to secure offshore oil concessions. Plaintiff sued for damages, claiming a violation of antitrust law. Defendant asserted the act-of-state doctrine as a defense and moved to dismiss. The district court granted defendant's motion. Plaintiff appealed, contending that the FCPA created a new exception to the act-of-state doctrine.

ISSUE

Does the FCPA abrogate the act-of-state doctrine in private suits based on foreign payments?

DECISION

No.

REASONS

In private suits, as opposed to governmental enforcement actions under the FCPA, the act-of-state doctrine remains necessary to protect the proper conduct of national foreign policy. In this case, a different action against Occidental, brought by the government, resulted in Occidental's consent to a permanent injunction prohibiting further payment in violation of the FCPA.

16 OVERSEAS PRIVATE INVESTMENT CORPORATION (OPIC)

The **Overseas Private Investment Corporation** (OPIC) is a hybrid, public and private agency that began functioning in 1971. All of the stock of OPIC is owned by the United States, and eight of the fifteen members of the board of directors are appointed by the President. The other directors are government officials. The general charge given to OPIC is to encourage and support qualified, private investments in developing countries that maintain friendly relations with the United States. Preferential consideration is given to investment projects in countries having per capita income below a specified amount, currently $680 (measured in 1979 dollars). Although OPIC offers several investment incentives, the program having the most significance for domestic firms is the Investment Insurance Program. This program provides domestic investors with coverage for the political risks of expropriation and confiscation, war, revolution, insurrection, civil strife, and inconvertibility of currency. Criteria for eligibility include:

1 The investor must be a United States citizen or a firm owned by a substantial number (at least 51 percent) of United States citizens.
2 The investment must be in a developing country that has entered into an investment guaranty agreement with the United States. (More than 115 countries have such agreements with the United States.)
3 The foreign host government must approve the project.
4 The project must obtain OPIC approval for serving the host country's economic and social needs.

OPIC has broad discretion to approve projects; preferential consideration is given to small businesses.

The bilateral investment guaranty agreements referred to previously provide that, in the event payment is made by the United States under the insurance contract, the foreign government will recognize the subrogation to the United States government of any claim that the investor might have against the foreign government. Upon receipt of payment under the insurance contract, the investor must transfer any claim against the foreign government to the United States federal government. Before making payment under any claim, OPIC requires that the investor exhaust all local remedies in the country where the claim arose.

17 OTHER PROBLEM AREAS

When resolving interstate domestic disputes, courts are often confronted with the problem of which state's law to apply to a case. Recall that this issue, the conflict-of-laws principle, was discussed in Chapter 2. On an international scale, the "conflicts" problem may be even more complex, because the transaction crosses national borders. For example, suppose a Minnesota seller contracts to sell goods to a French buyer. In the event of a lawsuit claiming breach of contract, should the court apply Minnesota law or French law? As explained in the earlier conflict-of-laws discussion, a court in the United States would probably base its determination of which law governed this transaction upon either the place where the contract was made, the place of performance, or the place with the most substantial contact with the contract. Further, suppose that the court concludes that the law of France should govern. A court in Minnesota probably could locate French legal materials so as to be able to determine how the case should be decided under French law. If, however, the buyer is from Cameroon, Yugoslavia, or Iceland, it is questionable whether the substantive law of these places could be obtained. Many of these problems can be avoided by inclusion of a choice-of-laws clause in the agreement between the parties. This clause contractually specifies which country's law to apply if litigation arises.

A related problem in international law is the enforceability of a judgment obtained in one country by the courts of another country. In the previous example, assume that the French buyer filed suit in France against the Minnesota seller and obtained a judgment ordering the seller to pay damages. To what extent would courts in the United States enforce the foreign judgment? Judgments obtained in one state are enforceable in the other states under the full faith and credit clause of the United States Constitution; however, the clause does not apply to judgments from other countries. In general, such foreign judgments may be enforceable if obtained under fair proceedings (that is, if the defendants were afforded essentially the same rights that would have been available in a proceeding in the United

States) and if enforcement of the judgment does not offend the public policy of the United States. The likelihood of successfully enforcing a foreign judgment will be enhanced if reciprocity, or comity, exists; that is, a foreign country that renders a judgment must be able and willing to enforce a similar judgment coming from a United States court.

18 ARBITRATION

The advantages of arbitration in domestic transactions are discussed in Chapter 4. These advantages may be more pronounced in international transactions because of the differences among legal systems and the additional expenses and delays involved in international litigation. Arbitration is increasingly used as a method of resolving international business disputes. Several organizations, including the International Chamber of Commerce, the American Arbitration Association, and UNCITRAL have developed sets of rules for international commercial arbitration. In addition, an ad hoc arbitration process is available under which the proceedings are conducted in a manner prescribed by the parties.

The case which follows illustrates some of the complexities of international commercial arbitration.

MITSUBISHI MOTORS v. SOLER CHRYSLER-PLYMOUTH
105 S.Ct. 3346 (1985)

FACTS

The parties entered into a contract for the distribution of automobiles. The contract contained a clause providing for arbitration of disputes arising from the contract. After a dispute arose, Mitsubishi filed suit, seeking an order to compel arbitration. Soler asserted a counterclaim under United States antitrust law; it contended that its counterclaim was not subject to arbitration.

ISSUE

Is the antitrust claim arbitrable?

DECISION

Yes.

REASONS

The previously followed doctrine asserted that rights conferred by antitrust law are inappropriate for enforcement by arbitration. However, concerns of international comity, respect for the capacities of foreign and transnational tribunals, and sensitivity to the need of the international commercial system for predictability in the enforcement of disputes require that the agreement to arbitrate be enforced.

19 CONCLUSION

International business transactions have become such a pervasive component of the global economy that no businessperson can afford to be uninformed as to the international legal environment. Enhanced communications and transportation will undoubtedly result in an increased level of international economic linkages. The laws applicable to international transactions will continue to evolve and adapt to the "shrinking" earth. This evolution and adaptation will likely result in continued efforts at cooperation through greater participation in international conventions, standardization of legal norms, and familiarity with the laws of other countries.

This chapter has provided a broad overview of selected topics of importance to the conduct of international business. Many other topics might also have been included, such as international income tax law, countertrade, the law pertaining to ocean beds and their underlying minerals, international financial institutions, and the selection of legal counsel in other countries. As with all legal topics, the initial exposure to the study must be thought of as an introduction and the beginning of a process rather than a completed task. All law evolves. International law is no exception.

REVIEW QUESTIONS

1 For each term in the left-hand column, match the most appropriate description in the right-hand column:

(1) Most-favored nation
(2) Confiscation
(3) Nationalization
(4) Dumping
(5) Sovereign compulsion
(6) Licensing
(7) Choice-of-law clause
(8) Expropriation

(a) A clause in a contract that designates the law that will be used to determine rights and obligations.
(b) A defense in antitrust actions when conduct is compelled by a foreign country.
(c) The practice of selling goods in one country at less than the comparable price in the country from which they are exported.
(d) Assumption of ownership of expropriated property by a foreign government.
(e) The seizure of foreign-owned property by a government.
(f) Failure to compensate fairly the owners of expropriated property.
(g) The transfer of intangible property rights in exchange for the payment of royalties.
(h) A provision requiring GATT members to treat one another at least as well as the country receiving most favorable treatment.

2 Draw a diagram (or flowchart) explaining the use of an irrevocable letter of credit. Use arrows to and from each party and indicate what document(s) each party gives and receives.

3 Explain the act-of-state doctrine.
4 Explain the doctrine of sovereign immunity.
5 You are the sole owner of a sewing-machine factory located in the country of Utobania. The government of Utobania nationalizes the factory and all equipment, using as its reason the assertion that you have exploited its citizens by paying them less than they deserved. The government refuses to pay you any compensation because, it claims, you have not reinvested enough of your profits in Utobania. Can you sue Utobania in the International Court of Justice? Why, or why not? Explain.
6 What are the main provisions of the Foreign Corrupt Practices Act? Explain each.
7 What is the Overseas Private Investment Corporation? What does it do? Explain.
8 Describe several ways in which a firm in the United States might conduct business abroad.
9 What is the European Community? What does it do? Explain.
10 Two Swedish sandal manufacturers enter into an agreement in Sweden that one will sell its products in the United States only east of the Mississippi River and the other will sell only west of the river. Does this agreement violate United States antitrust law? If so, would the Swedish firms be subject to punishment by the United States government? Explain.
11 When do the antidumping provision of United States law apply? Explain.
12 When will foreign judgments be enforced by courts of the United States? Explain.
13 What is the United Nations Commission on International Trade Law? What does it do? Explain.
14 What is the United Nations Conference on Trade and Development? What does it do? Explain.
15 How can international conflict-of-laws problems be minimized? Explain.

PART FIVE

PROTECTING EMPLOYEES

14
Worker Protection

15
Discrimination in Employment

16
Right to Union Activity

17
Unfair Labor Practices

CHAPTER **14**

WORKER PROTECTION

OVERVIEW

Worker-protection laws developed only in this century. Prior to 1900, workers had very little or no protection from dangerous job conditions, low pay, and the risk of firing. Today, however, many statutes protect the worker. They are part of a trend which will likely continue and grow.

This chapter addresses two primary issues of worker protection: job safety (including the handling of work-related injuries) and financial security. The Occupational Safety and Health Administration is the federal agency most responsible for job safety. When accidental employee injuries do occur in the course of employment, state workers' compensation laws impose strict liability on employers for death or disability benefits, medical expenses, and wage losses.

The Fair Labor Standards Act protects children in the workplace by limiting the types of employment children can have at various ages. This act also sets minimum-wage and overtime requirements on employers and is the first major federal act aimed at increasing workers' financial security.

Passed in the 1930s, the unemployment compensation law is one part of the Social Security Act. The other part is the employer-employee funding of retirement, disability, and health insurance programs. Together, they mark a major step in worker protection.

Private pension plans have helped advance the financial retirement security of millions of workers. This chapter covers the Employee Retirement

Income Security Act, which is the major federal law regulating private pension plans.

Concluding the chapter is a discussion of trends limiting employment-at-will, the right of employers to discharge most employees without regard to job security. These trends shed light on the larger picture of worker protection.

Important terms of this chapter include course of employment, defined benefit plan, defined contribution plan, discharge for proper cause, employment-at-will, exclusive remedy rule, fellow-servant rule, individual retirement account, minimum wage, qualified pension plan, and vested rights.

1 THE OCCUPATIONAL SAFETY AND HEALTH ACT

In General

Congress adopted the *Occupational Safety and Health Act* (OSHA) in 1970 to ensure safe and healthful working conditions for practically every employee in the United States. Special health and safety laws in such industries as construction, maritime, and coal mining had been previously adopted, but such far-reaching legislation as OSHA, with an impact of such magnitude on business, had never been considered at the national level.

OSHA requires that employers furnish to each employee a place of employment that is free from recognized hazards that are causing or are likely to cause death or serious physical harm. It also requires that the employer comply with occupational safety and health standards established under the act by the secretary of labor. This is done through an agency called The Occupational Safety and Health Administration (also known as OSHA). To accomplish its mission, OSHA investigators conduct unannounced inspections. During any investigation, an employer as well as an employee has the right to accompany the inspectors or have a representative do so. Remember that the Supreme Court has ruled that employers can require OSHA inspectors to produce a search warrant before they begin an inspection. Employers also, as required by regulations, must keep and preserve records relating to accidents and injuries.

OSHA regulates employees as well as employers. It requires that each employee comply with occupational safety and health standards and all rules, regulations, and orders issued under it which are applicable to his or her own actions and conduct.

The secretary of labor issues standards for healthful and safe employment. The Occupational Safety and Health Review Commission reviews citations of violations and proposed penalties. Orders of this commission are, of course, reviewable by a federal court of appeals, as in the case of other federal administrative agencies.

Enforcement

The most significant aspect of OSHA is its approach to enforcement by unannounced inspections. Inspections of businesses may be made either on the initiative of the department itself or upon the request of an employee or employees' representative. Inspections must be made during regular working hours and at other reasonable times within reasonable limits and in a reasonable manner. No advance notice of inspections can be given. Employees' representatives have the right to participate in walk-around inspections, and such representatives get compensation from the employer for the time involved. If an inspection reveals a violation, the employer receives a citation. If the violation presents a threat of serious or immediate harm, the secretary of labor can go into a federal district court and get a temporary injunction to restrain the danger. Having received a citation, the employer is next informed of the penalty. If the employer decides to contest the citation or penalty, it may appeal through the review commission and then into the federal court system.

In certain cases, OSHA regulations permit employees a right of "self-help." Because the act itself does not mention a self-help remedy, the following case challenged the remedy's legality.

WHIRLPOOL CORP. v. MARSHALL
100 S.Ct. 883 (1980)

FACTS

The secretary of labor passed a regulation under the Occupational Safety and Health Act. It provided that an employee could refuse to perform work that she or he reasonably feared would cause death or serious injury if she or he reasonably believed no less drastic alternative was available.

A Whirlpool Corporation employee refused to walk on a screen mat that was suspended twenty feet above the assembly line. Other employees had fallen partly or completely through the screen; on one occasion such a fall resulted in death. Because the employee refused to do the work commanded, he was sent home without pay. He sued.

ISSUE

Is the OSHA regulation that protects such a refusal to work valid?

DECISION

Yes.

REASONS

1. The objective of the act is to prevent deaths and serious injuries.
2. Although the statute generally does not allow an employee to walk off the job to protest OSHA violations, in circumstances such as these, less drastic measures would not sufficiently protect the employee.

Trends

In the 1970s, OSHA came under much criticism from industry groups. Its safety regulations were long and difficult to understand and apply. Many people considered OSHA inspectors to be biased against business and too quick to issue citations. The number of workers injured annually failed to go down and in some instances actually rose.

OSHA has tried a different approach in the 1980s. Its focus has changed somewhat from safety to health. Instead of an inflexible concern over the number of knotholes in ladders and the height of fire extinguishers from the floor, OSHA has devoted attention to workers' exposure to chemical and other health hazards. It has issued regulations limiting exposure to lead, asbestos, cotton dust, noise, and other potential causes of disability and disease. In 1986, OSHA put into effect a hazardous substance right-to-know standard. The rule requires chemical manufacturers, distributors, and importers to assess the hazards of their chemicals and pass along that information to their buyers. Employers receiving such notice must label the chemicals with appropriate warnings and train employees in their use.

A second change in OSHA has been a careful targeting of its resources. It presently concentrates inspections on industries which offer the greatest threat to worker health and safety (see Table 14-1). It has virtually eliminated inspections of certain employers, including insurance companies, retail stores, and other white-collar and service businesses, where the potential for danger to employees is low. To increase operating efficiency, OSHA has begun a program which allows approved labor-management committees to conduct workplace inspections and keep records. These committees free agency inspectors for other duties.

A final change in OSHA has been the effort to be seen as a helper of business, rather than its enemy. OSHA inspectors have been ordered to offer

TABLE 14-1 MOST AND LEAST DANGEROUS INDUSTRIES ACCORDING TO DAYS LOST TO OCCUPATIONAL INJURY OR ILLNESS*

Most dangerous		Least dangerous	
1	Truck transportation	1	Communications
2	Railroad equipment	2	Chemical products
3	Meat packing	3	Aircraft
4	Lumber and wood products	4	Electrical equipment
5	Newspapers	5	Petroleum refining
6	Rail transportation	6	Textile products
7	Water transportation	7	Apparel making
8	Paper products	8	Pipeline transportation
9	Government	9	Motor-vehicle products
10	Air transportation	10	Natural gas production

*Data from National Safety Council.

more help in correcting workplace hazards. The agency has also begun programs which exempt certain employers from regular OSHA inspections when they maintain exceptional safety records.

There are critics of the changes in OSHA. Union leaders have criticized OSHA as attempting to accommodate businesses instead of protecting workers. They point to a decline in the number of OSHA inspections initiated by workers' complaints. They view the significant reduction in the number of employers who contest OSHA complaints as evidence that OSHA is not pursuing cases concerning serious safety violations. Partly as a result of these criticisms, OSHA recently has begun to prosecute more vigorously those businesses that underreport workplace accidents in required reports to OSHA. Several major corporations have received large fines.

2 WORKERS' COMPENSATION ACTS

Introduction

Around the turn of the century, the tort system was largely replaced in the workplace by a series of workers' compensation acts. These statutes were enacted at both the state and federal level, and they imposed a type of strict liability on employers for accidental workplace injuries suffered by their employees. The clear purpose of these statutes was to remove financial losses of injury from workers and redistribute them onto employers and ultimately onto society. The following two sections examine present workers' compensation acts.

History

Workers' compensation laws are state statutes designed to protect employees and their families from the risks of accidental injury, death, or disease resulting from their employment. They were passed because the common law did not give adequate protection to employees from the hazards of their work. At common law, anyone was liable in tort for damages resulting from injuries caused to another as a proximate result of negligence. If an employer acted unreasonably and his or her carelessness was the proximate cause of physical injury suffered by an employee, the latter could sue and recover damages from the employer. However, the common law also provided the employer with the means of escaping this tort liability in most cases. It provided three defenses: (1) **assumption of the risk,** (2) **contributory negligence,** and (3) the **fellow-servant rule.**

For example, assume that employer E knowingly instructed workers to operate dangerous machinery not equipped with any safety devices, even though it realized injury to them was likely. W, a worker, had his arm mangled when it was caught in the gears of one of these machines. Even though E was negligent in permitting this hazardous condition to persist, if W were aware of the dangers which existed, he would be unable to recover damages because he knowingly *assumed the risk* of his injury. In addition, if the injury were caused by contributory negligence of the employee as well as the negligence of the employer, the action was defeated. And if the injury occurred because of the negligence of another employee, the negligent employee, rather than the employer, was liable because of the fellow-servant rule.

The English Parliament passed a workers' compensation statute in 1897. Today all states have such legislation, modeled to a greater or lesser degree on the English act. These laws vary a great deal from state to state as to the industries subject to them, the employees they cover, the nature of the injuries or diseases which are compensable, the rates of compensation, and the means of administration. In spite of wide variances in the laws of the states in this area, certain general observations can be made about them.

The Workers' Compensation System

State workers' compensation statutes provide a system to pay workers or their families if the worker is accidentally killed or injured or incurs an occupational disease while employed. To be compensable, the death, illness, or injury must arise out of and in the course of the employment. Under these acts, the negligence or fault of the employer in causing an on-the-job injury is not an issue. Instead, these laws recognize the fact of life that a certain number of injuries, deaths, and diseases are bound to occur in a modern industrial society as a result of the attempts of businesses and their employees to provide the goods and services demanded by the consuming public.

This view leads to the conclusion that it is fairer for the consuming public to bear the cost of such mishaps rather than to impose it on injured workers. Workers' compensation laws create strict liability for employers of accidentally injured workers. Liability exists regardless of lack of negligence or fault, provided the necessary association between the injuries and the business of the employer is present. The three defenses the employer had at common law are eliminated. The employers, treating the costs of these injuries as part of the costs of production, pass them on to the consumers who created the demand for the product or service being furnished.

Workers' compensation acts give covered employees the right to certain cash payments for their loss of income due to accidental on-the-job injuries. In the event of a married employee's death, benefits are provided for the surviving spouse and minor children. The amount of such awards usually is subject to a stated maximum and is calculated by using a percentage of the wages of the employee. If the employee suffers permanent partial disability, most states provide compensation both for injuries which are scheduled in the statute and those which are nonscheduled. As an example of the former, a worker who loses a hand might be awarded 100 weeks of compensation at $95 per week. Besides scheduling specific compensation for certain specific injuries, most acts also provide compensation for nonscheduled ones based upon the earning power the employee lost due to his or her injury. In addition to the above payments, all statutes provide for medical benefits.

As the result of inflation, many states have increased the amounts payable as workers' compensation benefits. However, the amounts paid in most states are substantially inadequate to provide a decent standard of living for injured workers. For example, even some of the more generous of these provide only about $100 per week for periods of temporary total disability and around $25,000 for death benefits.

In some states, employers have a choice of covering their workers' compensation risk with insurance or of being self-insured (that is, paying all claims directly) if they can demonstrate their capability to do so. Approximately 20 percent of compensation benefits are paid by self-insurers. In other states, employers pay into a state fund used to compensate workers entitled to benefits. In these states, the amounts of the payments are based on the size of the payroll and the experience of the employer in having claims filed against the system by its employees.

Workers' compensation laws are usually administered exclusively by an administrative agency called the industrial commission or board, which has quasi-judicial powers. Of course, the ruling of such boards is subject to review by the courts of the jurisdiction in the same manner as the actions of other administrative agencies.

Tests for Determining Workers' Compensation

The tests for determining whether an employer must pay workers' compensation to an employee are simply: (1) *"Was the injury accidental?"* and (2) *"Did the injury arise out of and in the course of employment?"* Because workers' compensation laws benefit workers, courts interpret them liberally to favor workers.

In recent years, cases have tended to expand employers' liability. For instance, courts have held that heart attacks (as well as other common ailments in which the employee has had either a preexisting disease or a physical condition likely to lead to the disease) are compensable as "accidental injuries." One ruling approved an award to a purchasing agent who became mentally ill because she was exposed to unusual work, stresses, and strains. Her "nerve-racking" job involved a business whose sales grew over sixfold in ten years. Factors contributing to her "accidental injury" included harsh criticism by her supervisor, long hours of work, and inability to take vacations due to the requirements of her position.

Likewise, the courts have been liberal in upholding awards which have been challenged on the ground that the injury did not arise "out of and in the course of employment." Courts routinely support compensation awards for almost any accidental injury which employees suffer while traveling for their employers. A recent Minnesota Supreme Court decision upheld a lower court award of compensation to a bus driver. On a layover during a trip, the driver had been shot accidentally in a tavern parking lot following a night on the town.

However, as the following case shows, not every workplace injury arises out of employment.

UNITED PARCEL SERVICE v. FETTERMAN
336 S.E.2d 892 (Va. 1985)

FACTS

Randall Fetterman, a driver for United Parcel Service, was unloading a truck when he noticed his shoelace was untied. Bending over to tie his shoe, he felt acute pain in his lower back. The injury kept him from work, and he applied for workers' compensation.

ISSUE

Did Fetterman's injury arise out of employment?

DECISION

No.

REASONS

1. An injury arises out of employment when there is a connection between the employee's injury and the conditions under which the employer requires the work to be performed. Excluded from compensation is an injury that comes from a hazard to which the employee would have been equally exposed apart from the employment.
2. The act of bending over to tie the shoe was unrelated to any hazard of the workplace. Every person who wears laced shoes must occasionally retie them. Since nothing particular to the work environment caused the injury, compensation is denied.

The outcome of this case is not obvious. Before the employer appealed to the Virginia Supreme Court, the workers' compensation board had granted the employee compensation. Suppose the employee had argued that his carrying an especially large package had caused him to stumble over his shoelaces. Then, does the untied lace arise out of employment? In another state, an employee received compensation for a back injury related to his decision to kill a roach on his employer's ceiling.

Exclusive Remedy Rule

Recently, some courts have been liberal in their interpretations of the **exclusive remedy rule.** This rule, which is written into all compensation statutes, states that an employee's sole remedy against an employer for workplace injury or illness shall be workers' compensation. In the past few years, courts in several important jurisdictions have created exceptions to this rule (see Table 14-2). Note that these exceptions recognize in part that workers' compensation laws do not adequately compensate badly injured workers.

Since workers' compensation laws apply only to accidentally injured workers, the exclusive remedy rule does not protect employers who intentionally injure workers. But the issue arises as to how "intentional" such an injury has to be. What if an employer knowingly exposes employees to a chemical which may cause illness in some employees over a long term?

Exclusions from Workers' Compensation Coverage

Even though all states have some form of workers' compensation, the statutes exclude certain types of employment from their coverage. Generally, domestic and agricultural employees are not covered. In addition, the law may not provide compensation for specified kinds of accidents or diseases. In about one-half the states, the statutes are compulsory. In the other half, employers may elect to be subject to the act or to lawsuits by employees or their survivors for damages. If the latter course is chosen, an employee seeking compensation for injuries must prove they resulted proximately from the negligence of the employer, as at common law, however, the case is *not* subject to the common-law defenses. In negligence, there is no statutory limit to the amount of damages recoverable.

The Future of State Workers' Compensation

Currently, many problems confront the state workers' compensation system. Fifty separate nonuniform acts make up the system. Many acts ex-

TABLE 14-2 EXCEPTIONS TO THE EXCLUSIVE REMEDY RULE*

1. Employee sues manufacturer of a product which causes work-related injury.
2. Employee sues fellow employee who causes work-related injury.
3. Employee sues insurer who breaches a duty to warn employer of dangerous work conditions.
4. Employee sues employer who intentionally inflicts injury, including mental distress, or who intentionally conceals a dangerous work condition.
5. Employee sues employer who is in a "dual capacity" with employee. Example: Employer manufactured product which injured employee in the workplace.
6. Employee sues employer who fraudulently conceals an employee's medical condition caused by exposure to workplace conditions.

*Not all exceptions exist in all states.

clude from coverage groups such as farm workers, government employees, and employees of small businesses. Many state legislatures have enacted changes in their compensation laws. However, states which have broadened coverage and increased benefits have greatly boosted the cost of doing business within their borders. This discourages new businesses from locating within these states and encourages those already there to move out.

In the last decade, workers' compensation payments have tripled. Many workers exaggerate their injuries to get compensation. On the other hand, compensation payments to seriously injured workers are often inadequate, and this has led to attempts to get around the exclusive remedy rule.

A major problem concerns slowly developing, occupational diseases. Many toxic chemicals cause cancer and other diseases only after workers have been exposed to them over many years. Often it is difficult or impossible for workers or their survivors to recover workers' compensation for such diseases. A university-conducted study released in 1984 showed that only about one-third of the average losses caused by asbestos diseases was compensated.

One solution to the problems confronting the workers' compensation system would be federal reform. Those advocating such reform have put forth several plans, but Congress has shown little inclination so far to adopt a uniform federal act. However, as the next section reveals, there are already federal compensation acts covering certain segments of the work force.

3 FEDERAL COMPENSATION ACTS

Congress has enacted several statutes which extend liability to certain kinds of employers for injuries, diseases, and deaths arising out of the course of employment. Railroad workers and other transportation workers are covered by the Federal Employers Liability Act (FELA). This statute does not provide for liability without fault, as in the case of workers' compensation, but it greatly increases the chances of a worker's winning a lawsuit against her or his employer by eliminating the defenses the employer would have had at common law. In a suit for damages based upon the negligence of the officers, agents, or employees of an employer, the contributory negligence of the injured employee does not prevent recovery. If it is present, however, the comparative responsibility rule reduces damages in proportion to the amount of the employee's negligence. This rule does not apply when the employer's violation of a statute enacted for the safety of the employee has contributed to the injury. Also, the common-law defense of assumption of the risk is not available to an employer.

The act further provides that a term in a contract of employment which attempts to exempt a covered employer from liability or prevent enforcement of the FELA is void. In addition, the legal rights of a deceased employee which are created by the statute survive for the benefit of the surviving spouse and children. Although fault of the employer must be proved for an employee to recover for injuries under the FELA, and a regular lawsuit must be filed in court, the act provides the worker with a distinct advantage over many workers' compensation systems. There is no limit or ceiling to the amount an employee can recover for injuries. It is clear that juries often are sympathetic to the injured worker, and verdicts in six or seven figures are not unusual. The Jones Act gives maritime employees the same rights against their employers as railway workers have against theirs under the FELA.

Other federal statutes require awards for on-the-job injuries or deaths of certain employees without regard to the fault of the employer, which is in the manner of state workers' compensation laws. These federal statutes provide formulas to use in computing the amounts of the awards for various kinds and degrees of disability, along with upper and lower limits for such awards. One statute is the Longshoremen's and Harbor Workers' Compensation Act. Congress extended this act to cover workers of private employers on United States defense bases.

4 WAGES AND HOURS OF WORK

Generally

Statutes setting **minimum wages** per hour and maximum hours of work exist on both the state and the federal level. Early state legislation of this type mainly concerned labor by children and women. At first, employers successfully attacked such legislation as being an unconstitutional invasion of the freedom of contract. Today we recognize that state governments possess the power to enact statutes of this type for social and economic purposes. Approximately 70 percent of the states have minimum-wage laws.

The federal government also regulates wages and hours. The Fair Labor Standards Act (FLSA), which was originally enacted in 1938, has been amended several times to increase the minimum wage, decrease maximum hours, and broaden its coverage. Originally, the FLSA required covered employers to pay their employees at least 25 cents an hour for a regular workweek of forty-four hours, to pay such employees at least time and one-half for all work performed over the forty-four-hour week, and to keep certain records for each worker which would demonstrate compliance or noncompliance with the act. It also restricted the use of child labor. The Supreme Court held the staute to be a constitutional exercise of the power of Congress under the commerce clause.

Minimum Wage

At the time of this book's writing, the minimum hourly wage is generally $3.35. The standard workweek is forty hours, with overtime pay at a rate of not less than one and one-half times the employee's regular rate of pay. Although this regular rate may not be less than the minimum wage, it can be and usually is more. If it is, the time and one-half is the higher rate. For example, an employee whose hourly rate is $4 receives $6 per hour for overtime. The wage and overtime provisions apply whether an employee is paid on a time, piece, job, incentive, or other basis. The FLSA does *not* require sick pay, holidays off, vacations, overtime pay for weekend or holiday work, or a limit on the hours of work for employees who are sixteen years of age or older.

Coverage

Not all types of employment were covered by the original FLSA, nor are they today. However, the amendments have expanded coverage greatly, along with the minimum wage, so that now it protects most workers. Although there are still some exempt businesses, their number is decreasing, and the trend is to require the minimum wage for all. Categories of persons who are presently not covered include many who do not need the protection, such as those engaged in the practice of a profession, managerial and supervisory personnel, and outside salespeople. Most of the time, persons engaged in such employment earn incomes far in excess of the FLSA minimums, anyway. Also not covered are certain workers employed by small farms and small businesses such as "mom and pop" retail establishments and other small independent stores which are intrastate in operation.

In addition, messengers, handicapped workers, and full-time students employed in similar service operations, institutions of higher education, or agriculture may be paid lower minimum wages, provided the employer first obtains special certificates from the administrator of the Wage and Hour Division of the Department of Labor. As the next case shows, the minimum wage also does not apply to individuals in training when the employer gains no benefit from the training itself.

DONOVAN v. TRANS WORLD AIRLINES
726 F.2d 415 (8th Cir. 1984)

FACTS

TWA maintains an academy where, among other things, it trains flight attendants. The flight-attendant trainees usually live in dormitories provided by TWA. The trainees neither expect nor receive monetary compensation during the four-week training sessions. The trainees spend approximately forty hours per week in training classes. TWA provides meals, lodging, ground transportation, and health and accident insurance during the four weeks. TWA does not pay minimum wage to the trainees. The secretary of labor sued to force payment of the minimum wage.

ISSUE

Are these trainees "employees," thereby requiring TWA to pay them minimum wages?

> **DECISION**
>
> No.
>
> **REASONS**
>
> 1. To qualify as an employee under the minimum-wage statute, an individual must work for the benefit of the employer.
> 2. TWA received no immediate benefit from its trainees during training.

One proposal to amend minimum-wage coverage applies to teenagers. It would allow employers to pay them less than minimum wage. This proposal is in response to widespread teenage unemployment, especially in the cities. The theory is that if employers could pay less than minimum wage, they would hire more teenagers. Unions oppose a reduction in the minimum wage.

Child Labor

Besides its wage and hour provisions, the FLSA contains sections which regulate the employment of child labor outside agriculture. Under these, eighteen is the minimum age for employment in occupations which are declared *hazardous* by the secretary of labor. These include such jobs as working in areas that involve exposure to radioactivity, operating various kinds of dangerous machinery, mining, and roofing. Otherwise, the basic minimum age for employment is sixteen, at which age children may be employed in any nonhazardous work.

The employment of fourteen- and fifteen-year-olds is limited to certain occupations such as sales and clerical work, under specific conditions of work, for limited hours, and outside school time only. Children under fourteen may not be employed, except for a few jobs which are specifically exempt. For example, children employed in agriculture outside of school hours, children employed by their parents in nonhazardous occupations, child actors, and newspaper deliveries are exempt. State laws on child labor must also be followed if they are more strict than the federal standards.

Penalties and Remedies

Willful violations of the provisions of the Fair Labor Standards Act may be prosecuted criminally by the attorney general. Violators may be punished by a fine of up to $10,000 for the first offense and, for subsequent offenses, a fine of up to $10,000 or imprisonment for up to six months, or both. Violators of the child-labor provisions can be fined a civil penalty of up to $1,000 for each violation. The act also empowers the federal district courts to issue injunctions restraining violations of it.

Finally, employees who are injured by a violation may bring a civil suit against their employer and recover unpaid wages or overtime compensation and an equal amount as "liquidated" damages, plus reasonable attorneys' fees and costs of the action. However, if the employer shows the court that she or he acted in good faith and had reasonable grounds to believe that she or he was not violating the law, the court may, in its discretion, award no liquidated damages, or limit them. The administrator of the Wage and Hour Division of the Department of Labor may supervise the payment of back wages, or the secretary of labor may, upon the written request of an employee, bring suit for back pay due the employee. In 1987, a federal court ordered a Texas utility company to pay employees $7.6 million in back overtime pay.

5 UNEMPLOYMENT COMPENSATION

Generally

Unemployment compensation is a federal-state program which provides for payments for temporary periods to workers who are unemployed through no fault of their own. It is a classic example of the use of the federal taxing power as a tool to pressure the states into adopting legislation deemed desirable by the federal government. The Social Security Act of 1935 imposed a federal tax on the wages paid by all employers who were not exempt. However, the act provided that taxed employers were entitled to a credit of up to 90 percent of this tax for any contributions they made to an approved state unemployment insurance plan. Although only Wisconsin had an unemployment compensation law in 1935, all the states enacted such statutes shortly after the Social Security Act.

The federal policy to encourage state unemployment insurance was a result of the mass unemployment in the depression during the 1930s. Then, millions were out of work for long periods, with about 25 percent of the labor force being unemployed. Partly, this mass unemployment was due to a self-feeding cycle. As workers were laid off, they lost their purchasing power and could consume less. Less consumption meant less need for production, so employers had to lay off more workers who lost their purchasing power and could consume less. Production continued to fall, so more workers became unemployed.

A major goal of unemployment compensation, besides the humanitarian one, was to break this vicious cycle.

Requirements of the Law

Today, the basic standard of the federal unemployment law imposes a tax on any person who pays $1,500 of wages during any three-month period of the current or preceding year. The tax is on the first $7,000 of wages at a

1985 rate of 6.2 percent. Up to 90 percent of this tax may be deducted for amounts paid to a state unemployment compensation fund.

The federal law grants a series of exemptions from the unemployment tax. Among the exempted are agricultural labor for certain small farming operations, family labor, labor for the United States government or for a state, and labor for a religious, charitable, or educational organization. The states may provide for wider coverage if they desire.

Only workers in a covered business can collect unemployment compensation, and then only if they meet certain tests. If they qualify, they draw payments as a matter of right, regardless of financial position, since need is not a factor. The laws require them either to have worked for a certain minimum number of weeks in a covered industry or to have earned a certain minimum amount of wages. These times and amounts vary from state to state. Generally, a worker must wait one week before applying and must register with the state employment agency and be ready, willing, and able to undertake suitable employment.

The maximum period during which benefits are payable varies from state to state and generally has ranged from twenty-six to thirty-nine weeks. The maximum amount of weekly payments for unemployment also varies widely. Usually it is computed as a percentage of the highest quarterly earnings in a base period.

All states have adopted **experience rating systems** which excuse employers who have a good record of maintaining stable employment from paying part or all of the state unemployment tax. Such systems have been adopted as a result of the provision which allows employers a credit against the federal tax not only for amounts paid the state but also for such amounts as they are excused from paying because of a good experience rating. Thus, businesses with a good rating pay less in unemployment taxes than ones with a higher unemployment experience.

As a result of the credit permitted by the experience rating system, the average unemployment tax rate nationwide has been considerably less than that provided for in the law. Experience rating has given employers the incentive to attempt to control their unemployment record and detect fraudulent claims filed by former employees. On the minus side, it means that taxes will be lower during times when the economy is in good condition and higher when general conditions are bad.

Disqualification from Receiving Compensation

State laws usually disqualify persons from receiving unemployment compensation for: (1) voluntarily leaving the job without good cause, (2) being discharged for misconduct, and (3) refusing suitable work while unemployed. In the following case, the Supreme Court considers whether federal law permits Missouri to deny unemployment compensation to women who voluntarily leave their jobs due to pregnancy.

> **WIMBERLY v. LABOR AND INDUSTRIAL RELATIONS COMM. OF MISSOURI**
> 107 S.Ct. 821 (1987)
>
> **FACTS**
>
> After having been employed by J. C. Penny Company for three years, Linda Wimberly requested a leave of absence because of her pregnancy. The company granted her a "leave without guarantee of reinstatement." Following the birth of her child, she notified the company that she wished to return to work, but she was told that there were no positions open. She then filed for unemployment compensation from the state. The state denied compensation on the basis that she had left work voluntarily. She sued.
>
> **ISSUE**
>
> Has Missouri denied Wimberly unemployment compensation "solely on the basis of pregnancy" in violation of federal law?
>
> **DECISION**
>
> No.
>
> **REASONS**
>
> 1. Most states regard job-leave due to pregnancy as a voluntary termination for good cause. A few states like Missouri, however, have decided that leaving a job for any reason, including pregnancy, disqualifies employees from unemployment compensation unless they leave for reasons directly related to the work or to the employer.
> 2. For a state to participate in the joint federal-state unemployment compensation program, it must meet the standards of the Federal Unemployment Tax Act. That act required that "no person shall be denied compensation under...state law solely on the basis of pregnancy or termination of pregnancy."
> 3. The plain meaning of the act is that Congress intended only to prohibit states from singling out pregnancy for unfavorable treatment in granting unemployment compensation. Missouri does not discriminate solely on the basis of pregnancy in granting compensation. Rather, it denies compensation to *all* persons who voluntarily leave employment for reasons unrelated to the work or to the employer. Since federal law does not require the states to give preferential treatment in granting unemployment compensation to pregnant women, Missouri has not violated that law.

Most states disqualify workers from receiving unemployment compensation if they are on strike because of a labor dispute. Sometimes, strikes affect workers who are not themselves on strike. In such cases, the workers can get unemployment compensation. The case which follows illustrates such a situation.

> **DUNAWAY v. DEPT. OF LABOR**
> 452 N.E.2d 1332 (Ill. 1984)
>
> **FACTS**
>
> Coal miner union members were under a valid collective-bargaining agreement with their employer. Another union, UMW, went on strike against a different employer. UMW put pickets at the first employer's mines. The nonstriking union members refused to cross the picket line, due in part to threats of harm. A work stoppage resulted and the nonstriking union members were temporarily unemployed.
>
> **ISSUE**
>
> Did the unemployment result from voluntary work stoppage and disqualify the employees from receiving unemployment compensation?
>
> **DECISION**
>
> No.
>
> **REASONS**
>
> 1. The general rule is that employees cannot collect unemployment benefits when their unemployment is a direct result of a labor dispute.
> 2. But that rule applies only when the labor dispute is with the employer in question.
> 3. This labor dispute was with a different employer.
> 4. If the labor dispute is with a different employer, and if employees refuse to cross the picket line due to threats, then resulting unemployment is involuntary and employees qualify for benefits.

What UMW did in the *Dunaway* case to the first employer is an illegal secondary boycott, which is an unfair labor practice. (See the discussion about this in Chapter 17.) UMW was eventually forced to remove pickets from the first employer.

6 SOCIAL SECURITY

In General

Social Security is a federal program for providing income when a family's earnings are reduced or stopped because of retirement, disability, or death. Under Social Security's Medicare provisions, hospital and medical insurance help protect persons who are sixty-five and older from high health-care costs. Every month, 36 million people receive Social Security benefits, which represent 27 percent of all expenditures made by the federal government.

Congress enacted the first Social Security Act in 1935. At first, it covered only certain workers in commerce and industry and provided them only with retirement benefits. Since then, a number of amendments have increased the kind and dollar amount of benefits to what they are today. These amendments have also greatly increased the number of persons covered so that now most self-employed persons, employees of nonprofit corporations, household and farm employees, federal employees, members of the armed forces, the clergy, and others are included also. Currently, nine out of ten workers in the United States are earning Social Security protection, and approximately one out of seven persons receives monthly Social Security checks.

The Social Security law requires that during their working years, covered employees, their employers, and self-employed persons pay Social Security taxes to the federal government. Employers must deduct their employees' share of the contribution to the Social Security system from their wages, match those payments, and send the combined amount to the IRS. Self-employed persons pay their tax each year when filing their individual income tax returns. Generally, employers must file an Employer's Quarterly Tax Return with the IRS and deposit Social Security taxes with an authorized commercial bank or Federal Reserve Bank at various times, usually at least once per month, depending on the amount of undeposited taxes at the time. A penalty is imposed for failure to make required deposits when due, without reasonable cause. Earnings of workers are taxable even if they are receiving Social Security benefits at the time.

Employers must keep all records pertaining to employment taxes for inspection by the IRS for a period of at least four years after the taxes are due or are paid. These records must include such things as the names, addresses, occupations, and Social Security numbers of the employees paid; the amounts and dates of the payments made to them; the period of their employment; duplicate copies of tax returns filed; and the dates and amounts of deposits made.

Criticisms and Problems of the Social Security System

In recent years, concern has grown over the financial health of the Social Security system. It appears underfunded, in spite of the fact that the amount of wages subject to Social Security tax, as well as its rates, have increased dramatically. In 1984, the tax was paid on the first $37,800 of personal income, an amount that was $29,700 in 1981. For 25 percent of all employees, Social Security tax is larger than federal income tax, and for small businesses it is the largest federal tax. The rates of taxation will rise gradually, at least through 1990 (see Table 14-3).

Critics of the system point to the fact that much of the burden of paying for increasing Social Security benefits is being imposed on the younger workers of today, at a time when many of them are raising families and attempting to purchase homes. The work force appears to be leveling off

TABLE 14-3 RATES OF SOCIAL SECURITY TAXATION THROUGH 1990*

Year	Employee and employer, each	Self-employed
1986	7.15%	14.30%
1987	7.15%	14.30%
1988	7.51%	15.02%
1989	7.51%	15.02%
1990	7.65%	15.30%

*The amount of income to which the tax applies will also likely rise, but Congress has not yet set it.

due to the trend toward zero population growth in the country. However, the number of Social Security beneficiaries will be increasing due to longer life expectancies and, at the turn of the century, to the retirement of persons born during the period after World War II, that is, the "baby boom" generation.

In 1983, Congress amended the Social Security Act to raise the retirement age for receiving full benefits. Beginning in the year 2000, the current retirement age of 65 will begin to rise. For persons born in 1960 and later, the retirement age will be 67. However, early retirement at reduced benefits will be available. That option may also be exercised at present.

Congress also has made taxable up to 50 percent of Social Security benefits for retirees whose incomes exceed a certain amount. Previously, all Social Security benefits were nontaxable. Even with these changes, however, there is still concern about the solvency of the Social Security system. In light of soaring medical costs, the Medicare trust fund of the Social Security system, which pays for retirement health costs, faces severe financial problems in the near future.

7 PRIVATE PENSION PLANS: INCENTIVES AND PROTECTION

Economic security in retirement has been a national policy goal for much of this century. The Social Security system is a good example. Encouragement of private pension plans is another part of this policy. In the past decade, the number of employer-established private retirement plans has more than doubled. Some 60 million employees are currently covered by private plans.

The law provides incentives for businesses and individuals to create private pension plans. It also protects employees who are part of such plans.

Incentives for Pension Plans: The "Qualified" Plan

There are many types of pension plans (as well as profit-sharing arrangements). One of the motivations for such plans, of course, is a genuine interest by a business in the retirement future of all its employees, along with a desire to attract and retain high-quality workers. Some plans have resulted mainly from union pressure and collective-bargaining agreements. In addition, those persons in control of a business have a personal interest in assuring their own financial futures.

A major financial incentive to the formation of private pension plans is favorable income tax treatment. If an employer has instituted a **qualified pension plan,** as defined by the Internal Revenue Code, it can claim income tax deductions from contributions made to fund the plan, and fund earnings from investments are not taxable. Employees need pay personal income tax only on payments received after retirement. Such payments often receive special retirement income treatment and come at a time when other sources of income are lower, putting the retired person in a lower tax bracket. Basically, to qualify for this special treatment, a plan must cover either a certain percentage of all employees (usually 70 percent) or cover classifications of employees which do not discriminate in favor of management (officers or highly compensated employees) or shareholders, as determined by the IRS.

Employee Retirement Income Security Act

Qualification of a pension plan by the IRS does not ensure that it is a good plan for employees. Prior to 1974, plans were sometimes improperly funded, and the money in them was irresponsibly invested. In other cases, many employees lacked **vested rights** (rights which cannot be taken away) in their company's pension plan. If they were discharged prior to retirement, they received no pension.

In 1974, Congress passed the Employee Retirement Income Security Act (ERISA) to protect employee rights in private pension plans. The act applies to both **defined benefit plans** and **defined contribution plans** (often called money-purchase plans). Defined benefit plans usually guarantee employees a certain retirement income based on years of service and salary or wage level. Actuarial calculations determine employers' funding obligations with such a plan. Under a defined contribution plan, employers contribute a percentage of an employee's pay (often 5 to 10 percent) to the pension fund. Retirement income is determined by the total of these contributions plus investment return.

The defined contribution plan allows employers to budget pension costs in advance. Because of this and because ERISA regulates funding requirements for defined benefit plans very heavily, the majority of employers favor defined contribution plans.

Pension Benefit Guaranty Corporation

An important provision of ERISA requires **plan termination insurance coverage** for all defined benefit plans. The idea is to make the plans pay annual premiums to insure the benefits to participants in the event that the plan is terminated and its assets are not sufficient to meet its obligations. The act creates the Pension Benefit Guaranty Corporation (PBGC) to provide this insurance. It ensures that vested benefits will be paid up to established maximums. The employer, not just the separate pension plan itself, is also made liable to reimburse PBGC for the insured benefits it pays, up to 30 percent of the employer's net worth. Without this requirement, claims could be made only against the pension trust's assets, but not against the employer when the pension trust failed.

The Fiduciary Obligation

Another aspect of ERISA is also designed to protect the assets of pension plans. Strict rules require plan **fiduciaries** (those who are placed in a position of trust and confidence with regard to another's assets) to exercise the degree of care that a prudent person would in handling his or her own affairs in the management of a fund's assets. Anyone who has any such control, as well as one who gives investment advice for a fee, is included in the act's definition of a fiduciary. Also, transactions between the plan and a party with a conflicting interest, like the employer, are forbidden. Under this rule, a loan between the plan and employer is prohibited, as is a sale of property between them. Investments by a plan in the securities of the employer are generally limited to 10 percent.

Vesting

ERISA also ensures employees' rights to benefits under pension plans. The law states that benefits from an employee's own contributions (if any) to a plan are fully and immediately vested when the contributions are made. Benefits from an employer's plan contributions must begin vesting before retirement under one of several ERISA standards. The most common standard selected by employees provides for full employee vesting after ten years of service. Another standard establishes a gradual five- to fifteen-year vesting.

Record-Keeping and Reporting Requirements

The record-keeping and reporting requirements under ERISA are substantial. The years of service and percentage of vesting of benefits of each participant must be recorded. If vested employees terminate before retirement, the plan administrator must furnish both the IRS and the Department of Labor with information on their vested benefits. A booklet (approved by the Department of Labor) must be prepared for distribution to plan participants. It must include a detailed plan description and a summary, understandable by the average participant. A very detailed annual report must be filed with the department and made available for examination by plan participants and for public inspection. The plan report generally must include financial statements, an opinion on them by an independent certified accountant, information on the plan's investments, assets, and transactions, and other data which are specified in great detail by the act.

Simplified Employee Pensions

The Revenue Act of 1978 permits employers to set up **simplified employee pensions.** This change was designed to appeal to employers, particularly smaller businesses, who do not wish to set up a full-blown pension plan of their own because of the expense and complications involved. Under this plan, employers can contribute up to a specified amount of an employee's income to an **individual retirement account** (IRA) for each employee. The contributions (including interest or other income from their investment) are not taxable to the employees until they begin drawing from their account in retirement, which can start anytime after age fifty-nine and one-half without penalty. Employees select their own investment vehicle when they open their IRAs. The approved list includes banks, savings and loans, credit unions, insurance companies, and mutual funds. The fact that the employee decides where the IRA is invested should result in greatly reduced liability risk on the part of the employer. The IRA belongs to the employee, so it vests immediately. Also, the fund goes along with the employee who changes jobs, and it continues to accumulate.

Businesses which adopt the simplified employee pensions plan may deduct contributions from their income tax. However, to qualify they must meet certain requirements. For example, all covered employees must receive the same *percentage* contribution. The percentage rate of contribution may be changed from year to year (for all workers), or, in a bad year, the employer may decide to make no contributions at all.

Individual Retirement Accounts

Any person under age seventy and one-half can set up and fund an individual retirement account. Within limits set by ERISA, the person can invest the IRA funds. IRA contributions up to $2000 annually are fully deductible from presently taxable income if the person is not covered by an employment retirement plan. For persons already covered by employment retirement plans (or whose spouses are covered), there are substantial limits on deductibility of IRA contributions at higher income levels.

Because the purpose of IRAs is to provide retirement income, there are substantial tax penalties for early withdrawal of funds. Withdrawals can be made without penalty beginning at age fifty-nine and one-half. If death occurs prior to that age, distributions can also be made to survivors without penalty. Along with pension plans, IRAs have helped reduce demands for an expanded Social Security program.

ERISA Trends

Most observers consider ERISA a success. Over half of the work force, both male and female, participate in private pension plans. Because of its success, ERISA might be amended to include retirement medical insurance. This step would help prop up the Social Security Medicare program, which could become insolvent if medical costs continue to rise and Congress fails to provide additional funding.

Even with its success, ERISA also faces problems. More than 1,000 private pension plans have fallen into insolvency, and the PBGC is operating at a deficit to meet the obligations of these plans to retired employees. One solution, which PBGC has proposed to Congress, is to raise the annual insurance premium which employers with defined benefit plans currently pay to PBGC.

A major problem of ERISA is the amount of paperwork required of employers who maintain pension plans. These employers must keep records and make reports to three separate governmental agencies: PBGC, the Labor Department, and the Treasury Department (IRS). Many smaller businesses cannot afford to do this and do not have pension plans. Only 15 percent of businesses with fewer than 25 employees cover their work force with a pension plan. A proposed solution would centralize authority in one agency, probably PBGC, thus reducing the paperwork burden.

8 TRENDS IN WORKER PROTECTION: LIMITATIONS ON EMPLOYMENT-AT-WILL

Historically, unless employees contracted for a definite period of employment (such as for one year), employers were able to discharge them without reason at any time. This is called the **employment-at-will** doctrine.

During the 1930s, employers began to lose this absolute right to discharge employees whenever they desired. The Labor-Management Relations Act prohibited employers from firing employees for union activities. Now, many federal laws limit employers in their right to terminate employees, even at-will employees (see Table 14-4). Some states have also prohibited employers by statute from discharging employees for certain reasons, such as for refusing to take lie-detector examinations.

Courts, too, have begun limiting the at-will doctrine. Under contract theory, several courts have stated that at-will employment contracts (which are not written and are little more than the agreement to pay for work performed) contain an implied promise of good faith and fair dealing by the employer. This promise, implied by law, can be broken in certain cases by unjustified dismissal of employees. As the following case illustrates, other

TABLE 14-4 FEDERAL STATUTES LIMITING EMPLOYMENT-AT-WILL DOCTRINE

Statute	Limitation on employee discharge
1 Labor-Management Relations Act	Prohibits discharge for union activity or for filing charges under the act
2 Fair Labor Standards Act	Forbids discharge for exercising rights guaranteed by minimum wage and overtime provisions of the act
3 Occupational Safety and Health Act	Prohibits discharge for exercising rights under the act
4 Civil Rights Act	Makes illegal discharge based on race, sex, color, religion, or national origin
5 Age Discrimination in Employment Act	Forbids age-based discharge of employees aged forty to seventy
6 Employee Retirement Income Security Act	Prohibits discharge to prevent employees from getting vested pension rights
7 Clean Air Act	Prevents discharge of employees who cooperate in proceedings against employer for violation of the act
8 Clean Water Act	Prevents discharge of employees who cooperate in proceedings against employer for violation of the act
9 Consumer Credit Protection Act	Prohibits discharge of employees due to garnishment of wages for any one indebtedness
10 Judiciary and Judicial Procedure Act	Forbids discharge of employees for service on federal grand or petit juries

courts have ruled that an employer's publication of personnel handbooks can change the nature of at-will employment.

SMALL v. SPRINGS INDUSTRIES, INC.
Sup.Ct. 357 S.E.2d 452 (S.C. 1987)

FACTS

Five years after plaintiff Small went to work for Spring Industries, Spring issued an employee handbook. It later sent a bulletin to all employees explaining the handbook's termination procedure. Prior to employee termination, the procedure outlined a four-step disciplinary process: verbal reprimand, a written warning, a final written warning, and discharge. Small had problems with her employer and was discharged after only one written warning. She sued.

ISSUE

Was the four-step disciplinary process part of an implied employment contract that Small had with her employer?

DECISION

Yes.

REASONS

1. Like most employment agreements, the agreement in this case was unilateral. The employer offered or promised to hire the employee under certain conditions. The employee accepted the offer by working for the employer.
2. The employer did not have to issue a handbook and bulletin, but it chose to do so. It certainly intended for employees to follow the rules and procedures outlined in these publications. Therefore, strong equitable and social policy reasons exist to prevent the employer from deviating capriciously from its own rules and procedures.
3. If company policies are not worth the paper they are printed on, it would be better not to mislead employees by issuing them. If policies are purely advisory and the company does not wish to be bound to them, it may so state and continue an employment-at-will relationship with employees.
4. A majority of states permit handbooks to alter the employment-at-will relationship. This state now joins that majority.

DISSENT

The employee did not allege any consideration to support the employer's implied promise to be bound by the handbook. The employee's continuing to work for the employer was not sufficient consideration.

Many contract and tort exceptions to employment-at-will have involved one of three types of employer behavior: (1) discharge of employee for performance of an important public obligation (such as jury duty); (2) discharge of employee for reporting employer's alleged violations of law (called "whistle blowing"); and (3) discharge of employee for exercising statutory rights. Most of the cases that limit at-will employment state that the employer has violated "public policy." What does it mean to say that an employer has violated public policy? Is it a court's way of saying that most people no longer support the employer's right to do what it did?

Limitations on employment-at-will doctrine show continued development of worker protection. Instead of dealing with worker safety and financial security, they concern a related issue: job security. It may be part of a trend which could ultimately lead to some type of broad, legally guaranteed job security. Many nations have much stricter laws promoting an employee's right to job security than does the United States. In recent years, unions have increasingly focused on job-security issues in their bargaining with employers.

REVIEW QUESTIONS

1 For each term in the left-hand column, match the most appropriate description in the right-hand column:

(1) Course of employment
(2) Defined benefit plan
(3) Defined contribution plan
(4) Discharge for proper cause
(5) Employment-at-will
(6) Exclusive remedy rule
(7) Fellow-servant rule
(8) Minimum wage
(9) Qualified pension plan
(10) Vested rights

(a) The law which states that an employee may only recover workers' compensation against an employer for an accidental injury.
(b) A common-law doctrine which held that an employer was not liable when one employee injured another.
(c) The legal concept that an employer may fire at any time an employee who is not under contract.
(d) A pension system which guarantees employees a certain retirement income based on years of service and salary.
(e) A pension system under which an employer pays a certain percentage of an employee's wage or salary to a fund but does not guarantee a certain level of retirement income.
(f) The pursuing of the employer's interest under the employer's direction.
(g) The firing of someone for failing to follow orders, tardiness, and so on, which makes that person ineligible for unemployment compensation.
(h) Rights which cannot legally be taken away.
(i) The lowest legal pay an employer can give for certain types of employment.
(j) A retirement income program under which employers can claim income tax deductions for contributions made to fund the program.

2 You are the owner of a small smelting plant. An employee informs you that an OSHA inspector has just arrived in the plant parking lot. Must you allow the inspector entrance to the plant? If OSHA issues your company a citation for violating its standards, what happens then? Discuss.

3 How did the assumption-of-risk, contributory-negligence, and fellow-servant doctrines make it difficult in the 1800s for injured employees to sue their employees for job-related accidents?

4 If Corgel fails to wear a hard hat as required by his employer and is injured by a falling screwdriver, can he recover workers' compensation from the employer?

5 Discuss exceptions to the exclusive-remedy rule. Why are ever greater numbers of injured employees trying to avoid the impact of the rule?

6 A railroad employee falls from a moving train and suffers back injury. Can the employee recover under workers' compensation? Explain.

7. While preparing her income tax return, Corrine Smythe finds that she worked 2,500 hours in 1987 in her job as a picker-packer. Her hourly wage was $8 and her employer paid her a total of $20,000 during the year. Suddenly, Smythe realizes that her employer has violated the Fair Labor Standard Act. Explain and tell what remedies she has under the act.
8. The foreman of a work crew employed by the Zenith Roof Company asks the company to hire his sixteen-year-old nephew as a roofer's assistant during the summer. How should the company respond to this request? Explain.
9. What tax incentive is there for businesses to have a low turnover of employees? Explain.
10. Claudia's employer fired her for theft of office supplies. Marco quit his job in hopes of becoming a writer. Are either of these two persons entitled to unemployment compensation?
11. Discuss the problems facing the Social Security system.
12. Consider defined benefit pension plans and defined contribution pension plans. From a financial viewpoint, which type will an employer usually prefer? An employee? Discuss.
13. Weitz, a retired industrial worker, gets $750 monthly under a defined benefit pension plan. He learns that his former employer is bankrupt and that there is not enough money in the pension plan to continue paying his benefits. What will likely happen to Weitz's retirement income?
14. Roebuck Manufacturing, a small equipment firm, has only thirty-five employees. Because of the expense and complication of setting up a regular defined benefit or contribution plan, it has not set up a pension plan for its employees. Then it learns of the "simplified employee pension." Discuss the advantages of this type of pension plan for a firm like Roebuck Manufacturing.
15. Turner was employed by the Apco Textile Company. He injured his back and missed a substantial period of work. When he sought workers' compensation, he was fired. Can he sue Apco for damages? Explain.

CHAPTER 15

DISCRIMINATION IN EMPLOYMENT

OVERVIEW

This chapter examines laws which require employers to give equal job opportunities to various groups. The laws prohibit discrimination based on race, sex, color, religion, and national origin. In many instances, they also forbid discrimination arising from age or handicap.

Note in your study that discrimination can be illegal even when it is *not* intentional. For example, a company's hiring policies which apply equally to all job applicants are illegal if they discriminate disproportionately and are not related directly to job performance. Realize that the courts, not the employer, will decide whether hiring policies are job-related.

At the federal level, the Equal Employment Opportunity Commission investigates and prosecutes complaints of illegal job discrimination. Employees can also often file discrimination charges with state agencies. When these regulatory bodies do not resolve differences between employees and their employer, the employees can take complaints of discrimination into the courts.

Key terms in this chapter are affirmative action, bona fide occupational qualifications, comparable worth, discrimination-in-effect, paper fortress, pattern and practice cases, reverse discrimination, Section 1981, and seniority system.

1 HISTORICAL DEVELOPMENT OF EMPLOYMENT DISCRIMINATION LAW

"That all men are created equal" was one of the "self-evident" truths recognized by the Founding Fathers in the Declaration of Independence. However, equality among all our citizens clearly has been an ideal rather than a fact. The Constitution itself recognizes slavery by saying that slaves should count as "three-fifths of all other Persons" for determining population in House of Representatives elections. And, of course, that all *men* are created equal says nothing about women, who did not even get a constitutionally guaranteed right to vote until 1920.

Nowhere have effects of inequality and discrimination been felt more acutely than in the area of job opportunity. Historically, common law permitted employers to hire and fire virtually at will, unless restrained by contract or statute. Under this system, white males came to dominate the job market in their ability to gain employment and their salaries and wages.

Although the Civil Rights Act of 1866 contains a provision which plaintiffs now widely use in employment discrimination cases, such use is recent. Passage of labor law in the 1920s and 1930s marks the first significant federal limitation on the relatively unrestricted right of employers to hire and fire. Then, in connection with the war effort, President Roosevelt issued executive orders in 1941 and 1943 requiring a clause prohibiting racial discrimination in all federal contracts with private contractors. Subsequent executive orders in the 1950s established committees to investigate complaints of racial discrimination against such contractors. Affirmative action requirements on federal contracts followed from executive orders of the 1960s.

The most important statute eliminating discriminatory employment practices, however, is the federal Civil Rights Act of 1964, as amended by the Equal Employment Opportunity Act of 1972.

2 THE CIVIL RIGHTS ACT: GENERAL PROVISIONS

The provisions of Title VII of the Civil Rights Act of 1964 apply to employers with fifteen or more employees. They also cover labor unions and certain others (see Table 15-1). The major purpose of these laws is to eliminate job discrimination against employees, job applicants, or union members based on race, color, religion, sex, or national origin. Discrimination for any of these reasons is a violation of the law, except that employers, employ-

TABLE 15-1　EMPLOYERS AND OTHERS COVERED BY TITLE VII

1. Private employers with fifteen or more employees
2. Labor unions with fifteen or more members
3. Employment agencies
4. State and local governments (but elected officials are not covered)
5. Public and private educational institutions
6. Federal government (in most instances)

ment agencies, and labor unions can discriminate on the basis of religion, sex, or national origin where these are **bona fide occupational qualifications (bfoq)** reasonably necessary to normal business operations. Title VII also permits discrimination if it results unintentionally from a seniority or merit system.

The types of employer action in which discrimination is prohibited include: (1) discharge, (2) refusal to hire, (3) compensation, and (4) terms, conditions, or privileges of employment. The following case establishes that Title VII applies even to partnership promotion at a law firm.

HISHON v. KING & SPALDING
52 L.W. 4627 (1984)

FACTS

Ms. Hishon was employed by the law firm of King & Spalding in 1972. Her employment ended in 1979 when the firm, a general partnership, decided not to invite her to become a partner. She sued, claiming sex discrimination under Title VII. The federal district court dismissed the complaint on the basis that Title VII did not apply to selection of partners by a partnership. The court of appeals affirmed.

ISSUE

Does Title VII apply to selection of partners by a partnership?

DECISION

Yes.

REASONS

1. Although selection to partnership is not a *right* of employment, it is a *privilege* or benefit of employment in this instance to be considered for partnership.
2. Title VII prohibits, among other things, sex discrimination as to "terms, conditions, or privileges of employment."
3. Title VII thus applies to this case.

Employment *agencies* are prohibited from either *failing to refer* or from *actually referring* an individual for employment on the basis of race, color, religion, sex, or national origin. This prohibition differs from the law binding *employers,* where it is unlawful only to fail or refuse to hire on discriminatory grounds—the affirmative act of hiring for a discriminatory reason is apparently not illegal. For example, assume that a contractor with a government contract seeks a qualified black engineer and requests an employment agency to refer such an individual. The agency complies with the request, and a black is referred and hired. Unless a white applicant was discriminated against, the employer probably did not commit an unlawful practice; but the employment agency, by referring an individual on the basis of his color, unquestionably *did* commit a unlawful practice under Title VII.

Employers, unions, and employment agencies are prohibited from discriminating against an employee, applicant, or union member because he or she has made a charge, testified, or participated in an investigation or hearing under the act, or otherwise opposed any unlawful practice.

Note that regarding general hiring, referrals, advertising, and admissions to training or apprenticeship programs, Title VII allows discrimination only on the basis of religion, sex, or national origin and only where these considerations are bona fide occupational qualifications. For example, it is legal for a Baptist church to refuse to engage a Lutheran minister. EEOC guidelines on sex discrimination consider sex to be a bona fide occupational qualification, for example, where it is necessary for authenticity or genuineness in hiring an actor or actress. The omission of *race* and *color* from this exception must mean that Congress does not feel these two factors are ever bona fide occupational qualifications.

Additional exemptions exist with respect to laws creating preferential treatment for veterans and hiring based on professionally developed ability tests that are not designed or intended to be used to discriminate. Such tests must bear a relationship to the job for which they are administered, however.

3 ENFORCEMENT PROCEDURES

Generally

The Civil Rights Act of 1964 created the Equal Employment Opportunity Commission. This agency has the primary responsibility of enforcing the provisions of the act. The EEOC is composed of five members, not more than three of whom may be members of the same political party. They are appointed by the President, with the advice and consent of the Senate, and serve a five-year term. In the course of its investigations, the Equal Employment Opportunity Commission has broad authority to hold hearings, obtain evidence, and subpoena and examine witnesses under oath.

Under the Equal Employment Opportunity Act of 1972, the EEOC can file a civil suit in federal district court and represent a person charging a violation of the act. However, it must first exhaust efforts to settle the claim. Remedies which may be obtained in such an action include reinstatement with back pay for the victim of an illegal discrimination and injunctions against future violations of the act by the defendant. Since discrimination complaints can take years to litigate to a conclusion, the size of back pay awards is often substantial (see Table 15-2). What can an employer

TABLE 15-2 SELECTED RECENT AWARDS IN EMPLOYEE DISCRIMINATION CASES

Defendant	Plaintiff(s)	Award or settlement
University of Minnesota	250 female faculty members	$40 million, plus $2 million attorneys' fees
General Motors	Females and minorities	$42.5 million
Nabisco	8,000 women	$5 million
Leeway Motor Freight	Eighty-two black employees	$2.8 million
Federated Department Stores	Three employees	$2.3 million, plus attorney fees
Burlington Northern, Inc.	4,000 black employees	$10 million
Kemper Group	Female employees	$3 million
State Farm	Black employees	$4 million
Northwest Airlines	Female employees	$52.2 million
Geneva Tire and Rubber Company	Two female employees	$118,000, plus $138,000 attorneys' fees
Alabama Power Company	Black employees	$1.7 million

accused of discrimination do to limit the amount of back pay awarded? Consider the next case.

FORD MOTOR CO. v. EQUAL EMPLOYMENT OPPORTUNITY COMM.
102 S.Ct. 3057 (1982)

FACTS

In 1973, the Ford Motor Company offered picker-packer positions to two of the three women employees who had earlier applied for such jobs but had been denied them discriminatorily. The women declined because Ford refused to grant job seniority dating from their original applications in 1971. The women were terminated in 1974, and a district court awarded them back pay, including the amount accumulating after the dates on which they declined Ford's offer of employment.

ISSUE

Can an employer stop the continuing accumulation of back pay liability simply by unconditionally offering the Title VII claimant the job previously denied?

DECISION

Yes. The employer need not offer seniority retroactive to the date of the alleged discrimination in order to toll back-pay liability.

REASONS

1. The rule adopted by the district court does not promote Title VII's primary goal of getting employment discrimination victims into jobs they deserve as quickly as possible. The rule threatens the interests of other innocent employees by disrupting established seniority.

2. On the other hand, the rule that a Title VII claimant's rejection of an employer's job offer ends the employer's ongoing liability for back pay powerfully motivates employers to put claimants to work as soon as possible. It also satisfies Title VII's compensation goal.

In enacting Title VII, Congress made it clear that it did not intend to preempt states' fair employment laws. Where state agencies begin discrimination proceedings, the EEOC must wait sixty days before it starts action. Furthermore, if a state law provides relief to a discrimination charge, the EEOC must notify the appropriate state officials and wait sixty days before continuing action.

An employee must file charges of illegal discrimination with the EEOC within 180 days after the alleged unlawful practice occurred. If the EEOC does not act within a certain time period, the employee may personally file a civil action in federal district court against the employer.

A Title VII plaintiff must initially show that actions taken by the employer were likely based on an illegal discriminatory basis, such as race. For example, a Title VII violation may be established by showing that the defendant's employment policies or practices, even though applied equally to all job applicants, were nevertheless discriminatory in effect against a particular group. That is, the defendant selected applicants for hire or promotion in a pattern significantly different from that of racial minorities or women available in the pool of applicants. The employer can defeat the plaintiff's case by showing that the policies used are job-related and based on a legitimate consideration. However, the plaintiff may still prove a violation by showing that other selection devices or practices would serve the employer's legitimate interest in picking the right person for the right job, without having undesirable discriminatory effects.

Even though the employer's practices do not have a disparate impact on minorities, a plaintiff may also prove his or her case by showing: (1) that he or she belongs to a minority, (2) that he or she applied and was qualified for a job for which the employer was seeking applicants, (3) that despite his or her qualifications, he or she was rejected, and (4) that the job remained open and the employer continued to seek applicants from persons with the plaintiff's qualifications. Here, too, the employer can prevail by showing a legitimate nondiscriminatory reason for the plaintiff's rejection. For example, an employer would not be expected to fill the position of cashier with an applicant who had a prior record of embezzlement.

Current Trends

In recent years, the EEOC has reduced the number of *pattern and practice* cases it chooses to file. Based on statistical profiles of employer work forces by race and sex, these cases show bias through statistical imbalances rather than discriminatory intent. However, the EEOC has continued to prosecute individual complaints vigorously. Note that private plaintiffs can still maintain pattern and practice cases and that a change in presidential administration might cause the EEOC once again to involve itself in such cases on a large scale.

4 DISCRIMINATION ON THE BASIS OF RACE OR COLOR

The integration of blacks into the mainstream of American society was the primary objective of the Civil Rights Act of 1964. Title VII, which deals with employment practices, was recognized by Congress as being the key to achieving this goal. Without equal employment opportunities, blacks can hardly enjoy other guaranteed rights, such as access to public accommodations.

Title VII prohibits discriminatory employment practices based on race or color which involve *recruiting, hiring,* and *promotion* of employees. Of course, intentional discrimination in these matters is illegal, but as previously stated, **discrimination-in-effect** is also forbidden. Such discrimination arises from an employer's policies or practices which apply equally to everyone but which discriminate in greater proportion against minorities and have no relation to job qualification. Table 15-3 gives examples of discrimination-in-effect. Often at issue in discrimination-in-effect cases is whether a discriminatory policy or practice relates to job qualification. Courts require proof, not mere assertion, of job relatedness before upholding an employer's discriminatory personnel test or other practice.

The law also prohibits discrimination in *employment conditions* and *benefits*. EEOC decisions have found such practices as the following to be violations: permitting racial insults in the work situation; maintaining all-white or all-black crews for no demonstrable reasons; providing better housing for whites than blacks; and granting higher average Christmas bonuses to whites than blacks for reasons that were not persuasive to the Commission.

TABLE 15-3 EXAMPLES OF DISCRIMINATION-IN-EFFECT

1. Denying employment to unwed mothers where minorities have a higher rate of illegitimate births than whites
2. Refusing to hire people because of poor credit rating when minorities are disproportionately affected
3. Refusing to hire people with arrest records when minorities have higher arrest rates than whites
4. Giving hiring priority to relatives of present employees when minorities are underrepresented in the work force
5. Using discriminatory personnel tests which have no substantial relation to job qualification

5 DISCRIMINATION ON THE BASIS OF NATIONAL ORIGIN

Title VII's prohibition against national origin discrimination protects Hispanics and other ethnic groups in the population. Discrimination concerning the speaking of a native language is a frequent source of national-origin lawsuits.

For instance, courts have ruled illegal an employer's rule against speaking Spanish during working time without the employer's showing a business need to understand all conversations between Hispanic employees. On the other hand, some courts have held that if jobs require contact with the public, requirements that employees speak some English *may* be a bona fide occupational qualification.

Direct foreign investment in the United States has doubled and redoubled in recent years. This increasing investment has presented some unusual issues of employment discrimination law. For instance, many commercial treaties with foreign countries give foreign companies operating in the United States the right to hire executive-level employees "of their choice." Does this mean that foreign companies in the United States can discriminate as to their managerial employees on a basis forbidden under Title VII? In 1982, the Supreme Court partially resolved this issue by ruling that the civil rights laws applied to a Japanese company which did business through a subsidiary incorporated in this country.

6 DISCRIMINATION ON THE BASIS OF RELIGION

As was noted, religious corporations, associations, or societies can discriminate in all their employment practices on the basis of religion, but not on the basis of race, color, sex, or national origin. Other employers cannot discriminate on the basis of religion in employment practices, and they must make reasonable accommodation to the religious needs of their employees if it does not result in undue hardship to them. In the following case, the Supreme Court provided guidance on how far employers must go reasonably to accommodate religious needs of their workers.

TRANS WORLD AIRLINES, INC. v. HARDISON
97 S.Ct. 2264 (1977)

FACTS

Hardison worked in an essential job in a TWA department which operated around the clock every day of the year. It was subject to a seniority system in a collective-bargaining agreement between TWA and the union. Hardison joined a church whose members refrained from working on Saturdays. Hardison was asked to work Saturdays for a fellow employee on vacation, but he refused. The union was not willing to violate seniority rules by changing work assignments for Hardison, and TWA rejected a proposal that Hardison work only four days a week. The position had to be filled on Saturdays, and to employ a substitute would have required TWA to pay premium wages. Hardison was discharged for insubordination. The district court ruled in favor of TWA when Hardison filed this action. The court of appeals reversed, holding that TWA had not made reasonable accommodation to Hardison's religious needs and thus had violated Title VII.

ISSUE

Under the facts, was TWA guilty of discriminating in employment on the basis of religion by not making reasonable accommodation to Hardison's religious needs?

DECISION

No.

REASONS

1. There were no volunteers to relieve Hardison on Saturdays, and to give him that day off, TWA would have had to abandon the seniority system and deprive another employee of his shift preference, at least in part because he did not adhere to a religion that observed the Saturday Sabbath.
2. Or, TWA would have had to pay a replacement premium wages. To require TWA to bear additional costs when no such costs are incurred to give other employees their desired days off would involve unequal treatment of employees on the basis of their religion. The Court will not readily interpret the statute to require an employer to discriminate against some employees to enable others to observe their Sabbath.

In another case, the Supreme Court let stand a lower-court ruling that an employee cannot be required to pay union dues if she or he has religious objections to unions. There, it held that a union had violated the Civil Rights Act by forcing the company to fire a Seventh Day Adventist who did not comply with a collective-bargaining agreement term that all employees must pay union dues. This was despite the union's contention that it had made "reasonable accommodation" to the worker's religious needs by offering to give any dues paid by him to charity.

7 DISCRIMINATION ON THE BASIS OF SEX

Civil Rights Act

Historically, states have enacted many laws designed to supposedly protect women. For example, many states by statute have prohibited the employment of women in certain occupations such as those which require lifting heavy objects. Others have barred women from working during the night or more than a given number of hours per week or day. A federal district court held that a California state law which required rest periods for women only was in violation of Title VII. Some statutes prohibit employing women for a specified time after childbirth. Under EEOC guidelines, such statutes are not a defense to a charge of illegal sex discrimination and do not provide an employer with a bona fide occupational qualification in hiring standards. Other EEOC guidelines forbid employers: (1) to classify jobs as male or female and (2) to advertise in help-wanted columns that are designated male or female, unless sex is a bona fide job qualification. Similarly, employers may not have separate male and female seniority lists.

Table 15-4 gives examples of prohibited acts of sex discrimination under Title VII.

Whether sex is a bona fide occupational qualification (and discrimination is thus legal) has been raised in several cases. The courts have tended to consider this exception narrowly. In the following instances involving hiring policy, *no* bona fide occupational qualification was found to exist: a rule requiring airline stewardesses, but not stewards, to be single; a policy of hiring only females as flight-cabin attendants; a rule against hiring females with preschool-age children, but not against hiring males with such children; and a telephone company policy against hiring females as switchmen because of the alleged heavy lifting involved in the job. In this latter instance, the court held that for a bona fide occupational qualification to exist, there must be "reasonable cause to believe, that is, a factual basis for believing, that all or substantially all women would be unable to perform safely and efficiently the duties of the job involved." The Supreme Court has indicated that for such a qualification to exist, sex must be provably relevant to job performance.

Pregnancy Discrimination Act

The Pregnancy Discrimination Act amended the Civil Rights Act in 1978. Under it, employers can no longer discriminate against women workers

TABLE 15-4   EXAMPLES OF ILLEGAL SEX DISCRIMINATION

1 A radio station's refusing to hire a female newscaster because "news coming from a woman sounds like gossip"
2 A bank's allowing males but not females to smoke at their desks
3 A utility company's allowing women to retire at age fifty, while requiring men to wait until age fifty-five
4 A company's failing to promote women to overseas positions because foreign clients were reluctant to do business with women
5 A hospital's firing a pregnant x-ray technician for health reasons instead of giving her a leave of absence
6 A company's failure to stop repeated, offensive sexual flirtations on the part of some of its employees

who become pregnant or give birth. Thus, employers with health or disability plans must cover pregnancy, childbirth, and related medical conditions in the same manner other conditions are covered. The law covers unmarried as well as married pregnant women. It also states that an employer cannot force a pregnant woman to stop working until her baby is born, provided she is still capable of performing her duties properly. And, the employer cannot specify how long a leave of absence must be taken after childbirth. Coverage for abortion is not required by the statute, unless an employee carries to term and her life is endangered, or she develops medical complications because of an abortion. If a woman undergoes an abortion, though, all other benefits provided for employees, such as sick leave, must be provided to her.

Note that sex discrimination applies to discrimination against men as well as against women. Consider the following case decided by the Supreme Court in 1983.

NEWPORT NEWS SHIPBUILDING AND DRY DOCK CO. v. EEOC
103 S.Ct. 487 (1983)

FACTS

Title VII was amended in 1978 by the Pregnancy Discrimination Act to prohibit sex discrimination on the basis of pregnancy. To comply with the act, an employer changed its health insurance plan to provide its female employees with hospitalization benefits for pregnancy-related conditions to the same extent as for other medical problems. Spouses of male employees, however, were given less comprehensive pregnancy coverage. EEOC guidelines indicated that the amended plan was unlawful, and the employer filed suit. The district court upheld the lawfulness of the plan and enjoined enforcement of the EEOC guidelines. The court of appeals reversed, finding that the plan illegally discriminated. The Supreme Court granted certiorari.

ISSUE

Did the employer's health insurance plan discriminate against the male employees because of sex, which is in violation of Title VII?

DECISION

Yes.

REASONS

1. Under the health insurance plan, the husbands of female employees received a fixed level of hospitalization benefits for all conditions. The wives of male employees receive the same coverage except for pregnancy-related conditions. When Congress enacted the Pregnancy Discrimination Act, it made it clear that exclusion of pregnancy-related conditions from a plan that covers other medical conditions is discrimination.

> 2. Therefore, the employer's plan unlawfully gives married female employees a benefits package that is more extensive than the coverage given married male employees.

Equal Pay Act

Other federal legislation which pertains to sex discrimination in employment includes the *Equal Pay Act of 1963*. Presently administered by the EEOC, the act prohibits an employer from discriminating on the basis of sex in the payment of wages for equal work performed. For jobs to be equal, they must require "equal skill, effort, and responsibility" and must be performed "under similar working conditions." Discrimination is allowed if it arises from a seniority system, a merit system, a piecework production system, or on any factor other than sex.

The focus of Equal Pay Act cases is whether the male and female jobs being compared involve "equal" work. Courts have recognized that *equal* does not mean *identical*, it means *substantially* equal. Thus, courts have ruled "equal" the work of male barbers and female beauticians and of male tailors and female seamstresses. Differences in male and female job descriptions will not totally protect employers against charges of equal pay infractions. The courts have held that "substantially equal" work done on different machines would require the employer to compensate male and female employees equally.

In 1983, the Supreme Court ruled that discriminatory male and female pay differences can also be illegal under Title VII. In *County of Washington v. Gunther,* the Court decided that plaintiffs can use evidence of such pay differences to help prove intentional sex discrimination, even where the work performed is not "substantially equal." Relying on the *Gunther* case, several lower courts have held that women must be paid equally with men who perform comparable work. For instance, a federal district court ruled that the state of Washington discriminated against secretaries (mostly women) by paying them less than maintenance and other personnel (mostly men). The **comparable worth** theory is highly controversial and has not yet been upheld by the Supreme Court.

EMPLOYMENT PRACTICES WHICH MAY BE CHALLENGED

8 TESTING AND EDUCATIONAL REQUIREMENTS

Employers have used a number of tools to help them find the right person for the right job in hiring and promoting employees. Among these are interviews, references, minimum educational requirements (such as a high school diploma), and personnel tests. Obviously, interviewers can be biased, even if they try not to be.

One study indicated that interviewers tended to select tall men for sales positions because interviewers *subconsciously* related height with potential sales success. References may not be so reliable, either. A previous employer's letter may reflect personal biases against an applicant that were not related to job performance.

At the other extreme, an employer may give a poor employee a top recommendation because of sympathy or fear of a lawsuit in case the letter is somehow obtained by the employee. Advocates of personnel tests in the selection process feel they are very valuable in weeding out the wrong persons for a job and picking the right ones. They believe reliance on tests results eliminates biases which interviewers or former employers who give references may have. However, as the following case indicates, even where "bottom line" employment practices of the employer favor the group alleging discrimination, test use may be illegal under Title VII.

CONNECTICUT v. TEAL
102 S.Ct. 2525 (1982)

FACTS

Connecticut law required that to obtain permanent status as a state agency supervisor, a written exam must first be passed. Thirty-four percent of the black candidates and 79 percent of the white candidates passed, but the plaintiff black employees failed the exam and alleged that the discriminatory test violated Title VII. The defendant, the state of Connecticut, entered evidence showing that more blacks than whites actually were promoted from the eligibility list and urged that this "bottom line" result was a complete defense to the discrimination suit. The defendant won in the trial court, but the court of appeals reversed the decision.

ISSUE

Does the "bottom line" theory prevent employees from establishing its discrimination case and provide the employer with a complete defense to such a case?

DECISION

No. The state of Connecticut's nondiscriminatory "bottom line" theory is rejected.

REASONS

1. In considering claims of disparate impact under Title VII, the focus has been consistently on employment and promotion requirements that create a discriminatory bar to *opportunities*. The focus has never been placed on the overall number of minority or female applicants actually hired or promoted. Such an interpretation would narrow unduly the broad scope of Title VII that Congress intended.
2. Therefore, the plaintiffs' statutory rights have been violated, unless the state of Connecticut can show that the examination given was not an

> artificial, arbitrary, or unnecessary barrier and that it measured necessary job-related skills.

As a result of court decisions and government enforcement guidelines, many companies have eliminated or sharply reduced testing as an employment tool, because compliance is too costly and time-consuming. Even if companies obtain what appears to be proper evidence that a given test is valid, the threat of a court challenge, with its costs and bad publicity, would still exist.

9 HEIGHT AND WEIGHT REQUIREMENTS

Minimum or maximum height or weight job requirements apply equally to all job applicants, but if they have the effect of screening out applicants on the basis of race, national origin, or sex, the employer must demonstrate that such requirements are validly related to the ability to perform the work in question. For example, maximum size standards would be permissible, even if they favored women over men, if the available work space were too small to permit larger persons to perform the duties of the job properly. Most size requirements have dictated minimum heights or weights, often based on a stereotyped assumption that a certain amount of strength probably was necessary for the work that smaller persons might not have. In one case, a 5-foot, 5-inch, 130-pound Hispanic man won a suit against a police department on the basis that the department's 5-foot, 8-inch minimum height requirement discriminated against Hispanics, who often are shorter than that standard. Later, he was hired when he passed the department's physical agility examination, which included dragging a 150-pound body 75 feet and scaling a 6-foot wall.

In the following case, the Supreme Court considered the legality of Alabama's statutory minimum height and weight requirements for prison guards, along with a Board of Corrections regulation which expressly limited prison jobs to men.

DOTHARD v. RAWLINSON
97 S.Ct. 2720 (1977)

FACTS

Rawlinson, a 22-year-old college graduate, applied for employment as a prison guard in Alabama. Although she had majored in correctional psychology, her application was rejected because she failed to meet the minimum 120-pound requirement of the applicable Alabama statute, which also established a height minimum of 5 feet, 2 inches. Rawlinson filed suit, challenging the height and weight requirements of the statute and Regulation 204 of the Alabama Board of Corrections, which provided that only males could be assigned as prison guards to maximum security institutions for "contact positions" that required physical closeness to inmates.

ISSUE

1. Do the height and weight requirements discriminate against women illegally?
2. Does Regulation 204 discriminate against women illegally?

DECISIONS

1. Yes.
2. No.

REASONS

1. The argument that the height and weight requirements have a necessary relationship to strength (which is essential to effective job performance as a prison guard) is without merit. A less discriminatory test which measures strength directly should be adopted.
2. However, Regulation 204 states a bfoq. In a prison system where violence is common each day, inmate access to guards is made easier by dormitory living arrangements. Since every institution is understaffed and a substantial portion of the inmates are sex offenders, there is little to stop inmate assaults on women guards. Therefore, the use of women as guards in "contact" positions poses a substantial security problem, directly linked to the sex of the prison guard.

Even though the Supreme Court found that sex was a bona fide occupational qualification in *Rawlinson,* note that the bfoq exception is narrowly interpreted.

10 APPEARANCE REQUIREMENTS

Employers often have set grooming standards for their employees. Those regulating hair length of males or prohibiting beards or mustaches have been among the most common. Undoubtedly, motivation for these rules stems from the feeling of the employer that the image it projects to the public through its employees will be adversely affected if their appearance is not "proper." It is unclear whether appearance requirements are legal or illegal, since there have been rulings both ways. Refusing to hire applicants because of a company policy prohibiting "handlebar" and "Fu Manchu" mustaches and bushy hairstyles was found illegal. Although the policies appeared neutral on their face, it was held that they had the effect of discriminating against blacks.

In another case, a black employee argued that he was wrongfully fired for breaking a company rule prohibiting beards. Dermatologists testified that the plaintiff had a condition called "razor bumps" (which occurs when the tightly curled facial hairs of black men become ingrown from shaving) and that the only known cure was for him not to shave. Although the federal appeals court found that the plaintiff was prejudiced by the employer's regulation, it held in favor of the company, ruling that its "slight racial impact" was justified by the "business purpose" it served. However, a conflicting opinion in still another case upheld an employee's right to wear a beard because of razor bumps.

11 AFFIRMATIVE ACTION PROGRAMS AND REVERSE DISCRIMINATION

Affirmative Action

Since the 1940s, a series of presidential executive orders have promoted nondiscrimination and affirmative action by employers who contract with the federal government. The authority for these orders rests with the President's executive power to control the granting of federal contracts. As a condition to obtaining such contracts, employers must agree contractually to take affirmative action to avoid unlawful discrimination in recruitment, employment, promotion, training, rate of compensation, and layoff of workers.

The **affirmative action** requirement means that federally contracting employers must actively recruit members of minority groups being underused in the work force. That is, employers must hire members of these groups when there are fewer minority workers in a given job category than one could reasonably expect, considering their availability. In many instances, employers must develop written affirmative action plans and set goals and timetables for bringing minority (or female) work forces up to their percentages in the available labor pool.

The Labor Department administers executive orders through its Office of Federal Contract Compliance Programs (OFCCP). The OFCCP can terminate federal contracts with employers who do not comply with its guidelines and can make them ineligible for any future federal business. For instance, it required Uniroyal, Inc., to give its female employees an estimated $18 million in back pay to compensate for past employment discrimination. The alternative was elimination of $36 million of existing federal contracts and ineligibility for future federal business.

In the early 1980s, the Labor Department eased OFCCP regulations on 75 percent of the firms which do business with the federal government. Firms with fewer than 250 employees and federal contracts of under $1 million no longer must prepare written affirmative action plans for hiring women and minorities. The OFCCP has also begun to limit its use of back-pay awards to specific individuals who can show an actual loss due to violation of OFCCP guidelines.

Reverse Discrimination

Not all affirmative action programs are imposed on employers by the government. Many employers have adopted programs voluntarily or through collective-bargaining agreements with unions. Sometimes these affirmative action programs have subjected employers to charges of **reverse discrimination** when minorities or women with lower qualifications or less seniority than white males are given preference in employment or training. Even though such programs are intended to remedy the effects of present or past discrimination or other barriers to equal employment opportunity, white males have argued that the law does not permit employers to discriminate against *them* on the basis of race or sex any more than it allows discrimination against minorities or women.

In *United Steelworkers of America v. Weber,* the Supreme Court ruled legal under Title VII a voluntary affirmative action plan between an employer and a union. The plan required that at least 50 percent of certain new work trainees be black. The Court noted that the plan did not require that white employees be fired or excluded altogether from advancement. It was only a temporary measure to eliminate actual racial imbalance in the work force.

The *Weber* case provoked much controversy. Some scholars questioned whether the Supreme Court might reverse *Weber* or limit its application. In further upholding affirmation action against charges of reverse discrimination, the next case seems to answer those questions.

JOHNSON v. SANTA CLARA COUNTY TRANSPORTATION AGENCY
55 LW 4379 (March 25, 1987)

FACTS

The Santa Clara County Transportation Agency (Agency) operated under a voluntary affirmative action plan for hiring and promoting minorities and women. When the Agency announced a job vacancy for a road dispatcher position, none of the 238 positions in the relevant job category was held by a woman. Under its affirmative action plan, the Agency finally selected a well-qualified woman for the road dispatcher position. Paul Johnson, one of the men passed over for the position, sued the Agency and alleged illegal discrimination under Title VII.

ISSUE

Did the Agency's decision to take the woman's sex into consideration in promoting her violate Title VII?

DECISION

No.

REASONS

1. Once a plaintiff shows that race or sex has been a factor in an employment decision, the employer must prove a nondiscriminatory reason for its decision. A valid affirmative action plan provides such a reason.

2. In justifying its affirmative action plan, an employer need not point to its own prior discrimination. Proving that minorities or women are significantly underrepresented in a job category is sufficient.
3. The Agency's plan did not unnecessarily limit the rights of male employees. It did not absolutely prohibit job promotion for them. It simply provided that the sex of employees might be one factor taken into account in appropriate circumstances.
4. An affirmative action plan need be temporary only if it sets aside specific job positions on the basis of race or sex. The Agency's plan sought only measureable annual improvements in traditionally segregated job categories.

The EEOC has issued guidelines intended to protect employers who set up affirmative action plans. This indicates that Title VII is not violated if an employer determines that there is a reasonable basis for concluding that such a plan is appropriate, and the employer takes "reasonable" affirmative action. For example, if an employer discovers that it has a job category where one might expect to find more women and minorities employed than are actually in its work force, the employer has a reasonable basis for affirmative action.

In an affirmative action move intended to help minority-owned businesses, Congress passed the 1977 Public Works employment plan. This requires that 10 percent of the work on federally funded, local, public works projects be performed by minority contractors or subcontractors. Contractor groups attacked the 10 percent requirement as an unconstitutional form of reverse discrimination, in violation of the Fifth and Fourteenth Amendments. However, in 1980 the Supreme Court upheld validity of the requirement.

12 SENIORITY SYSTEMS

Seniority systems give priority to those employees who have worked longer for a particular employer, or in a particular line of employment of the employer. Employers may institute seniority systems on their own, but in a union shop they are usually the result of collective bargaining. Their terms are spelled out in the agreement between the company and the union. Seniority systems often determine the calculation of vacation, pension, and other fringe benefits. They also control many employment decisions such as the order in which employees may choose shifts or qualify for promotions or transfers to different jobs. They also are used to select the persons to be laid off when an employer is reducing its labor force. As aresult of seniority, the last hired are usually the first fired. Decisions based on seniority have in recent years been challenged as violating the laws relating to equal employment opportunity. Challenges often arose when recently hired members of minority groups were laid off during periods of economic downturn. Firms with successful affirmative action programs often lost most of their minority employees.

Section 703(h) of the Civil Rights Act of 1964 provides that, not withstanding other provisions in the act, it is not an unlawful employment practice for an employer to apply different employment standards pursuant to a bona fide (good faith) seniority system if the differences are not the result of an *intention* to discriminate. The issue in the following case is whether a seniority system can be used if it has a discriminatory impact on minorities and was instituted after the adoption of an affirmative action plan.

MEMPHIS FIRE DEPT. v. SHOTTS
52 L.W. 4767 (1984)

FACTS

In 1980, the city of Memphis made a settlement in a class action suit in federal district court. The settlement agreed to affirmative action in the hiring and promotion of blacks in the fire department. In 1981, the city announced that budget deficits made it necessary to lay off a certain number of city employees under a last hired, first fired rule of the city's seniority plan. The district court ordered the city to modify its layoff plans so as to protect black firefighters hired or promoted by affirmative action. The court of appeals affirmed, and the Supreme Court agreed to hear the case.

ISSUE

Did the district court exceed its powers in requiring the city to modify layoff plans under its seniority plan to protect affirmative action?

DECISION

Yes.

REASONS

1. Title VII permits employers to apply a seniority plan to employees, even if such application discriminates against minorities, as long as the seniority plan is not a result of intentional racial discrimination. The seniority plan here was a bona fide plan.
2. If individual members of a plaintiff class show that they have been victims of discrimination, they may be granted competitive seniority, but none of the individuals here made such a showing.

OTHER STATUTES AND DISCRIMINATION IN EMPLOYMENT

13 CIVIL RIGHTS ACT OF 1866

An important federal law which complements Title VII of the 1964 Civil Rights Act is the Civil Rights Act of 1866. One provision of that act, known as **Section 1981,** provides that "all persons...shall have the same right to make and enforce contracts...as enjoyed by white citizens." Since union memberships and employment relationships involve contracts, Section 1981 bans racial discrimination in these areas.

The courts have interpreted Section 1981 as giving a private plaintiff most of the same protections against racial discrimination that the 1964 Civil Rights Act provides. In addition, there are at least two advantages to the plaintiff who files a suit based on Section 1981. First, there are no procedural requirements for bringing such a suit, while there are a number of fairly complex requirements plaintiffs must follow before bringing a private suit under Title VII. For instance, they must file charges of discrimination with the EEOC within 180 days after the illegal practice occurs, or they will lose their rights.

By using Section 1981, a plaintiff can immediately sue an employer in federal court but need not worry about losing rights if he or she fails to do so within 180 days. A second advantage to Section 1981 is that under it the courts can award damages to aggrieved plaintiffs. Although it permits recovery of back pay, Title VII does not allow for the assessment of damages. As a practical matter, parties alleging discrimination usually proceed under both Section 1981 and Title VII.

Note that Section 1981 does not cover discrimination based on sex, religion, national origin, age, or handicap. As interpreted by the courts, this section applies only to *racial* discrimination. However, what is race? The Supreme Court addressed that question in the following case.

SAINT FRANCIS COLLEGE v. AL-KHAZRAJI

55 LW 4626 (May 18, 1987)

FACTS

Al-Khazraji, a United States citizen born in Iraq, sued his employer, Saint Francis College. He alleged that he was improperly denied tenure as a professor because of his Arabian race.

ISSUE

Is being of Arabian ancestry a racial characteristic that brings one under the protection of Section 1981?

DECISION

Yes.

REASONS

1. Although Section 1981 does not use the word "race," it forbids only racial discrimination in the making of contracts.
2. The concept of race was different when Congress passed Section 1981 than it is today. Nineteenth-century encyclopedias and dictionaries, as well as

> the legislative history of Section 1981, show that the concept of race when Section 1981 was passed included the descendants of a particular "family, tribe, people, or nation." Race was not limited to major divisions of humanity based on physical characteristics and color.
> 3. If Al-Khazraji can prove that he was intentionally discriminated against because he was born an Arab, he will be protected under Section 1981.

Under this same type of analysis, the Supreme Court has also held that being of Jewish ancestry constitutes a race. Question: Does the *Al-Khazraji* case open the door for a white job applicant to sue a black employer for discrimination under Section 1981?

14 DISCRIMINATION ON THE BASIS OF AGE

Neither the Civil Rights Act nor the Equal Employment Opportunity Act forbids discrimination based on age. In 1967, however, Congress passed the Age Discrimination in Employment Act, which protects persons between forty and sixty-five years old from job discrimination against them because of their age. The act is enforced by the EEOC.

In 1986, Congress amended the act to prohibit mandatory retirement of employees at any age. Firefighters and police officers may still be forced into retirement under certain circumstances until 1993. Bona fide executives and high policymakers of private companies who will have pensions of at least $27,000 per year also can be forced into early retirement. The statute invalidates retirement plans and labor contracts that call for retirement in violation of the act.

In one case under the act, Standard Oil Company of California agreed to pay $2 million in back wages to 160 employees who had been laid off and were over forty. Thus, if persons over forty are just as qualified as younger workers to handle their jobs, they usually must be kept. To cut costs, some companies have discriminated against older, higher-ranking, and higher-paid employees by replacing them with younger, lower-salaried persons who are equally competent to handle the job. This cost-cutting is also illegal. One decision awarded three former department store executives $2.3 million for such discrimination. In another case, a firm transferred a sixty-year-old man to a job that required him to stand for long periods. When he died, his widow, arguing that the transfer was a subterfuge to induce him to retire, obtained a judgment against the firm for $750,000 in damages for illegal age discrimination.

An important area of age discrimination litigation exists when age is a bona fide occupational qualification. It is recognized that as people grow older their physical strength, agility, reflexes, hearing, and vision tend to diminish in quality. However, this generally provides no legal reason for discriminating against older persons as a class. Although courts will uphold job-related physical requirements if they apply on a case-by-case basis, they frequently find as illegal those policies which prohibit the hiring of persons beyond a maximum age, or which establish a maximum age beyond which employees are forced to retire for physical reasons. Thus, one court ruled that a mandatory retirement age of sixty-five was illegally discriminatory as applied to the job of district fire chief. To the contrary, another court ruled that the airlines could impose a maximum age for hiring a new pilot in light of a Federal Aviation Administration mandated retirement age for pilots.

Courts have disagreed on whether remedies for violation of the act include, in addition to reinstatement and wages lost, damages for the psychological trauma of being fired or forced to resign illegally. One federal district court awarded $200,000 to a victim of age discrimination who was an inventor and scientist, for the psychological and physical effects suffered from being forced into early retirement at age sixty. Also awarded were out-of-pocket costs of $60,000 and attorney's fees of $65,000. Note that "willful" violations of the act entitle discrimination victims to *double damages*.

Since the 1978 amendments to the act, age discrimination claims have grown rapidly. In recent years, they have more than doubled in number.

15 DISCRIMINATION ON THE BASIS OF HANDICAPS

To promote and expand employment opportunities for handicapped persons, both in the public and private sectors, Congress enacted the Rehabilitation Act of 1973. This statute requires each department and agency in the executive branch of the federal government to have an approved affirmative action plan for the hiring, placement, and advancement of qualified handicapped individuals. And under Section 503 of the Rehabilitation Act, every employer doing business with the federal government under a contract for over $2,500 must take affirmative action to hire and advance qualified handicapped persons at all levels, including executive. Section 503 affects about one-half the businesses in the United States and the twelve million or so employable handicapped persons in the population.

A handicapped person protected by the act is anyone with a physical or mental impairment which substantially limits a major life activity (such as a blind, deaf, paraplegic, or mentally retarded person), or one who has a *record of* such an impairment (this would include a rehabilitated mental patient or a person with a history of cancer or heart condition). *All* such handicapped persons are not covered, however. An individual must be "qualified," or capable of performing a particular job, with reasonable accommodation to his or her handicap. And an amendment to the act specifically provides that the term "handicapped individual" does not include any individual who is an alcoholic or drug abuser.

Both contractors and subcontractors must make "reasonable accommodation" to the physical and mental limitations of handicapped employees or applicants, unless it can be shown that such would involve an "undue hardship" to them. The cost of any necessary workplace accommodation and availability of alternatives bear upon the issue of undue hardship.

The Department of Labor's Office of Federal Contract Compliance Programs can enforce Section 503 of the act by forcing settlements of claims of discrimination by handicapped workers. Claims may be settled by hiring the claimants with payment of back wages and retroactive seniority, or the like. In an extreme case, the government contract with the offending employer can be terminated.

Section 504 of the Rehabilitation Act prohibits discrimination against a handicapped person under any program receiving federal financial assistance. Section 504 applies to a great many state and local government programs that receive federal grants. Private organizations receiving federal assistance are also affected. Although the next case was brought under Section 504, it has significance as well for private employers under Section 503. For the first time, the Supreme Court rules that a contagious disease can make one a "handicapped person."

NASSAU COUNTY SCHOOL BOARD v. ARLINE
107 S.Ct. 1123 (1987)

FACTS

Gene Arline was hospitalized for tuberculosis in 1957. Following her hospitalization, she began teaching elementary school in Florida. In 1977 and 1978, Arline had relapses of tuberculosis. The school board at first suspended her with pay. Finally, the board discharged her because of the tuberculosis. Arline brought suit under the Rehabilitation Act.

ISSUE

Does Arline's contagious tuberculosis make her a "handicapped person" protected under the Rehabilitation Act?

DECISION

Yes.

REASONS

1. Arline's tuberculosis affects her respiratory system and substantially limits one or more of her "major life activities." Her hospitalizations establish a record of impairment because of her disease.
2. The fact that she is contagious does not remove her from the Rehabilitation Act's coverage. Others' fear of her disease does not permit her employer's discrimination so long as she is "qualified" for her job.
3. Specific medical findings should be made to determine whether Arline is qualified for her job.

The *Arline* case is especially important because of the spread of AIDS. As of now, there are cases pending in the federal court system brought by employees with AIDS against their former employers.

16 OTHER FEDERAL LEGISLATION

Other federal legislation dealing with employment discrimination includes the National Labor Relations Act. The NLRB has ruled that appeals to racial prejucide in a collective-bargaining representation election constitute an unfair labor practice. The NLRB has also revoked the certification of unions which practice discriminatory admission or representation policies. Additionally, employers have an obligation to bargain with certified unions over matters of employment discrimination. Such matters are considered "terms and conditions of employment" and are thus mandatory bargaining issues. Note that the reverse discrimination issue in the *Weber* case (p. 438) arose because of an affirmative action plan in a collective-bargaining contract.

Finally, various other federal agencies may prohibit discriminatory employment practices under their authorizing statutes. The Federal Communications Commission, for example, has prohibited employment discrimination by its licensees (radio and TV stations) and has required the submission of affirmative action plans as a condition of license renewal.

17 STATE DISCRIMINATION LAWS

Federal laws concerning equal employment opportunity specifically permit state laws which impose additional duties and liabilities. In recent years, fair employment practices legislation has been introduced and passed by many state legislatures. At the time the federal Equal Employment Opportunity Act became effective, forty states had such laws, but their provisions varied considerably. A typical state act makes it an unfair employment practice for any employer to refuse to hire or otherwise discriminate against any individual because of his or her race, color, religion, national origin, or ancestry. If employment agencies or labor organizations discriminate against an individual in any way because of one of the foregoing reasons, they are also guilty of an unfair employment practice. State acts usually set up an administrative body, generally known as the Fair Employment Practices Commission, which has the power to make rules and regulations and hear and decide charges of violations filed by complainants.

In addition, many states have enacted equal pay statutes similar to the federal one, but these have not proved to be very effective.

18 AVOIDING UNFOUNDED DISCRIMINATION CLAIMS

Much discrimination in effect, and even intentional discrimination, occurs in employment situations. But most employers strive to obey equal employment laws. These employers still face discrimination claims, however, including many made by unsatisfactory employees who have been discharged or disciplined. How can employers protect themselves from unfounded discrimination claims in such instances? The best protection is a system of adequate documentation. Sometimes called the **paper fortress,** this documentation consists of job descriptions, personnel manuals, and employee personnel files.

Before handing anyone an employment application, the employer should insist that the person carefully study a job description. A well-written job description will help potential applicants eliminate themselves from job situations for which they lack interest or qualification. Applicant self-elimination helps employers later avoid having to dismiss disinterested or unqualified employees, which can lead to discrimination claims.

Once a new employee is hired, the employer should give the employee a personnel manual. This manual should include information about employee benefits and should also outline work rules and job requirements. The employer should go over the manual with the employee and answer any questions. Clear identification of employer expectations and policies helps provide a defense against discrimination claims if subsequent discipline or discharge of the employee becomes necessary. The employer should ask that the employee sign a form indicating receipt of the manual and the employer's explanation of its contents.

The employer should enter this form, with all other documentation relevant to an employee's work history, in the employee's personnel file. Regular written evaluations of employee performance should also be entered in the personnel file. A chronological record of unsatisfactory work performance is a very useful defense against an unjustified claim of employment discrimination following discipline or discharge.

Another piece of documentation which helps justify employer decisions in light of equal employment law is the written warning. Anytime an employee breaks a work rule or performs unsatisfactorily, the employer should issue the employee a written warning and should place a duplicate in the personnel file. The warning should explain specifically where the employee went wrong, that is, what work rule the employee violated, and it should give the employee the opportunity to place a letter of explanation in the personnel file. Employers should either have an employee sign that he or she has received a warning, or else note in the personnel file that the employee has received a copy of it.

Congress did not intend for equal employment laws to prevent employers from discharging unsatisfactory employees. Whatever the employee's race, sex, religion, or ethnic background, the employer should not hesitate to terminate the employee for unacceptable performance. In an actual termination conversation, however, the employer should provide the employee with specific reasons for discharge, taken from the personnel file. The employee should also be encouraged to succeed in other employment.

In combating unfounded discrimination claims, an adequate system of documentation is vital. However, other things are also important, such as having a specific company policy coupled with an effective employment program promoting nondiscrimination. Caterpillar has such a policy in its Code of Ethics.

An Effective Employment Program

We aspire to a high standard of excellence in human relationships. Specifically, we intend to select and place employees on the basis of qualifications for the work to be performed—without discrimination in terms of race, religion, national origin, color, sex, age, or handicap unrelated to the task at hand.

REVIEW QUESTIONS

1 For each term in the left-hand column, match the most appropriate description in the right-hand column:

  (1) Affirmative action   (a) Selection of employees for hire or promotion in a pattern significantly different from that of racial minorities or women available in the pool of job applicants
  (2) Comparable worth   (b) Documentation including job descriptions, personnel manuals, and employee personnel files
  (3) Paper fortress   (c) Job-related employment characteristics based on sex or religion
  (4) Seniority system   (d) A theory under which employees are paid equally based on jobs which are dissimilar but are rated equally
  (5) Reverse discrimination   (e) Taking active steps to seek out and employ groups traditionally underrepresented in the work force
  (6) Discrimination in effect   (f) A system to give priority to those employees who have worked longer for a particular employer
  (7) Bfoqs   (g) Prohibits contractual discrimination based on race
  (8) Section 1981   (h) Employment discrimination against white males

2 Historically, employers could discriminate against employees and job applicants for any reason. Discuss the series of legal developments that changed this historic right of employers in the employment discrimination area.

3 Jennings Company, which manufactures sophisticated electronic equipment, hires its assembly employees on the basis of applicants' scores on a standardized mathematics aptitude test. It has been shown that those who scored higher on the test almost always perform better on the job. However, it has also been dem-

onstrated that the use of the test in hiring employees has the effect of excluding blacks and other minority groups. Is this practice of the Jennings Company prohibited by the Civil Rights Act of 1964?

4. Martel, a competent male secretary to the president of ICU, was fired because the new president of the company believed it would be more appropriate to have a female secretary.

   (a) Has a violation of the law occurred?

   (b) Assume that a violation of the law has occurred and Martel decides to take an extended vacation after he is fired. Upon his return seven months later, Martel files suit in federal district court against ICU, charging illegal discrimination under the Civil Rights Act of 1964. What remedies will be available to him under the act?

5. A male supervisor at Star Company makes repeated offensive sexual remarks to female employees. The employees complain to higher management, which ignores the complaints. If the company does not discharge or otherwise penalize the employee, has it violated Title VII? Discuss.

6. The Acme Corporation has a hiring policy of giving preference to the relatives of present company employees. Does this policy violate Title VII? Explain what you need to know to answer this question fully.

7. ADCO, an advertising agency, asked an employment agency to refer females to it who might be suitable to play the role of Mother Nature in a TV commercial ADCO was preparing. The agency referred five women to ADCO, one of whom was selected for the part. Has either ADCO or the employment agency violated the Civil Rights Act?

8. Muscles-Are-You, Inc., a bodybuilding spa targeted primarily toward male bodybuilders, refused to hire a woman for the position of executive director. The spa's management stated that the executive director must have a "macho" image to relate well with the spa's customers. Discuss whether it is likely that the spa has violated Title VII.

9. Ortega, an employee of ABC, Inc., recently joined a church which forbids working on Saturdays, Sundays, and Mondays. Ortega requested that his employer change his work schedule from eight-hour days, Monday through Friday, to ten-hour days, Tuesday through Friday. Ortega's request was refused because the employer was in operation only eight hours per day, five days a week. After a month during which Ortega failed to work on Mondays, he was fired, since the employer said that "only a full-time employee would be acceptable" for Ortega's position. What are Ortega's legal rights, if any?

10. Assume that the degree of job difficulty for secretaries and maintenance personnel is approximately the same. If your state pays secretaries (mostly women) an average salary which is $2,000 below that of maintenance personnel (mostly men), has it violated employment discrimination laws?

11. Tartel, Inc., had been guilty of flagrant discrimination against blacks in its hiring, promotion, and compensation of employees before the Civil Rights Act of 1964 was passed. After the act, Tartel decided to remedy the situation and place blacks in 50 percent of all new openings created by expansion, or by the retirement, resignation, or death of persons in its almost exclusively white work force. Discuss the legality of Tartel's action.

12. Your company has traditionally hired males to do its assembly-line work. The

assembly-line positions include some jobs which require lifting and some that do not. Males are rotated between these jobs, all male workers being on the same pay scale. The company has recently started to hire females for the assembly line, but they only work in nonlifting positions. For this reason, they are paid a lower wage scale than the men. The women employees sue. Discuss the considerations a court deciding the case should take into account.

13 Cantrell, the controller of Xylec's, Inc., was forced to retire at age fifty-eight due to a general company policy. Although Cantrell had a company pension of $50,000 per year, she felt that her lifestyle would soon be hampered due to inflation, since the pension provided for no cost-of-living increases. What are Cantrell's rights, if any?

14 The owner of Harold's Restaurant refuses to hire a job applicant because he is Hispanic. Can the job applicant immediately sue the owner in federal district court? Explain.

15 Ralph Torrison is a systems analyst for the Silicon Corporation, a major defense contractor. When Ralph's co-workers learn that he has AIDS, six of them quit work immediately. Fearing that additional resignations will delay production, the company discharges Ralph. Discuss whether or not the company has acted legally.

16 You have just been hired as personnel manager of a medium-sized corporation. Discuss what steps you can take to shield your company from unfounded claims of employment discrimination.

CHAPTER 16

RIGHT TO UNION ACTIVITY

OVERVIEW

This chapter and the next one cover the topic of labor law and the rights of workers to bargain collectively. The subject matter is labor-management relations. The goal of labor law is successful collective bargaining. Collective bargaining is the process by which labor and management negotiate and reach agreements on matters of importance to both. The chapter emphasizes the rights of workers to engage in union activity.

This chapter considers the basic statutes which have been enacted by Congress to regulate labor-management relations. The next chapter examines various violations of these laws and the sanctions which may be imposed for such violations. Most of the legal principles involved in labor law have been developed at the federal level because of the need for national uniformity in this field. The National Labor Relations Board has the primary responsibility for enforcing these statutes, and you should pay special attention to this very important administrative agency.

This chapter introduces the following terms used in labor law: closed shop, collective bargaining, eighty-day cooling-off period, Landrum-Griffin Act, right-to-work law, Taft-Hartley Act, unfair labor practices, union shop, Wagner Act, and yellow-dog contract.

1 INTRODUCTION

Various statutes governing labor-management relations have been enacted by Congress to provide a framework in which management and labor can collectively make decisions on issues of importance to both. Such issues include wages to be paid workers, hours to be worked, and other terms and conditions of employment. This framework also recognizes that the public has an important stake in a workable system of **collective bargaining,** since it benefits not only employers and employees, but the public interest as well. Because collective bargaining only can be successful if the bargaining power of the parties is equal, most laws regulating labor-management relations seek to equalize this bargaining power. As a result, some laws add to the bargaining position of labor while others add to that of management.

At the outset, understand that the law encourages workers to join together and bargain as a group with employers. This encouragement of union activity is the logical result of the inequality of bargaining power between any single employee and a business. Unions have had a significant impact on wages, hours, and conditions of employment, not only in unionized industries, but also in those which are not. Labor laws generally require employers to bargain with unions. The depth of this policy requirement is demonstrated in the case which follows; it held that a successor company is required to bargain with the union representing its predecessor's employees.

FALL RIVER DYEING & FINISHING CORP. v. NATIONAL LABOR RELATIONS BOARD
107 S.Ct. 2225 (1987)

FACTS

Sterlingwale laid off all of its production employees in February 1982, and it finally went out of business in late summer. During this period, one of its former officers and the president of one of its major customers formed Fall River; he intended to engage in one aspect of Sterlingwale's business and take advantage of its assets and its work force. Fall River acquired Sterlingwale's plant, real property, equipment, and some of its remaining inventory, and began operating out of Sterlingwale's former facilities and hiring employees in September 1982, with an initial hiring goal of one full shift of workers. In October 1982, the union that had represented Sterlingwale's production and maintenance employees for almost thirty years requested Fall River to recognize it as the bargaining agent for its employees and begin collective bargaining. Fall River refused the request. At that time, a majority of petitioner's employees were ex-Sterlingwale employees, as also was true in mid-January 1983, when petitioner met its initial hiring goal of one shift of workers. By mid-April 1983, petitioner had reached two shifts, and, for the first time, ex-Sterlingwale employees were in the minority. The same working conditions existed as under Sterlingwale, and over half of petitioner's business came from ex-Sterlingwale customers.

ISSUE

Is Fall River required to bargain with the union that represents its predecessor's employees?

> **DECISION**
>
> Yes.
>
> **REASONS**
>
> 1. The general rule is that a new employer that succeeds to another's business has an obligation to bargain with the union that represents the predecessor's employees.
> 2. A "successor" employer's obligation to bargain is not limited to the situation where the union in question only recently was certified before the transition in employers. A union certified for more than one year has a rebuttable presumption of majority status. That status continues, despite the change in employers.
> 3. Although the new employer is not bound by the substantive provisions of the predecessor's bargaining agreement, it has an obligation to bargain with the union so long as it is, in fact, a successor of the old employer and so long as the majority of its employees were employed by its predecessor.
> 4. Fall River is a "successor" to Sterlingwale. The Board's approach in determining this question is based upon the totality of the circumstances. It requires that the Board focus on whether there is "substantial continuity" between the enterprises, with particular emphasis on the retained employees' perspective as to whether their job situations are essentially unaltered.

The major federal laws which govern labor-management relations are briefly described in Table 16-1. They are discussed in more detail later in this chapter.

FEDERAL LAWS BEFORE 1935

2 CLAYTON ACT

The first federal statute of any importance to the labor movement was the Clayton Act of 1914. It contained two sections relating to labor. The first attempted to prohibit federal courts from enjoining activities such as strikes and picketing in disputes over terms or conditions of employment. This provision was narrowly construed by the Supreme Court and has had little impact. The second section stated that antitrust laws regulating anticompetitive contracts did not apply to labor unions or their members in lawfully carrying out their legitimate activities. This exemption covers legitimate union practices. It does not cover activities unrelated to collective bargaining and union representation. A union that seeks by agreement with a nonlabor party to reduce competition for the benefit of such a party may be guilty of an antitrust violation.

The following case, which illustrates the labor-union antitrust exemption, is usually considered to be a landmark.

TABLE 16-1 FEDERAL LAWS GOVERNING LABOR-MANAGEMENT RELATIONS

Year	Statute	Summary of major provisions
1914	Clayton Act	Exempted union activity from the antitrust laws.
1926	Railway Labor Act	1. Governs collective bargaining for railroads and airlines. 2. Created the National Mediation Board to conduct union elections and mediate differences between employers and unions.
1932	Norris-LaGuardia Act	1. Outlawed yellow-dog contracts. 2. Prohibited federal courts from enjoining lawful union activities, including picketing and strikes.
1934	Wagner Act (National Labor Relations Act)	1. Created the National Labor Relations Board (NLRB). 2. NLRB conducts union certification elections. 3. Outlawed certain conduct by management as unfair to labor (unfair labor practices). 4. Authorized NLRB to hold hearings on unfair labor practices and correct wrongs resulting therefrom.
1947	Taft-Hartley Act	1. Outlawed certain conduct by unions as unfair labor practices. 2. Provided for an eighty-day cooling-off period in strikes which imperil national health or safety. 3. Allowed states to enact right-to-work laws. 4. Created the Federal Mediation and Conciliation Service to assist in settlement of labor disputes.
1959	Landrum-Griffin Act (Labor Management Reporting and Disclosure Act—LMRDA)	1. Bill of Rights for union members. 2. Requires reports to the Secretary of Labor. 3. Added to the list of unfair labor practices.

LOCAL UNION NO. 189, AMALGAMATED MEAT CUTTERS, AND BUTCHER WORKMEN OF NORTH AMERICA, AFL-CIO, ET AL. v. JEWEL TEA COMPANY, INC.
85 S.Ct. 1596 (1965)

FACTS

A union and several employers negotiated a collective-bargaining agreement which restricted the operating hours of food-store meat departments in Chicago, Illinois, to 9:00 *a.m.* through 6:00 *p.m.* Jewel Tea initially rejected the restriction, making a counteroffer which would have allowed Friday night operations. However, under threat of a union strike, it signed the contract. Jewel Tea then brought suit, alleging that the agreement was in violation of the Sherman Antitrust Act. The complaint stated that a prepackaged, self-service system of marketing meat eliminated the need to have a butcher on duty at all times; therefore, the limitation on operating hours was an unreasonable restraint of trade. It sought invalidation of the contract, treble damages, and attorneys' fees. The defendants claimed that this controversy was within the jurisdiction of the National Labor Relations Board (NLRB) and therefore exempt from the antitrust laws.

ISSUE

Is this agreement immune from attack under the labor exemption to the antitrust laws?

DECISION

Yes.

REASONS

1. The issue before the Supreme Court is whether the collective-bargaining agreement is exempt from the antitrust laws.
2. The national labor policy expressed in the National Labor Relations Act immunizes from the Sherman Act union-employer agreements on when, and on how long, employees must work. The agreement herein is thus exempt.

3 RAILWAY LABOR ACT

In 1926, Congress enacted the Railway Labor Act, which encouraged collective bargaining in the railroad industry to resolve labor disputes that might otherwise disrupt transportation. The act, which provided a means for dealing with labor disputes, was later extended to airlines; it applies to both air and rail transportation today. It established the three-member National Mediation Board, which must designate the bargaining representative for any given bargaining unit of employees in the railway or air transport industries. The Board generally does this by holding representation elections. The Railway Labor Act also outlawed certain **unfair labor practices**, such as refusing to bargain collectively.

In 1951, Congress amended the Railway Labor Act to permit the union shop. A union shop permits a union and an employer to require all employees in the bargaining unit to join the union as a condition of continued employment. The act does not permit a union to spend an objecting employee's dues to support political causes, however. The use of money for political purposes is unrelated to the desire of Congress to prevent "free-riders"— those who get the benefits of the union without paying a fair share of the costs. There are other expenditures which are improper, as the following case illustrates.

ELLIS v. BROTH. OF RY., AIRLINE AND S.S. CLERKS
104 S.Ct. 1883 (1984)

FACTS

The Railway Labor Act permits a union and an employer to require all employees to join the union as a condition of continued employment. A collective-bargaining agreement between a union and an airline required that all of the airline's clerical employees join the union or pay agency fees equal to members' dues. Plaintiff clerical employees objected to the use of their compelled dues or fees for specified union activities. The defendant union conceded that the statutory authorization did not permit a union to spend an objecting employee's money for union political or ideological activities. It had adopted a rebate program under which objecting employees were ultimately reimbursed for their shares of such expenditures.

The parties disagreed about the adequacy of the rebate scheme and the legality of charging objecting employees with union expenses for: (1) the national union's quadrennial Grand Lodge convention, (2) litigation not involving the negotiation of agreements or settlement of grievances, (3) union publications, (4) social activities, and (5) general organizing efforts. The trial court held that the union's existing rebate program adequately protected employees' rights. It ordered refunds for the expenditures at issue. The court of appeals ruled that because the challenged activities ultimately benefited the union's collective-bargaining efforts, no refund was required.

ISSUE

Are the nonunion members entitled to a rebate of their union fees?

DECISION

Yes, for reasons number 2 and 5 and part of number 3.

REASONS

1. The union's pure rebate approach is inadequate. Even if the union were to pay interest on the amount refunded, it would still obtain an involuntary loan for purposes to which the employee objected.
2. A union cannot be allowed to commit dissenters' funds to improper uses, even temporarily.
3. The statute authorizing the union shop makes it possible to require all members of a bargaining unit to pay their fair share of the union's costs of performing the function of exclusive-bargaining agent. It eliminates "free-riders," on whose behalf the union has been obliged to perform its statutory functions, who have refused to contribute to the cost thereof.
4. When employees object to being burdened with particular union expenditures, the test must be whether the challenged expenditures are necessarily or reasonably incurred in order to perform the duties of an exclusive representative of the employees in dealing with the employer on labor-management issues.
5. With regard to the specific union expenses challenged here, the plaintiff must help defray the costs of the national union's conventions, at which the members elect officers, establish bargaining goals, and formulate overall union policy. Such conventions are essential to the union's discharge of its duties as bargaining agent. Petitioners may also be charged for union social activities, which, though not central to collective bargaining, are sufficiently related to it to be charged to all employees. The statute also allows the union to charge objecting employees for its monthly magazine insofar as it reports to them about those activities the union can charge them for doing, but not insofar as the magazine reports on activities for which the union cannot spend dissenters' funds.

> 6. The law does not authorize charging objecting employees for the union's general organizing efforts, or for expenses of litigation that is not incident to negotiating and administering the contract or to settling grievances and disputes arising in the bargaining unit.

The National Mediation Board, unlike the National Labor Relations Board (NLRB), has no judicial power to hold hearings and issue cease and desist orders. Willful violations of the Railway Labor Act are punishable through criminal proceedings initiated by the Department of Justice in the regular federal court system. However, convictions are almost impossible to obtain because it is difficult to prove beyond any reasonable doubt that the commission of a given unfair labor practice was intentional.

When the parties to a dispute over proposed contract terms in the transportation industry cannot reach an agreement concerning rates of pay or working conditions, the National Mediation Board must attempt mediation of their differences. If mediation does not resolve their differences, the Board encourages voluntary arbitration. If the parties refuse arbitration and the dispute is likely to disrupt interstate commerce substantially, the Board informs the President, who then appoints a special emergency board. This emergency board also lacks any judicial power, but it encourages the parties to reach agreement by investigating the dispute and publishing its findings of fact and recommendations for settlement. During the investigation, which lasts thirty days, and for an additional thirty days after the report is issued, business is conducted without interruption. The parties, however, have no duty to comply with the special board's proposals. Thus, if no new collective-bargaining agreement is reached after the sixty-day period, lockouts by management and strikes by workers become legal.

In several cases since 1940, the Railway Labor Act has failed to resolve major disputes, necessitating special action by the President or the Congress. The transportation industry frequently has had its labor problems presented to the government for solution because the procedures of the Railway Labor Act are not such that all disputes can be resolved without irreparable damage to the public. It should be noted that the provisions previously discussed apply to assisting employers and unions in arriving at a collective-bargaining agreement where none currently is in force. The act requires compulsory arbitration of disputes concerning interpretation of existing contracts between the parties. This requirement is peculiar to the transportation industry.

4 NORRIS-LAGUARDIA ACT

In 1932, the Norris-LaGuardia Act was passed by Congress. The first major provision of the Norris-LaGuardia Act made **yellow-dog contracts** (those forbidding union membership) unenforceable. The second listed specific acts of persons and organizations participating in labor disputes which were not subject to federal court injunctions. These included: (1) striking or quitting work, (2) belonging to a labor organization, (3) paying strike or unemployment benefits to participants in a labor dispute, (4) publicizing the existence of a labor dispute or the facts related to it (including picketing), (5) peaceably assembling to promote their interests in a labor dispute, and (6) agreeing with others or advising or causing them to do any of the above acts without fraud or violence. These acts are given a liberal interpretation, as is illustrated by the following case which had its roots in international politics rather than in labor relations.

JACKSONVILLE BULK TERMINALS, INC. v. INTERNATIONAL LONGSHOREMEN'S ASSOC.
102 S.Ct. 2673 (1982)

FACTS

After President Carter announced certain trade restrictions with the Soviet Union because of its intervention in Afghanistan, the defendant union announced that its members would not handle any cargo bound to, or coming from, the Soviet Union. When an affiliated local union refused to load certain goods (not included in the presidential embargo) bound for the Soviet Union, the employer of the union brought suit against the international union, its officers and agents, and the local union. The employer alleged that the union's work stoppage violated the terms of a collective-bargaining agreement which contained a no-strike clause and a provision requiring arbitration of disputes. The district court granted a preliminary injunction pending arbitration. The court reasoned that the political motivation behind the work stoppage rendered inapplicable Section 4 of the Norris-LaGuardia Act, which prohibits injunctions against strikes "in any case involving or growing out of any labor dispute."

ISSUE

Does the Norris-LaGuardia Act prevent the use of an injunction to stop this activity?

DECISION

Yes.

REASONS

1. The plain language of the act, which prohibits injunctions for "any" labor dispute and defines "labor dispute" to include "any controversy concerning terms of conditions of employment," does not exempt labor disputes having their origin in political protests.
2. The critical element in determining the act's applicability is whether, as here, the employer-employee relationship is the focus of the controversy.
3. The existence of noneconomic motives does not make the act inapplicable.

Although the Norris-LaGuardia Act greatly restricts the use of injunctions in labor disputes, it does not prohibit them altogether. An injunction may be issued to enjoin illegal strikes, such as ones by public employees. When unlawful acts are threatened, they may be enjoined also. These unlawful acts must cause substantial, irreparable damage. The situation must be such that public authorities who have the duty to protect the employer's property cannot furnish adequate protection or are unwilling to do so. In addition, one seeking an injunction in a labor dispute must meet the test of a stringent clean-hands rule. No restraining order will be granted to any person who has failed to comply with any obligation imposed by law or who has failed to make every reasonable effort to settle the dispute.

Although the Norris-LaGuardia Act restricts the use of federal court injunctions in labor disputes, it does not limit the jurisdiction of state courts in issuing them. The Supreme Court has upheld the jurisdiction of a state court to enjoin a union's work stoppage and picketing in violation of a no-strike clause in its collective-bargaining agreement.

THE WAGNER ACT

5 GENERAL SUMMARY

The labor movement received its greatest stimulus for growth with the enactment in 1935 of the National Labor Relations Act (**Wagner Act**). Noting that a major cause of industrial strife was the inequality of bargaining power between employees and employers, the act stated that its policy was to protect by law the right of employees to organize and bargain collectively and to encourage the "friendly adjustment of industrial disputes."

The Wagner Act accomplishes this policy by providing that the right of employees to bargain collectively is a fundamental right. Section 7 of the law provides:

> Employees shall have the right to self organization, to form, join, or assist labor organizations, to bargain collectively through representatives of their own choosing, and to engage in concerted activities for the purpose of collective bargaining or other mutual aid or protection.

In summary, the Wagner Act:

1. Created the National Labor Relations Board (NLRB) to administer the act.
2. Provided for selection by employees through NLRB-supervised elections of a union with exclusive power to act as their collective-bargaining representative.
3. Outlawed certain conduct by employers which generally had the effect of either preventing the organization of employees or emasculating their unions where they did exist. These forbidden acts were defined as "unfair labor practices" and are discussed in the next chapter (Chapter 17) in detail.
4. Authorized the NLRB to conduct hearings on unfair labor practice allegations and, if they were found to exist, take corrective action including issuing cease and desist orders and awarding dollar damages to unions and employees.

6 THE NLRB

Today, the NLRB has five members appointed by the President, with the advice and consent of the Senate, who serve staggered terms of five years each. The President designates one member to serve as chairman. In addition, there is a General Counsel of the Board who supervises Board investigations and serves as prosecutor in cases before the Board. The General Counsel supervises operations of the NLRB so that the Board itself may perform its quasi-judicial function of deciding unfair labor practice cases free of bias. As part of this function, the Board has full authority over the Division of Administrative Law Judges. The administrative law judges are responsible for the initial conduct of hearings in unfair labor practice cases. The General Counsel is appointed by the President, with the advice and consent of the Senate, for a term of four years. The General Counsel has final authority in investigation of charges, issuance of complaints, and prosecution of such complaints, as well as the dismissal of charges.

The General Counsel also is responsible for the conduct of representation elections, since the Board has delegated this function to its regional directors, subject to a review of their actions. (The Board still determines policy questions, such as what types of employers and groups of employees are covered by the labor law.) In addition, the General Counsel is responsible for seeking court orders requiring compliance with the Board's orders, and represents the Board in miscellaneous litigation.

Congress gave the NLRB jurisdiction over any business "affecting commerce," with a few exceptions. However, certain employers and employees are specifically exempt from NLRB jurisdiction. These include employees of federal and state governments, political subdivisions of the states, and persons subject to the Railway Labor Act. Also excluded are independent contractors, individuals employed as agricultural laborers or domestic servants in a home, and those employed by their spouse or a parent. Finally, supervisors are not considered employees. This supervisor exception excludes all employees properly classified as "managerial." For example, university professors who control admissions, hire and fire faculty, and participate in budget preparation are supervisors, and they are not covered by the act. Professors who have no power to act in these areas are covered.

The supervisor or managerial exception raises difficult issues when applied to persons having access to confidential information. The mere fact that a person has access to confidential information of an employer does not make the person a supervisor. Only those persons with access to confidential information of the employer concerning labor relations are exempt. This labor-relations connection means that persons who serve in a confidential capacity to persons who formulate, determine, or effectuate labor policy are not covered by the act.

The NLRB has never been able to exercise fully the powers given it, because of budget and time considerations. It has limited its own jurisdiction to businesses of a certain size. Table 16-2 lists these businesses.

TABLE 16-2 NLRB JURISDICTION

1. *Nonretail operations* with an annual outflow or inflow across state lines of at least $50,000
2. *Retail enterprises* with a gross volume of $500,000 or more a year
3. *Enterprises operating office buildings* if the gross revenues are at least $100,000 per year
4. *Transportation enterprises* furnishing interstate services
5. *Local transit systems* with an annual gross volume of at least $250,000
6. *Newspapers* which subscribe to interstate news services, publish nationally syndicated features, or advertise nationally sold products and have a minimum annual gross volume of $250,000
7. *Communication enterprises* which operate radio or television stations or telephone or telegraph services with a gross volume of $100,000 or more per year
8. *Local public utilities* with an annual gross volume of $250,000 per year or an outflow or inflow of goods or services across state lines of $50,000 or more per year
9. *Hotel and motel enterprises* which serve transient guests and gross at least $500,000 in revenues per year
10. All enterprises whose operations have a substantial impact on *national defense*
11. *Nonprofit hospitals*
12. *Private universities and colleges*

As a result of the NLRB's policy, federal laws do not cover many small employers who are subject to both any applicable state law on labor relations and common law principles. Of course the Board may decide to take jurisdiction over any business that affects interstate commerce.

Each year the NLRB handles over 50,000 cases of all kinds. About two-thirds involve unfair labor practice charges. Most of these are filed by unions or workers against employers, but one-third involve charges against unions.

7 NLRB SANCTIONS

The Wagner Act directs the Board, upon finding that a person has committed an unfair labor practice, to issue an order requiring him or her to cease and desist such practices. The Board is also authorized to order corrective action if necessary to overcome any injury caused by the unfair labor practice. Such orders are subject only to limited judicial review. On such a review, the Board's order will not be disturbed unless it can be shown that it is an obvious attempt to achieve ends contrary to the policies of the law. The NLRB has no independent power to enforce its orders. If necessary, it seeks enforcement in the United States Courts of Appeal.

To illustrate the corrective action that may be taken, we use the example of an employee who has been discharged wrongfully; the NLRB may order the reinstatement of that employee with back pay and restoration of full seniority rights. In fact, even a purchaser of a business who acquires and operates it knowing that the seller discharged an employee in violation of the Wagner Act may be ordered by the NLRB to reinstate the employee with back pay. The NLRB may require an employer to bargain collectively with the appropriate union, or vice versa. It may order an employer to post notices at the plant assuring employees that it will no longer commit a particular unfair labor practice of which it has been found guilty. If an employer or union has committed an unfair labor practice which may have influenced the outcome of a representation election, the NLRB may set aside the election and hold another one free of such improper pressures on the employees.

At one time, the NLRB was willing to certify a union that lost an election if the employer was guilty of unfair labor practices to such an extent that the employer's conduct could be described as outrageous and pervasive. In 1984, the courts reversed this policy, and today the NLRB will not certify a union that loses an election. It will set aside the election and require the employees to vote again. A nonmajority bargaining order departs from the national policy of employee free choice. The law requires a union election victory or some other concrete proof of majority assent to union representation. At the present time, unions lose the majority of certification and decertification elections. This negative trend has developed since the late 1970s.

8 NLRB ELECTIONS

An employer may voluntarily recognize that its workers desire to have a certain union represent them and agree to bargain with the union. In the absence of such voluntary recognition, the selection of a union as collective-bargaining representative is made by a majority of the employees voting "in a unit appropriate for such purposes." Elections are by secret ballot and supervised by the NLRB. The Board decides what unit of employees is appropriate for purposes of collective bargaining and therefore which employees are entitled to vote in an election. It may select the total employer unit, craft unit, plant unit, or any subdivision of the plant.

Obviously, how the Board exercises its discretion in this regard may be crucial to the outcome of a given election. If all 100 workers at one plant operated by an employer desire to organize but 400 out of 500 at another of the employer's plants do not, designation of the total employer unit as appropriate would ensure that both plants would remain nonunion. The Board may deny some employees the right to vote, as the case that follows illustrates.

N.L.R.B. v. ACTION AUTOMOTIVE, INC.
105 S.Ct. 984 (1985)

FACTS

A union certification election was held, and the union received a plurality of the votes, but enough ballots were challenged on each side to place the outcome in doubt. The ballots challenged by the union included ones cast by the owner's wife and one by his mother, who worked at the corporation. The hearing officer recommended that the union's challenge be sustained, since the employees' family ties were sufficient to align their interests with management. The NLRB adopted this recommendation and, after all qualified votes were counted, certified the union as the exclusive-bargaining unit. The employer refused to bargain, and the union filed charges of unfair labor practices with the NLRB. The NLRB ordered the employer to bargain.

ISSUE

Does the NLRB have authority to exclude employees from a bargaining unit, based solely on their close family ties?

DECISION

Yes.

REASONS

1. Section 9(b) of the Act vests in the Board authority to determine "the unit appropriate for the purposes of collective bargaining." The Board's discretion in this area is broad, which shows Congress's recognition of the need for flexibility in shaping the bargaining unit to the particular case.
2. The Board has long hesitated to include the relatives of management in bargaining units because their interests are sufficiently distinguished from those of the other employees. The greater the family involvement in the ownership and management of the company, the more likely the employee-relative will be viewed as aligned with management and, hence, excluded.
3. The very presence at union meetings of close relatives of management could tend to inhibit free expression of views and threaten the confidentiality of union attitudes and voting.

Petitions

Before a representation election is conducted by the NLRB, a petition for such an election must be filed with the Board by either an employee, labor organization, or employer. If the petition is filed by either an employee or labor organization, it must allege either: (1) that a substantial number of employees want a collective-bargaining representative but their employer refuses to recognize their representative or (2) that a substantial number of employees assert that the union which has been certified by the Board, or which the employer currently recognizes as their bargaining representative, is no longer such. "Substantial" has been interpreted to mean that at least 30 percent of the employees must support the petition.

An employer may file a petition for selection of an initial representative without making and proving any allegations of fact. However, an employer who files a petition for an election to invalidate certification of an incumbent union must show that it doubts, in good faith, the continued support of the union by a majority of the employees.

The NLRB investigates a petition, and if it determines that there is an issue to be voted upon, it directs that a representation election be held by a secret ballot. After the results are tallied, the Board certifies either than no union has been selected by a majority of the employees or that a given one has. In some cases, two or more unions compete to qualify as the legal representative of the bargaining unit.

As was noted, employees may withdraw authority from a previously designated bargaining representative by secret ballot. If at least 30 percent of those in a bargaining unit allege that they desire their union's authority to be rescinded, the Board must hold an election to that effect. However, after any valid election has been conducted by the NLRB, another is not permitted for one year. Also, if an election has resulted in Board certification of a union, no new election may take place within one year of the certification. Also, an election is not allowed within the term of a collective-bargaining agreement, or three years after it has been signed, whichever period is shorter.

Cards

A union seeking to represent employees may solicit cards from them indicating their willingness that the union act in that capacity. The NLRB may issue a bargaining order based on such cards if the cards are unequivocal and clearly indicate that the employee signing the card is authorizing the union to represent him or her. The general counsel of the NLRB is not required to prove that the employees read or understood the cards. If a card states on its face that it authorizes collective bargaining, it will be counted for that purpose unless there is clear proof that the employee was told that it would not be used for that purpose. The employer could have relied upon the cards and agreed to bargain with the union.

Most cards simply request an election because of the belief that peer pressure may cause workers who do not actually favor the union to sign the cards. The secret ballot of the election process ensures freedom of choice for the workers. The refusal to accept a union based on cards is not an unfair labor practice, as was held in the case which follows.

LINDEN LUMBER DIVISION, SUMMER & CO. v. NLRB
95 S.Ct. 429 (1974)

FACTS

A union obtained authorization cards from a majority of employees and demanded that it be recognized as the collective-bargaining representative. The employer doubted the union's claimed majority status and suggested that the union petition the Board for an election. The union struck for recognition as the bargaining representative and filed a charge of unfair labor practice based on the refusal to bargain.

ISSUE

Is it an unfair labor practice to refuse to accept evidence of majority status other than the results of a Board election?

DECISION

No.

REASONS

1. An employer is not obligated to accept a card check as proof of majority status. The employer is also not required to justify his or her insistence on an election by making an investigation of employee sentiment and showing affirmative reasons for doubting the majority status.
2. An employer's petition for an election, although permissible, is not required.
3. Unless an employer has engaged in an unfair labor practice that impairs the electoral process, a union with authorization cards that purports to represent a majority of the employees, which is refused recognition, has the burden of taking the next step in invoking the Board's election procedure.

THE TAFT-HARTLEY ACT

9 MAJOR PROVISIONS

The Wagner Act opened the door for the rapid growth of the union movement. From 1935 to the end of World War II, the strength and influence of unions grew by leaps and bounds. Where, prior to the Wagner Act employers had the greater advantage in bargaining power, by 1946 many persons felt the pendulum had shifted and that unions with their ability to call nationwide crippling strikes had the better bargaining position.

As an attempt to balance the scale, the Labor-Management Relations Act of 1947 (the **Taft-Hartley Act**) was enacted to amend the Wagner Act. Its purposes were to ensure the free flow of commerce by eliminating union practices which burden commerce and to provide procedures for avoiding disputes which jeopardize the public health, safety, or interest. It recognized that both parties to collective bargaining need protection from wrongful interference by the other and that employees sometimes need protection from the union itself.

In attempting to balance bargaining power, the Taft-Hartley Act:

1 Created the Federal Mediation and Conciliation Service to assist in the settlement of labor disputes.

2 Restricted the right of unions to insist on a union membership.
3 Attempted to give employers freedom of speech in labor-management relations.
4 Provided for an **eighty-day cooling-off period** in strikes which imperil the national health or safety.
5 Allowed suits for breach of contract against a union.
6 Outlawed certain conduct by unions as unfair labor practices (see Chapter 17).

The Federal Mediation and Conciliation Service has a staff of trained specialists who work with the parties to a labor dispute in an attempt to resolve differences. These mediators often become public figures as a result of news coverage of major labor disputes.

10 UNION MEMBERSHIP

The second major change brought about by the Taft-Hartley Act was its provision which outlawed the **closed shop** but permitted the union shop in those states which did not outlaw it by enacting right-to-work legislation. In a closed-shop contract, the employer agrees that it will *not* hire any person who is *not* a member of the union. In a **union-shop** contract, the employer agrees to require membership in the union after an employee has been hired as a condition of his or her continued employment. Under the Taft-Hartley Act, such a requirement may not be imposed until the thirtieth day after employment begins. In addition, an employer may not compel union membership of an employee: (1) if such was not available on the same terms and conditions applicable to other members or (2) if the employee's membership was denied or terminated for reasons other than failure to pay dues and fees.

One of the most distasteful sections of the Taft-Hartley Act to unions is 14(b), which outlaws the union shop in states which have adopted a **right-to-work law.** Right-to-work laws prohibit agreements requiring membership in a labor organization as a condition of continued employment of a person who was not in the union when hired. Approximately twenty states have right-to-work laws today. Workers who do not belong to a union may not be required to pay representation fees to the union that represents the employees. However, such workers are subject to the terms of the collective-bargaining agreement, and the union must handle their grievances, if any, with management.

A union has the power to discipline its members and impose fines. However, unions may not fine employees who are not members or who resign. A union constitution may not prohibit resignations. Taft-Hartley had eliminated compulsory union membership through a closed shop. As a result, a union may not fine former members who have resigned, as was held in the following case.

> **PATTERN MAKERS' LEAGUE OF NORTH AMERICA v. N.L.R.B.**
> 105 S.Ct. 3064 (1985)
>
> **FACTS**
>
> A labor-union constitution provides that resignations are not permitted during a strike or when a strike is imminent. The union fined ten of its members who, in violation of this provision, resigned during a strike and returned to work. The NLRB held that these fines were an unfair labor practice.
>
> **ISSUE**
>
> Does Taft-Hartley prohibit a union from fining members who have tendered resignations which are invalid under the union constitution?
>
> **DECISION**
>
> Yes.
>
> **REASONS**
>
> 1. Taft-Hartley provides that a union commits an unfair labor practice if it "restrains or coerces" employees in the exercise of their statutory rights. When employee members of a union refuse to support a strike (whether or not a rule prohibits returning to work during a strike), they are refraining from concerted activity. Therefore, imposing fines on these employees for returning to work "restrains" the exercise of their rights.
> 2. Union restrictions on the right to resign are inconsistent with the policy of voluntary unionism.
> 3. A union has not left a worker's employment rights inviolate when it exacts an entire paycheck in satisfaction of a fine imposed for working. Congress sought to eliminate completely any requirement that the employee maintain full union membership. Therefore, the Board was justified in concluding that by restricting the right of employees to resign, the policy of voluntary unionism is impaired.

11 FREE SPEECH

Employers had complained that the Wagner Act violated their right of free speech. To meet this objection, Congress added the following provision:

> 8(c) The expressing of any views, argument, or opinion, or the dissemination thereof, whether in written, printed, graphic, or visual form, shall not constitute or be evidence of an unfair labor practice under any of the provisions of this Act, if such expression contains no threat of reprisal or force or promise of benefit.

This provision gives employers limited free speech, at best. It is difficult to make statements that cannot be construed as a threat or a promise. For example, if an employer predicts dire economic events as a result of unionization, such may be an illegal threat if the employer has it within his or her power to make the prediction come true. Whether particular language is coercive or not often depends on the analysis of the total background of facts and circumstances in which it was uttered. To be forbidden, the statements of an employer need not be proved to have been coercive in fact but only to have had a reasonable tendency to intimidate employees under the circumstances. At the present time, the NLRB takes the position that misleading statements will not automatically cancel election results, nor will inadvertent errors overturn elections. The purpose of this approach is to advance free speech by both sides.

An employer's threats to withdraw existing benefits of employees if they unionize is not speech protected by 8(c). For example, in one case the officer of a firm noted in a speech to employees of a plant where an election was forthcoming that the business could supply the same product from one of its nonunion plants. The NLRB held that this statement constituted a threat to provide better and more jobs at nonunion plants, and it set aside the election, which the union had lost. In another case, an illegal threat was ruled to be implied from management comments shortly before a representation election warning that annual pay raises would be subject to collective bargaining and thus delayed by a union victory. However, mere predictions and prophecies are protected. For example, an employer's speeches and handbills during the union's organizational campaign stated its intention to fight the union in every legal way possible and to "deal hard" with the union at arm's length if it were voted in, and warned that employees could be permanently replaced if the union called an economic strike. This language was held to fall within the protection of Section 8(c). The right of free speech guaranteed by the Taft-Hartley Act applies to labor unions as well as employers. However, there is a rule prohibiting either side from making election speeches on company time to massed assemblies of employees within twenty-four hours before an election.

12 EIGHTY-DAY COOLING-OFF PERIOD

The provision of the Taft-Hartley Act calling for an eighty-day "cooling-off period" after certain procedures have been followed begins: "Whenever in the opinion of the President of the United States, a threatened or actual strike or lockout affecting an entire industry or substantial part thereof engaged in trade, commerce, transportation, transmission, or communication among the several states or with foreign nations, or engaged in the production of goods for commerce, will, if permitted to occur or to continue, imperil the national health or safety, he may appoint a board..." Thus, the procedure starts with the President, recognizing the emergency characteristics of a strike, appointing a board of inquiry to obtain facts about the strike. The board then makes a study of the strike and reports back to the President. If the board finds that the national health or safety is indeed affected by the strike, then the President, through the Attorney General, goes to the federal court for an injunction ordering the union to suspend the strike (or company to suspend the lockout) for eighty days. During the eighty-day period, the Federal Mediation Service works with the two parties to try to achieve an agreement. If during this time the reconciliation effort fails, the presidential board holds new hearings and receives the company's final offer. The union members are then allowed to vote on this final proposal by the company. If they vote for the new proposal, the dispute is over and work continues as usual. If they vote against the proposal, the workers may again be called out on strike. At this point, the strike may continue indefinitely until the disagreement causing it is resolved by collective bargaining, or unless there is additional legislation by Congress to solve the problem. Experience has shown that many disputes are settled during the eighty-day period. The injunction provided for in the Taft-Hartley Act may not be used for all strikes but is limited to "national emergency" strikes. These must involve national defense or key industries or must have a substantial effect on the economy.

13 SUITS AGAINST UNIONS

Section 301 of the Taft-Hartley Act provides that suits for breach of a contract between an employer and a labor organization can be filed in the federal district courts, without regard to the amount in question. A labor organization is responsible for the acts of its agents and may sue or be sued. Any money judgment against it is enforceable only against its assets and not against any individual member. Moreover, individuals cannot be sued for actions such as violating no-strike provisions of a collective-bargaining contract. Thus, an employer may enforce a no-strike clause in a collective-bargaining agreement by obtaining an injunction against the union, or it may recover money damages from the union if it breaches such a contract clause. In addition, employees may sue their union and recover the money damages they suffer because of an illegal strike. If a union activity is both an unfair labor practice and breach of a collective-bargaining agreement, the NLRB's authority is not exclusive and does not destroy the jurisdiction of courts under Section 301 of the Taft-Hartley Act.

THE LANDRUM-GRIFFIN ACT

14 AS A "BILL OF RIGHTS"

The **Landrum-Griffin Act,** or Labor-Management Reporting and Disclosure Act (LMRDA), was passed in 1959 as a result of the widespread corruption, violence, and lack of democratic procedures in some labor unions that was revealed in congressional hearings conducted in the 1950s. Its requirements provide for union reform and a "bill of rights" for union members. LMRDA gives union members the following rights:

1 To nominate candidates, to vote in elections, to attend membership meetings, and to have a voice in business transactions, subject to reasonable union rules and regulations.
2 To have free expression in union meetings, business discussions, and conventions subject to reasonable rules and regulations.
3 To vote on an increase of dues or fees.
4 To sue and testify against the union.
5 To receive written, specific charges; to be given a reasonable time for defense; and to be accorded a full and fair hearing before any disciplinary action is taken by the union against them except for nonpayment of dues.
6 To be given a copy of the collective-bargaining agreement that they work under, upon request.

The rights and remedies granted to union members of this statute are in addition to any other rights members may have under other laws or under union constitutions and bylaws. In the event that a member's rights are violated, the statute allows him or her to bring civil actions for damages, including an injunction.

The case which follows is typical of those brought to protect the rights of the rank and file union members to control their union. In this case, the Secretary of Labor filed suit under the Landrum-Griffin Act, challenging the validity of an international union rule which limited eligibility for local union office to certain members.

LOCAL 3489 UNITED STEELWORKERS OF AMERICA v. USERY
97 S.Ct. 611 (1977)

FACTS

The international union had a constitutional provision which limited eligibility for local union office to members who had attended at least one-half of the regular meetings of the local for three years prior to an election. The Secretary of Labor filed suit to invalidate the election of officers of a local union.

ISSUE

Did the provision in the constitution of the international union violate Section 401(e) of the Landrum-Griffin Act?

DECISION

Yes.

REASONS

1. Unions may restrict candidacies for office by adopting reasonable qualifications. The LMRDA states that "every member in good standing shall be eligible to be a candidate and to hold office, subject to reasonable qualifications, uniformly imposed."

2. The anti-democratic effect of the meeting-attendance rule was to exclude 96.5 percent of the members from candidacy for union office. This was not a "reasonable qualification" consistent with the LMRDA's goal of free and democratic elections.

Some other restrictions which are related to union elections have been upheld. In the case which follows, the union was concerned about outside financial support for candidates in union elections. Note that union candidates are given less protection and have more restrictions placed upon them than do candidates for public office.

UNITED STEELWORKERS OF AMERICA v. SADLOWSKI
102 S.Ct. 2339 (1982)

FACTS

A union amended its constitution to include an "outsider rule." This rule prohibits candidates for union office from accepting campaign contributions from nonmembers. It also creates a committee to enforce the rule and makes the committee's decisions final and binding. Plaintiff is a union member who had been an unsuccessful candidate for union office before adoption of the rule. He had received much of the financial support for his campaign from sources outside the union. He filed suit, claiming the rule violated Section 101(a)(4) of the Labor-Management Reporting and Disclosure Act of 1959 (LMRDA). It provides that a union may not limit the rights of its members to institute an action in any court or administrative agency. He argued that the rule prohibited financing of campaign-related litigation. Plaintiff also contended on appeal that the rule violated the "freedom of speech and assembly" provision of Section 101(a)(2) of the LMRDA, which gives every union member the right to assemble freely with other members and express at union meetings his or her views about candidates in union elections or any business properly before the meeting.

ISSUE

Does the "outsider rule" violate LMRDA?

DECISION

No.

REASONS

1. The outsider rule is protected by Section 101(a)(2)'s proviso which gives a union authority to adopt "reasonable" rules regarding its members' responsibilities. Union rules need not meet the same standards as applied by the First Amendment to political candidates.
2. Congress adopted the freedom of speech and assembly provision to promote union democracy, particularly through fostering vigorous debate during election campaigns. Although the outsider rule may limit somewhat the

ability of insurgent union members to wage an effective campaign against incumbent officers, as a practical matter the impact may not be substantial. The record shows that challengers have been able to defeat incumbents or administration-backed candidates, despite the absence of financial support from nonmembers.
3. The purpose in adopting the outsider rule was to ensure that nonmembers would not unduly influence union affairs and union leadership would remain responsive to the membership. The policies underlying the LMRDA show that this is a legitimate purpose that Congress meant to protect.
4. The outsider rule does not violate Section 101(a)(4)'s right-to-sue provision. The rule simply does not apply when a member uses funds from outsiders to finance litigation.

The LMRDA protects rank and file union members. It does not protect job security or tenure of union officers or employees. For example, the courts have held that after a union election, the winner may remove appointive union officials. Union leaders may select staff members with compatible views.

15 LMRDA REPORTING REQUIREMENTS

The act also contains several provisions concerning the Secretary of Labor and reports required of unions. The purpose of these reports is to reveal practices detrimental to union members. For example, each union must adopt a constitution and bylaws and file them with the Secretary of Labor, together with the following information:

1 The name and address of the union office and the place where records are kept
2 The names and titles of officers
3 The amount of initiation fees required
4 The amount of dues charged
5 A detailed statement of procedures for: *(a)* qualification for office, *(b)* levying fees, *(c)* insurance plans, *(d)* disbursement of funds, *(e)* audits, *(f)* selection of officers, *(g)* removal of officers, *(h)* determining bargaining demands, *(i)* fines, *(j)* approval of contracts, *(k)* calling strikes, and *(l)* issuance of work permits

In addition, yearly financial reports must be filed which indicate:

1 Assets and liabilities
2 Receipts and sources of funds
3 Salaries of officers
4 Loans to members greater than $250
5 Loans to business enterprises
6 Other disbursements

Note that the above reports do not concern the operation of union welfare and pension-plan funds, which involve a great deal more money than union treasuries. The Welfare and Pension Plans Disclosure Act of 1958 (as amended in 1962), also known as the Teller Act, governs such funds. This act requires filing with the Secretary of Labor a description of every employee pension and welfare plan covered by it as well as annual reports detailing the operations of the funds. The act also gives the Secretary broad investigative and enforcing powers.

The Landrum-Griffin Act also requires reports on trusteeships. A trusteeship is a method of supervision or control whereby a labor union suspends the autonomy otherwise available to a subordinate body under its constitution and bylaws. In this report, the union must state the names and addresses of subordinate organizations, the date of establishing trusteeship, and the reasons for establishing the trusteeship.

In addition to the foregoing reports, union employees and officials must file a yearly report with the Secretary of Labor which contains information on possible areas of conflict of interest, such as stock holdings in companies with which the union has dealings and payments personally received from employers. Employers must file yearly reports with the Secretary which contain information concerning payments made to unions or union officials. An employer must also report on payments made to consultants whom it engages to deal with unions. Reports made to the Secretary of Labor become public information and may be used as the basis of criminal proceedings.

16 INTERNAL UNION ACTIVITIES

The Landrum-Griffin Act provides an elaborate system of regulation of internal union activities. These regulations cover union election procedures, management of union funds, trusteeships, and union personnel. The Secretary of Labor is given power to investigate alleged violations of any of the regulations and may institute criminal proceedings through the Attorney General.

The act requires that elections be held at minimum regular intervals to promote democracy. National unions must hold elections at least every five years, locals every three years, and intermediate bodies every four years. Elections must be by secret ballot of members, or of delegates who were chosen by secret ballot of members. Every candidate for union office must have access to membership lists. The union must provide adequate safeguards to ensure a fair election, and every candidate is given the right to post observers at the polls and counting place. All candidates must have equal opportunity to run for office without penalty or punishment by the organization. Union funds may not be used by any candidate in his or her campaign.

The act also recognizes the fiduciary responsibility of officers of unions.

All clauses in union constitutions which attempt to provide that union officers do not have liability for wrongful conduct are void as against public policy. A member of a union may, after he or she has exhausted union proceedings, sue for funds mishandled by union officers, and the member will be repaid the cost of bringing suit.

The act makes embezzlement of union funds a federal crime. The penalty is imprisonment for up to five years or a fine of up to $10,000, or both. Every union employee who handles funds must be bonded. No union may lend more than $2,000 to a union employee or official. Any person who willfully violates either of these two provisions is subject to imprisonment for one year, a fine of up to $10,000, or both. Unions are not permitted to pay the fines imposed on their officers or employees who are convicted of violating the act. However, the propriety of payments to cover legal fees in lawsuits is judged on an individual basis.

The Landrum-Griffin Act also makes it a federal offense to engage in extortionate picketing. This is picketing to force an employer to pay money to union officials or other individuals for their own personal use rather than for the benefit of the union membership generally.

17 LABOR LAW AND GOVERNMENT EMPLOYEES

Perhaps the most difficult problems in the labor field today involve government employees. Should such employees have the right to form unions and bargain collectively with the government units that employ them? If collective bargaining fails to reach satisfactory agreements, should government employees have the right to strike? The clear-cut trend in the law is to answer the first question affirmatively and the second negatively. Today, unions or employee organizations exist at all levels of government. However, in the absence of a statute giving them the right, there is no right to strike. This was reaffirmed when the air controllers who went on strike were discharged and their union decertified. A union without the right to strike is a "paper tiger." Without the right to strike, the power of public-employee unions is much less than that of unions in the private sector.

The right to strike is denied government workers because such strikes affect the public more adversely than those by employees in the private sector. Strikes by police, firefighters, teachers, sanitation workers, transportation workers, and other public employees who perform vital services obviously can be directly and immediately detrimental to the health, safety, and welfare of those whom they are supposed to serve.

Collective bargaining in public employment varies throughout the country. States vary from having no laws granting bargaining rights to public employees to having statutes with broad guarantees. A few states even give some public employees the right to strike. Unions of public workers are pressing for legislation that would give them the choice of striking or turning to binding arbitration if a dispute cannot be resolved. Other unions advocate the expansion of the present Wagner and Taft-Hartley Acts to cover state and local employees.

The difficulties of collective bargaining in the public sector are multiplied by the problem of funds needed to meet labor's demands, since one of the most significant differences between public and private labor relations is that there is no "bottom line" for cost in governmental bodies as there is in private corporations. Frequently, public officials have neither the funds to meet labor's demands nor the power to raise taxes without the consent of the voters. A school board may be very willing to grant pay increases, but unless voters will agree to the tax increases required, the money to do so is simply not available. For example, the faculty of Florida's state colleges and universities bargained for a raise of 10 percent. The legislature refused to fund it. In such a case, the collective-bargaining agreement must give way to the constitutional provisions on state funding. A possible solution to this dilemma is to integrate the bargaining process with the budgetary process.

Wisconsin has taken steps toward such integration. There, state employee contracts negotiated by the executive branch are subject to approval by a committee of the legislature, which binds the state if it is given. Rejection by the committee sends a contract back to bargaining.

It is expected that the number of public employees represented by unions will continue to grow. However, few of these will have the right to strike. Employees performing essential services are not likely to be granted this right, even though it is basic to the whole concept of unions. Employees performing nonessential services may acquire the right to strike, or, in some cases, actions will not be taken to stop such strikes even if they are technically illegal. The more important the job, the less likely a strike will be tolerated.

REVIEW QUESTIONS

1 Identify the federal statute which accomplished each of the following:
   a Exempted union activity from the antitrust laws
   b Created the National Labor Relations Board (NLRB)
   c Allowed states to enact right-to-work laws
   d Outlawed certain conduct by management as unfair to labor (unfair labor practices)
   e Governed collective bargaining for railroads and airlines
   f Prohibited federal courts from enjoining lawful union activities, including picketing and strikes
   g Bill of rights for union members
   h Provided for an eighty-day cooling-off period in strikes which imperil national health or safety
   i Outlawed yellow-dog contracts
   j Created the Federal Mediation and Conciliation Service

2 Two labor unions entered into an agreement with an employer that no union member should work for another company that was a competitor of the employer. The employer was the largest firm in its industry, and the other company was a new firm. Is the agreement exempt from the antitrust laws? Why, or why not?

3 Which of the following expenditures would be proper for a union collecting dues from nonmembers?
   a Political contributions
   b Convention expenses
   c Officers' salaries
   d Official publications
   e Social events
   f General organizing efforts

4 Assume that a company has a collective-bargaining agreement that includes a no-strike clause during its terms. Despite this, the union calls a strike. No violence has resulted from the strike. Will the Norris-LaGuardia Act prevent a *state court* from issuing an injunction that enforces the contract and orders the strike to cease? Explain.

5 Except for the members of the National Labor Relations Board, what position connected with the NLRB has the most power and responsibility? Briefly describe these powers and responsibilities.

6 Albert owns a small retail store with seven full- and part-time employees. One employee is fired for advocating that the employees form a union. If the employee files a complaint of an unfair labor practice with the NLRB, what will be the result? Why?

7 A railroad sought a preliminary injunction in a federal court against secondary picketing by a union that represents railroad employees. Does the federal court have jurisdiction to enter the injunction? Why, or why not?

8 The Yeshiva University Faculty Association filed a representation petition with the NLRB, seeking certification as bargaining agent for the full-time faculty. At this private university, the faculty's authority in academic matters at the university was absolute. The university opposed the petition on the ground that all of its faculty members were managerial or supervisory personnel and thus not "employees" within the meaning of the Wagner Act. Is the faculty entitled to conduct a union certification election? Explain.

9 The general counsel of the NLRB issued a bargaining order based on union authorization cards. The authorization cards were unequivocal and clearly stated that the employee authorized the union to represent him or her. The employer contended that the employees were orally told that signing the cards will only result in an election. Will the bargaining order be set aside? Why, or why not?

10 Pat lives in a state that has enacted a right-to-work law. The company which employs her has recognized the United Clerical Workers (UCW) as the bargaining representative of its workers. The union has sought to collect union dues or their equivalent from Pat. Is she required to pay them? Why, or why not?

11 ABC Company's employees voted by 51 percent in an election to have American Confederation act as their collective-bargaining representatives. Only four months later, 60 percent of the employees became disenchanted with American Confederation and wished to oust it. May they do so? Explain.

12 Four employees solicited union authorization cards from other employees. They informed those people solicited that union initiation fees would be waived if the cards were signed. Is this a ground for setting aside a union election victory? Explain.

13 Suppose a union threatens a nationwide strike that will shut down an industry indefinitely. Procedurally, how can the strike be prevented or delayed? For how long? Explain.

14 The Amalgamated Lead Workers' Union suspected that antiunion persons were infiltrating its ranks to overthrow the union. Accordingly, its board proposed a rule, which the membership adopted, that only those who had belonged to the union for at least two years would be eligible for union office. Walter, who had been in AML for only eighteen months, filed a petition to run for president, but it was refused because of the two-year requirement. Walter filed suit, challenging the rule. What was the result? Why?

15 The garbage collectors in Metropolis are city employees. They are represented by a union. Negotiations with the city manager have broken down and the garbage collectors have gone on strike. The city manager has notified all employees that anyone who does not return to work within twenty-four hours will be discharged. Those who do not return are then replaced with new employees. Will a court order the discharged workers to be rehired? Why, or why not?

CHAPTER 17

UNFAIR LABOR PRACTICES

OVERVIEW

The previous chapter introduced you to labor law. It emphasized that the Wagner Act declared certain practices by management to be unfair to labor unions and workers. The Taft-Hartley Act later declared certain practices by unions to be unfair and illegal. The Landrum-Griffin Act later added to both lists. This chapter discusses these unfair labor practices in detail.

As you study this chapter, keep in mind that the law encourages collective bargaining. It seeks to give employees a free choice in choosing whether or not to be represented by a union. The responsibility for determining whether or not a party has committed an unfair labor practice is with the NLRB, and its rules and decisions are given great deference. As you read this chapter, recognize how easy it is for both management and labor to commit an unfair labor practice.

The following additional legal terms are introduced in this chapter: compulsory bargaining issue, concerted activities, constructive discharge, featherbedding, hot-cargo contract, organizational picketing, secondary boycott, voluntary bargaining issue, work rules, and Wright-Line Doctrine.

1 INTRODUCTION

The term "unfair labor practice" was originally used to describe practices by management that were unfair to workers and their unions. The Wagner

Act listed five general categories of such violations. A later amendment added a sixth. These are summarized in Table 17-1.

An activity may be, and often is, a violation of more than one of the listed unfair labor practices. Indeed, most violations constitute interference with the right to engage in concerted activity (the first category). For example, retaliation against a union leader for filing charges would constitute a violation of both the first and fourth categories.

If management is guilty of an unfair labor practice, the NLRB has a broad range of remedies to use in eliminating the impact of the violation. If a union has lost a representation election, it may order a new one. If an employee has been wronged, for example, by a wrongful discharge, the Board can order the employee rehired with back pay. The NLRB has the capability of righting wrongs that have occurred.

As we noted in the prior chapter, the Taft-Hartley Act declared that certain actions by unions are also unfair labor practices. The Landrum-Griffin Act also expanded the list of unfair labor practices. The sections which follow give examples of violations by both parties—management and labor. The discussion of unfair labor practices by unions begins with section 10 of this chapter.

2 INTERFERENCE WITH EFFORTS OF EMPLOYEES TO FORM OR JOIN LABOR ORGANIZATIONS

In part, the first unfair labor practice listed is for an employer to interfere with the efforts of employees to form, join, or assist labor organizations. This is a catchall intended to guarantee the right to organize and join a labor union. It clearly prohibits "scare" tactics, such as threats by employers to fire those involved in organizing employees or to cut back on employee benefits if employees succeed in unionizing. In addition, less obvious activities are outlawed, such as requiring job applicants to state on a questionnaire whether they would cross a picket line in a strike, unless the questionnaire contains an assurance by the employer against reprisal. In one typical case, the company personnel director questioned two employees on

TABLE 17-1 UNFAIR LABOR PRACTICES BY EMPLOYERS

1. Interference with efforts of employees to form, join, or assist labor organizations, or to engage in concerted activities for mutual aid or protection
2. Domination of a labor organization or contribution of financial or other support to it
3. Discrimination in hiring or tenure of employees for reason of union affiliation
4. Discrimination against employees for filing charges or giving testimony under the act
5. Refusal to bargain collectively in good faith with a duly designated representative of the employees
6. Agreeing with a labor organization to engage in a secondary boycott

break about both the whereabouts of a union meeting and if the union was paying employees to sign authorization cards. These questions were a coercive interrogation and an unfair labor practice. An employer cannot engage in conduct calculated to erode employee support for the union.

Retaliation for union activity is discussed more fully in section 4 of this chapter. However, keep in mind that not every act of retaliation is an unfair labor practice. For example, the filing of a lawsuit may or may not be an unfair labor practice, depending on the outcome of the lawsuit. In the case which follows, the NLRB attempted to stop the lawsuit as an unfair labor practice but was not allowed to do so.

BILL JOHNSON'S RESTAURANTS, INC. v. N.L.R.B.
103 S.Ct. 2161 (1983)

FACTS

Helton, a waitress at Johnson's restaurant, filed unfair labor practice charges with the NLRB, alleging that she had been fired because of her efforts to organize a union. Later, Helton and other waitresses picketed the restaurant and distributed leaflets. The restaurant then filed a suit for damages and injunctive relief against Helton and the other demonstrators in an Arizona state court. It alleged that Helton and the other demonstrators had harassed customers, blocked access to the restaurant, created a threat to public safety, and libeled the restaurant by false statements in the leaflets.

On the following day, Helton filed a second charge with the NLRB, alleging that the civil suit was filed in retaliation for the defendant's protected, concerted activities and the filing of charges with the NLRB. An administrative law judge concluded that, on the basis of the record and from his observation of the witnesses, the evidence failed to support the allegations of the complaint in the state court action and that such action thus lacked a reasonable basis, and its prosecution was retaliatory, in violation of the National Labor Relations Act. The NLRB ordered the restaurant to withdraw its state court complaint.

ISSUE

Is filing the lawsuit in the state court an unfair labor practice?

DECISION

No.

REASONS

1. The NLRB may not halt the prosecution of a state court lawsuit, regardless of the plaintiff's motive, unless the suit lacks a reasonable basis in fact or law. Retaliatory motive and lack of reasonable basis are both essential prerequisites to the issuance of a cease and desist order against a state suit.
2. The filing and prosecution of a well-founded lawsuit may not be enjoined as

an unfair labor practice, even if it would not have been commenced but for the plaintiff's desire to retaliate against the defendant for exercising rights protected by the Wagner Act.
3. The act's provisions which guarantee employees the enjoyment of their rights to unionize, engage in concerted activity, and utilize the NLRB's processes without fear of coercion or retaliation by their employer are to be liberally construed.
4. However, countervailing considerations against allowing the NLRB to condemn the filing of a suit as an unfair labor practice include the First Amendment right of access to the courts and the state's compelling interests in maintaining domestic peace and protecting its citizens' health and welfare. Thus, the NLRB's interpretation of the act that the *only* essential element of a violation by the employer is retaliatory motive in filing a state court suit is untenable.
5. It is an enjoinable unfair labor practice to prosecute a baseless lawsuit with the intent of retaliating against an employee for the exercise of rights protected by the act. Such suits are not within the scope of First Amendment protection, and the state interests do not enter into play when the suit has no reasonable basis.
6. In determining whether a state court suit lacks a reasonable basis, the NLRB inquiry must preserve the state plaintiff's right to have a state court jury or judge resolve genuine material factual or state law legal disputes pertaining to the lawsuit. Therefore, the NLRB must await the results of the state court adjudication with respect to the merits of the state suit. If the state proceedings result in a judgment adverse to the plaintiff, the NLRB may then find that the lawsuit was filed with retaliatory intent and order appropriate relief.

Conferring Benefits

Even conferring of benefits by an employer may be an unfair labor practice. In one case, the employer reminded its employees by a letter sent two weeks before a representation election that the company had just instituted a "floating holiday" which they could take on their birthdays. The letter also announced a new system for computing overtime during holiday weeks, which had the effect of increasing wages for those weeks, and a new vacation schedule which let employees extend their vacations by sandwiching them between two weekends. The union lost the election, but the Supreme Court set it aside. It held that it was an unfair labor practice for the employer to engage in conduct immediately favorable to employees which is undertaken with the express purpose of impinging upon their freedom of choice for or against unionization and is reasonably calculated to have that effect. The danger inherent in well-timed increases in benefits is the suggestion of a fist inside the velvet glove. Employees are not likely to miss the inference that the source of benefits now conferred is also the source from which future benefits must flow and which may dry up if it is not obliged.

Work Rules

Company **work rules** often affect negatively workers' attempts to organize and join a union. These work rules may prohibit wearing buttons or insignia on work clothes. Unless the employer can establish a valid reason for such rules, they cannot be used to stop the wearing of union buttons or insignia. To punish a worker for violating such a work rule would constitute an unfair labor practice. Similarly, "no solicitation on the premises" rules which go beyond the actual necessity of the employer to ensure health, safety, or the like are not enforceable; the employer cannot use these to stop workers from organizing.

A rule which prohibits solicitation during "working time" is presumptively valid, but a rule which bans solicitation during "working hours" is presumptively invalid. It is an unfair labor practice to prohibit union activity and solicitation on company property during the employees' own time. The employer need not permit it when the employee is supposed to be working.

In one case, the NLRB held that a hospital's rule prohibiting solicitation by its employees at all times "in any area of the hospital which is accessible to or utilized by the public" was presumed to be invalid except in "immediate patient areas." These were defined as places such as patients' rooms, operating rooms, and places where patients receive treatment. The Supreme Court agreed with the Board that the hospital had not justified its rule as applied to its cafeteria, gift shop, and the lobbies and entrances on its first floor. However, union solicitation in the presence or within the hearing of patients in corridors and sitting rooms that adjoined patients' rooms and operating and treatment rooms might have an adverse effect on their recovery. Thus, the no-solicitation rule was not an unfair labor practice as applied to such areas, in addition to the "immediate patient-care areas."

Of course, the Wagner Act does not guarantee the rights of employees to solicit for *any* cause on an employer's property. Solicitation must be protected by Section 7 if it involves collective bargaining or an activity engaged in for other mutual aid or protection.

Written and Oral Statements Made to Employees

A difficult aspect is presented in those cases in which an employer is accused of an unfair labor practice as a result of something he has said or written. Such allegations may conflict with First Amendment guarantees of freedom of speech and the press. Moreover, as we noted in Chapter 16, the Taft-Hartley Act provides that the expression of views, arguments, or opinions is not evidence of an unfair labor practice if it contains no threats of reprisal or promises of benefits.

An employer may even predict that the consequences of unionization will be unfavorable if she or he does so in a way which contains no threat. The statement that "it is our definite view that if the union were to come in here, it would work to your serious harm" has been held privileged and noncoercive. However, if the employer predicts dire economic events as a result of unionization, such may be an illegal threat if he has it within his power to make the prediction come true.

It is extremely difficult to draw a clear-cut line between those statements of employers which are coercive and those which are noncoercive and thus privileged. Interpretations of the Board have varied with its membership over the years.

3 INTERFERING WITH CONCERTED ACTIVITIES

The first half of the first unfair labor practice refers to interference with efforts to form, join, or assist labor organizations. The second half covers "**concerted activities** for mutual aid or protection." A violation of the second half does not have to involve a union. It protects any group of employees acting for mutual aid and protection. This protection is limited, however, when an exclusive-bargaining representative has already been chosen. It does not protect individuals in other unions.

Concerted activity may directly involve a union and issues of importance to the workers and their union. The phrase is given a liberal interpretation to create a climate that encourages unionization, collective bargaining, and all that may flow therefrom. For example, some employees refused to work after a heated grievance meeting. They followed their supervisors onto the workroom floor and continued to argue loudly until they were ordered a second time to resume work. The employer issued letters of reprimand, alleging insubordination. This was an unfair labor practice. The employees were engaged in a protected activity. The protection of employee conduct at grievance meetings is extended to a brief "cooling-off period" following an employer's termination of such a meeting. Protection of employee participation in the meetings themselves would be seriously threatened if the employer could at any point call an immediate halt to the operation of the law simply by declaring the meeting ended.

The case which follows illustrates the extent to which the law protects workers in concerted activities.

> **EASTEX, INC. v. N.L.R.B.**
> 98 S.Ct. 2505 (1978)
>
> **FACTS**
>
> Employees tried to distribute a newsletter in nonworking areas of the company's plant during nonworking time. The newsletter included a section that urged employees to voice opposition to incorporation of states' right-to-work laws into a revised state constitution and a section criticizing a presidential veto of an increase in the federal minimum wage. The employer refused to allow distribution, and the NLRB held this was an unfair labor practice.
>
> **ISSUE**
>
> Does the law protect the distribution of this newsletter as a concerted activity?
>
> **DECISION**
>
> Yes.
>
> **REASONS**
>
> 1. The "mutual aid and protection" clause includes any employee and is not limited to support of employees in one particular unit.
> 2. Employees do not lose the protection of the clause when they go outside the immediate employee-employer relationship. The NLRB will define just how tenuous a relation a particular activity can bear to the employment relationship and still be a protected concerted activity.

Work Rules

Concerted activities often involve the refusal to follow work rules. If the employer has a rule with which the workers disagree, it is not uncommon for several of them to refuse to comply. Is it permissible to discipline such employees, or is discipline in such cases an unfair labor practice? The answer is often unclear and depends upon the facts in each case.

For example, a typical work rule used in industry is that a worker may not leave work without permission. In one case, the employer discharged seven employees for violating this rule. The employees on a particularly cold day had walked off the job from an uninsulated machine shop which on that day had no heat. On other occasions, protests had been made about the poor heat. The employees claimed to have acted as a group in protest against unfit working conditions, hoping that their concerted action would cause the employer to heat the shop properly. The employer justified the discharge action by claiming that the men left work without permission. The NLRB ruled that the action of the employees was protected concerted activity and that their discharge amounted to an unfair labor practice. The Supreme Court agreed and noted that employees do not:

...necessarily lose their right to engage in concerted activities...merely because they do not present a specific demand upon their employer to remedy a condition which they find objectionable. The language of [the law] is broad enough to protect concerted activities whether they take place before, after, or at the same time such a demand is made....Having no bargaining representative and no established procedures...the men took the most direct course to let the company know they wanted a warmer place in which to work.

However, in another case the Supreme Court held that it was not an unfair labor practice for a company to fire certain employees who picketed the company's store against union advice. There, the union had investigated charges that the company was racially discriminating against employees and had invoked the contract grievance procedure under the collective-bargaining agreement, by demanding that the joint union-management adjustment board be convened "to hear the entire case." The discharged employees had begun picketing the company because they felt that the grievance procedure being utilized was inadequate. In upholding the NLRB's decision, the court ruled that the law recognizes the principle of exclusive representation. Therefore, concerted activities by a minority of employees to bargain with their employer over issues of employment discrimination are not protected by the Wagner Act. Such employees may not bypass their exclusive-bargaining representative.

Interviews

The concerted-activity concept has been expanded in recent decisions. In one case, an employer was investigating theft by employees. One employee asked that a union representative be present during her interview. She was refused. The Supreme Court held that the employee had a right to representation when there was a perceived threat to her employment security. The presence of a representative assures other employees in the bargaining unit that they too can obtain aid and protection if they wish when there appears to be a threat to their job security. Refusing the assistance at the interview was an unfair labor practice.

A few years later, a nonunion employee sought to have a union representative present at an investigatory interview. The courts held that the employee had a right to this assistance. Just as a union member has this right, so does a nonunion employee. The right to representation is derived from the protection afforded to concerted activity for mutual aid or protection, not from a union's right to act as an employee's exclusive representative for the purpose of collective bargaining.

Sole Employee as Concerted Activity

The right to engage in concerted activity has been expanded to cover the actions of a sole employee under certain circumstances. If an employee has a grievance which may affect other workers, that employee has rights protected by the concerted activity language of the first unfair labor practice.

N.L.R.B. v. CITY DISPOSAL SYSTEMS, INC.
104 S.Ct. 1505 (1984)

FACTS

James Brown, a truck driver, was employed by City Disposal Systems, Inc., which hauls garbage for the city of Detroit. He was discharged when he refused to drive a truck that he honestly and reasonably believed to be unsafe because of faulty brakes. The collective-bargaining agreement provided: "[t]he Employer shall not require employees to take out on the streets or highways any vehicle that is not in safe operating condition or equipped with safety appliances prescribed by law. It shall not be a violation of the Agreement where employees refuse to operate such equipment unless such refusal is unjustified."

Brown filed a grievance with the union, but it declined to process it. He then filed an unfair labor practice charge which challenged his discharge. The NLRB found that Brown was discharged for refusing to operate the truck and that the discharge was an unfair labor practice. It found that an employee who acts alone in asserting a contract right is nevertheless engaged in concerted activity. He was ordered reinstated with back pay. The court of appeals reversed, holding that there was no concerted activity.

ISSUE

Was the employee grievance a form of concerted activity?

DECISION

Yes.

REASONS

1. An individual's reasonable and honest assertion of a right grounded in a collective-bargaining agreement is concerted activity and is protected by the Wagner Act.
2. If the employee's action is based on a reasonable and honest belief that he is being asked to perform a task that he is not required to perform under his collective-bargaining agreement, and if the action is reasonably directed toward the enforcement of a collective-bargaining right, the NLRB's judgment that the employee is engaged in concerted activity will be affirmed.
3. The fact that an activity is concerted does not necessarily mean that an employee may engage in the activity with impunity. If an employee has engaged in concerted activity in a manner that is overly abusive or violative of his collective-bargaining agreement, his actions will be unprotected.

4 DISCHARGE AND OTHER FORMS OF RETALIATION

One of the primary techniques used by management to discourage unionization and interfere with the right of workers to engage in concerted union activity is either to threaten to "fire" the workers or actually to discharge them if the union wins the election. Retaliation and the threat of retaliation are clearly unfair labor practices. However, the issues are often much more complicated. Is it an unfair labor practice to discharge a union organizer who is also an unsatisfactory employee? What is the effect of an employer's assisting others in making it impossible for the worker to continue his or her employment?

The latter issue was involved in the following case.

N.L.R.B. v. SURE-TAN, INC.
672 F.2d 592 (1982)

FACTS

After a union was certified, the employer sent a letter to the Immigration and Naturalization Service (INS), asking it to check the immigration status of five named employees. After a short investigation, INS agents discovered that each of the five employees listed in the letter was a Mexican national working illegally in the United States. The employees were arrested and later accepted the INS's grant of voluntary departure as a substitute for deportation. The NLRB found that the employer constructively discharged the employees for forming the union.

ISSUE

Was the employer guilty of an unfair labor practice?

DECISION

Yes.

REASONS

1. The employer was not legally obligated to report the employees. It did so to retaliate against them. The evidence showed antiunion bias.
2. The employees were constructively discharged. Two elements are required to establish a **constructive discharge.** The employer's conduct must have created working conditions that forced the employees to resign, and the employer must have acted to discourage membership in a labor organization.
3. The employees were reinstated with back pay. If they could not get back into the country, the back pay was to be for six months.

In cases involving mixed motivation for discharge, the NLRB follows a procedure known as the **Wright-Line Doctrine.** Under this doctrine, the NLRB's general counsel first introduces evidence that makes a prima facie showing sufficient to support the inference that the employer's opposition to protected conduct was a "motivating factor" in the employer's discharge decision. The NLRB can find an unfair labor practice based solely on the general counsel's proof of a prima facie case of discrimination. This is possible if the employer does not come forward with any evidence to support its allegations that the discharge has been for legitimate business reasons.

Once this prima facie case is established, the burden shifts to the employer to demonstrate that the same action would have taken place even in the absence of the protected conduct. The Board retains the burden to prove retaliatory discharge by a preponderance of the evidence.

The case which follows is typical of those involving mixed motivation for discharge and the application of the Wright-Line Doctrine. Note that the employer does not have the burden of proving that an unfair labor practice has not occurred. The weighing by the NLRB includes a careful consideration of the employer's "good" reason as well as the general counsel's evidence of improper motive.

N.L.R.B. v. TRANSPORTATION MANAGEMENT CORP.
103 S.Ct. 2469 (1983)

FACTS

The National Labor Relations Board found that Transportation Management Corp. (TMC) had discharged Santillo, one of TMC's bus drivers, for union activity. Santillo had attempted to organize TMC drivers and convince them to join the Teamsters' Union. TMC had argued that Santillo was dismissed for leaving his keys in the bus and taking unauthorized breaks.

In conducting the hearing, the NLRB applied its rule that the general counsel has the burden of persuading the Board by a preponderance of the evidence that an antiunion bias has contributed to the employer's decision to discharge the employee. Under this rule, the employer can avoid the conclusion that it violated the act by proving by a preponderance of the evidence that the employee would have been fired for permissible reasons even if he had not been involved in protected union activities. The Board concluded that TMC failed to carry its burden of persuading the Board that the employee's discharge would have taken place even if he had not been engaged in protected union activities.

ISSUE

Was it error to place the burden of proof on the employer to prove that the employee would have been fired even if not involved in union activities?

DECISION

No.

> **REASONS**
> 1. The burden of proof placed on the employer under the Board's rule is consistent with the rest of the statute; it provides that the Board must prove an unlawful labor practice by a preponderance of the evidence.
> 2. The Board's construction of the statute, which is not mandated by the act, extends to the employer what the Board considers to be an affirmative defense. However, it does not change or add to the elements of the unfair labor practice that the general counsel has the burden of proving. This is a permissible construction, and the Board's allocation of the burden of proof is reasonable.
> 3. The Board was justified in this case in finding that the employee would not have been discharged had the employer not considered his protected activities. Such finding was supported by substantial evidence on the record considered as a whole.

The NLRB has a rule regarding the discharge of supervisors. Under the rule, the discharge of a supervisor is unlawful only if it interferes with the rights of an employee. Supervisors are excluded from the definition of employee, and the employer is entitled to insist on the loyalty of supervisors. Supervisors are not free to engage in activities which would be protected if engaged in by other employees. The only exceptions to the rule are: (1) to discharge a supervisor for testifying before the Board or during the grievance process, (2) to discipline a supervisor for refusing to commit an unfair labor practice, or (3) to discharge a supervisor who has hired his own pro-union crew as a pretext for terminating the former crew.

Retaliation may take other forms than discharge. It may entail a reduction of benefits. For example, several workers were on sick leave when their union commenced a strike. The company discontinued accident and sickness payments to all workers who were sick but continued to make payments to workers who were disabled by job-related injuries. This distinction constituted an unfair labor practice. The sick workers were not required to repudiate the strike, and the employer may not presume support of the strike by silence.

5 DOMINATION OF A LABOR ORGANIZATION

Before the Wagner Act was passed, it was a fairly common practice for employers to sidetrack the desires and efforts of employees to organize by forming a "union" which was in fact controlled by the employer. The second unfair labor practice is the domination of a labor organization by employers or their contribution of financial or other support to it; the act puts an end to the use of such company unions.

Under the Wagner Act, any organization of employees must be completely independent of their employers. Neither the employers nor their supervisory personnel may promote or sponsor a particular organization for collective bargaining. In the case of a controversy between competing unions, employers must remain strictly neutral unless they already have a union-shop agreement in force with one of them. This section of the law was violated when it was agreed that an employee representative plan could not be amended if the employer disapproved. Such control of the form and structure of the employees' representative committee deprived them of the guaranteed freedom from control by their employer. It is an unfair labor practice for the employer to support a union by giving it a meeting place; providing refreshments for union meetings; permitting the union to use the employer's telephone, secretary, or copying machine; or allowing the union to keep cafeteria or vending-machine profits.

An employer's agreement to pay initiation fees and dues to a union for member employees is in violation when it is an inducement to join the union. This provision also prevents an employer from recognizing or bargaining with a union before it wins an election if there are two or more rival unions. Even when there is only one union, the employer is in violation by bargaining with it if it does not represent a majority of the employees.

6 DISCRIMINATION FOR UNION AFFILIATION

Under provisions designed to prevent the third unfair labor practice, an employer may neither discharge nor refuse to hire an employee either to encourage or discourage membership in any labor organization. The employer also may not discriminate regarding any term or condition of employment for such purposes. Thus, discrimination in wages, hours, work assignments, promotions, vacations, and the like against union members is forbidden. The law does not oblige an employer to favor union members in hiring employees. It also does not restrict him or her in the normal exercise of any employer's right to select or discharge employees. However, the employer may not abuse that right by discriminatory action which encourages or discourages membership in a labor organization. For example, a company may not go partially out of business because some of its employees have organized, nor may it temporarily close that portion of its business that has unionized. If a company closes one plant because a union is voted in, such action discourages union activity at other plants. Partial closings to "chill" unionism are unfair labor practices, as the case which follows indicates.

> **TEXTILE WORKERS UNION v. DARLINGTON MANUFACTURING CO.**
> 85 S.Ct. 994 (1965)
>
> **FACTS**
>
> Deering Milliken was a holding company for several separately incorporated textile mills. The Darlington plant was unionized despite fierce resistance by the employer. The company informed the workers that if the union won the election, the plant would be closed. When the workers voted for union representation, the board of directors liquidated the corporation, sold all plant machinery and equipment, and laid off their entire work force. The NLRB found that the plant had been closed because of antiunion bias and that the closing was a violation of Section 8(a)(3). It ordered the plant reopened, the workers rehired, and back pay paid.
>
> **ISSUES**
>
> 1. May an employer go out of business to avoid a union?
> 2. Was the employer guilty of an unfair labor practice in this case?
>
> **DECISIONS**
>
> 1. Yes.
> 2. Yes.
>
> **REASONS**
>
> 1. An employer can terminate its entire business for any reason, but it cannot terminate part of its business simply because a union has been chosen by its workers.
> 2. A partial or temporary closing of a plant or department is an unfair labor practice under Section 8(a)(3) if it is motivated by a purpose to chill unionism in any of the remaining plants or departments of a single employer and if the employer may reasonably have foreseen that the closing would likely have that effect.
> 3. To avoid being guilty of an unfair labor practice, the company would have to close all of its plants.

Many other examples of discrimination against union members and especially union leaders exist. In one example, a collective-bargaining agreement contained a no-strike clause but there was no provision requiring union officials to prevent illegal work stoppages. When union members and leaders refused to cross a picket line (established by a different union), the company suspended for five to ten days employees who were union members. The employees who were union leaders were suspended twenty-five days. The court held that the employer violated Section 8(a)(3) of the Wagner Act. To justify the more severe punishment imposed upon union leaders, there must be an affirmative duty that these leaders prevent illegal work stoppages. Since the contract contained no such duty, the company's action on the basis of an employee's union activity was discriminatory.

In cases such as these, the terms of the collective-bargaining agreement are very important. The union may agree to harsher penalties for union officials as a part of the bargaining process. For example, a wildcat strike was conducted in violation of a collective-bargaining agreement. A union official was suspended for ten days while the rank and file strikers were only suspended for five days. This was not an unfair labor practice. A contract may allow for selective discipline of union officials. The parties to a collective-bargaining agreement may seek to increase the effectiveness of a no-strike clause by providing for heightened efforts on the part of union officials to avoid or reduce the disruptive effects of strikes during the contract term. Provision of harsher penalties for union officials who disobey these duties may spur union officials to honor those duties. Allowing the parties to give effect to such contractual terms furthers the strong national labor policy of substituting peaceful dispute resolution for industrial strife and the equally strong policy of freedom of contract.

7 DISCRIMINATION: NLRB PROCEEDINGS

Under provisions to prevent the fourth unfair labor practice, employees are protected from being discharged or from other reprisals by their employers because they have sought to enforce their rights under the act. This prevents the NLRB's channels of information from being dried up by employers' intimidation of complainants and witnesses. An employer cannot refuse to hire a prospective employee because charges have been filed by him or her. Although supervisors are not regarded as "employees" within the meaning of the act, they have been held to be protected from discharge or reprisal for testifying in a labor proceeding. Such action would coerce those who are employees in the exercise of their rights to organize.

The main defense of any employer accused of reprisal is that he or she discharged or discriminated against the employee for some reason other than filing charges or giving testimony. Thus, most often such cases boil down to trying to prove what motivated the company in pursuing its course of action. If the company can convince the NLRB that the employee was discharged because of misconduct, low production, personnel cutbacks necessitated by economic conditions, or other legitimate considerations, the company will be exonerated. Otherwise, it will be found guilty of this unfair labor practice. Please refer to the discussion in section 4 of this chapter which deals with discharge and other forms of retaliation that constitute violations of the first unfair labor practice provision. Many cases violate more than one provision. Most cases involving the fourth category also involve the first.

8 THE DUTY TO BARGAIN COLLECTIVELY IN GOOD FAITH

It is now an unfair labor practice for both an employer and the representatives of employees to refuse to bargain collectively with each other. The Wagner Act did not define the term "to bargain collectively." Judicial decisions have added the concept "good faith" to it, so that it actually means to bargain in good faith. Thus, although an employer need not agree to any union demands, such conduct as the failure to make counterproposals to union demands may be evidence of bad faith. To comply with the requirement that they bargain collectively in good faith, employers and unions must approach the bargaining table with fair and open minds and a sincere purpose to find a basis of agreement. Refusing to meet at reasonable times with representatives of the other party, refusing to reduce agreements to writing, and designating persons with no authority to negotiate as representatives at meetings are examples of this unfair labor practice. The employer's duty to bargain collectively includes a duty to provide relevant information needed by a union for the proper performance of its duties as the employees' bargaining representative. For example, data about chemicals used by employees must be furnished so that the union and its members can be aware of dangers to health. Companies cannot refuse to provide unions with job-related nonproprietary safety and health information that does not disclose personal medical records. The union has an obligation to safeguard its members' health and safety.

A more fundamental issue than good faith is also inherent in the requirement that parties bargain collectively. That issue, simply stated, is: "About what?" Must the employer bargain with the union about all subjects and all management decisions in which the union or the employees are interested? Are there subjects and issues upon which management is allowed to act unilaterally?

In answering these questions, the law divides issues into two categories—**compulsory bargaining issues** and **voluntary bargaining issues.** Compulsory or mandatory bargaining issues are those concerned with wages, hours, and other terms and conditions of employment. Although the parties may voluntarily consider other issues, the refusal by either to bargain in good faith on such other permissive matters is not an unfair labor practice. Nor is it an unfair labor practice to refuse to bargain over the rights of former employees. For example, an employer eliminated medical benefits to retired workers when Medicare became effective. The union demanded to negotiate. This was not a mandatory bargaining issue. If a matter does not affect employees in a working relationship, it will be a mandatory issue of bargaining only if it vitally affects the terms and conditions of employment for those working.

In recent years, one of the most difficult legal issues in labor-management relations has been the impact on collective-bargaining contracts of bankruptcy proceedings. Employers frequently seek reorganization under Section 11 of the bankruptcy laws. Since collective-bargaining agreements are "executory contracts," the bankruptcy code permits a debtor in possession of its estate or the trustee in bankruptcy to modify or cancel such contracts. The Supreme Court in 1984, in a five-to-four decision, held that an employer could unilaterally cancel collective-bargaining agreements and change the wage structure of its employees without committing an unfair labor practice. The Supreme Court decision holding that a unilateral rejection or modification of a labor contract is not an unfair labor practice has been on the premise that such a rejection is a necessary part of reorganization. The dissenting justices believe that the duty to bargain collectively prohibits termination or modification unless the union is given timely notice, there is an order to meet and confer, and the agreement continues for sixty days after notice.

Subsequent to this decision, Congress has amended the bankruptcy laws to give more protection to workers. The law now requires employers filing for bankruptcy to have court approval before they repudiate a labor contract. As a result, employers seeking reorganization may unilaterally change the terms of their collective-bargaining agreement only with court approval. The terms of labor contracts remain compulsory bargaining issues. Courts before approving a petition to modify or reject a labor contract will require reasonable efforts to negotiate a voluntary modification and proof that collective bargaining cannot produce a prompt and satisfactory solution to the problem.

Classifying an issue as compulsory or voluntary is done on a case-by-case basis. For example, questions relating to fringe benefits are compulsory bargaining issues because they are "wages." The NLRB and the courts are called on to decide whether management and labor must bargain with each other on a multitude of issues, as the case which follows illustrates.

FORD MOTOR COMPANY v. NLRB
99 S.Ct. 1842 (1979)

FACTS

Ford had the contractual right to review the prices and quality of an in-plant cafeteria and vending-machine service provided by an independent company. The union wanted to negotiate over proposed increases in prices by the vendor, and Ford refused. The NLRB found this a violation of the duty to bargain in good faith.

ISSUE

Is this a compulsory bargaining issue?

DECISION

Yes.

REASONS

1. The Board's view should be given considerable deference. Courts will not reverse the NLRB if its determination is not unreasonable or based upon an unprincipled construction of the facts.
2. Requiring bargaining over this issue leads to peace and not disorder.
3. Because eating and the availability of food is a major consideration of the employee conditions, it is within the employment relationship. If disputes over food prices are likely to be frequent and intense, it follows that more, not less, collective bargaining is the remedy.

A party to labor negotiations may present a demand relating to a nonmandatory bargaining issue as long as its resolution is not a condition precedent to the resolution of mandatory bargaining issues. Tying a voluntary bargaining issue to a compulsory bargaining issue results in a failure to bargain in good faith and is, in effect, an unfair labor practice.

Courts tend to defer to the special expertise of the NLRB in classifying collective-bargaining subjects, especially in the area of "terms or conditions of employment." The courts have affirmed Board rulings which hold that issues such as union-dues checkoff, health and accident insurance, safety rules, merit-pay increases, incentive-pay plans, Christmas and other bonuses, stock purchase plans, pensions, paid vacations and holidays, the privilege of hunting on a reserved portion of a paper company's forest preserve, proposals for effective arbitration and grievance procedures, and no-strike and no-lockout clauses are compulsory bargaining issues. Industry practice is a major factor in many decisions.

The Board has recently changed its policy on the issue of whether the employer can unilaterally transfer operations from a unionized facility to an unorganized facility during the term of a collective-bargaining agreement. In 1982, the Board held that a unilateral transfer is an unfair labor practice. In 1984, the Board held that an employer does not violate the Wagner Act by relocating the work of a bargaining unit without the union's consent so long as the employer is willing to bargain in good faith over the proposed change. An employer may not unilaterally institute changes before reaching a good-faith impasse in bargaining. Although an employer may not modify the terms and conditions of the contract without the union's consent, if the contract does not specifically prohibit the change then the only obligation is to bargain in good faith on the issue.

Remember that neither the employer nor the union is required to make concessions to the other concerning a mandatory subject of bargaining. The law only demands that each negotiate such matters in good faith with the other before making a decision and taking unilateral action. If the parties fail to reach an agreement after discussing these problems, each may take steps which are against the wishes and best interests of the other party. For example, the employer may refuse to grant a wage increase requested by the union, and the union is free to strike.

9 AGREEING WITH A UNION TO ENGAGE IN A SECONDARY BOYCOTT

The unfair labor practice by employers of a **secondary boycott** was not one of the original five forbidden under the Wagner Act. Taft-Hartley attempted to limit the use by unions of the secondary boycott as an indirect weapon in a campaign to organize employees. It was an unfair labor practice for a union to induce the *employees* of an employer to strike, or engage in a concerted refusal to use, handle, or work on any goods or to perform any services, to force the employer to stop doing business with any other person. For example, assume that employer A sells supplies to manufacturer B, which are transported by trucking firm C, whose employees are nonunion. This Taft-Hartley provision makes it illegal for either a union attempting to organize the employees of C or the union representing the employees of A to induce the employees of A to strike or refuse to load C's trucks with supplies to require A to stop shipping its goods by C. This represents a swing of the pendulum back from the Norris-LaGuardia Act's liberalization of the use of secondary boycotts toward the policy of the law as it existed before that act. Then, secondary boycotts were viewed as illegal combinations in restraint of trade under the Sherman Act or as illegal conspiracies under the common law.

Taft-Hartley, however, was not successful in eliminating all secondary boycotts. Loopholes appeared in its proscriptions. For example, a **hot-cargo contract,** in which an *employer* voluntarily agrees with a union not to handle, use, or deal in non-union-produced goods of another person, was held to be legal. The union was prevented only from inducing the *employees* of the employer to strike or otherwise act to force their employer not to handle such goods. The Landrum-Griffin Act plugged this loophole and outlawed hot-cargo contracts. Its amendment to Taft-Hartley made it an unfair labor practice for any labor organization and any *employer* to enter into any contract or agreement whereby such employer agrees to refrain from handling, using, selling, transporting, or otherwise dealing in any of the products of any other employer, or to cease doing business with any other person. The secondary boycott provisions as they pertain to unions are discussed further in section 13 of this chapter.

UNFAIR LABOR PRACTICES BY UNIONS

10 INTRODUCTION

The Wagner Act did not contain any provisions relating to unfair labor practices by labor unions. It was, in effect, one-sided. The Taft-Hartley Act covered the missing side by declaring that certain conduct or activities by labor unions also were unfair labor practices and thus illegal. Six such activities were specified. The Landrum-Griffin Act in 1959 added two additional unfair labor practices by unions to those declared illegal by the Taft-Hartley Act.

The following table summarizes the actions and omissions by unions which are unfair labor practices:

Numbers 1, 4, 7, and 8 are discussed in subsequent sections. (Number 3 is the union duty to bargain in good faith. It was discussed in section 8 with the same duty of employers.) The second unfair practice by unions recognizes that if a legal union-shop agreement is in effect, a labor organization may insist that the employer observe its terms.

Unfair labor practice number 5 exists because employees in a union shop must join the union after they have been employed for a minimum period of thirty days. Since there is unequal bargaining power and the union sets its initiation fee and dues, the law requires that they be neither excessive nor discriminatory against new members.

11 RESTRAINING OR COERCING AN EMPLOYEE IN JOINING A UNION

This unfair labor practice includes misconduct by unions directed toward employees and employers. Also forbidden are any attempts by a union to influence an employer in selecting its representatives to bargain with the union. Most allegations of unfair labor practices filed against unions are brought under this provision. The law makes it illegal for a union to re-

TABLE 17-2 UNFAIR LABOR PRACTICES BY UNIONS

1. Restraining or coercing an employee to join a union or an employer in selecting representatives to bargain with the union
2. Causing or attempting to cause the employer to discriminate against an employee who is not a union member, unless there is a legal union-shop agreement in effect
3. Refusing to bargain with the employer if it is the NLRB-designated representative of the employees
4. Striking, picketing, and engaging in secondary boycotts for illegal purposes
5. Charging new members excessive or discriminatory initiation fees when there is a union-shop agreement
6. Causing an employer to pay for work not performed ("featherbedding")
7. Picketing to require an employer to recognize or bargain with a union which is not currently certified as representing its employees in certain cases
8. Agreeing with an employer to engage in a secondary boycott

strain or coerce employees in the exercise of their rights to bargain collectively, just as it is an unfair labor practice by employers to interfere with the same rights. Employees also are guaranteed the right to *refrain* from union activities unless required by a legal union-shop agreement in force between their employer and a labor organization. In the following case, the employer refused to bargain with a union which had won a representation election on the grounds that prior to the election the union had violated this provision.

N.L.R.B. v. SAVAIR MANUFACTURING CO.
94 S.Ct. 495 (1973)

FACTS

The union circulated "recognition slips" to employees before a representation election. If a worker signed a slip and the union was subsequently certified, those who signed could join the union without paying an initiation fee. The union won the election. The employer, however, refused to bargain because it felt the union committed an unfair labor practice.

ISSUE

Is the union guilty of an unfair labor practice that will set aside the election?

DECISION

Yes.

REASONS

1. By permitting the union to offer to waive an initiation fee for those employees signing a recognition slip prior to the election, the NLRB allows the union to buy endorsements and paint a false portrait of employee support during its election campaign.
2. The statutory policy of fair elections does not permit endorsements, whether for or against the union, to be bought and sold in this fashion.
3. Any procedure requiring "fair" elections must honor the right of those who oppose a union as well as those who favor it. The law is wholly neutral when it comes to that basic choice. Employees have the right not only to "form, join, or assist" unions but also the right "to refrain from any or all of such activities."

The second part of this provision prohibits a union from restraining or coercing an employer in the selection of its representatives for collective bargaining. It is violated if a union refuses to bargain with a proper representative of an employer and yet threatens a strike if bargaining does not succeed. However, if a strike called by a union is an economic one with the sole objective of obtaining certain contractual terms and is not based on the refusal to deal with the employer's representative, it is not coercion of the employer forbidden by this subsection.

Union fines levied against management personnel sometimes run afoul of this provision. If a union were able to retaliate against supervisors who engage in negotiations or grievance proceedings on behalf of management, management would be coerced in the selection of its representatives. However, supervisors that are not engaged in such activities are still subject to union discipline and fines, as the court held in the following case.

N.L.R.B. v. INTERN. BROTH. OF ELEC. WORKERS, LOCAL 340
107 S.Ct. 2002 (1987)

FACTS

A union went on strike when its contract with the employers expired. Two of its members (Schous and Choate) were supervisors and continued to work. The union fined Schous $8,200 and Choate $6,000 for violating its constitution. The violations involved working for employers that did not have a collective-bargaining agreement with the union. The employers filed unfair labor practice charges. They alleged that the union had violated Section 8(b)(1)(B) of the National Labor Relations Act (Act), which makes it an unfair labor practice for a union "to restrain or coerce...an employer in the selection of his representatives for the purposes of collective bargaining or the adjustment of grievances." The two supervisors were not directly involved in collective bargaining or in the grievance procedures, although they could be so involved in the future.

ISSUE

Are these fines an unfair labor practice by the union?

DECISION

No.

REASONS

1. Union discipline of a supervisor member is prohibited only when that member engages in collective bargaining, grievance adjustment, or some other closely related activity such as contract interpretation.
2. Union discipline is an unfair labor practice only when it may adversely affect the supervisor's future conduct in performing labor-management related duties. Such an adverse effect will exist only when the supervisor is disciplined for behavior that occurs while the supervisor has such duties.
3. The general impact of union discipline on the supervisor's loyalty to the employer is insufficient to be an unfair labor practice.
4. There was no collective-bargaining relationship between the employers and the union when the latter enforced its no-contract, no-work rule against its supervisor members. Thus, the possibility that the union's discipline of the

supervisors would coerce the employers is too attenuated to form the basis of an unfair labor practice charge.
5. An employer is not restrained or coerced in the selection of its representatives because a union member must accept union expulsion or other discipline to continue in a supervisory position. Since union members have a right to resign from a union at any time and avoid imposition of union discipline, the employer may require that its representatives leave the union.

12 CAUSING AN EMPLOYER TO DISCRIMINATE AGAINST A NONUNION MEMBER

As noted in the prior chapter, the Taft-Hartley Act made union security contracts calling for a closed shop illegal, even if both employer and employees are in favor of one. However, if a legal *union-shop* agreement is in effect, a labor organization may insist that the employer observe its terms. But even when a legal union-shop contract is in effect, the law prohibits a union from attempting to cause an employer to discriminate against an employee who has been denied membership, or had his or her membership terminated, for some reason other than failure to pay the dues and initiation fees uniformly required of all members. And, even if an employee is a member, the union may not cause the employer to discriminate against him or her for not following union rules. This prohibition was designed to prevent the use of the union shop as a means of intimidating employees who were at odds with union officials over their policies.

13 SECONDARY BOYCOTTS AND OTHER ILLEGAL STRIKES AND PICKETING

It is an unfair labor practice for a union to threaten, coerce, or restrain third persons not parties to a labor dispute for the purpose of causing the third person to cease using, selling, handling, transporting, or otherwise dealing in the products of any other producer, or to cease doing business with any other person. The purpose of this law, which restricts most strikes and picketing to the employer with which the union actually has a labor dispute, protects neutral parties from serious economic injury or even ruin. The case which follows illustrates some situations in which picketing a secondary employer may be legal and some in which it is not. If a foreseeable consequence of a strike, picketing, or boycott is to disrupt the business of a third person, the activity is an unfair labor practice.

N.L.R.B. v. RETAIL STORE EMP. UNION, ETC.
100 S.Ct. 2372 (1980)

FACTS

Safeco Title Insurance Co. underwrites real estate title insurance, doing business with several title insurance companies that derive over 90 percent of their gross incomes from the sale of Safeco insurance policies. After contract negotiations between Safeco and the union reached an impasse, the employees went on strike. The union picketed each of the title companies, urging customers to support the strike by canceling their Safeco policies. Safeco filed a complaint with the NLRB, charging that the union had engaged in an unfair labor practice by picketing to promote a secondary boycott against the title companies.

ISSUE

Was the NLRB correct in ruling that the union's picketing was an unfair labor practice?

DECISION

Yes.

REASONS

1. Product picketing that reasonably can be expected to threaten neutral parties with ruin or substantial loss simply does not square with the language or the purpose of the law.
2. Since successful secondary picketing would put the title companies to a choice between their survival and the severance of their ties with Safeco, the picketing plainly violates the statutory ban on the coercion of neutrals in a labor dispute. Such coercion, which has the object of forcing neutrals to cease dealing in the primary product or to cease doing business with the primary employer, is illegal.

The restrictions are not limited to strikes and picketing. Publicity must be directed at the basic employer and not at third parties which are uninvolved in the labor dispute. The law allows publicity that shows that a product produced by an employer is being sold by a third person. It does not allow publicity that is directed at parties that do not sell the products. Note that in the case which follows, the "product" is a building.

EDWARD J. DEBARTOLO CORP. v. N.L.R.B. ET AL.
103 S.Ct. 2926 (1983)

FACTS

High Construction Company (High) was a general building contractor retained by H. M. Wilson Company (Wilson) to construct a department store in a shopping center owned and operated by the DeBartolo Corporation (DeBartolo). Neither DeBartolo nor any other tenant in the mall had a right to control the manner in which High constructed the Wilson store.

A local building trade union complained that High, in the building of the Wilson store, was paying its employees substandard wages without fringe benefits. Union members passed out handbills that urged customers not to trade with any of the stores in the mall, even though only Wilson had a business relationship with High. DeBartolo filed an unfair labor practice charge with the NLRB. It held that the handbilling was exempted from the secondary boycott prohibition of Section 8(b)(4) by the "publicity proviso." The NLRB reasoned that the proviso applied, because all tenants would derive a substantial benefit from the new store.

ISSUE

Is the distribution of the handbills directed at all tenants by the union a permissible activity?

DECISION

No.

REASONS

1. The National Labor Relations Act, Section 8(b)(4), prohibits secondary boycotts. However, the section includes a provision that permits publicity which advises the public that a product being produced by an employer with whom a union has a primary dispute is being sold by another employer. (The building is a product, for purposes of this exemption.)
2. The only publicity exempted from the secondary boycott prohibition is publicity intended to inform the public that the primary employer's product is "distributed by" the secondary employer. Here, the NLRB's analysis would almost strip the distribution requirement of any limiting effect. It diverts the inquiry away from the relationship between the primary and secondary employers and toward the relationship between the two secondary employers. It then tests that relationship by a standard so generous that it would be satisfied by virtually any secondary employer that a union might want consumers to boycott.
3. The handbills did not merely call for a boycott of the department-store company's products; they also called for a boycott of the products being sold by the company's co-tenants. Neither DeBartolo nor any of the co-tenants had any business relationship with the building contractor, nor do they sell any product whose chain of production can reasonably be said to include the contractor. Hence, there is no justification for treating the products that the co-tenants distribute to the public as products produced by the contractor.

Another example of illegal secondary activity occurs when a union induces the employees of an employer to strike, or to engage in a concerted refusal to use, handle, or work on any goods or perform any services, to force the employer to stop doing business with a third person. For example, assume once more that A sells to manufacturer B supplies which are transported by trucking firm C, whose employees are nonunion. It is illegal for either a union attempting to organize the employees of C or the union representing the employees of A to induce the employees of A to strike or refuse to load C's trucks with supplies to require A to stop shipping its goods by C. Similarly, it is forbidden for the union of X's employees, when engaging in a dispute with X, to induce any employees of Y to strike to coerce Y to stop buying the products of X. Likewise, it would be a violation for the union of X's employees to induce the employees not to work on goods produced by "scab" labor at the nonunion plant Z, to induce X to use union-made goods instead.

It is also an unfair labor practice for both the employer involved and the union to enter into a hot-cargo contract. As previously noted, a hot-cargo contract is one in which an employer voluntarily agrees with a union that the employees should not be required by their employer to handle or work on goods or materials going to, or coming from, an employer designated by the union as "unfair." Such goods are said to be "hot cargo." These clauses were common in trucking and construction. The law thus forbids an employer and a labor organization to make an agreement whereby the employer agrees to stop doing business with any other employer.

It is also an unfair labor practice for a union to threaten or to coerce an employer to recognize or bargain with one union if another one has been certified as the representative of its employees. This provision was made to protect employers (and their employees) from the destructive rivalry between unions competing to be the bargaining representative of employees in a unit where they had already chosen one. Jurisdictional strikes are also unfair labor practices. A jurisdictional strike is one forcing an employer to assign work to employees in one craft union rather than another. Since the dispute is between the two unions and not with the employer, the law requires that such disputes be submitted to the NLRB by the unions. Note that it is not a violation for a union certified by the Board to represent the employees performing the particular work involved to force the employer to assign it to them.

14 REQUIRING EMPLOYEES TO PAY EXCESSIVE FEES

The unfair labor practice of requiring employees to pay excessive fees was included in the law to protect employees who, by reason of a union-shop agreement, were required to join a union as a condition of employment. It prohibits the charging of an excessive or discriminatory initiation fee as a requirement of becoming a member of the union.

Since the employees (especially *new* employees) have no choice about membership and no bargaining power, the law requires that the dues and fees be reasonable and not discriminatory. For example, in one case a union raised its initiation fee to $500 from the former $50 for all new employees who received a certain minimum starting salary. This fee was held to be excessive and discriminatory.

15 CAUSING AN EMPLOYER TO PAY FOR WORK NOT PERFORMED

Designating as illegal the unfair labor practice of requiring an employer to pay for work not performed was meant to prevent **featherbedding.** The law is quite limited in actual operation. The issue is: What are "services not performed or not to be performed"? Make-work rules have been approved by the courts as being outside the prohibition of this provision. It is not violated as long as some services are performed, even if they are of little or no actual value to the employer. In one such case, the Supreme Court held that it was permissible for a musicians' union to require a theater to employ a local orchestra to play overtures and intermissions as a condition of the union's consent to local appearances of traveling big-name bands. And in another decision, the Court approved the insistence by a union that newspaper publishers who used advertising mats as molds for metal castings from which to print advertisements pay union printers for setting up in type duplicates of these advertisements. The payments were found to be for work actually done, in spite of the fact that the duplicates were not used and ordinarily were just melted down.

16 PICKETING WHEN NOT CERTIFIED

The seventh provision makes it illegal in certain cases for union picketing to require an employer to recognize or bargain with the union if it is not currently certified as the duly authorized collective-bargaining representative. The purpose of the provision is to reinforce the effectiveness of the election procedures employed by the NLRB; it outlaws certain tactics used by unions backed by only a minority of the employees of a particular employer. Thus, picketing to force an employer to recognize an uncertified union has become illegal in the following cases:

1 When the employer lawfully has recognized another union as the collective-bargaining representative of its employees
2 When a valid representation election has been conducted by the NLRB within the past twelve months
3 When picketing has been conducted for a reasonable time, not in excess of thirty days, without a petition for a representation election being filed with the NLRB

Under item 3, however, the act does not prohibit so-called informational picketing. That is, picketing or publicity to truthfully advise the public, including consumers, that an employer has a nonunion business is not prohibited unless the effect of the picketing is to induce employees of another person to observe the picket line.

Certain kinds of **organizational picketing** have been made unfair by the Landrum-Griffin Act. Before, it was possible for a minority union to picket an employer for recognition as the collective-bargaining representative of its employees, when it was illegal for the employer to accept it as such. Though Congress felt that unions should be able to publicize the fact that certain employers are nonunion, it also felt that unions should not be permitted to attempt to force employers to violate the law. Purely recognitional picketing under the circumstances stated above is illegal. Purely informational picketing probably is legal.

The fact is, however, that often picketing has both purposes. Such dual-purpose picketing under the facts stated in cases 1 or 2 listed above is literally unlawful. However, dual-purpose picketing in case 3 is probably legal unless it inhibits deliveries of goods to the employer being picketed, or the like. Even if it does, the NLRB has ruled that such interruptions must be substantial enough to curtail the employer's business. The rules concerning the application of this provision of the statute have not been clearly enunciated by the NLRB (which has taken several positions) or the courts.

This part of the act also prohibits picketing by an uncertified union (in the situations enumerated) to force the *employees* of an employer to select that union as their collective-bargaining representative. When a charge of a violation is filed and there is reasonable cause to believe it is true, the proper officer of the Board must seek a temporary injunction that restrains further violation until the NLRB disposes of the matter.

17 THE UNION'S DUTY OF FAIR REPRESENTATION

None of the federal labor laws contains an *express* provision which requires a union to fairly represent the employees in a collective-bargaining unit after it has been certified as their exclusive bargaining representative. However, Supreme Court rulings have imposed an *implied* duty of fair representation on unions under both the Railway Labor Act and the National Labor Relations Act. Section 9(a) of the NLRA states that: "[r]epresentatives designated or selected for the purposes of collective bargaining by the *majority* of the employees in a unit appropriate for such purposes, shall be the *exclusive* representative of *all* the employees in such unit for the purposes of collective bargaining in respect to rates of pay, wages, hours of employment, or other conditions of employment…[emphasis added]." A similar provision is found in the Railway Labor Act. Thus, bargaining by a single employee with the employer about that employee's terms or conditions of employment is not permitted, even if the employee voted against the union. Collectively bargained agreements, bargained through the union and for the benefit of the group, are substituted by the act for employment contracts negotiated separately by individual employees. Because of the union's position as the *exclusive* representative, the Supreme Court has reasoned that the union must exercise fairly the power given it by statute on behalf of all for whom it acts.

In negotiating a collective-bargaining agreement with the employer, the union has an implied "duty of fair representation" to act reasonably, with honesty of purpose, and in good faith. The union can prove that it has met this duty by showing that its motives in settling for the terms in the contract which finally results have not been improper. The union is required to represent all the employees in the bargaining unit, including those who are nonunion, impartially and without hostile discrimination. A union has a great deal of discretion in bargaining and may work to obtain different terms for different employees or subgroups of employees, provided it does not have an improper motive for doing so.

The duty of fair representation not only applies to the *negotiation* of a collective-bargaining agreement but also to the *administration* of the agreement while it is in effect. That is, unions must also fairly represent employees in disputes with the employer about the *interpretation* and *application* of the terms of an existing contract. The law does not grant unions the same exclusive power in the processing of grievances as it does in negotiating contracts. Section 9(a) of the NLRA states that: "any individual employee or a group of employees shall have the right at any time to present grievances to their employer and to have such grievances adjusted, without the intervention of the bargaining representative, as long as the adjustment is not inconsistent with the terms of a collective bargaining contract...then in effect: *Provided*..., that the bargaining representative has been given an opportunity to be present at such adjustment." However, most collective-bargaining agreements provide that the union has final control over their grievance-arbitration processes.

An employee may file suit in state court against the union and its representatives for damages that result from breach of their duty of fair representation in processing his or her grievance against the employer. Unions must act honestly and in good faith in processing grievances as well as in negotiating collective-bargaining agreements. A union may not process a grievance in an arbitrary, indifferent, or careless manner. For example, failure to investigate a grievance probably would be arbitrary. However, even if a union violates its duty of fair representation, the damages attributable solely to the employer's breach of contract are its sole responsibility and are not charged to the union. The union is liable to the employee only for increases (if any) in those damages caused by its refusal to process the grievance. Thus, the award assessed against it may not be substantial. Some authorities feel that the current labor laws do not provide penalties severe enough to deter unions from breaching their duty of fair representation.

The cases in which unions have been found guilty of breaching the duty of fair representation include: failing to file a grievance of an employee within the time permitted by a collective-bargaining agreement; failing to present all available evidence in favor of an employee's case; and failure to notify the employee of the time of an arbitration hearing, knowing that no other witness would testify in his or her behalf.

REVIEW QUESTIONS

1. A firm parked a cart filled with groceries in the area where employees were casting ballots in a representation election. A sign on the cart said that the value of the food in it was the same as a year's union dues and suggested that the employees vote against the union. Is this an unfair labor practice? Why, or why not?
2. A company representative ordered an employee to remove his van from an employee parking lot unless he removed from the side of the van a 4-foot by 6-foot sign endorsing a candidate for president of the union local. The company had a rule which prohibited on company property vehicles displaying "any type of large sign or banner, political or otherwise." Vehicles with bumper stickers, window stickers, or similar ornamentation or devices commonly displayed on automobiles were allowed. Did the company commit an unfair labor practice? Why, or why not?
3. Union members selected a new chairman. The employer notified the new chairman that he would not be allowed the same privileges that had been granted the former chairman. Among the privileges taken were four hours of paid time per day to conduct union business. Is this change of policy an unfair labor practice? Why, or why not?
4. Two months after the conclusion of a union strike against a country club, the club's president invited the regular, full-time employees who had worked during the strike to an "appreciation party." The work schedules of at least three employees were adjusted so that they could attend the party. Employees who participated in the strike, and therefore were not invited, worked for the club at the party, which cost approximately $4,000. Was the club guilty of an unfair labor practice? Why, or why not?
5. An airline treated union flight attendants who worked during a strike more favorably than those who stayed on strike. In addition, trainees were given job preference over employees with more seniority. Are these unfair labor practices? Why, or why not?
6. Sally, a supervisor for May Candy Company, ordered Will, a worker, to come into her office for an interview regarding alleged serious breaches of company rules. Will complied, and when the interview confirmed Will's misconduct, he was fired. Will and the union filed charges of unfair labor practices with the NLRB against the May Candy Company because a union representative was not present during the interview. What should be the result? Why?
7. Burger King issued a ban on its employees' wearing any button on their uniforms. Only items using the Burger King logo could be worn by employees. Some counter employees wanted to wear union buttons. When they were not allowed to do so, they filed a complaint with the NLRB, alleging that an unfair labor practice had been committed. Is the ban on buttons an unfair labor practice? Why, or why not?
8. Some of the employees of a janitorial service business were trying to unionize it. The sole proprietor stated that he would never deal with a union and would go

out of the business if his workers voted one in. The union won the representation election, and true to his word, the owner closed his business and sold all its assets. Was he guilty of an unfair labor practice? Explain.

9 A chemical manufacturer was asked to provide the union representing its employees with the generic names of all substances used and produced at the manufacturer's plant. The union also sought information concerning occupational illness and accident data related to workers' compensation claims. The company refused to furnish the information. Is this refusal an unfair labor practice? Why, or why not?

10 For many years, the employer gave all employees a Christmas turkey. The practice continued after a union was certified. For economic reasons, the employer decided to cancel the practice. The union alleged that cancellation was an unfair labor practice and that cancellation could not be unilateral. The turkeys were not mentioned in the collective-bargaining agreement. Is the employer guilty of an unfair labor practice. Why, or why not?

11 A union prevailed in an NLRB election. The employer challenged it on the ground that a union agent made threatening statements to employees one hour before the election. The evidence established that the union agent said that if anyone helped the employer in a strike, he would be made an example of, and noted that during the last strike an individual who opposed the union was still in the hospital. Should the election be set aside? Why, or why not?

12 A union refused to discuss the inclusion of a clause in the collective-bargaining agreement being negotiated with a corporation whereby the union agreed not to strike during the term of the agreement. Is the union guilty of an unfair labor practice? Why, or why not?

13 XYZ Company has a legal union-shop agreement with the designated collective-bargaining representative of its employees. One of the members, Geraldine, was expelled from the union on a technicality, the real reason being her long-running feud with the union president. May the union require XYZ to fire Geraldine? Why, or why not?

14 A contractor subcontracted construction work to three companies, all of which employed union operating engineers. The union disputed the assignment by one of the subcontractors of an operation involving an electric welding machine to members of another labor organization. The union demanded jurisdiction over electric welding machines. The union went on strike when the employers neglected the demand, and its members physically prevented operation of the welding machine. Is this an unfair labor practice? Why, or why not?

15 Cosell Manufacturing canceled all orders for parts that it usually purchased from Madden Corporation, whose employees had no collective-bargaining representative. When asked the reason for the decision, Cosell's purchasing agent stated that her company had agreed with its employees' union that it would only buy its needs from unionized companies in the future. Is this agreement legal? Explain.

16 Ed was discharged for allegedly stealing property from his employer. He asked his union to have him reinstated because his discharge violated the collective-bargaining agreement in force. However, the union did not investigate the incident until it was too late to file a request for arbitration under the collective-bargaining agreement. Assuming that Ed is innocent of the charges, does he have any rights against the union? Explain.

PART SIX

PROTECTING PARTIES TO TRANSACTIONS

18
Investor Protection

19
Consumer Protection

20
Creditor and Debtor Protection

CHAPTER 18

INVESTOR PROTECTION

OVERVIEW

In Chapter 11 we discussed legal factors that should be considered when creating a business organization. This chapter can be viewed as a continuation of that topic as well as a continuation of Chapter 12 on the managers' liability. A clear understanding of securities regulation is essential if managers are to avoid the liability, both civil and criminal, discussed in this chapter. This chapter is also designed to acquaint investors with the laws designed to protect them.

This chapter examines the broad legal meaning given to the word *security*. In addition, federal and state securities laws are discussed. Such laws at the federal level regulate the sale of securities in interstate commerce as well as the operation of national securities exchanges. The following sections should give the reader an understanding of two major federal securities laws—the Federal Securities Act of 1933 and the Federal Securities Exchange Act of 1934. At the end of the chapter, states' securities laws, often called blue-sky laws, are described. These laws regulate the sale of securities in intrastate commerce.

As you study this chapter, remember that the regulation of securities began as part of the program to help the United States overcome the great depression of the early 1930s. You should also realize that these securities laws are designed to give potential investors sufficient information so that they can make intelligent investment decisions based on factural information rather than on other less certain criteria.

By the end of this chapter, you should be familiar with the meaning and application of the following terms: blue-sky laws, controlling person, insider, issuer, prospectus, registration statement, scienter, security, seller, shelf registration, tippee, and underwriter.

1 DEFINITION OF SECURITY

Because securities laws aim to protect uninformed people from investing their money without sufficient data, the term **security** includes within its broad definition much more than corporate stock. A security exists when one person invests money and looks to others to manage the money for profit. The securities laws apply to every investment contract in which a person receives some evidence of indebtedness or a certificate of interest or participation in a profit-sharing agreement. As a result, sales of oil well interests, interests in race horses, interests in limited partnerships, margin sales of coins, and even the sale of a business has been held to come within the scope of the securities laws. Courts seek positive answers to the following three questions when determining whether a person has purchased a security: (1) Is the investment in a common venture? (2) Is the investment premised on a reasonable expectation of profits? (3) Will these profits be derived from the entrepreneurial efforts of others?

The cases involving the sale of a business best illustrates these three questions. As a general rule, the sale of a business does not involve a security subject to the securities laws, because control of the business almost always goes to the buyer of the business. When managerial control passes, question number 3 above is answered in the negative. However, if managerial control does not pass to the buyer of all of the stock of a business, the sale will be of a security, subject to the securities laws.

The following case has become known as a landmark Supreme Court decision on the issue of what is a security. A careful reading of this interesting factual situation indicates the breadth of the definition of a security.

SECURITIES AND EXCHANGE COMMISSION v. W. J. HOWEY CO.
328 U.S. 293 (1946)

FACTS

W. J. Howey Company and Howey-in-the-Hills Service, Inc., are Florida corporations under common control and management. Howey Company offered to sell to the public its orange grove, tree by tree. Howey-in-the-Hills Service, Inc., offered these buyers a contract wherein the appropriate care, harvesting, and marketing of the oranges would be provided. Most of the buyers who signed the service contracts were nonresidents of Florida who had very little knowledge or skill needed to care for and harvest the oranges. These buyers were attracted by the expectation of profits.

ISSUE

Is a sale of orange trees by the Howey Company and a sale of services by Howey-in-the-Hills Service, Inc., a sale of a security?

DECISION

Yes.

REASONS

1. Under the Federal Securities Act of 1933, a security exists whenever one person invests money in a common enterprise with the expectation of profits resulting from the efforts of another person.
2. Upon examination of these orange-grove transactions, these essential requirements of a security were found to be present. Therefore, these sales of land and service contracts, when taken together, were subject to the registration requirements of the 1933 act.
3. Since these registration requirements were not satisfied, the controllers of these Howey companies have violated the Federal Securities Act of 1933.

Despite this broad definition of a security, the Supreme Court has made it clear that federal securities laws are not designed to provide a remedy for all fraudulent transactions. In recent years, the Court has held that securities laws do not necessarily apply: (1) to a compulsory pension plan into which the employee is not required to make contributions, or (2) to certificates of deposit insured by the federal government. In the first instance, the Court found that the employee was protected by the Employee Retirement Income Security Act, and in the second situation it found that the customer was insured by the Federal Deposit Insurance Corporation. In these areas where "an investor" is protected by other means, protection provided by the securities laws is less essential.

2 SECURITIES AND EXCHANGE COMMISSION

The Securities and Exchange Commission (SEC), which was created in 1934, administers the federal securities laws. The materials discussed in Chapter 7 on administrative agencies generally apply to the SEC. The SEC consists of five commissioners appointed by the President for a five-year term. In addition to these commissioners, the SEC employs staff personnel such as lawyers, accountants, security analysts, security examiners, and others.

The SEC has both quasi-legislative and quasi-judicial powers. Using its quasi-legislative power, it has adopted rules and regulations relating to financial and other information which must be furnished to the Commission.

It also has rules prescribing information which must be given to potential investors. The SEC also regulates the various stock exchanges, utility holding companies, investment trusts, and investment advisers.

The SEC is involved in a variety of investigations and rule-making activities. Typical of these are the following:

1. Investigating insider trading and stock manipulation, especially that connected with takeover attempts and rumors.
2. Investigating the leakage of information (factual and false) that can significantly affect stock prices.
3. Studying and investigating examples of suspected insider trading.
4. Adopting rules that govern stock-market newsletters published by brokerage firms. (The Supreme Court held that it could not regulate newsletters published independently of brokerage firms.)
5. Examining annual reports to ensure that proper accounting practices are followed and companies do not have "cooked books" that either "puff" earnings or exaggerate net worth.
6. Adopting rules that govern which shareholder-proposed resolutions must be submitted for a vote at corporate annual meetings. For example, the SEC requires that a shareholder must have invested $1,000 for at least one year before submitting a proposal. A proposal must get at least 5 percent of the vote the first time before it can be resubmitted.

FEDERAL SECURITIES ACT OF 1933: GOING PUBLIC

3 GENERAL PROVISIONS

The Federal Securities Act of 1933 was enacted by Congress to regulate the initial sale of securities to the public. This law makes it illegal to use the mails or any other interstate means of communication or transportation to sell securities without disclosing certain financial information to potential investors. The following sections discuss several aspects of the Federal Securities Act of 1933 in detail, including who is regulated, what documents are required, which transactions are exempted, when civil and criminal liability exists, and what defenses are available. As you read, remember that this law applies only to the initial sale of the security. Subsequent transfers of securities are governed by the Federal Securities Exchange Act of 1934, discussed in sections 11 through 16.

In essence, the 1933 act requires the disclosure of information to the potential investor or other interested party. The information given must not be untrue or even misleading. If this information is not accurate, liability is imposed upon those responsible. The Federal Securities Act of 1933 recognizes three sanctions for violations. There is the criminal punishment, the equitable remedy of an injunction, and civil liability, which may be imposed in favor of injured parties in certain cases. Proof of an intentional violation usually is required before criminal or civil sanctions are imposed. However, proof of negligence will support an injunction.

4 PARTIES REGULATED

The Federal Securities Act of 1933 regulates anyone who is involved with or who promotes the initial sale of securities. Typically, involved parties may include issuers, underwriters, controlling persons, and sellers. An **issuer** is the individual or business organization offering a security for sale to the public. An **underwriter** is anyone who participates in the original distribution of securities by selling such securities for the issuer or by guaranteeing their sale. (Often, securities brokerage firms or investment bankers have acted as underwriters with respect to a particular transaction.) A **controlling person** is one who controls or is controlled by the issuer, such as a major stockholder of a corporation. Finally, a **seller** is anyone who contracts with a purchaser or who exerts a substantial role which causes the purchase transaction to occur.

These parties who participate in or promote a sale of securities from an issuer to the public are subject to the Federal Securities Act of 1933, which protects a person from being defrauded by false or nonexistent information. The initial reading of the previous paragraph may not indicate the broad meaning given to the words "issuer," "underwriter," "controlling person," and "seller." However, the following case illustrates the wide application of the 1933 act.

JUNKER v. CRORY
650 F.2d 1349 (5th Cir. 1981)

FACTS

James Junker owned 162 shares of stock in Reco Investment Corporation. These shares were equal to 16.2 percent of the 1,000 shares Reco had outstanding. Reco became heavily indebted to another corporation known as Road Equipment Company, Inc. To resolve Reco's poor financial condition, Frederick Heisler, a lawyer for Reco, suggested and strongly recommended that Reco be merged into Road. Due to what he believed was an unreasonably low appraised value of Reco's stock, Junker voted against the proposed merger. However, the remaining shareholders of Reco approved the merger plan, and it was accomplished. Later, Junker discovered some negative news about Road's financial condition. This information was not revealed at the shareholders' meeting when the merger vote was taken. Junker sued Frederick Heisler, alleging a violation of the Federal Securities Act of 1933. Heisler defended the suit by arguing that he had no duty to reveal additional information.

ISSUE

Is Heisler, as an attorney but not as an officer or director, liable under the 1933 act?

> **DECISION**
>
> Yes.
>
> **REASONS**
>
> 1. Heisler qualifies as a seller and is subject to the disclosure requirements of the 1933 act.
> 2. A merger may amount to a purchase or sale of a security for purposes of the federal securities laws.
> 3. Mere participation in the events leading up to the transaction (merger) is insufficient to constitute one as a seller of a security. However, those in privity with the purchaser or those "whose participation in the buy-sell transaction is a substantial factor in causing the transaction to take place" are classified as sellers.
> 4. Heisler did attempt to persuade the Reco shareholders to approve the merger. He was an active negotiator in the transaction, acting as an implementor, not merely a counselor. Therefore, Heisler's actions brought him within the scope of the definition of seller under the 1933 act.

5 DOCUMENTS INVOLVED

In regulating the initial sale of securities, the Federal Securities Act of 1933 should be viewed as a disclosure law. In essence, this law requires that securities subject to its provisions be registered prior to any sale and that a prospectus be furnished to any potential investor prior to any sale being consummated. Thus, an issuer of securities who complies with the federal law must prepare: (1) a **registration statement** and (2) a **prospectus**.

Registration Statement

The Federal Securities Act of 1933 contains detailed provisions relating to the registration of securities and describes which selling activities are permitted at the various stages of the registration process. There are three distinct periods during the registration process: (1) the prefiling period, (2) the waiting period, and (3) the posteffective period. A registration becomes effective twenty days (the waiting period) after it is filed, unless the SEC gives notice that it is not in proper form or unless the SEC accelerates the effective date. Any amendment filed without the Commission's consent starts the twenty-day period running again.

During the prefiling period, it is legal for the issuer of a security to engage in preliminary negotiations and agreements with underwriters. It is illegal to sell a covered security during this period. Offers to sell and offers to buy securities also are prohibited during this prefiling period.

During the waiting period, it is still illegal to sell a security subject to the act. However, it is not illegal to make an offer to buy or to sell. Written offers to sell must conform to the prospectus requirements, but oral offers are permissible. Since contracts to sell are still illegal, offers cannot be accepted during the waiting period. As a result of these waiting periods, sellers may solicit offers for later acceptance, also.

Many offers during the waiting period are made in advertisements called "tombstone ads." These ads are brief announcements identifying the security and stating its price, by whom orders will be executed, and from whom a prospectus may be obtained. Almost any issue of *The Wall Street Journal* contains such ads. Offers may also be made during the waiting period by use of a statistical summary, a summary prospectus, or a preliminary prospectus. These techniques allow dissemination of the facts that ultimately are to be disclosed in the formal prospectus.

Prospectus

During the posteffective period, securities may be sold. A prospectus must be furnished to any interested investor, and it must conform to the statutory requirements. Like the registration statement, the prospectus contains financial information related to the issuer. Indeed, the prospectus contains the same essential information contained in the registration statement. The prospectus supplies the investor with sufficient facts (including financial information) so that he or she can make an intelligent investment decision. The SEC has adopted rules relating to the detailed requirements of the prospectus. The major requirements are detailed facts about the issuer and financial statements, including balance sheet and statements of operations of the issuer.

Theoretically, any security may be sold under the act, provided the law and the rules and regulations enacted under it are followed. The law does not prohibit the sale of worthless securities. An investor may "foolishly" invest his or her money and a person may legally sell the blue sky if the statutory requirements are met. In fact, the prospectus must contain the following, in capital letters and boldface type:

THESE SECURITIES HAVE NOT BEEN APPROVED OR DISAPPROVED BY THE SECURITIES AND EXCHANGE COMMISSION NOR HAS THE COMMISSION PASSED UPON THE ACCURACY OR ADEQUACY OF THIS PROSPECTUS. ANY REPRESENTATION TO THE CONTRARY IS A CRIMINAL OFFENSE.

6 SHELF REGISTRATION

Regarding initial sale of securities to the public, the most significant development in some time has been the SEC's relaxation of disclosure requirements. This trend is not a change in the 1933 law, but it is a new direction for the rules and regulations issued by the SEC pursuant to the 1933 act.

Rule 415 of the SEC, which provides for **shelf registration** of securities, allows companies to submit a single, comprehensive disclosure statement describing their long-term financing plans. These disclosure statements permit companies to sell securities whenever rapidly changing market conditions appear most favorable. Through Rule 415, the issuer of securities to the public no longer has to prepare a prospectus for the SEC's review every time it plans to sell securities.

Under SEC Rule 415 as modified, companies with less than $150 million in stock held by investors unaffiliated with the company can no longer use the shelf-registration method of selling securities to the public. The Rule 415 limitations are designed to protect investors who may not be able to get adequate financial data about these smaller, little-known companies in the short time between the announcement of a shelf issue and its sale.

7 EXEMPTIONS

Some statutory provisions exempt certain transactions, and others exempt certain securities from registration requirements. Provisions that exempt certain transactions limit the application of the law to transactions in which a security is sold in a public offering by the issuer, an underwriter, a controlling person, or a seller. Transactions by a securities dealer (as distinguished from an issuer or an underwriter) are exempt after forty days have elapsed from the effective date of the first public offer. If a company offers the security with no prior registration statements, this period is ninety days. This exemption allows a dealer to enter into transactions in securities after a minimum period has elapsed. In addition, brokers' transactions executed on any exchange or in the over-the-counter market are exempt.

Private Sales Transactions

Perhaps the most difficult issue in determining whether a sale is an exempt transaction is the concept of a public offering. Private sales are exempt. Sales to the general public are not. In determining whether or not a sale is being made to the general public, the SEC will examine: (1) the number of offerees, (2) their knowledge about the company in which they are investing, (3) the relationship between the offeror and offeree, (4) whether the security remains in the hands of the offeree or is resold, and (5) the amount of advertising involved. The issuer has the burden of proof to show that the sale is private and not public.

Specialized Securities

The law also exempts certain securities from its coverage. These include securities subject to regulation by governmental agencies other than the SEC, such as securities of banks and savings and loan institutions and intrastate offerings. The intrastate exemption covers securities that are offered and sold only to persons who reside within the state of incorporation. If the issuer is unincorporated, the purchasers must reside within the state of its residence and place of business. If the sale is to a resident planning to resell to a nonresident, the intrastate exemption is lost. The same is true if the mails or interstate systems of communication are used to sell the security. Remember that even if the sale is exempt under federal law, it is probably subject to a similar state law. Commercial paper arising out of current transactions with a maturity not exceeding nine months and securities issued by not-for-profit corporations are also exempt.

Size of Offering

The SEC can create additional exemptions. Typically, these exemptions depend on the dollar amount of securities sold and on who the investor-purchasers are. Furthermore, the exemptions change from time to time. In recent years, the SEC's trend has been to exempt larger offerings to help businesses raise capital. Currently, any business may sell up to $500,000 in securities during a twelve-month period without registering the offering, according to the 1933 act's requirements. The amount of this exemption increases to $5 million if the issuer believes that there are no more than thirty-five investor-purchasers who lack the sophistication to acquire and evaluate information about the security being sold.

No general advertising or solicitation is permitted in association with exempt transactions. Furthermore, all parties involved in the initial sales of securities from the issuer remain subject to the federal laws' antifraud and civil liability provisions. States also may require compliance with their securities laws, regardless of any applicable federal disclosure exemptions. Finally, the securities sold in these exempt transactions are restricted. In other words, before these securities can be resold, registration requirements must be satisfied unless the resale is part of another exempt transaction.

Table 18-1 summarizes the exemptions provided in the 1933 Securities Act and regulations issued by the SEC.

8 CRIMINAL LIABILITY

Under the Federal Securities Act of 1933, both civil and criminal liability may be imposed for violations. Criminal liability results from a willful violation of the act or fraud in *any* offer or sale of securities. Fraud also occurs

TABLE 18-1 EXEMPTIONS

Exempt securities	Exempt transactions
1 Securities up to $1.5 million in value during a twelve-month period (Regulation A)	1 Securities dealers' and brokers' transactions
2 Securities subject to governmental regulation other than the SEC (banks, savings and loan, not-for-profit corporations, etc.)	2 Private offering (not available to general public)
3 Securities sold only intrastate	3 $500,000 per twelve-month period for any business
	4 $5,000,000 per twelve-month period if there are thirty-five or fewer nonaccredited investors
	5 Unlimited offering if there are thirty-five or fewer nonaccredited investors who have expertise to evaluate investment opportunity

when any material fact is omitted, causing a statement to be misleading. The penalty is a fine up to $100,000, five years in prison, or both. Fraud in the sale of an exempt security is also a criminal violation if the mail is used or if an instrumentality of interstate commerce, such as the telephone, has been used.

The law requires that violations be willful. "Willful" means with intent to defraud. The government can meet its burden by proving that a defendant deliberately closed his or her eyes to facts he or she had a duty to see, or recklessly stated as facts things of which he or she was ignorant. The willfulness requirement can be satisfied by mere "proof of representation which due diligence would have shown to be untrue." In discussing the state of mind required for a criminal conviction of a lawyer or an accountant under the statute, one court observed:

> In our complex society the accountant's certificate and the lawyer's opinion can be instruments for inflicting pecuniary loss more potent than the chisel or the crowbar. Of course, Congress did not mean that any mistake of law or misstatement of fact should subject an attorney or an accountant to criminal liability simply because more skillful practitioners would not have made them. But Congress equally could not have intended that men holding themselves out as members of these ancient professions should be able to escape criminal liability on a plea of ignorance when they have shut their eyes to what was plainly to be seen or have represented a knowledge they knew they did not possess.

A person accused of intentionally violating the 1933 act usually cannot escape criminal liability by arguing that a nonexempt transaction involving the exchange of misinformation technically was outside the 1933 act's scope. The following case again demonstrates the broad application of the securities law to achieve its purpose.

> **RUBIN v. UNITED STATES**
> 101 S.Ct. 698 (1981)
>
> **FACTS**
>
> Rubin, a vice president of a corporation involved in energy exploration and production, was indicted for violating and conspiring to violate the Federal Securities Act of 1933, which prohibits fraud in the "offer or sale" of securities. Rubin allegedly made false representations to a bank while arranging for loans to his corporation. To secure the loans, Rubin pledged stock which he represented as being marketable and worth approximately $1.7 million. In fact, the stock was nonmarketable and practically worthless. Rubin denies that a sale occurred and claims that there could only be a sale by foreclosure upon default of the loans.
>
> **ISSUE**
>
> Does a pledge of stock as collateral for a bank constitute an "offer or sale" under the Federal Securities Act of 1933?
>
> **DECISION**
>
> Yes.
>
> **REASONS**
>
> 1. "Sale" or "sell" includes every contract of sale or disposition of a security for value. "Offer" includes every attempt or offer to dispose of, or solicitation of an offer to buy, a security or interest in a security for value.
> 2. Obtaining a loan secured by a pledge of stock unmistakably involves a "disposition of...interest in a security, for value." Although pledges transfer less than absolute title, the interest thus transferred nonetheless is an "interest" in a security.
> 3. It is not essential under the terms of the act that full title pass to a transferee for the transaction to be an "offer" or a "sale."
> 4. These provisions were enacted to protect against fraud and promote the free flow of information in the public discrimination of securities.

9 CIVIL LIABILITY

This portion of the chapter discusses three sections of the Federal Securities Act of 1933 that directly apply to civil liability of parties involved in issuing securities. The first section of importance (Section 11 of the act) deals with registration statements; the second (Section 12 of the act) relates to prospectuses and oral and written communication; and the third (Section 17 of the act) concerns fraudulent interstate transactions.

The civil liability provision dealing with registration statements imposes liability on the following persons in favor of purchasers of securities:

1 Every person who signed the registration statement

2 Every director of the corporation or partner in the partnership issuing the security
3 Every person who, with his or her consent, is named in the registration statement as about to become a director or partner
4 Every accountant, engineer, or appraiser who assists in the preparation of the registration statement or its certification
5 Every underwriter

Section 11: Registration Statement

The persons mentioned in the preceding paragraph are liable if the registration statement: (1) contains untrue statements of material facts, (2) omits material facts required by statute or regulation, or (3) omits information which if not given makes the facts stated misleading. This latter situation describes the factual situation of a statement containing a half-truth which has the net effect of being misleading. The test of accuracy and materiality is as of the date the registration statement becomes effective.

The SEC and the courts have attempted to define materiality. The term *material* limits information concerning those matters as to which an average prudent investor ought reasonably to be informed before purchasing the security registered. What are "matters as to which an average prudent investor ought reasonably to be informed?" They are matters which such an investor needs to know before he or she can make an intelligent, informed decision as to whether or not to buy the security. As a result, a material fact is one which, if correctly stated or disclosed, would have deterred or tended to deter the average prudent investor from purchasing the securities in question. The term does not cover minor inaccuracies or errors in matters of no interest to investors. Facts that tend to deter a person from purchasing a security are those that have an important bearing upon the nature or condition of the issuing corporation or its business.

A plaintiff-purchaser need not prove reliance on the registration statement to recover, but proof of actual knowledge of the falsity by the purchaser is a defense. Knowledge of the falsity by a defendant need not be proved, but except for an issuer, reliance on an expert, such as an accountant, is a defense. For example, a director may defend a suit based on a false financial statement by showing reliance on a CPA.

Section 12: Prospectus

The separate provision relating to liability in connection with prospectuses and communications imposes liability on sellers who fail to comply with the registration requirements of the act. This liability is imposed regardless of wrongful intent or conduct of those who fail to comply with the law. It also imposes liability on sellers who use a prospectus or make communications (by mail, telephone, or other instrumentalities of interstate commerce) that contain an untrue statement of material facts. Purchasers of such securities may sue for their actual damages or to rescind the purchase and obtain a refund of the price. Used when the purchaser still owns the security, this latter remedy requires privity of contract. There is no liability for aiding and abetting someone who violates these provisions.

Section 17: Fraudulent Transactions

This provision concerning fraudulent interstate transactions prohibits the use of any instrument of interstate communication in the offer or sale of any securities when the result is: (1) to defraud, (2) to obtain money or property by means of an untrue or misleading statement, or (3) to engage in a business transaction or practice that may operate to defraud or deceive a purchaser.

The requirement that a defendant-seller must act with intent (**scienter**) to deceive or mislead to prove a Section 17 violation also applies when an injunction is sought. Section 17 does not explicitly provide for the private remedy of monetary damages. Note that the references in this case to 1, 2, and 3 are the same as to 1, 2, and 3 in the first paragraph of Section 11.

AARON v. SECURITIES AND EXCHANGE COMMISSION
100 S.Ct. 1945 (1980)

FACTS

Two securities brokers, as employees of a broker-dealer firm, produced false information about the Lawn-A-Mat Chemical & Equipment Corporation. This false information was given to potential investors to induce the purchase of Lawn-A-Mat stock. Evidence of these brokers' wrongful actions was given to their supervisor, Peter Aaron. When he did nothing to prevent further distribution of false information, the SEC sought to enjoin Aaron from aiding and abetting continuous violations of Section 17(a) of the Federal Securities Act of 1933.

ISSUE

Is the SEC required to establish scienter as an element of a civil enforcement action to enjoin violations of Section 17(a) of the 1933 act?

DECISION

Yes, under Section 17(a)(1). No, under Section 17(a)(2) and Section 17(a)(3).

REASONS

1. Scienter *is* an element of violation of Section 17(a)(1) of the 1933 act which makes it unlawful to employ any device, scheme, or artifice to defraud.
2. Scienter is not an element of a violation of Section 17(a)(2) of the 1933 act, which prohibits any person from obtaining money or property by means of

any untrue statement of material fact or any omission to state a material fact.
3. Scienter is not an element of a violation of Section 17(a)(3) of the 1933 act, which makes it unlawful for any person to engage in any transaction, practice, or course of business which operates or would operate as a fraud or deceit.
4. Finally, the provisions of the 1933 act which authorize injunctive relief do not modify the substantive provisions so far as scienter is concerned.

10 DEFENSES

The Federal Securities Act of 1933 recognizes several defenses that may be used to avoid liability. Lack of materiality is a common defense. Determining whether or not a particular fact is material depends on the facts and the parties involved.

The statute of limitations is a defense for both civil and criminal liability. The basic period is one year. The statute does not start to run until the discovery of the untrue statement or omission. Or it does not start to run until the time such discovery would have been made with reasonable diligence. In no event may a suit be brought more than three years after the sale.

A defense similar to the statute of limitations is also provided. This statute provides that if the person acquiring the security does so after the issuer has made generally available an earnings statement covering at least twelve months after the effective date of the registration statement, then this person must prove actual reliance on the registration statement. However, this defense has little applicability in most cases.

A very important defense for experts such as accountants is the due diligence defense. The law provides that no person is liable who shall sustain the burden of proof that "as regards any part of the registration statement purporting to be made upon his authority as an expert that he had, after reasonable investigation, reasonable ground to believe and did believe, at the time such part of the registration statement became effective, that the statements therein were true and that there was no omission to state a material fact required to be stated therein or necessary to make the statements therein not misleading." In determining whether or not an expert such as an accountant has made a reasonable investigation, the law provides that the standard of reasonableness is that required of a prudent person in the management of his or her own property. The burden of proof of this defense is on the expert, and the test is as of the time the registration statement became effective. The due diligence defense, in effect, requires proof that a party was not guilty of fraud or negligence.

To better understand the materials concerning civil liability under the Federal Securities Act of 1933, study Table 18-2. It is intended as a summary of Sections 11, 12, and 17.

TABLE 18-2 CIVIL LIABILITY UNDER THE 1933 ACT

Section of 1933 act	Purpose of section	Plaintiff's required proof of defendant's scienter	Defendant's defense
Section 11	Creates liability for false or misleading registration statements	Not required to prove defendant's intent to deceive	1. Proof of no false or misleading information is a defense. 2. Proof that plaintiff knew of false or misleading nature of information is a defense. 3. Except for issuer, proof of reliance on an expert (attorney, accountant, etc.) is a defense. 4. Proof of good faith is *not* a defense.
Section 12	Creates liability for false or misleading prospectus	Not required to prove defendant's intent to deceive	Same as above
Section 17	In an interstate transaction it is: 1. unlawful to employ device, scheme, or artifice to defraud. 2. unlawful to obtain money or property by untrue statement or omission of material fact. 3. unlawful to engage in events which operate or would operate as a fraud or deceit.	1. Required to prove defendant's intent to deceive 2. Not required to prove defendant's intent to deceive 3. Not required to prove defendant's intent to deceive	1. Proof of no intent to deceive is a defense. Good faith is a defense. 2. Proof of no material misstatement of omission is a defense. Good faith is *not* a defense. 3. Proof of no involvement in unlawful activities is a defense. Good faith is *not* a defense.

FEDERAL SECURITIES EXCHANGE ACT OF 1934: BEING PUBLIC

11 GENERAL COVERAGE

Whereas the Federal Securities Act of 1933 deals with original offerings of securities, the Federal Securities Exchange Act of 1934 regulates transfers of securities after the initial sale. The 1934 act, which created the SEC, also deals with regulation of security exchanges, brokers, and dealers in securities.

It is illegal to sell a security on a national exchange unless a registration is effective for the security. Registration under the 1934 act differs from registration under the 1933 act. Registration under the former requires filing prescribed forms with the applicable stock exchange and the SEC. As a general rule, all equity securities held by 500 or more owners must be registered if the issuer has more than $1 million in gross assets. This rule picks up issues traded over the counter and applies to securities that might have qualified under one of the exemptions under the 1933 act.

Provisions relating to stockbrokers and dealers prohibit the use of the mails or any other instrumentality of interstate commerce to sell securities unless the broker or the dealer is registered. The language is sufficiently broad to cover attempted sales as well as actual sales. Brokers and dealers must keep detailed records of their activities and file annual reports with the SEC.

The SEC requires that issuers of registered securities file periodic reports as well as report significant developments which would affect the value of the security. For example, the SEC requires companies to disclose foreign payoffs or bribes to obtain or retain foreign business operations. Businesses must disclose their minority hiring practices and other social data that may be of public concern. Business has been forced by the SEC to submit certain shareholder proposals to all shareholders as a part of proxy solicitation. When a new pension law was enacted, the SEC required that financial reports disclose the law's impact on the reporting business. SEC activity concerning information corporations must furnish to the investing public is almost limitless. As a result, SEC regulations are of paramount significance to all persons concerned with the financial aspects of business. This area of regulation directly affects the accounting profession. Since the SEC regulates financial statements, the Commission frequently decides issues of proper accounting and auditing theory and practices.

How the Federal Securities Exchange Act of 1934 affects the businessperson, the accountant, the lawyer, the broker, and the investor is seen in the following sections. These sections cover some fundamental concepts of this law, such as civil liability in general and insider transactions in particular, as well as criminal violations and penalties under the 1934 act.

12 SECTION 10(b) AND RULE 10b-5

Most of the litigation under the Federal Securities and Exchange Act of 1934 is brought under Section 10(b) of the act and Rule 10b-5 promulgated by the SEC pursuant to the act. Section 10(b) and Rule 10b-5 declare that it is unlawful to use the mails or any instrumentality of interstate commerce or any national securities exchange to defraud *any person* in connection with the *purchase or sale* of any security. They provide a private remedy for defrauded investors. This remedy may be invoked against any person who indulges in fraudulent practices in the purchase or sale of securities. In actual practice, defendants in such cases tend to fall into four general categories: (1) insiders; (2) broker-dealers; (3) corporations whose stock is purchased or sold by plaintiffs; and (4) those, such as accountants, who "aid and abet" or conspire with a party who falls into one of the first three categories.

Section 10(b) and Rule 10b-5 are usually referred to as the antifraud provisions of the act. A plaintiff seeking damages under the provisions must establish: (1) the existence of a material misrepresentation or omission made in connection with the purchase or sale of a security, (2) the culpable state of mind of the defendant, (3) his or her reliance and due diligence, and (4) damage as a result of the reliance. Materiality under the 1934 act is the same as materiality under the 1933 act. Liability under Rule 10b-5 requires proof of scienter and not proof of simple negligence. It also requires proof of a practice that is manipulative or deceptive and not merely corporate mismanagement.

SANTA FE INDUSTRIES, INC. v. GREEN
97 S.Ct. 1292 (1977)

FACTS

Santa Fe sought to merge under the Delaware "short-form" merger statute and obtained independent appraisal values of the stock. The company complied with the statute and sent to each minority shareholder an information statement containing the appraisal values of the assets. It offered the minority shareholders $150 per share (the appraisal value was $125) for their stock. Respondents, minority shareholders, did not pursue their appraisal remedy in the state courts. Instead, they filed suit under Rule 10b-5, claiming that Santa Fe used a device to defraud and that the information statement failed to reveal that the stock was actually worth $772 per share.

ISSUE

Did Santa Fe violate Rule 10b-5?

DECISION

No.

> **REASONS**
>
> 1. Mere instances of corporate mismanagement or allegations that shareholders are treated unfairly by a fiduciary are not violations of Section 10(b) or Rule 10b-5.
> 2. Section 10(b) and Rule 10b-5 seek to prohibit conduct that is or can be viewed as manipulative or deceptive. No such deception is alleged to have occurred in this factual situation.
> 3. On the basis of the information provided, minority shareholders could either accept the price offered or reject it and seek an appraisal in state court. Furthermore, these minority shareholders were furnished all the relevant information on which to make their decision.

The concept of fraud under Section 10(b) encompasses untrue statements of material facts and the failure to state material facts necessary to prevent statements actually made from being misleading. In other words, a half-truth that misleads is fraudulent. Finally, failure to correct a misleading impression left by statements already made, or silence where there is a duty to speak, gives rise to a violation of Rule 10b-5 because it is a form of "aiding and abetting." Although there is no general duty on the part of all persons with knowledge of improper activities to report them, a duty to disclose may arise from the fact of a special relationship or set of circumstances such as an accountant certifying financial statements.

The application of Section 10(b) and Rule 10b-5 applies to all sales of any security if the requisite fraud exists and the interstate aspect is established. The rule requires that those standing in a fiduciary relationship disclose all material facts before entering into transactions. This means that an officer, a director, or a controlling shareholder has a duty to disclose all material facts. Failure to do so is a violation and, in effect, fraudulent. Privity of contract is not required for a violation, and lack of privity of contract is no defense. However, a defendant, such as the one in the following case, who proves he did not occupy a fiduciary position is relieved of liability, even if all material facts are not disclosed.

CHIARELLA v. UNITED STATES
100 S.Ct. 1108 (1980)

FACTS

A financial printer had been hired by certain corporations to print corporate-takeover bids. Chiarella, an employee of the printer, was able to deduce the identities of both the acquiring companies and the companies which were targeted for takeover. Without disclosing the knowledge about the prospective takeover bids, Chiarella purchased stock in the target companies and then sold his purchased shares for a profit immediately after the takeover attempts were made public. After the SEC began an investigation, Chiarella entered into a consent decree in which he agreed to return the profits he had made as a result of his activities.

Thereafter, Chiarella was indicted for violating Section 10(b) of the Federal Securities Exchange Act of 1934 and Rule 10b-5. Chiarella was convicted, and his conviction was affirmed by the Second Circuit Court of Appeals.

ISSUE

Was Chiarella in a position where he was obligated to disclose the nonpublic information he had learned?

DECISION

No.

REASONS

1. Not every instance of financial unfairness constitutes fraudulent activity under Section 10(b).
2. The element required to make silence fraudulent—a duty to disclose—is absent in this case. No duty could arise from Chiarella's relationship with the sellers of the target company's securities, for he had no prior dealings with them. Chiarella was not their agent; he was not a fiduciary; he was not a person in whom the sellers had placed their trust and confidence. He was, in fact, a complete stranger who dealt with the sellers only through impersonal market transactions.
3. When an allegation is based upon nondisclosure, there can be no fraud without a duty to speak. A duty to disclose under Section 10(b) does not arise from the mere possession of nonpublic market information.

Liability under Rule 10b-5 may be imposed on accountants even though they may perform only an unaudited write-up. An accountant is liable for errors in financial statements contained in a prospectus or other filed report even though unaudited if there are errors he or she knew or should have known. Even when performing an unaudited write-up, an accountant must undertake at least a minimal investigation into the figures supplied to him or her, and she or he cannot disregard suspicious circumstances.

A plaintiff in a suit under Rule 10b-5 must prove damages. The damages of a defrauded purchaser are usually out-of-pocket losses or the excess of "what was paid" over the value of "what was received." Courts in a few cases have used the "benefit of the bargain" measure of damages and awarded the buyer the difference between what he or she paid and what the security was represented to be worth. A buyer's damages are measured at the time of purchase. Buyers are not subject to setoffs for the tax benefits received during the period they owned the investments when they exercise their right of rescission.

Computation of a defrauded seller's damages is more difficult. A defrauding purchaser usually benefits from an increase in the value of the securities, while the plaintiff seller loses this increase. Courts do not allow defrauding buyers to keep these increases in value. Therefore, the measure of the seller's damages is the difference between the fair value of all that the seller received and the fair value of what he or she would have received had there been no fraud, except where the defendant received more than the seller's loss. In this latter case, the seller is entitled to the defendant's profit. As a result, defendants lose all profits flowing from the fraudulent conduct.

Plaintiffs under Rule 10b-5 are also entitled to consequential damages. These include lost dividends, brokerage fees, and taxes. In addition, courts may order payment of interest on the funds. Punitive damages are not permitted as they are in cases of common law fraud based on state laws. This distinction results from the language of the statute which limits recoveries to "actual damages."

As a general rule, attorneys' fees are not recoverable. This is consistent with the rule in most litigation. However, in class action suits, the attorneys can collect their fees out of the recovery. These fees in a class action suit will often exceed the usual hourly rate and will often be close to or equal to the contingent fee rate (one-third of the recovery).

13 INSIDER TRANSACTIONS

Section 16, one of the most important provisions of the Federal Securities Exchange Act of 1934, concerns insider transactions. An **insider** is any person: (1) who owns more than 10 percent of any security or (2) who is a director or an officer of the issuer of the security. Section 16 and SEC regulations require that insiders file, at the time of the registration or within ten days after becoming an insider, a statement of the amount of such issues of which they are the owners. The regulations also require filing within ten days after the close of each calendar month thereafter, if there has been any change in such ownership during such month (indicating the change). There are exemptions to the insider rules for executors or administrators of estates, and odd-lot dealers are also generally exempt.

The reason for prohibiting insiders from trading for profit is to prevent the use of information that is available to an insider but not to the general public. Because the SEC cannot determine for certain when nonpublic information is improperly used, Section 16 creates a presumption that any profit made within a six-month time period is illegal. These profits are referred to as "short-swing profits." Thus, if a director, officer, or principal owner realizes profits on the purchase and sale of a security within a six-month period, the profits inure and belong to the company or to the investor who purchased it from or sold it to an insider, resulting in the insider's profit and investor's loss. The order of the purchase and sale is immaterial. The profit is calculated on the lowest price in and highest price out during any six-month period. Unlike the required proof of intent to deceive under Section 10(b), the short-swing-profits rule of Section 16 does not depend on any misuse of information. In other words, short-swing profits by insiders, regardless of the insiders' state of mind, are absolutely prohibited.

14 NONPUBLIC INFORMATION

The SEC's concern for trading based on nonpublic information goes beyond the Section 16 ban on short-swing profits. Indeed, a person who is not technically an insider but who trades securities without disclosing nonpublic information may violate Section 10(b) and Rule 10b-5. The SEC takes the position that the profit obtained as the result of a trader's silence concerning information that is not freely available to everyone is a manipulation or deception prohibited by Section 10(b) and Rule 10b-5. In essence, a user of nonpublic information is treated like an insider if he or she can be classified as a **tippee**, or a temporary insider.

A tippee is a person who learns of nonpublic information from an insider. A tippee is liable for the use of nonpublic information, because an insider should not be allowed to do indirectly what he cannot do directly. In other words, a tippee is liable for trading or passing on information that is nonpublic. However, a person who learns of nonpublic information from a source other than an insider is not required to reveal that information prior to trading. Moreover, a tippee becomes liable under Section 10(b) only if the tippee breaches a fiduciary duty to the business organization or fellow shareholders. Therefore, if the tipper communicates nonpublic information for reasons other than personal gain, neither the tipper nor the tippee can be liable for a securities violation.

DIRKS v. SECURITIES AND EXCHANGE COMMISSION
103 S.Ct. 3255 (1983)

FACTS

Dirks, an investment analyst for a brokerage firm, discovered from a former officer of an insurance company that the company's assets were overstated because of fraudulent accounting practices. During his investigation, Dirks never personally dealt in the insurance company's securities. However, he talked about his investigation with his investing clients. These clients sold their interests before the fraud was publicly announced and the insurance company's securities declined in value. The SEC found that Dirks had violated Section 10(b) because he, as a tippee, failed to disclose the information gained from an insider to the public before that information was used to profit in trading.

ISSUE

Did Dirks violate Section 10(b)?

DECISION

No.

REASONS

1. Not every use of inside information violates the securities laws.
2. A tippee assumes a fiduciary duty to shareholders of a corporation not to

trade on material nonpublic information only when the insider has breached his fiduciary duty to the shareholders by disclosing the information to the tippee, and the tippee knows, or should know, that there had been a breach.

3. In determining whether or not a tippee is under an obligation to disclose or abstain, it is necessary to determine whether or not the insider's "tip" constitutes a breach of the insider's fiduciary duty. Whether or not disclosure is a breach of duty, therefore, depends largely on the purpose of the insider's disclosure.
4. The test to be used is whether or not the insider personally will benefit, directly or indirectly, from his or her disclosure. If there is no attempt to achieve a personal gain, there is no breach of duty to the stockholders. And absent a breach by the insider, there can be no derivative breach by the tippee.
5. The former officer of the insurance company disclosed the inside information to reveal the company's fraudulent practices; he never intended to, and did not, receive any monetary or personal gain. Since this insider did not breach a fiduciary duty, Dirks could not have participated in "passing on" the insider's breach of a fiduciary duty.

Despite this apparent loophole in the use of nonpublic information, it now appears that a person will be considered to be a temporary insider if the insider conveyed nonpublic information which was to be kept confidential. The following case illustrates the logic of finding a temporary insider liable under Section 10(b), even though there was no breach of a fiduciary duty.

SECURITIES AND EXCHANGE COMMISSION v. LUND
570 F. Supp. 1397 (C.D. Cal. 1983)

FACTS

Lund was the chief executive officer and chairman of the board of Verit Company. Horowitz was the chief executive officer and chairman of the board of P&F. To solicit investment funds, Horowitz told Lund about P&F's opportunity to participate in a Las Vegas gambling casino. Horowitz sought investment capital from Verit. After learning of these unannounced plans, Lund purchased 10,000 shares of P&F's stock. Three days later, P&F's plans to participate in the casino joint venture were announced, and the stock doubled in price. Lund sold his shares at a substantial profit. The SEC sued Lund for violating Section 10(b) of the Federal Securities Exchange Act of 1934.

ISSUE

Did Lund illegally use nonpublic information to gain a profit?

DECISION

Yes.

REASONS

1. It is clear that Horowitz did not breach his fiduciary duty to P&F or its shareholders by disclosing information to Lund about the joint venture. Horowitz had the legitimate business purpose of seeking investment capital.
2. Without a breach of fiduciary duty by Horowitz, Lund cannot be liable under Section 10(b) as a tippee. However, under certain circumstances "outsiders" may owe a fiduciary duty to disclose nonpublic information or abstain from trading. In essence, these people can be considered to be "temporary insiders."
3. The relationship between Horowitz and Lund was such as to imply that the information was to be confidential. Horowitz clearly did not expect Lund to make this information public or to use this information for his personal gain.
4. Under these circumstances, Lund's breach of his duty to disclose or abstain from trading is actionable as a violation of Section 10(b).

Insider rules are rigidly applied in ordinary sale and purchase transactions. However, courts have held that the provisions do not apply to certain "unorthodox" transactions that are not within the intent of the law. For example, it has been held that if a purchaser did not own 10 percent of the total stock prior to the purchase, then the purchase and later sale within six months is not subject to the law.

The SEC has always tried to curb "insider" transactions, but historically it has been difficult because of a limited civil sanction. Until 1984, the "insider" was liable only to return the profit illegally gained. In 1984, the law was changed. Today, the SEC may seek a civil penalty of three times the illegal profits. The SEC has used this increased penalty to further its campaign against the use of inside information which is a very serious, continuing problem. The following statement from Caterpillar's Code of Ethics illustrates an appropriate corporate policy on the use and nonuse of inside information.

Inside Information

Inside information may be defined as information about Caterpillar which isn't known to the investing public. Such information may have value—for example, certain financial data, technical materials, and future plans. Those with access to such information are expected to treat it confidentially, and in a fashion which avoids harm to Caterpillar.

Inside information may or may not be "material." Information is "material" if there is substantial likelihood that a reasonable investor would consider it important in making an investment decision about Caterpillar.

Those who have "material" inside information are expected to refrain from using it for personal gain. For example, they are required to refrain from personal trading of Caterpillar stock until the information has become public...or until it's no longer "material."

The preceding pertains to both: (1) all corporate officers, and (2) those who, by reason of their jobs, possess such information.

While Caterpillar may hire individuals who have knowledge and experience in various technical areas, we don't wish to employ such persons as a means of gaining access to trade secrets of others. New employees are asked not to divulge such trade secrets.

The concept of "inside information" extends outside the company, and requires ethical judgments by people involved. Beyond other conflict-of-interest rules which may apply, a Caterpillar employee having access to confidential company information that could affect the price of a supplier's, customer's, or competitor's stock shouldn't trade in such stock.

15 ADDITIONAL CIVIL LIABILITY

Section 18 of the Securities Exchange Act of 1934 imposes liability on any person who shall make or cause to be made any false and misleading statements of material fact in any application, report, or document filed under the act. This liability for fraud favors both purchasers and sellers. Plaintiffs must prove scienter, reliance on the false or misleading statement, and damage. Good faith is a defense. Good faith exists when a person acts without knowledge that the statement is false and misleading. In other words, freedom from fraud is a defense under an action predicated on Section 18. There is no liability under this section for simple negligence.

In addition to Section 18, the securities laws include many provisions that require reports to be filed with the SEC. These reporting provisions do not lead to a civil remedy for inaccurate reporting. This result is due in part to the specific civil remedy provided in Section 18.

Section 14(e) of the act prohibits fraudulent, deceptive, or manipulative acts or practices in connection with tender offers. This provision has been interpreted in the same way as Section 10(b). For a violation to occur, there must be a misrepresentation or nondisclosure of a material fact—in other words, fraud must be proven. Unfairness is not a violation.

SCHREIBER v. BURLINGTON NORTHERN, INC.
105 S.Ct. 2458 (1985)

FACTS

Burlington Northern, Inc., made a hostile tender offer for El Paso Gas Co. Although a majority of El Paso's shareholders subscribed, Burlington did not accept the tendered shares. Later Burlington and El Paso announced a new agreement, which was soon oversubscribed. The rescission of the first tender offer caused a reduced payment to those shareholders who had tendered during the first offer. Plaintiff filed suit, alleging a violation of Section 14(e) of the Securities Exchange Act of 1934, which prohibits "fraudulent, deceptive or manipulative acts or practices...in connection with any tender offer."

ISSUE

Was the withdrawal of the first tender offer, coupled with the substitution of the January offer, a "manipulative" distortion of the market for El Paso stock?

DECISION

No.

REASONS

1. The word "manipulative" is virtually a term of art when used in connection with the securities markets. It connotes intentional or willful conduct *designed to deceive or defraud* investors by controlling or artificially affecting the price of securities.
2. The term refers generally to practices, that are intended to mislead investors by artificially affecting market activity. It does not mean instances of corporate mismanagement, the essence of which is unfair treatment by a corporate fiduciary.
3. The purpose of the Federal law is to ensure that public shareholders who are confronted by a cash tender offer for their stock will not be required to respond without adequate information.

16 CRIMINAL LIABILITY

The 1934 act provides for criminal sanctions for willful violations of its provisions or the rules adopted under it. Liability is imposed for false material statements in applications, reports, documents, and registration statements. The penalty is a fine not to exceed $100,000, five years in prison, or both. Failure to file the required reports and documents makes the issuer subject to a $100 forfeiture per day. A person cannot be convicted if he proves that he has no knowledge of a rule or regulation, but, of course, lack of knowledge of a statute is no defense.

Criminal liability is important for officers and directors. It is also important for accountants. Accountants have been found guilty of a crime for failure to disclose important facts to shareholder-investors. Compliance with generally accepted accounting principles is not an absolute defense. The critical issue in such cases is whether the financial statements as a whole fairly present the financial condition of the company and whether they accurately report operations for the covered periods. If they do not, the second issue is whether the accountant acted in good faith. Compliance with generally accepted accounting principles is evidence of good faith, but such evidence is not necessarily conclusive. Lack of criminal intent is the defense usually asserted by accountants charged with a crime. They usually admit mistakes or even negligence but deny any criminal wrongdoing. Proof of motive is not required.

In the case of *United States v. Natelli,* 527 F.2d 311 (1975), the United States Court of Appeals for the Second Circuit discussed the element of criminal intent and the role of the jury in deciding if it exists. It noted that the failure to follow sound accounting practice is evidence that may prove criminal intent. It said in part:

It is hard to prove the intent of a defendant. Circumstantial evidence, particularly with proof of motive, where available, is often sufficient to convince a reasonable man of criminal intent beyond a reasonable doubt. When we deal with a defendant who is a professional accountant, it is even harder, at times, to distinguish between simple errors of judgment and errors made with sufficient criminal intent to support a conviction, especially when there is no financial gain to the accountant other than his legitimate fee....

...The arguments Natelli makes in this court as evidence of his innocent intent were made to the jury and presented fairly. There is no contention that Judge Tyler improperly excluded any factual evidence offered....

...We reject the argument of insufficiency as to Natelli, our function being limited to determining whether the evidence was sufficient for submission to the jury. We hold that it was.

...There are points in favor of Natelli, to be sure, but these were presented to the jury and rejected.

From the foregoing, it is clear that great deference is given to the findings of fact by the jury in criminal cases.

As with issues of civil liability, most cases involving potential criminal liability under the Federal Securities Exchange Act of 1934 are litigated under Section 10(b) and Rule 10b-5.

CONSIDERATIONS BEYOND THE FEDERAL SECURITIES LAWS

17 STATE "BLUE-SKY" LAWS

In addition to understanding the federal securities laws discussed in the previous sections, every person dealing with the issuance of securities should be familiar with state securities regulations. Throughout their history, these laws commonly have been referred to as **blue-sky laws,** probably because they were intended to protect the potential investor from buying "a piece of the attractive blue sky" (worthless or risky securities) without financial and other information about what was being purchased. The blue-sky laws can apply to securities subject to federal laws as well as to those securities exempt from the federal statutes. It is clearly established that the federal laws do not preempt the existence of state blue-sky laws. Because of their broad application, the blue-sky laws passed by the various states should be surveyed by any person associated with issuing or thereafter transferring securities.

Although the existence of federal securities laws has influenced state legislatures, enactment of blue-sky laws has not been uniform, Indeed, states typically have enacted laws that contain provisions similar to either: (1) the antifraud provisions, (2) the registration of securities provisions, (3) the registration of securities brokers and dealers provisions, or (4) a combination of these provisions of the federal laws. To bring some similarity to the various blue-sky laws, a Uniform Securities Act was proposed for adoption by all states beginning in 1956. Since that time, the Uniform Securities Act has been the model for blue-sky laws. A majority of states have used the uniform proposal as a guideline when enacting or amending their blue-sky laws.

Registration Requirements

Despite this trend toward uniformity, these state laws still vary a great deal in their methods of regulating both the distribution of securities and the securities industry within each state. One example of the variety of state regulation concerns the requirements of registering securities. States have chosen one of two types of regulations: (1) registration by notification or (2) registration by qualification. Registration by notification allows issuers to offer securities for sale automatically after a stated time period expires, unless the administrative agency takes action to prevent the offering. This is very similar to the registration process under the Federal Securities Act of 1933. Registration by qualification usually requires a more-detailed disclosure by the issuer. Under this type of regulation, a security cannot be offered for sale until the administrative agency grants the issuer a license or certificate to sell securities.

In an attempt to resolve some of this conflict over the registration procedure, the drafters of the Uniform Securities Act may have compounded the problem. This act adopts the registration-by-notification process for an issuer who has demonstrated stability and performance. Registration by qualification is required by those issuers who do not have a proven record and who are not subject to the Federal Securities Act of 1933. In addition, the Uniform Securities Act created a third procedure—called *registration by coordination*. For those issuers of securities who must register with the SEC, duplicate documents are filed with the state administrative agency. Unless the state official objects, the state registration becomes effective automatically when the federal registration statement is deemed effective.

Exemptions

To further compound the confusion about blue-sky laws, various exemptions of the securities or transactions have been adopted by the states. Four basic exemptions from blue-sky laws have been identified. Every state likely has enacted at least one and perhaps a combination of these exemptions. Among these common four are the exemption: (1) for an isolated transaction, (2) for an offer or sale to a limited number of offerees or purchasers within a stated time period, (3) for a private offering, and (4) for a sale if the number of holders after the sale does not exceed a specified number.

This second type of exemption probably is the most common exemption, since it is part of the Uniform Securities Act. Nevertheless, states vary on whether the exemption applies to offerees or to purchasers. There also is great variation on the maximum number of such offerees or purchasers involved. That number likely ranges between five and thirty-five, depending on the applicable blue-sky law. The time period for the offers or purchases, as the case may be, also may vary; however, twelve months seems to be the most common period.

Usually the applicable time limitation is worded to read, for example, "*any* twelve-month time period." In essence, this language means that each day starts a new time period running. For example, assume a security is exempt from blue-sky registration requirements if the issuer sells (or offers to sell) securities to no more than thirty-five investors during any twelve-month period. Furthermore, assume the following transactions occur, with each investor being a different person or entity:

On February 1, 1988, issuer sells to five investors.
On June 1, 1988, issuer sells to ten investors.
On September 1, 1988, issuer sells to ten investors.
On December 1, 1988, issuer sells to five investors.
On March 1, 1989, issuer sells to five investors.
On May 1, 1989, issuer sells to ten investors.

Only thirty investors are involved during the twelve-month period following February 1, 1988. However, forty investors are purchasers during the twelve months following June 1, 1988. Therefore, this security and the transactions involved are not exempt from the blue-sky law. Civil as well as criminal liability may result for failure to comply with applicable legal regulations.

Although blue-sky laws, because of their variation, may cause confusion, ignorance of the state legal requirements is no defense. This confusion is furthered when the businessperson considers the applicability of federal securities laws as well as the variety of blue-sky laws. To diminish this confusion, any person involved in the issuance or subsequent transfer of securities should consult with lawyers and accountants as well as other experts who have a working knowledge of securities regulations.

18 ETHICAL CONSIDERATIONS

Because of the importance of complying with the financial-reporting and disclosure requirements of the securities laws, many companies have developed explicit policies which recognize the legal and social obligations involved. Caterpillar's Code of Ethics, for example, includes the following statements:

Accounting Records and Financial Reporting

Accounting is called the "universal language" of business. Therefore, those who rely on the company's records—investors, creditors, and other decision makers and interested parties—have a right to information that is timely and true.

The integrity of Caterpillar accounting and financial records is based on validity, accuracy, and completeness of basic information supporting entries to the company's books of account. All employees involved in creating, processing, or recording such information are held responsible for its integrity.

Every accounting or financial entry should reflect exactly that which is described by the supporting information. There must be no concealment of information from (or by) management, or from the company's independent auditors.

Employees who become aware of possible omission, falsification, or inaccuracy of accounting and financial entries, or basic data supporting such entries, are held responsible for reporting such information. These reports are to be made as specified by corporate procedure.

A basic premise of Caterpillar's financial reporting is that conservatism in determining earnings is in the best long-term interests of the company and its shareholders. This means the accounting practices followed by Caterpillar are those which minimize: (1) the possibility of overstating reported earnings and (2) the likelihood of having unexpected or extraordinary adjustments in future periods.

Disclosure of Information

In a free society, institutions flourish and businesses prosper not only by customer acceptance of their products and services, but also by public acceptance of their conduct.

Therefore, the public is entitled to a reasonable explanation of operations of a business, especially as those operations bear on the public interest. Larger economic size logically begets an increased responsibility for such public communication.

In pursuit of these beliefs, the company will:

1 Respond to public inquiries—including those from the press and from governments—with answers that are prompt, informative, and courteous.
2 Keep investors, securities trading markets, employees, and the general public informed about Caterpillar on a timely, impartial basis.

REVIEW QUESTIONS

1 Identify the terms in the left-hand column by matching each with the appropriate statement in the right-hand column.

(1) Registration statement (a) An advertisement made during the waiting period. It announces the security, its price, by whom orders will be executed, and from whom a prospectus may be obtained.

(2)	Prospectus	(b)	A participant in the distribution of a security who guarantees the sale of an issue.
(3)	Tombstone ad	(c)	The individual or business organization that offers a security for sale.
(4)	Insider	(d)	The document that contains financial and other information. It must be filed with the SEC prior to any sale of a security.
(5)	Issuer	(e)	A party who controls or is controlled by the issuer.
(6)	Controlling person	(f)	A person who owns more than 10 percent of a security of an issuer or who is a director of an officer of an issuer.
(7)	Underwriter	(g)	Any person who contracts with a purchaser or who exerts a substantial role which causes a purchase transaction to occur.
(8)	Seller	(h)	A document or pamphlet that includes the essential information contained in the registration statement. It is filed with the SEC and made available to potential investors.

2 Under the provisions of the Federal Securities Act of 1933, there are three important time periods concerning when securities may be sold or offered for sale. Name and describe these three time periods.

3 Patrick, a promoter for a newly organized corporation, began to solicit purchasers of the corporation's stock. The corporation did not limit the number of potential shareholders, but it did not plan to sell more than $400,000 worth of securities. What is Patrick's responsibility, under the provisions of the Federal Securities Act of 1933, with respect to registering this offering?

4 Dahl purchased a fractional undivided interest in oil and gas leases. He also actively solicited friends and family to purchase the securities, which he knew were unregistered. He received no commission and did not know that failure to register was unlawful. The interests proved worthless, and Dahl sought his money back. Is he entitled to it? Why, or why not?

5 Investors in a limited-partnership tax shelter sued under Section 10(b) of the Securities and Exchange Act to rescind their purchase. The defendants sought to set off the amount to be refunded against the tax savings of each investor. May the defendants deduct this tax saving? Why, or why not?

6 A securities brokerage firm hired a public accounting firm to conduct audits and prepare financial statements for filing with the SEC. The brokerage firm failed and sued the accounting firm, alleging that the accounting firm breached its duty owed to customers by conducting an improper audit and certification. Is the law requiring such audits and reports a basis of a suit for damages? Why, or why not?

7 Betty, a buyer of unregistered securities from the "U-2-Can-B-Rich Co.," lost all her investment when the company filed for bankruptcy. What civil remedies does Betty have if these securities are subject to the Federal Securities Act of 1933?

8 Section 10(b) of the Federal Securities Exchange Act of 1934 and Rule 10b-5 are of fundamental importance in the law of securities regulations. What is the main purpose of this section and rule?

9 Donna, a corporate director, sold 100 shares of stock in her corporation on June

1, 1985. The selling price was $10.50 a share. Two months later, after the corporation had announced substantial losses for the second quarter of the year, Donna purchased 100 shares of the corporation's stock for $7.25 a share. Are there any problems with Donna's sale and purchase? Explain.

10 David, the president of a large corporation, participated in a managerial decision to expand business operations in the near future. Anticipating that the corporation's financial status would improve because of this decision, David purchased stock from Sandra, a shareholder who had no knowledge of the company's plans. The market value of the stock rose immediately after the decision was announced. Is David liable to Sandra for any profits made from this transaction? Why, or why not?

11 The Valley Loan Association (VLA) issued investment notes to various persons. The proceeds were used to make loans to customers of the association. VLA went bankrupt, and its president was charged with a criminal violation of the Federal Securities Law of 1933. He contended that the law was not applicable, because the notes were not securities. Was he correct? Why, or why not?

CHAPTER 19

CONSUMER PROTECTION

OVERVIEW

There have been more consumer protection laws passed since World War II than in the 175 years preceding the war. Two key factors seem primarily responsible for this rapid expansion of legal regulation. First, most of the past several decades has been a time of rising affluence, when the public has been willing to absorb costs of additional legal regulation, which inevitably come in the form of higher prices for goods and services. Second, the organization of well-financed consumer lobbying groups has led to legislative responses favorable to consumer interests.

Recent trends toward a more cautious federal approach to consumer protection reveal the conservative, market-oriented philosophy of a Republican administration. At the state level, however, consumer protection regulation continues to be increasingly active. Even at the federal level, there are a great number of existing laws which continue to be enforced. Many provide remedies which allow injured consumers to sue law violators.

This chapter divides consumer protection into federal and state laws. At the federal level, the Federal Trade Commission (FTC) is the primary regulatory agency. It enforces statutes which prohibit unfair and deceptive trade practices, various credit abuses, and misleading warranties.

At the state level, all states have unfair and deceptive acts and practices laws. State attorneys general usually administer these laws, which greatly resemble the federal FTC Act. The states also have a variety of consumer protection laws regulating specific businesses such as auto repair shops and health spas.

Significant terms in this chapter include bait-and-switch promotion, consumer, investigative consumer report, corrective advertising, industry guide, legal clinics, redlining, respondent, and trade practice regulation.

1 WHO IS A CONSUMER?

The laws discussed in this chapter protect consumers. Who is a **consumer?** Consider the following case:

ANDERSON v. FOOTHILL INDUSTRIAL BANK
674 P.2d 232 (Wyo. 1984)

FACTS

The Andersons charged Foothill Industrial Bank with misrepresenting the annual percentage rate of a loan, which is a violation of the Truth-in-Lending Act.

ISSUE

Did the bank violate the Truth-in-Lending Act?

DECISION

No.

REASONS

1. The Truth-in-Lending Act protects only consumers—natural persons who incur debt "primarily for personal, family, or household purposes."
2. According to their own statements, the Andersons obtained their loan to finance a mail-route business. Although part of the loan was used to pay off a second mortgage on their house, the loan was *primarily* used for a commercial, not a personal, purpose.

According to the *Anderson* case, consumers are natural (rather than corporate) persons who incur debt "primarily for personal, family, or household purposes." Most of the statutes in this chapter define "consumer" similarly.

Although the Federal Trade Commission Act protects businesses as well as consumers, the consumer protection mission of the Federal Trade Commission (FTC) is promoted by a special bureau called the Bureau of Consumer Protection. This body within the FTC is the regulatory center for federal consumer protection. The next sections examine activities of the FTC and the Bureau of Consumer Protection.

FEDERAL CONSUMER PROTECTION

2 THE FEDERAL TRADE COMMISSION

Created in 1914, the FTC is an "independent" regulatory agency charged with keeping competition free and fair, and with protecting consumers. The FTC obeys its mandate to promote competition through enforcement of the antitrust laws discussed in Chapters 21 to 23. It achieves its consumer protection goal by trade-practice regulation under that section of the FTC Act which prohibits using "unfair or deceptive acts or practices in commerce." It also administers several other consumer protection acts covered in this chapter and Chapter 20. (See Table 19-1.) In the final analysis, promoting competition and protecting consumers overlap considerably. A highly competitive economy produces better goods and services at lower prices, while **trade practice regulation** ensures fair competition by preventing those who would deceive consumers from diverting trade from those who compete honestly.

The FTC furthers consumer protection through trade practice regulation in several ways. For instance, it advises firms that request it as to whether a proposed practice is unfair or deceptive. Although not legally binding, an **advisory opinion** furnishes a good idea about how the FTC views the legality of a given trade practice. Sometimes the FTC also issues **industry guides,** which specify the agency's view of the legality of a particular industry's trade practices. Like advisory opinions, industry guides are informal and not legally binding. The Bureau of Consumer Protection plays

TABLE 19-1 CONSUMER PROTECTION LAWS THE FTC ADMINISTERS

Laws	Duties
FTC Act	To regulate unfair or deceptive acts or practices
Fair Packaging and Labeling Act	To prohibit deceptive labeling of certain consumer products and require disclosure of certain important information
Equal Credit Opportunity Act	To prevent discrimination in credit extension based on sex, age, race, religion, national origin, marital status, and receipt of welfare payments
Truth-in-Lending Act	To require that suppliers of consumer credit fully disclose all credit terms before an account is opened or a loan made
Fair Credit Reporting Act	To regulate the consumer credit reporting industry
Magnuson-Moss Warranty Act	To require the FTC to issue rules concerning consumer product warranties
Fair Debt Collection Practices Act	To prevent debt-collection agencies from using abusive or deceptive collection practices

the major role in issuing advisory opinions and industry guides on trade regulation issues.

In its function of protecting consumers, however, the FTC goes far beyond merely advising businesses about the legality of trade practices. It also prosecutes them for committing unfair or deceptive trade practices. Such prosecutions arise in one of two related ways. First, the Bureau of Consumer Protection may allege that an individual or company, called a **respondent,** has violated Section 5 of the FTC Act, which prohibits **unfair or deceptive acts or practices.** Over the years, the FTC's administrative law judges, and the commissioners who review decisions of the judges, have derived a body of quasi-judicial interpretations as to what constitutes unfair and deceptive acts.

Prosecutions may also arise from allegations under Section 5 that a respondent's actions violate a trade regulation rule of the FTC. At the recommendation of the Bureau of Consumer Protection, the five-member Commission adopts trade regulation rules in exercising its quasi-legislative power. These rules are formal interpretations of what the FTC regards as unfair or deceptive, and they have the force and effect of law. The rules usually deal with a single practice in a single industry, and they cover all firms in the affected industry. Examples of trade regulation rules include required disclosures of the "R" value for siding and insulation, and the familiar warning on cigarette packages and in ads.

Alleged trade practice violations may come to the attention of the Bureau of Consumer Protection in a variety of ways. A business executive may complain about another's acts that injure competition, or a consumer may direct the attention of the Bureau to unfair or deceptive acts of a business. Such complaints are filed informally, and the identity of the complainant is not disclosed. A letter signed by a complaining party provides a basis for proceedings if it identifies the offending party, contains all the evidence which is the basis for the complaint, and states the relief desired. Of course, other government agencies, Congress, or the FTC itself may discover business conduct alleged to be illegal. For instance, the Bureau of Consumer Protection maintains a special media monitoring unit which examines the media for trade practice violations.

The chief legal tools of the Bureau are the **consent order** and the **cease and desist order.** As discussed in Chapter 7, under the consent-order procedure, a party "consents" to sign an order which restrains the promotional activity deemed offensive and agrees to whatever remedy the Bureau imposes, if any. Most cases brought by the Bureau are settled by this procedure.

If a party will not accept a consent order, it will be prosecuted before an administrative law judge. If the party is found guilty, the judge issues a cease and desist order prohibiting future violations. Parties may appeal cease and desist orders to the full five-member commission and from there to the court of appeals if legal basis for further appeal is present.

3 FTC PENALTIES AND REMEDIES

Civil Fines

The basic penalty for trade practice violations under the FTC Act is a civil fine of not more than $10,000 per violation. The punishment function of fining violators is only an incidental one, as the FTC's main purpose is to prevent and deter trade practice violations.

To obtain fines, either the FTC or the Justice Department must ask the federal court to assess them. The exception is when companies agree to fines as part of a consent order. Fines may be assessed in three distinct situations: (1) for a violation of a consent or cease and desist order, (2) for a violation of a trade regulation rule, and (3) for a knowing violation of prior FTC orders against others.

This last situation requires some explanation. In 1975, Congress amended the FTC Act to permit the FTC to assess fines against parties who knowingly did what others in the past had been ordered to stop. The main purpose in this change in the law was to be fair to firms who had been ordered to stop a certain practice but whose competitors continued to do it. As changed, the law allows assessment of fines against such competitors once they know of the illegality of their practice. To establish knowledge, the FTC can mail copies of its orders against a respondent to other firms in a respondent's industry. Then, any further instance of the practice would be a knowing violation. In one penalty action, the FTC assessed a $100,000 fine against a toy manufacturer who knowingly continued a practice which the FTC had ordered another manufacturer to cease.

The FTC Act provides that "each separate violation of...an order shall be a separate offense." It also states that in the case of a violation through continuing failure to obey an order, each day the violation continues is a separate offense. Because of these provisions, the total fine against a violator may be considerably more than $10,000. As the following case illustrates, there can be disagreement about what constitutes a separate violation under the act.

UNITED STATES v. READER'S DIGEST ASSOCIATION, INC.
662 F.2d 955 (1981)

FACTS

In 1972, the *Reader's Digest* agreed to accept a consent order from the FTC which barred it from using or distributing simulated checks. In 1973 and 1975, the *Digest* engaged in four bulk-mailing sweepstakes promotions using "travel checks" and "cash-convertible bonds." In 1980, the district court found the *Digest* guilty of over 17 million violations of the FTC Act, one for each distributed letter, and assessed a penalty of $1,750,000.

ISSUES

1. Did each individual distribution constitute a separate violation of the consent order?
2. Was the district court's calculation of the penalty based on an improper analysis of the circumstances?

DECISION

1. Yes. Each individual mailing clearly violates the FTC Act and the consent order.
2. No. The record supports the findings of the district court.

REASONS

1. The statute states that there can be a penalty of no more than $10,000 for *each* violation of a cease and desist order and that each *separate* violation shall be a *separate* offense. Congress anticipated such potential liability for multiple violations when drafting the penalty provision.
2. The *Digest* clearly did not act in good faith by conducting a sweepstakes campaign in the face of an existing consent order prohibiting such distributions. The trial court had already found that such distributions had the capacity to deceive consumers and nothing more need be proved. There is also ample evidence to support the district court's finding that the *Digest* received substantial benefits from the illegal mailings.

Other Remedies

In addition to assessing penalty fines, the FTC has broad powers to fashion appropriate remedies to protect consumers in trade regulation cases. One remedy the FTC uses to accompany some of its orders is **corrective advertising.**

When a company has advertised deceptively, the FTC can require it to run ads that admit the prior errors and correct the erroneous information. The correction applies to a specific dollar volume of future advertising. The theory is that the future advertising, however truthful itself, will continue to be deceptive unless the correction is made because it will remind consumers of the prior deceptive ads. Corrective ads have forced admissions that a mouthwash does not reduce cold symptoms or prevent sore throats, that an oil-treatment product cannot decrease gasoline consumption, and that an aspirin-based drug cannot relieve tension.

Other remedies the FTC may use in its orders, or may seek to impose by court action under certain circumstances, include: (1) recission of contracts (each party must return what has been obtained from the other), (2) refund of money or return of property, (3) payment of damages to consumers, and (4) public notification of trade practice violations. When it is in the public interest, and when harm from an illegal practice is substantial and likely to continue, the FTC may ask the federal court to grant temporary or even permanent injunctions to restrain violators.

4 TRADITIONAL TRADE PRACTICE REGULATION

The FTC conducts trade practice regulation under its power to determine "unfair or deceptive acts or practices in commerce." Most of its cases have focused on deceptive practices. Often, as the following discussion reveals, proof of traditional deception relies more on a showing of legalistically inaccurate promotional language, rather than on consumer injury.

Price Misrepresentations

One common type of advertising traditionally attacked by the FTC makes prospective purchasers believe they will be getting a "good deal" in terms of price if they buy the product in question. For example, a seller of goods was ordered to refrain from advertising its products for sale using a price comparison in which its actual price was compared to a higher "regular" price or a manufacturer's list price. The Commission ruled that it is deceptive to refer to "regular price" unless the defendant has usually sold the items at the price recently in the regular course of business. Also, it was held deceptive to refer to the "manufacturer's list price" when that list price is not the ordinary and customary retail sales price of the item in the locality. This is in spite of the fact that manufacturers themselves suggest the retail prices to which the seller may compare its lower selling price. In ordering enforcement of the Commission's cease and desist order, the court of appeals said: "We do not understand the Commission to hold that use of the term 'manufacturer's list price' is unlawful per se; rather it is unlawful only if it is not the usual and customary retail price in the area."

Similar to price representations which offer "free" goods for the purchase of others is a **bait-and-switch promotion.** Here, the seller intends to use a product advertised at a low price only as bait to capture the interest of consumers and then switch their attention from it to products which the baiter really has desired to sell from the beginning.

Performance Misrepresentations

Besides involving misleading price representations, deceptive practices may result from fraudulent, false, or misleading advertising or other representations concerning the performance capability of goods or services being sold. False representations of the composition, quality, character, or source of products, by misbranding or otherwise, have been barred as deceptively misleading. For example, lumber dealers have been barred from advertising under names such as "California white pine" and "Western white pine" when their products were inferior to genuine "white pine," even though these terms were accepted and understood in the trade. Other cases falling into this category of violation are ones in which a seller suggested that a beauty aid "restored natural moisture necessary for a lively healthy skin," a claim which was false, and one in which cigars made of domestic tobacco were labeled "Havana."

False statements which misrepresent either a product or its price have also been ruled unfair or deceptive. Typical of these is one in which a product is endorsed by one who is misrepresented to be a "doctor" or "scientific expert." Disparaging the goods of others in an attempt to promote the sale of one's own is also an unfair practice. For example, the FTC restrained a manufacturer of stainless-steel cooking utensils from publishing questions such as the following: "Do you know that aluminum pans may be full of the most deadly bacteria known to science?" "Did you ever find maggots in your aluminum pans?"

Truthful Yet Deceptive Ads

Other cases have involved no actual misstatement but representations which, while true in themselves, were intended to mislead. Using a word while having a hidden or unusual interpretation in mind for the purpose of promoting sales is an example. If a manufacturer states that its product is "guaranteed for life," most people would probably believe that the guarantee was to run for the life of the purchaser. However, Parker Pen Company used this phrase in its advertising with the undisclosed intention that the lives in question were those of the pens they manufactured, thus making the guarantee worthless. Parker was restrained from making such "guarantees."

Using the technique of product-name simulation is also unfair. This occurs when a manufacturer or seller uses either the same name or one that is deceptively similar to another product of another manufacturer which has acquired consumer acceptance. This conduct, whether undertaken with the intent of exploiting the goodwill of a competitor or not, may confuse consumers. If the name selected is close enough to that of the established product, its use may be restrained by the FTC as being deceptive.

Even silence by a seller may result in deception of consumers, and the Commission may require that positive disclosures be made before further sales of the goods in question are permissible. For example, nondisclosure that books published were abridged or condensed was ruled as deceptive. In addition, distributing secondhand or rebuilt goods without indicating them as such and selling foreign goods without disclosing their origin have been restrained by the Commission in its efforts to protect consumers from unfair or deceptive trade practices.

Table 19-2 gives recent examples of FTC deceptive trade practice cases. Most of these cases are "traditional" in nature.

5 POLICY TRENDS AT THE FTC

Generally

After the 1970s, the consumer activist decade at the FTC, the 1980s has brought a more-restrained effort at consumer protection by the agency. During the 1970s, the FTC began broad-scale use of its rule-making powers. It passed or proposed sweeping rules on thermal insulation, eyeglasses,

TABLE 19-2 RECENT FTC DECEPTIVE PRACTICE CASES

Company	Order
American Home Products	Must not give the impression that pain relievers are something other than aspirin when they are not. Must disclose presence of aspirin when company's product is contrasted with another product containing aspirin. Required to prove claims of product superiority with two controlled clinical studies.
California-Texas Oil Co.	Must not make unsubstantiated claims about gasoline additives improving fuel mileage. Cannot use language that additives improve mileage "up to" 15 percent unless an appreciable number of consumers can achieve that performance under normal conditions.
Meredith Corp.	Company must stop misleading potential home buyers and sellers by ads which allege that obtaining a Better Homes real estate franchise is more difficult than it actually is.
Champion Home Builders Co.	Must pay $550,000 to consumers who purchased solar furnaces in which ad claims misrepresented amount of heat the furnaces would produce.
Heatcool	Company must run twelve months of corrective ads stating that its products "do not insulate better than comparable glass storm windows."
Sears	Must cease and desist from making claims that Lady Denmore dishwashers eliminate the need for scraping and prerinsing dishes. Cannot make claims for *any* major home appliance unless reliable substantiating evidence is available.

the funeral industry, franchising, business opportunities, vocational schools, food labeling, used cars, and children's advertising. These rules threw many affected businesses into such turmoil that Congress, prompted by heavy lobbying, acted to restrain the FTC.

In the 1980s, the FTC has backed away from its earlier enthusiasm for rule making. Prior to final adoption, the proposed food labeling and children's advertising rules were withdrawn from consideration. Under the Reagan FTC, the Bureau of Consumer Protection has focused its enforcement efforts on a case-by-case approach to regulation, rather than on rule making. And in line with the theory that the marketplace itself can cure many types of deceptive practices, the Reagan FTC has substantially reduced the number of deceptive trade practice cases from the levels of previous administrations.

Another development of the 1970s which has continued vitality in the 1980s is the FTC's **ad substantiation program.** It is now an unfair and deceptive trade practice for sellers to make affirmative claims about their products which they cannot prove. The claims themselves may even be true, but it is illegal to make them if there is no proof to support them. Thus, the FTC required a manufacturer of weight-loss tablets to prove claims that consumers could lose weight without restricting caloric intake. When the manufacturer could not substantiate the ads, it had to discontinue them. Occasionally, the FTC has applied ad substantiation to claims made by an entire industry, rather than to the claims of a specific advertiser.

One 1970s trend at the FTC which continues into the 1980s is the trade regulation emphasis on disclosure to consumers. For instance, the Commission forced a major encyclopedia company to disclose in its advertising that salespersons would call on anyone who returned response coupons. The Commission termed it "deceptive" for the company to fail to make this disclosure. The emphasis on disclosure underscores the belief that informed consumers can "regulate" many trade practices by voting with their dollars, if they possess sufficient information.

In recent years, the FTC has grappled with advertising problems presented by radio and television. The following case illustrates that in electronic media ads the FTC can go beyond words to analyze "aural-visual" imagery.

AMERICAN HOME PRODUCTS CORP. v. F.T.C.

695 F.2d 681 (1982)

FACTS

American Home Products (AHP) advertised that its product Anacin "contains more of the specific medication [doctors] recommend for pain than the leading aspirin, buffered aspirin, or extra-strength tablet." The FTC ruled that this and other claims were deceptive since they suggested that Anacin was more effective than the other medications. In fact, aspirin was the active ingredient in all of them. AHP appealed the ruling.

ISSUE

Did the FTC properly determine that the Anacin advertising was deceptive?

DECISION

Yes.

REASONS

1. The tendency of advertising to deceive must be judged by viewing it as a whole.
2. The FTC had the authority to analyze not only the work but also the "aural-visual" imagery of television advertising.
3. The reviewing court must uphold the FTC's ruling if it has been supported by "substantial evidence on the record."
4. There was substantial evidence on the record to support the FTC's conclusion that the challenged advertising claimed Anacin was more effective than the other medications.

New Deception Guidelines

Traditionally, the concept of deceptive trade practices includes all practices which have a "tendency or capacity" to mislead consumers. No actual harm to any specific group of consumers need to be shown. As of this writing, the courts have not changed the "tendency or capacity standard." The FTC, however, has.

In its new standard, the FTC has said that it will use three tests to determine whether to take action against trade practices. First, the FTC must conclude that the ad is "likely to mislead consumers." Second, misled consumers must be "acting reasonably in the circumstances." Third, the practice must be "material"; that is, it must potentially affect consumers' purchasing decisions.

In explaining its new standard, the FTC noted that certain practices are unlikely to deceive consumers acting reasonably. Generally, the FTC will not bring advertising cases based on subjective claims (taste, feel, appearance, smell) or on correctly stated opinion claims. It will also not pursue cases involving obviously exaggerated or puffing claims.

Under the guidelines, the FTC will likely ignore technically deceptive practices which cannot be shown to affect consumers' purchase decisions, such as an ad which falsely claims the "best prices in town." Although the FTC retains the authority to conclude on its own evaluation whether a practice affects consumers' decision making (is material), the new guidelines will probably cause it to turn increasingly to outside evidence provided by consumer testing.

6 INTRODUCTION TO FEDERAL CREDIT REGULATIONS

In addition to the FTC Act, the FTC administers several other consumer protection statutes as well. One of them, the Fair Debt Collection Practices Act, is discussed in Chapter 20 on debtor-creditor relations. Most of the other FTC-administered statutes concern credit regulation.

As the large number of credit cards in the average consumer's wallet indicates, credit buying has truly become a national pastime. Credit financing of consumer contracts has jumped astronomically in recent years. At the close of World War II, consumer credit outstanding amounted to only $2.5 billion, a figure which had changed little since the 1920s. Today, however, consumer credit debt has soared above the $350 billion mark. Both in absolute terms and as a percentage of GNP, credit debt has grown steadily since World War II. Considering the importance of credit buying to the consumer and business, it is no surprise that a number of laws regulating credit extension have been passed. The laws discussed in the following sections cover nondiscrimination in credit extension, the collection of information for credit reports, and the standardized disclosure of credit charges.

7 EQUAL CREDIT OPPORTUNITY ACT

In 1975, Congress passed the Equal Credit Opportunity Act (ECOA). The ECOA's purpose is to prevent discrimination in credit extension. In an economy in which credit availability is so important, the ECOA is a logical extension in a vital consumer area of the antidiscrimination laws found in the employment field.

ECOA Prohibitions

This act prohibits discrimination based on sex, marital status, race, color, age, religion, national origin, or receipt of welfare in any aspect of a consumer credit transaction. Although the ECOA forbids discrimination on the basis of all these different categories, it is aimed especially at preventing sex discrimination. As the divorce rate climbs, the age of first marriage grows later, and more women enter the work force, it is expected that sex discrimination in credit extension will increasingly become a subject for litigation.

The law prohibits one to whom the act applies from discouraging a consumer from seeking credit based on sex, marital status, or any other of the enumerated categories. A married woman, for example, cannot be denied the right to open a credit account separate from her husband's or in her maiden name. Unless the husband will be using the account or the consumer is relying on her husband's credit, it is illegal even to ask if the consumer is married. It is also illegal to ask about birth-control practices or childbearing plans or to assign negative values on a credit checklist to the fact that a woman is of childbearing age.

The ECOA applies to all businesses which regularly extend credit, including financial institutions, retail stores, and credit-card issuers. It also affects automobile dealers, real estate brokers, and others who steer consumers to lenders. And as the following case indicates, many courts are ruling that ECOA covers consumer leasing situations, which may substitute in place of credit-based sales.

BROTHERS v. FIRST LEASING
724 F.2d 789 (1984)

FACTS

Patricia Brothers attempted to lease an automobile for personal use from First Leasing. First Leasing required her to submit an application and, over her objections, also required an application from her husband. When a credit check on her husband revealed that he had previously filed for bankruptcy, First Leasing rejected Patricia Brothers's application. She sued, alleging a violation of ECOA.

ISSUE

Does ECOA apply to consumer leases?

RESULT

Yes.

REASONS

1. The purpose of ECOA is to end credit discrimination against certain groups, particularly women.
2. Along with the ECOA, the Consumer Leasing Act is part of an umbrella statute, the Consumer Credit Protection Act.
3. In enacting the Consumer Leasing Act, Congress expressly recognized that leasing was an alternative to credit-based installment sales of automobiles.
4. In view of the overriding national policy against discrimination, the term "credit" in the ECOA should not be given a narrow interpretation. The ECOA applies to consumer leases.

Responsibilities of the Credit Extender

In basing a credit decision on the applicant's income, the credit extender must consider alimony, child support, and maintenance payments as income, although the likelihood of these payments being actually made may be considered as well. The credit extender must also tell an applicant that she need not disclose income from these sources unless she will be relying on that income to obtain credit. In calculating total income, those subject to the law must include income from regular part-time jobs and public assistance programs.

Information on accounts used by both spouses must be reported to third parties, such as credit reporting agencies, in the names of both spouses. This provision of the law helps women establish a credit history and enables a woman who separates from her husband to obtain credit in her own right.

To date, much of the litigation surrounding the ECOA concerns the requirement that *specific* reasons be given a consumer who is denied credit. Several cases have imposed liability upon credit extenders who have failed to provide any reasons for credit denial or who merely informed the consumer that she had failed to achieve a minimum score on a credit rating system. Other cases have dealt with age and race discrimination. The government filed an action recently against a large consumer finance company which made extension of credit to the elderly conditional upon their obtaining credit life insurance. It has also been established that the practice of **redlining,** that is, refusing to make loans at all in certain areas where property values are low, can discriminate on the basis of race in granting mortgage credit.

ECOA Remedies and Penalties

Private remedies for violation of the ECOA are recovery of actual damages, punitive damages up to $10,000, and attorney's fees and legal costs. Actual damages can include recovery for embarrassment and mental distress. Punitive damages can be recovered even in the absence of actual damages. In addition to private remedies, the government may bring suit to enjoin violations of the ECOA and to assess civil penalties. In one case, the FTC assessed a $200,000 civil penalty against a major national oil company. The FTC charged that the company practiced race and sex discrimination by using ZIP codes as a factor in deciding whether to extend credit and by failing to consider women's alimony and child support income.

8 THE FAIR CREDIT REPORTING ACT

The Fair Credit Reporting Act (FCRA) applies to anyone who prepares or uses a credit report in connection with: (1) extending credit, (2) selling insurance, or (3) hiring or discharging an employee. It covers credit reports on consumers but not those on businesses. The purpose of the law is to prevent unjust damage to an individual because of inaccurate or arbitrary information in a credit report. It is also designed to prevent the undue invasion of individual privacy in the collection and selling of information about a person's credit record.

Consumer Rights Under FCRA

The law gives individual consumers certain rights whenever they are rejected for credit, insurance, or employment because of an adverse credit report. These rights include: (1) the right to be told the name of the agency making the report, (2) the right to require the agency to reveal the information given in the report, and (3) the right to correct the information or at least give the consumer's version of the facts in dispute.

This law does have one important limitation. It provides that a report containing information solely as to transactions or experiences between the consumer and the person making the report is not a "consumer report" covered by the act. To illustrate this limitation, assume that a bank is asked for information about its credit experience with one of its customers. If it reports only as to its own experiences, the report is not covered by the act. The act is designed to cover credit reporting agencies which obtain information from several sources, compile it, and furnish it to potential creditors. If the bank passed along any information it had received from an outside source, then its credit report would be subject to the provision of the act. Also, if the bank gave its opinion as to the creditworthiness of the customer in question, it would come under the act. The limitation is restricted to information relating to transactions or experiences, and the information furnished must be of a factual nature if the exception is the law is to be applicable.

Many businesses can avoid the pitfalls of being a credit reporting agency, but most businesses will be subject to the "user" provisions of this law. The "user" provision requires that consumers who are seeking credit for personal, family, or household purposes be informed if their application is denied because of an adverse credit report. They must also be informed of the source of the report and the fact that they are entitled to make a written request within sixty days as to the nature of the information received. If they request the information in the report, they are entitled to receive it so that they may challenge the accuracy of the negative aspects of its contents.

Investigative Consumer Reports

The act also contains a provision on **investigative consumer reports.** These are reports on a consumer's character, general reputation, mode of living, and so on, obtained by personal interviews in the consumer's community. No one may obtain such a report unless at least three days' advance notice is given the consumer that such a report will be sought. The consumer has the right to be informed of the nature and scope of any such personal investigation. Reports which are intended to be covered by this act are those usually conducted for insurance companies and employment agencies.

Observing Reasonable Procedures

In making investigations and collecting information, credit reporting agencies must observe *reasonable procedures,* or they will be liable to consumers. For example, when a consumer investigative report contained false information about a consumer's character—including rumored drug use, participation in demonstrations, and eviction from prior residences—a court found liability against the credit reporting agency. The agency's investigator had obtained the information from a single source, a person with a strong bias against the consumer, and he failed to double-check it. However, if an agency follows reasonable procedures, it is not liable to a consumer, even if it reports false information. Furthermore, several courts have ruled that the FCRA preempts state law. This prevents consumers from filing libel actions against agencies which report false information.

FCRA Penalties and Remedies

Anyone who violates the FCRA is civilly liable to an injured consumer. For instance, as the next case shows, a business that seeks a credit report for an improper reason may be liable under the FCRA.

ZAMORA v. VALLEY FEDERAL SAVINGS & LOAN ASSOCIATION
811 F.2d 1368 (10th Cir. 1987)

FACTS

An employee at the Valley Federal Savings and Loan Association was being considered for a branch manager position. When she got married, her employer obtained a credit report on her husband from the credit bureau. Her husband later filed suit, claiming that the employer knowingly obtained a credit report on him under false pretenses in violation of the FCRA.

ISSUES

1. Does the FCRA permit an employer to obtain a credit report on a spouse of an employee being considered for a security-sensitive position?
2. Did the employer knowingly obtain consumer information under false pretenses?

DECISIONS

1. No
2. Yes

> **REASONS**
> 1. The FCRA sets forth an exclusive list of permissible purposes for which a credit report may be obtained, including for "employment purposes." But nothing in the FCRA indicates that a report may be obtained on any person other than the actual individual considered for employment. Permitting a user of reports to obtain information on an employee's spouse would violate a right to privacy that Congress intended to protect.
> 2. The employer's policy did not allow a credit report to be requested on the spouse of a loan applicant. A vice president of the employer also acknowledged to the employee that getting the credit report on her spouse had been a mistake. From this evidence, the jury could properly conclude that the report had been obtained "knowingly." Further, requesting information for a purpose not permitted under the FCRA, while representing that the report will be used for permissible purposes ("employment purposes"), subjects the employer to civil liability for obtaining information under "false pretenses."

The government may also assess civil and criminal penalties against FCRA violators in certain instances.

9 THE TRUTH-IN-LENDING ACT

The Truth-in-Lending Act authorized the Federal Reserve Board to adopt regulations "to assure a meaningful disclosure of credit terms so that the consumer will be able to compare more readily the various credit terms available to him and avoid the uninformed use of credit." As previously mentioned, the FTC enforces these regulations.

Truth-in-Lending Coverage

The Truth-in-Lending Act covers all transactions in which: (1) the lender is in the business of extending credit in connection with a loan of money, a sale of property, or the furnishing of services; (2) the debtor is a natural person, as distinguished from a corporation or business entity; (3) a finance charge may be imposed; and (4) the credit is obtained primarily for personal, family, household, or agricultural purposes. It covers loans secured by real estate, such as mortgages, as well as unsecured loans and loans secured by personal property. Disclosure is necessary whenever a buyer pays in four installments or more.

Truth-in-Lending imposes a duty on all persons regularly extending credit to private individuals to inform them fully of the cost of the credit. It does not regulate the charges which are imposed.

Finance Charge and Annual Percentage Rate

The Truth-in-Lending philosophy of full disclosure is accomplished through two concepts, namely, the **finance charge** and the **annual percentage rate** (APR). The borrower uses these two concepts to determine the amount he or she must pay for credit and what the annual cost of borrowing will be in relation to the amount of credit received. Theoretically, a debtor armed with this information will be better able to bargain for credit and choose one creditor over the other.

The finance charge is the sum of all charges payable directly or indirectly by the debtor or someone else to the creditor as a condition of the extension of credit. Included in the finance charge are interest, service charges, loan fees, points, finder's fees, fees for appraisals, credit reports or investigations, and life and health insurance required as a condition of the loan.

Among the costs frequently paid by debtors which are not included in the finance charge are recording fees and taxes, such as a sales tax, which are not usually included in the listed selling price. These are items of a fixed nature, the proceeds of which do not go to the creditor. Other items of cost not included are title insurance or abstract fees, notary fees, and attorney's fees for preparing deeds.

The law requires that the lender disclose the finance charge, expressing it as an annual percentage rate, and specifies the methods for making this computation. The purpose is to ensure that all credit extenders calculate their charges in a uniform fashion. This enables consumers to make informed decisions about the cost of credit.

Financing Statement

The finance charge and annual percentage rate are made known to borrowers by use of a financing statement. This statement must be given to the borrower before credit is extended and must contain, in addition to the finance charge and the annual percentage rate, the following information:

1 Any default or delinquency charges that may result from a late payment
2 Description of any property used as security
3 The total amount to be financed, including a separation of the original debt from finance charges

As the following case indicates, the financing statement must disclose certain terms more conspicuously than others.

HERRERA v. FIRST NORTHERN SAVINGS & LOAN ASSN.
805 F.2d 896 (10th Cir. 1986)

FACTS

Plaintiffs entered into a real estate loan agreement with the defendant savings and loan association. The defendant gave plaintiffs the statement required by the Truth-in-Lending Act (TILA). The plaintiffs later sued the defendant for numerous alleged violations of TILA and asked for statutory damages, reasonable attorney's fees, and costs.

ISSUES

1. Did the defendant disclose the annual percentage rate (APR) more conspicuously than its other terms, as required by law?
2. Are the plaintiffs entitled to statutory damages, even though they suffered no actual damages?

DECISION

1. No.
2. Yes.

REASONS

1. TILA regulations state that "where the terms 'finance charge' and 'annual percentage rate' are required to be used, they shall be printed more conspicuously than other terminology required by this part." Defendant printed its APR term in capital letters, but the statement also contained thirty other terms printed in the same way. Reasonable minds cannot differ on whether the defendant printed the APR "more conspicuously" than other terms. The statement failed to meet the regulatory requirement.
2. Plaintiff need not show actual damages to recover the statutory penalty. A proven violation of the disclosure requirement is presumed to injure the borrower. It frustrates the purpose of permitting consumers to compare various available credit terms.

The court in the *Herrera* case awarded the plaintiffs a $1,000 statutory penalty, $1,930 in attorney's fees, and $20 in costs. A question arises: Why did the defendant savings and loan association pursue this case all the way to the court of appeals? Was it because the defendant had disclosed APRs to many other consumers on the same printed form?

Penalties and Remedies under Truth-in-Lending

There are both civil and criminal penalties for violation of Truth-in-Lending. The civil liability provisions make creditors liable to debtors for an amount equal to twice the finance charge, but not less than $100 nor more than $1,000, plus the costs and attorney's fees required to collect it.

Creditors may avoid liability in the event they make an error, provided they notify the debtor within sixty days after discovering the error and also correct the error. In this connection, the law allows for corrections in favor of the debtor only. Creditors cannot collect finance charges in excess of those actually disclosed.

The Truth-in-Lending Act also gives debtors the right to rescind or cancel certain transactions for a period of three business days from the date of the transactions or from the date they are given the notice of their right to rescind, whichever is later. For example, consumers may generally cancel transactions in which they give a security interest on their principal residence if they do so within the three-day period. If the transaction is rescinded, the borrower has no liability for any finance charge, and the security which he or she has given is void.

Truth-in-Lending Trends

In 1980, Congress passed the Truth-in-Lending Simplification Act. Two changes from the original act stand out. First, the law eliminates statutory penalties based on purely technical violations of the act. It restricts such penalties to failures to disclose credit terms that are of *material* importance in credit comparisons. Second, the Simplification Act requires the Federal Reserve Board to issue model disclosure forms. These are particularly important to small businesses that cannot afford legal counsel to help prepare such forms. Proper use of the forms proves compliance with the Simplification Act.

Studies conducted by the FTC show that many of those involved in credit extension, such as home builders and realtors, fail to make required Truth-in-Lending disclosures in their advertising. In several instances, the FTC has successfully undertaken programs to educate these businesses about their disclosure obligations under Truth-in-Lending.

10 THE MAGNUSON-MOSS WARRANTY ACT

Not all federal consumer protection laws involve deceptive trade practices or credit abuses. This section concerns federal regulation or express warranties. Remember from Chapter 10 that an express warranty makes a statement about a product or a promise about its performance. Many, perhaps most, problems that consumers have with the products they buy come from breaches of warranty.

Historically, one of the major problems with consumer warranties was that they contained highly technical legal language. Consumers did not understand that this language often placed severe limitations on their rights to exercise warranties. Many express warranties even actually deprived consumers of rights, such as the rights furnished by implied warranties.

Yet at the same time, manufacturers used consumer warranties promotionally to show that their products were "guaranteed."

In 1975, Congress passed the Magnuson-Moss Warranty Act to help correct warranty problems with consumer products. The law covers **express consumer warranties.** Warranties on such goods must disclose the terms of the warranty in simple and readily understood language. If a product costs more then $10, the warranty must be labeled "full" or "limited." The FTC has the responsibility to prepare regulations to accomplish the goals of the law.

Products covered by a *full* warranty must be repaired or replaced by the seller without charge and within a reasonable time in the event there is a defect. Manufacturers cannot impose requirements on buyers to obtain the repairs or replacements unless the requirements are reasonable. The law does not require manufacturers to give any warranty, but if one is given, its nature and extent must be in language that can be understood by the buyer. If a warranty is to be *limited,* the limitation must be conspicuous so that buyers are not misled. If a written warranty is given, there can be no disclaimer of implied warranties, although consequential damages may be limited.

To aid consumers in making intelligent purchase selections, sellers must make warranty information available to buyers prior to purchase. The information must be conspicuously displayed in association with the warranted product. The FTC has taken action against several sellers who have failed to observe this requirement.

The Magnuson-Moss Act also encourages sellers to set up informal dispute-settlement procedures to handle complaints made under the warranty. Although not requiring such procedures, the act requires that if they exist, consumers must pursue them prior to filing a lawsuit.

As a result of the law, many sellers have eliminated their warranties or have opted for the limited warranty. Some companies, rather than become involved with all the law's requirements, have stopped giving warranties. But the warranties which remain are more useful to consumers than before Magnuson-Moss.

STATE CONSUMER PROTECTION

11 STATE CONSUMER FRAUD LEGISLATION

A Justice Department study released in 1982 identifies fraud as a major problem in our economic system. "Consumer fraud is a serious and pervasive phenomenon which continues to plague the American marketplace," the study stated. In the last twenty-five years, all states have passed legislative acts to help deal with this problem.

Generally termed Unfair and Deceptive Acts and Practices (UDAP) statutes, these acts often resemble the FTC Act. They prohibit fraudulent, deceptive, and unconscionable trade practices. They seek to deter merchants from engaging in such practices and provide remedies to ensure that consumers will recover for damages and suffering.

Typically, a state's attorney general will administer a UDAP statute, although special agencies are sometimes used. These public authorities often have power to make rules and conduct investigations. If they uncover fraudulent activities, they can impose a variety of remedies (see Table 19-3). Remedies imposed by public authorities (public remedies) constitute the basic means of UDAP enforcement in most states.

To assist state enforcement efforts through public remedies, UDAP statutes provide a number of private remedies that injured consumers themselves can seek from dishonest merchants (see Table 19-4). Private litigation offers a powerful deterrent to consumer fraud and allows consumers to gain compensation for their injuries.

State Regulation of Specific Businesses

Recently, states have begun amending UDAP statutes or passing new legislation to regulate specific businesses. For instance, several states specifically regulate the auto-repair industry. This regulation came as a result of a United States Department of Transportation undercover study which concluded that consumers waste 53 percent of every dollar spent on auto repairs.

Another specific business targeted by state consumer protection statutes is apartment leasing. A number of states prohibit lessors from retaining consumers' security deposits on apartments unless they follow clearly outlined procedures. Door-to-door sales firms and health spas are also regulated in many states.

States have imposed a variety of procedures for controlling fraud in specific businesses. *Escrow accounts* restrict a seller's ability to get or keep money until he or she has given satisfactory performance. Failure to perform means that the escrow agent (frequently a bank) will return part or

TABLE 19-3 PUBLIC UDAP REMEDIES*

1 *Injunctions* prohibiting offensive practices
2 *Restitution* forcing fraudulent merchants to reimburse their victims
3 *Civil penalties* which must be paid to the state
4 *Revocation* of licenses and other forms of permission to do business within a state
5 Court appointment of a *receiver* who handles the defendant's assets and runs the defendant's business to benefit injured consumers
6 *Criminal fines* and/or *imprisonment*
7 *Assessment* of court costs or cost of the fraud investigation

*Not all states permit every remedy.

514   PART 6:   PROTECTING PARTIES TO TRANSACTIONS

TABLE 19-4   PRIVATE UDAP REMEDIES*

1 Recovery of *actual losses*
2 Recovery of *triple damages* or a *set minimum amount*
3 Assessment of *punitive damages*
4 Assessment of *attorney's fees* and *costs*
5 Authorization of *class actions* by injured consumers
6 *Injunctions* prohibiting offensive practices
7 *Rescission* which frees consumers from deceptive arrangements and requires reimbursement of deposits or prepayments

*Not all states permit every remedy.

all of a consumer's payment. *Bonding* provides a compensation fund for consumers. *Industry pools,* adopted in Hawaii for travel agencies, establish an industry-funded "pool," which is used to compensate defrauded consumers. *Registration* permits easy location of firms by public authorities. *Licensing* requires special training or competence before doing business.

Still other consumer protection regulations serve to prevent fraud or to limit losses in specific situations. *Mandatory disclosures* require merchants to provide certain written information before a sale becomes final. *Plain English* rules require consumer contract provisions to be written in a simply understood fashion. *Cooling-off periods* allow consumers a few days to cancel door-to-door sales agreements. *Limited duration* establishes a maximum length for service contracts and thus limits a consumer's future financial obligations. *Limited prepayments* limit the amount a merchant can require consumers to pay in advance.

Increasingly, state (and federal) pressure on specific businesses is forcing them to adopt procedures for mediating or arbitrating disputes with dissatisfied consumers. For instance, consumers who have engine problems with General Motors cars can turn to their local Better Business Bureau for arbitration. Arbitration decisions are binding on GM, although consumers retain the right to go into court if they disagree with the decisions. Most other car manufacturers also have arbitration-type procedures to resolve consumer dissatisfaction problems.

CONSUMER PRIVACY ETHICS AND THE FUTURE OF CONSUMERISM

12   CONSUMER PRIVACY

As society becomes more complex, as population growth creates overcrowding, and as the technology of information gathering becomes more sophisticated, the need for privacy increases. In recent years, the law has come to recognize the invasion of privacy as a tort (see Chapter 9) and even to extend a constitutional right of privacy. For example, a constitutional right of privacy has been asserted by the Supreme Court under the First and Fourth Amendments in cases involving the freedom of association, the possession in the home of pornographic materials, and the use of contraceptive devices. Most of the laws and cases which apply the concepts of privacy protect the individual from being overwhelmed by the intrusive power of the government and other large organizations, including businesses. Many laws directly affect us as "consumers," and almost all apply to protect us in our personal, rather than public, lives. Consumer protection regulation and privacy laws, then, have very much in common.

Several of the consumer protection laws discussed in this chapter contain provisions protecting personal privacy. Under the Fair Credit Reporting Act, for example, a potental employer, insurer, or creditor must inform the consumer that an investigative report is being obtained on him or her. This notice allows the consumer to terminate the contemplated transaction, thus ending the legitimate business reason for the report and preventing the report from being obtained legally.

One of the chief threats to individual privacy comes from the government and governmental agencies which investigate individuals or which collect information from individuals. Several federal statutes are directed specifically at this problem. The Privacy Act of 1974 places constraints on how certain kinds of information collected by the federal government can be used and limits those to whom the information may be released. It also provides a tort cause of action against those who violate the act. A second statute, the Right to Financial Privacy Act of 1978, requires all government agencies seeking depositor records from banks and other financial institutions to notify depositors of this fact. The individual depositor then has fourteen days to challenge an agency's legal basis for seeking the records. Depositors are allowed to sue the government agencies or financial institutions which fail to comply with the statute for actual and punitive damages, plus attorney's fees.

13 ETHICAL CONSIDERATIONS

Individual privacy is such an important part of individual freedom that both legal and ethical questions regarding privacy are bound to multiply in the computer age. While debate continues concerning the need for further federal privacy legislation, many states have passed their own privacy-related statutes. Several states guarantee workers access to their job personnel files and restrict disclosure of personal information to third parties. Almost half the states forbid businesses from requiring lie-detector tests as a condition of employment, although employers can still ask job applicants to submit voluntarily to the tests. Other state laws prohibit illegal interception of computer communications and regulate the privacy of data transmitted on cable television networks.

Responding to privacy issues, hundreds of companies have adopted privacy sections in their codes of ethics. Most of these sections concern personnel information. The following is an example from the Caterpillar Code of Ethics.

Privacy of Information about Employees

Information needed for administration of payrolls, benefit plans, and labor agreements—and for compliance with laws—has resulted in collection, by Caterpillar, of an increasing amount of personal data. We seek to minimize intrusiveness, and maximize fairness and confidentiality of such data.

Personal data will contain only such individually identifiable information as is necessary for business purposes and compliance with law. Such information is to be handled confidentially and securely. Company access to such information is limited to those who have legitimate, pertinent business purposes.

Entries to employee data files are to be factual, job-related, and accurate. Any information found to be in error will be corrected or eliminated: Company data about an employee will be made available, on request, to that employee...excepting for special, sensitive files such as those pertaining to career planning and litigation.

14 POLICY TRENDS: THE FUTURE OF CONSUMERISM

Consumerism and the litigation it breeds seem to be here to stay. The slowdown in the appearance of new consumer protection regulation should by no means, however, be taken as an end to the importance of consumer protection in general. As the laws discussed in this chapter indicate, there is substantial consumer regulation already enacted. And, as these existing laws are further implemented, their impact on the business community will likely continue to grow.

In a quiet way, a recent change in the marketing of legal services may also give a boost to the consumer movement. Low-cost assistance provided by **legal clinics,** which specialize in routine, high-volume services, is enabling many individuals to pursue consumer complaints which would previously have been too expensive for them to pursue. Hyatt Legal Services, the largest legal clinic, had 117 offices in 1983 and projected 300 or more by 1988.

Large chains like Sears and H&R Block are also beginning to open their facilities for use by attorneys in providing inexpensive legal advice. In addition, legal advertising is on the increase and will probably contribute significantly to the public's awareness of the availability of legal remedies for common consumer problems.

The increasing numbers of lawyers is one factor which will ensure that consumer litigation does not diminish. There are now approximately

600,000 lawyers in the United States, twice as many as practiced twenty years ago. We have three times as many lawyers per capita as England and twenty times as many as Japan.

Prepaid legal plans for workers and other developments will also help ensure a healthy future for consumerism. Millions of workers and their dependents are presently covered by prepaid legal plans. General Motors has recently covered its 400,000 employees with a legal service plan called for in a collective-bargaining contract.

Finally, the number of legal "hotlines," which provide legal advice by telephone, is growing rapidly. In several states, CIGNA Corp. offers credit-card holders unlimited telephone consultations for a low monthly fee.

REVIEW QUESTIONS

1. For each term in the left-hand column, match the most appropriate description in the right-hand column:

   (1) Bait-and-switch
   (2) Consumer
   (3) Corrective advertising
   (4) Consumer investigative report
   (5) Industry guides
   (6) Redlining
   (7) Legal clinics
   (8) Respondent
   (9) Trade practice regulation

   (a) A person who buys something for personal, family, or household use.
   (b) A report prepared on someone's personal life, as well as credit status.
   (c) A private person against whom an agency takes administrative action.
   (d) The practice of generally refusing credit to persons who live in certain areas.
   (e) Another name for FTC consumer protection activity.
   (f) The practice of attracting consumers to a store by advertising a specific product and then criticizing that product to persuade them to purchase another, higher-priced product.
   (g) Advertising which contains a message that counters prior deceptive advertising.
   (h) Law firms which specialize in inexpensive, mass legal services.
   (i) Informal, nonbinding FTC guidelines on a trade group's business practices.

2. The Mosquito-No Company claims that its electronic mosquito repellent will "eliminate all mosquito problems within a one-half acre area." The Federal Trade Commission doubts that this claim is correct. What will the FTC likely demand that the company do?

3. List the penalties and remedies available to the FTC for use against a business that has violated the FTC Act.

4. Jane Thomas applies for automobile financing at Kenwood Cars, Inc., a used-car dealership. The dealership obtains a credit report on her. On the basis of this report, the dealership denies her credit. The manager informs her that she will

have to get her husband to cosign her application if she wants dealership financing. She refuses, and sues Kenwood Cars, Inc., under the ECOA. What was result, and why?

5 The ABC Department Store refused credit to Mary Jane. Mary Jane has a good job and no debts. She cannot understand the refusal. What would you suggest Mary Jane do? Explain.

6 A potential employer requests information about a former employee of yours. Without complying with the requirements of the Fair Credit Reporting Act, can you tell the potential employer that the former employee: (a) was often late to work? (b) was caught drunk on the job? (c) has a general reputation in your community as a troublemaker? Explain.

7 Wes Tomic takes out a $50,000 loan with First Bank to open a small electronics business. Shortly after signing the final loan papers, Tomic finds out that he could have gotten his financing elsewhere at a lower interest rate. He then realizes that First Bank never furnished him a Truth-in-Lending financing disclosure form. Does he have rights against the bank, under the Truth-in-Lending Act? Discuss.

8 Under the Truth-in-Lending Act, what is a "finance charge?" What charges are and are not included as finance charges?

9 Discuss various legal remedies granted consumers under state UDAP statutes.

10 Mr. Jones, a black school principal, applies for a mortgage loan at a bank. After examining the application, the bank politely but firmly refuses the loan, explaining that property values in Mr. Jones's neighborhood are too low to support the amount he is seeking. Might Mr. Jones have some course of action against the bank? Under what law?

11 Discuss how privacy is protected by the various laws covered in this chapter.

12 Jan has a problem with the engine of his new Chevrolet. If the car dealer refuses to take care of the problem under the warranty, what can Jan do? Consider that he cannot afford to hire an attorney.

13 Discuss trends that suggest that the impact of consumer protection laws on the business community may continue to grow.

CHAPTER **20**

CREDITOR AND DEBTOR PROTECTION

OVERVIEW

In a private enterprise economy based on freedom of contract, there will always be creditors and debtors. Each group has legal rights. The problem is how to balance rights between creditors and debtors while keeping a fairly run economy. For instance, creditors can no longer put a debtor into prison for failure to pay debts, but creditors can seize a debtor's wages and property, which is a topic covered in Chapter 4.

This chapter discusses the laws that protect creditors and debtors. Creditor protection includes: (1) artisan's and mechanic's liens, which give unpaid creditors a claim against personal and real property which they have carried, stored, repaired, or improved; (2) bulk transfer law, which protects creditors when a merchant debtor sells a major part of its inventory out of the ordinary course of its business; (3) suretyship, which covers the legal rules applying when one promises to perform for a creditor if a debtor does not; (4) secured transactions in personal property, which covers Article 9 of the Uniform Commercial Code; and (5) secured transactions in real property, which focuses on mortgages.

Debtor protection includes: (1) usury laws, which regulate maximum interest rates on loans; (2) limitation on debt collection, which considers the Fair Debt Collection Practices Act; (3) the Bankruptcy Act, which specifies when debtors can have their debts discharged or adjusted; and (4) special consumer-debtor protection, which covers abolishment of the holder-in-due-course doctrine and the power of consumers to revoke credit-card charges.

Important terms in this chapter are artisan's lien, attachment, bulk transfer, contribution, financing statement, foreclosure, liquidation, mechanic's lien, real estate mortgage, perfection, purchase-money security interest, reimbursement, reorganization, right of redemption, surety, and usury.

CREDITOR PROTECTION

1 INTRODUCTION

Many laws protect creditors. As used in the following sections, a **creditor** is one who lends money or extends credit for goods or services.

In a private enterprise economy it is extremely important to all consumers that creditors have legal protection. First, legal protection makes creditors more willing to lend money and extend credit. Second, if there were no legal protection of creditors, they would have to charge higher interest and prices to all consumers to cover the greater losses suffered because of the lack of legal protection. The conclusion is that the creditor protection laws discussed in the following sections benefit consumers as well as creditors.

2 ARTISAN'S LIENS

A *lien* is an obligation for payment of money—also called a "security interest"—which attaches to property as a result of statute, common law, equity, or contract. Usually the property can be sold to satisfy the lien if the lien holder is not paid. Among others, there are tax liens, judgment liens, mortgage liens (see section 20-7), Article 9 liens (see section 20-6), mechanic's liens (see section 20-3), and artisan's liens.

Today, statutes in every state create **artisan's liens.** These liens are a class of liens which protect those who store, carry, or repair the goods of another for a price. For instance, if a common carrier, such as the railroad, is not paid for shipping and storing goods, it may sell the goods to satisfy the obligation. Likewise, failure to pay for repair of a television allows the person who performed the repairs to sell the television to satisfy the debt owed. In both instances, the creditor can sell the property because of the artisan's lien. Generally, the statute requires the creditor to give notice to the debtor before a sale takes place. Any surplus from the sale after the debt is paid must be returned to the debtor.

Usually, an artisan's lien lasts only as long as the creditor has possession of the property. Surrender of the property to the debtor means that the creditor loses the lien if someone buys the property from the debtor or legally seizes it. However, some statutes permit the creditor to record the artisan's lien with the proper records office. If the creditor records the lien, it has priority even against third parties who legally acquire it from the debtor. In fact, an artisan's lien is commonly superior to all claims on the property.

3 MECHANIC'S LIENS

Almost any contract for the improvement of real property creates a **mechanic's lien** in favor of the person who improves the property. For instance, a contractor who constructs a building has a lien on it for payment of what is owed. A landscaper, an architect, and a roofing repairer also have mechanic's liens for services rendered. These are all persons who contract directly with an owner to improve real property and who are known as "contractors."

Mechanic's liens also protect those who provide services or material to contractors who improve real property. These persons include building material suppliers and those hired by a contractor to work on the property. Note that these persons, called "subcontractors," contract with the primary contractor rather than with the property owner.

Mechanic's lien statutes usually specify that a lien must be recorded within sixty to ninety days following completion of work or delivery of materials to establish priority over third parties, such as mortgagees or buyers of the property. Subcontractors must also record within this period to be able to exercise a lien against the property owner, although contractors often have two to three years to record against the property owner. The difference in treatment between contractors and subcontractors arises because property owners may not know of the existence of the latter group. The mechanic's lien is lost if it is not recorded within the specified time periods.

Two problems deserve special comment. First, real estate purchasers should always check the records office for mechanic's liens. This check is part of the title search, which is routine for most real estate sales. But a title search cannot detect very recent mechanic's liens, because of the sixty- to ninety-day period allowed for recording them against third parties. Real estate purchasers should therefore try to determine whether any improvements or repairs have been made on the property within this statutory time period.

The second problem concerns the property owner. It is quite possible for the owner to pay a building contractor for work performed but the contractor to fail to pay material suppliers or workers. These suppliers or workers can exercise mechanic's liens against the property. The owner will have to pay again to avoid foreclosure of the liens. Of course, in these situations the building contractor is often uncooperative, unavailable, or bankrupt.

Property owners can protect themselves from this problem in several ways. It is often possible for an owner to get subcontractors, and even contractors, to *waive* (legally give up) their rights to mechanic's liens. Alternatively, an owner should get from the contractor a sworn statement listing all subcontractors. The owner can then pay the subcontractors directly or demand proof of payment for materials or services before paying the contractor.

An owner may rely upon the truthfulness of the contractor's sworn statement concerning the identity of and amount owed to subcontractors. If an owner gets a proper sworn statement, subcontractors who are not listed or who are listed for a smaller amount than they are owed can look for payment only to the contractor with whom they dealt.

4 BULK TRANSFERS

Bob Jackson, owner of Acme Hardware, is in financial trouble. His major creditor, First Bank, has refused to renew his loan and is requiring a $75,000 payment which he cannot meet. Several smaller creditors have called recently and demanded payment of long-overdue accounts. The significant possibility of lawsuits and bankruptcy hang over him. The only real asset he has left is the inventory of his store.

After considering his increasingly slim chances of staying in business, he phones the owner of City Hardware, a neighboring competitor, and offers to sell his entire inventory for a very reasonable price. His offer is quickly accepted. Later that week, Bob Jackson leaves town. He takes with him the $55,000 he got for his inventory and leaves no forwarding address.

When merchants get into financial difficulty, the last asset they have is often the inventory and equipment of their businesses. Sometimes they sell this asset to a competitor and neglect to pay their creditors. A special body of law addresses this problem. It is the law of bulk transfers found in Article 6 of the Uniform Commercial Code.

Article 6 defines a **bulk transfer** as a transfer (usually a sale) out of the ordinary course of business of all or a major part of the inventory (or inventory and equipment) of a merchant. Inventory is the stock that a merchant holds for resale. Note that the sale must be "out of the ordinary course of business" and that it must constitute a "major part" of the inventory. Regular sales to a merchant's customers are not included within the meaning of bulk transfer.

Creditor protection under Article 6 places a notice requirement on bulk buyers, that is, on those who buy a major part of a merchant's inventory out of the ordinary course of business. A bulk buyer must get from the merchant a schedule of the inventory sold and a sworn list of the merchant's creditors. The bulk buyer can rely upon the accuracy of this list. The buyer must then notify the listed creditors, personally or by registered mail, that a bulk sale will take place. Notice must be given at least ten days before the bulk buyer takes possession of the inventory or pays for it. Table 20-1 tells what information the bulk buyer must provide to the creditors.

The notice requirement of Article 6 gives a merchant's creditors plenty of time to stop a bulk sale by throwing the merchant into bankruptcy or otherwise protecting themselves. Should a bulk buyer fail to give required no-

TABLE 20-1 BULK BUYER'S NOTICE REQUIREMENTS TO CREDITORS OF SELLER

1. That a bulk transfer is about to be made
2. The names and business addresses of the bulk buyer and seller
3. Whether or not the seller's debts are to be paid in full from the proceeds of the sale

If the debts are not to be paid in full from the sale proceeds, the bulk buyer must further state:

4. The location and description of the property to be transferred and the estimated total of the seller's debts
5. The address where the schedule of property and list of creditors may be inspected
6. The sale price and the time and place for payment

If the transfer of property is to satisfy an existing debt, this must be stated instead.

tice, the merchant's creditors can seize the inventory property from the bulk buyer and sell it to satisfy their debts. In the example which introduced this section, City Hardware may lose the hardware inventory it purchased to the creditors of Bob Jackson.

Some states require the bulk buyer to apply proceeds of a bulk sale to satisfy the merchant's creditors. In these states, failure to apply proceeds to the merchant's debts creates personal liability on the bulk buyer for the value of the inventory property.

5 SURETYSHIP

Introduction

A savings and loan association bonds its employees for "faithful performance." If an employee embezzles money, the S&L can recover its loss from the bonding company. A retail store having a new warehouse built requires the builder to get a construction bond. If the builder fails to complete the warehouse when promised, the store can demand payment of this construction bond. A bank insists that a student's parents endorse her education loan note. If she does not repay the loan, the bank can get payment from the parents.

These situations all involve the law of suretyship, which is important in many commercial transactions. A **surety** is one who promises to perform some obligation upon breach or default of performance by another person. The parties to a suretyship are a *debtor* who owes a performance, a *creditor* to whom the performance is owed, and a surety who will have to perform if the debtor does not. Figure 20-1 illustrates this three-part relationship in the example of a student loan.

A suretyship is a contractual arrangement. The consideration given which binds the surety may come from one of several sources; for example, the debtor may pay the surety (the construction bond is an example), or the

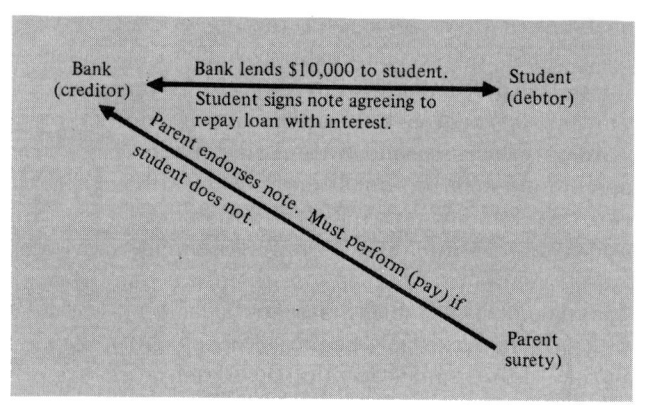

FIGURE 20-1 Suretyship Arrangement for a $10,000 Education Loan.

creditor may provide some other consideration to the surety (agreeing to extend an education loan to the surety's child).

If the surety signs the contract between the creditor and debtor, it is a true suretyship contract. The student-loan note endorsed by a parent is an example. Where the surety is not a party to the creditor-debtor contract, but contracts separately, the resulting arrangement is a **guaranty**. The construction bond is a guaranty, since the bonding company does not sign the building contract between the builder and the owner. The builder contracts separately with the bonding company. Usually, the law treats suretyship and guaranty contracts in identical fashion, so the rest of this discussion will call all such contracts "suretyship contracts."

Unless they state otherwise, suretyship contracts are **unconditional**. This means that once the debtor fails to perform, the creditor can immediately demand performance from the surety. **Conditional** suretyship contracts require that the creditor meet some condition before being entitled to the surety's performance. Often, the condition is that the creditor sue the debtor and get a judgment before demanding payment from the surety.

Once all conditions are properly met, the surety must perform. However, since commercial suretyship arrangements are frequently very complex, there may be dispute over the nature of the surety's required performance. The following case illustrates this.

NEW HAMPSHIRE INS. CO. v. GRUHN
670 P.2d 941 (Nev. 1983)

FACTS

An insurance company issued a surety bond to a mortgage company. The bond was to protect customers of the mortgage company. The surety contract bound the surety to "pay all damages suffered by any person...by reason of any fraud, dishonesty, misrepresentation or concealment of material facts."

A court found the mortgage company guilty of fraudulent misrepresentation and awarded the fraud victims $5,000 in punitive damages.

ISSUE

Is the surety liable for the $5,000 in punitive damages?

DECISION

No.

REASONS

1. The surety only agreed to pay all damages *suffered* by any victim.
2. The $5,000 was not suffered by the fraud victims; it was awarded to punish the mortgage company, not to compensate the victims.

Being a surety can expose one to a great deal of liability, although the consideration given the surety for undertaking the risk may be small or nothing. The defenses which the surety can raise when the creditor demands performance are thus very important.

DEFENSES AVAILABLE TO SURETY

Chapter 8 discussed defenses to an allegation of breach of contract. These defenses include *fraud, duress, illegality, lack of consideration, proper performance, mistake,* and *impossibility of performance*. Regarding these defenses, the basic rule in suretyship situations is that any time defenses are available to the debtor, they are also available to the surety. When the creditor demands that the surety perform, it is possible then for the surety to escape liability by establishing that the creditor defrauded the debtor, that the creditor did not perform properly for the debtor, or that some other defense exists.

The surety may also raise defenses which are not available to the debtor. If the creditor releases the debtor from liability, the surety is generally released as well. Likewise, if the creditor knows or learns of facts which increase the surety's risk, but fails to warn the surety (for example, if a bank fails to tell the bonding company that a bank employee had previously stolen money from the bank), the surety can later assert this to avoid liability. Also, recall from Chapter 8 that if a suretyship contract is not in writing, the surety can raise the statute of frauds as a defense.

If the creditor and debtor modify their contract so as to increase the risk to the surety, it discharges the surety from liability. Typical modifications which may release the debtor include substituting one debtor for another and legally changing the amount, place, or time of the debtor's payments.

Historically, any modification of the debtor's duties gave the surety a defense. In most states today, however, the modification must *materially increase* the risk to the surety, especially if the surety is a commercial insurance or bonding company. A "material" increase is one that is important or significant to the assumed risk.

Certain defenses available to the debtor cannot be raised by the surety. For example, the debtor's *infancy* or *incapacity* will not prevent the surety from being liable, although the debtor can assert these defenses if sued. The reason for this is obvious: the creditor may insist on having a surety to begin with because of the debtor's age or lack of capacity.

Rights Available to the Surety

Even if the surety is liable because of the debtor's failure to perform the contract properly, the surety has certain rights and remedies. For instance, the right of **set off** permits the surety to reduce the amount owed to the creditor. The sum can be reduced by any amount which the creditor owes the surety arising out of some other transaction.

In most cases, the rights of reimbursement and subrogation will be even more valuable to the surety. **Reimbursement,** or **indemnity,** refers to the duty of the debtor to reimburse the surety when the surety has had to pay the creditor. The surety may sue to enforce this right, although often the debtor has no money.

When the surety has performed for the debtor, the surety has the same rights against the debtor that the creditor had. Another way of saying this is that the surety has a right of **subrogation.** If the creditor is holding the debtor's property as collateral for a debt, the subrogation right will entitle the surety to the collateral when he or she pays the debt to the creditor. Should the creditor defeat the surety's subrogation right by returning the collateral to the debtor, the surety's obligation to the creditor reduces by an amount equal to the collateral's value.

Co-Suretyship

Sometimes more than one surety guarantees the same obligation of a debtor. This arrangement is called **co-suretyship.** Co-sureties share *joint and several liability*. The creditor whose debtor defaults on a $20,000 loan may recover the amount from either or both of the co-sureties, although, of course, the creditor may collect only $20,000 in all.

Co-sureties have the same rights of reimbursement and subrogation that single sureties have. In addition, they have the right of **contribution.** If both guarantee the $20,000 loan, and the creditor collects that amount from only one of them, the one who paid can recover $10,000 from the other co-surety.

A creditor who releases co-surety A from liability destroys co-surety B's right of contribution against co-surety A. As a result, the law reduces co-surety B's liability by the amount of the destroyed right of contribution. The next case examines whether this rule applies to co-sureties who have signed a promissory note.

KEYSTONE BANK v. FLOORING SPECIALISTS, INC.
518 A.2d 1179 (Pa. 1986)

FACTS

A corporation borrowed money from the Keystone bank. As representatives of the corporation, the president and vice president signed a promissory note for the amount owed. In their personal capacities, the president and vice president (and their wives) also signed a surety clause in the note, thus guaranteeing payment if the corporation defaulted on the debt. When the corporation failed to pay, the bank sued and got judgment liens against the real property owned by the sureties. Subsequently, the bank released its lien against certain real property owned by the corporate president and his wife so they could sell it. When the bank sought a writ of execution against the home of the corporate vice president and his wife, these persons asserted that the bank's release of the lien against the co-sureties' property discharged them from liability.

ISSUES

1. Does the common law of suretyship apply to a surety who signs a promissory note?
2. Should the vice president and his wife be discharged of liability?

DECISIONS

1. Yes.
2. Undecided.

REASONS

1. Promissory notes are subject to the provisions of the Uniform Commercial Code. The code clearly indicates that sureties who guarantee payment of promissory notes shall have the protections of the common law.
2. When there are several sureties for a debt, the common law states that each surety owes to his or her co-surety a duty to pay a proportional share of their common debt. Should a co-surety pay more than a proportional share of the debt, he or she is entitled to contribution from the other co-surety. If the creditor injures the co-surety's right of contribution by releasing the other co-surety from liability, this act also releases the injured co-surety from liability to the extent that contribution is destroyed. This case must be returned to the trial court for a determination of whether and to what extent the right of contribution is destroyed.

6 SECURED TRANSACTIONS IN PERSONAL PROPERTY

The topic of **secured transactions** concerns how a debtor puts up personal property as collateral to ensure repayment of a loan or an extension of credit. If the debtor does not repay, the creditor may seize and sell the property to satisfy the debt. Secured transactions are extremely important to the smooth running of our economic system. Banks and other financial institutions are much more willing to lend money when valuable property secures the loan. Manufacturers are more likely to extend credit to retailers—and retailers are more likely to sell on credit to consumers—when their risk is secured by more than a simple promise to pay.

Article 9 of the Uniform Commercial Code controls secured transactions nationwide, except in Louisiana. It applies to *personal property* (as opposed to real property). The various types of personal property, which are very important to Article 9, are set out in Table 20-2.

Why Have a Secured Interest?

If a debtor fails to repay a loan or credit, the creditor can always sue the debtor, get a judgment, and, if necessary, sell the debtor's property to satisfy the judgment. Why then is it desirable to have a security interest? There are two main reasons.

First, if the creditor has a proper security interest in personal property and the debtor defaults in payment, the creditor can simply seize the personal property and sell it to satisfy the debt. This bypasses the complicated, expensive litigation process.

TABLE 20-2 TYPES OF PERSONAL PROPERTY COVERED BY ARTICLE 9

1 Tangible property
   a Consumer goods: those bought for personal or family use
   b Inventory: goods bought for resale or lease
   c Equipment: goods bought for use in a business (does not include inventory)
   d Farm products: crops, livestock, or supplies produced or used in a farming operation
2 Intangible property
   a Account: any right to payment for leased or sold goods or services
   b General intangible: personal property such as royalty rights, copyrights, and patent rights
3 Documentary property
   a Instruments: certificates of deposit, promissory notes, checks, and other negotiable instruments
   b Documents of title: documents which represent ownership rights to goods held by a warehouse, freight carrier, or other keeper of property

Second, a secured creditor often has priority over many other parties who may also want the property which has the security interest on it. Judgment creditors, lien holders, trustees in bankruptcy, and buyers of the property are all worthy opponents of a secured creditor. The *rules of priority,* which are discussed later, determine whether the secured creditor will triumph over these opponents. Note, however, that the unsecured creditor has no priority at all.

Attachment of a Security Interest

To be enforceable, a security interest in the property must first attach. **Attachment** occurs when three elements are present:

1 There must be an *agreement* that there should be a security interest. This agreement is usually in writing and signed by the debtor. Often, it is part of a sales or credit contract.
2 The creditor must give *value* to the debtor. Goods sold on credit or money from a loan is the usual form of value given by the creditor.
3 The debtor must have *rights in the property,* which is collateral for the security interest.

The next case considers what it means for the debtor to have rights in the collateral.

FIRST NATIONAL BANK OF SANTA FE v. QUINTANA
733 P.2d 858 (N.M. 1987)

FACTS

Manesas and Archuleta entered into an agreement to buy a restaurant and equipment from a restauranteur. The First National Bank of Santa Fe loaned them $59,000 and took out a security agreement on the equipment that they intended to get from the restauranteur. A financing statement was filed. When the buyers did not go through with their purchase of the restaurant and equipment, the defendant, Dan Quintana, bought it. He then entered a contract to sell the restaurant and equipment to Manesas and Archuleta, who took possession of the restaurant and equipment. Manesas and Archuleta never paid either the bank or Quintana. Quintana seized the restaurant and equipment from them, and the bank sued Quintana for the equipment and damages, alleging priority under a perfected security agreement.

ISSUE

Did Manesas and Archuleta have rights in the restaurant equipment to which the bank's security interest might attach?

DECISION

No.

> **REASONS**
>
> 1. For a security interest to attach, the debtor must have rights in the collateral. Mere possession of the collateral does not prove that the debtor has rights.
> 2. Manesas and Archuleta did not comply with the conditions set forth by their contract with defendant, Quintana. They did not pay him the full down payment required by the contract. Thus, the contract "was never consummated," and Manesas and Archuleta had no rights in the restaurant equipment to which the bank's security interest might attach.

It seems obvious that the debtor cannot put up property to secure a loan when he or she has no rights to that property. Yet, Article 9 permits a security interest in **after-acquired property,** property in which the debtor has no rights when the security interest initially attaches but which is acquired at a future date. An example is when a bank lends a merchant money to buy inventory, and the security agreement contains an after-acquired property clause. Any inventory goods which the merchant later acquires become subject to the bank's security interest. Article 9 says that as soon as the merchant acquires the property and has rights in it, the bank's security interest immediately attaches.

Perfection of a Security Interest

Attachment alone seldom gives a secured creditor maximum priority over others who want the secured property. **Perfection** must also take place. The creditor perfects the security interest in one of several ways.

Attachment does give perfection when the creditor has a **purchase-money security interest** in consumer goods. A purchase-money interest arises when the credit or loan extended is used to acquire the property which is subject to the security interest. Most often this type of perfection is found in credit sales of retail goods. A merchant who sells a television on credit obtains a perfected security interest in the television through mere attachment of the security interest.

Possession is an alternate means of establishing perfection of a security interest. The pawnbroker is a good example of a creditor who has a perfected security interest through possession. Note that the interest remains perfected only as long as possession exists. An exception is that a secured party that perfects by possession continues to have perfection for twenty-one days when releasing negotiable instruments or documents back to the debtor so the debtor can obtain their payment.

A special type of possession is **field warehousing.** Field warehousing enables a creditor to possess inventory goods even though they remain at the debtor's place of business. For a small sum, the creditor rents a portion of the debtor's business premises and temporarily hires one of the debtor's employees. The secured goods are placed in the rented area and roped off from the rest of the debtor's premises. Signs are posted to indicate the creditor's possession.

The legal test for possession by field warehousing is whether the creditor has *sole dominion and control* over the secured property. As used here, "dominion" means the right to possess. Field warehousing of inventory is sometimes necessary because inventory which is in the debtor's possession can be sold free and clear of any security interest to buyers in the ordinary course of the debtor's business.

The last method for getting perfection is by filing a **financing statement** in the appropriate records office. A proper financing statement is signed by the debtor and secured creditor, gives their addresses, and contains an adequate description of the secured property. An "adequate description" is one that informs others as to which of the debtor's properties are covered by the security interest. The appropriate place for filing the financing statement varies according to the state.

Sometimes a debtor in possession of secured property sells it or transforms it into something else. Thus, a retailer might sell secured inventory and get paid for it, or a manufacturer might take secured raw materials and turn them into finished products. In these situations, payments for inventory or finished products from raw materials are called **proceeds.** A secured creditor continues to have a perfected security interest in finished products from raw materials if a financing statement covers "proceeds." Even if there is no mention of proceeds, the perfected security interest in proceeds continues for ten days. A slightly different provision is made for cash or check proceeds.

The law requires perfection to obtain maximum priority for the secured creditor. This is because perfection gives notice to other creditors and parties of the existence of the secured interest. Certainly, possession by the creditor gives notice that there may be a security interest in property. A financing statement provides notice by being publicly available. As to purchase-money security interests in consumer goods, one suspects that with widespread consumer credit sales almost any consumer goods may be subject to security interests.

Priorities of Security Interests

Article 9 contains many rules regarding priorities of security interests. The best way to illustrate these priorities is through a series of examples:

1 John and Mary each hold an attached security interest in the same property. Neither has perfected. The interest which attached first has priority.

2 First Bank has an attached (but not perfected) security interest in Farmer Brown's prize bull. Judgment creditor Smith, who had lent

money to Farmer Brown, gets a writ of execution and seizes the bull. First Bank sues to recover the bull. First Bank loses. It has no priority over other creditors of the debtor.

3 First Bank has an attached (but not perfected) security interest in Acme Manufacturers' bottling equipment. Second Bank has a security interest in the same equipment which is both attached and perfected. Even if First Bank's interest attaches first, Second Bank has priority because a perfected interest prevails over a merely attached one.

4 In example 3, suppose that both First Bank and Second Bank have perfected security interests. The first to perfect has priority.

5 TV Barn sells a television on credit to John Consumer and perfects its purchase-money security interest through attachment alone. TV Barn has priority over John's judgment creditors and a trustee in bankruptcy. It does not have priority over a television repairperson's lien, or over a neighbor who does not know of the security interest and buys the set from John in good faith.

6 In example 5, if TV Barn had perfected by filing a financing statement, it would have priority over the claim of John's neighbor. It would not have priority over liens of repair, storage, or transportation, because these liens always triumph over Article 9 security interest.

7 First Bank has perfected its security interest in Computer Retail's inventory by filing a finance statement. Mary buys a computer out of this inventory. So long as she buys it as a customer in Computer Retail's *ordinary course of business,* she takes it free and clear of the security interest.

8 In example 7, another computer store which bought Computer Retail's entire stock would be subject to First Bank's security interest. This sale is not in the ordinary course of Computer Retail's business.

9 Best Builder Corp. gets a $50,000 loan from Second Bank. Second Bank takes possession of and holds as secured collateral a $75,000 promissory note which a client owes Best Builder. Later, Second Bank returns the promissory note to Best Builder so that it can collect payment of the note from its client. For a twenty-one-day period following release of the note for collection, Second Bank continues to have priority over judgment creditors of Best Builder or a trustee in bankruptcy. The bank does not have priority over someone who buys the note from Best Builder in good faith, for value, and without actual notice of Second Bank's perfected security interest.

10 Note that in example 9, Second Bank's priority is limited to $50,000, the value it has lent to Best Builder. A judgment creditor or trustee in bankruptcy could get the remaining $25,000 represented by the promissory note.

11 First Bank perfects its security interest in inventory belonging to

Hernandez's Department Store. Later, Imperial Chair Mfg. perfects a purchase-money security interest in chairs it sells to Hernandez's, and Imperial notifies First Bank of its perfected interest. When Hernandez's goes bankrupt, First Bank seizes the inventory, including the chairs. Imperial sues to recover the chairs. As long as Imperial perfected its purchase-money security interest and gave First Bank notice before Hernandez's received the chairs, Imperial has priority. This result is an exception to the rule that the first to perfect has priority.

12 In example 11, if the purchase-money collateral were equipment, a different rule would apply. Imperial has priority over First Bank as long as it perfects its interest within ten days after Hernandez receives the equipment. No notice to First Bank is required.

13 Venture Capital, Inc., sets up a field warehouse on certain inventory of its debtor, Associated Manufacturers. When Associated goes into bankruptcy, the trustee seizes this inventory and Venture sues to recover it. As long as Venture has sole dominion and control over the field-warehouse inventory, it has priority over the trustee, judgment creditors, or a buyer of the inventory.

Article 9 covers other types of priority, but the listed examples cover most priority situations.

Rights upon Default

If the debtor fails to repay a loan or pay for goods or services sold on credit, the debtor is in *default* under the contract. At this point, the secured creditor may repossess the collateral, if it is in the debtor's possession, and sell it. The creditor may also propose to the debtor that the creditor keep the collateral property in satisfaction of the debt owed. However, when the collateral is consumer goods, and 60 percent of the cash price or loan has been repaid, the secured creditor must sell the goods within ninety days.

If the collateral is accounts receivable, instruments, or documents, the creditor may collect whatever comes due on the collateral. For instance, a bank with a security interest in a merchant's accounts receivable could, upon default, notify the merchant's debtors to pay their accounts directly to the bank.

In selling collateral in its possession, a secured creditor may sell the collateral in any "commercially reasonable manner." If possible, the secured creditor must notify the debtor of the time and place of a public sale, or the time after which a private sale will be made.

The secured creditor applies the proceeds gotten from sale of the collateral in the following order: (1) expenses of the creditor in repossessing and selling the property; (2) satisfaction of the debt owing the creditor; (3) satisfaction of debt owing to holders of subordinate security interests (such as one whose security interest was perfected after that of the selling secured creditor); and (4) return of what remains, if anything, to the debtor. Note that the debtor continues to be liable to the creditor if proceeds from sale of the collateral do not satisfy the debt owed.

Failure to sell the collateral in a commercially reasonable manner, or violation of some other Article 9 procedure concerning handling of the collateral, can cause the creditor problems. It can make it impossible for the creditor to recover the rest of the debt should sale proceeds not cover all indebtedness. Or the creditor may be liable to the debtor for failing to return a reasonable surplus in such situations. In cases involving a consumer, there is a statutory penalty which the consumer can seek against a creditor who fails to comply with Article 9 requirements regarding default.

7 SECURED TRANSACTIONS IN REAL PROPERTY

More families in the United States own homes than in any other major country of the world. Few families would be able to own homes, however, were lenders unwilling to lend major sums for home purchase. Lenders, in turn, are willing to make such loans only because they can secure them. The usual method of securing home-purchase loans is the **real estate mortgage.**

Lien and Title Theory

Most commonly, the real estate mortgage places a **lien** against the home or business property purchased with the loan given. If the debtor, called the **mortgagor,** fails to repay the loan, the creditor, or **mortgagee,** can foreclose the mortgage and sell the property. In a few states, the mortgagor grants **title** (ownership) to the mortgagee subject to the condition of repayment of the loan. When the mortgagor pays off the loan, title returns to the mortgagor.

Promissory Note and Mortgage Deed

The mortgage arrangement usually consists of a **promissory note** and a **mortgage deed.** The note promises repayment of the loan at a fixed or variable interest rate. The mortgagee must file the mortgage deed, which is the legal document establishing the security interest, in the appropriate records office. Failure to file and record means that the security interest is not perfected against third parties who buy the property from the mortgagor. The mortgagee also lacks protection against later mortgagees who record their mortgage deeds first.

Recall from Chapter 8 that a mortgage must be in writing to be enforceable. The statute of frauds requires it because a mortgage is considered a sale of an interest in land.

Rights and Duties of Mortgagor and Mortgagee

The mortgage agreement specifies many of the rights and duties of the mortgagor and mortgagee. The law imposes others. Table 20-3 sets out a list of common rights and duties of mortgagor and mortgagee.

For the mortgagee, the most important right is the right of **foreclosure**. If the mortgagor defaults in repaying the loan, the mortgagee can cut off the debtor's rights to the property (foreclose) and sell the property to satisfy the debt. The usual procedure is for the mortgagee to sue in an equity court to get foreclosure. The court will then order the property sold.

If there is more than one mortgage on the property, the first mortgage must be completely satisfied by proceeds from the foreclosure sale before any money goes to satisfy subsequent mortgages. Then, any surplus amount goes to the mortgagor. The buyer at a foreclosure sale takes the property free and clear of the subsequent mortgages.

Foreclosure usually results when the mortgagor does not meet the scheduled monthly payments under the mortgage note. It can happen, however, when the mortgagor fails to pay taxes. Many mortgage agreements have **due-on-sale** clauses. If the mortgagor sells the property, the entire remaining balance of the loan is due. Mortgagees place due-on-sale clauses in mortgage agreements so they can force renegotiation of interest rates when the property is sold. However, exercise of the due-on-sale clause can lead to foreclosure if renegotiation is unsuccessful.

A significant right of the mortgagor is the common law **right of redemption** (also called "equity of redemption"). When the mortgagor has defaulted on the mortgage agreement, and before an equity court orders the property sold, the mortgagor can redeem it or get it back free of the lien.

TABLE 20-3 RIGHTS AND DUTIES OF MORTGAGOR AND MORTGAGEE

Mortgagor	Mortgagee
1 Retains possession of the property	1 Has a lien against the property in most states
2 May lease the property and keep all rents	2 Has priority over all claims except tax liens if mortgagee records properly
3 Can sell the property	
4 Must pay taxes on and insure the property	3 Can sell mortgage rights to a third party
5 Cannot "waste" the property, that is, reduce its value through exploitation or failure to maintain	4 Can foreclose the mortgage if the mortgagor defaults
6 Can redeem the property	5 Must terminate lien or return title when mortgagor repays loan

The mortgagor must pay the entire debt owed, plus interest and costs. Even after a foreclosure sale, most states grant the mortgagor a statutory right to redeem the property for a period of time, often one year.

Sale of Mortgaged Property

In the United States, homes are resold every five years on the average. Most of these homes have mortgages on them. The law permits mortgagors to sell their mortgaged property, subject to provisions such as the due-on-sale clause.

Most buyers of mortgaged property assume the mortgage. An **assumption of mortgage** occurs when the new buyer agrees to accept liability for making the mortgage payments and complying with other mortgage provisions. If proceeds from a foreclosure sale are not enough to pay the mortgage debt, the buyer who assumes the mortgage is personally liable for the deficiency.

Since the original mortgagor remains as a surety on the mortgage debt, the mortgagee can recover the deficiency from him or her if the buyer does not pay it. However, several states prohibit mortgage lenders from recovering deficiencies on purchase-money residential mortgages.

If a buyer of mortgaged property does not asume the mortgage, the property is still **subject** to the mortgage. Should the mortgagor not meet the payments, the mortgagee can foreclose against the property in the hands of the buyer.

DEBTOR PROTECTION

8 INTRODUCTION

Mounting credit debts and swings of the economy between boom and recession cause many debtors to be unable to repay their debts on time. Several laws protect debtors when this happens. These laws recognize that creditors should not be allowed to take advantage of debtors. They attempt to balance fairness to individual debtors against the benefits produced by an efficient market system. Appreciate, then, that laws protecting individual debtors can raise the cost of goods and services to everyone, since creditors who face bad debts or increased costs of debt collection will spread these costs to their other customers.

The next four sections discuss laws which: (1) limit the interest a creditor may charge to a debtor, (2) regulate the methods of legitimate debt collection, (3) discharge debtors from their debts, and (4) allow debtors to assert certain defenses against third parties. Note that some of these laws protect only consumer debtors; others protect business debtors as well.

9 USURY

The law has traditionally attempted to protect debtors by limiting the amount of interest that may be charged upon borrowed money or for the extension of the maturity of a debt. Contracts by which the lender is to receive more than the maximum legal rate of interest are *usurious*. **Usury** laws usually provide for criminal penalties and, in addition, may deny a lender the right to collect any usurious interest. However, a few states permit recovery of interest at the legal rate.

The usury laws of most states are better known for permitting exceptions to the general principles than for applying them. Debtors who need the protection of usury laws usually find that their creditors are legally entitled to charge far in excess of the stated legal maximum rate because of some statutory exception. For example, it is not usurious in most states to collect the legal maximum interest in advance or to add a service fee that is no larger than reasonably necessary to cover the costs of making the loan—such as inspection, legal, and recording fees. Both of these practices have the effect of increasing the actual rate of interest paid.

A seller of goods may also add a finance or carrying charge on long-term credit transactions in addition to the maximum interest rate. A different means of avoiding usury is to have a "credit" price that differs from the "cash" price. Another is to charge extra interest for delinquent payments. Some states permit special lenders such as pawnshops, small loan companies, or credit unions to charge in excess of the otherwise legal limit. In addition, as the next case shows, usury statutes often apply only to consumer, rather than to business, loans.

RADFORD v. COMMUNITY MORTGAGE AND INVESTMENT CORP.
312 S.E.2d 292 (Va. 1984)

FACTS

The plaintiffs, a self-employed man and his wife, borrowed money to pay past-due income taxes. They borrowed a total of $68,556 from the defendant corporation. The loan had interest of 19.67 percent, a usurious rate. The loan was secured by a mortgage on the plaintiffs' home. After the plaintiffs defaulted, the defendant began foreclosure on the mortgage. The plaintiffs sued, claiming that the interest rate on the loan was usurious. The defendant claimed exemption from the usury statute because the statute excluded business loans from its protection.

ISSUE

Was this a business loan and accordingly exempt from the usury statute?

DECISION

No.

REASONS

1. Once the usurious rate was shown, the defendant had the burden of proof to show that it was a business loan.
2. The facts displayed that the defendant knew the loan was to pay the plaintiffs' income taxes.
3. The income taxes were personal, and not business, obligations.

When usury is suspected, courts examine very carefully the details and true intent of a transaction. For example, a court may decide that a transaction is a usurious "sale," even though the contract calls it a "lease."

Supporters of an unrestricted marketplace advocate legislation to abolish interest rate limits on consumer credit. They have proposed several plans to Congress.

10 DEBT COLLECTION

In a consumer-credit-oriented economy, the collection of bad debts is very important. At present, there are more than five thousand collection agencies in the United States engaged in collecting unpaid accounts, judgments, and other bad debts. Annually, creditors turn over bills totaling more than $5 billion for collection to such agencies.

Fair Debt Collection Practices Act

Due to complaints that some debt-collection agencies used techniques of harassment, deception, and personal abuse to collect debts, Congress in 1978 passed the Fair Debt Collection Practices Act (FDCPA). The act covers only *consumer* debt collections. It applies to agencies and individuals whose primary business is the collection of consumer debts for others. It also applies to the Internal Revenue Service and attorneys who collect consumer debts on behalf of their clients. Creditor collection efforts are exempt from the act.

One of the first actions of a debt collector will usually be to locate the debtor. This action, known as "skip-tracing," may require that the collector contact third parties who know of the debtor's whereabouts. The FDCPA permits the collector to contact third parties, such as neighbors or employers, but it limits the way in which this contact may be carried out. The collector may not state that the consumer owes a debt nor contact any given third party more than once, except in very limited circumstances. When the collector knows that an attorney represents the debtor, the collector may not contact any third parties, except the attorney, unless the attorney fails to respond to the collector's communication.

Having located the debtor, the collector will next seek to get payment on

TABLE 20-4
FDCPA'S RESTRICTIONS ON COLLECTION METHODS OF COLLECTION AGENCIES

The collector cannot:
1. Physically threaten the debtor
2. Use obscene language
3. Represent himself of herself as an attorney unless it is true
4. Threaten to debtor with arrest or garnishment unless the collector can legally take such action and intends to do so
5. Fail to disclose his or her identity as a collector
6. Telephone before 8:00 A.M. or after 9:00 P.M. in most instances
7. Telephone repeatedly with intent to annoy
8. Place collect calls to the debtor
9. Use any "unfair or unconscionable means" to collect the debt

the overdue account. However, the FDCPA restricts methods that can be used in the collection process. Table 20-4 outlines these restrictions.

FDCPA Remedies and Enforcement

If the consumer debtor desires to stop the debt collector from repeatedly contacting him or her about payment, the debtor need only notify the collector in writing of this wish. Any further contact by the collector following such notification violates the act. The collector's sole remedy now is to sue the debtor. Violations of the FDCPA entitle the debtor to sue the debt collector for actual damages, including damages for invasion of privacy and infliction of mental distress, plus court costs and attorney's fees. In the absence of actual damages, the court may still order the collector to pay the debtor up to $1,000 for violations. Class action suits, as well as individual ones, are permitted under the act.

State Laws Regulating Debt Collection

Congress specified that the FDCPA does not preempt state laws regulating debt collections so long as they are more strict than FDCPA standards. As the following case illustrates, these laws may apply to debt collections by *creditors* as well as by collection agencies.

JACKSONVILLE STATE BANK v. BARNWELL
481 So.2d 863 (Ala. 1985)

FACTS

Plaintiff Barnwell borrowed money from the defendant bank to purchase a mobile home. He put up the mobile home as collateral. Later, it burned in a fire. The home was not covered by insurance. When Barnwell failed to make further payments on his debt, the bank began a series of telephone calls to him. The bank placed between twenty-eight and thirty-five calls to Barnwell at home and work. His supervisor reprimanded him about the calls, and he requested that the bank not call him at work. The calls continued. Then the bank sent an agent to Barnwell's place of employment. The agent caused a commotion and called Barnwell vulgar names in front of his fellow employees. Barnwell became anxious and had to be hospitalized. He sued the bank.

ISSUE

Do the bank's actions constitute an invasion of privacy?

DECISION

Yes.

REASONS

1. A person has a right to be free from the invasion of privacy. Invasion of a debtor's privacy by a creditor has been described as "the wrongful intrusion into one's private activities in such a manner as to outrage or cause mental suffering, shame, or humiliation to a person of ordinary sensibilities."
2. When the creditor takes actions that exceed the bounds of reasonableness, the debtor has an action against the creditor for injuries suffered.
3. The bank deliberately harassed Barnwell with numerous telephone calls at home and work. Its agent also intentionally embarrassed and threatened him. The jury properly found that these actions by the bank were outrageous to a person of ordinary sensibilities.

11 BANKRUPTCY

In 1978, Congress revised the federal bankruptcy laws. This marks the first time in over fifty years that these laws have been substantially revised. Since the 1978 Bankruptcy Act became effective, the number of bankruptcies has skyrocketed. Personal bankruptcies climbed from 228,000 in 1979 to over twice that number in 1984. Although a recession prompted part of that increase, the Federal Reserve Board of Atlanta estimated that, nationwide, as much as 75 percent of the increase was due to the liberal provisions of the new law. Annually, the courts discharge more than $6 billion of nonmortgage consumer debt.

Although the force of the consumer movement helped prompt the new changes in the bankruptcy laws, the laws apply to both consumers and businesses. Under the present laws, corporations and partnerships cannot be discharged of their debts, but all individuals, whether consumers or entrepreneurs, can be.

A principal change in the new laws has been the institution of a bankruptcy court. Previously, most bankruptcy proceedings were handled by legal officials appointed under the authority of the federal district court.

Because the new federal bankruptcy judges do not have lifetime appointments, there is serious question as of this writing about the constitutionality of their creation.

Bankruptcy Proceedings

Bankruptcy proceedings begin upon the filing of either a voluntary or involuntary petition to the court. A **voluntary petition** is one filed by the debtor; an **involuntary petition** is filed by one or more creditors of the debtor. The creditors who sign the involuntary petition must be owed at least $5,000. If the court finds in an involuntary proceeding that the debtor is **unable to pay his or her debts as they mature,** the court will order "relief" against the debtor. Relief may also be ordered if someone has been appointed to control the debtor's property (for example, a receiver) within the previous 120 days for the purpose of satisfying a judgment of other lien.

Two alternatives are possible in a bankruptcy proceeding against an individual. The individual's property will be either **liquidated** and the debts discharged, or the debts will be **adjusted.** An individual who has secured debts (mortgages, security interests against personal property, and so on) of less than $350,000 and unsecured debts of under $100,000 can have his or her debts adjusted by the court. The amount and repayment schedule of the debts will be arranged by the court to permit the debtor to repay the creditors. Creditors cannot require the court to adjust the debts. The decision must be that of the debtor. Most debtors choose to have their debts discharged and their property liquidated, rather than to seek an adjustment, since they remain obligated to pay a portion of adjusted debts.

Even when a debtor's property is liquidated, federal law exempts a substantial portion of the property from the liquidation process. Individual states, however, may reduce the amounts of the federal exemptions through legislation.

Corporations and partnerships can also have all their assets liquidated and distributed to creditors. However, especially for large businesses, an alternative to liquidation is **reorganization.** A main part of the reorganization is a plan which is proposed by the businesses and considered by a committee of creditors prior to court approval. The plan rearranges the business's liabilities and equities (ownership assets). Parts of the business may be sold, and always the existing ownership interests in the business are reduced. In effect, the creditors often become owners in the business.

Trustee in Bankruptcy

The **trustee in bankruptcy** is an important person in the bankruptcy proceeding. The trustee is someone elected by the creditors to represent the debtor's estate in taking possession of and liquidating (selling off) the debtor's property. Broad powers are granted the trustee. The trustee can: (1) affirm or disaffirm contracts with the debtor which are yet to be performed; (2) set aside fraudulent conveyances, that is, transfers of the debtor's property for inadequate consideration or for the purpose of defrauding creditors; (3) void certain transfers of property by the debtor to creditors which prefer some creditors over others; (4) sue those who owe the debtor some obligation; and (5) set aside statutory liens against the debtor's property which take effect upon the beginning of bankruptcy proceedings. With the court's authorization, the trustee can also run the debtor's business during the liquidation process.

Creditor Priority

Under bankruptcy laws, certain creditors receive priority over others in the distribution of a debtor's assets. The law divides creditors into priority classes, as set forth in Table 20-5. The amounts owing to each creditor class must be satisfied fully before the next lower class of priority can receive anything. Note that secured creditors who hold mortgages or Article 9 security interests in the debtor's property usually have priority over the bankruptcy creditor classes.

Discharge

From the debtor's point of view, the purpose of bankruptcy is to secure a **discharge** of further obligation to the creditor. Certain debts, however, cannot be discharged in bankruptcy. They include those arising from taxes, alimony and child support, intentional torts (including fraud), breach of fiduciary duty, liabilities arising from drunken driving, government fines, and debts not submitted to the trustee because the creditor has lacked knowledge of the proceedings. Education loans which become due within five years of the filing of the bankruptcy petition are also nondischargeable.

TABLE 20-5 PRIORITY OF BANKRUPTCY CREDITORS

1. Creditors with claims that arise from the costs of preserving and administering the debtor's estate (such as the fee of an accountant who performs as audit of the debtor's books for the trustee)
2. Creditors with claims that occur in the ordinary course of the debtor's business after a bankruptcy petition has been filed
3. Employees who are owed wages earned within ninety days, or employee benefits earned within 180 days of the bankruptcy petition (limited to $2,000 per employee)
4. Consumers who have paid deposits or prepayments for undelivered goods or services (limited to $900 per consumer)
5. Government (for tax claims)
6. Creditors who have other claims (general creditors)

As the following case indicates, an exception to this rule exists when repayment of the loan constitutes an "undue hardship." Consider the difference the court makes between "hardship" and "undue hardship."

MATTER OF TOBIN
18 B.R. 560 (1982)

FACTS

Mr. Tobin is a twenty-seven-year-old male whose employment produces $432 per month. However, the prospect for improved future employment is clouded by a prior criminal conviction. In a petition for bankruptcy, Mr. Tobin claims that under these circumstances repayment of a student loan would constitute an undue hardship.

ISSUE

In consideration of the debtor's financial situation, would the repayment of a student loan constitute an undue hardship, justifying discharge of the debt?

DECISION

No.

REASONS

1. The repayment of the student loan would unquestionably produce a hardship upon the defendant, but under the circumstances the repayment would not constitute an "undue" hardship.
2. Mr. Tobin's relocation in another city, his continued education, the lack of dependents, and his fiancee's income all indicate that his financial situation may be less severe in the future.
3. The debt should not be discharged.

In addition to having certain debts denied discharge, the debtor may fail to receive a discharge from *any* of his or her debts if the courts find that the debtor has concealed property, falsified or concealed books of record, refused to obey court orders, failed to explain satisfactorily any losses of assets, or been discharged in bankruptcy within the prior six years. As mentioned previously, corporations and partnerships as legal entities cannot receive a discharge of their debts. Of course, the individuals behind these businesses can always form a new corporation or partnership.

Trends in Bankruptcy

A major bankruptcy trend in recent years has been the increasing frequency with which large businesses have gone through bankruptcy reorganization. Some see this trend as a management strategy of even financially healthy businesses for avoiding potential liabilities or forcing renegotiation of burdensome contracts. For instance, the Manville Corporation entered bankruptcy reorganization to attempt to force a favorable settlement of the thousands of asbestos-related lawsuits which it faces. Another reason for this trend is that the 1978 revision of the bankruptcy laws has made it easier for existing management to take a business through reorganization while staying in control of the business. Texaco, Inc., chose reorganization following the multibillion-dollar judgment obtained against it by Pennzoil.

Other companies have sought reorganization to relieve themselves of obligations imposed by collective-bargaining contracts with unions. After the Supreme Court ruled in 1984 that bankruptcy did affect performance of collective-bargaining contracts, Congress changed the law. Now, bankruptcy reorganization can reject a collective-bargaining contract only if the union has refused to accept necessary contractual modifications "without good cause," and, on balance, the court decides that the situation "clearly favors" rejection.

Another important bankruptcy development affects a consumer's ability to get a discharge of debts through liquidation. Congress amended the law in 1984 to give courts power to refuse to allow consumers to seek the relief of discharge when relief would amount to a "substantial abuse" of the bankruptcy process.

This change in the law recognizes a problem of the bankruptcy process. Historically, consumers with few assets, but well-paying jobs, could get discharged of their debts by surrendering their few assets to liquidation. Creditors argued that debt discharge was unfair in this situation since credit is usually extended to consumers based on their ability to repay out of future earned income.

With the change in the law, courts can deny consumers a discharge of debts through liquidation. When liquidation and discharge relief would be a "substantial abuse," a consumer's only bankruptcy relief will be an adjustment of debts. In this type of relief, the court can consider a consumer's future earning power in deciding what percentage of the consumer's debts must be repaid. It is likely that courts will find that a substantial abuse exists when consumers can reasonably pay for debts out of future income.

12 ADDITIONAL PROTECTION FOR CONSUMER-DEBTORS

A lawsuit is not always an adequate remedy for an injured party to a contract. For instance, it is usually not practical for consumers to sue a seller of goods or services over breaches of contract involving only a few hundred dollars. Attorney's fees are high, and small claims' court awards are difficult to enforce. From consumers' viewpoints, it would be better if they could simply refuse to pay for unsatisfactory products or services. However, many times consumers have already paid for what they obtained or have promised to pay.

If consumers have already paid for products or services, they have little recourse except to initiate legal proceedings when others refuse to perform their contractual obligations properly. But what occurs in a situation in which consumers have signed credit agreements and have merely *promised* to pay? It appears that consumers can simply refuse to pay until the obligations owed them have been performed satisfactorily. In the past, however, this was not usually the case.

The Holder-in-Due-Course Doctrine and Its Abolishment

Until fairly recently, most credit contracts contained clauses which stated that consumers agreed not to assert any contractual defenses against third parties. These clauses meant that if a merchant sold a consumer's credit contract to a collection agency, the agency could legally collect the contract price from the consumer in spite of the fact that the merchant had breached the contract, or had even defrauded the consumer. In addition to a credit agreement, many times the consumer had also signed a promissory note. (A promissory note is an easily transferrable, special type of commercial instrument or paper.) Because of the **holder-in-due-course** doctrine, third parties who bought notes and other forms of commercial paper could usually enforce them free of all personal defenses the consumer might have against the merchant, such as that purchased goods were defective or were never delivered.

In the mid-1970s, the FTC acted to protect consumers who made purchases on credit. It adopted a rule which abolishes the holder-in-due-course concept and which declares illegal contract provisions cutting off defenses against third parties. The rule applies only to *consumer* transactions. The rule also specifies that the consumer-debtor's right to assert claims and defenses against collection agencies, banks, and other third parties must actually be set forth in any installment credit contract used to finance retail purchases.

Rejection of Disputed Credit-Card Charges

A related law now protects consumers in instances in which credit-card charges have been made and contractual disputes arise. Under the federal Fair Credit Billing Act, a consumer can withhold from any credit-card payments the amount of a disputed charge made to a seller of goods or services. This right applies to any charge of more than $50 when the charge is made in the consumer's home state or within 100 miles of his or her home. The procedure requires that the consumer first attempt to resolve the contractual dispute with the seller. When this fails, the consumer can send the bank which issues the credit card a written notice of the problem which states that negotiations have been unfruitful. The consumer can then withhold the amount of the disputed charge from credit-card payments to the bank.

As a practical matter, banks recredit a consumer's account for the amount of a disputed charge (if it has been already deducted) and charge back against the seller's bank. The seller's bank then charges back against the seller. The seller might sue the consumer, but once again, litigation costs make such a course of action unlikely in cases which involve relatively small amounts of money.

REVIEW QUESTIONS

1. For each term in the left-hand column, match the most appropriate description in the right-hand column:

   (1) Lien
   (2) Attachment
   (3) Bulk transfer
   (4) Foreclosure
   (5) Liquidation
   (6) Real estate mortgage
   (7) Perfection
   (8) Purchase-money security interest
   (9) Surety
   (10) Usury

   (a) The sale of all or most of the inventory of a merchant out of the ordinary course of business.
   (b) A legal claim against property to secure a debt or obligation.
   (c) The lending of money at an illegal interest rate.
   (d) A security interest in property arising from the credit extended to buy the property.
   (e) Occurs when a security agreement exists, the creditor has given value to the debtor, and the debtor has rights in the collateral.
   (f) The cutting off of a debtor's rights in property.
   (g) A security interest in land.
   (h) One who gives a collateral promise to answer for another's debt.
   (i) In bankruptcy, the selling off of a debtor's property to get cash to pay the creditors.
   (j) This is usually necessary before the secured creditor has priority over other creditors.

2. Arrow Sales recently had built a new warehouse. A roofing subcontractor contracts the warehouse manager and demands $15,000 in payment for his work and materials. The manager responds that Arrow Sales had no contract with the roofing subcontractor and that all subcontractors must look to the general contractor for payment. When told that the general contractor has filed for bankruptcy, the manager replies that Arrow Sales paid the general contractor in full for the work and that all subcontractors will have to get paid from the general contractor's estate. Is the manager correct? Explain.

3. To set yourself up in business, you are considering buying the inventory of a local hardware store which is going out of business. What must you be sure to do before paying for the inventory or taking delivery of it?

4. First Bank promotes its bonded teller to vice president. If First Bank forgets to notify the bonding company of the promotion and the new vice president embezzles money, is the bank still protected by the bond? Explain.

5 If Smith guarantees a $20,000 debt and Smyth guarantees $10,000 of the same debt, what is Smith's right of contribution against Smyth if Smith has to pay the entire $20,000?
6 Under what circumstances is it possible to perfect a security interest by attachment alone?
7 Clela buys a car from Adam's Auto Co. Adam's inventory was subject to a security interest held by Second Bank. If Adam's does not repay its loan to Second Bank, can Second Bank recover the car from Clela? Explain.
8 If Eli takes mortgaged propery "subject to the mortgage," will he be liable if a foreclosure sale of the property later fails to pay off the debt which the mortgage secured?
9 Why is it true that the usury laws of most states are better known for permitting exceptions to general usury principles than for applying them?
10 Discuss the FDCPA's restrictions on collection methods of collection agencies.
11 The Zenith Credit Bureau telephones Dan and his family almost daily about payment of a $3,500 debt which Dan owes to Equipment Suppliers, Inc. The phone calls are causing stress for Dan's family. Dan cannot afford to pay the debt at present, and he needs a listed telephone number for his business. Is there anything Dan can do legally to stop the calls from Zenith?
12 Willson Manufacturing, Inc., has gone into bankruptcy liquidation. Bankruptcy creditors include employees, suppliers, the electric utility, and the government (for back income tax). In what order will these various creditors be paid out of the debtor's estate?
13 Targett Company manufactures pharmaceuticals. Recently, one of its drugs has been found to cause birth defects. Hundreds of lawsuits have been filed against Targett. Amounts claimed in damages against Targett exceed insurance limits. The lenders who finance Targett are becoming nervous. Its stock prices have fallen on the stock exchange. Targett is considering bankruptcy relief. What relief is available, other than liquidation? Why might it be attractive to Targett's management? Explain.
14 Sims borrows money from a local finance company to help send her daughter to college. The loan contract Sims signs contains a clause that waives any defenses she may have against the finance company if the contract is assigned to a third party. Discuss the legality of this clause.
15 Susan joins a newly opened exercise spa. She pays the annual $200 membership fee with her bank credit card. One week later, the spa locks its doors and goes out of business. Repeated phone calls and letters to the spa's management, which demand a refund of her money, go unanswered. What is now Susan's best course of legal action for getting back her $200?

PART SEVEN

PROTECTING SOCIETY

21
Protecting Competition

22
Sherman Act Enforcement

23
Clayton Act and FTC Act Enforcement

24
Environmental Laws and Pollution Control

CHAPTER 21

PROTECTING COMPETITION

OVERVIEW

This chapter and the next two discuss antitrust laws. These are laws which are intended to make our competitive economic system work. In other words, the goal of these statutes is workable competition and all of the benefits that are intended to flow from it.

This chapter introduces the basic statutes designed to protect competition: the Sherman Antitrust Act of 1890 and the Clayton Act of 1914. It also discusses activities that are exempt from the antitrust laws, such as those required by state governments.

There are three major sanctions available to enforce the antitrust laws. First, it is a crime to violate many of the provisions. Second, courts of equity may use the injunction remedy either to prevent violations or to correct the impact of past violations. Last and most important, persons who suffer injury as a result of noncompliance may sue wrongdoers for triple damages. As you study this chapter, keep in mind the great importance of this triple damage remedy and the fact that antitrust cases frequently involve millions of dollars. These remedies are enforced by the Department of Justice, the Federal Trade Commission, and private individuals.

One of the important distinctions in this chapter is the distinction between violations that are *per se illegal* and those that are subject to the *rule of reason*. The concept of per se illegality means that proof of an activity is proof of a violation without any evidence of its economic impact. The following terms are introduced in this chapter: *Illinois Brick* Doctrine, monopoly, Noerr-Pennington Doctrine, nolo contendere, *Parker v. Brown* Doctrine, per se illegality, restraint of trade, rule of reason, Sherman Act, state action exemption, and triple damages.

1 THE MEANING OF ANTITRUST

A "trust" is a fiduciary relationship concerning property in which one person, known as the trustee, holds legal title to property for the benefit of another, known as the beneficiary. The trustee has the duty to manage and preserve the property for the use and enjoyment of the beneficiary. Trusts are generally legal, and the so-called "antitrust laws" are not aimed at trusts which serve legitimate and socially desirable purposes, such as promoting education or caring for spendthrift or incompetent children.

In the last part of the nineteenth century, the trust device was used extensively to gain monopolistic control of different types of business. Through it, a group of corporations having the same type of business could unite in following common business policies and eliminate competition among themselves by controlling production, dividing the market, and establishing price levels. The trust device allowed all or at least a majority of the stock of several companies to be transferred to a trustee. Stockholders were issued trust certificates which named them as beneficiaries of the trust and entitled them to dividends declared on the stock they had transferred. The trustee then was in a position to control the operation and policy making of all the companies, since it held the stock and could vote for directors of its own choosing in each. Technically, the companies were still separate businesses, but in substance they were united under one guiding hand.

The first statutes attempting to control monopolistic combinations were enacted about the time this trust device was in vogue; hence, these laws came to be known as antitrust laws, although they were aimed at protecting the public from any type of monopoly or activity in restraint of trade. The term *antitrust laws* is used to describe all laws that attempt to regulate competition. The goal of such laws is to ensure that our competitive economic system works and achieves its goals of lower prices, product innovation, and equitable distribution of real income among consumers and the factors of production. In other words, the antitrust laws are designed to ensure a system of workable competition.

2 STATUTES INVOLVED

There are several statutes involved in the field of antitrust law. The basic statute is the **Sherman Antitrust Act** of 1890. Prior to that time, states had enacted the first antitrust laws. These proved to be largely ineffective in preventing monopolistic practices, for a number of reasons. Among these were lack of enforcement facilities and the fact that **monopolies** were really a national problem. The federal government entered the scene in 1887 with the enactment of the Interstate Commerce Act (ICA) to control the railroads, where the obvious danger of monopoly had first appeared. This was followed in 1890 by the Sherman Act, which Congress passed under its constitutional authority to regulate interstate commerce.

The Sherman Act attacks two types of anticompetitive business behavior to further the policy of preserving competition. Section 1 covers contracts, combinations, and conspiracies in restraint of trade or commerce. Contracts in restraint of trade usually result from words, but combinations usually result from conduct. A conspiracy is usually established by words, followed by some act carrying out the plan of the conspiracy.

Section 2 of the act is directed at monopoly and attempts to monopolize any part of interstate or foreign commerce. The law supplies a means to break up existing monopolies and prevent others from developing. It is directed at single firms and does not purport to cover shared monopolies or oligopolies.

In 1914, Congress decided that the Sherman Act was too general and that it needed to be made more specific. It enacted the Clayton Act, which is actually an amendment to the Sherman Act. The Clayton Act contains several important sections, many of which were later amended. In this text, we will review the provisions and the appropriate amendments in the chapters and sections, as indicated:

	Clayton Act section	Subject matter	Text coverage
Section 2	As amended by the Robinson-Patman Act (1936)	Price discrimination	Chapter 23; sections 2–9
Section 3		Tying and exclusive contracts	Chapter 23; sections 10–13
Section 4		Triple damage suits	Chapter 21; section 8 and 9
Section 7	As amended by the Celler-Kefauver Amendment (1950)	Mergers and acquisitions	Chapter 23; sections 14–20
Section 8		Interlocking directorates	Chapter 23; section 2

In 1914, Congress also passed the Federal Trade Commission Act (FTC Act). This act created the Federal Trade Commission (FTC). The FTC was created to have an "independent" administrative agency charged with keeping competition free and fair. It enforces the Clayton Act provisions on price discrimination, tying and exclusive contracts, mergers and acquisitions, and interlocking directorates. In addition, it enforces Section 5 of the Federal Trade Commission Act. This act originally made "unfair methods of competition" in commerce unlawful. The Wheeler-Lea amendments of 1938 added that "unfair or deceptive acts or practices in commerce" were also unlawful under Section 5. The role of the FTC in antitrust enforcement will be discussed in Chapter 23.

3 EXEMPTIONS TO THE SHERMAN ACT

There are numerous business activities that are exempt from the Sherman Act. Some of these exemptions were created by the original statute; others, by the Clayton Act and other amendments; and still others, by the courts. Each of these exemptions is based upon some other form of regulation and a policy that overrides the goals of the Sherman Act. Among activities and business for which there are statutory exceptions are insurance companies, farmers' cooperatives, shipping, milk marketing, and investment companies. Activities required by state law are exempt. In addition, normal activities of labor unions are exempt. These exemptions are narrowly construed and do not mean that every activity of a firm is necessarily exempted simply because most activities are exempted. For example, it has been held that an agreement between an insurance company and a pharmaceutical organization which regulates the price of prescription drugs given to policyholders of the insurance company was not exempt—it was not the business of insurance that was involved in the transaction. It is the business of insurance that is exempt and not the business of insurance companies. Similarly, the courts have eliminated from exemptions people who belong to organizations but do not actually participate in the industry declared to be exempt. Likewise, a union would forfeit its exemption when it agreed with one set of employers to impose a certain wage scale on other employer bargaining units. It is only the usual and legitimate union activity that is exempt.

4 THE STATE ACTION EXEMPTION

In a 1943 case known as *Parker v. Brown,* the Supreme Court created a **state action exemption** to the Sherman Act. This state action exemption, usually referred to as the ***Parker v. Brown* Doctrine**, was based on the reasoning that the Sherman Act does not apply to state government. Since that time, numerous cases have attempted to define the limits of this exemption. Although the courts are still deciding cases and adding to the body of law applicable to the doctrine of *Parker v. Brown,* several principles limiting its application are evident. They may be summarized as follows:

1 When a state acts in its sovereign capacity, it is immune from federal antitrust scrutiny.
2 Although municipalities are state subdivisions, they do not enjoy the deference due a state. A municipality will be immune from antitrust liability only if it acts as an instrumentality of the state, through which the state has clearly and affirmatively chosen to implement its policies.
3 When a state agency or subdivision claims immunity from federal law, it must first identify a clearly expressed state policy that authorizes its actions. The legislation must contain an affirmative showing of intent

to replace competition with regulation, though it need do no more than authorize the challenged conduct.
4 So long as the resulting anticompetitive activities are a foreseeable consequence of state delegation, the state policy of replacing competition with regulation has been clearly articulated. The party claiming the state action defense must show that the legislature contemplated the action complained of.
5 A state need not actively supervise a municipality, since a municipality, unlike a private party, has no incentive to act other than in the public interest. When the challenged actor is a private party, both forseeability and supervision must be demonstrated, according to the case which follows.

CALIFORNIA RETAIL LIQUOR DEALERS ASSOC. v. MIDCAL ALUMINUM, INC., ET AL.
100 S.Ct. 937 (1980)

FACTS

A California statute required all wine producers and wholesalers to file price schedules or fair trade contracts with the state. No wholesaler may sell wine to a retailer at a price different from that set by either method, subject to fines, license suspension, or license revocation. California was divided into three trading areas for application of this wine-pricing scheme. A single fair-price contract or schedule for each brand governed all wholesale transactions in that brand within a particular area. With state regulations, the wine prices quoted by a single wholesaler would bind all wholesalers for that area.

The defendant was accused of selling wine for prices less than those set by a particular price schedule. He admitted such sales, but contended that the state's wine-pricing system was a violation of the Sherman Act. The California Retail Liquor Dealers Association contended that the pricing program was shielded from the Sherman Act by the state action doctrine of *Parker v. Brown*.

ISSUE

Is the wine-pricing scheme established by California statute a violation of the Sherman Act?

DECISION

Yes.

REASONS

1. Resale price maintenance constitutes illegal restraint of trade. Under California's wine-pricing system, producers can dictate prices charged by wholesalers, clearly preventing price competition.
2. For antitrust immunity under *Parker v. Brown*: (a) the challenged restraint on trade must be "clearly articulated and affirmatively expressed as state policy" and (b) the policy must be one "actively supervised" by the state itself.

> 3. The California wine-pricing system meets the first standard but not the second. The state does not set prices or review the reasonableness of price schedules, nor does it regulate the terms of fair-trade contracts. There is not sufficient state involvement to grant immunity under the state action exemption.

Notwithstanding the aforesaid limitations, there are many state laws which do create immunity from antitrust sanctions, not only for the state, but also for private parties that comply with state laws. When a state acting in its sovereign capacity seeks to limit competition and replace it with regulations supervised and enforced by the state, *Parker v. Brown* will prevent antitrust liability. For example, Kansas City, Missouri, granted an exclusive license to one company to provide ambulance services. This was held to be a valid state action. The city established the ambulance system pursuant to state authority, and it clearly expressed state policy.

In another case, an unsuccessful candidate for admittance to the Arizona Bar alleged a conspiracy by the Bar examiners in violation of the Sherman Act. He contended that the grading scale was dictated by the number of new attorneys desired rather than by the level of competition and answers on the exam. The courts held that this activity was exempt from the Sherman Act. The grading of bar examinations is, in reality, conduct of the Arizona Supreme Court and thus exempt. Action by the courts is just as immune as actions by the legislature.

5 THE NOERR-PENNINGTON DOCTRINE

Another exemption from the Sherman Act is known as the **Noerr-Pennington Doctrine**. This doctrine exempts from the antitrust laws concerted efforts to lobby government officials, regardless of the anticompetitive purposes. The doctrine is applicable even though the activity to be influenced is a commercial enterprise. The doctrine is based on the First Amendment. For example, Budget Rent-A-Car filed suit against Hertz and National Rent-A-Car because the defendants lobbied officials at three state-owned airports to limit the number of car-rental operations. They lobbied for restrictions that would have made it more difficult for Budget to compete. For example, they sought a restriction that would require equal fees for all agencies. They also requested that nationwide reservation systems be required, and that each firm have a specified number of years' experience at a specified number of airports. This lobbying was exempt from the Sherman Act. The Noerr-Pennington Doctrine is based on the free flow of information and the First Amendment right to petition government for a redress of grievances. The doctrine does not have a commercial exception, and it applies to attempts to influence government on behalf of business.

Attempts to influence nongovernmental bodies, such as associations that set standards within an industry, are not protected by this exception. For example, a federal court in 1987 held that, by virtue of the Noerr-Pennington Doctrine, attempts to influence private associations which set product-safety standards that are often incorporated into state and local statutes are not immune from antitrust scrutiny.

SANCTIONS

6 THE CRIMINAL SANCTION

The Sherman Act as amended by the Clayton Act recognizes four separate legal sanctions. First, it is a federal crime to violate the Sherman Act. Second, violations may be enjoined by the courts. Third, injured parties may collect triple damages. Finally, any property owned in violation of Section 1 of the act that is being transported from one state to another is subject to seizure by and forfeiture to the United States. This last remedy has rarely been used.

In addition to these sanctions, the law allows the government to demand information from suppliers, consumers, and target companies in noncriminal investigations. The data obtained may be used to establish proof of market share or other relevant statistics. The information may then be used to obtain injunctions.

The punishment imposed by the criminal law may be a fine, imprisonment, or both, for any person or corporation that violates its provisions. Although originally such violations were only misdemeanors, today crimes under the Sherman Act are felonies. An individual found guilty may be fined up to $100,000 and imprisoned up to three years. A corporation found guilty may be fined up to $1 million for each offense.

In criminal cases, the defendant has three possible pleas to enter to an indictment charging a violation—"guilty," "not guilty," or "**nolo contendere.**" This last plea of "no contest" allows sentencing just as if the defendant had pleaded or been found guilty. It has the advantage to a defendant of avoiding the cost of trial and the effect of a guilty plea or finding in a subsequent civil suit. Criminal convictions create prima facie cases for triple damages, but this effect can be avoided by the nolo contendere plea. Acceptance of nolo contendere pleas (the plea is not a matter of right, but discretionary with the trial court) tends to discourage triple damage suits because of the difficulties private parties face in proving Sherman Act violations. The cost of investigation and preparation of antitrust suits is usually substantial, and, therefore, private litigants benefit greatly from either a guilty plea or a conviction. As a result, the government today often opposes pleas of nolo contendere.

The criminal sanction has historically been the least used of Sherman

Act remedies. However, in recent years it has been used more often. In 1987, the Justice Department had 150 grand juries looking into allegations of criminal price-fixing and bid-rigging in industries that ranged from defense contracting and gasoline retailing to soft-drink and kosher food preparation. As a general rule, it is used in price-fixing cases when there is proof of specific intent to restrain trade or to monopolize. If a firm has been charged civilly and found guilty, the government is required to bring criminal charges if the evidence suggests continuing violations. Many first-offense cases are handled civilly rather than criminally. However, criminal prosecution is likely to result if practices similar to those engaged in have been held to be a violation in a prior case. Action undertaken with knowledge of a prior decision will supply the requisite criminal intent.

Criminal prosecutions under the Sherman Act do require proof of criminal intent. There is no presumption of wrongful intent. The major use of the criminal sanction is in price-fixing cases. For example, criminal cases have been brought against road builders of interstate highways because of rigged bids, and against various real estate firms for fixing the price of real estate commissions. These criminal cases were brought to deter others from similar practices.

7 THE INJUNCTION

The Sherman Act empowers courts to grant injunctions at the request of the government or a private party that will prevent and restrain violations or continued violations of its provisions. An injunction may prevent anticompetitive behavior or it may even force a breakup of a corporation. For example, it was used to split the former American Telephone & Telegraph Company (Ma Bell) into eight organizations—one national company for long-distance telephone service and seven regional companies for local service. The remedy is also used to prevent acquisitions and stop practices that are deemed to be anticompetitive.

The injunction remedy is frequently used when the success of a criminal prosecution is doubtful. It takes less proof to enjoin an activity (preponderance of the evidence only) than it does to convict of a crime (beyond a reasonable doubt). There have been cases involving this remedy even after an acquittal in a criminal case. In effect, the court ordered the defendant not to do something which it had been found innocent of doing.

Under Section 16 of the Clayton Act, private parties "threatened [with] loss or damage by a violation of the antitrust laws" may seek injunctive relief. This private remedy is in addition to suits for triple damages. To obtain an injunction, a private party must prove a threat of an antitrust injury—an injury of the type the antitrust laws were designed to prevent. These are the same types of injuries that may result in triple damages. As the case which follows illustrates, loss of profits due to increased competition is not such an injury.

CARGILL, INC. v. MONFORT OF COLORADO, INC.
107 S.Ct. 484 (1986)

FACTS

Monfort is the country's fifth-largest beef packer. Excel Corporation is the second-largest packer. Excel operates five integrated plants and one fabrication plant. It is a wholly owned subsidiary of Cargill, Inc., a large privately owned corporation with more than 150 subsidiaries in at least thirty-five countries.

On June 17, 1983, Excel signed an agreement to acquire the third-largest packer in the market, Spencer Beef, a division of the Land O'Lakes agricultural cooperative. Spencer Beef owned two integrated plants and one slaughtering plant. After the acquisition, Excel would still be the second-largest packer, but it would command a market share almost equal to that of the largest packer, IBP, Inc.

The meat-packing business is highly competitive, with low profit margins. Monfort brought an action to enjoin the prospective merger, on the ground that it violated Section 7 of the Clayton Act.

ISSUES

1. Must a plaintiff seeking an injunction prove a threat of antitrust injury?
2. If so, does loss or damage due to increased competition constitute such an injury?

DECISIONS

1. Yes.
2. No.

REASONS

1. Antitrust laws were enacted for the protection of competition, not competitors.
2. To seek injunctive relief under Section 16, a private plaintiff must allege threatened loss or damage "of the type the antitrust laws were designed to prevent and that flows from that which makes defendants' acts unlawful."
3. The threat of loss of profits due to possible price competition following a merger does not constitute a threat of antitrust injury.
4. The antitrust laws do not require the courts to protect small businesses from the loss of profits due to continued competition, but only against the loss of profits from practices forbidden by the antitrust laws.

Many antitrust cases are settled by agreement of the government and the defendants. In the past, it was sometimes alleged that political considerations played a part in such settlements. Therefore, the law now requires that all contacts between government and company officials, except for those between the lawyers involved, be reported when a proposed negotiated settlement of an antitrust case is made public. In addition, out-of-court settlements must be approved by the court, and the judge must find that the settlement is in the national interest before it can be approved. In the case involving AT&T, the trial judge balked at accepting the settlement agreed upon by the parties. It was later approved after some modifications.

8 TRIPLE DAMAGES

The third remedy (created by the Clayton Act amendment in 1914) affords relief to persons injured by another's violation of the Sherman Act. Such victims are given the right, in a civil action, to collect three times the damages they have suffered, plus court costs and reasonable attorney's fees. Normally, the objective of awarding money damages to individuals in a private lawsuit is to place them in the position they would have enjoyed, as nearly as this can be done with money, had their rights not been invaded. The **triple damage** provisions of the antitrust laws, however, employ the remedy of damages to punish a defendant for a wrongful act in addition to compensating the plaintiff for actual injury. Today it is perhaps the most important remedy of all, because it allows one's competitors as well as injured members of the general public to enforce the law if government fails to do so.

In recent years, there have been several developments relating to triple damages. After the Supreme Court held that, under the Sherman Act, foreign governments are persons, Congress by statute provided that foreign nations may sue only for actual damages when they have purchased products for which prices have been fixed. The Court has held that local governments and nonprofit organizations may be sued under the law when they participate in activities which violate the Sherman Act. Such cases may arise when local government operates a business such as a utility, or when a professional association causes its members to take certain actions. In these cases, liability is imposed by use of the doctrine of respondeat superior and antitrust liability is imposed for unlawful conduct of agents within the scope of their actual or apparent authority.

The law authorizes the attorney general of a state to file triple damage suits on behalf of the citizens of a state. Such suits are similar to a class action suit. For example, either the consumers involved or the attorney general on their behalf may sue for triple damages when consumers have paid higher prices for products and the higher prices resulted from antitrust violations. Damages under the antitrust laws are not limited to commercial losses or to those of a competitive nature. The term "property" is given a broad definition and includes anything of a material value, including money.

REITER v. SONOTONE CORP.
99 S.Ct. 2326 (1979)

FACTS

Reiter purchased a hearing aid and filed suit for triple damages, alleging price-fixing. Sonotone Corp. contended that Reiter was not injured in her business or property and, therefore, was not entitled to triple damages.

ISSUE

Is the payment of a higher price for a product an injury to property?

DECISION

Yes.

REASONS

1. The word "property" is given a broad and inclusive meaning and includes anything of material value.
2. Money is property, and Reiter lost money.
3. The remedy of triple damages is not limited to business losses, but it includes losses to consumers.

The triple damage remedy is perhaps the most important of all the sanctions available. Successful triple damage suits may impose financial burdens on violators far in excess of any fine that could be imposed as a result of a criminal prosecution. This significant liability may be far in excess of the damages caused by any one defendant, because the liability of defendants is based on tort law and is said to be joint and several. For example, assume that ten companies in an industry conspire to fix prices and that the total damages caused by the conspiracy equal $100 million. Also, assume that nine of the defendants settle out of court for $25 million. The remaining defendant, if the case is lost, would owe $275 million ($3 \times 100 - 25$). The case which denied any right of contribution in such circumstances follows. It should be noted that Congress is considering legislation to change this decision because of its impact on a few companies which face liabilities approaching a billion dollars.

TEXAS INDUSTRIES, INC. v. RADCLIFF MATERIALS, INC.
102 S.Ct. 2061 (1981)

FACTS

A manufacturer of ready-mix concrete, which was defending a Sherman Act triple damage suit, filed a third-party complaint against alleged co-conspirators seeking contribution should it be held liable in the original action.

ISSUE

Is there a right of contribution?

DECISION

No.

REASONS

1. Federal courts have no common law or statutory authority to compel

contribution among co-conspiring antitrust violators. The "far-reaching" policy questions about the creation of such a remedy must be left to Congress.
2. There is no implied congressional intent to create such a cause of action, and there is an absence of any reference to contribution in the legislative history or of any possibility that Congress was concerned with softening the blow on joint wrongdoers in this setting.
3. It is clear that the Sherman Act and the provision for triple damage actions under the Clayton Act were not adopted for the benefit of the participants in a conspiracy to restrain trade. The very idea of triple damages reveals an intent to punish past, and to deter future, unlawful conduct, not to ameliorate the liability of wrongdoers.

9 THE ILLINOIS BRICK DOCTRINE

Who is entitled to collect triple damages? Is everyone in the chain of distribution entitled to use Section 4 of the Clayton Act and recover damages? The leading case on this point involved a company called Illinois Brick. The case has become so well known in antitrust law that the legal principle which it announced is simply referred to as the *Illinois Brick* **Doctrine.** This doctrine announced that courts generally restrict the recovery of triple damages to direct purchasers, and they do not allow recoveries by indirect purchasers.

ILLINOIS BRICK CO. v. ILLINOIS

97 S.Ct. 2061 (1977)

FACTS

A manufacturer of concrete blocks sold its product to companies who, in turn, sold them to general contractors for use as building materials in completed structures. Plaintiff, who had purchased a completed building containing concrete block, sued the manufacturer, contending that there was price-fixing in concrete blocks. The defendant contended that plaintiff was an indirect purchaser and, therefore, not entitled to recover triple damages.

ISSUE

Is an indirect purchaser entitled to collect triple damages?

DECISION

No.

REASONS

1. The right to recover damages based on price-fixing cannot be passed on by the direct purchaser from the price-fixer to others.
2. The overcharged direct purchaser is the injured party in a price-fixing case.

3. A defendant is not entitled to the use of a pass-on defense; therefore, the plaintiff is not entitled to sue on the pass-on theory.
4. The principal basis for the decision is the uncertainty and difficulty in analyzing the extent to which the higher price is passed on. The evidentiary complexities and uncertainties involved in the pass-on theory make it impossible to allow such suits. The damages would be pure speculation.

The *Illinois Brick* decision continues to require further interpretation and application. Several courts have held that *Illinois Brick* does not preclude consumers from suing manufacturers who allegedly conspire with middlemen to fix retail prices. These courts recognize that the claim is not based on pass-through damages but is instead a form of retail price fixing.

Not every case fits into the *Illinois Brick* mold. In one instance, an employee sued for wrongful discharge for refusing to participate in a Sherman Act violation. The employee had standing to sue, because the damage problems of the pass-on theory are not present in such cases. The case which follows illustrates another exception to *Illinois Brick*.

BLUE SHIELD OF VIRGINIA, ET AL. v. McCREADY
102 S.Ct. 2540 (1982)

FACTS

As a county employee in Virginia from 1975 to 1978, McCready received partial compensation in the form of coverage under a prepaid health plan purchased from Blue Shield. This health plan provided reimbursement for a portion of any outpatient psychotherapy administered by *psychiatrists*. The plan did not reimburse for treatment by *psychologists* unless they were supervised by and billed through a physician.

McCready submitted several claims to Blue Shield. These claims were denied because they were not billed through a physician. He then filed a class action suit on behalf of all Blue Shield subscribers denied reimbursement for psychological services, alleging that Blue Shield and the Neuro-psychiatric Society of Virginia, Inc., had engaged in unlawful conspiracy to exclude psychologists from receiving compensation under Blue Shield plans, which was in violation of the Sherman Act, Section 1. Plaintiff sought triple damages. Defendants contended that plaintiff was not in the class of persons entitled to triple damages.

ISSUE

Is the plaintiff entitled to triple damages?

DECISION

Yes.

REASONS

1. The language of Section 4 of the Clayton Act is very broad. Although a person may not recover damages for injuries that are *too remote* from the

alleged antitrust violation, that restriction is a vague concept. In deciding which injuries are too remote, the Court looks: (*a*) to the physical and economic connection between the alleged violation and the injury, and (*b*) the relationship of the injury to the injuries "about which Congress was likely to have been concerned in making defendant's conduct unlawful and in providing a private remedy under Section 4."

2. Here, the remedy is not restricted to psychologists, who were as a group the target of the conspiracy. The specific means to exclude the psychologists was to deny reimbursement claims of subscriber-patients, such as the plaintiff.

3. Defendant's injury, resulting from an anticompetitive scheme, was of a type for which Congress intended to provide a private remedy under Section 4 of the Clayton Act.

10 PROOF OF SHERMAN ACT VIOLATIONS

Plaintiffs seeking triple damages must satisfy the interstate commerce element to have a Sherman Act claim. They must allege facts which show that the activity is either in interstate commerce or that it has a substantial effect on interstate commerce. A plaintiff need not allege and prove a change in the volume of interstate commerce but only that the activity had a substantial and adverse or not insubstantial effect on interstate commerce. In a recent case involving the medical profession, it was held that the Sherman Act is applicable to staff privileges at a hospital. The impact on interstate commerce is readily apparent.

Difficulties may arise in proving the existence of a contract, combination, or conspiracy among competitors when they indulge in cooperative action to control the market in some fashion. Must an actual oral or written offer and acceptance be established? If the market behavior of competitors is consciously parallel, will it be implied that they are conspiring together? If one party reacts to another's conduct, does this prove a conspiracy? In the case that follows, there was evidence that a manufacturer terminated a distributor in response to other distributors' complaints about price-cutting. Is this sufficient to prove a conspiracy in violation of Section 1 of the Sherman Act? If there is evidence that tends to prove that a manufacturer and others had a conscious commitment to a common silence designed to achieve an unlawful objective, the issue becomes one of fact for a jury.

MONSANTO v. SPRAY-RITE SERVICE CORPORATION
104 S.Ct. 1464 (1984)

FACTS

Monsanto manufactures agricultural herbicides. Spray-Rite was a wholesaler distributor of agricultural chemicals and an authorized Monsanto distributor. Monsanto canceled Spray-Rite's distributorship after receiving complaints from other distributors that Spray-Rite was cutting prices. Spray-Rite sued for triple damages, alleging a conspiracy between Monsanto and other distributors in violation of Section 1 of the Sherman Act. Monsanto contended that the distributorship was terminated because Spray-Rite had failed to hire trained salespeople and promote sales adequately, not because of the complaints. In a jury trial, the court instructed the jury that Monsanto's conduct was per se unlawful if it was in furtherance of a conspiracy to fix prices. The jury found the conspiracy to exist. The court of appeals affirmed, stating that proof of termination following competitor complaints is sufficient to: (a) support an inference of concerted action and (b) make the issue one for the jury.

ISSUE

Is proof of termination following a competitor's complaint enough to make the issue of liability a jury question?

DECISION

No.

REASONS

1. There are two distinctions in distributor-termination cases. First, there is the distinction between concerted and independent actions: concerted activity is illegal; independent action is not. A manufacturer can announce its resale prices in advance and refuse to deal with those who fail to comply (Colgate Doctrine). A distributor is free to acquiesce in the manufacturer's prices to avoid termination without being part of a conspiracy.
2. The second distinction is between concerted action to set prices and concerted action on nonprice restrictions. The former are illegal per se, and the latter are judged under the rule of reason.
3. A price-fixing agreement cannot be inferred from the existence of complaints from other distributors or even from the fact that termination came in response to such complaints. Something more than evidence of complaints is needed to prove price-fixing.
4. There must be evidence that tends to exclude the possibility that the manufacturer and nonterminated distributors were acting independently. There must be evidence that reasonably tends to prove that the manufacturer and others had a conscious commitment to a scheme designed to achieve an unlawful objective.
5. Using this standard, there was sufficient evidence for the jury to find the conspiracy. Even though the court of appeals was wrong in its reasons, it reached the correct result.

11 THE RULE OF REASON AND PER SE ILLEGALITY

The **rule of reason** as applied to the Sherman Act was enunciated in the case of *Standard Oil Co. v. United States*.[1] The court in that case held that contracts or conspiracies in **restraint of trade** were illegal only if they con-

---

[1] 221 U.S. 1 (1911).

stituted *undue* or *unreasonable* restraints of trade, and that only *unreasonable* attempts to monopolize were covered by the Sherman Act. As a result, acts which the statute prohibits may be removed from the coverage of the law by a finding that they are *reasonable*. The rule of reason gives flexibility and definition to the law. The rule does not open the field of antitrust inquiry to any argument in favor of a challenged restraint that may fall within the realm of reason. Instead, it focuses directly on the challenged restraint's impact on competitive conditions. The fact that prices fixed are reasonable is no defense. Monopolistic practices that promote trade are still illegal.

The *test of reasonableness* is whether challenged contracts or acts are unreasonably restrictive of competitive conditions. Unreasonableness can be based either: (1) on the nature or character of the contracts or (2) on surrounding circumstances giving rise to the inference or presumption that they were intended to restrain trade and enhance prices. Under either branch of the test, the inquiry is confined to a consideration of impact on competitive conditions. If an agreement promotes competition, it may be found legal. If it suppresses or destroys competition, it is unreasonable and illegal.

For purposes of the rule of reason, Sherman Act violations may be divided into two categories. Some agreements or practices are so plainly anticompetitive and so lacking in any redeeming virtues that they are conclusively presumed to be illegal without further examination under the rule of reason. These agreements have such a pernicious effect on competition that elaborate inquiry as to the precise harm they may cause or a business excuse for them are unnecessary. They are said to be illegal per se. It is not necessary to examine them to see if they are reasonable. They are conclusively presumed to be unreasonable. Of course, the other category consists of agreements and practices that are illegal only if they impose an unreasonable restraint upon competitors.

The concept of **per se illegality** simplifies proof in cases in which it is applied. When an activity is illegal per se, courts are not required to conduct a complicated and prolonged examination of the economic consequences of the activity to determine whether it is unreasonable. If it is illegal per se, proof of the activity is proof of a violation and proof that it is in restraint of trade.

The most common example of an agreement that is illegal per se is one that fixes prices. In other words, an unreasonable contract or combination in restraint of trade is established by simply proving the existence of a price-fixing agreement. Similar contracts to those fixing the price at which conspirators sell their product have been held unreasonable per se. Thus, agreements among competitors to divide up territories, to fix the market price of a product or service they are buying, or to limit the supply of a commodity are outlawed without proof of any unreasonable effects. Group boycotts are usually held to be illegal per se. In studying antitrust cases, you should note those activities to which the illegal per se concept is applied and those to which the rule of reason is applied. Courts develop this distinction on a case-by-case basis, as is done in the following case:

CATALANO, INC. v. TARGET SALES, INC.
100 S.Ct. 1925 (1980)

FACTS

Beer retailers (plaintiffs) brought suit, alleging that their wholesalers had engaged in an unlawful conspiracy to restrain trade. The wholesalers refused to sell beer unless the retailers paid cash in advance or at the time of delivery. They had an agreement that none of them would grant short-term credit, even though such credit had been extended in the past.

ISSUE

Is the wholesalers' agreement per se illegal under the Sherman Act?

DECISION

Yes.

REASONS

1. Under the Sherman Act, a combination formed for the purpose of raising, depressing, fixing, pegging, or stabilizing the price of a commodity in interstate or foreign commerce is illegal per se.
2. Credit terms must be characterized as an inseparable part of the purchase price; therefore, an agreement to terminate the practice of giving credit is tantamount to an agreement to eliminate discounts, and it thus falls squarely within the traditional per se rule against price-fixing.
3. The fact that a practice may turn out to be harmless in a particular set of circumstances will not prevent its being declared unlawful per se.
4. An agreement among competing wholesalers to refuse to sell unless the retailer makes payment in cash or upon delivery is "plainly anticompetitive," and it is merely one form of a price-fixing agreement which lacks any "redeeming value." Therefore, it is conclusively presumed illegal without further examination under the rule of reason.

12 ENFORCEMENT

The antitrust laws are enforced by: (1) the Department of Justice, (2) the FTC, and (3) private parties. The Department of Justice alone has the power to bring criminal proceedings. The Department shares power with the FTC and private parties in civil proceedings. The civil proceedings may use either the injunctive remedy or the triple damage remedy.

A separate division of the Justice Department deals with antitrust. The Antitrust Division is headed by an assistant attorney general, appointed by the President and confirmed by the Senate. The Antitrust Division is essentially a large law office with several hundred lawyers whose basic function is litigation. It conducts investigations as well as tries and settles cases. By statute, the Division has the power to subpoena information and discover documents. Grand juries are routinely impaneled to assist the Division in gathering evidence when the criminal sanction is likely to be used.

Chapter 23 discusses the role of the Federal Trade Commission in enforcing the antitrust laws and especially the unfair methods of competition provision of the FTC Act. Previous sections dealing with the triple damage remedy have covered the role of private persons in the enforcement process.

Antitrust enforcement by state government is rapidly expanding. As previously noted, a state attorney general may bring triple damage suits under the Sherman Act as well as suits for an injunction. In addition, state legislators have enacted antitrust laws that cover both products and services. These laws cover intrastate activities and are designed to prevent loss of competition in local communities. For example, recent cases have involved agreements by golf course operators to fix the price of green fees and golf cart rentals. Another case involved a real estate subdivider whose contracts of sale required that his real estate firm be used as the broker on a subsequent sale. For several years, the federal government awarded grants to aid state governments in antitrust enforcement. The impact of such local enforcement is likely to be much greater in the future.

REVIEW QUESTIONS

1 For each term in the left-hand column, match the most appropriate description in the right-hand column:

(1) Nolo contendere
(2) Noerr-Pennington Doctrine
(3) Per se illegality
(4) State action exemption
(5) The rule of reason
(6) Illinois Brick Doctrine

(a) Only direct purchasers from a price-fixer are entitled to collect triple damages.
(b) A rule that states that contracts or conspiracies are illegal only if they constitute undue or unreasonable restraints of trade, or if they unreasonably attempt to monopolize.
(c) Certain acts, in themselves, are unreasonable and, therefore, illegal under the Sherman Act.
(d) Concerted efforts to lobby governmental bodies are exempt from the antitrust laws.
(e) The antitrust laws do not cover activities mandated by state and local laws.
(f) A plea of "no contest" to a charge of a criminal violation of the law.

2 A city used federal funds to build a sewage-treatment facility. It refused to supply sewage-treatment services to neighboring towns, but it did supply services to landowners who agreed to be annexed to the city. Neighboring towns brought suit under the Sherman Act. What was the result? Why?

3 Three rating bureaus that represent common carriers in five southeastern states provided a forum for carriers to discuss and agree on rates for intrastate transportation of commodities. These rates are then proposed to the various state

public-service commissions for approval. The United States instituted action to enjoin this activity. The defendants asserted the state action exemption. What was the result? Why?

4. The National Basketball Association and the National Basketball Players Association entered into a collective-bargaining agreement. The agreement limits to one year the period during which a team has exclusive rights to negotiate with and sign draftees. It permits a salary cap, under which a team that has reached its maximum allowable team salary may sign a first-round draft choice only to a one-year contract for $75,000. It also prohibits the use of player corporations, which had been formed by players to enter into contracts with teams. Wood filed suit, alleging that the agreement violates the Sherman Act. Is he correct? Why, or why not?

5. A complaint alleged that private individuals conspired with city officials to legalize the operation of poker clubs in certain areas of a city. The conspiracy was allegedly carried out by advocating the adoption of a local zoning ordinance which authorized the clubs in a specified area. What defense will likely be asserted? Explain.

6. The four largest real estate brokers in Atlanta conspired to fix real estate commissions. They were indicted by a federal grand jury and ultimately entered a plea of nolo contendere. The usual commission rate prior to the conspiracy was 5 percent. The agreed-upon rate was 7 percent.

   a. What punishment may be imposed on the individuals involved?
   b. If the brokers are incorporated, what punishment may be imposed?
   c. If a suit for triple damages is filed, what proof is required? Explain.
   d. Assume that you had sold your house for $150,000 during the period the conspiracy was in effect. How much could you collect from your broker that was involved?

7. A former employee alleged that his employer and other lithograph label manufacturers conspired to fix prices, allocate customers, and boycott anyone who interfered with their plans. As a result, he was forced to leave his job for refusing to participate in the scheme. He claimed he was unable, after his resignation, to find another job in the label industry. He sued for triple damages under Section 4 of the Clayton Act. The defendants contended that the plaintiff lacked standing to sue. What was the result? Why?

8. A group of gasoline dealers, through concerted action, refused to sell gasoline to the general public for several days. The purpose of the action was to influence the government to raise the maximum retail price of gasoline. When charged with an antitrust violation, they contended that they were exercising their right of free speech and that it was exempt from the antitrust law for activities aimed at influencing the government. Are they guilty? Why, or why not?

9. Assume that a Sherman Act violation is not illegal per se. What is the significance of this legal conclusion? Explain.

10. The plaintiff operated a motion-picture theater in a neighborhood shopping center. It filed suit against film distributors because they restricted first-run motion pictures to downtown theaters. The jury found the defendant not guilty of restraining competition. The plaintiff contended that the court should have held the defendant guilty as a matter of law. Was he correct? Why, or why not?

CHAPTER **22**

SHERMAN ACT ENFORCEMENT

OVERVIEW

Chapter 21 introduced you to the Sherman Act and the sanctions which may be used to enforce its provisions. This chapter illustrates typical violations under both Sherman Act provisions. The sections illustrating activities in restraint of trade (Section 1 of the Sherman Act) cover in detail such illegal contracts, combinations, and conspiracies as price-fixing, both horizontal and vertical, and concerted activities among competitors. Price-fixing is said to be horizontal when it is done among competitors, and vertical when a manufacturer fixes a price for either its wholesalers or retailers.

The latter portions of this chapter discuss Section 2 of the Sherman Act, which deals with monopoly and attempts to monopolize. These cases are brought either by the government or by a competitor seeking triple damages. As you study this chapter, keep in mind the importance of the distinction between the rule of reason and per se illegality. Also, note that many of the cases seek triple damages.

The following terms are introduced in this chapter: Colgate Doctrine, consignment, fee schedule, price-fixing, resale price-maintenance, and vertical price-fixing.

1 ACTIVITIES IN RESTRAINT OF TRADE

Section 1 of the Sherman Act is directed at contracts, combinations, and conspiracies in restraint of trade. An express agreement is not required to create a contract in restraint of trade. Such contracts may be implied. For example, discussion of price with one's competitors taken together with conscious parallel pricing would establish a violation.

Joint activities by two or more persons that may constitute a contract, combination, or conspiracy in restraint of trade are limitless. The most common form of violation is **price-fixing.** Agreements relating to territories of operation as well as any other agreement among competitors may be a violation. For example, an agreement by several competitors to buy exclusively from a single supplier is a violation of Section 1. Competition is required when buying as well as when selling. A group boycott may be a violation, even though the victim is just one merchant whose business is so small that its destruction makes little difference to the economy. An attempt to extend the monopolistic economic power of a patent or copyright to unrelated products or services may be a violation. Providing credit to one corporation on the condition that products be purchased from a separate corporation likewise may be illegal.

The acceptance of an invitation to participate in a plan that is in restraint of interstate commerce is sufficient to establish an unlawful conspiracy. Circumstantial evidence may be used to prove a conspiracy. For example, the simultaneous price increases by three major cigarette producers at a time of declining sales were admissible evidence without direct proof of communication among them.

The sections which follow illustrate typical Section 1 cases. The usual remedy is a suit for triple damages. However, some of the examples involve criminal violations and others are cases involving injunctions.

2 PRICE-FIXING

Price-fixing agreements among competitors are illegal per se. The term "price-fixing" is not given a literal interpretation. For example, if partners set the price of their goods or services, they have engaged in "price-fixing," but not the type envisioned by the Sherman Act. The price-fixing covered by the Sherman Act is that which threatens free competition. It is no defense to a charge of price-fixing that the prices fixed are fair or reasonable. It also is no defense that price-fixing is engaged in by small competitors to allow them to compete with larger competitors. The per se rule makes price-fixing illegal whether the parties to it have control of the market or not, and whether or not they are trying to raise or lower the market price. It is just as illegal to fix a low price as it is to fix a high price. It is just as illegal to fix the price of services as it is to fix the price of goods. Maximum fee agreements are therefore just as illegal as minimum fee agreements in the service sector. Price-fixing in the service sector has been engaged in by professional persons as well as by service workers, such as automobile and TV repair workers, barbers, and refuse collectors. For many years it was contended that persons performing services were not engaged in trade or commerce. It was also contended that there was a "learned profession" exception to the Sherman Act.

In the mid-1970s, the Supreme Court rejected these arguments and held that the Sherman Act covered services, including those performed by the learned professions such as law.

GOLDFARB ET UX. v. VIRGINIA STATE BAR ET AL.
95 S.Ct. 2004 (1975)

FACTS

Plaintiffs contracted to buy a home in Fairfax County, Virginia. They were unsuccessful in finding a lawyer who would perform the required title examination for less than the fee prescribed in a **minimum fee schedule** published by the Fairfax County Bar Association and enforced by the Virginia State Bar. They brought a class action suit, seeking injunctive relief and damages, and alleging that the minimum fee schedule constituted price-fixing, which was in violation of Section 1 of the Sherman Act.

ISSUE

Are minimum fee schedules subject to Section 1 of the Sherman Act?

DECISION

Yes.

REASONS

1. A rigid price floor resulted from the defendants' activities. The schedule was enforced through the threat of professional discipline.
2. The title examination is an integral part of an interstate transaction and, therefore, it affects commerce.
3. There is no evidence that Congress intended a sweeping exclusion for learned professions.
4. The fact that the state bar is a state agency for some limited purposes does not create an antitrust shield that allows it to foster anticompetitive practices for the benefit of its members.

As a result of the foregoing case, the cost of legal services for real estate transactions in the area involved was reduced significantly. Price competition in the service sector is lowering such prices, and the threat of triple damage suits is forcing the abandonment of price-fixing activities by many groups which had actively engaged in them prior to 1975.

Some professional groups have attempted to avoid laws restricting price-fixing through the use of ethical standards. Others have attempted to determine the price of services indirectly by using formulas and relative value scales. For example, some medical organizations have determined that a given medical procedure would be allocated a relative value on a scale of one to ten. Open-heart surgery might be labeled a nine and an appendectomy a three. All members of the profession would then use these values in determining professional fees. Such attempts have been uniformly held to be illegal.

The case which follows is typical of those in which an ethical standard came into conflict with the Sherman Act's ban on limiting competition. Although such ethical standards are not illegal per se, they are nevertheless anticompetitive and a violation of the Sherman Act. Although not a form of price-fixing, the ethical standards in this case prevented price competition.

NATIONAL SOCIETY OF PROFESSIONAL ENGINEERS v. U.S.
98 S.Ct. 1355 (1978)

FACTS

The National Society of Professional Engineers adopted a rule in its code of ethics which prohibited competitive bidding by members. This was done to minimize the risk that competition would result in inferior engineering work which would endanger the public safety. The United States brought a civil suit to nullify the canon of ethics.

ISSUE

Is the canon a violation of Section 1 of the Sherman Act?

DECISION

Yes.

REASONS

1. The act does not require competitive bidding; it prohibits unreasonable restraints on competition.
2. It is the restraint that must be justified under the rule of reason. Petitioner's attempt to do so on the basis of the potential threat that competition poses to the public safety and the ethics of its profession is nothing less than a frontal assault on the basic policy of the Sherman Act.
3. Even assuming occasional exceptions to the presumed consequences of competition, the statutory policy precludes inquiry into the question of whether competition is good or bad.

---

3 RESALE PRICE MAINTENANCE: VERTICAL PRICE-FIXING

Manufacturers sometimes seek to control the ultimate retail price for their products. These efforts result in part from the desire to maintain a high-quality product image, the assumption being that a relatively high price establishes quality. These efforts are also based on a desire to maintain adequate channels of distribution. If one retailer is selling a product at prices significantly below those of other retailers, there is a strong likelihood that the other retailers will not continue to carry the product.

At one time, retail price maintenance was based on state fair trade laws. Congress had authorized states to enact fair trade laws as an exception to the Sherman Act. These fair trade laws allowed manufacturers to enter into contracts with one or more retailers, setting the minimum price for products. The provisions of these contracts were then binding on all sellers in that state, and in effect nonsigners of the contract could not sell below the agreed-upon price without being in breach of contract. In the 1970s, the fair trade exception to the Sherman Act was repealed, and state fair trade laws and the contracts entered into pursuant to them were thus illegal.

Although most **resale price-maintenance** schemes run afoul of the Sherman Act, it is possible for a manufacturer to effectively control the resale price of its products. The primary method of legally controlling the retail price is for a manufacturer to simply announce its prices and refuse to deal with those who fail to comply. This practice is commonly referred to as the **Colgate Doctrine.** The Colgate Doctrine recognizes that independent action by a manufacturer is not a per se violation of the Sherman Act. The *Monsanto* case on page 564 illustrated that although price-fixing is illegal per se, there must be concerted action and not simply a refusal to deal with distributors who do not comply with the announced price policy. The Colgate Doctrine will justify resale price maintenance only if there is no coercion or pressure other than the announced policy and its implementation. If the manufacturer sits down with the distributor or retailer and gets an agreement that the parties will comply, then there is a violation of Section 1 of the Sherman Act. The Colgate Doctrine only allows the announcement of prices and refusal to deal with those who do not comply.

Other methods of maintaining retail prices have been attempted. For example, real estate leases and equipment leases sometimes contain provisions allowing the lessor to set the prices to be charged by the lessee. Such leases are illegal because there is usually coercion present. Another example of attempted retail price maintenance is the use of a **consignment** contract. In a consignment, the consignor retains title to the property and the consignee has possession. The consignee is paid a commission if he or she sells the property. Since the property belongs to the consignor, she or he is entitled to determine the price for its product. Art objects and racehorses are frequently sold on consignment. However, the consignment technique may not be used to subvert the antitrust laws, as the following case suggests.

SIMPSON v. UNION OIL CO.
377 U.S. 13 (1964)

FACTS

Union Oil requires lessees of its retail service stations to sign "consignment" agreements which allow Union Oil to set the prices at which the retailer sells gasoline. The agreement provides that title to the gas remain in Union Oil until sold by the retailer and that all property taxes be paid by Union Oil. Retailers were then to be paid by a commission on sales made and had to pay all the costs of operating the station. Simpson, a retailer of Union Oil gasoline, sold gasoline at 2 cents below the price set by Union, and because of this, Union refused to renew his lease. Simpson sued for triple damages, claiming the consignment contract violated the Sherman Act.

ISSUE

Is the consignment agreement illegal under the Sherman Act?

DECISION

Yes.

REASONS

1. Section 1 of the Sherman Act prohibits most resale price-maintenance agreements.
2. Although consignment agreements serve useful purposes, they only control and allocate the risks and rights between the parties and do not necessarily control the rights of others. Therefore, no matter how lawful it is under private contract law, a consignment agreement must comply with federal antitrust policy.
3. Dealers are independent businesspeople—they have all characteristics of entrepreneurs except setting prices. Their return is affected by the rise and fall of market price. These agreements allow Union Oil to impose noncompetitive prices on retailers by the use of coercive consignments.

Not every consignment of common goods which attempts to control retail price is illegal. For example, a bakery consigned its products to wholesalers under an arrangement by which the bakery fixed the wholesale prices to be paid by retailers who receive the goods from the distributors. This was not a violation. The case was distinguishable from *Simpson v. Union Oil Co.* The prices were wholesale prices, and the bakery bore the burden of risk during the consignment period.

Whether or not *vertical price-fixing* should be illegal per se has been a matter of debate among economists and politicians. There is a possibility that a vertical restraint imposed by a single manufacturer or wholesaler may stimulate interbrand competition as it reduces intrabrand competition. Nevertheless, Congress in 1984 adopted a resolution condemning vertical price-fixing. The resolution indicated Congress's attitude that vertical price-fixing is just as bad as horizontal price-fixing and, therefore, should be illegal per se. Since Congress has spoken, vertical price-fixing is just as illegal as horizontal price-fixing.

4 CONCERTED ACTIVITIES BY COMPETITORS

Concerted activities among competitors take a variety of forms and appear in diverse circumstances. Some arise out of a desire to protect a channel of distribution or a marketing system. Others result from attempts to keep marginal competitors in business, which is, in fact, one goal of the antitrust laws. Thus, some cases dealing with concerted activities actually involve conflicts between various competing goals of the antitrust laws.

In the next case, the concerted activity among competitors took the form of an exchange of price information. Economic theory was used to support the assumption that prices would be more unstable and lower if the information had not been exchanged. Conduct directed at price stabilization is per se anticompetitive.

UNITED STATES v. CONTAINER CORPORATION OF AMERICA
89 S.Ct. 510 (1969)

FACTS

Manufacturers of corrugated containers entered into an agreement whereby each one agreed to exchange information upon request as to the most recent price charged or quoted to a consumer. The government brought a civil antitrust action, claiming that this agreement was price-fixing in violation of Section 1 of the Sherman Act.

ISSUE

Is an agreement to exchange price information a violation of the Sherman Act?

DECISION

Yes.

REASONS

1. The exchange of price information has the effect of keeping prices within a fairly narrow range.
2. Stabilization of prices as well as raising them is in violation of Section 1 of the Sherman Act.

Typical of the cases involving concerted activities was a 1981 suit filed against the National Association of Broadcasters, charging that its "overcommercialization" rules improperly regulated the amount and format of advertising on television, which was in violation of the Sherman Act. The code had the effect of curtailing and restricting the quantity of broadcast time available for television advertising and the number and format of advertisements that could be broadcast. The challenged rules put varying limits on the amount of "nonprogram material" aired every hour. In prime time, the hourly limit was nine and one-half minutes, plus thirty seconds for promotional announcements. At other times, it was generally sixteen minutes; however, children's shows were allowed nine and one-half minutes on weekends and twelve minutes during the week. Other rules limited the number of consecutive announcements and the number of interruptions within programs. A consent decree was entered which stopped the practice. The rules on the number of broadcasts were not per se violations. However, a rule prohibiting more than one product being advertised in a commercial lasting less than sixty seconds was a per se violation.

In 1984, the televising of college football games was the subject matter of a significant antitrust suit. It was filed by two football powers, the University of Georgia and the University of Oklahoma. The case has had a significant impact on college football and on the revenues that support college athletics.

NATIONAL COLLEGIATE ATHLETIC ASSOCIATION v. BOARD OF REGENTS OF THE UNIVERSITY OF OKLAHOMA AND UNIVERSITY OF GEORGIA ATHLETIC ASSOCIATION
104 S.Ct. 272 (1984)

FACTS

The National Collegiate Athletic Association (NCAA) adopted a plan for the televising of college football games for the 1982–1985 seasons. The plan was intended to reduce the adverse effect of live television upon football game attendance. It limited the total amount of televised football games and the number of games that any one college could televise. No member of the NCAA was permitted to make any sale of television rights, except in accordance with the plan. The NCAA had agreements with ABC and CBS which granted each network the right to telecast games for a specified "minimum aggregate compensation" to the participating NCAA members.

The College Football Association (CFA) was organized to promote the interests of major football-playing colleges within the NCAA structure. Its members claimed that they should have a greater voice in the formulation of football television policy than they had in the NCAA. The CFA accordingly negotiated a contract with NBC that would have allowed a more liberal number of television appearances for each college and would have increased the revenues realized by CFA members. In response, the NCAA announced that it would take disciplinary action against any CFA member that complied with the CFA-NBC contract. Two universities that belonged to both the NCAA and CFA then filed suit to enjoin such action, contending that the plan violated Section 1 of the Sherman Act.

ISSUE

Does the NCAA plan controlling college football violate the Sherman Act?

DECISION

Yes.

REASONS

1. Competition in "live" college football television was restrained in three ways: (*a*) the NCAA fixed the price for particular telecasts; (*b*) its exclusive network contracts were tantamount to a group boycott of all other potential broadcasters, and its threat of sanctions against its members constituted a threatened boycott of potential competitors; and (*c*) its plan placed an artificial limit on the production of televised college football.
2. The activity is not illegal per se, even though it involves horizontal price-fixing. It is subject to the rule of reason, because some horizontal restraint is essential if the product is to be available at all.
3. The NCAA television plan raised prices and reduced output without regard to consumer preference. No affirmative defense was established to justify these restraints.
4. The NCAA plan did not protect live attendance, since games could be televised during all hours that college football games are played. Moreover, by seeking to insulate live ticket sales from the full spectrum of competition because of its assumption that the product itself is insufficiently attractive to draw live attendance when faced with competition from televised games, the NCAA forwarded a justification that is inconsistent with the Sherman Act's basic policy. The rule of reason does not support a defense based on the assumption that competition itself is unreasonable.
5. The NCAA asserted as a further justification for its television plan that it had an interest in maintaining a competitive balance among amateur athletic teams; however, this was not related to any neutral standard or to any readily identifiable group of competitors. The television plan was not even arguably tailored to serve such an interest. It did not regulate the amount of money that any college may spend on its football program or the way the colleges may use their football program revenues; instead, it simply imposed a restriction on one source of revenue that is more important to some colleges than to others. There is no evidence that such restriction produces any greater measure of equality throughout the NCAA than would a restriction on alumni donations, tuition rates, or any other revenue-producing activity.

5 JOINT OPERATIONS

Competitors sometimes attempt to share some activities or join together in the performance of some function. Joint research efforts to find a cure for cancer or to find substitutes for gasoline would seem to provide significant benefits to society. A sharing of technology may be beneficial also. Joint efforts in other areas may reduce costs and improve efficiency. For example, several professional football teams share the information of a college scouting organization. This practice is currently being challenged in the courts by the players' association. Joint operations may violate the Sherman Act, as the following case illustrates.

CITIZEN PUBLISHING CO. ET AL. v. UNITED STATES
89 S.Ct. 927 (1969)

FACTS

The only two daily newspapers of general circulation in Tucson, Arizona, the *Citizen* and the *Star,* signed a joint operating agreement. Under this agreement, each paper retained its own news and editorial department and its corporate identity. Tucson News, Inc. (TNI), owned equally by both parties, was formed to manage all other departments for each paper. The agreement eliminated competition between the parties through three control devices: (*a*) *price-fixing*—distribution, sales and placement of advertising were all handled by TNI, while subscription and advertising rates were set jointly; (*b*) *profit pooling*—all profits were commingled and distributed pursuant to an agreed ratio; and (*c*) *market control*—neither paper nor its stockholders could engage in the other competing business, that is, publishing, in the Tucson metropolitan area. The United States brought suit, charging unreasonable restraint of trade or commerce in violation of the Sherman Act.

ISSUE

Does the joint operating agreement violate the Sherman Act?

DECISION

Yes.

REASONS

1. Price-fixing is illegal per se.
2. Profit pooling at a set ratio reduces, and possibly eliminates, incentive to compete, violating the Sherman Act.
3. The market control arrangement is a "division of fields," prohibited by the Sherman Act.
4. The failing-company defense, held to permit otherwise illegal mergers, is unavailable here since neither the *Star* nor the *Citizen* were in immediate danger of going out of business.

5. The First Amendment is not involved, for there is no regulation of news gathering or dissemination. In fact, freedom of the press is being protected from undue restraints on competition.

6 AGREEMENTS RELATING TO TERRITORY

Territorial agreements may be either horizontal or vertical. A horizontal agreement would be entered into by a group of similar businesses for the purpose of giving each an exclusive territory. For example, if all Oldsmobile dealers in state X agreed to allocate each an exclusive territory, a horizontal arrangement would exist. It would be illegal per se under the Sherman Act. This is true even if the arrangement is made by a third party. For example, an agreement among competing cable television operators to divide the market in Houston, Texas, was a per se violation, even though the agreement required city council approval.

A vertical agreement is one between a manufacturer and a dealer or distributor. It assigns the dealer or distributor an exclusive territory, and the manufacturer agrees not to sell to other dealers or distributors in that territory in exchange for an agreement by the dealer that it will not operate outside the area assigned. Such agreements are usually part of a franchise or license agreement, and while they are not per se violations, they may nevertheless be illegal. The case which follows explains why such agreements are subject to the rule of reason.

CONTINENTAL T.V., INC. v. GTE SYLVANIA, INC.
97 S.Ct. 2549 (1977)

FACTS

The defendant, a manufacturer of television sets, marketed its products through a retail franchise system that required franchisees to sell its products only from the locations at which it was franchised. The plaintiff, a disenchanted franchisee, claimed that defendant had violated Section 1 of the Sherman Act by entering into and enforcing these agreements.

ISSUE

Are territorial restrictions per se violations?

DECISION

No.

REASONS

1. Territorial restrictions are subject to the rule of reason.
2. Vertical restrictions reduce intrabrand competition but promote interbrand competition. As such, inquiries as to the harm, if any, on competition are required.

3. There was also no evidence that the vertical restrictions in this case are likely to have a pernicious effect on competition.

A vertical territorial restriction may be illegal and may result in the awarding of triple damages. If a plaintiff can establish that the interbrand market structure is such that intrabrand competition is a critical source of competitive pressure on price, a plaintiff may recover triple damages. The plaintiff is required to show the nature and effect of the territorial restriction were it to adversely affect market competition.

MONOPOLY

7 SECTION 2: THE RATIONALE

Competition tends to keep private markets working in ways that are socially desirable. It encourages an efficient allocation of resources, stimulates efficiency and product innovation, and may even encourage the conservation of scarce resources. Competition also tends to limit private economic power and substitutes individual decisions for government regulation. Of course, a competitive system that allows easy entry and withdrawal from the marketplace is consistent with individual freedom and economic opportunity. Therefore, it is not surprising that the Sherman Act attacks monopoly and attempts to monopolize.

In *United States v. Aluminum Company of America*[1] Circuit Judge Learned Hand commented on the purposes and philosophy of Section 2 of the Sherman Act. In holding that Alcoa was guilty of a violation of Section 2 for having intentionally acquired and maintained control of over 90 percent of the domestic "virgin" ingot market in aluminum, even though Alcoa had not misused such monopoly power to obtain exorbitant profits, Judge Hand said:

> ...it is no excuse for "monopolizing" a market that the monopoly has not been used to extract from the consumer more than a "fair" profit. The Act has wider purposes. Indeed, even though we disregard all but economic considerations, it would by no means follow that such concentration of producing power is to be desired, when it has not been used extortionately. Many people believe that possession of unchallenged economic power deadens initiative, discourages thrift and depresses energy; that immunity from competition is a narcotic, and rivalry is a stimulant, to industrial progress; that the spur of constant stress is necessary to counteract an inevitable disposition to let well enough alone. Such people believe that competitors, versed in the craft as no consumer can be, will be quick to detect opportunities for saving and new shifts in production, and be eager to profit by them. In any event the mere fact that a producer, having command of

[1]148 F.2d 416 (1945).

the domestic market, has not been able to make more than a "fair" profit, is no evidence that a "fair" profit could not have been made at lower prices.... True, it might have been thought adequate to condemn only those monopolies which could not show that they had exercised the highest possible ingenuity, had adopted every possible economy, had anticipated every conceivable improvement, stimulated every possible demand. No doubt, that would be one way of dealing with the matter, although it would imply constant scrutiny and constant supervision, such as courts are unable to provide. Be that as it may, that was not the way that Congress chose; it did not condone "good trusts" and condemn "bad" ones; it forbade all. Moreover, in so doing, it was not necessarily actuated by economic motives alone. It is possible, because of its indirect social or moral effect, to prefer a system of small producers, each dependent for his success upon his own skill and character, to one in which the great mass of those engaged must accept the direction of a few....

Judge Hand indicated that, besides the economic reasons behind the Sherman Act's proscription of monopoly,

...there are others, based upon the belief that great industrial consolidations are inherently undesirable, regardless of their economic results. In the debates in Congress Senator Sherman himself...showed that among the purposes of Congress in 1890 was a desire to put an end to great aggregations of capital because of the helplessness of the individual before them....Throughout the history of these statutes it has been constantly assumed that one of their purposes was to perpetuate and preserve, for its own sake and in spite of possible cost, an organization of industry in small units, which can effectively compete with each other....

In 1958, Justice Black in *Northern Pacific Ry. Co. v. United States,* 356 U.S. 1, discussed the purpose of the Sherman Act. He stated in part:

The Sherman Act was designed to be a comprehensive charter of economic liberty aimed at preserving free and unfettered competition as the rule of trade. It rests on the premise that the unrestrained interaction of competitive forces will yield the best allocation of our economic resources, the lowest prices, the highest quality and the greatest material progress, while at the same time providing an environment conducive to the preservation of our democratic political and social institutions.

8 SECTION 2: THE APPROACH

Under Section 2, it is a violation for a firm to: (1) monopolize, (2) attempt to monopolize, or (3) conspire to monopolize any part of interstate or foreign commerce. Attempts to monopolize cases require proof of intent to destroy competition or achieve monopoly power. This is most difficult and, as a result, there have been few cases concerning attempts to monopolize. A conspiracy to monopolize requires proof of specific intent to monopolize and at least one overt act to accomplish it. Proof of monopoly power or even that it was attainable is not required. This conspiracy theory is usually joined with the allegation of actual monopoly in most cases.

A firm has violated Section 2 if it followed a course of conduct through which it obtained the power to control price or exclude competition. The mere possession of monopoly power is not a violation. There must be proof that the power resulted from a deliberate course of conduct or proof of intent to maintain the power by conduct. Proof of deliberateness is just as essential as is proof of the power to control price to exclude competition.

Section 2 Sherman Act cases require proof of market power—the power to affect the price of the firm's products in the market. Whether such power exists is usually determined by an analysis of the reaction of buyers to price changes by the alleged monopolist seller. Such cases require a definition of the relevant market and a study of the degree of concentration within the market. Barriers to entry are analyzed, and the greater the barriers, the greater the significance of market share. The legal issues in such cases require structural analysis.

In defining the relevant market, the courts examine both product market and geographic market. A relevant market is the smallest one wide enough so that products from outside the geographic area or from other producers in the same area cannot compete with those included in the defined relevant market. In other words, if prices are raised or supply is curtailed within a given area while demand remains constant, will products from other areas or other products from within the area enter the market in enough quantity to force a lower price or increased supply?

Some monopoly cases involve homogeneous products, whereas others involve products for which there are numerous substitutes. For example, aluminum may be considered a product that is generally homogeneous. If a firm has 90 percent of the virgin aluminum market, a violation would be established. However, if a firm had 90 percent of the Danish coffeecake market, the decision is less clear, because numerous products compete with Danish coffee cakes as a breakfast product. The relevant product is often difficult to define because of differences in products, substitute products, product diversification, and even product clusters.

UNITED STATES v. GRINNELL CORPORATION
86 S.Ct. 1698 (1966)

FACTS

The government filed a civil suit under Section 2 of the Sherman Act, claiming Grinnell Corporation had a monopoly over the central station hazard-detecting devices. These are security devices to prevent burglary and to detect fires. They involve electronic notification of the police and fire departments at a central location. Grinnell, through three separate companies, controlled 87 percent of that business. It argued that it faces competition from other modes of protection from burglary, and therefore it did not have monopoly power.

ISSUE

Did Grinnell violate the Sherman Act?

DECISION

Yes.

REASONS

1. Grinnell has monopoly power in the market with 87 percent control if the proper market was chosen. The geographic market is the nation. The product market is central station hazard-detecting systems.
2. The court must consider whether there are "substitutes" that should be considered in determination of market share. None of the substitutes for the accredited central station service meet the interchangeability test.
3. The market power was achieved by unlawful and exclusionary practices that establish the violation.

Section 2 cases may involve a variety of proofs and many different forms of economic analysis. The degree of market concentration, barriers to entry, structural features such as market shares of other firms, profit levels, the extent to which prices respond to changes in supply and demand, whether or not a firm discriminates in price between its customers, and the absolute size of the firm are all factors usually considered by courts in monopoly cases. In addition, courts examine the conduct of the firm. How did it achieve its market share? Was it by internal growth or acquisition? Does the firm's current conduct tend to injure competition? These and other issues are important aspects in any finding of the existence of monopoly power. Note that in the case which follows the illegal conduct was the failure to cooperate with a competitor. This conduct was designed to eliminate the competitor, and it resulted in liability for triple damages.

ASPEN SKIING CO. v. ASPEN HIGHLANDS SKIING CORP.
105 S.Ct. 2847 (1985)

FACTS

Plaintiff owns one of the four major mountain facilities for downhill skiing at Aspen, Colo. It filed a triple-damage suit against the defendant, which owns the other three major facilities, alleging a violation of Section 2 of the Sherman Act. In the early years of Aspen skiing, there were three major facilities operated by three independent companies, including these parties. Each competitor offered both its own tickets for daily use of a mountain and an interchangeable six-day, all-Aspen ticket, which provided convenience to skiers who wanted flexibility as to what mountain they might ski each day. The defendant acquired the second of the three original facilities and opened a fourth. It also offered a weekly multiarea ticket which covered only its mountains, but eventually the all-Aspen ticket outsold the multiarea ticket. Over the years, the method for allocation of revenues from the all-Aspen ticket to the competitors developed into a system based on random-sample surveys to determine the number of skiers who used each mountain. However, for the 1977–1978 ski season, plaintiff was required to accept a fixed percentage of the ticket's revenues as a condition of defendant's participation. When plaintiff refused to accept a lower percentage for the next season—considerably below its historical average, based on usage—defendant discontinued its sale of the all-Aspen ticket; instead, the defendant sold six-day tickets which covered only its own mountains, and took additional actions that made it extremely difficult for plaintiff to market its own multiarea package to replace the joint offering. Plaintiff's share of the market declined steadily thereafter.

ISSUE

Is this a violation of Section 2 of the Sherman Act?

DECISION

Yes.

REASONS

1. Although even a firm with monopoly power has no general duty to engage in a joint marketing program with a competitor, the absence of an unqualified duty to cooperate does not mean that every time a firm declines to participate in a particular cooperative venture, that decision may not have evidentiary significance, or that it may not give rise to liability in certain circumstances.
2. The question of intent is relevant to the offense of monopolization in determining whether the challenged conduct is fairly characterized as "exclusionary," "anticompetitive," or "predatory." In this case, the monopolist elected to make an important change in a pattern of distribution of all-Aspen tickets that had originated in a competitive market and had persisted for several years.
3. It must be assumed that the jury concluded that there were no "valid business reasons" for defendant's refusal to deal with plaintiff.
4. The evidence showed that, over the years, skiers developed a strong demand for the all-Aspen ticket, and that they were adversely affected by its elimination.
5. Plaintiff was injured by the steady decline of its share of the relevant market after the ticket was terminated.

As previously noted, proof of monopoly power alone is not enough. Some monopolies are lawful. If monopoly power is "thrust upon" a firm or if it exists because of a patent or franchise, there is no violation of Section 2 if the firm does not engage in conduct that has the effect or purpose of protecting, enforcing, or extending the monopoly power. The power must either have been acquired or used in ways that go beyond normal, honest industrial business conduct for a violation to exist. In other words, the power must have been *deliberatively* acquired or used. A firm is guilty of monopolization when it acquires or maintains monopoly power by a course of deliberate conduct that keeps other firms from entering the market or from expanding their share of it. Deliberativeness is not difficult to prove in most cases.

Conduct that proves deliberativeness may be anything in restraint of trade. For example, predatory conduct would prove deliberativeness. Conduct which is exclusionary in purpose and effect will also do so. For example, if a firm through its leases tends to exclude its competitors from a market, the case is made, even though the conduct is less than predatory. In some cases, the courts have concluded that proof of monopoly power creates a prima facie case. If the firm seeks to deny that power was deliberately achieved or maintained, it may rebut the presumption by proving that power is attributable solely to a reason that is not illegal or against public policy. For example, proof that power arose from a patent or franchise would rebut the presumption.

Monopolistic conduct is often described as predatory. "Predatory" means that a firm seeks to advance its market share by injuring its actual or potential competitors by means other than improved performance. It may be for the purpose of driving out competitors, for keeping them out, or for making them less effective. Pricing policies are frequently examined for proof of predatory conduct. Profit-maximizing pricing; limit pricing, whereby the price is limited to levels that tend to discourage entry; and the practice of price discrimination all may tend to prove monopoly power and predatory conduct.

WILLIAM INGLIS & SONS BAKING CO., ET AL. v. ITT CONTINENTAL BAKING CO., INC., ET AL.

668 F.2d 1014 (9th Cir. 1981)

FACTS

Inglis was a family-owned bakery, manufacturing and distributing rolls in northern California. Continental is a national wholesale bakery, operating in part in northern California, competing with Inglis. Both companies marketed their products under "private" and "advertised" labels, the principal difference being the higher price of advertised labels. Inglis filed suit for triple damages, alleging that Continental had engaged in discriminatory and below-cost pricing for its private label bread in an effort to eliminate competition in the northern California market. Continental argued that its pricing fluctuations were necessitated by overall market conditions and that it reduced its prices in response to competitors lowering their prices. Continental also claimed that various retail stores, such as Safeway, were establishing their own bakeries, increasing an already highly competitive situation.

ISSUE

Was there sufficient evidence for a jury to find that Continental had engaged in discriminatory and below-cost pricing for the purpose of eliminating competition and attempting to monopolize the wholesale bread market in northern California?

DECISION

Yes.

REASONS

1. To find an "attempt to monopolize" in violation of Section 2 of the Sherman Act, a court must find:
   a Specific intent to control prices or destroy competition in commerce
   b Predatory or anticompetitive conduct aimed at accomplishing this unlawful purpose
   c Dangerous probability of success
2. To establish the fact of predatory pricing, a plaintiff must prove that the defendant lowered prices below costs to reduce or eliminate competition with the intent to then raise costs to experience long-term benefits for itself. In addition, the defendant must have had no sufficient justification for such low pricing outside of reducing competition.
3. Here, a jury could reasonably conclude that Continental had lowered its prices below cost in an effort to eliminate competition.

9 ETHICAL CONSIDERATIONS

The antitrust violations discussed in this chapter raise several ethical questions which are coextensive with or complementary to the legal issues involved. Is it ethical to develop or to enforce a code of professional ethics running counter to the requirements of the law? What are the ethical implications of retaining corporate executive officers who are found guilty of price-fixing?

Formal Code of Ethics

The first question—can a code of ethics be unethical?—must be answered affirmatively. It is clear that a law can be unethical, such as one stating that all people of a certain race may not own property or have civil rights, or that human slaves may be bought and sold. One can imagine scores of examples of possible laws which would violate commonly accepted ideas of what is right. But one hopes that a democratic approach to creation of law prevents such "unethical" law, or stated another way, that the law encourages or at least tolerates ethical behavior.

A code of ethics derived by any group to affect or control the conduct of group members is akin to private law. It is the group's opinion of proper conduct within the group's domain. It is possible for any code of conduct, even one labeled a code of ethics, to sanction acts contrary to law or to the ethics of society as a whole. Thus, we see professional groups in both the *Goldfarb* and *National Society of Professional Engineers* cases discussed in section 2 laying down standards of professional conduct which are anticompetitive in the extreme. By preventing price competition, the conduct encouraged as "ethical" for both attorneys and engineers amounted to unreasonable restraints of trade in violation of Section 1 of the Sherman Act. One suspects that these "ethical" approaches to "professional competition" were designed and used less to protect the public from shoddy work and more to protect the professionals from the rigors of the marketplace. Whether or not a conscious decision has been made to avoid the obligations imposed by law or ethics, a group's code which abrogates standards established by society at large is subject to legal challenge, social criticism, or both.

Informal Codes of Ethics

Whether or not a corporation creates a formal code of ethics, it has one. If found nowhere else, a code is established by the activities encouraged (or condoned by inaction) in the corporate hierarchy. The ethical attitudes and sensitivities of the corporation's leaders appear to be crucial in determining the ethical character of a corporation. Consider, for example, why price-fixing by competitors in industry has been so common. An alarmingly high percentage of both large and small businesses has engaged in price-fixing at various times in the more than ninety years it has been a crime. Companies prominent both nationally and in their respective industries have been convicted of it. Some have even been regular, repeat offenders. It has been estimated that price-fixing costs consumers $60 billion annually. Like other crimes committed for corporate rather than direct personal gain, price-fixing has soiled businesses' general reputation and depressed public confidence in executives. So why have price-fixing violations continued? Until recently, the profits to be made through price-fixing were often high compared to the risks of being caught or the penalties imposed. Today's threat of triple damage actions together with greater criminal fines and the likelihood of prison terms may counterbalance the economic incentives to conspire with competitors. Of course, many factors contribute to price-fixing, including similarities of products sold, degree of price competition, profit margins, the industry's production capacity, character of market demand, and the level in the corporation where prices are determined. The most important determinant may be whether the company treats price-fixing as improper conduct. Is there emphasis on short-run returns and an uncaring attitude about how those profits are achieved? Is there formal, or even informal, training about what market conduct is approved and what is prohibited by the company? Are executives or other employees convicted of price-fixing discharged or allowed to resign, or are they welcomed back to the corporate bosom with open arms? If employees who violate the law "on behalf of" the corporation are treated differently from those who violate the law "against" the corporation (embezzlement), a message is being sent through the corporate structure that criminal conduct on behalf of the company will be tolerated.

Internal Sanctions

If a company were serious about not price-fixing, it would act as though it meant it by imposing corporate penalties for price-fixing. Law compliance programs and training to help employees deal with ethical dilemmas would also affirm the corporation's attitude toward misconduct. However, a real threat to job security for price-fixers might go further than any education program or code of ethics ever could. Giving lip service to corporate integrity while at the same time tolerating unlawful conduct to reach a profit on the bottom line signifies either corporate hypocrisy or blindness. Either leads one to the conclusion that the company is ethically insensitive.

10 CATERPILLAR CODE OF COMPETITION

As an illustration of a corporate statement concerning competitive conduct, the following detailed provision of the Caterpillar code is included. It should be noted that Caterpillar appears to be using United States law to establish ethical norms for its conduct throughout the world.

Competitive Conduct

Fair competition is fundamental to the free enterprise system. We support laws prohibiting restraints of trade, unfair practices, or abuse of economic power. And we avoid such practices everywhere—including areas of the world where laws don't prohibit them.

In large companies like Caterpillar, particular care must be exercised to avoid practices which seek to increase sales by any means other than fair merchandising efforts based on quality, design features, productivity, price, and product support.

In relationships with competitors, dealers, suppliers, and customers, Caterpillar employees are directed to avoid arrangements restricting our ability to compete with others—or the ability of any other business organization to compete freely and fairly with us, and with others.

There must be no arrangements or understandings, with competitors, affecting prices, terms upon which products are sold, or the number and type of products manufactured or sold—or which might be construed as dividing customers or sales territories with a competitor.

In the course of our business, we may sell engines and other items to companies which are also competitors in other product areas. Related information from such customers will be treated with the same care we would expect Caterpillar data to be accorded, in a similar situation.

Relationships with dealers are established in the Caterpillar dealership agreements. These embody our commitment to fair competitive practices, and reflect customs and laws of various countries where Caterpillar products are sold. Our obligations under these agreements are to be scrupulously observed.

Caterpillar aims to increase its sales—to excel and lead. We intend to do this through superior technical skill, efficient operations, sound planning, and effective merchandising.

We believe that fair competition is good for the marketplace, customers and Caterpillar.

REVIEW QUESTIONS

1 Doctors in a county medical society fixed *maximum* fees to be charged patients for various medical services. Arizona filed suit to enjoin the use of maximum fee schedules. What was the result? Why?

2 National associations of repossessors established fee schedules to be used in charging for their services. Repossessors were to be hired by lenders such as automobile dealers to take possession of items that were bought with loans that were later defaulted. The Justice Department sought to enjoin the use of the fee schedules. What was the result? Why?

3 Members of a real estate brokers' association voted to raise their commission rate from 6 to 7 percent. The bylaws of the association provided for expulsion of any member charging less than the agreed-upon commission. If broker X continues to charge 6 percent, can she be expelled legally? Why, or why not?

4 A cemetary required all customers purchasing grave lots to purchase burial vaults. Is this a violation of any law? Explain.

5 Under Blue Shield's prepaid dental services plan, dentists become participants by agreeing to accept reimbursement from Blue Shield, but the plan limits reimbursement to a percentage of the usual charges of dentists. Subscribers are permitted to use nonparticipating dentists, who can charge them the difference between what Blue Shield will pay and what the dentists charge. This practice is known as balance billing. Participating dentists agree not to engage in that practice. As a result, a participating dentist agrees to sell services at a discount. The benefits of becoming a participating dentist are direct payment from Blue Shield and increased patronage from Blue Shield subscribers who seek to avoid balance billing. A dental organization encouraged its members not to participate in the plan. Is this a violation of the antitrust laws? Why, or why not?

6 A New York statute provided that liquor retailers must charge at least 112 percent of the wholesaler's "posted" bottle price in effect at the time the retailer sells or offers to sell the item. The law did not provide for active supervision by the state itself. A retailer challenged the validity of the state law. (*a*) What theory will support the challenge? (*b*) What defense will be asserted? Decide the case.

7 The American Society of Anesthesiologists has an ethical standard which prevents its member doctors from working for salaries at hospitals. It insists on fee-for-service arrangements. Is such a standard a violation of the Sherman Act? Explain.

8 There was a contract between the manufacturer of paint and a retailer of paint in which they agreed not to compete on the retail level. Is this a per se violation of the Sherman Act? Why, or why not?

9 Assume that all the producers of a product agree to limit their advertising budgets to 10 percent of gross sales. The resultant savings is used to reduce the price of the product to the consumer. Is the agreement legal? Explain.

10 An association of real estate brokers which operated a multiple-listing service denied membership to part-time brokers. Zippy filed suit against the association, contending the denial was a violation of the antitrust laws. What was the result? Why?

11 Standard Oil entered into exclusive-supply contracts with the operators of 5,937 independent retail service stations in seven western states. In these contracts,

the dealers had agreed to purchase from Standard Oil not only all of their requirements for petroleum products but also all of their tubes, tires, and batteries. Are these "T.B.A," contracts illegal? Why, or why not?

12 A shopping center leased a service-station location to a major oil company. The lease contained a provision that the lessor would not lease any other part of the shopping center for use as a service station. Does the lease violate the Sherman Act? Why, or why not?

13 A buying association for small- and medium-sized regional supermarket chains allocated territories to its members in which they had exclusive or de factor exclusive licenses to sell the association's private-label brands, and a veto over admission of new members. No price-fixing was involved. It was contended that such practices actually increase competition by enabling members of the association to compete successfully with larger regional and national chains. Is this arrangement a violation of the Sherman Act? Why, or why not?

14 A newspaper publisher produced the only paper serving a three-county area. It informed all of its advertisers that they must boycott the local radio station before the newspaper would sell them advertising space. Is this a Sherman Act violation? Why, or why not?

CHAPTER 23

CLAYTON ACT AND FTC ACT ENFORCEMENT

OVERVIEW

In 1914, Congress decided to make the Sherman Act more specific. It did so by enacting the Clayton Act. This chapter is primarily concerned with three provisions of the Clayton Act—Section 2 on price discrimination, Section 3 on tying and exclusive contracts, and Section 7 on mergers and acquisitions. There will also be a brief discussion of Section 8 on interlocking directorates.

Congress also in 1914 adopted the FTC Act which created the FTC as an administrative agency to assist the Justice Department in enforcing the antitrust laws. This chapter will discuss this role of the FTC.

Section 2 of the Clayton Act, which deals with the subject of price discrimination, was amended in 1936 by a statute known as the Robinson-Patman Act. The materials in this chapter dealing with price discrimination are based on that statute. The basic goal of the Robinson-Patman amendment is to ensure that all retailers can buy a manufacturer's goods at the same price.

Section 3 of the Clayton Act seeks to preserve competition by limiting special contractual arrangements whereby the effect may be substantially to lessen competition. These special arrangements include contracts which seek to connect one product with another, contracts which contain reciprocal arrangements in which each party is a buyer and a seller, and provisions foreclosing buying or selling with others. These latter exclusive-dealing contracts are quite common. In studying the material in this chapter, keep in mind that most violations are subject to the rule of reason, and it is only when coercion or force is present that per se violations may occur.

Section 7 covers a very important area of antitrust—acquisition of one business by another. Such acquisitions may lead to monopoly power or may only involve a lessening of competition. They can make the goals of our competitive economic system difficult to attain.

There are thousands of acquisitions each year, and many involve very large businesses. The extent to which Section 7 is enforced varies from time to time, and its enforcement or lack thereof often has significant economic consequences.

The following legal terms are introduced in this chapter: bank merger acts, conglomerate merger, consolidation, exclusive dealing, failing-company doctrine, geographic extension merger, geographic market, good-faith meeting of competition, greenmail, Herfindahl-Hirschman Index, horizontal merger, interlocking directorates, market extension merger, merger guidelines, potential-entrant doctrine, predatory pricing, price discrimination, product extension merger, product market, reciprocal dealing, Robinson-Patman amendment, shark repellent, tender offer, tying contract, vertical merger, and white knight.

1 INTRODUCTION

After it had been in effect for a time, the Sherman Act was criticized as being inadequate. For one thing, it did little to prevent practices which only tended to reduce competition or which were simply conducive to creating monopolies. As interpreted with the rule of reason, the Sherman Act did not apply to situations likely to lead to the destruction of competition but which fell short of an actual monopoly or combination in unreasonable restraint of trade. Also, the rule of reason and lack of specificity in the Sherman Act practically required that courts decide each alleged violation on its own merits on a case-by-case basis. Also, there were a few interpretations by the courts that were contrary to the will of Congress. For example, the Supreme Court held that the law applied to labor unions.

The foregoing factors led to the passage of the Clayton Act and the Federal Trade Commission Act in 1914. One purpose of the Clayton Act was to exclude labor unions and nonprofit agricultural organizations from the scope of antitrust legislation.

The Clayton Act declares that certain enumerated practices in commerce are illegal. These are practices that might adversely affect competition but which are not clear violations of the Sherman Act. The enumerated practices do not have to actually injure competition to be wrongful; they are outlawed if their effect may substantially lessen competition or tend to create a monopoly. The Clayton Act makes it possible to attack in their incipiency many practices which, if continued, eventually could destroy competition or create monopoly.

The sections of the Clayton Act discussed in detail later in this chapter are:

- Section 2—price discrimination
- Section 3—tying and exclusive contracts
- Section 7—mergers and acquisitions

Section 8 of the Clayton Act also has antitrust significance. It is aimed at **interlocking directorates.** It prohibits a person from being a member of the board of directors of two or more corporations at the same time, when one of them has capital, surplus, and undivided profits which total more than $1 million, where elimination of competition by agreement between such corporations would amount to a violation of any of the antitrust laws.

As corporations have tended to diversify and as the number of conglomerates has increased substantially, it has not been difficult to find some form of competition between two companies which are ostensibly involved in quite different fields. For example, a director on the board of a business which manufactures aluminum who also served on the board of a steel company was found to be in violation, even though the companies are in different industries, because aluminum and steel compete under certain circumstances.

Violations of the original Clayton Act were not crimes, and the act contained no sanction for forfeiture of property. However, it did provide that the Justice Department might obtain injunctions to prevent violations. Those persons injured by a violation could obtain injunctive relief in their own behalf and, in addition, were given the right to collect three times the damages they suffered plus court costs and reasonable attorney's fees. The discussion in Chapter 21 relating to triple damage suits was based on Section 4 of the Clayton Act.

The Clayton Act expanded Sherman Act provisions by allowing private individuals to obtain injunctions in cases of threatened loss due to violations of any of the antitrust laws. It also greatly eased the burden of proof which normally must be shouldered by a plaintiff in triple damage suits. A final decision in favor of the United States to the effect that a defendant has violated the antitrust laws was made prima facie evidence of such violation. This means that if a business is found to be guilty of a Sherman Act violation, a suit for triple damages need not prove violation of the law other than by showing a copy of the court order which finds the defendant guilty.

CLAYTON ACT—SECTION 2

2 HISTORICAL PERSPECTIVE

Section 2 of the Clayton Act as originally adopted in 1914 declared that it is unlawful for a seller to discriminate in the price charged different purchasers of commodities when the effect may be to lessen competition substantially or create a monopoly in any line of commerce. However, "discrimination in price...on account of differences in the grade, quality, or quantity of the commodity sold, or that makes only due allowance for differences in the cost of selling or transportation..." was not illegal. This latter provision so weakened Section 2 that it was very difficult if not impossible to prevent **price discrimination.**

In the 1920s and early 1930s, various techniques such as quantity discounts were used by large-volume retailers, especially chain stores, to obtain more favorable prices than those available to smaller competitors. In addition to obtaining quantity discounts, some large businesses created subsidiary corporations that received brokerage allowances as wholesalers. Another method used by big business to obtain price advantages was demanding and obtaining larger promotional allowances than were given to smaller businesses. The prevalence of the foregoing practices led to the enactment in 1936 of the **Robinson-Patman amendment** to Section 2 of the Clayton Act. This statute attempted to eliminate the advantage that a large buyer could secure over a small buyer solely because of the large buyer's quantity purchasing ability. The legal principles in the sections which follow are based on the Robinson-Patman amendment.

3 PREDATORY PRICING

The Robinson-Patman amendment made it a crime for a seller to sell at lower prices in one geographic area than elsewhere in the United States to eliminate competition or a competitor, or to sell at unreasonably low prices to drive out a competitor. The statutory language declared predatory pricing to be illegal.

Predatory pricing means pricing below marginal cost by a company willing and able to sustain losses for a prolonged period to drive out competition. (It is assumed that the price will later be increased when the competitor is destroyed.) Predatory pricing also involves charging higher prices on some products to subsidize below-cost sales of other products or cutting prices on a product below cost in just one area to wipe out a small local competitor.

Historically, price-cutting was generally deemed predatory when a price was below total costs, including long-term fixed costs. However, some economists have argued that pricing is predatory only if companies slash prices below average variable costs—the short-run expenditures, such as for labor and materials, needed to produce some more units of a product. With long-term fixed costs excluded, prices legally can be cut to a much lower level without the price-cutter being guilty of predatory conduct.

Today a prima facie case of predatory pricing is established by proof that a price is below average variable costs. Such pricing is proof of anticompetitive conduct, unless evidence of justification is admitted to show some other reason for the low price. If a price is below average total costs but above average variable costs, a plaintiff must offer proof that the price has been predatory. Only when prices are below average variable costs is a prima facie case established. As a result of the variable-cost test, many cases which allege predatory pricing do not succeed.

There are several recognized exceptions to the laws prohibiting sales below cost. For example, sales for legitimate purposes, such as for liquidation of excess, obsolete, or perishable merchandise, may be legal, even if the prices used are below unit cost.

4 PRICE DISCRIMINATION

The goal of the Robinson-Patman amendment is to ensure equality of price to all customers of a seller of commodities for resale when the result of unequal treatment may be to lessen competition substantially or tend to create a monopoly in any line of commerce or injure competition with any person. An injury to competition may be established by showing an injury to a competitor victimized by the discrimination. It is a violation to knowingly receive a benefit of such discrimination. Therefore, the law applies to both buyers and sellers. It is just as illegal to receive the benefit of price discrimination as it is to give a lower price to one of two buyers. In price-discrimination cases, a determination of fact is required as to the relevant market and the probable anticompetitive effects of the discrimination. The relevant market determination has two aspects—product market and geographic market.

The Robinson-Patman amendment forbids any person engaged "in commerce" to discriminate in price when the goods involved are for resale. It does not apply to a sale by a retailer to consumers. The term "commerce" is defined as "trade or commerce among the several states and with foreign nations...." This means that the Robinson-Patman amendment extends only to transactions in goods in interstate commerce. It does not extend to transactions that only affect intrastate commerce. In addition, the law is applicable only to the sale of commodities. It does not cover contracts that involve the sale of services or the sale of advertising such as television time.

The law protects competitors from one another. As a general rule, there is no exemption for state purchases to compete with private enterprise. However, the Nonprofit Institutions Act provides that the Robinson-Patman amendment does not apply to purchases of supplies for their own use by schools, colleges, universities, public libraries, churches, hospitals, and charitable institutions not operated for profit. This exemption is limited to goods purchased for their own use. If the goods are resold, there is no governmental exemption.

The Robinson-Patman amendment gives the FTC jurisdiction and authority to regulate quantity discounts. It also proscribes certain hidden or indirect discriminations by sellers in favor of certain buyers. Section 2(c) prohibits an unearned brokerage commission related to a sale of goods. For example, it is unlawful to pay or to receive a commission or discount on sales or purchases except for actual services rendered. Section 2(d) outlaws granting promotional allowances or payments on goods bought for resale unless such allowances are available to all competing customers. For example, a manufacturer who gives a retailer a right to purchase three items for the price of two as part of a special promotion must give the same right to all competitors in the market. Section 2(e) prohibits giving promotional facilities or services on goods bought for resale, unless they are made available to all competing customers. The act does not expressly require that any anticompetitive effects be demonstrated to prove a violation of these provisions.

5 PROOF REQUIRED

Price discrimination is not illegal per se. Only those differences in prices that may adversely affect competition are prohibited. A plaintiff seeking triple damages because of price discrimination must prove that the effect of the discrimination is to injure, destroy, or prevent competition with any person who grants or knowingly receives the benefit of the discrimination, or with customers of either of them. A plaintiff seeking damages for a Robinson-Patman violation must prove actual injury attributable to the violation. It is not enough to prove a price differential, as there are no automatic damages.

J. TRUETT PAYNE CO. v. CHRYSLER MOTORS CORP.
101 S.Ct. 1923 (1981)

FACTS

The plaintiff, a former automobile dealer, brought suit against the defendant automobile manufacturer, alleging that the defendant's "sales incentives" programs over a certain period violated the Robinson-Patman amendment. Under these programs, Chrysler paid a bonus to its dealers if they exceeded their sales quotas. Plaintiff alleged that its quotas were higher than those of its competitors, that it ultimately received fewer bonuses than did its competitors, and that the net effect was that it paid more for its automobiles than did its competitors. It sought as damages the amount of the price difference multiplied by the number of cars purchased.

ISSUE

Is the plaintiff entitled to "automatic damages" upon a showing of a substantial price discrimination?

DECISION

No.

REASONS

1. By its terms, Section 2(a) of the Clayton Act as amended by the Robinson-Patman amendment is a preventative statute. It does not require that the price discrimination must, in fact, have harmed competition.

> 2. In contrast, Section 4 of the Clayton Act is essentially a remedial statute; under it, a plaintiff must make a showing of actual injury attributable to something the antitrust laws were designed to prevent in order to recover treble damages.
> 3. Proof of a violation of Section 2(a) establishes only that injury may result; therefore, proof of a violation does not mean that a disfavored purchaser has been actually "injured" within the meaning of Section 4. A plaintiff must prove more than a violation of Section 2(a). (The Court remanded the case so that the court of appeals could consider the sufficiency of the evidence of injury.)

Plaintiffs can satisfy the injury requirement of the Robinson-Patman amendment in one of two ways. First, they may use a market analysis to show a substantial possibility of injury to competition. Second, they may prove actual injury to a competitor coupled with predatory intent.

Proof of injury to a sole competitor is not enough. If there is no proof of injury to competition, there must be proof of predatory intent. Proof of predatory intent may be by circumstantial evidence.

6 LEVELS OF COMPETITION

Robinson-Patman cases vary somewhat, depending on the level of competition. Courts recognize primary-level cases (competition among sellers); secondary-level cases (competition among customers of sellers); and third-level cases (when there is a wholesaler between the manufacturer and the retailer). Figure 23-1 illustrates these levels.

In primary-level cases, proof of an adverse competitive effect is required. Primary-level cases usually involve territorial price discrimination—the charging of different prices by a multimarket seller in different geographic areas—to drive out its direct competitors. The case which follows illustrates this type of violation.

UTAH PIE CO. v. CONTINENTAL BAKING CO. ET AL.
87 S.Ct. 1326 (1967)

FACTS

The plaintiff, Utah Pie, operated a frozen dessert pie plant in Salt Lake City, selling the pies in Utah and surrounding states. The defendants are larger companies, which market fruit pies and other products on a greater scale than the plaintiff. Each defendant had entered the Salt Lake City frozen pie market before Utah Pie, and supplied the market from their respective California operations. The defendants sold pies cheaper in this market than elsewhere. The plaintiff brought suit, alleging discriminatory pricing schemes designed to lessen competition, which were in violation of the Robinson-Patman amendment.

```
                Manufacturer              Manufacturer
                     X                         Y
```

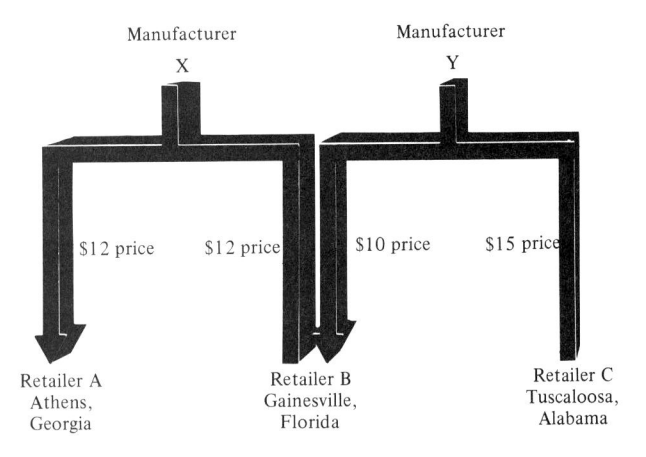

```
    $12 price    $12 price        $10 price      $15 price

   Retailer A    Retailer B      Retailer C
   Athens,       Gainesville,    Tuscaloosa,
   Georgia       Florida         Alabama
```

1. X and Y are primary level competitors. Y's sale to B is a primary line violation.
2. A, B, and C are secondary level competitors. Y's sale to B is also a secondary line violation.
3. If the retailers A, B, and C each purchased the goods through a wholesaler, they would be considered third-level competitors, and the price discrimination would be a third-line violation.

FIGURE 23-1 Levels of Competition: Robinson-Patman Violation Analysis

ISSUE

Is this a Robinson-Patman violation?

DECISION

Yes.

REASONS

1. Each of the defendants reduced the price of frozen dessert pies sold in the Salt Lake City, Utah, market. These prices were invariably lower than prices charged in other markets around the country, even where closer to operation bases.
2. A jury would be justified in finding that these pricing techniques were intended to affect competition in the Utah region in a discriminatory manner, forcing the petitioner to either lower prices itself or lose a percentage of its business.
3. The law protects competitors as well as customers.

In secondary-level competition cases, it is presumed that competition is adversely affected if directly competing customers of manufacturers and producers are charged different prices. Note, this establishes the violation but not the injury. Secondary-level cases require proof that both buyers compete in the same geographic area.

Cases have expanded the levels of competition to include injuries to competitors of the customer of the buyer. In the case which follows, there were actually four levels in the distribution system.

PERKINS v. STANDARD OIL COMPANY OF CALIFORNIA
89 S.Ct. 1871 (1969)

FACTS

Plaintiff was a distributor of oil and gas in Washington. Between 1955 and 1957, the defendant oil company charged the plaintiff a higher price for its gasoline and oil than it charged to its own branded dealers who competed with the plaintiff. The defendant also charged a lower price to Signal Oil, a wholesaler whose gas eventually reached a competitor of Perkins. Perkins sought triple damages for price discrimination.

ISSUES

Is the injury suffered from the discriminatory sales to Signal within the coverage of the act?

DECISION

Yes.

REASONS

1. An injured party may recover damages under the Robinson-Patman amendment if it can show a causal connection between the price discrimination and the injury suffered, regardless of the "level" in the chain of distribution on which the injury occurs.
2. The defendant's conduct is not immunized simply because the product passed through an additional formal exchange before reaching the plaintiff's competitor. The plaintiff's competitive harm is not less because of the presence of an additional link in the distribution chain.

---

7 DEFENSES

The statute recognizes certain exceptions or defenses:

1. Price differentials based on differences in the cost of manufacture, sale, or delivery of commodities are permitted (cost justification defense).
2. Sellers may select their own customers in bona fide transactions and not in restraint of trade.
3. Price changes may be made in response to changing conditions, such as actual or imminent deterioration of perishable goods, obsolescence of seasonal goods, distress sales under court process, or sales in good faith in discontinuance of business in the goods concerned (changing conditions defense).

4 A seller in good faith may meet the equally low price of a competitor (**good-faith meeting-of-competition** defense).

The cost justification defense is used to overcome a prima facie case of price discrimination established by a plaintiff. The burden of showing cost justification is upon the person charged with a violation. The cost justification defense has proved largely illusory in practice. Because of the complexities in determining what is "cost," this defense very rarely was successful in the past. One obvious problem is that of bringing forth acceptable evidence of cost. As a practical matter, proof of cost involves both direct costs and indirect costs. Indirect costs are based on assumptions, and accountants may make different ones. Therefore, there are disputes over the technique to determine actual cost, and proof of it is difficult, if not impossible. The status of the act is such that only the most prosperous and patient business firms can afford pursuit of this often illusory defense.

8 GOOD-FAITH MEETING-OF-COMPETITION DEFENSE

A very important affirmative defense justifying price discrimination is the good-faith meeting of competition. Section 2(b) of the Robinson-Patman amendment permits a defendant to demonstrate that a given price discrimination was not unlawful by "showing that his lower price or the furnishing of services or facilities to any purchaser or purchasers was made in good faith to meet an equally low price of a competitor, or the services or facilities furnished by a competitor." This defense may be established by proof of a price reduction to meet a competitor's price. It may also be established by proof that price was not increased in one market to meet competition in that market when prices were raised in other markets. In other words, the defense may result from active conduct (lowering prices), or it may be passive (not increasing prices).

"Good faith" is not easily defined. It is a flexible and pragmatic, not a technical or doctrinaire, concept. The standard of good faith is simply the standard of the prudent businessperson responding fairly to what he or she reasonably believes is a situation of competitive necessity. The facts and circumstances in each case govern its interpretation and application. Thus, the same method of meeting competition may be consistent with an inference of good faith in some circumstances, inconsistent with such an inference in others.

Although the term "good faith" cannot be quantified, it is clear that this defense cannot be established when the purpose of a seller's price discrimination is to eliminate competition. The seller may offer discriminatory prices to customers whether or not it has done business with them in the past, but these discriminatory prices must not knowingly be lower than those offered by competitors.

The timing of the price offers must be such that it is apparent they are made to meet an individual competitive situation and are not part of a general system of competition. The seller must have knowledge of the prices it is meeting, to the extent that a reasonable person would believe a lower price was necessary. Actual knowledge of a competitor's exact price is not required.

The overriding consideration concerning the good-faith requirement is the motive of the discriminating seller. The good-faith concept should be used solely to test the seller's adherence to the basic objectives of the meeting-competition proviso: facilitating price reductions in genuine response to competitive market pressures to equalize a competitive opportunity.

The good-faith meeting-of-competition defense is available to buyers as well as sellers. The buyers' liability is based on the sellers' liability, and as the next case shows, if the seller has a defense, so does the buyer.

GREAT ATLANTIC & PACIFIC TEA CO., INC. v. F.T.C.
99 S.Ct. 925 (1979)

FACTS

In an effort to achieve cost savings, a food-store chain (A&P) entered into an agreement with its long-time supplier, Borden, under which Borden would supply "private label" (as opposed to "brand label") milk to A&P stores in the Chicago area. When the contract came up for renewal, A&P refused Borden's initial offer and solicited orders from other companies, resulting in a lower offer from one of Borden's competitors. After being informed of this, Borden submitted a new offer which was substantially better than its competitor's, and it was accepted. The FTC charged A&P with violating Section 2(f) of the Robinson-Patman amendment by knowingly inducing or receiving illegal price discriminations from Borden.

ISSUE

Did A&P violate Section 2(f) of the Robinson-Patman amendment?

DECISION

No.

REASONS

1. A buyer who has done no more than accept the lower of two prices competitively offered does not violate Section 2(f), provided the seller has a meeting-competition defense and thus cannot be liable under Section 2(b).
2. A buyer cannot be liable if a prima facie case could not be established against a seller under Sections 2(a) or 2(b), or if the seller has an affirmative defense.
3. The meeting-competition defense is established when the seller has a good-faith belief that the granting of a lower price would, in fact, meet the equally low price of a competitor.
4. Since good faith rather than certainty is required, the defense is established even if the seller has unknowingly beaten the price of his competition.

5. Borden did act in good faith here because it was in danger of losing a long-standing customer in the Chicago area if it failed to resubmit a bid. Since it had a defense, so did the buyer.

9 THE FUTURE OF SECTION 2

The FTC is the sole governmental agency that now brings actions to enforce the Robinson-Patman amendment. It brings very few cases, and it has recently encouraged repeal of the law. This lack of enforcement results, in part, from the opinion of many economists that the Robinson-Patman amendment has resulted in higher prices than would exist in a more competitive market. Moreover, there is evidence that the statute offers little economic protection to small businesses; rather, it promotes high prices, restricts entry, and encourages inefficiency in the distribution of goods. Some commissioners of the FTC believe that the underlying philosophy of the amendment is no longer relevant and that the law is unpoliceable. Violations are an everyday occurrence.

Enforcement by way of trade damage suits by victims of price discrimination has also been greatly reduced in recent years as a result of two judicial decisions. First, the decision which holds that the statute does not apply to intrastate businesses but only to businesses engaged in interstate commerce has eliminated a significant percentage of all total cases. Second, the holding that a plaintiff must prove actual damages and that proof of price-differential is insufficient proof of damages as a practical matter has discouraged many cases. It is very difficult today to collect triple damages based on a Robinson-Patman violations. The lack of effective private enforcement may eventually lead to the repeal of this law that many people believe is outdated.

THE CLAYTON ACT—SECTION 3

10 TYING ARRANGEMENTS—GENERALLY

Section 3 of the Clayton Act makes it unlawful to lease or sell commodities or to fix a price charged on the condition that the lessee or purchaser should not use or deal in the commodities of a competitor of the lessor or seller when the effect may be to substantially lessen competition or tend to create a monopoly in any line of commerce. The same issues concerning the relevant market and probable anticompetitive effects are involved in determining a violation of Section 3 of the Clayton Act as in a case of alleged price discrimination under Section 2. Under Section 3, the law covers tying contracts, reciprocal dealings, and exclusive arrangements.

A **tying contract** is one in which a commodity is sold or leased for use only on condition that the buyer or lessee purchase a different product or service from the seller or lessor. The arrangement tying a product may even be to a loan of money, as the following case illustrates:

FORTNER ENTERPRISES, INC. v. UNITED STATES STEEL CORP. ET AL.
89 S.Ct. 1252 (1969)

FACTS

Fortner Enterprises, Inc., brought suit against United States Steel Corp. to restrain violations of the Sherman Act. Specifically, the plaintiff alleged that corporations and individuals seeking loans from the defendant for the purchase and development of land in the Louisville, Kentucky, area were required to erect a prefabricated house on each lot purchased with the loan proceeds. These houses were to be purchased from U.S. Steel only, at artificially high prices. The plaintiff was seeking triple damages for lost profits and injunctive relief.

ISSUE

Is there sufficient evidence of an illegal tying arrangement to warrant a trial on the merits?

DECISION

Yes.

REASONS

1. The loans and prefabricated houses offered represent "tying products." The prefabricated homes, "tied products," could not be bought without the loans.
2. Such tying arrangements are illegal whenever a party has sufficient economic power over the tying product to substantially restrain competition in the tied-product market.
3. "Sufficient economic power" does not require a complete monopoly or even a dominant position, only an appreciable restraint on competition, and not solely upon the plaintiff.
4. The annual sales foreclosed by the tying arrangements totaled in excess of $3 million over a three-year period. This is sufficient to require a trial on the merits.

Tying arrangements may be violations of both Section 1 of the Sherman Act and Section 3 of the Clayton Act. Although most tying arrangements are subject to the rule of reason, some tying arrangements are illegal without proof of anticompetitive effects. They are unreasonable in and of themselves (a per se violation) whenever: (1) a party has sufficient economic power with respect to the tying product to restrain free competition appreciably in the market for the tied product; (2) some coercion is shown; and (3) a "not insubstantial" amount of interstate commerce is affected.

The per se rule for tying contracts does allow a defendant to justify undertaking the tie. A tie-in may be justified if it is implemented for a legitimate purpose and if no less restrictive alternative is available.

A common form of tying arrangements is known as "full-line forcing." In full-line forcing, the buyer or lessee is compelled to take a complete product line from the seller. Under these arrangements, the buyer cannot purchase only one product of the line. A typical illegal agreement under this concept is one in which a gasoline company requires its dealers to purchase a stated amount of regular gasoline and premium-priced gasoline to obtain no-lead gasoline. Another example is for an automobile manufacturer to require that only its radios be sold with its new cars.

11 RECIPROCAL DEALINGS

A **reciprocal dealing arrangement** exists when two parties face each other as both buyer and seller. One party offers to buy the other's goods, but only if the second party buys other goods from the first party. For example, if one party is both a food wholesaler and a provider of goods used in processing foods, food processors may be faced by a reciprocal requirement. The first party may agree to buy the processor's products only if the processor buys the processing goods from it.

Reciprocity cases are quite similar to tying cases, and courts treat them in a similar manner. In each case, one side of a transaction has special power in the marketplace. It uses this power to force those with whom it deals to make concessions in another market. In tying arrangements, a seller with economic power forces the purchaser to purchase something else to obtain the desired item. In reciprocal dealings, a buyer with economic power forces a seller to buy something from it to sell its goods. In both cases, the key is the extension of economic power in one market to another market. Thus, the standard for judging reciprocal arrangements is the same as the standard for judging tie-in arrangements, as previously discussed. A reciprocal arrangement may be a per se violation if it is coercive and not justified by legitimate business objectives for which there is no better alternative.

Most cases involving reciprocity threaten foreclosure only of small percentages of any market. Nevertheless, courts apply the per se rule. Reciprocity cases are complicated by the fact that they can occur without an actual agreement. A seller may buy from a would-be customer in the hope that doing so will create goodwill and will lead eventually to sales. It is a natural thing for a seller to show appreciation by purchasing from its buyers.

12 EXCLUSIVE DEALINGS

An **exclusive-dealing** contract contains a provision that one party or the other (buyer or seller) will deal only with the other party. For example, a seller of tomatoes agrees to sell only to Campbell's Soup. A buyer of coal may agree to purchase only from a certain coal company. Such agreements tend to foreclose a portion of the market from competitors.

A similar arrangement is known as a *requirements contract*. In a requirements contract, a buyer agrees to purchase all of its needs of a given contract from the seller during a certain period of time. The buyer may be a manufacturer who needs the raw materials or parts agreed to be supplied, or it may be a retailer who needs goods for resale. In effect, the buyer is agreeing not to purchase any of the product from competitors of the seller.

Franchise contracts often require that the franchisee purchase all of its equipment and inventory from the franchiser as a condition of the agreement. These provisions are commonly inserted because of the value of the franchiser's trademark and the desire for quality control to protect it. For example, Baskin-Robbins ice cream may require its franchisees to purchase all of their ice cream from Baskin-Robbins. The legitimate purpose is to maintain the image of the franchise and the product. Customers expect the same ice cream from every retail operation. Such agreements, while anti-competitive, are legal, because the legitimate purpose outweighs the anti-competitive aspects.

However, a franchiser is not able to license its trademark in such a manner that it can coerce franchisees to give up all alternate supply sources, because such agreements are unreasonable restraints of trade. The quality-control aspect is not present for items such as packaging materials and food items in which special ingredients or secret formulas are not involved; thus, the purpose of the "exclusive source of supply" provision is only to limit competition. Although franchise agreements are not per se violations, they are subject to the rule of reason. The case which follows is a landmark case which involves franchise agreements.

SIEGAL, ET AL. v. CHICKEN DELIGHT, INC., ET AL.
448 F.2d 43 (9th Cir. 1971)

FACTS

A class action suit was brought against defendant corporation for alleged violations of Section 1 of the Sherman Act, stemming from *tying arrangements* included in franchise agreements. Under the tie-in, potential franchisees were required to purchase a specified amount of cooking equipment and other items at a higher cost than competitors' products.

ISSUE

Does the forced purchase of tangible items necessary to a business, in conjunction with the licensing of a franchise, constitute a significant restraint of trade in violation of the Sherman Act?

DECISION

Yes.

REASONS

1. Defendant's unique trademark, combined with the imposed tie-in, were sufficient to bring the case within the Sherman Act.
2. Defendant's trademark or franchise license is a distinct product. Thus, the requisite purchase of cookers and other equipment was "tied to" the trademark and license, denying potential franchisees access to the tied product market.
3. The fact that the defendant did not have a monopoly on the market for the tying product—the license and trademark—does not mean it lacked "sufficient economic power" to bring the case within the Sherman Act's protections; such power is now presumed to be where the tying product is patented or copyrighted.

13 ETHICS AND SECTION 3

Caterpillar has a special part of its ethics code which deals with the relationship with suppliers. Reciprocity is forbidden, and exclusive dealings are rare. The specific statement is as follows. Note that compliance with this standard will probably prevent any legal problems from occurring.

Relationships with Suppliers

Caterpillar's superior relationships are a vital, highly valued aspect of our worldwide operations. These relationships are based on a commitment to deal fairly and reasonably.

We aim at creation and maintenance of long-lasting company-supplier relationships. But as a general rule, neither Caterpillar nor a supplier should be overly dependent on the other, from a long-term standpoint.

Selection of suppliers and purchase of materials and services are determined by evaluations of quality, cost/price benefit, delivery capability, service, and maintenance of adequate supply sources. Other things being equal, our intention is to buy from sources as near to the using facility as possible.

Supplier competitiveness for Caterpillar business is encouraged throughout the world...as is company-supplier cooperation toward maximizing the value of Caterpillar products. No supplier is asked to buy Caterpillar products in order to compete for business, or continue as a supplier.

Suppliers may trade with Caterpillar's competitors and still merit our purchases. Further, Caterpillar personnel shall avoid arrangements or understandings prohibiting a supplier from selling products in competition with us, except where: (1) the supplier makes the product with tooling or materials owned by Caterpillar or (2) the product is one in which the company has a proprietary interest which has been determined to be legally protectable. Such an interest might arise from an important contribution by Caterpillar to the concept, design, application, or manufacturing process.

THE CLAYTON ACT—SECTION 7

14 INTRODUCTION

A business may acquire other businesses in a variety of ways. For example, two corporations may join together and create a third corporation, with the two original companies being dissolved. This is technically known as a "consolidation." One business may acquire and absorb another business, with the acquired business being dissolved. This is technically known as a "merger." Another method for one company to acquire another is for the former to purchase a controlling interest in the stock of the latter. The subsidiary is controlled by the parent company's electing the board of directors and controlling policy. When the stock of a company is controlled, both companies continue to exist, and no dissolution occurs. A fourth method of acquisition is for one business to purchase the assets of another. The selling company then ceases to continue its former business activities, and the purchased assets are integrated into the buying company.

In the material which follows, technical consolidations, mergers, and other acquisitions are generally referred to as mergers. Mergers are usually classified as *horizontal, market extension, vertical,* or *conglomerate*. A **horizontal merger** usually combines two businesses in the same field or industry. The acquired and acquiring companies have competed with each other, and the merger reduces the number of competitors and leads to greater concentration in the industry. The term **market extension merger** describes an acquisition in which the acquiring company extends its markets. This market extension may be either in new products (**product extension**) or in new areas (**geographic extension**). For example, if a brewery which did not operate in New England were to acquire a New England brewery, this would be a geographic market extension merger.

A **vertical merger** brings together a company which is the customer of the other in one of the lines of commerce in which the other is a supplier. Such a combination ordinarily removes or has the potential to remove the merged customer from the market, as far as other suppliers are concerned. It also may remove a source of supply, if the acquiring company is a customer of the acquired one. A **conglomerate merger** is one in which the business involved neither compete nor are related as customer and supplier in any given line of commerce. Some people consider product extension and geographic extension mergers to be conglomerate ones with many characteristics of horizontal ones. In any event, there is a great deal of similarity in the legal principles applied to market extension and to conglomerate mergers.

Theoretically, a merger or acquisition may be challenged under the Sherman Act. A horizontal merger would amount to a violation of the Sherman Act if it were a combination in unreasonable restraint of trade, if it were to result in monopolization of a line of commerce, or if it were an attempt to monopolize. A Sherman Act case requires detailed economic analysis of markets and market structure as well as the characteristics of the firms involved in a merger. Since Section 7 cases require less-detailed proof and analysis, the Sherman Act is seldom used to prevent a merger.

A great deal of merger litigation involves banks. Such mergers are subject to both the Sherman Act and the Clayton Act. In addition, they are subject to the provision of the **Bank Merger Acts** of 1960 and 1966. Under these laws, bank mergers are illegal unless they are approved by one of the agencies which regulates banks. If a merger involves a national bank, the approval of the comptroller of the currency is required. If the banks involved in a merger are state banks that are members of the Federal Reserve System, the approval of the Federal Reserve Board is necessary. Other mergers of banks insured by the Federal Deposit Insurance Corporation require approval of that agency.

If a bank merger is approved by one of the three appropriate regulatory agencies, it may nevertheless be challenged under the antitrust laws by the Justice Department within thirty days. The filing of a suit by the Justice Department stops the merger until the case is decided.

15 GENERAL PRINCIPLES

As originally enacted in 1914, the Clayton Act covered horizontal mergers. In 1950, Congress passed the Celler-Kefauver amendment, which substantially broadened the coverage. First of all, this amendment plugged a loophole, in that the original Section 7 only prohibited certain acquisitions of stock by one corporation of another. Technically, the same end could be accomplished and was permitted under it through an acquisition of assets. Therefore, the acquisition of assets was also prohibited. Second, the Celler-Kefauver amendment prohibited all acquisitions in which the effect lessened competition substantially in any line of commerce in any section of the country. Thus, the amendment added vertical and conglomerate mergers to the coverage of Section 7. In 1980, Congress expanded coverage by substituting "person" for "corporation," and included not only businesses engaged in interstate commerce, but businesses engaged in activities which affect commerce. The word "person" includes sole proprietorships and partnerships.

The language of Section 7 neither adopts nor rejects any particular tests for measuring relevant markets. Both the product market and geographic market of the companies involved are factual issues to be considered by the courts. In determining the relevant "line of commerce" (product market) and the relevant "section of the country" (geographic market) affected by the merger in question, the actual outcome of the litigation is frequently decided. The more narrowly the product line or geographic area is defined, the greater the impact a merger or acquisition will have on competition. Thus, the relevant market decision frequently determines the issue as to the probable anticompetitive effects of the merger. It is also obvious that a decision which enlarges the line of commerce may be equally important in establishing that a merger is *not* anticompetitive. Trial courts and reviewing courts frequently disagree as to what constitutes relevant markets in any given case. Reviewing courts today give great deference to trial court findings on these issues.

In addition to determining the relevant market affected by a given merger, courts must also find that within that market the effect of the merger "may be substantially to lessen competition, or to tend to create a monopoly" before a violation is established. Some cases have held that a small percentage increase in market share is sufficient to establish the prohibited effect. The degree of market concentration prior to the merger and the relative position of the merged parties are important factors in such cases. Where there has been a history of tendency toward concentration in an industry, slight increases in further concentration are prohibited because of the policy of the law to curb such tendencies in their incipiency. The following case illustrates the great uncertainty that exists as to the legality of many mergers and acquisitions. Note that the law deals with probabilities and is designed to arrest anticompetitive tendencies at their incipiency.

UNITED STATES v. VON'S GROCERY CO.
384 U.S. 270 (1966)

FACTS

Von's Grocery, a retail grocery chain doing business in the Los Angeles area, acquired a direct competitor, Shopping Big Food Store. As a result, Von's became the second largest grocery chain in Los Angeles, with sales of over $172 million annually, which amounted to 7.5 percent of the market. Before the merger, both companies were rapidly growing, aggressive competitors. The Los Angeles market was characterized by an increasing trend toward concentration through acquisitions and a marked decline in the number of single-store owners. The government brought this action, claiming that the merger was illegal under Section 7 of the Clayton Act.

ISSUE

Was the merger illegal under Section 7 of the Clayton Act?

DECISION

Yes.

REASONS

1. A merger between two of the most successful and largest companies in a relevant market may substantially lessen competition, especially when the merger has taken place in a market characterized by a long and continuous trend toward fewer and fewer competitors.
2. The primary purpose of antitrust law is to prevent the concentration of

> economic power in the hands of a few and to preserve competition among a large number of sellers. Therefore, Congress under Section 7 sought to preserve competition among many small businesses by arresting in its incipiency a trend toward concentration.

The Supreme Court has adopted a narrow view of the application of Section 7. It can be used only against mergers of companies actually engaged in interstate commerce. As a result, most service industries are exempt from the law, because such businesses are usually involved only in intrastate commerce.

16 SPECIAL DOCTRINES

The law recognizes two special doctrines in the merger area. These are commonly referred to as the "potential-entrant doctrine" and "the failing-company doctrine." The **potential-entrant doctrine** recognizes that there may be injury to competition as the result of a loss of a potential competitor. Of course, potential competitors that actually join a market increase competition. In addition, the mere presence of a potential competitor may affect a market by influencing the conduct of those actually competing. For example, the existence of a potential entrant may inhibit price increases. Actual competitors may price their goods just below the level that would attract the potential entrants to the market.

The potential-entrant doctrine finds that the prohibited effect may exist when an acquisition or merger involves a potential entrant into a market. An acquisition of a competitor by a potential competitor is thus illegal when the effect may be to substantially lessen competition. The potential-entrant doctrine has been used to prevent product extension mergers as well as geographic extension mergers. The potential-entrant doctrine is applied not only because if entry does occur there is an additional competitor, but also because the mere presence of a potential competitor at the edge of the market has positive effects on those companies actually competing.

In the 1920s, the Supreme Court created a **failing-company exception** to the law restricting mergers. It held that when a company is failing, the statutory prohibitions on anticompetitive mergers are set aside. The company in the case in which the exception was decided had in one year turned a surplus of $4 million into a deficit of $4.4 million.

The failing-company doctrine allows for special approval of mergers that would otherwise be unlawful. There are three general conditions which must be met. First, the acquisition candidate must be on the brink of bankruptcy. Second, corporate reorganization under Chapter 11 of the bankruptcy laws must not be a viable alternative. Finally, the doctrine requires proof that there is no other merger partner that would raise fewer antitrust problems.

Historically, the courts have been quite strict in interpreting the failing-company doctrine. They have required clear and convincing proof of the foregoing conditions. However, the Justice Department and the FTC have been more lenient in deciding which cases to oppose. The Justice Department's attitude has always been to recognize the doctrine and not to challenge those involving companies in serious financial difficulty. It has tended to consider the long-term prospects of a company, and if the future looks bleak, it has tended not to challenge the acquisition of a failing company.

As more and more companies have diversified and acquired subsidiaries, the failing-company doctrine has been applied to failing divisions and failing subsidiaries. If a company is about to close down an operation and a competitor is willing to take it over, society is probably better off if the law allows the sale or divestiture of the division rather than have it no longer exist as an economic unit. A sale which increases concentration is preferable to the death of the unit. At least the employees still have a job, and a new owner may be able to restore the division or organization to a profitable entity.

17 ENFORCEMENT

Section 7 of the Clayton Act is enforced by the Justice Department, the FTC, and individuals and affected firms. It is both a tool to prevent hostile takeovers and a law that is enforced by government. The basic remedy used by the Justice Department is the injunction. The FTC may prevent a merger by use of a cease and desist order, or it may order a divestiture through a decision which finds unfair methods of competition.

The injunction is a major sanction used by government and individuals in the merger field. A preliminary injunction prevents consummation of a merger until all legal issues are resolved. Preliminary injunctions are issued whenever there is a strong likelihood that the merger is illegal if there is potential for serious injury to the public from the proposed merger. After a trial, a preliminary injunction either is made permanent or is dissolved. If it is dissolved, the parties are free to proceed with the merger.

The injunction remedy is also used after mergers have been consummated. Such mandatory injunctions may require a divestiture of a merged firm or even a sale of stock in the event there is only partial ownership. Sometimes an acquisition or merger is challenged many years after it was consummated. While an acquisition of stock or assets may be perfectly legal at that time, it later may become illegal because it "threatens to ripen into a prohibited effect" of substantially lessening competition. The test of illegality is the time of the challenge.

The remedy of triple damages, in effect, allows one's competitors and other individuals directly affected to enforce the antimerger provisions of the Clayton Act. There have been numerous triple damage suits brought by one competitor against another and by a takeover candidate against its "suitor." Such suits may seek damages because of inadequate prices or for the costs of fending off a hostile takeover.

The FTC looks at market share as an important indication of anticompetitive effects of mergers. Other factors considered are barriers to entry and technological changes. If the barriers to entry are low, market share is less important. The FTC has indicated that it will give great weight to the Justice Department guidelines, which are discussed in more detail in Section 19.

The FTC also examines the companies involved. Market power is more important than market share. Market share may understate competitive significance. For example, a firm with a small market share may have unique competitive potential. Since mergers may improve the efficiency of a firm, this factor is considered in deciding whether or not to challenge an acquisition. However, if the challenge is made, increased efficiency is no defense. The failing-division as well as the failing-company doctrine are also considered by the FTC. The fact that a company or a part of one may go out of business is obviously a factor to consider, unless someone else seeks to take it over and keep it as a competitor.

Most cases involving Section 7 are settled by agreement. Many consent decrees in merger cases contain an arrangement that the company involved will not acquire any other firm for a stated period of time. Such decrees frequently provide that the divesting company will not engage in a certain line of business for a stated period, as well. The usual number of years in such cases is ten, although some have been for as long as twenty.

The Justice Department has used Section 7 of the Clayton Act as a basis for attacking foreign acquisitions. For example, it was used to prevent the Gillette Company from acquiring a German manufacturer of electric razors. The theory was that the German company was a potential competitor in the domestic shaving instrument market. Thus, the power of United States courts applies to foreign as well as to domestic mergers.

18 TENDER OFFERS

It should be recognized that many acquisitions and mergers are not the result of a mutual agreement. Many takeovers are, in fact, hostile, at least insofar as the management of the acquired firms is concerned. Hostile takeovers occur as a result of **tender offers** by the acquiring firm to the shareholders of the acquired firm. The management of the firm to be acquired often objects to the takeover, for very obvious reasons. Hostile takeovers usually result in wholesale changes in management, and existing management is simply fighting for survival. Moreover, if roadblocks are placed in the path of a merger, the price may be raised and other offerors may even enter the picture. It is common for existing management to contend that an offering price is too low even though the offering price is substantially in excess of current market price. Existing management frequently raises legal objections to a proposed takeover, even though the Justice Department and the FTC do not.

To discourage hostile takeovers, a variety of techniques have been developed and are being adopted by various corporations and state governments interested in protecting local businesses. Among the techniques are the following:

1 *Fair pricing bylaws*: These require that all shareholders be paid the same price for their stock in the event of a takeover.
2 *Staggered terms for directors*: These bylaws make it more difficult to gain control of the board of directors. Since fewer directors are elected each year, more votes are required to elect a director.
3 *Special stock issues*: These give special voting rights to a limited group of shareholders likely to oppose a takeover.
4 *Stronger voting guidelines*: These require a large percentage of all shareholders to approve a merger or takeover. Some of these percentages are as high as 95 percent.
5 *Golden parachutes*: These contracts protect executives by guaranteeing them cash settlements equal to several years' salaries if a takeover occurs.
6 *Corporate restructuring*: Corporations sometimes take "poison pills," in the form of increased debt, to avoid a takeover. The debt may be used to buy back stock. Valuable units are also sometimes sold to make a business less attractive.

These techniques have been described as **shark repellents,** because the company attempting a hostile takeover is viewed as a shark. They are needed by existing management, because the price offered is usually significantly higher than the existing market price of the stock. The fair-price bylaw stops someone from buying majority control at one price and paying a lower price or not purchasing the shares of other shareholders. The proposal for staggered terms for directors is designed to prevent someone from buying 5 percent or 10 percent of a company's stock and threatening a proxy fight unless management agrees to buy back the raider's stock at a premium. This latter technique is often described as **greenmail** to indicate that it is, in fact, a form of blackmail by which individuals or companies force someone to pay them off to avoid a takeover.

The *golden parachute* phenomenon does not prevent many mergers and acquisitions. However, it does give management the security of knowing that it will be well rewarded financially if a takeover occurs. There have been so many agreements providing golden parachutes in recent months that the SEC is seriously considering rules that limit such agreements. Under the terms of some agreements, a corporate president may receive several million dollars in the event the business is taken over by another organization. Some agreements call for the opening of the parachute on less than a total change of ownership and management.

Another technique used to fight takeovers is often referred to as the **white knight.** The white knight is another firm that makes a competing offer at a price significantly higher than the tender offer. The white knight is a friendly takeover candidate, and its presence creates a bidding war. The use of the white knight is in recognition that the company is likely to lose its independence, and, therefore, the best arrangement is a friendly rather than a hostile buyer.

Another technique used to discourage hostile takeovers is known as the *lockup.* In a lockup, the target company agrees either to sell part of its stock or part of its company to an acquirer of its choice. The lockup usually involves a white knight, and it frequently means that the most attractive part of the company is gone, thus discouraging the hostile takeover. The net effect of a lockup is to favor one bidder over another and to stack the deck in favor of one. Sometimes the lockup simply involves an option to someone to purchase a significant portion of the business.

Congress is considering several means of curbing unfriendly takeovers. Some people contend that the antitrust laws should be tightened to restrict unfriendly takeovers as a predatory practice. Others contend that the employees should be given the power to veto unfriendly takeovers. Finally, there is substantial support for new laws prohibiting greenmail. In some recent situations, greenmail has rewarded certain individuals and companies they control with windfall profits of $30 million to $40 million. A buyer can achieve such a windfall by acquiring a substantial block of stock and forcing management to rebuy it at a premium. One of the notable examples of greenmail in recent years involved Walt Disney. In this situation, one group made millions of dollars and significantly depressed the value of Disney stock in the process.

19 FTC PREMERGER NOTIFICATION

The application of Section 7 to any given merger is discretionary with the Justice Department and the FTC. Both have issued guidelines as to which mergers are likely to be challenged, but they have reserved the right to bring action against mergers and acquisitions they feel will probably lessen competition or tend to create a monopoly. To assist in enforcement, the FTC, pursuant to a 1976 statute, has adopted a premerger notification rule. This rule requires that prior notice be given to the Justice Department and to the FTC of all pending mergers subject to the rule. Once the notice is given in advance of the acquisition, either agency may institute appropriate action to prevent it.

The application of the premerger notification rules are determined by the size of the firms involved and the size of the transaction. The rules cover transactions involving at least 15 percent of either the assets or the voting securities of the firm to be acquired when the value of the purchase exceeds $15 million. The value of the assets is determined by fair market value, not by book value. The value of the securities is current value, not par value.

If we assume that the transaction is within the required size, we find that the premerger rules are applied if the acquiring party has either annual net sales or total assets of $100 million or more, and if the acquired firm is engaged in manufacturing and has annual net sales or total assets of $5 million or more. If the acquired firm is not engaged in manufacturing, the rule applies if the acquired firm has total assets of $5 million, irrespective of the size of sales. To prevent avoidance of the rules by having the smaller firm acquire the larger, the rules are also applicable whenever an acquired firm has annual sales of $10 million or more and the acquiring firm has annual sales of $100 million or more.

The notification requires a brief description of the proposed acquisition, the amount of securities or assets being acquired, and the manner of acquisition. It will include the sales information, broken down by industry, product class, and product. Copies of all SEC filings, together with market information and facts relative to other acquisitions by both firms, must be submitted.

20 JUSTICE DEPARTMENT MERGER GUIDELINES

In 1982, the Justice Department issued new **merger guidelines.** The guidelines are designed primarily to indicate when the Justice Department is likely to challenge a merger. These latest guidelines are more permissive than the ones announced in the 1960s, and most of their attention is directed at horizontal acquisitions. Under the new guidelines, the legality of vertical and conglomerate mergers is judged solely on their impact on future direct competition. Horizontal mergers are examined for the postmerger market concentration and the increase in concentration resulting from the merger.

An index known as the **Herfindahl-Hirschman Index** (HHI) is used to test the legality of horizontal acquisitions. The index is computed by squaring the market share of each firm in a market and adding the results. If the sum is 1,000 or less, the merger probably will not be challenged, as the market is considered to be unconcentrated, having the equivalent of at least ten equally sized firms. If the sum is between 1,000 and 1,800, a careful examination of the moderately concentrated market will be made to determine if acquisition is likely to harm competition. Harm will likely be found if the merger adds 100 points to the index. If less than fifty points are added, the Justice Department is unlikely to challenge the merger. The amount a merger will add is equal to twice the product of the merging firms' market share.

Notwithstanding the foregoing use of the HHI, the Justice Department is likely to challenge the merger of any firm with 1 percent of the market with the leading firm if the latter has 35 percent or more of the total market and is approximately twice as large as the second largest firm. In addition to examining market concentration and market share, the Justice Department also examines ease of entry, the nature of the product, conduct of firms in the market, and market performance in deciding if a merger will be challenged. Keep in mind that the HHI is only a guide and a general prediction of which mergers and acquisitions will actually be challenged. A sample HHI calculation is shown in Table 23-1.

In 1984, the Justice Department revised the merger guidelines to clarify some aspects of them. The revision explains the techniques to be used in defining and measuring a market. It also lists the factors that may affect the significance of concentration and market share data in evaluating horizontal mergers. The guidelines also indicate that foreign competition will be included in the relevant market data, even though there are import quotas. Import quotas are treated as a separate factor to be considered.

The revised guidelines indicate that if entry into a market is so easy that existing competitors could not succeed in raising prices for any significant period of time, the Department is unlikely to challenge mergers in that market. The Department is more likely to challenge a merger in the following circumstances:

1 Firms in the market previously have been found to have engaged in horizontal collusion in regard to price, territories, and customers, and the characteristics of the market have not changed appreciably since the most recent finding.
2 One or more of the following types of practices are adopted by substan-

TABLE 23-1 EXAMPLE OF HHI CALCULATION

Assumptions: In a market of ten firms, with market shares as stated, Firm No. 4 seeks to merge with Firm No. 8.

Firm no.	Assumed market share	Premerger index	Assumed merger of no. 4 + no. 8 index
1	20	400	400
2	18	324	324
3	16	256	256
4	12	144	289
5	10	100	100
6	8	64	64
7	6	36	36
8	5	25	—
9	3	9	9
10	2	4	4
	Increase of +120	1,362	1,482

Note that the increase in the index is equal to the product of the market share of the merging firms times 2 (12X5X2 = 120).

tially all of the firms in the market: (*a*) mandatory delivered pricing; (*b*) exchange of price or output information in a form that could assist firms in setting or enforcing an agreed price; (*c*) collective standardization of product variables on which the firms could compete; and (*d*) price protection clauses.

3 The firm to be acquired has been an unusually disruptive and competitive influence in the market.

Two other items of the revised guidelines are worthy of note. First, the Department recognizes that increased efficiency is generally desirable. Some mergers that might otherwise be challenged may be reasonably necessary to achieve significant net efficiencies. If the parties to the merger establish by clear and convincing evidence that a merger will achieve such efficiencies, those efficiencies will be considered in deciding whether to challenge the merger. Efficiency claims will be rejected if comparable savings can reasonably be achieved through other means.

Second, the guidelines recognize the failing-company doctrine and note that it has been ambiguous. The guidelines indicate that the Justice Department is unlikely to challenge an anticompetitive merger in which one of the merging firms is allegedly failing when: (1) the allegedly failing firm probably would be unable to meet its financial obligations in the near future; (2) it probably would not be able to reorganize successfully in bankruptcy; and (3) it has made unsuccessful good-faith efforts to elicit reasonable acquisition offers that would keep it in the market and pose a less severe danger to competition. Similarly, the "failure" of a division is an important factor affecting the likely competitive effect of a merger.

THE FEDERAL TRADE COMMISSION ACT

21 INTRODUCTION

The FTC was created in 1914 to have an "independent" administrative agency charged with keeping competition free and fair. It enforces the Clayton Act provisions on price discrimination, tying and exclusive contracts, mergers and acquisitions, and interlocking directorates. In addition, it enforces Section 5 of the Federal Trade Commission Act. This act originally made "unfair methods of competition" in commerce unlawful. The Wheeler-Lea amendments of 1938 added that "unfair or deceptive acts or practices in commerce" were also unlawful under Section 5. The FTC has broad, sweeping powers and a mandate to determine what methods, acts, or practices fall within the vague category of being "unfair or deceptive" and are thus unlawful. Such decisions are made on a case-by-case basis. A discussion of unfair methods of competition follows in the next section. Since unfair or deceptive acts or practices were prohibited to protect consumers and not competition, they were discussed in Chapter 19, which deals with consumer protection. That chapter also discussed many of the other consumer protection statutes for which the FTC has enforcement responsibility.

The FTC issues trade regulation rules which deal with business practices in an industry. For example, the FTC has said the American Medical Association must allow doctors to advertise. The FTC also periodically issues "trade practice rules and guides," sometimes referred to as industry guides. These rules are the FTC's informal opinion of legal requirements applicable to a particular industry's practices. Although compliance with the rules is voluntary, they provide the basis for the informal and simultaneous abandonment by industry members of practices thought to be unlawful. "Guidelines" are administrative interpretations of the statutes which the Commission enforces, and they provide guidance to both the FTC staff and businesspeople evaluating the legality of certain practices. Guidelines deal with a particular practice and may cut across industry lines.

The primary function of the FTC is to prevent illegal business practices rather than to punish violations. It prevents wrongful actions by use of cease and desist orders. Whereas violations of these orders may be punished by a fine of $10,000 per day, with each day being a new violation, the punishment factor is only incidental to the FTC's primary prevention role. As noted in Chapter 7 on administrative law, most FTC cases are settled by consent orders. In such cases, the respondent need not admit a law violation but agrees *not* to do the complained-of act in the future.

22 UNFAIR METHODS OF COMPETITION

Although the original Section 5 of the FTC Act outlawed unfair methods of competition in commerce and directed the FTC to prevent the use of such, it offered no definition of the specific practices which were unfair. The term "unfair methods of competition" was designed by Congress as a flexible concept, the exact meaning of which could evolve on a case-by-case basis. It can apply to a variety of unrelated activities. It is generally up to the FTC to determine what business conduct is "unfair." Great deference is given to the FTC's opinion as to what constitutes a violation and to the remedies it desires to correct anticompetitive behavior.

Business conduct in violation of any provision of the antitrust laws may also be ruled illegal under Section 5 of the FTC Act. Further, anticompetitive acts or practices which *fall short* of transgressing the Sherman or Clayton Acts may be restrained by the FTC as being "unfair methods of competition."

If a business practice is such that it is doubtful that the evidence is sufficient to prove a Sherman of Clayton Act violation, the FTC may nevertheless proceed and find that the business practice is unfair. Thus, business practices which could not be prevented in a judicial proceeding may be stopped by FTC cease and desist orders.

In FTC cases, the concepts of per se illegality and the rule of reason are used to determine the elements of proof required. While proof of relevant markets may be required, the FTC looks at the reality of the situation to see if elaborate market analysis is required. In the case which follows, the court did not require the FTC to examine the effects on the three-county market in great detail. The court more or less simply recognized that the markets for dental services tend to be localized.

F T C v. INDIANA FEDERATION OF DENTISTS
106 S.Ct. 2009 (1986)

FACTS

To evaluate patient claims, dental health insurers required dentists to submit x-rays with claim forms. The x-rays were reviewed to make sure that the services performed were necessary and proper. A group of Indiana dentists formed a federation which adopted a "work rule" which forbid its members to submit x-rays to dental insurers. The federation included almost every dentist in three Indiana communities.

ISSUE

Is the federation work rule an "unfair method of competition," in violation of Section 5 of the Federal Trade Commission Act?

DECISION

Yes.

REASONS

1. The federation's policy of requiring its members to withhold x-rays amounts to a conspiracy in restraint of trade, which is unreasonable and, hence, unlawful under Section 1 of the Sherman Act.
2. The restraint is subject to the rule of reason, and the activity is obviously unreasonable. The federation's policy takes the form of a horizontal agreement among the participating dentists. It withholds from the dentists' customers a particular service that they desire—the forwarding of x-rays along with claim forms to insurance companies.
3. A refusal to compete with respect to the package of services offered to customers, no less than a refusal to compete with respect to the price term of an agreement, impairs the ability of the market to advance social welfare. The market cannot ensure the provisions of desired goods and services to consumers at a price approximating the marginal cost of providing them.

REVIEW QUESTIONS

1 For each term in the left-hand column, match the most appropriate description in the right-hand column:

(1) Horizontal merger
(2) Conglomerate merger
(3) Requirements contract
(4) Full-time forcing
(5) Predatory pricing
(6) Exclusive-dealing contract
(7) Reciprocal dealing
(8) Tying contract
(9) Cease and desist order
(10) Interlocking directorate
(11) Shark repellents
(12) Potential-entrant doctrine
(13) Vertical merger

(a) When an individual is a member of the board of directors of two or more competing corporations at the same time.
(b) When a commodity is sold or leased for use only on condition that the buyer or lessee purchase certain additional products or services from the seller or lessor.
(c) A contract whereby a buyer agrees not to purchase an item or items of merchandise from competitors of the seller.
(d) A buyer agrees to purchase all of his of her business needs of a product from the seller during a certain period.
(e) The administrative equivalent of a court injunction, which is issued by an administrative agency with quasi-judicial powers to restrain future violations of the law.
(f) An arrangement that exists when two parties face each other as both buyer and seller.
(g) To sell at prices below average variable cost to close out competition.
(h) A doctrine which allows an acquisition to proceed because the company to be acquired would likely to go out of business because of financial difficulty.
(i) Techniques used to prevent hostile takeovers.
(j) Contracts requiring payment of large salaries to corporate officials in the event the firm is acquired and the officials are replaced.
(k) A form of tying arrangement in which the buyer or lessee is compelled to take a complete product line from the seller as a condition of being permitted to purchase the main product of the line.
(l) A merger which combines two businesses which formerly competed with each other in a particular line of commerce.
(m) A merger which brings together a customer in a line of commerce and a supplier.

(14) Failing-company doctrine (n) A merger in which the businesses that are combined neither compete nor are related as customer and supplier in any given line of commerce.

(15) Golden parachute (o) A doctrine that makes certain acquisitions illegal if the acquiring company might enter the product or geographic market of the acquired company and compete with it were it not for the acquisition.

2 Copp Paving Company sued Gulford for triple damages, alleging a violation of the Robinson-Patman amendment. Copp operates an asphaltic concrete "hotplant" in California. The plant manufactures asphalt for surfacing highways, including interstate highways, in California. Its whole operation is in intrastate commerce. Does the complaint allege a valid claim? Why, or why not?

3 Alice, who recently received a degree in business, has been named general sales manager of a building materials manufacturer. She has called a meeting of the sales force, and among other matters Alice has made the following statement: "We will cut prices so low our competitors will be cut off at the knees." If this policy is carried out, will any law be violated? Explain.

4 In the same situation as question 3, Alice later called on the corporation's most important customer. While informing this customer of its special importance, Alice said: "To you, Larry, and to you alone, the price we charge will always be below cost." If this policy is carried out, will it be in violation of any law? Explain.

5 A class action suit was brought against defendant corporation for alleged violations of Section 1 of the Sherman Act, stemming from *tying arrangements* included in fast-food franchise agreements. Under the tie-in, potential franchisees were required to purchase a specified amount of cooking equipment and other items at a higher cost than competitors' products. What was the result? Why?

6 A cemetery sold bronze markers for grave sites. It learned that it was paying $10 per marker more than a local monument dealer. It sued the manufacturer for triple damages and offered proof of the price differential and that it had purchased 1,000 markers. How much is it entitled to collect? Why?

7 The American Medical Association adopted a code of ethics which prohibited all advertising by physicians. Included in the prohibition were ads that indicated that physicians would make house calls. The FTC challenged the ethical rules under Section 5 of the FTC Act. What was the result? Why?

8 A department store solicited and received contributions from vendors toward the cost of the store's one-hundredth anniversary celebration. The store gave the vendors no direct promotional services for vendors' products. Is the store in violation of Section 2 of the Clayton Act as amended? Why, or why not?

9 Weinberg is on the board of directors of both Sears Roebuck & Company and B. F. Goodrich. Sears and Goodrich each have capital, surplus, and undivided profits in excess of $1 million. They compete with each other on the retail level in ninety-seven communities in the sale of appliances, hardware, automotive supplies, sporting goods, tires, radios, television sets, and toys. Is Weinberg acting illegally? Why, or why not?

10 In 1984, Standard Oil of California acquired the Gulf Oil Corporation for $13.4 billion, and it also acquired the Getty Oil Company for $10.1 billion. The Justice

Department and the FTC decided not to challenge the acquisition. Could these mergers still be challenged? Explain.

11 In an industry, there were ten competitors, each with the following market shares:

1–20%	6–10%
2–18%	7– 8%
3–16%	8– 5%
4–15%	9– 3%
5–12%	10– 1%

Number 7 decides to merge with number 9. Will the merger be challenged under the 1982 guidelines? Explain.

12 The Stroh's Brewing Company has made a tender offer of $17 per share for all shares of the Schlitz Brewing Company. Stroh's is the nation's seventh largest brewer, with approximately 5 percent of the United States beer market. Schlitz is the third-ranked beer nationally, with approximately 8 percent of the market. Prior to the Stroh's tender offer, the G. Heilemann Company had attempted to acquire Schlitz. Heilemann had 7.5 percent of the market, and its merger attempt was rejected by the Justice Department.

The beer industry in the United States is dominated by Anheuser Busch and the Miller Brewing Company. Together, they account for approximately 50 percent of the nation's beer sales. Schlitz's beer market has declined in recent years, except in the southeastern states where Schlitz holds 13.5 percent of the market and Stroh's 6.9 percent. Is it likely that the Justice Department will challenge Stroh's tender offer? Explain.

13 Maxwell House, Inc. (the second-largest producer of coffee in the United States, with 36 percent of the United States market), proposes to merge with Yuban, Inc. (the tenth-largest producer of coffee in the United States, with 5 percent of the United States market). The coffee-producing industry is highly concentrated—the four largest firms have 76 percent of the United States market. Maxwell House has agreed to this merger, despite the fact that Yuban has suffered financial losses in seven of the last ten years and for the past four years consecutively. Is it likely that the merger will be challenged? Explain.

14 Coca-Cola entered into an agreement to buy Dr. Pepper, and Pepsi-Cola entered into an agreement to purchase 7-Up. The proposed acquisitions would give Coca-Cola and Pepsi-Cola 80 percent of the domestic soft-drink market. Royal Crown challenges the acquisition. Will the FTC stop the mergers? Why, or why not?

15 The Brown Shoe franchise agreement provided that the retail franchisees would restrict their purchases of shoes to the Brown Shoe lines. In return, the retail operators would be given valuable benefits that were not granted to retail operators who did not execute the agreement. Can the FTC stop the use of the Brown Shoe franchise agreement as an unfair trade practice? Why, or why not?

CHAPTER **24**

ENVIRONMENTAL LAWS AND POLLUTION CONTROL

OVERVIEW

This chapter examines environmental laws and pollution control. Note that environmental regulation remains the single most expensive area of government's regulation of the business community. Over the next decade, industry will spend several hundred billion dollars on pollution control.

We can separate environmental laws into three main divisions: (1) government's regulation of itself, (2) government's regulation of business, and (3) suits by private individuals. Table 24-1 illustrates this breakdown.

Administering environmental laws at the federal level is the Environmental Protection Agency (EPA). Since many of the laws provide for joint federal-state enforcement, the states also have strong environmental agencies. Policies are set at the federal level, and the states devise plans to implement them.

Important terms in this chapter include: bubble concept, emissions reduction banking, environmental impact statement, manifest system, public and private nuisance, point source, prevention of significant deterioration, primary and secondary air quality standards, scoping, and Superfund.

1 THE NATIONAL ENVIRONMENTAL POLICY ACT

The way government regulates the environmental impact of its decision making interests the business community greatly. The federal government,

CHAPTER 24: ENVIRONMENTAL LAWS AND POLLUTION CONTROL **625**

TABLE 24-1 POLLUTION CONTROL LAWS

Government's Regulation of Itself
  National Environmental Policy Act
  State environmental policy acts
Government's Regulation of Business
  Clean Air Act
  Clean Water Act
  Noise Control Act
  Pesticide control acts
  Solid Waste Disposal Act
  Toxic Substances Control Act
  Natural Resource Conservation and Recovery Act
  Other federal, state, and local statutes
Suits by Private Individuals
  Public and private nuisance
  Strict liability for ultrahazardous activity
  Negligence
  Trespass
  Citizen enforcement provisions of various statutes

for instance, pays private enterprise over $40 billion annually to conduct studies, prepare reports, and carry out projects. In addition, the federal government is by far the nation's largest landholder, controlling one-third the entire area of the United States. Private enterprise must rely on governmental agencies to issue permits and licenses to explore and mine for minerals, graze cattle, cut timber, or conduct other business activities on government property. Thus, any congressional legislation which influences the decision making concerning federal funding or license granting also affects business. Such legislation is the **National Environmental Policy Act** (NEPA).

NEPA became effective in 1970. The act is divided into two titles. Title I establishes broad policy goals and imposes specific duties on all federal agencies, and Title II sets up the Council on Environmental Quality (CEQ). As the CEQ's role under NEPA consists mainly in gathering and assessing information, issuing advisory guidelines, and making recommendations to the President on environmental matters, this section will center on Title I.

The Environmental Impact Statement

Title I of NEPA imposes specific "action-forcing" requirements on federal agencies. The most important requirement demands that all federal agencies prepare an **environmental impact statement** (EIS) prior to taking certain actions. An EIS must be included "in every recommendation or report on proposals for legislation and other major Federal actions significantly affecting the quality of the human environment." This EIS is a "detailed statement" that estimates the environmental impact of the proposed action. Any discussion of such action and its impact must contain information on adverse environmental effects which cannot be avoided, any irreversible use of resources necessary, and available alternatives to the action (see Figure 24-1).

There have been hundreds of cases that interpret the EIS requirements. In the following case, the Supreme Court decides whether psychological fear caused by the risk of accident at a nuclear power plant is an "environmental effect."

METROPOLITAN EDISON CO. v. PEOPLE AGAINST NUCLEAR ENERGY
103 S.Ct. 1556 (1983)

FACTS

Residents near the Three Mile Island nuclear plants challenged the Nuclear Regulatory Commission's decision to restart one of the plants. The plant had been closed for refueling at the time the other plant suffered a serious accident. The residents contended that the Commission failed to consider the psychological harm which reopening the plant and exposing the community to the risk of nuclear accident might cause.

ISSUE

Does NEPA require an agency to evaluate the psychological effects of the risk of a nuclear power plant accident?

DECISION

No.

REASONS

1. Where an agency action significantly affects the quality of the human environment, NEPA requires preparation of an EIS.
2. NEPA does not require the agency to consider *every* effect of proposed action, but only the effect on the *environment*.
3. Congress intended the term *environment* to mean "physical environment."
4. A "risk" of an accident is not an effect on the physical environment.

Council on Environmental Quality Guidelines

Several regulatory guidelines issued by the CEQ have made the EIS more useful. One guideline directs the federal agencies to engage in **scoping.** Scoping requires that even before EIS preparation, agencies must designate which environmental issues of a contemplated action are most significant. It encourages impact statements to focus on more substantial environmen-

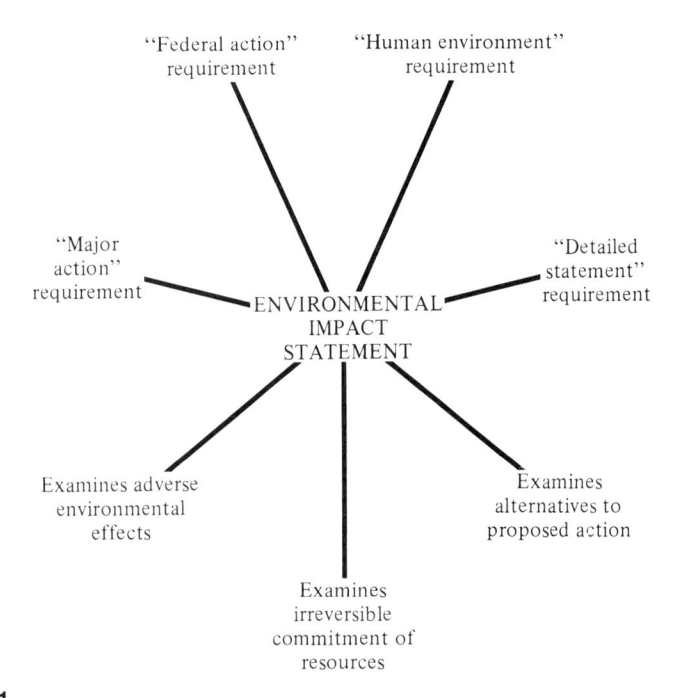

FIGURE 24-1

Environmental Impact Statement components:
- "Federal action" requirement
- "Human environment" requirement
- "Major action" requirement
- "Detailed statement" requirement
- Examines adverse environmental effects
- Examines alternatives to proposed action
- Examines irreversible commitment of resources

tal concerns and reduce the attention devoted to trivial issues. It also allows other agencies and interested parties to participate in the scoping process. This helps ensure that formal impact statements will address matters regarded as most important.

Another guideline directs that EISs be "clear, to the point, and written in plain English." This deters the use of technical jargon and helps those reading impact statements to understand them. The CEQ has also limited the length of impact statements, which once ran to more than 1,000 pages, to 150 pages, except in unusual circumstances.

Criticisms of the EIS

Critics of NEPA and the CEQ guidelines raise several issues in regard to the current EIS process. Some critics point out that the present process fails to consider the economic injury caused by abandoning or delaying projects. They also contend that those preparing EISs are forced to consider far too many alternatives to proposed federal action without regard to their economic reasonableness. Other critics maintain that most impact statements are too descriptive and not sufficiently analytical. They fear that the EIS is "a document of compliance rather than a decision-making tool." A final general criticism of the EIS process notes the limits of its usefulness. As follow-ups on some EISs have shown, environmental factors are often so complex that projections concerning environmental effects amount to little more than guesswork.

Although NEPA applies only to federal actions, many states have enacted similar legislation to assist their decision making. Many interpretive problems found on the national level are also encountered at the state level. In addition, as the states frequently lack the resources and expertise of the federal government, state EISs are often even less helpful in evaluating complex environmental factors than are those prepared by federal agencies.

GOVERNMENT'S REGULATION OF BUSINESS

2 INTRODUCTION

More and more companies are hiring environmental managers to deal with environmental compliance issues. This trend reflects the continuing importance of the government's regulation of private enterprise and its impact on the environment. Congress may fine-tune environmental acts, but the national commitment to a cleaner environment is here to stay.

For businesses which have borne the enormous expense of environmental cleanup, there is one bright note. When adjusted for inflation, real spending for pollution control is beginning to decline. The reason for the decline is that much of the initial expense of pollution control equipment has already been met.

3 THE ENVIRONMENTAL PROTECTION AGENCY

The modern environmental movement began in the 1960s. As it gained momentum, it generated political pressure, which forced government to reassess its role in environmental issues. One of the first steps taken at the federal level in response to this pressure was the establishing of the **Environmental Protection Agency** (EPA) in 1970. At the federal level, the EPA coordinates public control of private action as it affects the environment.

Today, the EPA is an enormous bureaucracy with a number of major responsibilities (see Table 24-2). Most importantly, it administers federal laws which concern pollution of the air and water, solid waste and toxic substance disposal, pesticide regulation, and radiation. The following sections examine these laws.

4 THE CLEAN AIR ACT: BASIC STRUCTURE

In 1257, Queen Eleanor of England was driven from Nottingham Castle because of harsh smoke from the numerous coal fires in London. Coal had

TABLE 24-2 RESPONSIBILITIES OF THE EPA

1. Conducting research on the harmful impact of pollution
2. Gathering information about present pollution problems
3. Assisting states and local governments in controlling pollution through grants, technical advice, and other means
4. Advising the CEQ about new policies needed for protection of the environment
5. Administering federal pollution laws

come into widespread use in England during this time after the cutting of forests for fuel and agricultural purposes. By 1307, a royal order prohibited coal burning in London's kilns under punishment of "grievous ransoms." This early attempt at controlling air pollution does not appear, however, to have been very effective. As recently as the London smog of 1952, 4,000 people died of air-pollution–related causes, including coal smoke.

The key federal legislation for controlling air pollution in the United States is the Clean Air Act. This legislation directs the EPA administrator to establish air quality standards and to see that these standards are achieved according to a definite timetable. So far, the administrator has set primary and secondary air quality standards for particulates, carbon monoxide, sulfur dioxide, nitrogen dioxide, hydrocarbons, and lead. **Primary standards** are those necessary to protect public health. **Secondary standards** guard the public from other adverse air pollution effects such as injury to property, vegetation, and climate, and damage to esthetic values. In most instances, primary and secondary air quality standards are identical.

Government regulation of private action under the Clean Air Act is a joint federal and state effort. The EPA sets standards and the states devise implementation plans, which the EPA must approve, to carry them out. The states thus bear principal responsibility for enforcing the Clean Air Act, with the EPA providing standard setting, coordinating, and supervisory functions. However, the EPA may also participate in enforcement. The administrator can require the operator of any air pollution source to keep such records and perform such monitoring or sampling as the EPA deems appropriate. In addition, the EPA has the right to inspect these records and data. Various criminal and civil penalties and fines back up the Clean Air Act. In addition, industries that do not obey cleanup orders face payment to the EPA; payment amounts to the economic savings they realize from their failure to install and operate proper antipollution equipment.

Air Pollution Sources

For control purposes, the Clean Air Act amendments divide air pollution sources into two categories: **stationary** and **mobile** (transportation). Under the state implementation plans, major stationary polluters, such as steel mills and utilities, must reduce their emissions to a level sufficient to bring down air pollution to meet primary and secondary standards. Polluters follow timetables and schedules in complying with these requirements. To achieve designated standards, they install a variety of control devices, including wet collectors (scrubbers), filter collectors, tall stacks, electrostatic precipitators, and afterburners. New stationary pollution sources, or modified ones, must install the best system of emission reduction which has been adequately demonstrated. Under the act's provision, citizens are granted standing to enforce compliance with these standards.

The act requires both stationary and mobile sources to meet a timetable of air pollution standards for which control technology may not exist at the time. This "technology-forcing" aspect of the act is unique to the history of governmental regulation of business, yet it has been upheld by the Supreme Court.

UNION ELECTRIC CO. v. EPA
427 U.S. 246 (1975)

FACTS

Plaintiff electric utility company sought review of the EPA administrator's approval of the Missouri state implementation plan under the Clean Air Act. Plaintiff's grounds were that it was impossible to comply with the emission limitations imposed by the Missouri plan.

ISSUE

Has plaintiff stated sufficient grounds to require review of the plan's approval?

DECISION

No.

REASONS

1. None of the eight criteria which the plan must satisfy for approval permit consideration of technological or economic problems.
2. The congressional purpose behind the Clean Air Act requires technology-forcing.
3. Thus, technological difficulty does not state grounds for review of the plan.

Technology-forcing does not always succeed. It is neither always possible nor always feasible to force new technological developments. In recognizing this fact, developers of the Clean Air Act have allowed the EPA in many instances to grant **compliance waivers** and **variances** from its standards.

5 THE CLEAN AIR ACT: POLICY TRENDS

In the past few years, the EPA has moved to make its regulatory practices more economically efficient. All new pollution control rules are now subjected to cost-benefit analysis. The EPA has also developed specific policies to achieve air pollution control in an economically efficient manner.

The Bubble Concept

Traditionally, the EPA has regulated each individual pollution emission **point source** (such as a smokestack) within an industrial plant or complex. Increasingly, however, the EPA is encouraging the states, through their implementation plans, to adopt an approach called the **bubble concept.** Under the bubble concept, each plant complex is treated as if it were encased in a bubble. Instead of each pollution point source being licensed for a limited amount of pollution emission, the pollution of the plant complex as a whole is the focus of regulation. Businesses may suggest their own plans for cleaning up multiple sources of pollution within the entire complex, as long as the total pollution emitted does not exceed certain limits. This approach permits flexibility in curtailing pollution and provides businesses with economic incentives to discover new methods of control. The following case shows that the Supreme Court has upheld the EPA's authority to approve the bubble concept, even in states where pollution exceeds air quality standards.

CHEVRON U.S.A. INC. v. NATURAL RESOURCES DEFENSE COUNCIL
104 S.Ct. 2778 (1984)

FACTS

The Clean Air Act places certain requirements on states that do not achieve the EPA's air quality standards. In general, states cannot issue emission permits for "new or modified major stationary sources" of pollution unless very strict conditions are met. In 1981, the EPA defined the term "stationary sources" to include treating an entire plant as a single stationary source. This allowed states to implement the bubble concept. It meant that companies could build new smokestacks within a plantwide "source" without getting new emission permits, as long as total pollution under the "bubble" did not rise. The Natural Resources Defense Council challenged the EPA's definition of "stationary sources." The court of appeals ruled that the EPA's definition, which permitted states to use the bubble concept, was inappropriate in areas where air quality violated EPA standards.

ISSUE

Is the court of appeals correct in its rejection of the EPA's definition of "stationary sources" under the Clean Air Act?

> **DECISION**
>
> No.
>
> **REASONS**
>
> 1. The Clean Air Act and legislative history are ambiguous about the meaning of "stationary sources."
> 2. The court of appeals's interpretation of the term as not applying to plantwide areas is a reasonable one, but it is not the only definition possible.
> 3. The EPA's definition is also permissible.
> 4. Courts must not substitute their interpretation of an ambiguous regulatory statute for that of the regulatory agency established by Congress to act under the statute.

Emissions Reduction Banking

A number of states are now developing EPA-approved plans for **emissions reduction banking.** Under such plans, businesses can cut pollution beyond what the law requires and "bank" these reductions for their own future use or to sell to other companies as emission offsets. Eventually, we may be headed for a "marketable rights" approach to pollution control, where the right to discharge a certain pollutant would be auctioned off to the highest bidder. This approach would promote efficiency by offering to those who have the greatest need for pollution rights the opportunity to obtain them by bidding highest for them.

Prevention of Significant Deterioration

Another important policy of the Clean Air Act is the **prevention of significant deterioration.** Under this policy, pollution emission is controlled, even in areas where the air is cleaner than prevailing primary and secondary air quality standards require. In some of these areas, the EPA permits construction of new pollution emission sources according to a strictly limited scheme. In other areas, it allows no new pollution emission at all. Critics of this policy argue that it prevents industry from moving into southern and western states, where air quality is cleaner than standards require.

The Permitting Process

One of the most controversial issues involving the Clean Air Act concerns the delay and red tape caused by the permitting process. Before a business can construct new pollution emission sources, it must obtain the necessary environmental permits from the appropriate state agency. Today, the estimated time needed to acquire the necessary permits to build a coal-fired electrical generating plant is five to ten years. This is nearly twice the length of time it took in the early 1970s. The formalities of the permitting process, the lack of flexibility in state implementation plans, the requirement that even minor variations in state implementation plans be approved by the EPA—all of these factors contribute to delay. Both the EPA and Congress are considering ways to streamline the permitting process.

In spite of the controversy generated by the Clean Air Act, evidence indicates that the overall air quality in the United States is steadily improving. The 16,000 quarts of air we each breathe daily are cleaner and healthier in most places than they were a decade ago. Yet an estimated 80 million persons in the United States still breath air that violates one or more primary air quality standards. Note, also, that air pollution is an international problem and that not all countries of the world have, or can afford, our air quality standards. This situation exists especially in developing nations of the world, which are striving to reach our standard of living.

Recognition of New Air Pollutants

In drawing up air quality standards in the 1970s, the EPA regulated only six pollutant groups. Since that time, however, environmental scientists have discovered scores of other potentially dangerous air pollutants, including asbestos, formaldehyde, and benzene. Partially in response to lawsuits by environmental organizations, the EPA has been forced to recognize that the Clean Air Act applies to these pollutants. As of this writing, the exact role of the EPA in regulating many of these pollutants has not been determined.

An environmental problem about which there is growing awareness is indoor air pollution. Paints, cleaning products, furniture polishes, gas furnaces, and stoves all emit pollutants that can be harmful to human health. Radioactive radon seeping into homes and buildings from the ground has now been recognized as a major health hazard. Some studies have found that indoor levels of certain pollutants far exceed outdoor levels, whether at work or home. Although the Clean Air Act does not apply to such pollution, the possibility of new regulation covering indoor pollution is always a possibility.

6 THE CLEAN WATER ACT

Business enterprise is a major source of water pollution in the United States. Almost one-half of all water used in this country is for cooling and condensing purposes in connection with industrial activities. The resulting discharge into our rivers and lakes sometimes takes the form of heated water, called thermal effluents. In addition to thermal effluents, industry also discharges chemical and other effluents into the nation's waterways.

The principal federal law regulating water pollution is the Clean Water

Act. As with the Clean Air Act, the Clean Water Act is administered primarily by the states in accordance with EPA standards. If the states do not fulfill their responsibilities, however, the federal government, through the EPA, can step in and enforce the law. The Clean Water Act applies to all navigable waterways, intrastate as well as interstate. As the following case shows, the term "navigable" has been interpreted very broadly.

QUIVIRA MINING CO. v. EPA
765 F.2d 126 (1985)

FACTS

The EPA issued permits to Quivira Mining Company and Homestake Mining Company. The permits limited these companies' rights to discharge pollutants into Arroyo del Puerto and San Mateo Creek. The companies challenged the EPA's power to regulate discharges into these nearly dry "gullies," asserting that the EPA could only regulate discharges into "navigable waters" under the Clean Water Act.

ISSUE

Can the EPA regulate pollutant discharge into Arroyo del Puerto and San Mateo Creek under the Clean Water Act?

DECISION

Yes.

REASONS

1. Under the Clean Water Act, Congress clearly intended to regulate waters of the United States to the fullest extent permitted by the commerce clause.
2. Substantial evidence supports the finding that at certain times there is a connection between Arroyo del Puerto, San Mateo Creek, and navigable-in-fact waters.
3. There is a sufficient impact on interstate commerce to justify regulation.

The Clean Water Act sets goals to eliminate water pollution. Principally, these goals are to make the nation's waterways safe for swimming and other recreational use and clean enough for the protection of fish, shellfish, and wildlife. The law sets strict deadlines and strong enforcement provisions, which must be followed by industry, municipalities, and other water polluters. Enforcement of the Clean Water Act revolves around its permit discharge system. Without being subject to criminal penalties, no polluter can discharge pollutants from any point source (that is, a pipe) without a permit, and municipal as well as industrial dischargers must obtain permits. The EPA has issued guidelines for state permit programs and has approved those programs that meet the guidelines.

Under the Clean Water Act, industries have a two-step sequence for cleanup of industrial wastes discharged into rivers and streams. The first step requires polluters to install best practicable technology (BPT). The second demands installation of best available technology (BAT). Various timetables apply in achieving these steps, according to the type of pollutant being discharged. In 1984, the EPA announced application of the bubble concept to water pollution in the steel industry.

In addition to the Clean Water Act, the EPA administers two other acts related to water pollution control. One, the Marine Protection, Research, and Sanctuaries Act of 1972, requires a permit system for the discharge or dumping of various material into the seas. The other is the Safe Water Drinking Act of 1974, which has forced the EPA to set maximum drinking-water contaminant levels for certain organic and inorganic chemicals, pesticides, and microbiological pollutants.

The Clean Water Act and other current statutes do not reach one important type of water pollution: *non-point source* pollution. Much water pollution comes not from industrial and municipal point source discharges, but from runoffs into streams and rivers. These runoffs often contain agricultural fertilizers and pesticides as well as oil and lead compounds from streets and highways. In 1987, Congress authorized $400 million for the National Non-Point Source Pollution Program to study the problem.

7 THE NOISE CONTROL ACT

The Preamble to the Constitution establishes as a constitutional purpose the assurance of "domestic tranquillity." This phrase has been legally defined as the state or character of being quiet, or "quietness." Nearly two hundred years since the Constitution's ratification, however, our society is noisier than ever, despite the fact that excessive noise has been implicated not only in causing deafness but also in contributing to high blood pressure, heart disease, stress, and emotional disturbance. The EPA estimates that some seventy million Americans presently live with neighborhood noise levels sufficiently high to cause annoyance and dissatisfaction. A recent Census Bureau survey reports that street noise was the most frequently mentioned neighborhood problem.

To combat the growing effects of noise pollution, Congress passed the Noise Control Act of 1972. In the opening sections of the act, Congress lists, as the major sources of noise, transportation vehicles and equipment, machinery, appliances, and other products used in commerce. The act aims at controlling the noise emission of these manufactured items rather than at limiting outside noise levels.

Under the act, the EPA must set limits on noise emission for any product which is identified as a major source of noise or which falls into certain specified categories. In setting these standards, the EPA must consider the noise levels necessary to protect public health and welfare, the best available technology, and the cost of compliance. The EPA has set or proposed standards for trucks, motorcycles, buses, air compressors, rock drills and pavement breakers, bulldozers, front-end loaders, power mowers, and air conditioners.

Most of the standards will take effect over a several-year period and apply only to new products. Manufacturers of these products are held to warrant to purchasers that their products comply with the standards, and no state or local government may enact or enforce noise emission levels which differ from them. For any product which the EPA determines emits noise capable of adversely affecting the public welfare or which is sold on the basis of its effectiveness in reducing noise, the agency must require that notice of this product's noise level be given to each prospective purchaser.

The act prohibits: (1) commercial distribution by a manufacturer of a product not complying with designated noise levels, (2) the removal from a product of a required noise control device, (3) the use of the product after removal, (4) the distribution of a product without a required notice of noise level and removal of this notice, and (5) the importation of a product not in compliance with designated noise levels. The EPA enforces these prohibitions through both criminal and civil remedies. It may also require manufacturers to maintain records and conduct tests of their products.

In the early 1980s, implementation and enforcement of the Noise Control Act slowed considerably. It remains to be seen whether noise control in the future will gain a significant role in environmental regulation.

8 THE PESTICIDE CONTROL ACTS

Pests, especially insects and mice, destroy over 10 percent of all crops grown in the United States, causing several billion dollars of damage annually. In many underdeveloped countries, however, a much greater percentage of total crop production is lost to pests, as high as 40 to 50 percent in countries such as India. Perhaps the principal reason for our lower rate of crop loss is that the United States uses more pesticides per acre than any other country.

The widespread, continual application of pesticides presents environmental problems, however. Not only is it dangerous to wildlife, particularly birds and fish, but it may eventually threaten our agricultural capacity itself. Rapidly breeding pests gradually become immune to the application of pesticides, and researchers may not always be able to invent new poisons to kill them.

Federal regulation of pesticides is accomplished primarily through two statutes: the Federal Insecticide, Fungicide, and Rodenticide Act of 1947, as amended, and the Federal Environmental Pesticide Control Act of 1972 (FEPCA). Both statutes require the registration and labeling of agricultural pesticides, although FEPCA coverage extends to the application of pesticides as well.

Under the acts, the administrator of the EPA is directed to register those pesticides which are properly labeled, which meet the claims made as to their effectiveness, and which will not have unreasonable adverse effects on the environment. The phrase "unreasonable adverse effects on the environment" is defined as "any unreasonable risk to man or the environment, taking into account the economic, social, and environmental costs and benefits of the use of any pesticide." In addition to its authority to require registration of pesticides, the EPA classifies pesticides for either general use or restricted use. In the latter category, the EPA may impose further restrictions that require application only by a trained applicator or with the approval of a trained consultant.

The EPA has a variety of enforcement powers to ensure that pesticide goals are met, including the power to deny or suspend registration. In the 1980s, the EPA has used this power and banned several pesticides suspected of causing cancer.

There are two chief criticisms of pesticide control: one coming from affected businesses; the other, from the environmental movement. Pesticide manufacturers complain that the lengthy, expensive testing procedures required by the FEPCA registration process delay useful pesticides from reaching the market and inhibit new research. On the other hand, many in the environmental movement contend that our country's pesticide control policy is hypocritical in that the FEPCA does not apply to pesticides which United States manufacturers ship to foreign countries. Companies can sell overseas what they cannot sell in this country.

9 THE SOLID WASTE DISPOSAL ACT

Pollution problems cannot always be neatly categorized. For instance, solid waste disposal processes often create pollution in several environmentally related forms. When solid waste is burned, it can cause air pollution and violate the Clean Air Act. When dumped into rivers, streams, and lakes, solid waste can pollute the water beyond amounts permitted under the Clean Water Act. Machinery used in solid waste disposal can also be subject to the regulation of the Noise Control Act.

By all accounts, solid waste pollution problems during the last twenty-five years have grown as the pollution has risen and as we have become more affluent and productive. Currently, total solid wastes produced yearly in the United States exceed 5 billion tons, or almost 25 tons for every individual in the population. Half this amount is agricultural waste, another third is mineral waste, and the remainder is industrial, institutional, and residential waste. Some wastes are toxic and hazardous, while others stink or attract pests. All present disposal problems of significant proportion.

The Solid Waste Disposal Act represents the primary federal effort in solid waste control. Congress recognized in this act that the main responsibility for nontoxic waste management rests with regional, state, and local management and limited the federal role in this area. Under this act, the federal role in nontoxic waste management is limited mainly to promoting research and providing technical and financial assistance to the states.

In responding to solid waste disposal problems, state and local governments have taken a variety of approaches. These include developing sanitary landfills, requiring that solid waste be separated into categories that facilitate disposal and recycling, and granting tax breaks for industries using recycled materials. A report by the Council of State Governments noted that there are over a thousand community recycling centers and that over a hundred cities and countries have waste-to-energy facilities. Nine states with 25 percent of the nation's population have beverage container deposit laws, the so-called "bottle bills."

Some companies have incorporated waste disposal provisions into their codes of ethics, as the following excerpt from the Caterpillar Code of Ethics illustrates.

Waste Disposal

Proper means for disposal of municipal and industrial wastes are essential to society. For example, continued operation of Caterpillar facilities depends upon availability of landfills and contract services for disposal.

When practical, Caterpillar reuses or recycles byproducts of manufacturing processes. But in some cases, reuse and recycling aren't practical. It then becomes necessary that waste materials be handled and disposed of in a manner consistent with the public interest, as expressed in applicable laws and regulations.

Aside from government regulations, we shall make certain that disposition of Caterpillar wastes is carried out in a manner consistent with the ethical business practices set forth in the Code. When contractors are involved, they should demonstrate necessary technical competence, maintain a high level of performance, and otherwise meet Caterpillar standards regarding long-lasting supplier relationships.

In 1976, Congress amended the Solid Wastes Disposal Act with the National Resource Conservation and Recovery Act. The next section discusses this act and other statutes related to toxic wastes.

10 TOXIC AND HAZARDOUS SUBSTANCES: INTRODUCTION

According to the opinion research organization Yankelovich, Skelly and White, the control of toxic and hazardous chemicals "ranks first" on the public's list of where the government's regulation of industry is needed. In the last several years, regulation of such chemicals has been expanding rapidly. We can divide public control of private action in this area into three categories: (1) regulation of the use of toxic chemicals, (2) regulation of toxic and hazardous waste disposal, and (3) regulation of toxic and hazardous waste cleanup.

11 TOXIC SUBSTANCES CONTROL ACT

Even as the Clean Air and Water Acts are slowly beginning to diminish many types of air and water pollution, attention is being drawn to another environmental problem which is potentially the most serious of all: toxic substances. Hardly a day passes without the news media reporting some new instance of alleged threat to human health and well-being from one or another of the chemical substances so important to manufacturing, farming, mining, and other aspects of modern life.

Threats to human welfare from toxic substances are not new to history. Some people suggest that poisoning from lead waterpipes and drinking vessels may have depleted the ranks of the ruling class of ancient Rome and thus contributed to the downfall of the Roman Empire. More recently, some think that the "mad hatters" of the nineteenth-century fur and felt trades likely suffered brain disorders from inhaling the vapors of mercury used in their crafts. Today, however, the presence of toxic substances in the environment is made more serious by the fact that over 70,000 industrial and agricultural chemical compounds are in commercial use, and new chemicals, a significant percentage of which are toxic, are being introduced into the marketplace at the rate of over 1,000 substances annually.

To meet the special environmental problems posed by the use of toxic chemicals, Congress in 1976 enacted the Toxic Substances Control Act (TSCA). Prior to passage of the TSCA, there was no coordinated effort to evaluate effects of these chemical compounds. Some of these compounds are beneficial to society and present no threat to the environment. Some, however, are both toxic and long-lasting, a fact which in the past has been uncovered only after these compounds were introduced into wide use and became important to manufacturing and farming. The primary purpose of the TSCA is to force an early evaluation of suspect chemicals before they become economically important.

The EPA collects information under TSCA sections which require that manufacturers and distributors report to the EPA any information they possess which indicates that a chemical substance presents a "substantial risk" of injury to health or to the environment. The TSCA further demands that the EPA be given advance notice before the manufacture of new chemical substances or the processing of any substance for a significant new use. Based on the results of its review, the EPA can take action to stop or limit introduction of new chemicals if they threaten human health or the environment with unreasonable risks.

The law also authorizes the EPA to require manufacturers to test their chemicals for possible harmful effects. Since not all the 70,000 chemicals in commerce can be tested simultaneously, the EPA has developed a priority scheme for selecting substances for testing based on whether or not the chemicals cause cancer, birth defects, or gene mutations.

In view of the beneficial role that many chemical substances play in all aspects of production and consumption, Congress directed the EPA through the TSCA to consider the economic and social impact, as well as the environmental one, of its decisions. In this respect the TSCA is unlike the Clean Air Act, which requires that certain pollution standards be met without regard for economic factors.

12 NATURAL RESOURCE CONSERVATION AND RECOVERY ACT

The congressional Office of Technology Assessment reports that more than a ton of hazardous waste per citizen is dumped annually into the nation's environment. A major environmental problem has been how to ensure that the generators of toxic wastes dispose of them safely. In the past, there have been instances where even some otherwise responsible companies have placed highly toxic wastes in the hands of less-than-reputable disposal contractors.

To help ensure proper handling and disposal of hazardous and toxic wastes, Congress in 1976 amended the Solid Waste Disposal Act by the Resource Conservation and Recovery Act (RCRA). Under the RCRA, a generator of wastes has two primary obligations. The first is to determine whether its wastes qualify as hazardous under RCRA. The second is to see that such wastes are properly transported to a disposal facility which has an EPA permit or license.

The EPA lists a number of hazardous wastes, and a generator can determine if a nonlisted waste is hazardous in terms of several chemical characteristics specified by the EPA. The RCRA accomplishes proper disposal of hazardous wastes through the **manifest system.** This system requires a generator to prepare a manifest document which designates a licensed facility for disposal purposes. The generator then gives copies of the manifest to the transporter of the waste. After receiving hazardous wastes, the disposal facility must return a copy of the manifest to the generator. In this fashion, the generator knows the waste has received proper disposal.

Failure to receive this manifest copy from the disposal facility within certain time limits requires the generator to notify the EPA. Under RCRA, the EPA has various investigatory powers. The act also prescribes various recordkeeping requirements and assesses penalties for failure to comply with its provisions.

As amended in 1986, RCRA is moving the handling of toxic wastes away from burial on land to treatments that destroy or permanently detoxify wastes. By 1990, RCRA requirements will cost business an estimated $20 billion annually.

13 THE SUPERFUND

After passage of TSCA and RCRA in 1976, regulation of toxic and hazardous substances was still incomplete. These acts did not deal with problems of the cleanup costs of unsafe hazardous waste dumps or spills, which are often substantial. Many dump sites are abandoned and date back as far as the nineteenth century. Even current owners of unsafe dump sites are frequently financially incapable of cleaning up hazardous wastes. The same applies to transporters and others who cause spills or unauthorized discharges of hazardous wastes.

In 1980, Congress created the Comprehensive Environmental Response, Compensation, and Liability Act to address these problems. Known as the **Superfund,** this act has allotted billions of dollars for environmental cleanup of dangerous hazardous wastes. Taxes on the petroleum and chemical industries finance most of the fund.

The act requires anyone who releases unauthorized amounts of hazardous substances into the environment to notify the government. Whether it is notified or not, the government has the power to order those responsible to clean up such releases. Refusal to obey can lead to a suit for reimbursement for any cleanup monies spent from the Superfund plus punitive damages of up to triple the cleanup costs. The government can also recover damages for injury done to natural resources. To date, the biggest Superfund case involved Shell Oil and the United States Army. These parties agreed to clean up a site outside Denver. Total costs may exceed $1 billion.

The Superfund imposes a type of strict liability on those responsible for unauthorized discharges of hazardous wastes. Thus, no negligence need be proved. An additional strict liability falls on generators of hazardous wastes. They are strictly liable for *any* illegal discharge of hazardous waste as long as they have a contractual relationship with the responsible parties. For example, a chemical company whose transporter of wastes causes an unauthorized release of toxic chemicals, or whose disposal facility dumps chemicals illegally, is strictly liable for any resulting injury.

Finally, take note that both the Clean Air Act and the Clean Water Act also contain provisions related to government suits to recover costs for the cleanup of toxic chemicals. Suits under the Superfund and other acts are growing rapidly (see Table 24-3) and will be a major area of environmental litigation in coming years. By the end of 1986, responsible parties had already spent more than $619 million in Superfund-required cleanup.

14 RADIATION

In 1979, the nuclear power plant accident at the Three Mile Island installation in Pennsylvania and subsequent evacuation of thousands of nearby residents focused the nation's attention on the potential hazards of radiation pollution.

TABLE 24-3 RECENT HAZARDOUS WASTE SETTLEMENTS

Company	Amount	Location
Alcoa	$5.6 million	Greenup, IL
Diamond Shamrock	$12 million	Newark, NJ
Occidental	$30 million	Niagara Falls, NY
Shell Oil (and United States Army)	Up to $1 billion	Denver, CO
Ten companies	$50 billion	Baton Rouge, LA
Waste Management	$10.5 million	Vickery, OH
Westinghouse	$90 million	Bloomington, IN

Although no single piece of legislation comprehensively controls radiation pollution and no one agency is responsible for administering legislation in this technologically complex area, overall responsibility for such control rests with the Nuclear Regulatory Commission. The EPA, however, does have general authority to conduct testing and provide technical assistance in the area of radiation pollution control. Also, the Clean Air Act, the Federal Water Pollution Control Act, and the Ocean Dumping Act all contain sections applicable to radiation discharges into the air and water.

SUITS BY PRIVATE INDIVIDUALS

15 INTRODUCTION

Achieving environmental goals requires coordinated strategy and implementation. As private citizens, individuals and groups of individuals lack both the power and foresight necessary to control pollution on a broad scale. There is a role, however, for the private control of private action in two principal areas.

First, most of the environmental laws, such as the Clean Air and Water Acts, contain "citizen enforcement" provisions. These provisions grant private individuals and groups the standing to sue to challenge failures to comply with the environmental laws. In many instances, private citizens can sue polluters directly to force them to cease violating the law. Private citizens also have standing to sue public agencies (for example, the EPA) to require them to adopt regulations or implement enforcement against private polluters which the environmental laws require. Between 1984 and 1987, citizen-enforcement actions, especially actions against polluters, grew rapidly.

A second area of private control of private action lies in tort law and its state codifications. When pollution directly injures private citizens, they may sue offending polluters under various theories of tort law. Thus, the traditional deterrence of tort law contributes to private control of private action. The next section further develops tort law's role in pollution control.

16 TORT THEORIES AND POLLUTION

Examination of tort law and pollution control reveals little understanding of the interdependence between ourselves and our environment. Instead, tort theories, as they have been applied to environmental problems, focus on the action of one person (or business) as it injures the health or interferes with the property rights of another. In other words, tort law attacks the pollution problem by using the established theories of nuisance, negligence, and trespass.

Nuisance

The principal tort theory used in pollution control has been that of nuisance. The law relating to nuisance is somewhat vague, but in most jurisdictions the common law has been put into statutory form. Several common elements exist in the law of nuisance in most states. To begin with, there are two types of nuisances: public and private.

A **public nuisance** arises from an act which causes inconvenience or damage to the public in the exercise of rights common to everyone. In the environmental area, air, water, and noise pollution can all constitute a public nuisance if they affect common rights. More specifically, industrial waste discharge which kills the fish in a stream may be held a public nuisance, since fishing rights are commonly possessed by the public. Public nuisance actions may be brought only by a public official, not private individuals, unless the latter have suffered some special damage to their persons or property as a result of the public nuisance.

Any unreasonable use of one's property so as to cause substantial interference with the enjoyment or use of another's land establishes a common law **private nuisance**. The unreasonableness of the interference is measured by a balancing process in which the character, extent, and duration of harm to the plaintiff is weighed against the social utility of the defendant's activity and its appropriateness to its location. Since society needs industrial activity as well as natural tranquillity, people must put up with a certain amount of smoke, dust, noise, and polluted water if they live in concentrated areas of industry. But what may be an appropriate industrial use of land in a congested urban area may be a private nuisance if it occurs in a rural or residential location.

Take note that the proving of nuisance does not demand that a property owner be found negligent. An unreasonable use of one's land does not mean that one's *conduct* is unreasonable.

Other Tort Decisions

Private plaintiffs in pollution cases frequently allege the applicability of tort doctrines other than that of nuisance. These doctrines, however, do overlap that of nuisance, which is really a field of tort liability rather than a type of conduct.

One such doctrine is that of trespass. A defendant is liable for **trespass** if, without right, she or he intentionally enters land in possession of another, or causes something to do so. The entrance is considered intentional if the defendant knew that it was substantially certain to result from her or his conduct. Thus, airborne particles which fall on a plaintiff's property can constitute a trespass. In recent years, many courts have merged the theories of nuisance and trespass to such an extent that before plaintiffs can recover for a particle trespass, they must prove that the harm done to them exceeds the social utility of the defendant's enterprise.

Negligence doctrine is sometimes used by private plaintiffs in environmental pollution cases. The basis for the negligence tort lies in the defendant's breach of his or her duty to use ordinary and reasonable care toward the plaintiff, which proximately (foreseeably) causes the plaintiff injury. A factory's failure to use available pollution control equipment may be evidence of its failure to employ "reasonable care."

Finally, some courts recognize the applicability in pollution cases of **strict liability tort doctrine**. This tort liability arises when the defendant injures the plaintiff's person or property by voluntarily engaging in ultrahazardous activity which necessarily involves a risk of serious harm that cannot be eliminated through the exercise of the utmost care. No finding of fault, or failure of reasonable care, on the defendant's part is necessary. This doctrine has been employed in situations involving the use of poisons, such as in crop dusting and certain industrial work, the storage and use of explosives, and the storage of water in large quantities in a dangerous place.

Increasing numbers of private plaintiffs are suing companies for pollution-related harm. In one recent case, a chemical company settled with three plaintiffs for $2.7 million.

Damages

An important issue in pollution-related tort cases concerns what damages are recoverable. Exposure to pollution frequently does not cause immediate harm. It merely increases the potential for harm (that is, disease). The next case examines what damages are recoverable in such an instance.

AYERS v. TOWN OF JACKSON
525 A.2d 287 (N.J. 1987)

FACTS

Residents living near the Town of Jackson, New Jersey, had their well water contaminated. For up to six years before the pollution was discovered, toxic pollutants from the town's landfill seeped into the aquifer which supplied water. For twenty additional months, residents could not use running water from their wells. They sued, and the trial court found the town negligent under the New Jersey Tort Claims Act.

ISSUE

Can the residents recover damages for: (1) the deterioration in the quality of life during the twenty months they were deprived of running water, (2) the emotional distress caused by the knowledge that they had drunk polluted water for up to six years, (3) the increased risk of disease, and (4) the cost of continued medical testing?

DECISIONS

1. Yes.
2. No.
3. No.
4. Yes.

REASONS:

1. Although the New Jersey Tort Claims Act prohibits recovery of damages for "pain and suffering," it allows the residents to recover for a deterioration in the quality of life. Being deprived of running water for months is an inconvenience associated with invasion-of-property interest.
2. Emotional distress is a type of "pain and suffering," the recovering of damages for which is prohibited by the act.
3. An increased risk of disease caused by exposure to toxic pollutants is an injury under the act. However, courts have been reluctant to give damages for such injury unless proof that harm (that is, disease) will occur is substantial. Since the residents did not quantify their risk of future disease or other harm, they cannot recover damages for this injury.
4. Well-established legal principles and important public health policy permit damages to be awarded to cover continued medical testing for those persons negligently exposed to toxic pollutants.

If a resident later develops disease caused by exposure to the toxic pollutants, could the resident still sue the town and recover damages? Note that the *Ayers* case was brought under the New Jersey Tort Claims Act because the defendant was a governmental body. Under common law negligence, the residents could have recovered damages for pain and suffering injury. Still a problem even under common law is whether damages can be awarded when negligence causes potential future harm rather than immediate injury.

17 TRENDS

Introduction

A *Wall Street Journal*▲NBC News survey conducted in 1987 suggests strong nationwide support for environment cleanup. A 61 percent majority favored more government regulation of the environment. Only 6 percent thought there should be less environmental regulation.

Cleanup efforts mean environmental regulation, and after being much criticized in the early 1980s, the EPA has shown renewed commitment to achieving regulatory goals. Criminal prosecutions of environmental law violators have increased. The EPA is paying new attention to the presence of toxic chemicals in the air and water. It also has a new administrator to lead it.

Meanwhile, researchers almost daily report new instances of how technological civilization affects life on our planet. For every allegation of pollution-caused environmental harm, however, there are usually countertheories raised, which maintain that the harm is not as significant as alleged, or else argue that the harm arises from causes unrelated to industrial pollution. Lack of unanimous scientific opinion on many environmental issues underscores their great complexity. It also reveals a key controversy at the heart of environmental regulation: *How much certainty of harm is required to justify regulatory intervention?*

Acid Rain

The concern over *acid rain* illustrates the problem. In the eastern United States and Canada, rain with a high acid content is killing fish in lakes and posing a significant threat to forests and certain crops. Considerable theory and research points to midwestern industrial sulfur emissions as causing acid rain problems. Pressure is mounting in Congress to legislate limitations on these emissions. On the other hand, other scientific opinion warns against overly hasty legislative "solutions" to acid rain. It points out that much acid rain is caused naturally.

Ozone

In 1987, representatives from forty-five nations met and agreed to limit production and use of chlorofluorocarbons. Scientists have asserted that these manufactured chemicals used in aerosol spray cans and refrigeration are destroying the *ozone layer* of the upper atmosphere. Destruction of ozone could lead to hundreds of thousands of cases of cataracts and skin cancer in humans, plus unknown serious damage to animal and plant life.

Greenhouse Effect

Overshadowing acid rain and ozone destruction as future pollution concern is increasing atmospheric concentrations of carbon dioxide. The National Academy of Sciences notes that global carbon dioxide levels have increased 6 percent since 1960. The increase is due largely to the burning of fossil fuels such as oil and coal.

Higher carbon dioxide levels will likely lead to warmer global temperatures, the so-called *greenhouse effect*. Changing climate patterns and rising sea levels are possible results. But the timing and magnitude of the greenhouse effect is hotly debated. Is regulatory intervention justified? Will the United States join with other nations seeking to limit the growth of fossil-fuel consumption? These are some of the questions which the business students of the 1980s will quite possibly face during their business careers. Present answers to these questions are unknown. Only one conclusion is clear-cut: We possess immense technological power today to change the environment for better and for worse, both intentionally and inadvertently.

REVIEW QUESTIONS

1 For each term in the left-hand column, match the most appropriate description in the right-hand column:

(1)	EIS	(a)	An unreasonable use of one's land which interferes with the use or enjoyment of another's land.
(2)	Point source	(b)	Treating several point sources at a plant as one source.
(3)	Prevention of significant deterioration	(c)	A process which must be followed by federal agencies before undertaking major actions which significantly affect the environment.
(4)	Superfund	(d)	A smokestack, pipe, or other opening which discharges pollution.
(5)	Nuisance	(e)	The Comprehensive Environmental Response, Compensation, and Liability Act.
(6)	Bubble concept	(f)	The tracking process for toxic waste disposal.
(7)	Manifest system	(g)	Air pollution levels necessary to protect human health.
(8)	Primary air quality standards	(h)	The policy of preventing additional pollution in certain areas which have air cleaner than required by primary standards.

2 Discuss why the way government regulates the environmental impact of its decision making is of significant interest to the business community.
3 Your firm has been hired to build a large government facility near a residential neighborhood. A committee of residents has been formed to oppose the building. You have been asked to assist in writing the EIS. What factors must your EIS take into consideration?
4 Outline criticisms of the EIS process. Why are state EISs often less helpful in evaluating complex environmental factors than are those prepared by federal agencies?
5 The Avila Timber Company has asked for and been granted permission by the Department of the Interior to cut 40 acres of timber from the 10,000-acre Oconee

National Forest. Prior to the actual logging, a local environmental group files suit in federal district court, contending that the Department of Interior has not filed an EIS. Can the group challenge the department's action? Analyze whether an EIS should be filed, in light of the facts given.

6 An EIS prepared for the Army Corps of Engineers by a private consulting firm concludes that the value of the farmland which will be submerged by a proposed dam is greater than the navigational benefits which the dam will bring. Is the Corps prohibited from building the dam because of this conclusion? Discuss.

7 What does it mean to say that the Clean Air Act is "technology-forcing"? What happens when an industry cannot meet the technological standards set by the EPA?

8 The Akins Corporation wishes to build a new smelting facility in Owens County, an area where air pollution exceeds primary air standards. What legal difficulties may they face? What solutions might you suggest for these difficulties?

9 What is the difference between "effluents" and "emissions"?

10 What is the difference between an individual point-source approach and a bubble-policy approach to dealing with factory pollution? For the factory owner, what are the advantages of employing the bubble concept?

11 Bug Control Incorporated desires to produce a new pesticide for control of fire ants. Before beginning manufacture, what process must it follow under the pesticide control acts?

12 Your company has decided to produce a new chemical which has great promise in manufacture of synthetic fabrics. It is recognized that if this chemical is used incorrectly or disposed of improperly, there may be risk to human health or to the environment. What steps must your company take prior to actual production to avoid legal difficulties with the EPA?

13 As a manufacturer of paints, you need to dispose of certain production byproducts which are highly toxic. Discuss the process which the law requires you to follow in disposing of these products.

14 An abandoned radioactive waste site is discovered by local authorities. The waste came from a company which manufactured radium watch faces and which is now out of business. Who will pay to clean up these radioactive wastes? Discuss.

APPENDIX

THE CONSTITUTION OF THE UNITED STATES OF AMERICA

We the People of the United States, in Order to form a more perfect Union, establish Justice, insure domestic Tranquility, provide for the common defence, promote the general Welfare, and secure the Blessings of Liberty to ourselves and our Posterity, do ordain and establish this Constitution for the United States of America.

ARTICLE 1

Section 1

All legislative Powers herein granted shall be vested in a Congress of the United States, which shall consist of a Senate and House of Representatives.

Section 2

The House of Representatives shall be composed of Members chosen every second Year by the People of the several States, and the Electors in each State shall have the Qualifications requisite for Electors of the most numerous Branch of the State Legislature.

    No Person shall be a Representative who shall not have attained to the Age of twenty five Years, and been seven Years a Citizen of the United

States, and who shall not, when elected, be an Inhabitant of that State in which he shall be chosen.

Representatives and direct Taxes shall be apportioned among the several States which may be included within this Union, according to their respective Numbers, which shall be determined by adding to the whole Number of free Persons, including those bound to Service for a Term of Years, and excluding Indians not taxed, three fifths of all other Persons. The actual Enumeration shall be made within three Years after the first Meeting of the Congress of the United States, and within every subsequent Term of ten Years, in such Manner as they shall by Law direct. The Number of Representatives shall not exceed one for every thirty Thousand, but each State shall have at Least one Representative; and until such enumeration shall be made, the State of New Hampshire shall be entitled to chuse three, Massachusetts eight, Rhode Island and Providence Plantations one, Connecticut five, New-York six, New Jersey four, Pennsylvania eight, Delaware one, Maryland six, Virginia ten, North Carolina five, South Carolina five, and Georgia three.

When vacancies happen in the Representation from any State, the Executive Authority thereof shall issue Writs of Election to fill such Vacancies.

The House of Representatives shall chuse their Speaker and other Officers; and shall have the sole Power of Impeachment.

Section 3

The Senate of the United States shall be composed of two Senators from each State, chosen by the Legislature thereof, for six Years; and each Senator shall have one Vote.

Immediately after they shall be assembled in Consequence of the Election, they shall be divided as equally as may be into three Classes. The Seats of the Senators of the first Class shall be vacated at the Expiration of the second Year, of the second Class at the Expiration of the fourth Year, and of the third Class at the Expiration of the sixth Year, so that one third may be chosen every second year; and if Vacancies happen by Resignation, or otherwise, during the Recess of the Legislature of any State, the Executive thereof may make temporary Appointments until the next Meeting of the Legislature, which shall then fill such Vacancies.

No Person shall be a Senator who shall not have attained to the Age of thirty Years, and been nine Years a Citizen of the United States, and who shall not, when elected, be an Inhabitant of that State for which he shall be chosen.

The Vice President of the United States shall be President of the Senate, but shall have no Vote, unless they be equally divided.

The Senate shall chuse their other Officers, and also a President pro tempore, in the Absence of the Vice President, or when he shall exercise the Office of President of the United States.

The Senate shall have the sole Power to try all Impeachments. When sitting for that Purpose, they shall be on Oath or Affirmation. When the President of the United States is tried, the Chief Justice shall preside: And no Person shall be convicted without the Concurrence of two thirds of the Members present.

Judgment in Cases of Impeachment shall not extend further than to removal from Office, and disqualification to hold and enjoy any Office of honor, Trust or Profit under the United States: but the Party convicted shall nevertheless be liable and subject to Indictment, Trial, Judgment and Punishment, according to Law.

Section 4

The Times, Places and Manner of holding Elections for Senators and Representatives, shall be prescribed in each State by the Legislature thereof: but the Congress may at any time by Law make or alter such Regulations, except as to the Places of chusing Senators.

The Congress shall assemble at least once in every Year, and such Meeting shall be on the first Monday in December, unless they shall by Law appoint a different Day.

Section 5

Each House shall be the Judge of the Elections, Returns and Qualifications of its own Members, and a Majority of each shall constitute a Quorum to do Business; but a smaller Number may adjourn from day to day, and may be authorized to compel the Attendance of absent Members, in such Manner, and under such Penalties as each House may provide.

Each House may determine the Rules of its Proceedings, punish its Members for disorderly Behaviour, and, with the concurrence of two thirds, expel a Member.

Each House shall keep a Journal of its Proceedings, and from time to time publish the same, excepting such Parts as may in their Judgment require Secrecy; and the Yeas and Nays of the Members of either House on any question shall, at the Desire of one fifth of those Present, be entered on the Journal.

Neither House, during the Session of Congress, shall, without the Consent of the other, adjourn for more than three days, nor to any other Place than that in which the two Houses shall be sitting.

Section 6

The Senators and Representatives shall receive a Compensation for their Services, to be ascertained by Law, and paid out of the Treasury of the United States. They shall in all Cases, except Treason, Felony and Breach of the Peace, be privileged from Arrest during their Attendance at the Session of their respective Houses, and in going to and returning from the same; and for any Speech or Debate in either House, they shall not be questioned in any other Place.

No Senator or Representative shall, during the Time for which he was elected, be appointed to any civil Office under the Authority of the United States, which shall have been created, or the Emoluments whereof shall have been encreased during such time; and no Person holding any Office under the United States, shall be a Member of either House during his Continuance in Office.

Section 7

All Bills for raising Revenue shall originate in the House of Representatives; but the Senate may propose or concur with Amendments as on other Bills.

Every Bill which shall have passed the House of Representatives and the Senate, shall, before it become a Law, be presented to the President of the United States; If he approve he shall sign it, but if not he shall return it, with his Objections to that House in which it shall have originated, who shall enter the Objections at large on their Journal, and proceed to reconsider it. If after such Reconsideration two thirds of that House shall agree to pass the Bill, it shall be sent, together with the Objections, to the other House, by which it shall likewise be reconsidered, and if approved by two thirds of that House, it shall become a Law. But in all such Cases the Votes of both Houses shall be determined by Yeas and Nays, and the Names of the Persons voting for and against the Bill shall be entered on the Journal of each House respectively. If any Bill shall not be returned by the President within ten Days (Sundays excepted) after it shall have been presented to him, the Same shall be a Law, in like Manner as if he had signed it, unless the Congress by their Adjournment prevent its Return, in which Case it shall not be a Law.

Every Order, Resolution, or Vote to which the Concurrence of the Senate and House of Representatives may be necessary (except on a question of Adjournment) shall be presented to the President of the United States; and before the Same shall take Effect, shall be approved by him, or being disapproved by him, shall be repassed by two thirds of the Senate and House of Representatives, according to the Rules and Limitations prescribed in the Case of a Bill.

Section 8

The Congress shall have Power to lay and collect Taxes, Duties, Imposts and Excises, to pay the Debts and provide for the common Defence and general Welfare of the United States; but all Duties, Imposts and Excises shall be uniform throughout the United States;

To borrow Money on the credit of the United States;

To regulate Commerce with foreign Nations, and among the several States, and with the Indian Tribes;

To establish an uniform Rule of Naturalization, and uniform Laws on the subject of Bankruptcies throughout the United States;

To coin Money, regulate the Value thereof, and of foreign Coin, and fix the Standard of Weights and Measures;

To provide for the Punishment of counterfeiting the Securities and current Coin of the United States;

To establish Post Offices and post Roads;

To promote the Progress of Science and useful Arts, by securing for limited Times to Authors and Inventors the exclusive Right to their respective Writings and Discoveries;

To constitute Tribunals inferior to the supreme Court;

To define and punish Piracies and Felonies committed on the high Seas, and Offenses against the Law of Nations;

To declare War, grant Letters of Marque and Reprisal, and make Rules concerning Captures on Land and Water;

To raise and support Armies, but no Appropriation of Money to that Use shall be for a longer Term than two Years;

To provide and maintain a Navy;

To make Rules for the Government and Regulation of the land and naval Forces;

To provide for calling forth the Militia to execute the Laws of the Union, suppress Insurrections and repel Invasions;

To provide for organizing, arming, and disciplining, the Militia, and for governing such Part of them as may be employed in the Service of the United States, reserving to the States respectively, the Appointment of the Officers, and the Authority of training the Militia according to the discipline prescribed by Congress;

To exercise exclusive Legislation in all Cases whatsoever, over such District (not exceeding ten Miles square) as may, by Cession of particular States, and the Acceptance of Congress, become the Seat of the Government of the United States, and to exercise like Authority over all Places purchased by the Consent of the Legislature of the State in which the Same shall be, for the Erection of Forts, Magazines, Arsenals, dock-Yards, and other needful buildings;—And

To make all Laws which shall be necessary and proper for carrying into Execution the foregoing Powers, and all other Powers vested by the Constitution in the Government of the United States, or in any Department or Officer thereof.

Section 9

The Migration or Importation of such Persons as any of the States now existing shall think proper to admit, shall not be prohibited by the Congress prior to the Year one thousand eight hundred and eight, but a Tax or Duty may be imposed on such Importation, not exceeding ten dollars for each Person.

The Privilege of the Writ of Habeas Corpus shall not be suspended, unless when in Cases of Rebellion or Invasion the public Safety may require it.

No Bill of Attainder or ex post factor Law shall be passed.

No Capitation, or other direct, Tax shall be laid, unless in Proportion to the Census or Enumeration herein before directed to be taken.

No Tax or Duty shall be laid on Articles exported from any State.

No Preference shall be given by any Regulation of Commerce or Revenue to the Ports of one State over those of another: nor shall Vessels bound to, or from, one State, be obliged to enter, clear, or pay Duties in another.

No Money shall be drawn from the Treasury, but in Consequence of Appropriations made by Law; and a regular Statement and Account of the Receipts and Expenditures of all public Money shall be published from time to time.

No Title of Nobility shall be granted by the United States: And no Person holding any Office of Profit or Trust under them, shall, without the Consent of the Congress, accept of any present, Emolument, Office, or Title, of any kind whatever, from any King, Prince, or foreign State.

Section 10

No State shall enter into any Treaty, Alliance, or Confederation; grant Letters of Marque and Reprisal; coin Money; emit Bills of Credit; make any Thing but gold and silver Coin a Tender in Payment of Debts; pass any Bill of Attainder, ex post facto Law, or Law impairing the Obligation of Contracts, or grant any Title of Nobility.

No State shall, without the Consent of the Congress, lay any Imposts or Duties on Imports or Exports, except what may be absolutely necessary for executing its inspection Laws: and the net Produce of all Duties and Imposts, laid by any State on Imports or Exports, shall be for the Use of the Treasury of the United States; and all such Laws shall be subject to the Revision and Controul of the Congress.

No State shall, without the Consent of Congress, lay any Duty of Tonnage, keep Troops, or Ships of War in time of Peace, enter into any Agreement or Compact with another State, or with a foreign Power, or engage in War, unless actually invaded, or in such imminent Danger as will not admit of delay.

ARTICLE II

Section 1

The executive Power shall be vested in a President of the United States of America. He shall hold his Office during the Term of four Years, and, together with the Vice President, chosen for the same Term, be elected, as follows:

Each State shall appoint, in such Manner as the Legislature thereof may direct, a Number of Electors, equal to the whole Number of Senators and Representatives to which the State may be entitled in the Congress: but no Senator or Representative, or Person holding an Office of Trust or Profit under the United States, shall be appointed an Elector.

The Electors shall meet in their respective States, and vote by Ballot for two Persons, of whom one at least shall not be an Inhabitant of the same State with Themselves. And they shall make a List of all the Persons voted for, and of the Number of Votes for each; which List they shall sign and certify, and transmit sealed to the Seat of the Government of the United States, directed to the President of the Senate. The President of the Senate shall, in the Presence of the Senate and House of Representatives, open all the Certificates, and the Votes shall then be counted. The Person having the greatest Number of Votes shall be the President, if such Number be a Majority of the whole Number of Electors appointed; and if there be more than one who have such Majority, and have an equal Number of Votes, then the House of Representatives shall immediately chuse by Ballot one of them for President; and if no Person have a Majority, then from the five highest on the List the said House shall in like Manner chuse the President. But in chusing the President, the Votes shall be taken by States, the Representation from each State having one Vote; A quorum for this Purpose shall consist of a Member or Members from two thirds of the States, and a Majority of all the States shall be necessary to a Choice. In every Case, after the Choice of the President, the Person having the greatest Number of Votes of the Electors shall be the Vice President. But if there should remain two or more who have equal Votes, the Senate shall chuse from them by Ballot the Vice President.

The Congress may determine the Time of chusing the Electors, and the Day on which they shall give their Votes; which Day shall be the same throughout the United States.

No Person except a natural born Citizen, or a Citizen of the United States, at the time of the Adoption of this Constitution, shall be eligible to the Office of President; neither shall any Person be eligible to that Office who shall not have attained to the Age of thirty five Years, and been fourteen Years a Resident within the United States.

In Case of the Removal of the President from Office, or of his Death, Resignation, or Inability to discharge the Powers and Duties of the said Office, the Same shall devolve on the Vice President, and the Congress may by Law provide for the Case of Removal, Death, Resignation or Inability, both of the President and Vice President, declaring what Officer shall then act as President, and such Officer shall act accordingly, until the Disability be removed, or a President shall be elected.

The President shall, at stated Times, receive for his Services, a Compensation, which shall neither be encreased nor diminished during the Period for which he shall have been elected, and he shall not receive within that Period any other Emolument from the United States, or any of them.

Before he enter on the Execution of his Office, he shall take the following Oath or Affirmation:—"I do solemnly swear (or affirm) that I will faithfully execute the Office of President of the United States, and will to the best of my Ability, preserve, protect and defend the Constitution of the United States."

Section 2

The President shall be Commander in Chief of the Army and Navy of the United States, and of the Militia of the several States, when called into the actual Service of the United States; he may require the Opinion, in writing, of the principal Officer in each of the executive Departments, upon any Subject relating to the Duties of their respective Offices, and he shall have Power to grant Reprieves and Pardons for Offenses against the United States, except in Cases of Impeachment.

He shall have Power, by and with the Advice and Consent of the Senate, to make Treaties, providing two thirds of the Senators present concur; and he shall nominate, and by and with the Advice and Consent of the Senate, shall appoint Ambassadors, other public Ministers and Consuls, Judges of the supreme Court, and all other Officers of the United States, whose Appointments are not herein otherwise provided for, and which shall be established by Law: but the Congress may by Law vest the Appointment of such inferior Officers, as they think proper, in the President alone, in the Courts of Law, or in the Heads of Departments.

The President shall have Power to fill up all Vacancies that may happen during the Recess of the Senate, by granting Commissions which shall expire at the End of their next Session.

Section 3

He shall from time to time give to the Congress Information of the State of the Union, and recommend to their Consideration such Measures as he shall judge necessary and expedient; he may, on extraordinary Occasions, convene both Houses, or either of them, and in Case of Disagreement between them, with Respect to the Time of Adjournment, he may adjourn them to such Time as he shall think proper; he shall receive Ambassadors and other public Ministers; he shall take Care that the Laws be faithfully executed, and shall Commission all the Officers of the United States.

Section 4

The President, Vice President and all civil Officers of the United States, shall be removed from Office on Impeachment for, and Conviction of, Treason, Bribery, or other high Crimes and Misdemeanors.

ARTICLE III

Section 1

The judicial Power of the United States, shall be vested in one supreme Court, and in such inferior Courts as the Congress may from time to time ordain and establish. The Judges, both of the supreme and inferior Courts, shall hold their Offices during good Behaviour, and shall, at stated Times, receive for their Services, a Compensation, which shall not be diminished during their Continuance in Office.

Section 2

The judicial Power shall extend to all Cases, in Law and Equity, arising under this Constitution, the Laws of the United States, and Treaties made, or which shall be made, under their Authority;—to all Cases affecting Ambassadors, other public Ministers and Consuls;—to all Cases of admiralty and maritime Jurisdiction;—to Controversies to which the United States shall be a Party;—to Controversies between two or more States;—between a State and Citizens of another State;—between Citizens of different States;—between Citizens of the same State claiming Lands under Grants of different States, and between a State, or the Citizens thereof, and foreign States, Citizens or Subjects.

In all Cases affecting Ambassadors, other public Ministers and Consuls, and those in which a State shall be Party, the supreme Court shall have original Jurisdiction. In all the other Cases before mentioned, the supreme Court shall have appellate Jurisdiction, both as to Law and Fact, with such Exceptions, and under such Regulations as the Congress shall make.

The Trial of all Crimes, except in Cases of Impeachment, shall be by Jury; and such Trial shall be held in the State where the said Crimes shall have been committed; but when not committed within any State, the Trial shall be at such Place or Places as the Congress may by Law have directed.

Section 3

Treason against the United States, shall consist only in levying War against them, or in adhering to their Enemies, giving them Aid and Comfort. No Person shall be convicted of Treason unless on the Testimony of two Witnesses to the same overt Act, or on Confession in open Court.

The Congress shall have Power to declare the Punishment of Treason, but no Attainder of Treason shall work Corruption of Blood, or Forfeiture except during the Life of the Person attainted.

ARTICLE IV

Section 1

Full Faith and Credit shall be given in each State to the public Acts, Records, and judicial Proceedings of every other State. And the Congress may by general Laws prescribe the Manner in which such Acts, Records and Proceedings shall be proved, and the Effect thereof.

Section 2

The Citizens of each State shall be entitled to all Privileges and Immunities of Citizens in the several States.

A Person charged in any State with Treason, Felony, or other Crime, who shall flee from Justice, and be found in another State, shall on Demand of the executive Authority of the State from which he fled, be delivered up, to be removed to the State having Jurisdiction of the Crime.

No Person held to Service or Labour in one State, under the Laws thereof, escaping into another, shall, in Consequence of any Law or Regulation therein, be discharged from such Service or Labour, but shall be delivered up on Claim of the Party to whom such Service or Labour may be due.

Section 3

New States may be admitted by the Congress into this Union; but no new State shall be formed or erected within the Jurisdiction of any other State; nor any State be formed by the Junction of two or more States, or Parts of States, without the Consent of the Legislatures of the States concerned as well as of the Congress.

The Congress shall have Power to dispose of and make all needful Rules and Regulations respecting the Territory or other Property belonging to the United States; and nothing in this Constitution shall be so construed as to Prejudice any Claims of the United States, or of any particular State.

Section 4

The United States shall guarantee to every State in this Union a Republican Form of Government, and shall protect each of them against Invasion; and on Application of the Legislature, or of the Executive (when the Legislature cannot be convened) against domestic Violence.

ARTICLE V

The Congress, whenever two thirds of both Houses shall deem it necessary, shall propose Amendments to this Constitution, or, on the Application of the Legislatures of two thirds of the several States, shall call a Convention for proposing Amendments, which, in either Case, shall be valid to all Intents and Purposes, as Part of this Constitution, when ratified by the Legislatures of three fourths of the several States, or by Conventions in three fourths thereof, as the one or the other Mode of Ratification may be proposed by the Congress; Provided that no Amendment which may be made prior to the Year One thousand eight hundred and eight shall in any Manner affect the first and fourth Clauses in the Ninth Section of the first Article; and that no State, without its Consent, shall be deprived of its equal Suffrage in the Senate.

ARTICLE VI

All Debts contracted and Engagements entered into, before the Adoption of this Constitution, shall be as valid against the United States under this Constitution, as under the Confederation.

This Constitution, and the Laws of the United States which shall be made in Pursuance thereof; and all Treaties made, or which shall be made, under the Authority of the United States, shall be the supreme Law of the Land; and the Judges in every State shall be bound thereby, any Thing in the Constitution or Laws of any State to the Contrary notwithstanding.

The Senators and Representatives before mentioned, and the Members of the several State Legislatures, and all executive and judicial Officers, both of the United States and of the several States, shall be bound by Oath or Affirmation, to support this Constitution; but no religious Test shall ever be required as a Qualification to any Office or public Trust under the United States.

ARTICLE VII

The Ratification of the Conventions of nine States, shall be sufficient for the Establishment of this Constitution between the States so ratifying the Same.

AMENDMENT I [1791]

Congress shall make no law respecting an establishment of religion, or prohibiting the free exercise thereof; or abridging the freedom of speech, or the press; or the right of the people peaceably to assemble, and to petition the Government for a redress of grievances.

AMENDMENT II [1791]

A well regulated Militia, being necessary to the security for a free State, the right of the people to keep and bear Arms, shall not be infringed.

AMENDMENT III [1791]

No Soldier shall, in time of peace be quartered in any house, without the consent of the Owner, nor in time of war, but in a manner to be prescribed by law.

AMENDMENT IV [1791]

The right of the people to be secure in their persons, houses, papers, and effects, against unreasonable searches and seizures, shall not be violated, and no Warrants shall issue, but upon probable cause, supported by Oath or affirmation, and particularly describing the place to be searched, and the persons or things to be seized.

AMENDMENT V [1791]

No person shall be held to answer for a capital, or otherwise infamous crime, unless on a presentment or indictment of a Grand Jury, except in cases arising in the land or naval forces, or in the Militia, when in actual service in time of War or public danger; nor shall any person be subject for the same offense to be twice put in jeopardy of life or limb; nor shall be compelled in any criminal case to be a witness against himself, nor be deprived of life, liberty, or property, without due process of law; nor shall private property be taken for public use, without just compensation.

AMENDMENT VI [1791]

In all criminal prosecutions, the accused shall enjoy the right to a speedy and public trial, by an impartial jury of the State and district wherein the crime shall have been committed, which district shall have been previousy ascertained by law, and to be informed of the nature and cause of the accusation; to be confronted with the Witnesses against him; to have compulsory process for obtaining witnesses in his favor, and to have the Assistance of counsel for his defense.

AMENDMENT VII [1791]

In Suits at common law, where the value in controversy shall exceed twenty dollars, the right of trial by jury shall be preserved, and no fact tried by a jury, shall be otherwise re-examined in any Court of the United States, then according to the rules of the common law.

AMENDMENT VIII [1791]

Excessive bail shall not be required, nor excessive fines imposed, nor cruel and unusual punishments inflicted.

AMENDMENT IX [1791]

The enumeration in the Constitution, of certain rights, shall not be construed to deny or disparage others retained by the people.

AMENDMENT X [1791]

The powers not delegated to the United States by the Constitution, nor prohibited by it to the States, are reserved to the States respectively, or to the people.

AMENDMENT XI [1798]

The Judicial power of the United States shall not be construed to extend to any suit in law or equity, commenced or prosecuted against one of the United States by Citizens of another State, or by Citizens or Subjects of any Foreign State.

AMENDMENT XII [1804]

The Electors shall meet in their respective states and vote by ballot for President and Vice-President, one of whom, at least, shall not be an inhabitant of the same state with themselves; they shall name in their ballots the person voted for as President, and in distinct ballots the person voted for as Vice-President, and they shall make distinct lists of all persons voted for as President, and of all persons voted for as Vice-President, and of the number of votes for each, which lists they shall sign and certify, and transmit sealed to the seat of the government of the United States, directed to the President of the Senate;—The President of the Senate shall, in the presence of the Senate and House of Representatives, open all the certificates and the votes shall then be counted;—The person having the greatest number of votes for President, shall be the President, if such number be a majority of the whole number of Electors appointed; and if no person have such majority, then from the persons having the highest numbers not exceeding three on the list of those voted for as President, the House of Representatives shall choose immediately, by ballot, the President. But in choosing the President, the votes shall be taken by states, the representation from each state having one vote; a quorum for this purpose shall consist of a member or members from two-thirds of the states, and a majority of all the states shall be necessary to a choice. And if the House of Representatives shall not choose a President whenever the right of choice shall devolve upon them, before the fourth day of March next following, then the Vice-President shall act as President. The person having the greatest number of votes as Vice-President, shall be the Vice-President, if such number be a majority of the whole number of Electors appointed, and if no person have a majority, then from the two highest numbers on the list, the Senate shall choose the Vice-President; a quorum for the purpose shall consist of two-thirds of the whole number of Senators, and a majority of the whole number shall be necessary to a choice. But no person constitutionally ineligible to the office of President shall be eligible to that of the Vice-President of the United States.

AMENDMENT XIII [1865]

Section 1

Neither slavery nor involuntary servitude, except as a punishment for crime whereof the party shall have been duly convicted, shall exist within the United States, or any place subject to their jurisdiction.

Section 2

Congress shall have power to enforce this article by appropriate legislation.

AMENDMENT XIV [1868]

Section 1

All persons born or naturalized in the United States, and subject to the jurisdiction thereof, are citizens of the United States and of the State wherein they reside. No State shall make or enforce any law which shall abridge the privileges or immunities of citizens of the United States; nor shall any State deprive any person of life, liberty, or property, without due process of law; nor deny to any person within its jurisdiction the equal protection of the laws.

Section 2

Representatives shall be appointed among the several States according to their respective numbers, counting the whole number of persons in each State, excluding Indians not taxed. But when the right to vote at any election for the choice of electors for President and Vice President of the United States, Representatives in Congress, the Executive and Judicial officers of a State, or the members of the Legislature thereof, is denied to any of the male inhabitants of such State, being twenty-one years of age, and citizens of the United States, or in any way abridged, except for participation in rebellion, or other crime, the basis of representation therein shall be reduced in the proportion which the number of such male citizens shall bear to the whole number of male citizens twenty-one years of age in such State.

Section 3

No person shall be a Senator or Representative in Congress, or elector of President and Vice President, or hold any office, civil or military, under the United States, or under any State, who, having previously taken an oath, as a member of Congress, or as an officer of the United States, or as a member of any State legislature, or as an executive or judicial officer of any State, to support the Constitution of the United States, shall have engaged in insurrection or rebellion against the same, or given aid or comfort to the enemies thereof. But Congress may by a vote of two-thirds of each House, remove such disability.

Section 4

The validity of the public debt of the United States, authorized by law, including debts incurred for payment of pensions and bounties for services in suppressing insurrection or rebellion, shall not be questioned. But neither the United States nor any State shall assume or pay any debt or obligation incurred in aid of insurrection or rebellion against the United States, or any claim for the loss or emancipation of any slave; but all such debts, obligations and claims shall be held illegal and void.

Section 5

The Congress shall have power to enforce, by appropriate legislation, the provisions of this article.

AMENDMENT XV [1870]

Section 1

The right of citizens of the United States to vote shall not be denied or abridged by the United States or by any State on account of race, color, or previous condition of servitude.

Section 2

The Congress shall have power to enforce this article by appropriate legislation.

AMENDMENT XVI [1913]

The Congress shall have power to lay and collect taxes on incomes, from whatever source derived, without apportionment among the several States, and without regard to any census or enumeration.

AMENDMENT XVII [1913]

The Senate of the United States shall be composed of two Senators from each State, elected by the people thereof, for six years; and each Senator shall have one vote. The electors in each State shall have the qualifications requisite for electors of the most numerous branch of the State legislatures.

When vacancies happen in the representation of any State in the Senate, the executive authority of such State shall issue writs of election to fill such vacancies: *Provided,* That the legislature of any State may empower the executive thereof to make temporary appointments until the people fill the vacancies by election as the legislature may direct.

This amendment shall not be so construed as to affect the election or term of any Senator chosen before it becomes valid as part of the Constitution.

AMENDMENT XVIII [1919]

Section 1

After one year from the ratification of this article the manufacture, sale, or transportation of intoxicating liquors within, the importation thereof into, or the exportation thereof from the United States and all territory subject to the jurisdiction thereof for beverage purposes is hereby prohibited.

Section 2

The Congress and the several States shall have concurrent power to enforce this article by appropriate legislation.

Section 3

This article shall be inoperative unless it shall have been ratified as an amendment to the Constitution by the legislatures of the several States, as provided in the Constitution, within seven years from the date of the submission hereof to the States by the Congress.

AMENDMENT XIX [1920]

The right of the citizens of the United States to vote shall not be denied or abridged by the United States or by any State on account of sex.

Congress shall have power to enforce this article by appropriate legislation.

AMENDMENT XX [1933]

Section 1

The terms of the President and Vice President shall end at noon on the 20th day of January, and the terms of Senators and Representatives at noon on the 3d day of January, of the years in which such terms would have ended if this article had not been ratified; and the terms of their successors shall then begin.

Section 2

The Congress shall assemble at least once in every year, and such meeting shall begin at noon on the 3d day of January, unless they shall by law appoint a different day.

Section 3

If, at the time fixed for the beginning of the term of the President, the President elect shall have died, the Vice President elect shall become President. If a President shall not have been chosen before the time fixed for the beginning of his term, or if the President elect shall have failed to qualify, then the Vice President elect shall act as President until a President shall have qualified; and the Congress may by law provide for the case wherein neither a President elect nor a Vice President elect shall have qualified, declaring who shall then act as President, or the manner in which one who is to act shall be selected, and such person shall act accordingly until a President or Vice President shall have qualified.

Section 4

The Congress may by law provide for the case of the death of any of the persons from whom the House of Representatives may choose a President whenever the right of choice shall have devolved upon them, and for the case of the death of any of the persons from whom the Senate may choose a Vice President whenever the right of choice shall have devolved upon them.

Section 5

Sections 1 and 2 shall take effect on the 15th day of October following the ratification of this article.

Section 6

This article shall be inoperative unless it shall have been ratified as an amendment to the Constitution by the legislatures of three-fourths of the several States within seven years from the date of its submission.

AMENDMENT XXI [1933]

Section 1

The eighteenth article of amendment to the Constitution of the United States is hereby repealed.

Section 2

The transportation or importation into any State, Territory, or possession of the United States for delivery or use therein of intoxicating liquors, in violation of the laws thereof, is hereby prohibited.

Section 3

This article shall be inoperative unless it shall have been ratified as an amendment to the Constitution by conventions in the several States, as provided in the Constitution, within seven years from the date of the submission hereof to the States by the Congress.

AMENDMENT XXII [1951]

Section 1

No person shall be elected to the office of the President more than twice, and no person who has held the office of President, or acted as President, for more than two years of a term to which some other person was elected President shall be elected to the office of the President more than once. But this Article shall not apply to any person holding the office of President when this Article was proposed by the Congress, and shall not prevent any person who may be holding the office of President, or acting as President, during the term within which this Article becomes operative from holding the office of President or acting as President during the remainder of such term.

Section 2

This article shall be inoperative unless it shall have been ratified as an amendment to the Constitution by the legislatures of three-fourths of the several States within seven years from the date of its submission to the States by the Congress.

AMENDMENT XXIII [1961]

Section 1

The District constituting the seat of Government of the United States shall appoint in such manner as the Congress may direct:

A number of electors of President and Vice President equal to the whole number of Senators and Representatives in Congress to which the District would be entitled if it were a State, but in no event more than the least populous State; they shall be in addition to those appointed by the States, but they shall be considered, for the purposes of the election of President and Vice President, to be electors appointed by a State; and they shall meet in the District and perform such duties as provided by the twelfth article of amendment.

Section 2

The Congress shall have power to enforce this article by appropriate legislation.

AMENDMENT XXIV [1964]

Section 1

The right of citizens of the United States to vote in any primary or other election for President or Vice President, for electors for President or Vice President, or for Senator or Representative in Congress, shall not be denied or abridged by the United States or any State by reason of failure to pay any poll tax or other tax.

Section 2

The Congress shall have power to enforce this article by appropriate legislation.

AMENDMENT XXV [1967]

Section 1

In case of the removal of the President from office or of his death or resignation, the Vice President shall become President.

Section 2

Whenever there is a vacancy in the office of the Vice President, the President shall nominate a Vice President who shall take office upon confirmation by a majority vote of both Houses of Congress.

Section 3

Whenever the President transmits to the President pro tempore of the Senate and the Speaker of the House of Representatives his written declaration that he is unable to discharge the powers and duties of his office, and until he transmits to them a written declaration to the contrary, such powers and duties shall be discharged by the Vice President as Acting President.

Section 4

Whenever the Vice President and a majority of either the principal officers of the executive departments or of such other body as Congress may by Law provide, transmit to the President pro tempore of the Senate and the Speaker of the House of Representatives their written declaration that the President is unable to discharge the powers and duties of his office, the Vice President shall immediately assume the powers and duties of the office as Acting President.

Thereafter, when the President transmits to the President pro tempore of the Senate and the Speaker of the House of Representatives his written declaration that no inability exists, he shall resume the powers and duties of his office unless the Vice President and a majority of either the principal officers of the executive department or of such other body as Congress may by law provide, transmit within four days to the President pro tempore to the Senate and the Speaker of the House of Representatives their written declaration that the President is unable to discharge the powers and duties of his office. Thereupon Congress shall decide the issue, assembling within forty-eight hours for that purpose if not in session. If the Congress, within twenty-one days after receipt of the latter written declaration, or, if Congress is not in session, within twenty-one days after Congress is required to assemble, determines by two-thirds vote of both Houses that the President is unable to discharge the powers and duties of his office, the Vice President shall continue to discharge the same as Acting President; otherwise, the President shall resume the powers and duties of his office.

AMENDMENT XXVI [1971]

Section 1

The right of citizens of the United States, who are eighteen years of age or older, to vote shall not be denied or abridged by the United States or by any State on account of age.

Section 2

The Congress shall have power to enforce this article by appropriate legislation.

GLOSSARY

Abatement Decrease, reduction, or diminution.
Ad infinitum without limit; endlessly.
Adjudication The judicial determination of a legal proceeding.
Administrative law The branch of public law dealing with the operation of the various agency boards and commissions of government.
Ad valorem According to value.
Affidavit A sworn written statement made before an officer authorized by law to administer oaths.
Affirmative action program A program designed to promote actively the position of minority workers with regard to hiring and advancement.
Affirmative defense A matter which, assuming the complaint to be true, constitutes a defense to it.
A fortiori Even more clearly; said of a conclusion that follows with even greater logical necessity from another which is already included in the argument.
Amicus curiae A friend of the court who participates in litigation though not a party to the lawsuit.
Annuity A contract by which the insured pays a lump sum to the insurer and later receives fixed annual payments.
Appellant The party seeking review of a lower court decision.
Appellee The party responding to an appeal. The winner in the trial court.
Arbitration Submission of a dispute to an extrajudicial authority for decision.
Arguendo For the sake of argument.
Artisan's lien The lien which arises in favor of one who has expended labor upon, or added value to, another's personal property. The lien allows the person to pos-

sess the property as security until reimbursed for the value of labor or materials. If the person is not reimbursed, the property may be sold to satisfy the claim.

Assault and Battery Assault: The intentional creation of immediate apprehension of injury or lack of physical safety. Battery; An intentional, unpermitted, offensive contact or touching.

Assumption of the risk Negligence doctrine which bars the recovery of damages by an injured party on the ground that such party acted with actual or constructive knowledge of the hazard causing the injury.

Attachment The term *attachment* has three meanings. First, attachment is a method of acquiring in rem jurisdiction of a nonresident defendant who is not subject to the service of process to commence a lawsuit. By "attaching" property of the nonresident defendant, the court acquires jurisdiction over the defendant to the extent of the value of the property attached. Second, attachment is a procedure used to collect a judgment. A plaintiff may have the property of a defendant seized, pending the outcome of a lawsuit, if the plaintiff has reason to fear that the defendant will dispose of the property before the court renders its decision. Third, attachment is the event which creates an enforceable security interest under the Uniform Commercial Code (UCC). In order that a security interest attach, there must be a signed, written security agreement, or possession of the collateral by the secured party; the secured party must give value to the debtor; and the debtor must maintain rights in the collateral.

Bait-and-switch An illegal promotional practice in which a seller attracts consumer interest by promoting one product, the "bait," then once interest has been attracted switches it to a second, higher-priced product by making the "bait" unavailable or unattractive.

Beneficiary A person entitled to the possession, use, income, or enjoyment of an interest or right to which legal title is held by another; a person to whom an insurance policy is payable.

Beyond a reasonable doubt The burden of proof required in a criminal case. The prosecution in a criminal case has the burden of proving the defendant is guilty, and the jury must have no reasonable doubt about the defendant's guilt. See also *Burden of proof*.

Bilateral contract An agreement which contains mutual promises, with each party being both a promisor and a promisee.

Bill of particulars In legal practice, a written statement furnished by one party to a lawsuit to another, describing in detail the elements upon which the claim of the first party is based.

Biodegradable Capable of being decomposed by organic action.

"Blue sky" laws Statutes designed to protect investors in stock and other securities by the regulation of transactions in securities, generally by requiring registration and disclosure of pertinent financial information.

Bona fide In good faith; innocently; without fraud or deceit.

Brief A written document produced by a party for a reviewing court which contains the facts, propositions of law, and argument of a party. It is in this document that the party argues the desired application of the law and any contentions as to the rulings of the lower court.

"Bubble" concept A procedure by which the Environmental Protection Agency (EPA) allows a business to treat its entire plant complex as though encased in a bubble. The business suggests its own methods of cleanup, provided the total pollution does not exceed certain limits.

Bulk transfer A transfer made outside the ordinary course of the transferor's business involving a major part of the business' inventory. Bulk transfers are subject to Article 6 of the UCC.

Burden of proof The term *burden of proof* has two meanings. It may describe the party at a trial with the burden of coming forward with evidence to establish a fact. The term also describes the party with the burden of persuasion. This party must convince the judge or jury of the disputed facts in issue or else lose that issue. There are various degrees of proof. See also *Beyond a reasonable doubt, Clear and convincing proof,* and *Preponderance of the evidence.*

Cause of action This phrase has several meanings but it is commonly used to describe the existence of facts giving rise to a judicially enforceable claim.

Caveat emptor Let the buyer beware; rule imposing on a purchaser the duty to inform him or herself as to defects in the property being sold.

Cease and desist order An administrative agency order directing a party to refrain from doing a specified act.

Certiorari The name of a writ by which an appellate court may exercise discretionary review of the ruling of an inferior tribunal.

Chancery Court of equity.

Chattel An item of personal property.

Chose in action A right to recover personal property not presently in the possession of the owner.

Civil law That area of law dealing with the rights and duties of private parties as individual entities, to be distinguished from criminal law. Sometimes the phrase refers to the European system of codified law.

Class action suit An action brought on behalf of other persons similarly situated. For example, a class action may be brought on behalf of all purchasers of a defective product. Class actions are popular because they often involve matters in which an individual would not have a sufficient financial interest to warrant the expense of a lawsuit.

Clear and convincing proof The burden of proof in a civil suit which requires a party to prove the facts beyond a well-founded doubt. This standard is more than a preponderance of the evidence, but less than beyond a reasonable doubt, which is required in a criminal case.

Colgate doctrine The doctrine stating that although price-fixing is illegal per se, there still must be a concerted action rather than simply a refusal to deal with distributors who do not comply with the manufacturer's price policy. A seller has the right to select its customers and to refuse to deal with those that do not charge its suggested price.

Collateral estoppel The doctrine which bars further inquiry into factual matters which have been conclusively adjudicated at a previous trial or hearing.

Collective bargaining The process of good-faith negotiation between employers and employee representatives concerning issues of mutual interest.

Commerce clause Article I, Section 8, Clause 3 of the Constitution of the United States, granting Congress the authority to regulate commerce with foreign nations, among the several states, and with the Indian tribes.

Common law That body of law deriving from judicial decisions as opposed to legislatively enacted statutes and administrative regulations.

Comparable worth A doctrine requiring equal pay for jobs which, although different, produce substantially equal value for the employer.

Comparative negligence A doctrine which compares the plaintiff's contributory fault with the defendant's fault and allows the jury to reduce the plaintiff's verdict by the percentage of the plaintiff's fault.

Complaint In legal practice, the first written statement of the plaintiff's contentions, which initiates the lawsuit.

Compulsory bargaining issue Mandatory bargaining issues regarding wages, hours, or other terms or conditions of employment. Refusal to engage in good faith bargaining with regard to these issues is an unfair labor practice.

Condition precedent In the law of contracts, a condition precedent is an event that must occur before a duty of immediate performance of the promise arises. Contracts often provide that one party must perform before there is a right to performance by the other party. For example, completion of a job is often a condition precedent to payment for that job. One contracting party's failure to perform a condition precedent permits the other party to refuse to perform, cancel the contract, and sue for damages.

Conflicts-of-law principles Rules of law the courts use to determine which substantive law applies when there is an inconsistency between laws of different states or countries.

Conglomerate merger The merger resulting when merging companies have neither the relationship of competitors nor that of supplier and customer.

Consideration An essential element in the creation of a contract obligation which creates a detriment to the promisee or a benefit to the promisor.

Consignment A delivery by the owner of goods to another for disposition usually by sale by the latter for a commission.

Consolidation The process by which two or more corporations are joined to create a new corporation.

Conspiracy A combination or agreement between two or more persons for the commission of a criminal act.

Consumer investigative report A report on a consumer's character, general reputation, mode of living, etc., obtained by personal interviews in the community where the consumer works or lives.

Contingent fee An arrangement whereby an attorney is compensated for services in a lawsuit according to an agreed percentage of the amount of money recovered.

Contract A legally enforceable promise.

Contribution The right of one who has discharged a common liability to recover from another also liable, the proportionate share of the common liability.

Contributory negligence A failure to use reasonable care by the plaintiff in a negligence suit.

Conversion An unlawful exercise of dominion and control over another's property which substantially interferes with property rights.

Corrective advertising A Federal Trade Commission (FTC) remedy which requires companies that have advertised deceptively to run ads that admit the prior errors and correct the erroneous information.

Counterclaim Any claim filed by the defendant in a lawsuit against the plaintiff in the same suit.

Covenant An agreement or promise in writing by which a party pledges that something has been done or is being done. The term is often used in connection with real estate to describe the promises of the grantor of the property.

Criminal law That area of law dealing with wrongs against the state as representative of the community at large, to be distinguished from civil law, which hears cases of wrongs against persons.

Damages Monetary compensation recoverable in a court of law.
D.B.A. Doing business as.
Decree The decision of a court of equity.
Defined benefit plan A money-purchase plan which guarantees a certain retirement income based on the employee's service and salary under the Employee Retirement Income Security Act. The benefits are fixed, and the contributions vary.
Defined contribution plan A money-purchase plan which allows employers to budget pension costs in advance under the Employee Retirement Income Security Act. The contribution is fixed and the benefits vary.
Demurrer In common law pleading a formal statement by the defendant that the facts alleged by the plaintiff are insufficient to support a claim for legal relief.
Deposition Sworn written testimony of a witness taken outside of court; a discovery procedure.
Dicta Statements made in a judicial opinion which are not essential to the decision of the case.
Directed verdict A motion for a directed verdict requests that the judge direct the jury to bring in a particular verdict if reasonable minds could not differ on the correct outcome of the lawsuit. In deciding the motion, the judge will view in the light most favorable to the nonmoving party, and if different inferences may be drawn by reasonable men, then the court can not direct a verdict. In essence, a directed verdict removes the jury's discretion.
Discovery Procedures by which one party to a lawsuit may obtain information relevant to the case from the other party or from third persons.
Discrimination in effect The discriminatory result of policies which appear to be neutral.
Dissolution Termination of the existence of a business entity.
Divestiture The antitrust remedy which forces a company to get rid of assets acquired through illegal mergers or monopolistic practices.
Docket A book containing a brief summary of all acts done in court in the conduct of each case.
Domicile That place that a person intends as his or her fixed and permanent legal residence; place of permanent abode, as contrasted with a residence, which may be temporary; a person can have a number of residences but only one domicile; the state of incorporation of a corporation.
Double jeopardy A constitutional doctrine which prohibits an individual from being prosecuted twice in the same tribunal for the same criminal offense.
Due process Fundamental fairness. As applied to judicial proceedings, adequate notice of a hearing and an opportunity to appear and defend in an orderly tribunal.
Duty A legal obligation imposed by the law.

Easement The right of one other than the owner of land to some use of that land.
Ejusdem generis Of the same kind of class; a doctrine of legislative interpretation.
Embezzlement The fraudulent appropriation by one person, acting in a fiduciary capacity, of the money or property of another.

Eminent domain Authority of the state to take private property for public use.

Emissions reduction banking The policy stating that businesses that lower pollution beyond the requirements of the law may use the additional reductions in the future.

En banc Proceedings by or before the court as a whole rather than any single judge.

Enjoin To require performance or absention from some act through issuance of an injunction.

Environmental impact statement A filing of documents required by the National Environmental Policy Act which forces governmental agencies to consider the environmental consequences of their actions.

Equal protection A principle of the Fifth and Fourteenth Amendments to the Constitution that individuals under like circumstances shall be accorded the same benefits and burdens under the law of the sovereign.

Equity A body of law which seeks to adjust conflicting rights on the basis of fairness and good conscience. Courts of equity or chancery may require or prohibit specific acts where monetary damages will not afford complete relief.

Escrow A deed, bond, or deposit which one party delivers for safekeeping by a second party who is obligated to deliver it to a third party upon the fulfillment of some condition.

Estoppel The legal principle that one may not assert facts inconsistent with one's own prior actions.

Exclusive dealing contract A contract under which a buyer agrees to purchase a certain product exclusively from the seller or in which the seller agrees to sell all his product production to the buyer.

Exculpatory clause A provision in a contract whereby one of the parties attempts to relieve itself of liability for breach of a legal duty.

Executory contract An agreement which is not completed. Until the performance required in a contract is completed, it is executory.

Exemplary damages Punitive damages. Monetary compensation in excess of direct losses suffered by the plaintiff which may be awarded in intentional tort cases where the defendant's conduct deserves punishment.

Failing company doctrine A merger between a failing company and a competitor may be allowed, although such a merger would be illegal if both companies were viable competitors.

False imprisonment The tort of an intentional, unjustified confinement of a nonconsenting person who knows of the confinement.

Fee schedule A plan, usually adopted by an association, which establishes minimum or maximum charges for a service or product.

Fellow-servant doctrine The doctrine which precludes an injured employee from recovering damages from his employer when the injury resulted from the negligent act of another employee.

Felony A criminal offense of a serious nature, generally punishable by death or imprisonment in penitentiary; to be distinguished from a misdemeanor.

Fiduciary One having a duty to act for another's benefit in the highest good faith.

Financing statement An established form that a secured party files with a public officer such as the Secretary of State to perfect a security interest under the Uniform Commercial Code (UCC). It is a simple form which contains basic information such as a description of the collateral, names, and addresses. It is designed to give notice that the debtor and secured party have entered into a security agreement.

Firm offer An offer in signed writing by a merchant to buy or sell goods; it gives assurances that the offer will be held open as governed by the Uniform Commercial Code (UCC).

Foreclosure If a mortgagor fails to perform his or her obligations as agreed, the mortgagee may declare the whole debt due and payable, and she or he may foreclose on the mortgaged property to pay the debt secured by the mortgage. The usual method of foreclosure authorizes the sale of the mortgaged property at a public auction. The proceeds of the sale are applied to the debt.

Forum non conveniens The doctrine under which a court may dismiss a lawsuit in which it appears that for the convenience of the parties and in the interest of justice the action should have been brought in another court.

Fraud A false representation of fact made with intent to deceive another which is justifiably relied upon to the injury of that person.

Full-line forcing An arrangement in which a manufacturer refuses to supply any portion of the product line unless the retailer agrees to accept the entire line.

Garnishment A legal proceeding whereby a creditor may collect directly from a third party who is obligated to the debtor.

Geographic extension merger A combining of companies involved with the same product or service which do not compete in the same geographical regions or markets.

Geographic market The relevant section of the country affected by a merger.

Going bare A professional practicing (in her or his field of expertise) without liability insurance.

Good faith Honesty in dealing; innocence; without fraud or deceit.

Good-faith meeting of competition A bona fide business practice which is a defense to a charge of violation of the Robinson-Patman Act. The Robinson-Patman Act is an amendment to the Clayton Act, which outlaws price discrimination that might substantially lessen competition or tend to create a monopoly. This exception allows a seller in good faith to meet the equally low price, service, or facility of a competitor. The good-faith exception cannot be established if the purpose of the price discrimination has been to eliminate competition.

Greenmail Forcing a corporation to buy back its own stock at an inflated price to avoid a takeover.

Guardian One charged with the duty of care and maintenance of another person, such as a minor or incompetent under the law.

Guardian ad litem A guardian appointed to prosecute or defend a lawsuit on behalf of an incompetent.

Habeas corpus The name of a writ which orders one holding custody of another to produce that individual before the court for the purpose of determining whether such custody is proper.

Hearsay evidence Evidence of statements made or actions performed out of court which is offered to prove the truth thereof.

Hearsay rule The exclusion, with certain exceptions, of evidence not within the personal knowledge of the witness.

Herfindahl-Hirschman Index An index used by the Justice Department to test the legality of horizontal acquisitions. The index is computed by squaring the market share of each firm in a market and adding the results.

Holder in due course One who has acquired possession of a negotiable instrument through proper negotiation for value, in good faith, and without notice of any defenses to it. Such a holder is not subject to personal defenses which would otherwise defeat the obligation embodied in the instrument.

Horizontal merger Merger of corporations that were competitors prior to the merger.

Hot-cargo contract An agreement whereby an employer agrees to refrain from handling, using, selling, transporting, or otherwise dealing in the products of another employer or to cease doing business with any other person.

Illinois brick doctrine The standing-to-sue requirement of the Sherman Act which requires that the plaintiff be directly injured by the defendant's violation. Damages are not passed through the channels of distribution.

Immunity Status of exemption from lawsuits or other legal obligations.

Implied in fact contract A legally enforceable agreement inferred from the circumstances and conduct of the parties.

Indemnify To reimburse another for a loss suffered.

Indictment A document issued by a grand jury formally charging a person with a felony.

Industry guide An opinion of the FTC defining the agency's view of the legality of an industry's trade practice.

Infliction of mental distress An intentional tort to the emotions which causes both mental distress and physical symptoms as a result of the defendant's outrageous behavior.

Injunction A court order directing a party to do or to refrain from doing some act.

In personam The jurisdiction of a court to affect the rights and duties of a specific individual.

In rem The jurisdiction of a court to affect property rights with respect to a specific thing.

Intangible property Something which represents value but has no intrinsic value of its own, such as a note or bond.

Interference in contractual relations A business tort in which persons are induced to breach binding agreements.

Interlocking directorates A situation in which the same persons are members of the board of directors of two or more competing corporations at the same time.

Interpleader A legal procedure by which one holding a single fund subject to conflicting claims of two or more persons may require the conflicting claimants to come into court and litigate the matter between themselves.

Interrogatory A written question propounded by one party to a lawsuit to another; a type of discovery procedure.

Inter se Between themselves.

Intestate A person who dies without a will.

Invasion of privacy A tort based on misappropriation of name or likeness, intrusion upon physical solitude, or public disclosure of objectionable, private information.

Joint tenancy A form of ownership in which each of two or more owners have an undivided right to possession of the property. Upon the death of an owner his or her interest passes to the surviving owners because of survivorship.

Judgment Official adjudication of a court of law.

Judgment notwithstanding the verdict The decision of a court which sets aside the verdict of a jury and reaches the opposite result.

Judicial activist An activist judge tends to abide by the following judicial philosophies: (1) The political process cannot adequately handle society's difficult issues; (2) the courts can correct society's ills through the decision-making process; (3) following precedent is not crucial; and (4) "judge-made law" is often necessary to carry out the legislative intent of the law. See also *Judicial restraint*.

Judicial restraint A judge who abides by the judicial restraint philosophy (1) believes that the political process, and not the courts, should correct society's ills, (2) decides an issue on a narrow basis, if possible, (3) follows precedent whenever possible, and (4) does not engage in "judge-made law," but interprets the letter of the law. See also *Judicial activist*.

Judicial review The power of courts to declare laws enacted by legislative bodies and actions by the Executive to be unconstitutional.

Jurisdiction The power and authority of a court or other governmental agency to adjudicate controversies and otherwise deal with matters brought before it.

Jurisprudence The science of the law; the practical science of giving a wise interpretation of the law.

Jury instruction A statement made by the judge to the jury informing them of the law applicable to the case which the jury is bound to accept and apply.

Laches Defense to an equitable action based on the plaintiff's unreasonable delay in bringing the action.

Legacy Personal property disposed of by a will. Sometimes the term is synonymous with bequest. The word devise is used in connection with real property distributed by will.

Libel A defamatory written statement communicated to a third party.

Lien A claim to an interest in property in satisfaction of a debt or claim.

Limited partnership A partnership in which one or more individuals are general partners and one or more individuals are limited partners. The limited partners contribute assets to the partnership without taking part in the conduct of the business. Such individual are liable for the debts of the partnership only to the extent of their contributions.

Liquidation The process of winding up the affairs of a business for the purpose of paying debts and disposing of assets. May be voluntary or under court order.

Long-arm statute A state statute which gives extraterritorial effect to process (summons) in specified cases. It allows state courts to obtain jurisdiction in civil actions over defendants who are beyond the border of the state provided the defendants have minimum contact with the state sufficient to satisfy due process.

Malfeasance Doing of some wrongful act.

Mandamus A court order directing the holder of an office perform his or her legal duty.

Market extension merger An acquisition in which the acquiring company increases its market through product extension or geographical extension.

Material breach A substantial failure, without excuse, to perform a promise which constitutes the whole or part of a contract.

Mayhem Unlawfully depriving a human being of a member of his body.

Mechanic's lien A lien on real estate that is created by statute to assist suppliers and laborers in collecting their accounts and wages. Its purpose is to subject the owner's land to a lien for material and labor expended in the construction of buildings and other improvements.

Merger The extinguishment of a corporate entity by the transfer of its assets and liabilities to another corporation which continues in existence.

Merger guidelines Guidelines issued by the government indicating which mergers and acquisitions will likely be challenged under the antitrust laws.

Ministerial duty An example of a definite duty regarding which nothing is left to discretion or judgment.

Misdemeanor A criminal offense of less serious nature than a felony, generally punishable by fine or jail sentence.

Misfeasance A misdeed or trepass.

Misrepresentation Any untrue manifestation of fact by word or conduct; it may be unintentional.

Monopoly Exclusive control of a market by a business entity.

Mortgage A transfer of an interest in property for the purpose of creating a security for a debt.

Motion The process by which the parties make written or oral requests that the judge issue an order or ruling.

Mutual mistake A situation in which parties to a contract reach a bargain on the basis of an incorrect assumption common to each party.

Negligence A person's failure to exercise reasonable care which foreseeably causes another injury.

Nexus A logical connection. In tax law, a connection between the tax and the activity or property being taxed.

NLRB National Labor Relations Board.

Noerr-Pennington doctrine This doctrine exempts from the antitrust laws concerted efforts to lobby government officials regardless of the anticompetitive purposes. It is based on the First Amendment freedom of speech.

No-fault laws Laws barring tort actions by injured persons against third-party tort-feasors and requiring such persons to obtain recovery from their own insurers.

Nolo contendere A plea entered by the defendant in a criminal case which neither admits nor denies the crime allegedly committed but which if accepted by the court permits the judge to treat the defendant as guilty.

Noscitur a sociis The principle that the scope of general words is delimited by specific accompanying words; a rule of legislative interpretation.

Notary public A public officer authorized to administer oaths and certify certain documents.

Notice Communication sufficient to charge a reasonable person with knowledge of some fact.

Nuisance A physical condition constituting an unreasonable and substantial interference with the rights of individuals or the public at large.

Oligopoly Control of a commodity or service in a given market by a small number of companies or suppliers.

Option A contractual arrangement under which one party has for a specified time the right to buy certain property from or sell certain property to the other party.

Ordinance The legislative enactment of a city, county, or other municipal corporation.

Organizational picketing Picketing by members of a union seeking to represent workers and to obtain recognition as the exclusive bargaining agent for them. Under the Landrum-Griffin Act, purely recognitional picketing under some circumstances is illegal, while purely informational picketing may be legal.

Ownership The bundle of rights to possess and use property because of title to the property.

Pari materia, in Concerning the same subject matter. A rule of statutory construction that two such statutes will be construed together.

Parker v. Brown doctrine The name given to the state action exemption to the Sherman Act. See *State action exemption*.

Parol evidence Legal proof based on oral statements; with regard to a document, any evidence which is extrinsic to the document itself.

Parol evidence rule Parol evidence is extrinsic evidence. In contracts, the parol evidence rule precludes the introduction of evidence of prior written or oral agreements which may vary, contradict, alter, or supplement the present written agreement. There are several exceptions to this rule. For example, when the parties to an agreement do not intend for that agreement to be final and complete, then parol evidence is admissible.

Patent To be patentable, inventions must be nonobvious, novel, and useful. A patent creates a 17-year protection period during which there is a presumption of validity if the patent is properly registered with the Patent Office.

Per capita By or for each individual.

Per curiam By the court; said of an opinion expressing the view of the court as a whole as opposed to an opinion authored by any single member of the court.

Peremptory challenge The power granted each party to reject a limited number of potential jurors during voir dire examination. No reason for the rejection need be given.

Perjury The giving of false testimony under oath.

Per se In itself.

Per se illegal Under the Sherman Act, agreements and practices are illegal only if they are unreasonable. The practices which are conclusively presumed to be unreasonable are per se illegal. If an activity is per se illegal, only proof of the activity is required, and it is not necessary to prove an anticompetitive effect. For example, price-fixing is per se illegal. See also *Rule of reason*.

Personal property Physical or intangible property other than real estate.

Plaintiff The person who initiates a lawsuit.

Pleadings The process by which the parties to a lawsuit present formal written statements of their contentions to create the issues of the lawsuit.

Plenary Entire; complete in all respects.

Point source Any source of air pollution which must be licensed under the Clean Air Act.

Potential entrant doctrine In antitrust law, a doctrine that prohibits mergers and acquisitions by a firm that is only a potential competitor in a market.

Precedent A prior judicial decision relied upon as an example of a rule of law.

Predatory pricing A seller lowering prices in one geographic area in order to eliminate competition.

Prejudicial error An error in judicial proceedings which may have affected the result in the case.

Preponderance of the evidence This means that evidence, in the judgment of the jurors, has greater weight and overcomes the opposing evidence and presumptions.

Price discrimination A seller charging different purchasers different prices for the same goods at the same time.

Price-fixing An agreement or combination by which the conspirators set the market price of a product or service either being sold or purchased, whether high or low.

Prima facie On the face of it; thus, presumed to be true unless proved otherwise.

Primary air quality standards The standards necessary to protect human health. Secondary air quality standards are stricter standards necessary to protect various environmental amenities.

Privilege A special advantage accorded by law to some individual or group; an exemption from a duty or obligation generally imposed by law.

Privity Interest derived from successive relationship with another party; a contractual connection.

Procedural law The body of rules governing the manner in which legal claims are enforced.

Product extension merger A merger that extends the products of the acquiring company into a similar or related product but one which is not directly in competition with existing products.

Promissory estoppel Court enforcement of an otherwise unbinding promise if injustice can only be avoided by enforcement of the promise. A substitute for consideration.

Pro tanto So far as it goes.

Proximate cause The doctrine which limits an actor's liability to consequences which could reasonably be foreseen to have resulted from the act.

Punitive damages Monetary damages in excess of a compensatory award, usually granted only in intentional tort cases where defendant's conduct involved some element deserving punishment; exemplary damages.

Purchase money security interest A security interest that is taken or retained by the seller of the collateral to secure all or part of the collateral's price.

Qualified pension plan A private retirement plan which gains favorable income tax treatment from the Internal Revenue Service (IRS). A qualified pension plan allows for the deduction of contributions made to fund the plan. Also, earnings from fund investments are not taxable, and employees defer personal income tax liability until payments are received after retirement. To qualify, the plan must cover a high percentage of workers and must not discriminate in favor of management or shareholders.

Quantity discount The practice of giving a lower per unit price to businesses that buy a product in volume than to their competitors that do not.

Quasi-contract A quasi-contract, often referred to as an implied-in-law contract, is not a true contract. It is a legal fiction that the courts use to prevent unjust enrichment and wrongdoing. Courts permit the person who conferred a benefit to recover the reasonable value of that benefit. Nonetheless, the elements of a true contract are not present.

Quasi-judicial Administrative actions involving factual determinations and the discretionary application of rules and regulations.

Quid pro quo The exchange of one thing of value for another.
Quitclaim deed The transfer by deed of all of rights, title, and interest in property.
Quo warranto An action brought by the government to test the validity of some franchise, such as the privilege of doing business as a corporation. By what authority are you acting?

Ratio decidendi Logical basis of judicial decision.
Real property Land and fixtures to land.
Reciprocal agreement A contract in which two parties agree to mutual actions so that each party can act as both a buyer and a seller. The agreement violates the Clayton Act if it results in a substantial lessening of competition.
Redlining An act or refusal to act which results in a discriminatory practice. For example, refusing to make loans in low-income areas can discriminate against minorities in granting credit.
Release Relinquishment of a right or claim against another party.
Remand Return of a case by an appellate court for further action by the lower court.
Remedy The action or procedure that is followed in order to enforce a right or to obtain damages for injury to a right; the means by which a right is enforced or the violation of a right is prevented, redressed, or compensated.
Reorganization The legal process in bankruptcy proceedings for restructuring debt and shareholder equity.
Replevin An action for the recovery of goods wrongfully taken or kept.
Res A thing, object, or status.
Resale price maintenance Manufacturer control of a brand or trade-name product's minimum resale price. This is vertical price-fixing.
Rescind To cancel or annul a contract and return the parties to their original positions.
Rescission The equitable remedy which annuls a contract and returns the parties to the position each occupied before the making of the contract. A party entitled to rescind a contract may choose to affirm it instead. The contract is voidable but not void. A contract which is void doesn't exist, and there is nothing to affirm.
Res judicata The doctrine which deems a former adjudication conclusive and prevents a retrial of matters decided in the earlier lawsuit.
Respondeat superior The doctrine imposing liability on one for torts committed by another person who is in his or her employ and subject to his or her control.
Respondent The party answering a suit in equity or an appeal.
Restraint of trade Monopolies, combinations, and contracts that impede free competition.
Reverse Overturn or vacate the judgment of a court.
Reverse discrimination The advancement and recruitment of minority workers ahead of similarly qualified nonminority workers.
Right of redemption The right to buy back. A debtor may buy back or redeem his or her mortgaged property when he or she pays the debt and all costs.
Right-to-work law A state statute which outlaws a union shop contract—one by which an employer agrees to require membership in the union sometime after an employee has been hired as a condition of continued employment.
Robinson-Patman Act The amendment to Section 2 of the Clayton Act covering price discrimination. As originally adopted, the Robinson-Patman Act outlawed

price discrimination in interstate commerce that might substantially lessen competition or tend to create a monopoly.

Rule of reason Under the Sherman Act, contracts or conspiracies are illegal only if they constitute an unreasonable restraint of trade or attempt to monopolize. An activity is unreasonable if it adversely affects competition. An act is reasonable if it promotes competition. The rule of reason requires that an anticompetitive effect be shown. See also *Per se illegal*.

Sanctions Penalties imposed for violation of a law.

Scienter With knowledge; particularly, guilty knowledge.

Secondary boycott Conspiracy or combination to cause the customers or suppliers of an employer to cease doing business with that employer.

Security Under the securities law, an investment in which the investor does not participate in management but relies on others for a financial return.

Seniority plan A system giving priority to employees based on the length of time the employee has worked for the employer. An employer may apply different standards pursuant to a good faith seniority system if the differences are not the result of an intention to discriminate.

Separation of powers The doctrine which holds that the legislative, executive, and judicial branches of government function independently of one another and that each branch serves as a check on the others.

Shark repellant Corporate action to make a threatened acquisition unattractive to the acquiring company.

Sherman Act An 1890 Congressional enactment designed to regulate anticompetitive behavior in interstate commerce.

Slander An oral defamatory statement communicated to a third person.

Specific performance Equitable remedy which requires defendants in certain circumstances to do what they have contracted to do.

Standing The doctrine which requires the plaintiff in a lawsuit to have a sufficient legal interest in the subject matter of the case.

Stare decisis The doctrine which traditionally indicates that a court should follow prior decisions in all cases based on substantially similar facts.

State action exemption The Sherman Act exemption of the sovereign action of a state which replaces competition with regulation if the state actively supervises the anticompetitive conduct.

Status quo The conditions or state of affairs at a given time.

Statute A legislative enactment.

Statute of frauds Legislation which states that certain contracts will not be enforced unless there is a signed writing evidencing the agreement.

Strict liability The doctrine under which a party may be required to respond in tort damages without regard to such party's use of due care.

Subpoena A court order directing a witness to appear or to produce documents in his or her possession.

Subrogation The right of a party secondarily liable to stand in the place of the creditor after he or she has made payment to the creditor and to enforce the creditor's right against the party primarily liable in order to obtain indemnity from him.

Substantive law A body of rules defining the nature and extent of legal rights.

Summary judgment A judicial determination that no genuine factual dispute exists and that one party to the lawsuit is entitled to judgment as a matter of law.

Summons An official notice to a person that a lawsuit has been commenced against him or her and that he or she must appear in court to answer the charges.

Superfund The Comprehensive Environmental Response, Compensation, and Liability Act of 1980.

Supremacy clause Article VI, U.S. Constitution, which states that the Constitution, laws, and treaties of the United States shall be the "supreme law of the land," and shall take precedence over conflicting state laws.

Surety One who incurs a liability for the benefit of another. One who undertakes to pay money in the event that his principal is unable to pay.

Tangible property Physical property.

Tender offer An invited public offer by a company or organization to buy shares from existing stockholders of another public corporation under specified terms.

Testator One who dies leaving a will.

Title Legal evidence of ownership.

Tort A civil wrong other than a breach of contract.

Treason Breach of allegiance to one's government, specifically by levying war against such government or by giving aid and comfort to the enemy.

Treble damages An award of damages allowable under some statutes equal to three times the amount found by the jury to be a single recovery.

Trespass An act done in an unlawful manner so as to cause injury to another; an unauthorized entry upon another's land.

Trust A fiduciary relationship whereby one party (trustee) holds legal title for the benefit of another (beneficiary).

Trustee One who holds legal title to property for the benefit of another.

Truth-in-lending A federal law which requires disclosure of total finance charges and the annual percentage rate for credit in order that borrowers may be able to shop for credit.

Tying contract A contract which ties the sale of one piece of property (real or personal) to the sale or lease of another item of property.

Ultra vires Beyond the scope of corporate powers granted in the charter.

Unconscionable In the law of contracts, provisions which are oppressive, overreaching, or shocking to the conscience.

Usury A loan of money at interest above the legal rate.

Venue The geographical area over which a court presides. Venue designates the court in which the case should be tried. Change of venue means to move to another court.

Verdict Findings of fact by the jury.

Vertical merger A merger of corporations where one corporation is the supplier of the other.

Vertical price-fixing An agreement between a seller and a buyer (for example, between a manufacturer and a retailer) to fix the resale price at which the buyer will sell goods.

Voidable Capable of being declared a nullity, though otherwise valid.

Voir dire The preliminary examination of prospective jurors for the purpose of ascertaining bias or interest in the lawsuit.

Voluntary bargaining issues Either party may refuse to bargain in good faith regarding matters other than wages, hours, and other terms and conditions of employment. This refusal does not constitute an unfair labor practice. An issue over which parties may bargain if they choose to do so.

Waiver An express or implied relinquishment of a right.

Warrant A judicial authorization for the performance of some act.

Warranty of merchantability A promise implied in a sale of goods by merchants that the goods are reasonably fit for the general purpose for which they are sold.

White knight A slang term which describes the inducement of a voluntary acquisition when an involuntary acquisition is threatened. The voluntary acquisition group is a white knight since it saves the corporation from an unfriendly takeover.

Workers' compensation A plan for the compensation for occupational diseases, accidental injuries, and death of employees which arise out of employment. Compensation includes medical expenses and burial costs and lost earnings based on the size of the family and the wage rate of the employee.

Wright-Line doctrine Establishes procedures for determining the burden of proof in cases involving mixed motivation for discharge.

Writ of certiorari A discretionary proceeding by which an appellate court may review the ruling of an inferior tribunal.

Writ of habeas corpus A court order to one holding custody of another to produce that individual before the court for the purpose of determining whether such custody is proper.

Yellow-dog contract An agreement in which a worker agrees not to join a union and that discharge will result from a breach of the contract.

INDEX

INDEX

Page references in **boldface** indicate tables.

Aaron v. Securities and Exchange Commission, 473–474
Abel v. Eli Lilly and Co., 230–231
Abortions, employee, 382
Abstention:
 decisions applying judicial, **36**
 doctrine of, 61
 judicial (judicial restraint), 32–36
Acceptance of offer to contract, 190–191
Accord and satisfaction, 194
Accountants:
 fraud by, 271
 liability of, 269–271, 470, 479, 485
 malpractice and, 269–271
 out-of-court malpractice settlements by, **269**
Accumulated-earnings technique of corporations, 294
Acid rain, 646
Acquired immune deficiency syndrome (AIDS), 395

Acquisitions (*see* Mergers)
Act-of-state doctrine, 300, 336, 337
Activism, judicial, 32–36
 decisions applying, **35**
Actual authority, 303–304
 of agents, 303–304, 315
 of partnerships, 315
Adams, John, quoted, 8
Adams Express Co. v. Beckwith, 43
Adjustment of debts, 541
Administrative agencies, 154–179
 advisory opinions of, 159, 494
 chart, **158**
 costs of regulation by, 174–177
 criticisms of, 174, **175**
 damage suits against personnel of, 164, 171–173
 Equal Access to Justice Act and, 173–174
 exhaustion of remedies by, 168–170
 fact determination by, 170–171
 fraudulent statements and, 159–160

Administrative agencies (*Cont.*):
 functions of, 155–161, 463–464
 influencing decisions by, 163–174
 judicial review of decisions by, 163–174
 major federal agencies, **156**
 organization of, 161–163
 organizational chart, **162**
 procedural aspects review of, 167–168
 rule making review of, 165–166
 under Seventh Amendment, 144
 (*See also specific agency*)
Administrative law judges, 163, 172
Advertising:
 ad substantiation program, 501
 corrective, 497
 deceptive, 498–500
 false, 224
 performance misrepresentation, 498–499
 price misrepresentation, 498
 product name simulation, 499

687

688 INDEX

Advertising *(Cont.)*:
  recent deceptive practice cases, **500**
  under Robinson-Patman amendment, 596
  of securities, 467, 469
  television, 501–502, 577, 596
  tombstone ads, 467
  truthful yet deceptive, 499–500
Advisory councils, 162
Advisory opinions:
  of administrative agencies, 159, 494
  by Federal Trade Commission, 494
Affirmative action:
  Civil Rights Act, Title VII and, 389
  for disabled persons, 393–395
  Equal Employment Opportunity Commission guidelines for, 389
  seniority systems and, 389–390
Affirmative defenses, 232
After-acquired property, 530
Age discrimination, 392–393
Age Discrimination in Employment Act (1967), 392
Agency, 302–303
  (*See also* Agents)
Agents, 303
  actual authority of, 303–304, 315
  apparent authority of, 304–305
  contract negotiation and, 315, 318–319
  foreign, 326–327
  liability of, 306–308, 310, 318–319
  in partnerships, 315
  principals and, 318–319
  ratification, 305–306
Aggravated negligence, 229
AIDS (acquired immune deficiency syndrome), 395
Air pollution:
  air quality standards, 629, 631–632
  bubble concept and, 631–632
  Clean Air Act, 628–633

Air pollution *(Cont.)*:
  emissions reduction, 628–630, 632
  history of, 628–629
  indoor, 633
  laws concerning, 628–630
  mobile sources, 629–630
  new pollutants, 633
  primary air quality standards, 629
  secondary air quality standards, 629
  sources of, 629–632
  stationary sources, 629–632
Alcoa, 581–582
Allied Structural Steel Co. v. Spannaus, 107–108
Alter ego doctrine, 290–291
Alternative liability, 230
Amendments to Constitution, 102
  (*See also* Bill of Rights; First Amendment; Fourteenth Amendment)
American Arbitration Association, 340
American Home Products, **500**
American Home Products v. F.T.C., 501–502
American Law Institute, 248
American Telephone and Telegraph Company (AT&T), breakup of, 558
American Textile Manufacturers Institute, Inc. v. Donovan, 176
Analytical school of legal thought, 7
Anderson v. City of Bessemer City N.C., 89–90
Anderson v. Foothill Industrial Bank, 493
Answer to complaint, 79
Antidumping laws, 334–335
Antitrust laws, 552
  enforcement of, 567–568, 612–613, 615–616, 618–619
  exemptions from, 593
  injunctions and, 568
  international transactions and, 335–336

Antitrust laws *(Cont.)*:
  Justice Department and, 567–568, 609, 612, 613, 616, 618
  liability and, 263, 561–562
  Noerr-Pennington Doctrine, 556–557
  nolo contendere plea and, 557
  price-fixing and, 312
  private parties and, 557–559
  products liability insurance and, 263
  property under, 560
  state, 552–553, 568
  state action exemption, 554–556
  triple damages under, 557, 558, 560–562, 594, 612–613
  unfair methods of competition, 618–620
  unions exemption to, 402–404, 593
  (*See also* Clayton Act; Federal Trade Commission; Federal Trade Commission Act; Mergers; Sherman Antitrust Act)
Apparent authority, 304–305, 310
Appeals court (*see* Reviewing courts)
Appearance requirements for employees, 386–387
Appellant, 70
  briefs by, 88–89
Appellate procedure, 88–89
  in defamation cases, 220
  (*See also* Reviewing courts)
Appellee, 70
  briefs by, 88–89
Apportionment, 123
Arbitration, 91–94, 104–105
  American Arbitration Association, 340
  awards, 93
  with brokerage firms, 92
  of consumer disputes, 514
  international transactions and, 328, 340
  issue of arbitrability, 93
  proceedings, 93–95

INDEX **689**

Arbitration *(Cont.)*:
  statutory, 95
  submission to, 93
Arguments:
  closing, 84–85
  oral, to reviewing court, 88–89
Aristotle, quoted, 62
Arkansas Writers' Project, Inc. v. Ragland, 131
Arrest, false (malicious prosecution), 218
Articles of Incorporation, 281–282
Artisan's liens, 520–521
Asbestos, 633
Aspen Skiing Co. v. Aspen Highlands Skiing Corp., 584–585
Assault and battery, 215
Assembly and association, freedom of, 136–138
Assignment of contracts, 203–204
  diagram, **203**
Assumption of mortgage, 536
Assumption of risk, 214, 233–234, 260, 349
At-will employment, doctrine of, 311–312, 367–369
  statutes limiting, **368**
AT&T Tech., Inc. v. Communications Workers, 93–94
Attachment of security interest, 529–530
Attorney-client privilege, 10, 86
Attorneys *(see* Lawyers)
Authority:
  actual, 303–304, 315
  apparent, 304–305, 310
  express, 303
  implied, 304, 315
  ostensible, 304–305, 310
Authors under copyright laws, 225–226
Awards in arbitration, 93
Ayers v. Town of Jackson, 644–645

Bail Reform Act of 1984, 15
Bait-and-switch promotions, 498
Baltimore Gas & Electric v. Natural Resources Defense Council, 170–171

Banco Nacionál de Cuba v. Sabbatino, 330–331
Bank Merger Acts (1960, 1966), 609
Bankruptcy, 540–544
  collective-bargaining contracts and, 442–443, 544
  courts, 540–541
  creditor priority in, 542
  discharge of debt in, 542–543
  involuntary petition for, 541
  proceedings, 541
  Supreme Court rulings on, 442–443, 554
  trends in, 543–544
  trustee in, 541–542
Bankruptcy Act (1978), 105, 540
Banks:
  confirming, 326
  issuing, 326
  mergers of, 609
Bargaining for consideration, 193
Battery and assault, 215
Beaches, 141–142
Beckman v. Vassall-Dillworth Lincoln-Mercury, 63
Beliefs, right to, 137
Beneficiaries, 552
  third-party, 204–205
Bentham, quoted, 40
Benzene, 633
Best available technology (BAT), 635
Best evidence rule, 87
Best practicable technology (BPT), 635
Beyond a reasonable doubt standard, 85, 161
Bfoq *(see* Bona fide occupational qualifications)
Bhopal, India, 328
Bilateral contracts, 185–186
  acceptance of, 190
Bilateral (mutual) mistake, 191–192
Bill Johnson's Restaurants, Inc., v. N.L.R.B., 429–430
Bill of lading, 326
Bill of Rights, 127–153

Bill of Rights *(Cont.)*:
  Benjamin Cardoza on, 145
  Fourth Amendment, 138–140
  Fifth Amendment, 140–143, 147
  Sixth Amendment, 143–144
  Seventh Amendment, 144
  (See also First Amendment; Fourteenth Amendment)
Black, Hugo:
  Northern Pacific Ry. Co. v. United States, 582
  Tinker v. Des Moines Independent Community School Dist., 128
Black, Jeremiah, *Ex Parte Milligan*, 30
Blackmun, Harry J., 36
Blue Shield of Virginia, et al. v. McCready, 563–564
Blue-sky laws, 486–488
Bok, Derek, quoted, 65
Bona fide occupational qualifications (Bfoq), 374
  age as, 392–393
  sex as, 381, 386
Bork, Robert H., 36
Bosley v. Andrews, 43
Bottom line theory of employment practices, 384
Boycotts, secondary, 361, 445, 449–452
Branti v. Finkel, 137
Breach of contract:
  inducing, 221
  material, 207
  remedies for, 187–188
  remedies illustration, **188**
Breakdown of products, issue of, 252–253
Brennan, William J., Jr., 36
Bribery, 320, 337
Bridgman v. Curry, 205
Briefs, 88
Brokerage firms, arbitration and, 92
Brothers v. First Leasing, 504
Bubble concept of pollution regulation, 631–632
Building permits, 141–142

Bulk transfers, 522–523
   notice requirements for, **523**
Burden of persuasion, 85
Burden of proof, 85
Bureau of Consumer Protection, 494–495
Burger, Warren, *United States v. Nixon*, 32
Business crime, 12
Business organizations, 275–323
   advantages of, 277, 278, 292, 293
   business entertainment, 294
   continuity of, 285–287
   control, 295–299
   creation of, 279–287
   disadvantages of, 277–278, 292, 293
   forms of, 276–277
   illegal conduct of, 310–312
   legal capacity of, 277
   liability in, 284, 288–291, 310–313, 315–318
   regulation of, 4, 136, 513–514, 628–642
   sale of, 462
   taxation of, 292–295
   (*See also* Agents; Closely held corporations; Corporations; Limited partnership; Partnerships)
Business torts, 220–222
Buy and sell agreements, 286, 298
Bystanders, strict liability protection of, 249

California Retail Liquor Dealers Assoc. v. Midcal Aluminum, Inc., et al., 555–556
California-Texas Oil Co., **500**
Cancer, 637, 646
Capacity to contract, 195–196
Captive insurers, 262–263
Cardoza, Benjamin:
   on Bill of Rights, 145
   on judicial process, 46–48
   MacPherson v. Buick, 243–244
   Ultramares Corp. v. Touche, 269

Care, duty of (*see* Duty, of care)
Carey v. National Oil Corporation, 331–332
Cargill, Inc. v. Monfort of Colorado, Inc., 559
Case law, 20, 28, 38
   conflict-of-law principles, **45**
   judicial process and, 45–46
   precedent in, 41–43
   problems of, 39–41
   products liability, 263–264
   selection of applicable, 43–45
Catalano, Inc. v. Target Sales, 567
Cataracts, 646
Caterpillar Tractor Company, Peoria, Ill., Code of Worldwide Business Conduct and Operating Principles:
   accounting records, 489
   board stewardship, 318
   business ethics, 24
   code compliance reporting, 24–25
   competitive conduct, 589
   disclosure of information, 489
   effective employment program, 397
   financial reporting, 489
   inside information, 483–484
   local laws and, 23–24
   privacy of information about employees, 516
   product quality, 267
   provisions of, 23–25
   public officials, 320
   relationships with suppliers, 607
   waste disposal, 638
Causation:
   in products liability cases, 254–255
   proximate, 214, 231–232, 247
Cause in fact, 229–231
Caveat emptor, 243
Cease and desist orders, 160
   for trade practice violations, 495
Celler-Kefauver amendment (1950), 609

Central American Common Market, 334
Certificate of limited partnership, 284
Certification mark, 223
Certiorari, petition of writ of, 53, 58, 59
   new court proposal for, 67
Challenges to perspective jurors, 83
Champion Home Builders Co., **500**
Chancery, courts of, 62–63
Change of venue, 78
Chevron U.S.A. Inc. v. Natural Resources Defense Council, 631–632
Chiarella v. United States, 478–479
Child labor, regulation of, 357
Child pornography, 134
Chlorofluorocarbons, ;646
Choice-of-law clause, 328, 339
Church and state, separation of (freedom of religion), 128–130
Circuit court, 52–53
Citizen Publishing Co., et al. v. United States, 579–580
Citizens St. Bank v. Timm Schmidt & Co., 270
Citizenship:
   diversity of, 54, 56–58, 60–61, 67
   under Fourteenth Amendment, 144–145
Civil actions, 62
Civil law, 20
   burden of proof in, 85
   conflict-of-laws principles applied to, 44–45, 60
   Fourteenth Amendment issues in, 138–140
   securities regulation as, 469, 471–474, **475**, 484–485
   (*See also* Contracts; Property; Torts)
Civil liability, 312
Civil rights, 59, 147
Civil Rights Act:
   of 1866, 373

Civil Rights Act of 1866 *(Cont.):*
   Section 1981, 390–392
   of 1871, Section 1983, 227
      areas of potential liability under, **227**
   of 1964, Title VII, 373–375, 377, 378
      affirmative action and, 389
      personnel tests and, 384
      persons covered by, **373**
      Pregnancy Discrimination Act, 381–383
      salary differences, 383
      seniority system and, 390
      sex discrimination and, 380–383
Class action suits, 73–75
   opt-out *vs.* opt-in, 74
Clayco Petroleum Corp. v. Occidental Petroleum Corp., 337–338
Clayton Act (1914), 402–404, **553**, 592–618
   Celler-Kefauver amendment, 609
   competitor acquisition, 611
   effect of mergers and, 610
   enforcement of, 612–613, 618
   ethics and, 607
   exclusive-dealing contracts, 605–607
   geographic market, 609–610
   history of, 594–595
   Illinois Brick Doctrine and, 562–564
   interlocking directorates, 594
   interstate commerce and, 611
   intrastate commerce and, 611
   Justice Department and, 612, 613
   potential entrant doctrine, 611
   product market, 609–610
   reciprocal dealing arrangements, 605
   relevant market decision and, 609–610
   Section 2, 594–603
   Section 3, 603–607
   Section 4, 560–564, 598

Clayton Act (1914) *(Cont.):*
   Section 7, 608–618
   Section 8, 594
   Section 16, 558
   service industry and, 611
   Supreme Court ruling on, 611
   tender offers and, 613–615
   triple damages, 560–564, 598, 612–613
   tying arrangements, 603–605
   (*See also* Robinson-Patman amendment)
Clean Air Act, 628–633
   exemptions to, 630
   permitting process, 632–633
   policy trends, 631–633
   prevention of significant deterioration, 632
   technology-forcing under, 630
Clean hands doctrine, 64
Clean Water Act, 633–635
   best available technology (BAT), 635
   best practicable technology (BPT), 635
   permit discharge system, 634–635
Clear and convincing proof, 85, 161
Closed shop, 415
Closely held corporations, 276
   buy and sell agreements in, 286
   control of, 296–299
   liability in, 290
   taxation of, 294
Closing argument, 84–85
Codes, 19–20
   competitive conduct and, 573, 587–589
   of ethics, 21–23, 573, 587–589
   (*See also* Caterpillar Tractor Company, Peoria, Ill., Code of Worldwide Business Conduct and Operating Procedures)
Colgate Doctrine, 574
Collateral:
   collateral contracts, 199–200
   rights in, 529
   secured transactions, 528–534

Collective bargaining, 401
   bankruptcy reorganization and, 442–443, 544
   classifications by National Labor Relations Board, 444
   compulsory issues, 442
   Supreme Court rulings on, 442–443, 554
   voluntary issues, 442
   (*See also* Labor laws)
Collective mark, 223
Color, discrimination based on (*see* Racial discrimination)
Commerce, Department of, 335
Commerce clause, 113–124
   discrimination against, 120, 121
   employee salaries regulating, 116
   foreign commerce under, 114, 122–123
   interstate commerce under, 114–116, 120–121
   limitations on, 116
   state police power and, 113–114, 117–121
   taxation and, 121–124
   undue burden concept, 118, 120
Commercial impracticability, 207–208
Commercial speech, 135–136
   Supreme Court ruling on, 136
Common carriers, limited liability of, 235
Common law, 20, 28
   contracts and, 185
   liability for injuries under, 349
   libel and, 132
   pollution and, 643–645
   suits at, 144
Common Market, 333
Comparable worth, 383
Comparative responsibility (comparative negligence, comparative fault), 232, 260
Compensation, unemployment, 358–361
   (*See also* Worker's compensation)

Compensatory damages, 236–237
Competition, 551–569
  concerted activities by competitors, 576–578
  regulation as substitute for, 157
  unfair, 222, 618–620
  (*See also* Antitrust laws)
Complaints, 79
Complete performance of contract, 206
Compliance waivers from Clean Air Act standards, 630
Comprehensive Environmental Response, Compensation, and Liability Act (1980), 641
Compulsory bargaining issues, 442
Computer programs, patentability of, 225
Computer technology, exporting of, 326
Concert of action theory, 230–231
Conditional suretyship contracts, 524
Conditions in contracts (precedent, subsequent, concurrent), 206
Confirming bank, 326
Confiscation of property, 329
Conflict of interest, 316
Conflict-of-laws principles, 39, 44–45, 60, 339
  samples, **45**
Conglomerate mergers, 608
Connecticut v. Teal, 384–385
Consent, voluntary, to contracts, 191–193
Consent orders, 161
  in Bureau of Consumer Protection cases, 495
Consideration in contracts, 193–195
Consignment, 574
Consol. Edison v. Public Service Com'n., 133–134
Consolidation, 608
Conspiracy to monopolize, 582–583

Constitution, U.S., 19, 101–126, 183
  amendments to, 102
  contract clause, 107–108
  external affairs and, 105, 107
  full faith and credit clause, 113
  import-export clause, 109–111
  interpretation of, 28
  judicial review and, 31–36
  jury system in, 29
  organization of, 101–102
  Preamble to, 635
  privileges and immunities clause, 111–113
  on property confiscation, 329
  separation of powers in, 102–104
  states' relation article, 111–113
  supremacy clause, 104–105
  taxing power under, 108–109, 121–124
  (*See also* Bill of Rights; Commerce Clause)
Constitutional relativity, 43
Constitutional torts, 227
  Section 1983, **227**
  Supreme Court ruling on, 227
Constitutions, 19, 38
Constructive discharge, 436
Consumer Leasing Act, 504
Consumer Product Safety Commission (CPSC), **156**, 157
Consumer protection, 492–518
  arbitration and, 514
  Bureau of Consumer Protection, 494–495
  consumer credit debt, 503, 544
  for consumer-debtors, 544–546
  consumer fraud, 512
  consumers, 493
  contracts and, 209
  credit extension discrimination, 503–505
  disclosure, 501
  federal, 494–512
  investigative consumer reports, 506–507
  Magnuson-Moss Warranty Act, 264, **494**, 511–512

Consumer protection (*Cont.*):
  policy trends, 516–517
  of privacy, 514–516
  redlining, 505
  state, 512–514
  Unfair and Deceptive Acts and Practices (UDAP) statutes, 512–513
  (*See also* Credit regulations; Federal Trade Commission; Trade practice regulation)
Contagious diseases, 394–395
Contempt of court, 65
Continental T.V., Inc. v. GTE Sylvania, Inc., 580–581
Contingent fee system, 66
Continuity of business organizations, 285–287
Contract clause of Constitution, 107–108
Contractors, 521
Contracts, 15–16, 39, 183–211
  acceptance of offer, 190–191
  agent-negotiated, 315, 318–319
  assignment of, 203–204
  assignment diagram, **203**
  bankruptcy and, 442–443, 544
  bilateral, 185–186, 190
  breach of, 187–188, 207, 221
  with brokerage firms, 92
  capacity to contract, 195–196
  choice-of-law clause, 328, 339
  classification of, 185–187
  collateral, 199–200
  collective-bargaining, 442–443, 544
  common law and, 185
  conditional suretyship, 524
  conditions affecting performance of, 206
  consideration, 193–195
  consignment, 574
  consumers and, 209
  credit agreements, 544, 545
  discharge of, **207**
  duty of performance of, 206
  elements of, 183, 188–191, 193–198

Contracts *(Cont.)*:
  exclusive-dealing, 605–607
  under fair trade laws, 574
  federal, 373, 387
  hot-cargo, 445, 452
  illegal, 196–198, 250
  implied warranty of merchantability in, 249–251
  importance of, 184–185
  impossibility of performance of, 207–208
  impracticability of performance of, 207–208
  intentional interference with, 221–222
  international, 328
  interpretation of, 201–203
  labor, 442–443, 544
  language of, 328
  levels of performance of, 206–207
  liability and, 303–307, 315, 316–319
  list of, **10**
  model contract of agency, 327
    nondiscrimination and, 373, 387
  offer to contract, 188–190
  parole evidence rule and, 201
  performance of, 206–208
  policy trends, 208–209
    remedies illustration, **188**
  requirements contracts, 204, 606
  in restraint of trade, 570–571
  sale of goods, 184, 185, 194, 200, 326, 333–335
  sources of, 185
  statute-of-frauds requirement exemptions, **200**
  suretyship, 523–527
  termination of offer for, **190**
  third-party beneficiaries of, 204–205
  time limitations for, 200
  tying, 603–605
  unauthorized, 305
  unconditional suretyship, 524
  voluntary consent to, 191–193
  written, 198–201

Contracts *(Cont.)*:
  yellow-dog, 406–407
  (*See also* Warranties; *specific types of contracts*)
Contribution, right of, 315, 526
  denial of, 561–562
Contributory negligence, 214, 232–233, 260, 349
Controlling person, 465
Convention on the International Sale of Goods (CISG), 333
Conventions (agreements), 327
Conversion, 218–219
Cooley v. The Board of Wardens of Port of Philadelphia, 117
Cooling-off period, eighty-day, 415, 417–418
Copyright Act (1976), 225
Copyright law, 225–226
Copyright protection, 327
Corporations, 276
  accumulated-earnings techniques of, 294
  advantages of, 278, 293
  buy and sell agreements in, 286
  continuity of, 286
  control of, 296
  corporate tax rates, 292
  corporate veil, 291
  costs of, 281
  creation of, 281–283
  defamation of, 219
  disadvantages of, 278, 293
  in diversity of citizenship cases, 54, 56–58
  double taxation of, 293–295
  ethical considerations for, 320–321
  under Fifth Amendment, 142
  foreign, 379
  freedom of speech of, 133
  intrastate commerce and, 282
  liability in, 290–291, 316–318
  litigation and, 278
  multinational, 325
  naming of, 281
  professional, 276
  punitive damages against, 238–239

Corporations *(Cont.)*:
  stock in, 282
  Subchapter S, 276, 294–295
  takeovers of, 321
  taxation of, 292–295
  torts and, 316–318
  (*See also* Closely held corporations; Directors, corporate; Mergers)
Corrective advertising, 497
Cost justification defense, 601
Costs:
  administrative agency regulation, 174–177
  below-price, 577–578, 586–587, 595–596
  contingent fee system, 66
  of corporations, 281
  of courts, 60
  Equal Access to Justice Act and, 173
  of legal services, 66, 173, 572
  of litigation, 30, 66, 70, 263–264
  for pollution clean-up, 640
  of products liability litigation, 263–264
  (*See also* Price-fixing; Pricing)
Co-suretyship, 526–527
Council on Environmental Quality (CEQ), 625
  guidelines, 626–627
Council for Mutual Economic Aid (COMECON), 333–334
Counterfeiting of products, 223–224
County of Washington v. Gunther, 383
Course of dealing, prior, 191
Course (scope) of employment:
  in respondeat superior cases, 234–235, 308–310
  in workers' compensation cases, 351–352
Courts, 27–67
  administrative agency decisions review in, 163–174
  bankruptcy, 540–541
  of chancery, 62–63
  circuit, 52–53

Courts (Cont.):
  classifications of, 51, 53–54
  contempt of, 65
  contracts and, 185
  costs, 60
  creation of, 51–52
  delays in, 65–67
  district, 53, 56
  in England, 62
  inferior trial, 53
  judges in, 28–29
  judicial process in, 45–48
  judicial review in, 31–36, 163–174
  justices in, 28–29
  law as principles used by, 5
  of law versus equity, 62–63
  legislation interpretation by, 36–38
  legislative function of, 28
  legislative history examination by, 37
  small-claims, 50, 53–54
  statutory construction by, 37–38
  superior, 53
  for tort cases, 56
  trial, 50, 52–53
  weighing process of, 120, 121, 129
  (See also Case law; Federal Courts; Jurisdiction; Jury; Litigation; Reviewing courts; State courts; Supreme Court, U.S.)
Crandell v. Larkin and Jones Appliance Co., 259
Credibility of witnesses, 89
Credit, 503–505
Credit-card payments, law on, 545–546
Credit regulations, 503
  Equal Credit Opportunity Act, **494**, 503–505
  Fair Credit Reporting Act, **494**, 505–508
  Fair Debt Collection Practices Act, **494**
  Fair Packaging and Labeling Act, **494**

Credit regulations (Cont.):
  Truth-in-Lending Act, 493, **494**, 508–511
  Truth-in-Lending Simplification Act, 511
  (See also Federal Trade Commission Act)
Creditor, 520
  donee, 204–205
Creditor priority:
  under bankruptcy laws, 542
  for secured creditors, 529, 531–533
Creditor protection, 519–536
  artisan's liens, 520–521
  attachment of security interest, 529–530
  bulk transfer notice requirements, **523**
  bulk transfers and, 522–523
  co-suretyship, 526–527
  default, 533–534
  education loan suretyship arrangement, **524**
  mechanic's liens, 521–522
  perfection of security interest, 530–531
  priorities of security interests, 531–533
  property covered by Article 9, **528**
  secured transactions: in personal property, 528–534
    in real property, 534–536
  surety defenses, 525–527
  surety rights, 526
  suretyship, 523–527
Criminal law, 11–15, 56
  burden of proof in, 85
  crime task force, 15
  federal crime, 224
  Fourth Amendment issues in, 138–140
  jurisdiction of cases, 77
  liability based on, 312–315, 485–486
  offenses, **12**
  problems of, 14–15
  proposed changes in, 15
  punishments, 11, 12

Criminal law (Cont.):
  in securities regulation, 469–471, 485–486
  Sherman Antitrust Act sanction, 557–558
  Sixth Amendment issues in, 143–144
  white-collar crime, 13–14
Cross-examination, 83
  right of, 86
Cyanide poisoning case, 12, 314

Damages, 65, 66
  administrative agency personnel and, 164, 171–173
  under antitrust laws, 557, 558, 560–564
  compensatory, 236–237
  Illinois Brick Doctrine and, 562–564
  mitigate, 187
  nolo contendere plea and, 557
  passion theory of, 562–564
  in pollution cases, 644–645
  in products liability cases, 238, 249
  punitive, 237–239
  structured settlements, 239
  tort case awards, **237**
  in tort cases, 236–239, 249
  (See also Triple damages)
Death penalty, 168
Debt, consumer, 503, 544
Debtor protection, 519–520, 536–546
  collection agency restrictions, 539
  for consumer-debtors, 544–546
  for credit-card charges, 545–546
  debt adjustment, 541
  debt collection, 538–540
  Fair Debt Collection Practices Act, 538–539
  holder-in-due-course doctrine, 545
  state laws, 539–540
  usury laws, 537–538
  (See also Bankruptcy)
Debtors in suretyship, 523–524

Deceptive acts, 494, 618–619
Deceptive advertising, 498–500
  recent cases, **500**
Decrees, 65
  enforcement of, 90–91
Deed, mortgage, 534–535
Deep pocket concept, 303, 309
Defamation, 132, 219–220
  of corporations, 219
  job references and, 220
Default, creditor's rights upon, 533–534
Defects, product, 252–254
  as cause of harm, 254–255
  design defects, 253–254
  in hands of defendant, 254
  production defects, 253
  unreasonable dangerousness from, 255–257
  (*See also* Products liability)
Defendants, 70–71
  in invasion of privacy cases, 217
  journalists as, 132
  jurisdiction over, 75–77
  nolo contendere plea by, 557
  pleadings filed by, 79–80
  in products liability cases, 259–261
    chart, **257**
    defect in hands of, 254
    defenses, 259–261
    parties involved, 257–258
  punitive damages against, 237–239
  re ipsa loquitor and, 229, 246–247
  venue and, 78
Defenses:
  affirmative, 232
  cost justification, 601
  defendant's product liability, **260**
  due diligence, 474
  good-faith meeting of competition, 601–603
  misuse, 261
  to negligence, 214, 232–234, 260, 349–350
  in products liability cases, 259–261

Defenses *(Cont.):*
  under Robinson-Patman amendment, 600–603
  in securities cases, 474, **475**
  state-of-the-art, 260–261
  of surety, 525–527
Defined benefit plans, 364
Defined contribution plans, 364
Definiteness requirements:
  for administrative agency authority, 165–166
  for contracts, 189
Delays in courts, 65–66
  solutions to, 66–67
Delivery, legal meaning of, 202
Department of Commerce, 335
Department of Justice (*see* Justice Department)
Deposited acceptance rule, 190–191
Depression (1030s), unemployment during, 358
Derivative suits, 297, 318
DES (diethylstilbestrol) cases, 230–231
Design defects, 253–254
  unreasonably dangerous doctrine and, 255–257
Diamond v. Diehr and Lutton, 225
Dicta, 40
Direct examination, 83
Direct sales, international, 326
Directed verdict, 80
Directors, corporate: conflict of interest and, 316
  control of corporation and, 296
  derivative suits and, 297
  golden parachutes and, 320–321
  initial, 282
  liability of, 313–318
  staggered terms of, 614
Dirks v. Securities and Exchange Commission, 481–482
Disabled persons, discrimination against, 393–395
Disaffirmation of contracts by minors, 196

Discharge of contracts, 207–208
  events leading to, **207**
Discharge of debt in bankruptcy, 542–543
Discharge of employees, 311–312
  employment-at-will doctrine, 311–312, 367–369
  limitations, **368**
  for pregnancy, 359–360
  for proper cause, 359–360
  as unfair labor practice, 436–438
Disclosure:
  to consumers, 501
  under Truth-in-Lending Act, 508–511
  (*See also* Federal Securities Exchange Act)
Discovery procedures, 81–82
  with journalist-defendants, 132
Discrimination:
  in credit extension, 503–505
  in employment, 372–399
    affirmative action and, 387, 389–390, 393–395
    based on age, 392–393
    based on appearance, 386–387
    avoiding, 395–397
    Civil Rights Act of 1866, Section 1981, 390–392
    based on disability, 393–395
    discrimination-in-effect, 378
      examples of, **378**
    by employment agencies, 374–375
    enforcement of laws against, 375–378
    Equal Pay Act, 383
    based on height, 385–386
    historical development of laws on, 372–373
    National Labor Relations Board proceedings and, 441
    based on national origin, 379
    for nonunion membership, 446–448
    personnel tests, 383–384

Discrimination, in employment *(Cont.)*:
  based on race, 378, 386–387, 390–392
  recent cases awards, **376**
  based on religion, 379–380
  reverse discrimination, 387–389
  seniority systems and, 389–390
  based on sex, 380–383
  state laws on, 395
  Supreme Court rulings on, 379–382, 385–386, 389
  for union affiliation, 439–441
  unions and, 395
  based on weight, 385–386
  (*See also* Civil Rights Act of 1964, Title VII)
Discrimination-in-effect, 378
  examples of, **378**
Diseases:
  contagious, 394–395
  occupational, 354
Dismissal, motion of, 79
Disparagement, trade (injurious falsehood), 220–221
Dissolution of business organizations, 285
District courts, 53, 56
Diversity of citizenship cases, 54, 56–58
  law applicable to, 60–61
  proposed elimination from federal courts, 67
Dixon v. Love, 146–147
Doctrine:
  of abstention, 61
  of sovereign compulsion, 336
  of unconscionability, 250
Documentary property, **528**
Documents:
  Fifth Amendment and, 142
  paper fortress, 396
  rules of evidence concerning, 87
  for securities, 466–468, 471–473
Donee beneficiary, 205
Donovan v. Trans World Airlines, 356–357
Dothard v. Rawlinson, 385–386

Double jeopardy, 140, 141, 145
Double taxation of corporations, 293–295
Douglas, William O., quoted, 41
Dram shop acts, 235
Dual federalism, 103, 104
Due diligence defense, 474
Due-on-sale clauses, 535
Due process:
  in administrative agencies, 163, 165, 167
  under constitutional amendments, 145–148
  double standard, 148
  in service of process, 75–77
  Supreme Court ruling on, 145–146
Dump sites, unsafe, 641
Dumping, 334
Dun & Bradstreet, Inc. v. Greenmoss Builders, Inc., 219–220
Dunaway v. Dept. of Labor, 361
Duress, 186
Duty:
  of care, 227–228
  by accountants, 269
  breach of, 229, 246
  by corporate directors, 316–318
  in pollution cases, 644
  by professionals, 268, 269
  by seller, 246
  of loyalty, 315, 316, 318–320
  of performance: of contracts, 206
  for promises or representations, 251–252
  of seller, in products liability:
    based upon conduct of seller, 246–248
    based upon promises or representations, 251–252
    based upon quality of product, 248–249

East African Economic Community, 334
Eastex, Inc. v. N.L.R.B., 433
Economic Community of West African States, 334

Economic factors in tort law development, 213–214
Economic influences on behavior, 21
Economy, regulation of, 147–148
Edward J. DeBartolo Corp. v. N.L.R.B., et al., 450–451
Effluents, 633
Eighty-day cooling-off period, 415, 417–418
Electronic surveillance, 139
Eli Lilly and Company v. Sav-On Drugs, Inc., 282–283
Ellis v. Broth. of Ry., Airline and S.S. Clerks, 404–406
Eminent domain, 141, 329
Emissions reduction, Clean Air Act, 628–630
Emissions reduction banking, 632
Employee Retirement Income Security Act (ERISA, 1974), 364–366
  reporting requirements under, 365–367
Employees:
  business-related crimes of, 313–315
  concerted activities by, 432–435
  employment-at-will doctrine, 311–312, 367–369
  government, 423–424
  privacy issues relating to, 516
  in respondeat superior cases, 234–235, 308–310
  trade secrets and, 222, 319
  warnings to, 396
  (*See also* Discharge of employees; Discrimination, in employment; Labor laws; Worker protection)
Employment agencies, discrimination by, 374–375
Employment-at-will doctrine, 311–312, 367–369
  statutes limiting, **368**
Enforcement of court decisions, 90–91, 339–340
English courts, history of, 62

Environmental impact statement (EIS), 625–628
  criticisms of, 627–628
  examples of, **627**
Environmental laws, 624–648
  bubble concept of, 631–632
  Clean Air Act, 628–633
  Clean Water Act, 633–635
  Comprehensive Environmental Response, Compensation, and Liability Act, 641
  Federal Environmental Pesticide Control Act, 636–637
  Federal Insecticide, Fungicide, and Rodenticide Act, 636–637
  Marine Protection, Research, and Sanctuaries Act, 635
  marketable rights approach, 632
  National Environmental Policy Act, 624–628
  National Nonpoint Source Pollution Program, 635
  Natural Resource Conservation and Recovery Act, 640
  Noise Control Act, 635–636
  point sources, 631, 634
  private suits and, 642–645
  radiation and, 641–642
  regulation of business by, 628–642
  Safe Water Drinking Act, 635
  Solid Waste Disposal Act, 637–638
  Superfund, 641
  Supreme Court rulings on, 626, 630, 631
  Toxic Substances Control Act, 639–640
  trends in, 645–647
  (*See also* Pollution)
Environmental Protection Agency (EPA), **156**, 157, 628
  Clean Air Act and, 628–630
  Clean Water Act and, 633–635
  current trends in, 646
  Fourth Amendment and, 139
  Noise Control Act and, 635–636

Environmental Protection Agency (EPA) *(Cont.)*:
  pesticide control acts administered by, 636–637
  responsibilities of, **629**
  under Toxic Substances Control Act, 639–640
Eppler, Guerin & Turner, Inc. v. Kasmir, 306–307
Equal access to Justice Act (1982), 173–174
Equal Credit Opportunity Act (ECOA, 1975), **494**, 503–505
  credit extender responsibilities, 504–505
  penalties under, 505
  prohibitions, 503–504
Equal Employment Opportunity Act (1972), 375
Equal Employment Opportunity Commission (EEOC), **156**, 174, 375, 377–378
  affirmative action guidelines by, 389
  amendments to, 392
  sex discrimination and, 381–383
Equal Pay Act (1963), 383
Equal protection clause, 148–151
  analysis, **149**
Equal work, concept of, 383
Equity, law of, 62–65
Equity of redemption (right of redemption), 535
Esquire Radio & Electronics, Inc. v. Montgomery Ward & Co., 195
Establishment clause, 129
Estoppel, 304
  partnership by, 280–281
  promissory, 194–195
Ethics, 22–25
  Clayton Act and, 607
  codes of, 21–23, 573, 587–589
  competitive conduct and, 573, 587–589
  corporate, 320–321
  of privacy, 515–516

Ethics *(Cont.)*:
  Sherman Antitrust Act and, 573
  (*See also* Caterpillar Tractor Company, Peoria, Ill., Code of Worldwide Business Conduct and Operating Principles)
European Community (EC), 333
European Economic Community (EEC), 333
Evidence:
  administrative agencies' use of, 170
  preponderance of, 85, 161
  presentation of, 83–84
  rules of, 9–10, 86–88, 201
Examination of witnesses, 83
  right of, 86
Exclusive-dealing contracts, 605–607
Exclusive remedy rule, 353
  exceptions to, **353**
Executed contracts, 185
Executive privilege, claim of, 31–32
Executory contracts, 185
Exemplary (punitive) damages, 237–239
Exhaustion of remedies, 168–170
Ex Parte Milligan, 30
Expense accounts, taxation of, 294
Experience rating systems, 359
Export Administration Act, 326
Exporting, 326
Express authority, 303
Express contracts, 185
Express warranties, 251, 512
Expression, freedom of, 133–135
Expropriation, 329
External affairs, 105, 107

Failing-company doctrine, 611–612
Failure to warn, 228, 255–257
Fair Credit Billing Act, 545
Fair Credit Opportunity Act, **494**, 503–505

Fair Credit Reporting Act
(FCRA), **494**, 505–508
consumer rights under, 506
investigative consumer
reports, 506–507
penalties under, 507–508
reasonable procedures, 507
Fair Debt Collection Practices
Act (FDCPA, 1978), **494**,
538–539
collection agency restrictions,
539
enforcement of, 539
Fair Labor Standards Act
(FLSA), 355–358
Supreme Court ruling on, 355
violations of, 357–358
Fair Packaging and Labeling
Act, **494**
Fair trade laws, 574
*Fall River Dyeing & Finishing
Corp. v. National Labor
Relations Board*, 401–402
False advertising, 224
False arrest (malicious prosecution), 218
False imprisonment, 217–218
Falsehood, injurious, 220–221
F.C.C. v. Midwest Video, 166
Featherbedding, 453
Federal Administrative Procedure Act, 168
Federal agencies (*see* Administrative agencies; *specific agency*)
Federal Aviation Administration (FAA), **156**
Federal Communications
Commission (FCC), **156**
First Amendment and, 132
judicial review of, 166
Federal courts, 44, 50, 54–56
class action suits in, 74
district courts, 56
diversity of citizenship cases
in, 54, 56–58, 60–61, 67
law in, 60–61
reviewing courts, 58–59
rules of evidence for, 87–88
substantive law in, 60–61

Federal courts *(Cont.):*
system, **55**
transfer of cases to, 59
(*See also* Supreme Court, U.S.)
Federal crimes, 224
Federal Employers Liability Act
(FELA), 354–355
Federal Environmental Pesticide Control Act (FEPCA,
1972), 636–637
Federal Insecticide, Fungicide,
and Rodenticide Act (1974),
636–637
Federal laws:
on consumer protection, 494–512
products liability revisions of,
265
on workers' compensation,
354–355
(*See also* Labor laws)
Federal Mediation and Conciliation Service, 414
Federal question cases, 54–55
doctrine of abstention in, 61
Federal Reserve Board (FRB),
156
Federal Securities Act (1933),
464–475
civil liability under, 469, 471–474, **475**
criminal liability under, 469–471
defenses recognized by, 474,
475
documents required by, 466–468, 471–473
exemptions from, 468–469
general provisions of, 464–465
parties regulated by, 465–466
Rule 415, 467–468
willful violation of, 470
(*See also* Securities and Exchange Commission)
Federal Securities Exchange Act
(1934), 476–486
Chiarella decision, 478–479
civil liability under, 484–485
criminal liability under, 485–486

Federal Securities Exchange Act
(1934) *(Cont.):*
fraud under, 484
general provisions under, 476
nonpublic information under,
478–479, 481–484
Section 10(b) and Rule 10b-5,
477–480, 484
Section 14(e), 484
Section 16, 480
Section 18, 484–485
(*See also* Securities and Exchange Commission)
Federal Trade Commission
(FTC), **156**, 494–503, 553,
618–619
advisory opinions by, 494
antitrust laws and, 612, 613,
615–616, 618–619
credit laws and, 503–511
holder in due course doctrine
abolished by, 545
laws administered by, **494**,
503–512, 612, 613, 618–619
Magnuson-Moss Act and, 511–512
penalties under, 496–498
per se illegality and, 620
policy trends, 500–503
premerger notification rule of,
500–503, 615–616
proof required by, 620
prosecution by, 495
purposes of, 494–495
Robinson-Patman amendment
enforcement by, 603
trade practice regulation by,
494, 498–503, 619
use of rule of reason, 620
Federal Trade Commission
(FTC) Act (1914), **494**, 496,
553, 618–620
Section 5, 495, 553, 619–620
Wheeler-Lea amendments to,
553, 618
Federalism, 103, 104
Fellow-servant rule, 349–350
Felonies, 12
list of, **12**

Fiduciary relationships, 303
  duty of loyalty in, 315, 316, 318–320
  in pension plans, 365
  trusts, 552
Field warehousing, 530–531
Fifth Amendment, 140–143, 147
Final decree, 65
Financing statement, perfection of security interest through, 531
Firm offer, 194
First Amendment, 128–138
  Hugo Black on, 128
  commercial speech under, 135–136
  Federal Communication Commission and, 132
  freedom of assembly and association under, 136–138
  freedom of press under, 131–132, 219
  freedom of religion under, 128–130
  freedom of religion and business, **130**
  freedom of speech under, 133–135
  governmental interference, 131
  Noerr-Pennington Doctrine based on, 556–557
  taxation and, 131
First National Bank of Santa Fe v. Quintana, 529–530
Fitness for particular purpose, implied warranty of, 252
Food and Drug Administration (FDA), **156**, 168
Football, 577–578
Ford Motor Co. v. Equal Employment Opportunity Comm., 376–377
Ford Motor Co. v. NLRB, 443–444
Ford v. Revlon, Inc., 216
Foreclosure, 535
Foreign acquisitions, 613
Foreign agents, 326–327
Foreign Assistance Act of 1964, 330

Foreign commerce, 114
  taxation on, 122–123
Foreign companies in U.S., hiring practices of, 379
Foreign Corrupt Practices Act (FCPA), 336–338
Foreign Sovereign Immunities Act, 331
Foreign subsidiaries, liability and, 328
Foreseeability, 231, 247, 261
Formaldehyde, 633
Fortner Enterprises, Inc. v. United States Steel Corp., et al., 604
Forum non conveniens, 78
Fourteenth Amendment, 144–151
  due process clause, 145–148
  equal protection analysis, **149**
  equal protection clause, 148–151
  incorporation of, 145
Fourth Amendment, 138–140
Franchise agreements, 104–105, 606–607
  products liability and, 258
  vertical territorial agreements, 580–581
Francis, Connie, 228
Frankfurter, Felix, *United States v. Mine Workers*, 7–8
Fraud, 12–14, 186, 310
  by accountants, 271
  administrative agencies and, 159–160
  consumer, 512
  under Section 10(b) and Rule 10b-5, 477–480
  in securities cases, 469–470, 473–474, 477–480, 484
  theory of, 169
Frauds, statute of, 198–201
  exceptions to, **200**
Free exercise clause, 129
Freedom of assembly and association, 136–138
Freedom of Information Act, 132
Freedom of press, 131–132, 219
Freedom of religion, 128–130

Freedom of speech, 133–135
  Hugo Black on, 128
  commercial speech, 135–136
  for corporations, 133
  for employers, 416–417, 431–432
Frolic and detour, 234
Full faith and credit clause, 113
Full-line forcing, 605
Full warranty, 512

Garland Co., Inc. v. Roofco Co., 199–200
General Agreement on Tariffs and Trade (GATT), 334
General Counsel, 162
General jurisdiction trial court, 52–53
General partnerships (*see* Partnerships)
Geographic extension mergers, 608, 611
Geographic market, 583
Germann v. F.L. Smithe Mach. Co., 247–248, 256, 261
Getty Oil, 221
Golden parachutes, 320–321, 614–615
Goldfarb et ux. v. Virginia State Bar, et al., 572
Good faith, 602
Good-faith meeting of competition defense, 601–603
Goods, contracts for sale of, 184, 185, 194, 200
  Convention on the International Sale of Goods, 333
  international, 326, 333–335
  under Robinson-Patman amendment, 596
  statute-of-frauds requirements exception, **200**
  (*See also* Products; Uniform Commercial Code)
Government:
  employees of, 423–424
  privacy of consumer and, 515
  (*See also* Administrative agencies)
Grand jury, 29, 140, 141

Great Atlantic & Pacific Tea Co., Inc. v. F.T.C., 601–603
Greenhouse effect, 646–647
Greenmail, 614
Greenman v. Yuba Power Products, Inc., 245
Gross National Product (GNP) of United States, 325
Guarantees (*see* Warranties)
Guaranty, 524
Guidelines of administrative agencies, 158–159

Habitability, implied warranty of, 250–251
Hand, Learned:
 on negligence, 229
 United States v. Aluminum Company of America, 580–581
Handgun case, 235, 236
Handicaps, discrimination based on, 393–395
Hanson v. Funk Seeds International, 250
Harlan, John Marshall:
 Reynolds v. Sims, 33–34
 on separation of powers, 103–104
Havens Realty Corp. v. Coleman, 72–73
Hazardous substances (*see* Toxic substances)
Health and safety provisions for workers:
 contagious diseases, 394–395
 occupational diseases, 354
 (*See also* Occupational Safety and Health Act; Occupational Safety and Health Administration; Workers' compensation)
Hearsay rule, 86
Heatcool (company), **500**
Height requirements for employment, 385–386
Henningsen v. Bloomfield Motors, 244
Herfindahl-Hirschman Index (HHI), 616–617

Herfindahl-Hirschman Index (HHI) (*Cont.*):
 sample calculation, **617**
Herrera v. First Northern Savings & Loan Assn., 510
Hishon v. King & Spalding, 374
Historical school of legal thought, 7
Hobbs Act, 164
Hobie v. Unemployment Appeals Com'n of Florida, 129–130
Hodel v. Indiana, 115–116
Holder in due course, 203, 545
Holmes, Oliver Wendall, quoted, 5, 46
Homogeneous products, 583
Horizontal mergers, 608–609
 guidelines for, 616, 617
Horizontal territorial agreements, 580
Hostile takeovers, tender offers in, 613–615
Hot-cargo contracts, 445, 452
Hours and wages, statutes on, 355–358
 violations of, 357–358
Housing, implied warranty of habitability for, 250–251

Illegal conduct, 310–312
Illegal contracts, 196–198, 250
 examples of, **197**
Illegality, per se (*see* Per se illegality)
Illinois Brick Co. v. Illinois, 562–564
Illinois Brick Doctrine, 562
Immunity:
 of government officials, 172–173
 judicial, 29, 172, 227
Implied authority, 304
 of partnerships, 315
Implied contracts, 185
Implied warranties, 244
 of fitness for particular purpose, 252
 of habitability, 250–251
 of merchantability, 249–251
Import-export clause, 109–111

Imported goods, federal power over, 114
Impossibility of performance of contracts, 207–208
Impracticability of performance of contracts, 207–208
Imprisonment, false, 217–218
In personam, 77
In rem, 77
In re Uranium Antitrust Litigation, 335–336
Incidental beneficiary, 205
Income taxes:
 of corporations, 292–295
 double taxation, 293–295
 of partnerships, 292
 pension plans and, 364
Incorporation, Articles of, 281–282
Incorporation of Bill of Rights by Fourteenth Amendment, 145
Incorporators, 281
Indemnification, 261–262
Indemnity (reimbursement), 526
Independent contractor, 310
India, 328, 329
Individual retirement accounts (IRAs), 366–367
Industries:
 least dangerous, **348**
 most dangerous, **348**
Industry guides by Federal Trade Commission, 494, 619
Inferior trial courts, 53
 small-claims court, 53–54
Infliction of mental distress, intentional, 215–216
Infringement:
 copyright, 225–226
 patent, 224–225
 trademark, 223
Injunctions:
 in merger cases, 612
 under Sherman Antitrust Act, 558–560
 against strikes, 406–408, 417–418
 under Taft-Hartley Act, 417–418

Injuries to persons and property:
  contagious diseases, 394–395
  occupational diseases, 354
  (*See also* Occupational Safety
    and Health Act; Occupa-
    tional Safety and Health
    Administration; Torts;
    Workers' compensation)
Injurious falsehood, 220–221
Insider transactions, 13, 480
  Caterpillar Tractor Company,
    Peoria, Ill., Code of World-
    wide Business Conduct
    and Operating Principles
    on, 483–484
  on *Chiarella* decision, 478–479
  tippees (temporary insiders),
    481–483
Inspections by Occupational
  Safety and Health Adminis-
  tration, 346–349
Insurance:
  antitrust laws and, 263
  captive insurers, 262–263
  plan termination coverage for
    pension plans, 364
  under Pregnancy Discrimina-
    tion Act, 382
  for products liability, 262, 263
  against punitive damages, 239
  risk retention program, 262–
    263
  self-insurance, 262
  Sherman Antitrust Act ex-
    emption, 554
*Insurance Company of North
  America v. Pasakarnis*, 232–
  233
Intangible property, 17, 18, **528**
Intent, 214–215
Intentional infliction of mental
  distress, 215–216
Intentional interference with
  contractual relations, 221–
  222
Intentional torts, 17, 214–227
  assault and battery, 215
  business torts, 220–222
  constitutional torts, 227
  conversion, 218–219

Intentional torts *(Cont.):*
  under copyright law, 225–226
  defamation, 132, 219–220
  false advertising, 224
  false imprisonment, 217–218
  injurious falsehood, 220–221
  intentional infliction of mental
    distress, 215–216
  intentional interference with
    contractual relations, 221–
    222
  invasion of privacy, 217
  malicious prosecution, 218
  under patent law, 224–225
  scope of employment issue
    and, 234–235
  Section 1983, **227**
  trade secrets and, 222
  trademarks and, 223–224
  trespass, 218, 644
  types of, **215**
Interest rates, laws limiting,
  537–538
Interference with contractual
  relations, intentional, 221–
  222
Interlocking directorates, 594
Interlocutory decree, 65
Internal Revenue Code, corporate taxation and, 294–295
Internal Revenue Service (IRS),
  155–156
  qualification of pension plans
    by, 364
International Chamber of Commerce, 328, 340
International Civil Aviation Organization, 334
International Court of Justice
  (ICJ), 332
International investments, 325
International Labour Organiza-
  tion, 334
International Monetary Fund,
  334
International Trade Commis-
  sion, 335
International transactions, 324–
  342
  antidumping laws, 334–335

International transactions
  (Cont.):
  antitrust laws and, 335–336
  arbitration and, 328, 340
  bribery, 337
  contracts, 328
  direct sale, 326
  domestic laws and, 334–340
  use of foreign agents, 326–327
  Foreign Corrupt Practices Act
    and, 336–338
  foreign subsidiaries, 327–328
  Investment Insurance Pro-
    gram, 338–339
  joint ventures, 328–329
  language and, 328
  legal institutions and, 332–334
  licensing, 327
  methods of conducting, 325–
    332
  Overseas Private Investment
    Corporation and, 338–339
  risks of, 326, 329–332
  taxation and, 326
Interpretation of law, 28, 36–38
Interrogatories (written questions), 81–82
Interstate commerce, 114–115,
  120–121
  Clayton Act and, 611
  discrimination against, 120,
    121
  Federal Securities Act and,
    475
  Robinson-Patman amendment
    and, 603
  securities transactions and,
    472–474
  Sherman Antitrust Act and,
    564–565
  taxation of, 121–124
  undue burden on, 118, 120
Interstate Commerce Act (ICA,
  1887), 553
Interstate Commerce Commis-
  sion (ICC), **156**
Intoxicated persons, capacity to
  contract by, 196
Intrastate commerce, 114–115
  Clayton Act and, 611

Intrastate commerce *(Cont.):*
  by corporations, 282
  laws favoring, 121
  Robinson-Patman amendment and, 603
Invasion of privacy, 217
Inventions, patents on, 224–225
Inventory:
  bulk transfer of, 522–523
  bulk transfer notice requirements, **523**
  field warehousing of, 530–531
Investigative consumer reports, 506–507
Investigative function of administrative agencies, 159
Investment Insurance Program, 338–339
Investor protection, 461–491
  (See also Securities)
Involuntary petition for bankruptcy, 541
IRAs (individual retirement accounts), 366–367
Irrevocable letter of credit, 326
Issuer of securities, 465
Issuing bank, 326

Jacksonville Bulk Terminals, Inc. v. International Longshoremen's Assoc., 407
Jacksonville State Bank v. Barnwell, 539–540
Japan, 329
J&K Computer Systems, Inc. v. Parrish, 319
Job discrimination
  (see Discrimination, in employment)
Johnson v. Santa Clara County Transportation Agency, 388–389
Joint operations, 579–580
Joint and several liability, 239
  in antitrust cases, 561–562
  of co-sureties, 526
  of partnerships, 288–289, 315
  of tortfeasors, 230, 231
Joint ventures, 328–329
Jones Act, 355

Journalist-defendants in libel cases, 132
J. Truett Payne Co., v. Chrysler Motors Corp., 597–598
Judges, 28–29
  administrative law, 163, 172
  Benjamin Cardozo on, 46–48
  trial, 89
Judgments:
  enforcement of, 90–91, 339–340
  motions for, 80
Judicial abstention (restraint), 32–36
  decisions applying, **36**
Judicial decisions as source of law, 20
Judicial immunity, 29, 172
  Section 1983 exception to, 227
  Supreme Court ruling on, 29
Judicial interpretation, 28, 38
Judicial procedures, 11
Judicial process, 45–48
  Benjamin Cardozo on, 46–48
  case law and, 45–46
  in courts, 45–48
Judicial restraint, 32–36
  decisions applying, **36**
Judicial review, 28, 31–36
  of administrative agency decisions, 163–174
  attitudes toward, 32–36
  Constitution, U.S., and, 31–36
  in courts, 45–48
  exhaustion of remedies, 168–170
  of fact determination, 170–171
  of procedural aspects, 167–168
  of rule making, 165–166
  separation of powers and, 31–32
Judiciary *(see* Courts)
Junker v. Crory, 465–466
Junkyard case, 139–140
Jurisdiction, 50–51
  in criminal suits, 77
  diversity of citizenship factor, 54, 56–58
  general, 50–53
  limited, 50–51, 53, 75
  in litigation procedure, 75–77

Jurisdiction *(Cont.):*
  primary, 169–170
  standing to sue and, 71
Jurisdictional rule of reason, 335
Jurisdictional strikes, 452
Jury, 29–30
  in Bill of Rights, 143–144
  challenges to, 83
  in Constitution, U.S., 29
  directed verdict and, 80
  grand, 29, 140, 141
  instructions to, 29
  petit, 29
  in securities cases, 485–486
  selection of, 82–83
  trial by, 29–30, 82–83, 143–144
  unanimous verdicts, 30
  verdict of, 30, 79–80
Jury duty:
  exclusion from, 143
  problems of, 30
Justice, law as, 6
Justice Department:
  antitrust laws and, 567–568, 609, 612, 613, 616–618
  bank mergers and, 609
  Clayton Act, Section 7 and, 612, 613
  failing-company doctrine and, 612, 618
  merger guidelines of, 616–618
  study of consumer fraud by, 512
Justices, 28–29
  opinions by, 89

Kassel v. Consolidated Freightways Corp., etc., 120–121
Kelly v. R.G. Industries, Inc., 235, 236
Keystone Bank v. Flooring Specialists, Inc., 527
Kramer v. McDonald's System, Inc., 284–285

Labor laws:
  Clayton Act (1914), 402–404
  on collective bargaining, 401

Labor laws *(Cont.):*
  federal laws governing labor-management relations, **403**
  government employees and, 423–424
  Labor-Management Relations Act (Taft-Hartley Act, 1947), **403**, 414–418, 445
  Labor-Management Reporting and Disclosure Act [LMRDA (Landrum-Griffin Act, 1959)], **403**, 418–424, 446
  Landrum-Griffin Act [Labor-Management Reporting and Disclosure Act (LMRDA, 1959)], **403**, 418–424, 446
  National Labor Relations Act (Wagner Act, 1934), **403**, 408–414, 427–428, 451, 454–455
  Norris-LaGuardia Act (1932), **403**, 406–408
  Railway Labor Act (1926), **403**, 404–406, 454
  right-to-work law, 415
  Taft-Hartley Act (1947), **403**, 414–418, 445
  Wagner Act (National Labor Relations Act, 1934), **403**, 408–414, 427–428, 451, 454–455
  (See also Unfair labor practices; Unions; Unions, unfair labor practices by)
Labor-Management Relations Act (Taft-Hartley Act, 1947), **403**, 414–418, 445
Labor-Management Reporting and Disclosure Act [LMRDA (Landrum-Griffin Act, 1959)], **403**, 418–424, 446
  reporting requirements, 421–422
  union elections and, 422–423
Labor unions *(see* Unions)
Land, sales of interests in, 198–199
Land-use regulations, 141–142
Land Management v. Department of Envir. Prot., 279
Landrum-Griffin Act [Labor-Management Reporting and Disclosure Act (LMRDA, 1959)], **403**, 418–424, 446
  reporting requirements, 421–422
  union elections and, 422–423
Lanham Act (1946), 223–224
  Section 43(a), 224
Latin American Free Trade Association, 334
Law, 4–6
  versus other behavioral influences, 21–22
  business decisions and, 4
  classifications of, 10–11
    subdivisions, **10**
  development of, 27–28
  versus equity, 62–65
  ethics and, 22–25
  in federal courts, 60–61
  interpretation of, 28, 38
  judicial decisions as source of, 20
  justice as, 6
  as principles used by courts, 5
  private, 10
  procedural, 10–11
  on products liability, 263–264
  products liability reforms, **266**
  public, 10
  rule of, 7–8
  as scheme of social control, 5–6
  schools of thought concerning, 6–7
  sources of, 19–21, 27
  substantive, 10–11
  (See also Case law; Civil law; Common law; Criminal law; *specific areas of law)*
Lawsuits *(see* Litigation)
Lawyers, 8–10
  attorney-client privilege, 10, 86
  cost of, 66
  criminal liability of, 470
  increased number of, 4, 516–517
Lawyers *(Cont.):*
  litigation and, 278
  mock trials by, 30
  price-fixing by, 572
  in products liability cases, 264
  in securities cases, 480
Layoff plans, seniority system and, 389
Leases, retail price maintenance and, 574
Legal capacity of business organizations, 277
Legal clinics, 516
Legal entity, partnership as, 277
Legal justice, 7
Legal services, costs of, 66, 173, 572
Legal thought, schools of, 6–7
Legality of contracts, violations of, 196–198
  examples of illegal contracts, **197**, 250
Legislation, 19–20
  interpretation of, 28, 36–38
Legislative branch:
  in Constitution, U.S., 102
  control over administrative agencies by, 164–165
Legislative history, courts' examination of, 37
Legislative veto, 32
Less than fair value (LTFV), 335
Lessors, products liability of, 258
Letter of credit, irrevocable, 326
Liability:
  of accountants, 269–271, 470, 479, 485
  of agents, 306–308, 310, 318–319
  alternative, 230
  antitrust laws and, 269, 561–562
  for back pay, 376–377
  based on contracts, 303–307, 318–319
  based on criminal law, 312–315
  of business organizations, 284, 288–291, 310–313, 315–318

Liability *(Cont.)*:
  civil, 312, 469, 471–474, **475**, 484–485
  of closely held corporations, 290
  of common carriers, 235
  under common law, 349
  of corporate directors, 316–318
  of corporations, 290–291, 316–318
  of co-sureties, 526
  criminal, 312–315, 469–471, 485–486
  deep pocket concept, 303, 309
  under Federal Securities Act, 469–474, **475**
  under Federal Securities Exchange Act, 484–486
  foreign subsidiaries and, 328
  of lawyers, 470
  limited, 235
  of limited partnerships, 284, 288
  managerial, 315–321
  of negligence, 318
  of partnerships, 288–289, 315
  of principles, 303–304, 310
  principles of fault, 316
  respondent superior doctrine and, 234–235, 308–310
  under securities laws, 469–471, **475**, 484–486
  of shareholders, 290–291, 318
  statutes and, 312
  to third party, 307
  based on torts, 230, 231, 307–312, 315–318
  vicarious, 234–235, 308–310
  (*See also* Defenses; Joint and several liability; Products liability; Service liability; Strict liability)
Libby, McNeil & Libby v. United Steelworkers, 192–193
Libel, 132, 219
  common-law presumption, 132
Licensing, 327, 328
Liens, 520, 534
  artisan's, 520–521
  mechanic's, 521–522

Limited jurisdiction, courts of, 53, 75
  small-claims court, 53–54
Limited liability of corporations, extent of, 290
Limited partnership, 276
  certificate of, 284
  creation of, 284–285
  dissolution of, 286
  liability of, 284, 288
  security agreements and, 284–285
Limited-power test for administrative agencies, 165
Limited warranty, 512
Lincoln, Abraham:
  cases of, 218
  quoted, 8
Linden Lumber Division, Summer & Co. v. NLRB, 413–414
Liquidation of property, debt discharge through, 541
Litigation, 69–97
  appellate procedure, 88–89
  versus arbitration, 91–94, 104–105
  burden of proof in, 85
  class action suits, 73–75
  conduct of trial in, 82–85
  corporations and, 278
  cost of, 28, 30, 66, 70, 263–264
  damage suits against administrative agency personnel, 164, 171–173
  in defamation cases, 219–220
  derivative suits, 297
  discovery procedures, 81–82
  enforcement of decisions in, 90–91
  environmental, 642–645
  jurisdiction of courts in, 75–77
  lawyers and, 278
  versus mediation, 91
  motions, 79–80
  National Labor Relations Board (NLRB) and, 409
  versus negotiated settlement, 187
  parties to, 70–71
  pleadings, 79

Litigation *(Cont.)*:
  for products liability, 263–264
  range of, 3–4
  res judicata, 91
  rules of evidence in, 9–10, 86–88, 201
  surrender of right to, as consideration, 193–194
  as unfair labor practice, 429–430
  against unions, 418
  venue in, 78
  (*See also* Courts; Reviewing courts; Standing to sue)
Loans:
  repayment of, as undue hardship, 543
  usurious, 537–538
Lobbying under Noerr-Pennington Doctrine, 556–557
Local 3489 United Steelworkers of America v. Usery, 419–420
Local Union No. 189, Amalgamated Meat Cutters, and Butcher Workmen of North America, AFL-CIO, et al. v. Jewel Tea Company, Inc., 403–404
Lockup, 615
Long-arm statutes, 76, 146
Longshoreman's and Harbor Workers' Compensation Act, 355
Losses of businesses, taxation and, 292, 293
Loyalty, duty of, 315, 316, 318–320
Lupien v. Malsbenden, 280

McDonald's, 327
MacPherson v. Buick, 243–244
Magnuson-Moss Warranty Act (1975), 264, **494**, 511–512
Maine v. Taylor, 119
Malice, 132, 219–220
Malicious prosecution, 218
Malpractice, 17, 286
  accounting profession and, 269–271

Malpractice (Cont.):
  out-of-court settlements by accounting firms, **269**
Management:
  federal laws governing labor-management relations, **403**
  golden parachute and, 614–615
  hostile takeovers and, 614–615
  of large corporations, 296
  liability of, 265–267, 288, 315–321
  National Labor Relations Board jurisdiction exemption for, 409–410
  planning by, for products liability, 265–267
  (See also Labor laws)
Mandatory retirement, 392
Marbury v. Madison, 31
  Warren Burger's citation of, 31
Marine Protection, Research, and Sanctuaries Act (1972), 635
Market analysis, 598
Market extension merger, 608
Market power, 583–584, 613
Market share theory, 231, 613
  in Herfindahl-Hirschman Index, 616–617
Markets, 583, 609–610
  competition and, 620
  mergers and, 617–618
Marshall, John, *Marbury v. Madison*, 31
Marshall, Thurgood, 36
Mason v. Hosta, 197
Master and servant, 303
  versus independent contractor, 310
  versus proprietor, 310
  respondeat superior doctrine concerning, 234–235, 308–310
Materiability, test of, 192
Material breach of contract, 207
Material facts, 472
Matter of Tobin, 543
Maxims of equity, 63–64
Mechanic's liens, 521–522

Mediation, 91
Meeting-competition defense, 601–603
Memphis Fire Dept. v. Shotts, 390
Mental distress, intentional infliction of, 215–216
Mentally incompetent persons, capacity to contract by, 196
Merchantability, implied warranty of, 249–251
Meredith Corp., **500**
Mergers, 608–618
  of banks, 609
  competitor acquisition, 611
  conglomerate, 608
  effect of, 610
  failing-company exception for, 611–612, 618
  Federal Trade Commission and, 500–503, 615–616
  foreign acquisitions, 613
  geographic extension, 608, 611
  golden parachute, 614–615
  greenmail, 614
  guidelines for, 616–618
  horizontal, 608–609, 616, 617
  hostile takeovers, 613–615
  injunctions in, 612
  Justice Department and, 616–618
  lockup, 615
  market extension, 608
  premerger notification rule for, 500–503, 615–616
  product extension, 608, 611
  shark repellents, 614–615
  under Sherman Antitrust Act, 608–609
  statutes involved with, 609
  tender offers, 613–615
  triple damages and, 612–613
  types of, 608–609
  vertical, 608
  white knight, 615
  (See also Clayton Act)
Metropolitan Edison Co. v. People Against Nuclear Energy, 626
Michelin Tire Corp. v. Wages, 110–111

Middle East, 327
Minimum contacts, concept of, 76, 77, 146
Minimum fee schedule, 572
Minimum rationality in equal protection clause:
  analysis, **149**
  versus strict scrutiny, 148–151
Minimum wages, 355–356
Minority shareholders, 297–299
Minors, contractual promises by, 196
Mirror image rule, 191
Misdemeanors, 12
  list of, **12**
Misrepresentation, 186, 252–253
Misuse defense in products liability, 261
Mitigate, 187
Mitsubishi Motors v. Soler Chrysler-Plymouth, 340
Mobile air pollution sources, 629–630
Mock trials, 30
Model contract of agency, 327
Monopoly, 552–553
  competitor cooperation, 584–585
  conspiracy of, 582–583, 586–587
  deliberativeness in, 585–586
  predatory conduct, 586–587
  regulation and, 157
  under Sherman Antitrust Act, Section 2, 553, 581–587
  (See also Antitrust laws)
Monsanto v. Spray-Rite Service Corporation, 564–565
Montgomery Ward case, 195
Mortgage:
  assumption of, 536
  deed, 534–535
  real estate, 534–535
  sale of property, 536
Mortgagee, 535–536
  rights and duties of, **535**
Mortgagor, 535–536
  rights and duties of, **535**
Most-favored nation status, 334
Motions, 79–80

Motions *(Cont.)*:
 for directed verdict, 80
 to dismiss, 79
 for judgment, 80
 for summary judgment, 80
Multinational corporations, 325
Musmanno, Justice, *Bosley v. Andrews*, 43
Mutual mistake, 191–192

Name simulation, product, 499
Naming of business organizations:
 corporations, 281
 partnerships, 281
Nassau County School Board v. Arline, 394–395
National Association of Broadcasters, 577
National Collegiate Athletic Association v. Board of Regents of the University of Oklahoma and University of Georgia Athletic Association, 577–578
National Conference of Commissioners on Uniform State Laws, 39
National Environmental Policy Act (NEPA, 1970), 170–171, 624–628
National Labor Relations Act (Wagner Act, 1934), **403**, 408–414
 unfair employer labor practices under, 428, 451, 454–455
National Labor Relations Board (NLRB), **156**, 395, 408–410
 collective-bargaining classifications by, 444
 employment discrimination and, 441
 jurisdiction of, **410**
 jurisdictional exemptions from, 409–410
 litigation and, 409
 organizational picketing and, 454
 proceedings of, 441
 sanctions imposed by, 410–411

National Labor Relations Board (NLRB) *(Cont.)*:
 supervisors and, 409, 438
 unfair labor practices and, 410–411, 429–431, 433–438, 441, 443–448, 450–451, 454
 unilateral transfer of operations and, 444–445
 union elections and, 409, 411–414
 use of Wright-Line Doctrine, 437
 work rules and, 431, 433–434
National Labor Relations Board (NLRB) cases:
 Bill Johnson's Restaurants, Inc. v. N.L.R.B., 429–430
 Eastex, Inc. v. N.L.R.B., 433
 Edward J. DeBartolo Corp. v. N.L.R.B., et al., 450–451
 Ford Motor Company v. NLRB, 443–444
 N.L.R.B. v. City Disposal Systems, Inc., 435
 N.L.R.B. v. Intern. Broth. of Elec. Workers, Local 340, 448–449
 N.L.R.B. v. Retail Store Emp. Union, Etc., 405
 N.L.R.B. v. Savair Manufacturing Co., 447
 N.L.R.B. v. Sure-Tan, Inc., 436
 N.L.R.B. v. Transportation Management Corp., 437–438
 Pattern Makers' League of North America v. N.L.R.B., 416
National Mediation Board, 404, 406
National Non-Point Source Pollution Program, 635
National origin, discrimination based on, 379
National Society of Professional Engineers v. U.S., 573
Nationalization, 329, 332
Natural Resource Conservation and Recovery Act (1976), 640

Natural school of legal thought, 7
Navarro Savings Association v. Lee, 57
Necessaries of life, minors' contracts for, 196
Negligence, 17, 66, 227–234
 by accountants, 269–271
 aggravated, 229
 assumption-of-risk, 214, 233–234, 260, 349
 cause in fact, 229–231
 contributory negligence, 214, 232–233, 260, 349
 defenses, 214, 232–234, 260, 349–350
 duty of care, 227–228
 elements in, 214, 227–232, 246–248
 elements of, **228**
 Learned Hand on, 229
 history of, 213–214, 243, 244
 liability of, 318
 in pollution cases, 644, 645
 proximate causation, 214, 231–232, 247
 seller conduct in, 246–248
 unreasonable behavior, 228–229, 246
Negotiated settlement, 187
Nerve center test, 58
New Hampshire Ins. Co. v. Gruhn, 524–525
New Jersey Tort Claims Act, 645
Newport News Shipbuilding and Dry Dock Co. v. EEOC, 382–383
News media, First Amendment and, 131–132, 219
New York v. Burger, 140
Nexus, 121–123
N.L.R.B. v. Action Automotive, Inc., 411–412
N.L.R.B. v. City Disposal Systems, Inc., 435
N.L.R.B. v. Intern. Broth. of Elec. Workers, Local 340, 448–449
N.L.R.B. v. Retail Store Emp. Union, Etc., 450
N.L.R.B. v. Savair Manufacturing Co., 447

N.L.R.B. v. Sure-Tan, Inc., 436
N.L.R.B. v. Transportation Management Corp., 437–438
Noerr-Pennington Doctrine, 556–557
Noise Control Act (1972), 635–636
Nolo contendere plea, 557
Nonconduct, liability for, 228
Nonprofit Institutes Act, 596
Nonpublic information, 481–484
  Chiarella decision and, 478–479
  short-swing profits and, 480
Norris-LaGuardia Act (1932), **403**, 406–408
Northern Pacific Ry. Co. v. United States, 582
Nuclear Regulatory Commission (NRC), **156**, 170–171, 642
Nuisance, 643

Obscenity, 134–135
Occupational Safety and Health Act (OSHA, 1970), 346–349
  enforcement of, 347
  Fourth Amendment and, 139
Occupational Safety and Health Administration (OSHA), **156**, 164, 176, 346–349
Occupational Safety and Health Review Commission, 346
O'Connor, Sandra Day, 36
Offer to contract, 188–190
  acceptance of, 190–191
  rules of consideration and, 194–195
  termination of, **190**
Office of Federal Contract Compliance Programs (OFCCP), 387, 394
Officers, corporate (*see* Directors, corporate)
Omnibus Crime Control and Safe Streets Act, 139
Onassis, Jacqueline Kennedy, 217
Opening statements, 83
Opinions by reviewing court justices, 89

Oral agreements:
  under parole evidence rule, 201
  statute-of-frauds requirement exemptions, **200**
  unenforceable, under statute of frauds, 198–201
Oral argument to reviewing court, 88–89
Organization of Petroleum Exporting Countries, 334
Organizational picketing, 454
Organizational standing, 72
Organizations, business (*see* Business organizations; Corporations)
OSHA (*see* Occupational Safety and Health Act; Occupational Safety and Health Administration)
Ostensible (apparent) authority, 304–305, 310
Overbreadth doctrine, 135
Overseas Private Investment Corporation (OPIC), 338–339
Overtime pay, 356, 358
Ownership, 18
Ozone, 646

Palmateer v. International Harvester Co., 311–312
Paper fortress, 396
Parker v. Brown, doctrine of, 554–555
Parole evidence rule, 87, 201
Part performance, doctrine of, 198–199
Partnerships, 276
  actual authority of, 315
  advantages of, 277, 292
  agents in, 315
  buy and sell agreements in, 286
  Civil Rights Act (1964), Title VII and, 374
  conduct of parties, 279–281
  control in, 295–296
  creation of, 279–281
  disadvantages of, 277–287, 292
  dissolution of, 285–286
  by estoppel, 280–281
  implied authority of, 315

Partnerships (*Cont.*):
  as legal entities, 277
  liability in, 288–289, 315
  naming of, 281
  partner selection, 374
  profit sharing in, 280
  taxation of, 292
  torts and, 315
  trading, 295, 315
  (*See also* Limited partnerships)
Patent law, 224–225
  Supreme Court ruling on, 225
Pattern Makers' League of North America v. N.L.R.B., 416
Pattern and Practice case, 377–378
Pay (*see* Salaries)
Pennzoil, 221, 544
Pension Benefit Guaranty Corporation (PBGC), 364–365, 367
Pension plans, 363–367
  Employee Retirement Income Security Act and, 364–366
  fiduciary obligation in, 365
  individual retirement accounts (IRAs), 366–367
  Internal Revenue Service and, 364
  Pension Benefit Guaranty Corporation (PBGC), 364–365, 367
  qualified, 363–364
  simplified, 366
  vested rights in, 364, 365
Per se illegality, 565–567
  Federal Trade Commission and, 620
  of horizontal territorial agreements, 580
  of price-fixing, 566, 571
  under Sherman Antitrust Act, 571, 580, 604
  of tying agreements, 604–605
Peremptory challenges, 83
Perfection of security interest, 530–533
Performance of contracts:
  conditions effecting, 206

Performance of contracts *(Cont.):*
  duty of, 206
  impossibility of, 207–208
  impracticability of, 207–208
  levels of, 206–207
Periodic payment (structured settlement), 239
Perkins v. Standard Oil Company of California, 600
Personal injury cases:
  contingent fee arrangement in, 66
  tort reform and, 239
  (See also Torts)
Personal property, 12, 18, 39
  covered by Article 9, **528**
  attachment of security interest, 529–530
  default, 533–534
  perfection of security interest, 530–531
  priorities of security interests, 531–533
  secured transactions in, 528–534
Personnel files, 395–397
Personnel handbooks, 368–369, 395–397
Pesticide control acts, 636–637
Petit jury, 29
Petition:
  for bankruptcy, 541
  for writ of certiorari, 53, 58, 59, 67
Phillips Petroleum Co. v. Shutts, 74–75
Philosophies of law, 6–7
Picketing, 449–454
  organizational, 454
  as right, 134
Piercing the corporate veil, 291
Pioneer Realty and Land Company v. Mortgage Plus, 189
Place of activities test, 58
Plain English statutes, 209
Plaintiffs, 70
  damage awards to, 236–239
  in disparagement cases, 220–221

Plaintiffs *(Cont.):*
  in injury cases, 214, 228–229, 232–234, 236–239
  pleading by, 79
  in products liability cases, 252–257
    defect as cause of harm, 254–255
    defect in hands of defendant, 254
    design defect, 253–254
    elements of, **252**
    product defect, 252–254
    unreasonable dangerousness of product, 255–257
  under Robinson-Patman amendment, 598, 603
  standing to sue, 71, 72
Plan termination insurance coverage for defined benefit plans, 364
Pleadings, 79
Point sources of pollution, 631, 634
Police power:
  commerce clause and, 113–114, 117–122
  possible subjects for government regulation, **117**
Pollution:
  acid rain, 646
  common law tort theories and, 643–645
  cost to clean up, 640
  damage awards, 644–645
  duty of care in, 644
  future concerns, 645–647
  greenhouse effect, 646–647
  negligence in, 644, 645
  noise, 635–636
  nonpoint-source, 635
  of ozone layer, 646
  pesticide, 636–637
  pollution control laws, **635**
  radiation, 641–642
  runoffs, 635
  from solid waste, 637–638
  support for clean up, 645–646
  from toxic substances, 638–641

Pollution *(Cont.):*
  (See also Air pollution; Environmental laws; Water pollution)
Pornography, 134–135
Possession, 18
  perfection of security interest by, 530
Potential entrant doctrine, 611
Pound, Roscoe, quoted, 6
Precedent, 20, 41–43
  state, 43–45
  weight given to, 41–43
Predatory conduct, 586
  in pricing, 595–596
Preemption, 105, **106**
  through commerce clause, 118
Pre-existing obligation rule, 194
Preferred stock, 296
Pregnancy, unemployment compensation and, 359–360
Pregnancy Discrimination Act (1978), 381–383
Premerger notification rule, 615–616
Preponderance of evidence, 85, 161
President:
  in Constitution, U.S., 102
  executive privilege, claim of, 31–32
  under Taft-Hartley Act, 417
Press, freedom of, 131–132, 219
Pretrial conference, 81
Price-fixing, 12, 17, 571–573
  antitrust laws and, 312, 566
  company attitudes toward, 588–589
  criminal sanction for, 558
  exchange of price information, 576
  by lawyers, 572
  per se illegality of, 566, 571
  by professionals, 572–573
  in service sector, 572–573
  Sherman Antitrust Act and, 566
  triple damages and, 560–564
  vertical, 573–576, 582

Pricing:
  average variable cost test for, 595–596
  below costs, 577–578, 586–587, 595–596
  Clayton Act, Section 2 and, 595
  fixed cost, 595–596
  predatory, 586, 595–596
  price discrimination, 595–597
  resale price maintenance, 573–576, 582
  under Robinson-Patman amendment, 596–597
  territorial price discrimination, 598–599
  variable-cost, 595–596
Primary air quality standards, 629
Primary jurisdiction, 169–170
Principals, 303
  agents and, 318–319
  liability of, 303–304, 310
Prior consideration, 193
Prior restraints:
  freedom of expression and, 135
  freedom of press and, 132
Priorities:
  of bankruptcy creditors, 542
  of security interests, 529, 531–533
Privacy, 514–516
  invasion of, 217
  Supreme Court ruling on, 515
Privacy Act (1974), 515
Private law, 10
Private nuisance, 643
Private property, 147
Privilege, executive, claim of, 31–32
Privileged communications (privilege), 10, 86, 187
  press-informant, 132
Privileges and immunities clause, 111–113
  of Fourteenth Amendment, 145–146
Privity doctrine, 243
  abolition of, 243–244

Procedural aspects of administrative agency judicial review, 167–168
  exhaustion of remedies, 168–170
Procedural due process, 146
Procedural law, 10–11
  in federal courts, 60–61
  list of, **10**
Proceeds:
  perfected security interest in, 531
  from sale of collateral, 533
Product extension merger, 608, 611
Product market, 583
Production defects, 253
Products:
  counterfeiting of, 223–224
  geographic market, 583, 609–610
  homogeneous, 583
  name simulation, 499
  product market, 583, 609–610
  quality, 267
  substitute, 583
Products extension merger, 608, 611
Products liability, 12, 17, 39, 235, 242–272
  antitrust laws and, 263
  basic theories of, 245–249
  case law and, 263–264
  causation in, 254–255
  damage awards, 238, 249
  defect as cause of harm, 254–255
  defect in hands of defendant, 254
  defendant's case in, 257–267
  defendant's defenses, 259–261
  defenses for, 261
  design defect, 253–254
  duty: based upon conduct of seller, 246–248
    based upon promises or representation, 251–252
    based upon quality of product, 248–249
  federal laws on, 265

Products liability (Cont.):
  franchise agreements and, 258
  historical development of, 243–245, 263–264
  indemnification in, 261–262
  in industrial accidents, 261
  insurance for, 262, 263
  lawyers and, 264
  legislative revision of, 264–265
  of lessors, 258
  litigation in, 263–264
  management planning for, 265–267
  parties involved in, 257–258
  plaintiff's case in, 252–257
    elements of, **252**
  possible reforms, **266**
  prevention of, **266**
  product defect, 242–254
  product-safety standards, 557
  production defect, 253
  punitive damages and, 238
  Risk Retention Act of 1981, 262–263
  self-insurance for, 262
  tort reform and, 239
  trends in, 263–264
  unreasonable dangerousness of product, 255–257
Professional corporations, 276
Professionals:
  duty of care by, 268, 269
  liability of, for malpractice, 17, 268–271
  price-fixing by, 12, 17, 572–573
Profits:
  nonpublic information and, 480
  in partnerships, 280
  short-swing, 480
  taxation and, 292, 293
Promissory estoppel, 194–195
Promissory note, 527, 534, 545
Proof:
  burden of, 85
  clear and convincing, 85, 161
Property, 17–19
  after-acquired, 530
  under antitrust laws, 560

Property *(Cont.):*
  under Article 9, **528**
  artisan's liens on, 520–521
  confiscation of, 329
  Constitution, U.S., on, 329
  conversion of, 218–219
  documentary, **528**
  intangible, 17, 18, **528**
  land-use regulations, 141–142
  liens on, 520–522, 534
  liquidation of, 541
  list of, **10**
  mechanic's liens on, 521–522
  ownership, 18
  sale of mortgaged, 536
  secured transactions in, 528–536
  tangible, 17, 18, **528**
  title search, 521
  (*See also* Personal property; Real property)
Proprietorship, sole, 276
Prosecution, malicious, 218
Prosecutors, immunity of, 173
Prosser, William, on proximate causation, 231
Protected (structured) settlement, 239
Protection (*see* Consumer protection; Creditor protection; Debtor protection; Worker protection)
Proxies, 296
Proximate causation, 214, 231–232, 247
  William Prosser on, 231
Public hearings of administrative agencies, 163
Public law, 10
Public nuisance, 643
Public-policy considerations for business, 310–312, 369
Public utilities, 133
Public Works employment plan (1977), 389
Publication, service by, 77
Punitive damages, 237–239
Purchase-money security interest, 530

Qualified pension plans, 363–364
Quality, product, 267
Quasi-contract, 186–187
Quasi-judicial function:
  of administrative agencies, 160, 163, 167–168, 173
  of Securities and Exchange Commission, 463–464
Quasi-judicial proceedings of administrative agencies, 160–161
Quasi-legislative function:
  of administrative agencies, 158, 163, 164–166
  of Securities and Exchange Commission, 463–464
Quivira Mining Co. v. EPA, 634

Racial discrimination, 378
  affirmative action and, 387, 389
  appearance requirements and, 386–387
  Civil Rights Act of 1866, Section 1981 and, 390–392
  reverse, 387–389
  seniority systems and, 389–390
Racketeer Influenced and Corrupt Organizations Act (RICO), 13–14, 92
Radford v. Community Mortgage and Investment Corp., 537–538
Radiation, 641–642
Radon, 633
Railway Labor Act (1926), **403**, 404–406, 454
  union expenditures and, 404–406
Ratification, 305–306
Reader v. Dertina & Associates Marketing, 291
Reagan, Ronald, administration of, Federal Trade Commission under, 501
Real estate mortgages, 534
Real property, 17, 18
  mechanic's liens on, 521–522

Real property *(Cont.):*
  secured transactions of, 534–536
Realist school of legal thought, 7
Reason, rule of, 565–567, 620
Reasonable care, duty of (*see* Duty, of care)
Reasonable doubt, standard of, 85, 161
Reciprocal dealing arrangements, 605
Redemption, right of, 535
Redirect and recross-examination, 83
Redlining, 505
Regulation:
  of business, 4, 136, 513–514, 628–642
  cost of, 174–177
  of economy, 147–148
  of monopoly, 157
  taxation for, 109
  (*See also* Administrative agencies; Commerce clause; Consumer protection; Environmental laws; Securities; Trade practice regulation)
Rehabilitation Act (1973), 393
  Section 504, 394
Rehnquist, William, 36
Reimbursement (indemnity), 526
Reiter v. Sonotone Corp., 560–561
Relevancy, rule of, 87
Relevant market, 583, 609–610
Religion:
  discrimination based on, 379–380
  freedom of, 128–130
Remedial statutes, 37
Renberg v. Zarrow, 287
Reorganization, 541, 543–544
  collective-bargaining agreements and, 442–443, 544
Repeal by implication, 38
Representational standing, 71–73
Requirements contracts, 204, 606

Res ipsa loquitur, 229, 246–247
Res judicata, 91
Resale price maintenance, 573–576, 582
Respondeat superior, 234–235, 308–310
Respondents, 495
Restatement (2d) of Foreign Relations, 330
Restraint of trade, laws on (see Antitrust laws; Sherman Antitrust Act)
Retail price maintenance, 574
Retirement, mandatory, 393
Retirement benefits:
  pension plans, 363–367
  Social Security, 361–363
Revenue Act (1978), 366
Reverse discrimination, 387–389
Reviewing courts, 53, 56
  federal, 58–59
  final, 50
  intermediate, 50
  judicial restraint exercised by, 34
  justices of, 28–29, 89
  oral arguments to, 88–89
  special court, 56
  state, 53
  (See also Judicial review)
Revised Uniform Limited Partnership Act, 289–290
Reynolds v. Sims, 33–34
RICO (Racketeer Influenced and Corrupt Organizations Act), 13–14, 92
Right of contribution, 315, 526
  denial of, 561–562
Right to Financial Privacy Act (1978), 515
Right of redemption, 535
Right-to-work law, 415
Risk, assumption of, 214, 233–234, 260, 349
Risk Retention Act of 1981, 262–263
  1986 amendment, 263
Robinson-Patman amendment (1936), 595
  advertising under, 596

Robinson-Patman amendment (1936) (Cont.):
  competition levels under, 598–600
  cost justification defense, 601
  defenses under, 600–603
  enforcement of, 603
  exemptions under, 596
  good-faith meeting of competition defense, 601–603
  interstate commerce and, 603
  intrastate commerce and, 603
  plaintiffs under, 598, 603
  predatory pricing under, 595
  price discrimination under, 596–597
  primary line competition, 598
  proof required under, 597–598, 603
  repeal of, 603
  secondary line competition, 599–600
  states applicability to, 596
  triple damages under, 603
  violation analysis, **599**
Roe v. Wade, 41
Roosevelt, Franklin D., 373
Rubin v. United States, 471
Rule of law, 7–8
Rule of reason, 565–567, 620
Rules of consideration, offer to contract and, 194–195
Rules of evidence, 9–10, 86–88, 201

Safe Water Drinking Act (1974), 635
Safety and health provisions for workers:
  contagious diseases, 394–395
  occupational diseases, 354
  (See also Occupational Safety and Health Act; Occupational Safety and Health Administration; Workers' compensation)
Saint Francis College v. Al-Khazraji, 391–392
Salaries:
  back pay, 376–377

Salaries (Cont.):
  commerce clause and, 116
  of corporate officials, 293–294
  differences in, 383
  Equal Pay Act (1963), 383
  minimum wages, 355–356
  overtime pay, 356, 358
  wages and hours statutes, 355–358
  violations, 357–358
Sale of goods contracts, 184, 185, 194, 200
  international, 326, 333–335
  statute-of-frauds requirement exemptions, **200**
Sale of interests in land, 198–199
Sampson v. Hunt, 316–317
Sanford v. Kobey Bros. Const. Corp., 308
Santa Fe Industries, Inc. v. Green, 477–478
Satisfaction and accord, 194
Scalia, Antonin, 36
Schools of legal thought, 6–7
Schreiber v. Burlington Northern, Inc., 484–485
Scienter, required proof of, 472–473, **475**
Scope of employment issue:
  in respondeat superior cases, 234–235, 308–310
  in workers' compensation cases, 351–352
Scoping process, 626–627
Searches and seizures, 138–140
Sears, Roebuck and Company, **500**
Second Restatement of Torts, 248–249
  Section 204A, 248–249, 258
Secondary air quality standards, 629
Secondary boycotts, 361, 445, 449–452
Secured transactions, 528–534
  default, 533–534
  financing statement, 531
  perfection of security interest, 530–531

Secured transactions *(Cont.)*:
  in personal property, 529–534
  priorities of security interests, 531–533
  property covered by Article 9, **528**
  in real property, 534–536
  security investment attachment, 529–530
Securities, 462–463
  advertising of, 467, 469
  blue-sky laws, 486–488
  Caterpillar's Code of Ethics and, 483–484, 488–489
  criminal law and, 469–471, 485–486
  defenses and, 474, **475**
  documents for, 466–468, 471–473
  exemptions concerning, 463, 468–469, 487–488
  fraud and, 469–470, 473–474, 479–480, 484
  insider transactions, 478–479, 481–484
  interstate, 472–474
  intrastate, 469
  issuer of, 465
  lawyers and, 480
  liability in connection with, 469–474, **475**, 484–486
  offerings of, 468, 469, 484
  parties involved in, 465
  private offerings of, 468
  prospectus, 467, 472–473
  public offerings of, 468
  registration of, 466–467, 471–472, 474, 476, 487
  reselling of, 469
  selling of, 465, 479–480
  shelf registration, 467–468
  size of offering, 469
  specialized, 469
  Supreme Court ruling on laws concerning, 463
  unorthodox transactions, 483
  (*See also* Federal Securities Act; Federal Securities Exchange Act)

Securities and Exchange Commission (SEC), **156**, 157, 463–464
  arbitration arrangement by, 92
  exempt transactions determined by, 468–469, **470**
  Federal Securities Exchange Act and, 476–480
  Fourth Amendment and, 139
  functions of, 463–464
  insider transactions and, 480
  Rule 10B-5 and, 477–480
  securities registration and, 466–468
  (*See also* Federal Securities Act; Federal Securities Exchange Act)
Securities and Exchange Commission v. Lund, 482–483
Securities and Exchange Commission v. W. J. Howey Co., 462–463
Security interests:
  artisan's liens, 520–521
  liens, 520–522, 534
  mechanic's liens, 521–522
  (*See also* Secured transactions)
Self-incrimination, compulsory, 142
Sellers:
  Clayton Act, Section 2 and, 595
  conduct negligence, 246–248
  disputed charges made to, 545–546
  duty of care by, 246
  price discrimination by, 595
  of securities, 465
  (*See also* Federal Trade Commission; Products liability; Robinson-Patman amendment; Service liability)
Seniority systems, 389–390
Separation of church and state (freedom of religion), 128–130
Separation of powers, 102–104
  John Marshall Harlan on, 103–104
  judicial review and, 31–32
Servant, 303

Servant *(Cont.)*:
  and master (*see* Master and servant)
Service of process, 75–76
  extraterritorial, 76
Service industry:
  Clayton Act and, 611
  price-fixing in, 572–573
  under Robinson-Patman amendment, 596
Service liability, 17, 235, 268–271
  punitive damages and, 238
  (*See also* Products liability)
Service mark, 223
Set-off, right of, 526
Seventh Amendment, 144
Sex discrimination, 380–383
  Civil Rights Act, Title VII and, 380–383
  in credit extension, 503–504
  examples, **381**
  Pregnancy Discrimination Act, 381–383
Shareholders:
  control of corporation and, 296
  death of, 286
  liability of, 290–291, 318
  minority, 297–299
  taxation and, 293–295
  withdrawal of, 286
Shark repellents, 614–615
Shearson/American Express, Inc., and Mary Ann McNulty v. Eugene McMahon et al., 92
Sherman Antitrust Act (1890), 336, 553, 570–591
  Caterpillar code and, 589
  concerted activities by competitors, 576–578
  criminal sanction under, 557–558
  ethical standards and, 573, 587–589
  exemptions to, 554, 556–557
  horizontal territorial agreements, 580
  injunction under, 558–560
  interstate commerce and, 564–565

Sherman Antitrust Act (1890) (Cont.):
    joint operations, 579–580
    mergers under, 608–609
    monopoly under, 553, 581–587
    Noerr-Pennington Doctrine and, 556–557
    per se illegality under, 565–567, 571, 580, 604
    price-fixing and, 566, 571–576
    proof of violations of, 564–565
    resale price maintenance, 573–576, 582
    rule of reason applied to, 565–567
    sanctions under, 557–568
    Section 1, 333, 553, 570–581
    Section 2, 333, 553, 581–587
    state action exemption, 554–556
    Supreme Court rulings on, 560, 572
    territorial agreements, 580–581
    triple damages under, 558, 560–562, 584–585
    tying agreements under, 604
    vertical price-fixing, 573–576, 582
    vertical territorial agreements, 580–581
    (*See also* Clayton Act)
Shield law, 132
Shoplifting cases, false imprisonment in, 217–218
Short-swing profits, 480
Siegal, et al. v. Chicken Delight, Inc., et al., 606–607
Silence versus acceptance in contracts, 191
Simplified employee pensions, 366
Simpson v. Union Oil Co., 575
Sindell v. Abbott Laboratories, 231
Sixth Amendment, 143–144
Skip-tracing, 538
Slander, 219
Small-claims court, 50, 53–54
Small v. Springs Industries, Inc., 368–369

Smith v. Jones, 169
Social control, law as scheme of, 5–6
Social justice, 6
Social Security, 361–363
    problems of, 362–363
    taxation rates, **363**
Social Security Act (1935), 358, 362
    amendments to, 362
Sociological school of legal thought, 7
Sole dominion and control over secured property, 531
Sole proprietorship, 276
Solid Waste Disposal Act, 637–638
    National Resource Conservation and Recovery Act amendment, 640
Sony Corporation of America v. Universal City Studios, Inc., 226
South America, 329
Southland Corp. v. Keating, 104–105
Sovereign immunity doctrine, 331, 336
Special business relationship, 228
Speech, freedom of, 133–135
    Hugo Black on, 128
    commercial speech, 135–136
    for employers, 416–417, 431–432
Standard Oil Co. v. United States (1911), 565–566
Standing to sue, 71–73
    administrative agencies and, 164, 168, 171–173
    at common law, 144
    in environmental cases, 642–645
    limitations on, 71
    plaintiffs in, 71, 72
Stanfield v. Laccoarce, 309–310
Stare decisis, 20, 41–43
    John Paul Stevens on, 42
    Byron White on, 41–42
State action exemption, 554–556

State courts, 50–53
    class action suits in, 73
    doctrine of abstention and, 61
    injunctions of, 408
    reviewing courts, 53, 58–59
    small-claims court, 53–54
    system, **52**
    transfer of cases from, 59
State Farm Mutual Automobile Ins. Co. v. Queen, 202–203
State laws, 38
    antitrust, 552–556, 568
    blue-sky, 486–488
    for business regulation, 513–514
    conflict-of-laws principles, **45**
    on consumer fraud, 512–513
    contract clause and, 107–108
    on debt collection, 539–540
    on discrimination, 395
    equal protection analysis, **149**
    equal protection challenges to, 148–151
    National Conference on Commissioners on Uniform State Laws, 39
    preemption cases, 105, **106**
    on privacy, 514–516
    products liability revisions of, 265
    resolution of variations in, 43–45, 60
    supremacy clause and, 104–105
    on unemployment compensation, 358–361
    Unfair and Deceptive Acts and Practices (UDAP) statutes, 512–513
    on wages and hours, 355–358
    on workers' compensation, 349–354
State-of-the-art defense, 260–261
State police power, commerce clause and, 113–114, 117–121
    possible subjects for government regulation, **117**
State sovereignty, 116

States' relation article, 111–113
  full faith and credit clause, 113
  privileges and immunities clause, 111–113
Stationary air pollution sources, 629–630
  bubble concept and, 631–632
Statute of frauds, 198–201
  exceptions to, **200**
Statute of limitations, 80
  for product liability suits, 254
  in securities cases, 474
Statute of respose, 266
Statutes, 38
  interpretation of, 28, 38
  liability and, 312
  long-arm, 76, 146
  Plain English, 209
  remedial, 37
  uniform, 38–39
  validity of, 59
Statutory arbitration, 95
Statutory construction by courts, 37–38
Statutory torts of unfair competition, 222
Stevens, John Paul, 36
  on stare decisis, 42
Stock:
  acquisition of, 608
  in corporations, 282, 296
  preferred, 296
  (*See also* Securities)
Stockholders (*see* Shareholders)
Strict construction, 32–36
  decisions applying, **36**
  statutory, 37–38
Strict liability, 234–239
  arguments for adoption of, **245**
  to bystanders, 249
  for discharge of hazardous wastes, 641
  history of, 213–214, 244–245
  implied warranty and, 244, 249–251
  by lessors, 258
  in pollution cases, 641, 644
  in product cases, 244–245, 248–251, 255–259

Strict liability (*Cont.*):
  respondeat superior, doctrine of, 234–235, 308–310
  in service cases, 268
  unreasonable dangerousness and, 255–257
  in used-products cases, 258–259
  for workers' accidental injuries, 349–350
Strict scrutiny in equal protection clause:
  analysis, **149**
  versus minimum rationality, 148–151
Strikes:
  eighty-day cooling-off period, 415, 417–418
  illegal, 449–452
  injunctions against, 406–408, 417–418
  jurisdictional, 452
  Norris-LaGuardia Act and, 406–408
  organizational picketing, 454
  by public employees, 423–424
  publicity and, 450
  secondary boycotts, 361, 445, 449–452
  under Taft-Hartley Act, 417–418
  unemployment compensation and, 360–361
Structured settlements, 239
Subchapter S corporation, 276, 294–295
Subcontractors, 521
Submission to arbitration, 93
Subrogation, 261, 526
Subsidiaries, foreign, 327–328
Substantial performance of contract, 206
Substantive due process, 146
Substantive versus procedural law, 10–11
  in federal courts, 60–61
Substitute products, 583
Suits (*see* Litigation)
Summary judgment, motions for, 80

Summons, 75–76
Superfund (Comprehensive Environmental Response, Compensation, and Liability Act, 1980), 641
Superior court, 53
Supervisors, National Labor Relations Board and, 409, 438
Supremacy clause, 104–105
Supreme Court of N.H. v. Piper, 112
Supreme Court, U.S. 147
  antimerger laws and, 611
  failing-company exception created by, 611
  judicial activism versus judicial restraint, 32–36
  nomination to, 36
  rulings: bankruptcy and collective-bargaining contracts, 442–443, 544
    Clayton Act, 611
    commercial speech, 136
    constitutional right of privacy, 515
    constitutional torts, 227
    discrimination in employment, 379–382, 385–386, 389
    due process clause, 145–146
    electronic surveillance, 139
    environmental laws, 626, 630, 631
    Fair Labor Standards Act, 355
    judicial immunity, 29
    patent law, 225
    securities laws, 463
    separation of powers, 102–104
    Sherman Antitrust Act, 560, 572
    state court injunctions, 408
    unfair labor practices, 431, 433–434, 443, 453
    warrantless inspections, 346
  (*See also specific cases*)
  writ of certiorari petitions to, 53, 58, 67
Suretyship, 523–527

INDEX 715

Suretyship *(Cont.)*:
  conditional contracts, 524
  co-suretyship, 526–527
  debtors in, 523–524
  defenses of surety in, 525–527
  education loan arrangement, **524**
  liability of, 526
  rights of surety in, 526
  unconditional contracts, 524

Taft-Hartley Act (1947), **403**, 414–418, 445
  injunctions under, 417–418
  President under, 417
  strikes under, 417–418
Takeovers:
  of corporations, 321
  hostile, 613–615
Tangible property, 17, 18, **528**
Taxable situs, 123
Taxation, 108–109
  of business entertainment, 294
  of business losses, 292, 293
  of closely held corporations, 294
  commerce clause and, 121–124
  under Constitution, U.S., 108–109, 121–124
  corporate tax rates, 292
  of corporations, 292–295
  double taxation, 293–295
  of expense accounts, 294
  fairness of, 122
  First Amendment and, 131
  of foreign commerce, 122–123
  import-export clause and, 109–111
  individual retirement accounts (IRAs) deductibility, 366
  of international transactions, 326
  of interstate commerce, 121–124
  of partnerships, 292
  pension plans and, 364
  profits and, 292, 293
  regulation for, 109
  of shareholders, 293–295
  Social Security, 361–363
  Social Security rates, **363**

Taxation *(Cont.)*:
  state, 121–124
  of undistributed earnings, 294
  unemployment, 358–359
  (See also Income taxes)
Technology:
  exporting of, 326
  licensing of, 327
Technology-forcing under Clean Air Act, 630
Television:
  advertising, 501–502, 577, 596
  college football games on, 577–578
  limited freedom of, 132
Teller Act (Welfare and Pension Plans Disclosure Act, 1958), 422
Temporary injunction, 65
Temporary insiders (tippees), 481–483
Tender offers in mergers, 613–615
Termination of offer to contract, **190**
Territorial agreements, 580–581
Test of materiability, 192
Test of reasonableness, 566
Tests, personnel, 383–384
Texaco, Inc., 221, 544
Texas Industries, Inc. v. Radcliff Materials, Inc., 561–562
Textile Workers Union v. Darlington Manufacturing Co., 440
Theory of fraud, 169
Third party, 303
  accountants and, 270–271
  consumer-debtor defenses against, 545
  debt collector's contracts with, 538
  liability to, 270–271, 307
  third-party beneficiaries, 204–205
  (See also Agents)
Timberlane Lumber Company v. Bank of America, 336
Tinker v. Des Moines Independent Community School Dist., 128

Tippees (temporary insiders), 481–483
Title, 18, 534
Title search, 521
Tombstone ads, 467
Torts, 16–17, 212–241
  compensatory damages, 236–237
  constitutional, 227
  corporations and, 316–318
  courts heard in, 56
  damages for, 236–239, 249
  history of, 213–215, 243–245, 349–350
  liability based on, 230, 231, 307–312, 315–318
  New Jersey Tort Claims Act, 645
  nuisance, 643
  partnerships and, 315
  pollution as, 643–645
  punitive damages, 237–239
  recent damage awards, **237**
  structured settlements, 239
  tort reform, 239
  (See also Intentional torts; Negligence; Products liability; Service Liability; Strict liability)
Total activity test, 58
Toups v. Sears, Roebuck & Co., 256
Toxic substances, 638–641
  Comprehensive Environmental Response, Compensation, and Liability Act, 641
  disposal of, 641
  dump sites, 641
  laws regulating, 638–640
  manifest system, 640
  National Resource Conservation and Recovery Act, 640
  recent settlements, **642**
  right-to-know standard, 348
  Superfund and, 641
Toxic Substance Control Act (TSCA, 1976), 639–640
Trade:
  fair trade laws, 574
  regulation of, 619

Trade *(Cont.)*:
  restraint of, 570–571
  trade damage suits, 603
Trade Agreements Act of 1979, 334–335
Trade disparagement (injurious falsehood), 220–221
Trade practice regulation, 494, 619
  cease and desist orders, 495
  civil fines for violations, 496–497
  by Federal Trade Commission, 494, 498–503, 619
  penalties for violations, 496–498
  prosecution of violations, 495
  recent deceptive practice cases, **500**
  traditional, 498–500
  trends in, 500–503
Trade secrets, 222, 319
Trademarks, 223–224
  lost, due to general use, **224**
Trading with the Enemy Act, 326
Trading partnership, 295, 315
Trans-Am Builders, Inc. v. Woods Mill Ltd., 289
Trans World Airlines, Inc. v. Hardison, 379–380
Traynor, Roger, *Greenman v. Yuba Power Products, Inc.*, 245
Treaties, 105, 107
Treaty of Rome (1957), 333
Trespass, 213, 218, 644
Trial courts, 50, 52–53
  small-claims court, 53–54
Trial judges, 28–29, 89
Trials:
  under Bill of Rights, 143–144
  for breach of contract, 187
  conduct of, 82–85, 201
  cross-examination in, 83, 86
  directed verdict in, 80
  by jury, 29–30, 82–83, 143–144
  mock, 30
  motions during, 79–80
  pretrial conference, 81

Trials *(Cont.)*:
  rules of evidence in, 9–10, 86–88, 201
  verdicts in, 79–80
  witness examination, 83, 86
Triple damages:
  under antitrust laws, 557, 558, 560–564, 594, 612–613
  under Clayton Act, 562–564, 598, 612–613
  exceptions to, 562–564
  Illinois Brick Doctrine and, 562–564
  mergers and, 612–613
  price-fixing and, 560–564
  under Robinson-Patman amendment, 603
  under Sherman Antitrust Act, 558, 560–562, 584–585
Trustees, 552
  in bankruptcy, 541–542
Trusts, 552
Truth-in-Lending Act, 493, **494**, 508–511
  annual percentage rate (APR), 509
  coverage of, 508
  finance charge, 509
  financing statement, 509–510
  penalties under, 510–511
Truth-in-Lending Simplification Act, 511
Tudor Engineering Co. v. Mouw, 64–65
Tuttle v. Raymond, 238
Tying arrangements, 603–605

UCC (*see* Uniform Commercial Code)
Ultrahazardous activity, 235
Ultramares Corp. v. Touche, 269
Unanimous verdicts, 30
Unconditional suretyship contracts, 524
Unconscionability, doctrine of, 250
Underwriters, 465
Undistributed earnings, taxation of, 294

Undue burdens on interstate commerce, 118, 120
Undue hardship, question of, 543
Undue influence, 186
Unemployment compensation, 358–361
  disqualification from receiving, 359–361
  pregnancy and, 359–360
  strikes and, 360–361
  taxation, 358–359
Unfair acts or practices, 495, 618–619
Unfair and Deceptive Acts and Practices (UDAP) statutes, 512–513
  private remedies under, **514**
  public remedies under, **513**
Unfair competition, 222
Unfair employment practices (*see* Discrimination in employment)
Unfair labor practices, 427–457
  concerted activities interference, 432–435
  conferring benefits, 430–431
  discrimination: for nonunion membership, 446–448
    for union affiliation, 439–441
  domination of labor organization, 438–439
  employee discharge, 436–438
  employer practices, **428**
  interviews, 434
  under labor laws, 454–455
  litigation as, 429–430
  National Labor Relations Board and, 410–411, 429–431, 433–438, 441, 443–448, 450–451, 454
  proceedings and, 441
  refusal to bargain collectively in good faith, 442–445
  secondary boycotts, 361, 445, 449–452
  statements to employees, 431–432
  supervisors discharge, 438

INDEX **717**

Unfair labor practices *(Cont.)*:
  Supreme Court rulings on, 431, 433–434, 443, 453
  union-related efforts interference, 428–432
  union shop and, 446
  work rules, 431, 433–434
  (*See also* Unions, unfair labor practices by)
Unfair methods of competition, 618–620
Uniform Commercial Code (UCC), 39, 185
  after-acquired property, 530
  Article 2, 333
  Article 6, 522–523
  Article 9, 528, 530–534
  bulk transfers, 522–523
  contracts and, 184, 189, 191, 194, 202–204, 207–208
  default requirements under, 534
  express warranty, 251
  implied warranty: of fitness for particular purpose, 252
    of merchantability, 249–251
  priorities of security interests under, 531–533
  property covered by Article 9, **528**
  Section 2-313, 251
  Section 2-314, 249–251
  Section 2-315, 252
  secured transactions, 528–534
Uniform Limited Partnership Act, 288
Uniform Partnership Act, 277
Uniform Securities Act, 488
Uniform statutes, 38–39
Unilateral contracts, 185–186
  acceptance of, 190
Unilateral mistake, 192–193
Union Carbide, 328
Union Electric Co. v. EPA, 630
Unions, 400–426
  antitrust laws exemptions of, 402–404, 593
  bankruptcy reorganization and, 442–443, 544

Unions *(Cont.)*:
  bill of rights for members, 418–421
  cards for elections, 413–414
  closed shop, 415
  discrimination and, 395
    of employees and, 395, 439–441, 446–448
    for union affiliation, 439–441
  domination of, 438–439
  duty of fair representation by, 454–456
  elections of, 409, 411–414, 419–420, 422–423, 447
  federal laws on, 402–408
  federal laws governing labor-management relations, **403**
  fines imposed by, 415
  improper expenditures in, 404–406
  internal activities of, 422–423
  joining, 446–448
  litigation against, 418
  member discipline by, 415
  membership of, 415–416
  nonmembership, 446–448
  outsider rule, 420–421
  petitions for elections, 412–413
  of public employees, 423–424
  religious objections to, 380
  reporting requirements for, 421–422
  solicitation by, 431
  under Taft-Hartley Act, 415–416
  trusteeships, 422
  unfair labor practices by, 361, 410, 445–446
    coercion, 446–448
    excessive fees, 452–453
    featherbedding, 453
    under labor laws, 451, 454–455
    organizational picketing, 454
    picketing, 449–454
    restraint, 446–448
    secondary boycotts, 449–452

Unions, unfair labor practices by *(Cont.)*:
  union rivalry and, 452
  (*See also* Labor laws; Unfair labor practices)
  union shop, 404–406, 415, 446, 452
  (*See also* Labor laws; National Labor Relations Board; Strikes)
United Nations (UN), 332–333
United Nations Commission on International Trade Law (UNCITRAL), 332–333, 340
United Nations Conference on Trade and Development (UNCTAD), 333
United Parcel Service v. Fetterman, 352
United States v. Aluminum Company of America (Alcoa), 336, 581–582
United States v. Container Corporation of America, 576
United States v. Doe, 142–143
United States v. Grinnell Corporation, 583–584
United States v. Mine Workers, 7–8
United States v. Natelli, 485–486
United States v. Nixon, 32
United States v. Park, 314
United States v. Reader's Digest Association, Inc., 496–497
United States v. Von's Grocery Co., 610–611
United States v. Yermian, 159–160
United Steelworkers of America v. Sadlowski, 420–421
United Steelworkers of America v. Weber, 388
Unreasonable behavior:
  in negligence, 228–229, 246
  under Sherman Antitrust Act, 565–567
Unreasonably dangerous doctrine, product defect and, 255–257

Used-products cases, liability in, 258–259
Usury laws, 537–538
Utah Pie Co. v. Continental Baking Co., et al., 598–599

Variances from Clean Air Act standards, 630
Venue, 78
Verdict:
  directed, 80
  judgment opposite to, 79–80
Vertical mergers, 608
Vertical price-fixing, 582
Vertical territorial agreements, 580–581
Vested rights in pension plans, 364, 365
Veto, legislative, 32
Vicarious liability, 234–235, 308–310
Vickers v. North Am. Land Development, 304–305
Violent Crime, task force on, 15
Va. St. Bd. of Pharm. v. Va. Cit. Cons. Council, 135–136
Void contracts, 186
  examples of illegal contracts, **197**
  illegal, 196–198, 250
  by minors, 196
Voir dire examination, 82
  challenges and, 83
Voluntary bargaining issues, 442
Voluntary consent to contracts, 191–193
Voluntary petition for bankruptcy, 541
Von's Grocery case, 610–611

Wages (*see* Salaries)
Wagner Act (National Labor Relations Act, 1934), **403**, 408–414
  unfair employer labor practices under, 428
  unfair union labor practices under, 451, 454–455
Walker v. Armco Steel Corp., 60–61

Wall Street Journal, The, 219
Wanamaker, Justice, *Adams Express Co. v. Beckwith*, 43
Wardair Canada, Inc. v. Florida Dept. of Revenue, 122–123
Warnings:
  to employees, 396
  with potentially dangerous products, 255–257
Warranties:
  express, 251, 512
  of fitness for particular purpose, 252
  of habitability, 250–251
  implied, 244, 249–252
  liability for, 244, 249–251
  limited, 512
  Magnuson-Moss Warranty Act, 264, **494**, 511–512
  of merchantability, 249–251
  Supreme Court rulings on, 346
  under Uniform Commercial Code, 249–251, 252
Warren, Earl, quoted, 35
Waste disposal, 637–638
  of toxic substances, 641–642
Water pollution:
  Clean Water Act, 633–635
  effluents, 633
  permit discharge system, 634–635
  Safe Water Drinking Act, 635
Watergate affair, 31–32
Webb-Pomerene Act, 336
Weighing process of courts, 120, 121, 128, 129, 136
Weight requirements for employment, 385–386
Welch v. Bancorp Management Advisors, Inc., 221–222
Welfare and Pension Plans Disclosure Act (Teller Act, 1958), 422
Westinghouse Electric Corp., 187–188
Wheeler-Lea amendments to Federal Trade Commission Act, 553, 618
Whirlpool Corp. v. Marshall, 347
White, Byron, 36

White, Byron (*Cont.*):
  Roe v. Wade, 41–42
  on stare decisis, 41–42
White-collar crime, 13–14
White knight, 615
Willful violation of securities law, 470
Willful and wanton negligence, 229
William Inglis & Sons Baking Co., et al. v. ITT Continental Baking Co., Inc., et al., 586–587
Wimberly v. Labor and Industrial Relations Comm. of Missouri, 360
Witnesses:
  credibility of, 89
  examination of, 83, 86
Women, crime committed by, 13
Woodruff v. Georgia State University, 51
Work rules, 431, 433–434
Worker protection, 345–371
  contract law and, 208–209
  Employee Retirement Income Security Act and, 364–366
  employment-at-will doctrine, 311–312, 367–369
  employment-at-will limitations, **368**
  job references, 220
  least dangerous industries, **348**
  most dangerous industries, **348**
  occupational diseases, 354
  pension plans, 363–367
  qualified pension plans, 363–364
  simplified employee pension plans, 366
  Social Security, 361–363
  Social Security taxation rates, **363**
  strict liability for accidental injuries, 349–350
  unemployment compensation, 358–361
  wages and hours statutes, 355–358

Worker protection, wages and hours statutes *(Cont.):*
  violations, 357–358
  (*See also* Occupational Safety and Health Act; Occupational Safety and Health Administration)
Workers' compensation, 261, 263
  exclusive remedy rule, 353
  exceptions, **353**
  federal laws, 354–355
  history of, 349–350

Workers' compensation *(Cont.):*
  problems of, 353–354
  state laws, 349–354
  system of, 350–351
  tests for determining, 351–352
World court, 332
World-Wide Volkswagen Corp. v. Woodson, 76–77
Wright-Line Doctrine, 437–438
Writ of certiorari, petition for, 53, 58, 59
  new court proposal for, 67

Written contracts, situations requiring, 198–201
  exceptions to, **200**

Yellow-dog contracts, 406–407

Zamora v. Valley Federal Savings & Loan Association, 507–508
Zapata Corporation v. Maldonado, 297–298